ROTISSERIE®
LEAGUE
BASEBALL

ROTISSERIE®
LEAGUE
BASEBALL

1995 Edition

Edited by
Glen Waggoner

The Rotisserie League
Lee Eisenberg • Rob Fleder • Peter Gethers
Daniel Okrent • Michael Pollet • Cary Schneider
Robert Sklar • Cork Smith • Harry Stein
Glen Waggoner • Steve Wulf

Little, Brown and Company
Boston New York Toronto London

Contents

ROTISSERIE® LEAGUE BASEBALL

Introduction

A Game Ravitched by Fehr

by Steve Wulf

It was our fault. Don't blame the owners, don't blame the players, don't blame Ravitch, don't blame Fehr, don't blame Selig ... all right, you can lay some of it off on old Kenesaw Molehill. But the lion's share of the responsibility for the just-incompleted 1994 baseball season lies with us, your humble Rotisseservants. You see, we were the ones who pioneered the concept of the salary cap.

When the founding fathers drew up the first Rotisserie constitution in 1980, we were motivated by a desire to make our game as much like the real game of franchise building as possible. *We wanted to be like them.* Rosters, trades, free agency, September call-ups were all built into our system; you had to carry two catchers, even if one of them was Biff Pocoroba. One of our digressions—improvements, if you will—from standard operating procedure was a ceiling on how much each franchise could spend in order to assemble its team. The "salary cap" was established to prevent one owner from bidding outrageous amounts of money. If we hadn't had it, there's no telling how much money Dan (Mr. Baseball) Okrent would have spent to pursue his elusive pennant.

Cut to 1994. The owners provoke the players union into striking because they want a salary cap. *They wanted to be like us.* This is not mere speculation. Over the years, Rotisserie baseball has become a strong, loud window-pane check in the Lindsay Nelson jacket that is sports. (You may want to stop reading right there to stand up and applaud that metaphor.) Rotisserie is played everywhere nowadays, in Eastern law offices, Southern firehouses, Western hospitals, and Midwestern auto dealerships—like Bud Selig Ford in Milwaukee and Marge Schott Chevrolet in Cincinnati. There was a time, not too long ago, when members of the Philadelphia Phillies front office—owner Bill Giles, included—were spending so much time dealing with *Rotisserie* matters that their fantasy talk had to be confined to lunch hours. San Diego Padres owner Tom Werner, who did a classic Rotisserie dump in 1993, is a player. So is the son of Peter Angelos, the Baltimore Orioles owner.

Major league executives also like our game because of another of its digressions: no agents. But it was the salary cap the Selig-mites really coveted, so much so that they were willing to ruin the greatest season in memory. (The Fehr-mongers were equally stupid, striking at the two-thirds point of the season, and for what reason? To improve their bargaining position?)

So we lost all those delicious possibilities involving Matt Williams and the Cleveland Indians and Ken Griffey and the Colorado Rockies and Tony Gwynn and the New York Yankees and Frank Thomas and The Baseball Network. By the time it became clear that the season would have to be shortened—even a little—it was damn the owners, damn the players, damn the torpedoes, damn baseball. But then it dawned on some of us that Rotisserie baseball might somehow be responsible for placing the forbidden fruit of the salary cap before the Lords of Baseball. Damn us.

Closer to home, the strike did almost as much to give the 1994 gonfalon to the Eisenberg Furriers as Peter's Smoked Fish did (see page 248). Just when the second-place Wulfgang thought it was gaining on the Furriers, the season ended. I had mortgaged my future for the present, and the present went past too quickly. Eddie Williams, we hardly knew ye.

Worse still, the strike nearly soured me on the whole Rotisserie experience. Trying to block out the trauma, I started to forget who my own players were. The image of Jeff Bagwell would nightly haunt me, like Banquo's ghost. I stopped reading *Baseball America*. I watched an NFL game *until its conclusion*. Most telling of all, I wept quietly in a seedy deli on Seventh Avenue in Manhattan one day last October when I gave my sons money to buy beverages of their choice, and they emerged from the back of the store with cans of . . . it still hurts to write this . . . Yoo-Hoo.

But we find redemption, as well as Yoo-Hoo, in the strangest of places. I found mine on a plane flight to the West Coast. While we were 35,000 feet above St. Louis, I began perusing *The Sporting News*, which is published 35,000 feet below, and I happened upon this item in the Pittsburgh Pirates notes: "The Pirates' outfield in 1995 is likely to be Al Martin, Jacob Brumfield, and Midre Cummings." "Jacob Brumfield?" I thought. I own Jacob Brumfield. I can protect Jacob Brumfield. *I didn't* give up everything last year. I still have the starting center fielder for the Pittsburgh Pirates.

So, armed with renewed hope and Jacob Brumfield, I once again look forward to a brand-new season of Rotisserie baseball. And in order to wash away the blood of the salary cap ("Out, out, damned Schott!"), I have proposed a measure that I think will improve the game, a measure we devoutly wish that the major league owners will someday want to adopt:

Car dealers from the Midwest are prohibited from owning franchises in our league.

1

The Inner Game

Play Ball!

Winter came a little early this year, so Rotisserie players have had longer than usual to contemplate the intellectual infrastructure and emotional subtexts of their game's inner game. What else were we supposed to do? You got no box scores, you spend a lot of time studying your navel.

The results of all that heavy thinking were so electrifying, so provocative, and so well typed that we decided to move this chapter up in the batting order. In eight previous editions, this space was occupied by our beloved Offical Constitution, now to be found in Chapter 7 (see page 283). In its place we offer three samples of cutting-edge, ahead-of-the-curve, post-deconstructionist analysis guaranteed to illuminate your path to the pennant. The only other things you will need to be assured of victory are some power, a strong bullpen, plenty of speed, and Greg Maddux.

As a Founding Father of Rotisserie League Baseball, **Lee Eisenberg** should need no introduction. But he does, since for the last three seasons the First Furrier has been living in a cave in eastern Tennessee, and none of us is sure what he looks like anymore. We naturally assumed that he was still putting in quality time with his computer printouts, his player lists, and his team's official by-laws, *The Prince* by Machiavelli. The evidence for that was his runaway victory in last year's truncated pennant race, a triumph lowlighted by The Trade (see Chapter 5), the most lopsided baseball deal since Babe Ruth left Boston. Here he weighs in with a screenplay for a nine-part documentary on Rotisserie League Baseball that will be aired by all the networks and PBS during the next baseball strike.

Last year **Mark Batterman** graced these pages with a shrill diatribe called **The K-Factor**, in which he demanded that Strikeouts be substituted for Ratio as a Rotisserie scoring category. Why would we permit such an outrage? Because we believe in free speech . . . because we celebrate cultural diversity in a pluralistic society . . . and because each year we have a certain number of pages to fill in order to justify charging you the price of a box seat at most major league ballparks for this book. It was a mistake. Not because of the bags of letters we received in support of Batterman's heresy, but because it encouraged him. That's right, he's back—this time in tandem with longtime Rotisserie running mate **Ken Kuta**. Like Batterman, Kuta was a founding member of the (now defunct) Farrah Fawcett-Major League.

Also like Batterman, Kuta dabbles in TV production in sunny Southern California. For his protection, we will not reveal the names of the sitcoms he has helped perpetrate over the years, but we will note that his primary contribution to Rotisserie lore—before now—was his team's name, the Kuta Kintes.

This year, Batterman and Kuta offer for our edification **Fast Track to the Cellar,** a compendium of the most common—and most lethal—mistakes that Rotisserie owners can make. They should know.

Our third contributor, **Andrew Stavisky,** had the supreme good fortune to see his very first major league baseball game in Fenway Park on October 21, 1975. The date sound familiar? We'll spare you the trouble of looking it up: it was the sixth game of the 1975 World Series between Boston and Cincinnati, otherwise known as The Greatest World Series Game Ever. That's right, young Andy was there for El Tiante's dipsy-doo contortions that kept the Red Sox alive, for Bernie Carbo's dramatic three-run homer that tied the game in the eighth, and for Carlton Fisk's immortal dance at home plate in the twelfth inning as his fly ball sailed over the Green Monster, inches inside the foul pole.

There's just one little problem. Andy was *there*, but he didn't exactly *see* Fisk's home run. Seems that as Fisk stepped up to the plate in the twelfth, Andy decided it was a good time to tie his shoe: all he saw was the backs of the fans in front of him. Amazing. Only eight years old, and already evidence of a Rotisserie mind in the making.

Now all grown up, Andy—excuse us, *Mr.* Stavisky—is still only 28, exactly the same age Peter Gethers was at the first-ever Rotisserie auction draft back in 1980. But there the similarity between the two ends. Mr. Stavisky—soon to be Dr. Stavisky—is a serious person, a scholar, with a Master of Arts in the sociology of sports. He is currently a graduate student working on his Ph.D. in the Department of Kinesiology at the University of Maryland. His doctoral dissertation will be a policy analysis of gender discrimination in intercollegiate athletics, but he was unable to finish that in time for inclusion in this year's book. Instead, we have an essay based on a paper he delivered at an academic conference last fall. The topic: "Rotisserie Baseball: Regaining Control in a McDonaldized Society."

Naturally, we are pleased that the academic community is finally taking notice of Rotisserie baseball and giving it the scholarly attention it deserves. Frankly, it's about time. We are confident that this essay, **Rotisserie 1, Big Mac 0,** will lay the groundwork for our ultimate goal—to have Rotisserie Studies recognized as a fully accredited academic department in every college and university in the country.

ATTENTION, NEWCOMERS!
Not so fast there. Before jumping into The Inner Game, have a gander at The Rules, Simplified (see pages 27–28). Then memorize the sacred Rotisserie Constitution in Chapter 7 (pages 283–300). Only then, after you are sure what you're getting into, is it safe to proceed.

Debasedball
A Documentary History of Rotisserie League Baseball, 1980–August 12, 1994

PRODUCED, DIRECTED, AND OVERWRITTEN

By Lee Eisenberg

Narrated by Daniel Schorr

VOICES

Glen Waggoner	*Garth Brooks*
Dan Okrent	*Fabio*
Valerie Salembier	*John Bobbitt*
Harry Stein	*Jeremy Irons*
Peter Gethers	*Roger Grimsby*
Cary Schneider	*Calvin Peete*
Bob Sklar	*Charlton Heston*
Cork Smith	*Macaulay Culkin*
Rob Fleder	*Carroll O'Connor*
Jay Lovinger	*Dom DeLuise*
Steve Wulf	*Shirley Povich*
Dominick Abel	*George Plimpton*
Michael Pollet	*Jackie Mason*

CONSULTANTS

Eliot Asinov	Mickey Herskowitz	Anne Rice
Murray Chass	Tommy Hilfiger	Ed Rollins
Alan Dershowitz	The Judds	Jonas Salk
Peter Drucker	Ted Kazanski	Peggy Siegal
ESPN's Peter Gammons	C. Everett Koop	Arthur Sulzberger Jr.
Pierre Franey	Andy Musser	Andres Thomas
Carlos Fuentes	Pablo Neruda	Jeff "Tain" Watts
Murray Gell-Mann	Rowland Office	George Will
Lewis V. Gerstner	Dean Ornish	George C. Wolfe
Nadine Gordimer	Gene Orza	Tom Wolfe
Elliott Gould	Peter Pascarelli	Miles Wolff
Mandy Grunwald	Harvey Penick	Youppi!
Stephen Hawking	Faith Popcorn	Steve Zabriskie

TOP OF THE FIRST

Narrator: It was the greatest game for baseball fans since baseball . . . and the worst game for baseball fans since baseball. It was a game played in the nation's dining rooms, on cornfields, in church pews, in paneled rec rooms, on kitchen tables, on conference tables, in hotel lobbies, in home offices, in airport club lounges, in barracks, and in backstreet pool halls haunted by the ghost of Edward Hopper. It was played by farm boys and fraternity boys, by doctors and lawyers, by millionaires and by everyday people who couldn't afford adequate health insurance if they changed jobs or had pre-existing conditions. It was a game whose diehard fans could be so long-winded that Mario Cuomo once fell asleep drafting what some have said was the greatest Rotisserie team ever drafted by a governor of Italian descent whose family once ran a simple grocery in the Bronx.

BOTTOM OF THE FIRST

Narrator: *[after pause for breath]* Or was it Brooklyn?

TOP OF THE SECOND

Narrator: Stories, myths, verse plays, sonnets, elegies, and limericks abound as to when the game was invented, who first set down its elaborate and elegant rules and customs—

Fabio: I did! *I* thought of it! *Le roi de la rotisserie, c'est moi!* *[a beat]* Dan Okrent, Worthington, Massachusetts, 1983.

Narrator: Some say a primitive form of the game was played in England in the Middle Ages. *[visual of a knight with his kishkas trickling out of his chain mail]* Instead of major league ballplayers they used prominent jousters of the day.

Garth Brooks: I don't think this can be sustained. *[a beat]* Glen Waggoner, editor, 1995 edition of *Rotisserie League Baseball*.

BOTTOM OF THE SECOND

Narrator: Still others say it was born in some long forgotten *shtetl*, where an oppressed but unsinkable people conceived it as a way of escaping the pathos of everyday reality. . . .

Garth Brooks: Can you blame them? Ever been to the Upper West Side of Manhattan? *[a beat]* Glen Waggoner.

Narrator: In the early 1980s a first-generation participant wrote to his son . . .

Jackie Mason: Jeremy, my darling boy. Please walk Max and give him some kibble when you get up in the morning. The draft is tomorrow morning and, as usual, I'm completely fahkocked and fatootzed. I didn't even start making my lists until late this evening, after you went to bed, my bubbe-leh. Please get me up no later than seven-thirty. *[a beat]* Michael Pollet, Pollet and Pollet, "Attorney-at-Law."

TOP OF THE THIRD

Murray Chass: *[graphic: Baseball "Writer," New York Times]* The game, at least when I first heard about it, this was—what?—years after it became popular, changed how fans thought about baseball—and not for the better. You can't overestimate what schmucks these Rotisserie people are. It's hard to know who to blame. I know Okrent asks for, and gets, much of the credit, but I can't help but think that the number nerds like Bill James who threw like girls and liked to sit around at card tables in their basements crunching numbers and picking their zits had something to do with it, too. These are the people who took baseball out of the hands of the sportswriters and turned it over to the smart-assed bean counters and magazine types.

BOTTOM OF THE THIRD

Narrator: *[music in background: "Star Spangled Banner" as played by Ferrante and Teisher—or is it Gold and Fizdale? Come to think of it, when was the last time you saw all four of them in the same room?]* The early drafts were spellbinding. Ten separate hearts pounded as one in the chests of the owners, while the cream cheese in the corners of their mouths went unwiped for the entire length of the auction. These April marathons lasted six, seven, even *eight* hours. Maybe nine. Ten, quite possibly. *Eleven* hours wouldn't be a stretch. Make that an even dozen. *Twelve* incredible hours they sat there. Sometimes it was *dark* when they finished!

Calvin Peete: I remember the year we walked out of the lobby of Cork's building and it was already dusk. No, actually, I think it was already dark. I think that was the year before we moved to Jersey. *[a beat]* Cary Schneider, Montclair, New Jersey.

TOP OF THE FOURTH

Narrator: Ronald Reagan was in the White House. *Thirtysomething* was on TV. Chelsea Clinton was already born. And Pinky Lee was already dead. (But how could they tell?) The grip the game held was awesome—that is, for those select few whose race, gender, and religious orientation fit the founders' idea of who might qualify as a "chosen" franchise owner in the original Rotisserie League . . . and who might not.

Jeremy Irons: Whaddya talkin'? Cut this PC bullshit! First of all, Waggoner's not even Jewish! *[a beat]* Harry Stein.

BOTTOM OF THE FOURTH

John Bobbitt: *[squeakily]* No! *You're* bullshit! *He's* right! They were—they *are*—a bunch of uptight, short, neurotic, full-of-themselves, little dick faces! Waggoner went along as their beard, the *shabbas goy!* Big deal, one Christian. I ask you, how many *women* have they let in? One. *Me*. I was their Jackie Robinson of gender, the token female, and I lasted— what?—a year or two? Ridiculed my every move. Like the time I raised Gene Richards's (or was it Gene Barry's?) salary to $39! The way they sniggered and guffawed and kept trying to peek inside my blouse whenever I reached across the table for the *Baseball Register*. *[a beat]* Valerie Salembier, to her attorney, a sexual harassment litigator, 1994.

TOP OF THE FIFTH

Tommy Hilfiger: *[graphic: "Clothing Designer"]* I've thought quite a bit about why so many people play Rotisserie baseball and . . . I forgot what I was going to say. . . .

Narrator: The competition in the new league proved fierce. It was a game for which hope sprung . . . sprang? . . . springed? . . . eternal every April, and, for most, came crushing? . . . crashing? . . . careening? . . . to earth after the All-Star break. Except for the one lucky winner, October was the cruelest month of all.

BOTTOM OF THE FIFTH

Narrator: Their names are engraved on a cheap piece of plastic that's screwed onto a tacky little Formica base that's designed to look like real "wood." It's called the Wigge Cup, so named for Larry Wigge, who like so many whose lives came to be identified with this game, is the entirely forgettable writer who eventually became a hockey scribe for the now defunct (or if it isn't, it should be) *Sporting News*. The Wigge Cup is emblematic of Rotisserie baseball's highest achievement. *[music swells: Herbie Mann's "Comin' Home"]* A championship season.

Macaulay Culkin: Like, you know, I look at these names on the trophy and I can't believe I've been letting these people pick their noses around my dining room table all these years. *[a beat]* Cork Smith, Commissioner for Life.

TOP OF THE SIXTH

Youppi!: *[graphic: "Mascot, Montreal Expos"]* You know, I can remember, as a boy, I used to lie in bed and memorize the names of the Rotisserie League's winning teams! *Zut alors!* It all seemed so *real* to me! I couldn't wait to buy the book every year to find out the final standings, the point totals, which team had the best ratio, what trades were made! My favorite team?! *Je ne c'est pas!* The Sklar Gazers, maybe, don't ask me *pourquoi!* Even today—*mon dieu!*—most nights before closing my eyes at night I can recite every past winner. . . !

BOTTOM OF THE SIXTH

George Plimpton: I'll wager a pound sterling that in the seventh inning they're going to do something frightfully inane like sing "Take Me Out to the Ball Game." *[a beat]* Dominick Abel, New York City.

T0P OF THE SEVENTH

Pablo Neruda: Take me out to the ball game . . .

Elliott Gould: . . . take me out to the crowd.

Mandy Grunwald: Buy me some peanuts and Crackerjack . . .

Tom Wolfe: . . . I don't care if I never get back.

Faith Popcorn: So it's root, root, root, for the home team . . .

ESPN's Peter Gammons: . . . if they don't win it's a shame.

Anne Rice: For it's ONE . . .

Lewis V. Gerstner: . . . TWO . . .

Arthur Sulzburger Jr.: . . . THREE strikes you're out at the . . .

Nadine Gordimer: . . . old ball game!

BOTTOM OF THE SEVENTH

Narrator: By the early 1990s, the Rotisserie League had grown far beyond its original ten, mostly Hebraic, teams—or should I say tribes? It is estimated that today between 500,000 and 2,000,000 Americans, from Natchez to Mobile, from the redwood forests to the Gulf Stream waters, gather each April to play America's former national pastime's national pastime. *[pregnant pause]* Then came August 12, 1994 . . .

TOP OF THE EIGHTH

Murray Gell-Mann: It was like being sucked into a black hole, a quark of fate.

Alan Dershowitz: It made me want to put Bud Selig on the stand and cross-examine the tongue out of his face.

The Judds: I broke down and cried. I broke down and cried, too.

BOTTOM OF THE EIGHTH

Andres Thomas: All that was left of baseball that year was 18½ hours of Ken Burns. Thank God for that, at least. Okrent was unquestionably the best. Nice red sweater, too. And, if you want my opinion, I actually think he looks better without the beard. Señora Thomas thought he looked a little like Warren Beatty. Anyhow, it's no wonder someone that intelligent and articulate has never won a Rotisserie championship. He obviously has better things to think about. I was so impressed with him and the rest of the series that I sent a check to PBS and told them to keep the tote bag.

TOP OF THE NINTH

Narrator: It was over. Just like that, the curtain dropped on what would have been an extraordinary season. A paunchy outfielder for the Padres was flirting with .400. A bald third-sacker for the Giants was pushing Maris and Ruth. And a little weasely furmeister, sitting atop the standings with an eight-point lead, was half-hoping for the season to end at least a little early so, like a raccoon at a dump site, he would be assured of his

---

tainted quarry. And, indeed, that's what happened. For the first time since, like a really long time ago, there was no World Series. The season just stopped, and the boys of summer went home. There was nothing left for a crestfallen nation to do but wait around for O.J.'s jury selection.

BOTTOM OF THE NINTH

Narrator: On the night of December 16, 1994, an object was found amidst a pile of refuse near a nuclear waste burial site between Oak Ridge and Knoxville, Tennessee. It was some kind of trophy. A tiny plastic baseball player was glued precariously to a crappy "wood-like" base. Engraved around the sides of the object were a list of names and dates:

- 1980 Getherswag Goners
- 1981 Wulfgang
- 1982 Eisenberg Furriers
- 1983 Stein Brenners
- 1984 Sklar Gazers
- 1985 Cary Nations
- 1986 Stein Brenners
- 1987 Fleder Mice
- 1988 Stein Brenners
- 1989 Cary Nations
- 1990 Stein Brenners
- 1991 Glenwag Goners
- 1992 Glenwag Goners
- 1993 Wulfgang
- 1994 Eisenberg Furriers

Narrator: No one knows how the trophy got there. The only living thing in the area was some kind of woodland creature, a possum or perhaps a ferret, its eyes aglow in the still, dank night. Whatever it was, it wasn't talking, except to let out a strange kind of hissing sound. It seemed to be saying, *Yesssss!*

Tommy Hilfiger: Oh, now I get it. It was Marv Albert, right?

Fade Out

Music Rises Over Credits

Solo acoustic guitar rendition of the "Star Spangled Banner," as played by Blind Lemon Horowitz.

Fast Track to the Cellar, or, the 24 Most Common Rotisserie Mistakes

By Mark Batterman and Ken Kuta

It doesn't matter what you call it: the cellar, the doormat, or the south end of a pony going north—last place sucks. We know. Been there. Done that. We've suffered the abuse from our fellow owners during those long, harsh, cold winter months. (Thank God we live in Southern California. Last place in Minnesota must be really brutal.) Happily, we've also taken the Yoo-Hoo shower and had the joy of watching the Farrah Fawcett-Major League pennant wave proudly over our home park while we graciously shoved our fellow owners' faces into it.

Old Blue Eyes said it best, "We've been up and down and over and out and we know one thing." And that one thing is that the thrill of victory is better than the agony of defeat. So from the Rotisserie school of hard knocks—from two veteran Rotisserie guys who know intimately the ins and outs of screwing the pooch—here are the 24 mistakes you *must* avoid at all costs if you want a shot at winning it all.

1. **Don't do enough research.** If you don't know who's who, what's what, and why's why, you've got as much chance of grabbing the flag as Cecil Fielder has of stealing a base. Trust us. You need research and lots of it. And it's got to be in an accessible form at the high-pressure draft table. Notes scribbled across this book, in the margins of Mazeroski, and on Opening Day rosters in *USA Today* won't cut it. You need lists. Lots of lists. Lists by position, lists by stat category, lists of who is available, lists of who is not. You need lists of guys who steal, lists of big boomers, and lists of $1 guys named Luís. Then you need to be able to get to all of your lists instantly. That's right, you need a list of your lists.

2. **Do too much research.** This is Mistake Number One for the obsessive-compulsive. You know who you are. And if you don't, there is a simple test: if you have already made a list of the lists recommended above, then you should seek help *before* the draft.

3. **Don't believe your research.** You're at the table, you know everything from Andy Benes's strikeout ratio to John Kruk's truss size. The George Steinbrenner next to you bids $25 on Kevin Gross. Kev broke your heart last year. You know there's a lot of pitching left. You know you shouldn't do it, but the George wannabe won the pennant last year, and if he

---

thinks old Kevin's worth 25 clams then . . . Stop! Your compass just pointed south!

4. **Don't read the spring training box scores.** You can name every player on every 40-man roster. You know every team's depth chart through Double-A ball. You have memorized Mazeroski. You subscribe to *Baseball America* and study every word of agate type. You can do all that, but unless you read the spring training box scores in *USA Today*, you can't know which rookies are being given long looks, whether players who underwent surgery last fall are healthy or toast, and if this is the year that Jeff Conine plays first if Mattingly moves to DH. We're not suggesting you have to go so far as to watch exhibition baseball on TV— even we draw the line somewhere. But staying on top of spring training is essential. This is the world's greatest fantasy game; ultimately real players with real lives do real things on the real diamond. If you don't take that into account, you're living in the past. And you don't need our help to win at Strat-O-Matic.

5. **Don't track the draft.** Not only do you need accurate lists going into the draft, you need lists that enable you to track player sales *during* the draft. When Darren Lewis is the last everyday outfielder available, you've got to know it. If you don't and you pass at $31 because "that's way more than this stiff is worth" you'll be stuck with a starting outfield of Kevin Bass, Billy Bean, and Jacob Brumfeld. Wave bye-bye as they push you down the cellar stairs. This leads us to . . .

6. **Don't spend all your money at the table.** The biggest mistake. Period. No matter what, spend it all. You didn't bid that $32 on Darren Lewis and you left the table only spending $257? Good going, Buckwheat. The $3 you get back from the Commissioner is just enough to send a congratulations card to the guy in first. Sometimes you just have to pay what the market demands. (We understand this, even if major league owners don't.) This game is a paranoiac balance between getting something for nothing and getting nothing because you didn't spend something.

7. **Believe this is a game about baseball.** Forget the romance of the National Pastime. Take a moment, swallow hard, and repeat after us: "This is a game for stat nerds . . . This is a game for stat nerds . . . This is a game for stat nerds." We're buying commodities at an open auction. It's not hard. Just think of the players as pork bellies.

8. **Don't be flexible at the table.** You keyed on McGriff and Matt Williams. You've bought Hal Morris and Mark Grace. You didn't want to; you didn't mean to. But they came up so early and went so cheap you couldn't let them pass. What do you do now? No worries. Grab Tony Gwynn for $32, sock away all the available BA at the table, and trade for power at the end of April. Waffling may not work if you're President of the United States, but it can save your Rotisserie ass.

9. **Have rigid, cast-in-stone player values.** Go back and review mistakes 5 and 6. Buy all the books, yeah-yeah. Read what the so-called experts

have to say about how much you should spend, doo-wa, doo-wa. Now throw it all away. Those guys ain't sitting at your draft. The only reality is now.

10. **Spend too much money on starting pitching.** It may be 90% of the game of baseball, but that's not the game we're playing. (Repeat after us, "This is a game for stat nerds.") We know that pitching represents 40 of the possible 80 points (48 of 96 if you were nuts enough to expand when the NL did or misguided enough to play American League from the git-go). Remember the law of supply and demand? The fine print says that there's always more pitching available than hitting. Sure you've got to spend a buck or two on Greg Maddux, José Rijo, or Randy Johnson to dance a victory jig, but if you spend more than 30% of your budget on pitching you'll never be able to buy an offense, and the only music you'll be dancing to is Taps.

(Of course, if this offends your sensibilities and you want to make Rotisserie baseball more fun and challenging, plus restore starting pitching to its rightful place of importance, you can jump on the ever increasing bandwagon, correct a major flaw in the game, and replace ratio with strikeouts! Ah, but that's another article for another day— specifically, "The K-Factor" by Mark Batterman in this space in last year's book.)

11. **Have a cockeyed theory.** Rule number two for the obsessive-compulsive crowd, in which you out-think yourself into a wacko strategy, flush all common sense down the locker room toilet, and leave the table guaranteed 13 b-i-i-i-g points. Here's one: the All Relievers Strategy. It goes like this: You corner the market in Saves, give up on Wins, and since these guys are great, you ace ERA and Ratio. Bring on the Yoo-Hoo! Not so fast. You see, grasshopper, one dark night you will have three closers going and they will all give up 10 hits and 6 earned runs and walk five in a row. Can you say "good-bye ERA and Ratio?" Can you say "hello" to the aforementioned 13 points in pitching?

Or let's say your All Relievers Strategy seems to be working: You have 31 pitching points, your loaded offense is on fire, and you're knock-knock-knocking on first-place door. Then, a couple of hours before the Trade Deadline, the team owner in third place rings you up and calls your attention to "The Fenokee IP Requirement" (see page 288) in this book. When did those $#@&^! add that, you cry. Obviously some time in the last few years since you walked into a bookstore and bought a new annual edition, but the precise year doesn't matter. What matters is you are now going to be punished for your sins—not the least of which was thinking you could win with such a wacko theory in the first place. If you walk this path, you walk with Daniel Okrent and the other outer-fringe Rotissestrategists. If you walk this path, you walk into last place.

12. **Spend more than $3 on catchers.** There's Piazza and Daulton, Hoiles and Tettleton. There's a handful of 'tweeners named Rodriguez and Lopez, Alomar and Wilkins. Everybody else is worth a buck. Paying for the blue-chippers commits too much payroll to a high injury-risk posi-

tion. Chasing the 'tweeners drives their prices way beyond reason. But hanging back for the one-buck backstops means you'll sometimes get five bucks worth of value. Take that extra cash and bid higher on Bagwell or Baerga.

13. **Draft too many rookies in Ultra.** Okay, good work, you've got *Baseball America's* top 10 AA players for your 13-man Reserve roster. But 80 stolen bases in Little Rock won't help you this July when all you need is one utility infielder from San Pedro de Macoris to make a trade for a pitcher—any pitcher—so you can cut Mike Moore or Mike Morgan from your active roster.

14. **Blow off draft day.** It's not called the best day of the year for nothing. We're begging you. Please avoid buying NHL playoff tickets for 2 P.M. when your draft starts at 11 A.M. And never, ever drink the league's free beer. Nothing sobers you faster than hearing your own voice say, "Darryl Strawberry, fifty-four dollars."

15. **Fall in love with your players.** No one is indispensable. The guy you've got to have, no matter what the cost, costs too much. Hey, get real. We're talking a bunch of filthy rich post-adolescents who spit tobacco, go to work in pajamas, and scratch their crotches in public, not Claudia Schiffer. Okay?

16/17. **Overvalue your guys and/or Be reluctant to pull the trade trigger.** We consider these two mistakes in tandem because if, say, you're the lucky sumbitch who got Jeff Kent at $12 (substitute your own personal draft coup), there are two major ways you can blow your temporary advantage. Let's say that Jeff blasts 10 moonshots in the first few weeks of the season. Great! Not! Because those 10 dingers put him on a pace to top Roger Maris by Labor Day, through most of May you're convinced the only fair trade for Babe Kent is Gary Sheffield *and* Deion Sanders. Then in June, even though you're only getting one point in steals, you can't pull the trigger on Super Kent for Delino DeShields 'cuz your friend's buddy's sister (a cousin of a former *New York Times* sports reporter) says "Dallas Green believes Jeff's good for at least 40 this year." The problem is, the only 40 old Jeff is good for is the 40 points you're stuck at because you have no speed. Wow. Isn't it amazing how fast you can fall from first to eighth?

18. **Worry about salaries at the wrong time.** We agree that salaries are important, but only when we're talking about yours versus that jerk at the desk next to you. Stop worrying about next year. After draft day the only numbers that matter are points. Who cares if you've got Albert Belle at $15 with one year left on his contract when your sitting in fifth? Trade him now to a "rebuilding" team for Puckett at $44 and Clemens at $35. Rebuilding is for ants.

19. **Don't make a trade 'cuz "they'd never make it in the majors."** Repeat after us: "This is a game for stat nerds."

20. **Listen to your significant other and/or kids.** Lets face it, RLB can

be hell on the old home life. But, hey, it comes with the turf—natural or Astro—when you step onto the field. Anyone who isn't ready to sacrifice a relationship or two to the Rotisserie gods ain't man (or woman) enough to carry Junior's jock. But don't take our word for it: Go ask Steve Garvey or Wade Boggs. The next time your spouse pleads that you just can't trade Craig Biggio for Kevin Mitchell because "Craig's got such a cute butt," say "Yes, dear," but pick up that phone and grab those extra dingers. It will be okay. There could be other relationships in your life, but how often do you have a chance to clinch a pennant?

21. **Call your team "the Sox."** There's such a thing as tradition. Call your team by a proper Rotisserie name. Even a lame proper Rotisserie name. Make a pun on your name. Do it! There's no such thing as a bad pun in Rotisserie nomenclature. But there are too many Manny's Maulers and Bill's Sox out there. This may have no effect on your winning or losing, but you'll get a whole lot more respect if you call your team Andy's Griffins or Sherman's March.

22. **Be a baseball fan.** You live on Chicago's North Side. You've just got to have a Cubbie or two on your team for when you go to Wrigley. Oh, what the hell, go after 'em all. Who wants to be in the money anyway?

23. **Follow these rules.** What's the old adage? "Those who can, do. Those who can't, . . ."

24. **Follow this book.**

PRE-SEASON CHECKLIST

✓ 1. Call Roti•Stats for info about stats service: 800-884-7684.
✓ 2. Join the RLBA (see page 274).
✓ 3. Send in for Free Opening Day Update (see page 277).
✓ 4. Fill out Rotiserrie Owners Survey (see page 267).
✓ 5. Outfit entire neighborhood in Rotisserie Caps and T-shirts (see page 279).
✓ 6. Sign up to Beat the Founding Fathers at Their Own Game (see page 276)
✓ 7. Cancel all business and social plans for two weeks prior to auction draft.

Rotisserie 1, Big Mac 0
By Andrew Stavisky

[Author's Note: The following essay is an adaptation of the paper "Rotisserie Baseball: Regaining Control in a McDonaldized Society," presented at the North American Society for Sport Sociology Conference in Savannah, Georgia, on November 10, 1994.]

"I think he [major league player] will definitely play better under new management."

—*One Rotisserie owner to another discussing a possible trade*

INTRODUCTION

In Rotisserie years, I am a relative newcomer. I, along with my partner, Paul Talkov, a New York City dentist, own the Stav Maniacs, a two-year-old expansion team in the Syracuse University Baseball League—so named because the league founders were primarily graduates of the Syracuse School of Communications (including ESPN's Mike Tirico [the Microphones] and Phillies announcer Todd Kalas [the TKO's]). In our first year the Stav Maniacs finished a respectable sixth in a 12-team league. In last years' strike-shortened season we moved up to fourth place—by half a point, thanks to a Jeff Brantley save on the eve of the strike. Next season (assuming there is a season) we plan to win the whole thing.

As a sport sociologist, I spend my days trying to make sense of the social world, particularly concerning phenomena that are in some way sport related. Rotisserie baseball, which was innocently developed 15 years ago by a group of middle-aged baseball fans, aka the Founding Fathers, as "The Greatest Game for Baseball Fans Since Baseball," has mushroomed into a national phenomenon, creating along the way numerous cottage industries such as statistics services, television pay-per-view specials, newsletters, books, and periodicals. This pastime, which has affected thousands of fantasy "owners" in dramatic fashion, seemed like a social phenomenon worth further examination. To my knowledge no one before now has embarked on an "academic" exploration of the subject. What follows, then, is a brief look at my initial investigation into the world of Rotisserie baseball.

THEORETICAL BACKGROUND

Rotisserie baseball is more than simply an innocuous diversion. It is the manifestation of a new level of sport fandom—a participatory consumership, if you will, where participants (owners) have moved from the role of passive spectators (fans), where they may have an emotional investment in a particular team but have no actual involvement in the event or control over its outcome, to the role of active participants, where their ability to apply their knowledge has empowered the fantasy owners with the perception that their actions (*e.g.*, the ability to select players, scout talent, make trades, *etc.*) in some way affect the outcome of their teams' performance.

Dave Thomas—the community psychologist, not the Wendy's guy—designed a list of individual and community needs that he uses when developing community programs in his native New Zealand. Thomas explains that programs must fulfill these needs or they will be unsuccessful in the long run. Included in this list are: a) *Meaningful Social Identities*—a sense of place, attachment to a location, a feeling of belonging; b) *Shared Belief System*— helps people make sense of the world and life events; c) *Opportunities for Social Participation*—opportunities for memberships in social groups, social contact, social stimulation; d) *Supportive Social Environment*—opportunities for self-disclosure and emotional support; e) *Perception of Control*—a feeling that one has some control over important aspects or domains in one's life; and f) *Self-Efficacy*—opportunities to develop specific skills, sense of competence in carrying out activities that are personally or socially important. While Thomas probably knows little about baseball, his schemata is relevant to the Rotisserie world. I would argue that baseball fandom offers fulfillment of the first four needs, encompassing meaning in life and social connectedness. Baseball spectatorship, however, does not fulfill the remaining two needs. For that, fans must look elsewhere.

The next step, then, is to explain where this need for perceived control and for self-efficacy arises. Max Weber, the great German social philosopher of the late 19th and early 20th century, offers insight to this question, and in doing so provides the platform for understanding the impact of and impetus for Rotisserie baseball in American culture, including a theoretical foundation for discerning why the need to regain one's perception of control and self-efficacy is likely the main motivation for Rotisserie owners' involvement in fantasy baseball.

Weber explained that by the turn of the century nearly all phases of human communal experience—science, education, the military, arts, religion, medicine, and even such ancillary activities as entertainment, leisure, and sport—were being transformed from a traditional to a rational model epitomized by bureaucratization, modernization, and organization. According to Weber, the trends of modernized society were moving toward the creation of an "Iron Cage" of rationality: a seamless web of rationalized institutions from which individuals would eventually find no escape, leading to the loss of perceived control and self-efficacy.

George Ritzer, a contemporary disciple of Weber, suggests in his book *The McDonaldization of Society* that today's model of rationalization (bureaucratization) is the fast-food restaurant McDonald's. Ritzer explains that in our increasingly mobile society, where people are constantly rushing from one place to another, "McDonaldization" not only affects the restaurant business but practically every social institution, including education, work, travel, leisure activities, politics, and the family. At the heart of McDonaldization lie four dimensions that operate synergistically to propel the elements of this model.

The first dimension of McDonaldization is *efficiency*, the quest for the ideal method for getting from one point to another. In the particular case of McDonald's, efficiency pertains to finding the fastest way to feed its customers, resulting in the development of the fast-food meal, which has evolved to the degree where one can even remain in his/her car and receive his/her food from a drive-through window. Ritzer argues that this efficient fast-food model has proliferated into an array of other social institutions such as journalism (*USA Today*), tax services (H&R Block), dieting (Nutri-System), exercise (Holiday Spas), automobile services (Midas Muffler), eye care (Pearle Vision Center), and amusement parks (Walt Disney World), to name just a few. Rotisserie baseball is also a product of this quest for efficiency—namely, how can player performance and productivity most effectively be represented? The use of statistics in Rotisserie baseball serves a dual efficiency function: to most effectively measure player performance while simultaneously most effectively measuring Rotisserie teams' performances. The development of Rotisserie Ultra, for example, was a result of trying to more efficiently represent player production.

The second dimension of McDonaldization is an emphasis on things easily *quantified* and *calculated*. Often with this consideration is a tendency to equate quantity with quality—to believe that bigger (or more) is better. The reasoning: If billions of customers have been served, the food must be good. McDonaldized institutions can be obsessed with quantification and calculability. For instance, in the entertainment industry, the success (and often the quality) of a movie is determined by how much money it earns in the box office. Likewise, the success of television programs is determined not by its educational, artistic, or social value but by its ratings. Ritzer explains that even the hallowed halls of academics are not immune from McDonaldization. Professional advancement for faculty (particularly at research institutions) is determined not by teaching ability but by quantifiable measures such as number of publications and number of works cited. Sports have become increasingly obsessed with statistics as a way to measure production and success—earned run average, total bases, batting average, quarterback rating, free-throw percentage, plus/minus rating, and so on. Each sport has sought ways to increase scoring—increase quantification—as a requisite to its success in attracting spectators. Rotisserie baseball also places a premium on quantification and calculability, while ignoring the more esoteric, aesthetic, subjective, and non-quantifiable qualities of the game—those qualities, for instance, that were highlighted in Ken Burns's recent PBS documentary, *Baseball*. If a characteristic is not measurable, it has no value in Rotisserie baseball.

The third dimension of McDonaldization is *predictability*. People in a rationalized society feel the need to know what to expect at all times. In the fast-food restaurant, for example, a customer knows that a Big Mac will be the same at a McDonald's in Alabama as it will in Alaska or even Argentina. In fact, Ritzer argues that much of the success of *USA Today*—McPaper, as it was popularly dubbed shortly after its launch—is its predictability, as the structure and makeup of the paper is highly predictable from one day to the next. Unlike a newspaper like the *New York Times* or the *Wall Street Journal,* where feature stories have depth and substance, the stories in *USA Today* are predictably short and easy to digest (news McNuggets, if you will). Similarly, Rotisserie baseball also seeks predictability in determining specific value for each player in several statistical categories. Theoretically, the owners who can most effectively predict player performance within the defined categories will select the most productive and ultimately successful teams.

The fourth dimension of McDonaldization is increased *control* by the institution over the individual, and replacement of human with non-human technology. Ritzer illustrates that McDonaldization involves the search for the means to exert increasing control over both employees and customers. While this institutional control seeks to maximize efficiency, predictability, and quantification, the primary consequence is that the rational system becomes a dehumanizing system, which, as Ritzer contends, epitomizes the irrationality of rationality.

Ritzer explains that the consequences of McDonaldization may depend on an individual's attitude toward the Iron Cage: his/her ability to navigate through the increasingly confining web of rationalized institutions. Some people evidently like a McDonaldized world and encourage its continued expansion throughout society. Others may like certain aspects of McDonaldization but seek to escape its bars whenever possible, often through non-rationalized forms of leisure and recreation. There are still others for whom McDonaldization truly is an Iron Cage, from which there are few, if any, escape routes. Ritzer suggests that the secret to coping with McDonaldization is to take advantage of the best that the McDonaldized world has to offer without becoming imprisoned by that world. Essentially, to survive in a McDonaldized society, as the walls of rationalization begin closing in, individuals must find some outlet to create a non-rationalized niche for oneself.

Drawing on these ideas, I would argue that Rotisserie baseball offers its "owners" the best of both worlds as Ritzer defines them: an irresistibly McDonaldized subculture that offers efficiency, quantification, and predictability, while simultaneously allowing its participants the real opportunity to apply their baseball knowledge in ways that let them retain their perception of control and feelings of self-efficacy. Rotisserie baseball thus provides for the final two individual and community needs, not afforded by merely being a spectator, that Thomas argues are critical if one is to feel a sense of balance in his/her life. Rotisserie baseball, consequently, may properly be seen as an essential contributor to one's ability to survive in a McDonaldized society.

METHODOLOGY

In order to address some of these theoretical issues, I developed a multifaceted questionnaire that was designed to obtain both relevant demographic information as well as information pertaining to owners' involvement in Rotisserie/fantasy baseball. Of 130 questionnaires mailed to Rotisserie owners, 111 were returned by the stipulated deadline (an 85% return rate). Rotisserie owners were solicited in essentially two ways. First, I posted a note on the fantasy baseball network on the Internet and received over 70 responses to my note by e-mail. I then mailed each of the respondents a survey with a self-addressed stamped envelope. Second, I solicited owners of the league I am involved with and also owners in other leagues in an informal grapevine manner. Therefore, while I found some interesting results in my study—as will soon be displayed—these results are suggestive rather than definitive, and in no way generalizable—absent corroboration by a more rigorously constructed survey—to a general Rotisserie/fantasy baseball community.

RESULTS

1. Number of years in your league: 5
2. Number of leagues involved in: 1.4
3. Particpation in other fantasy sports leagues:

Sport	Number of Respondents	Percentage
Football	29	26%
Basketball	11	10%
Hockey	4	3%
Auto Racing	1	<1%

4. Type of Fantasy Rotisserie League:

   Traditional Rotisserie: 69%
   Non-traditional Rotisserie: 25%
   E-mail League: 9%
   Rotisserie Ultra: 14%

5. Characteristics of League:

   Auction: 72%
   Draft: 29%
   Retention of Players: 53%

6. League Entry Fee:

   Mean (average) $88
   Median (point where half under and half over) $58
   Minimum $0
   Maximum $500

7. First-Place Winnings:

   Mean $572
   Median $350
   Minimum $0
   Maximum $3,500

On a scale of 1 to 6, with 1 being low and 6 being high, indicate how you would rate yourself on each of the following:
   (Note: mean response reported)

8. Interest in major league baseball: 5.4
9. Extent to which you influence the success of your Rotisserie/fantasy team: 4.7
10. Extent to which your involvement in Rotisserie/fantasy baseball conflicts with your work/school time: 2.4

11. Extent to which you are satisfied with your job: 4.4
12. Interest in your favorite major league team: 4.7
13. Overall knowledge of baseball: 5.3
14. Extent to which you influence events in your daily life: 4.7
15. Extent that involvement in Rotisserie/fantasy baseball conflicts with time spent with family/spouse/significant other: 2.1
16. Extent to which you control your performance at work/school: 4.8
17. On the same scale of 1 to 6, rate each of the following according to its contribution to your success in Rotisserie/fantasy baseball:

    a. Luck 4.2
    b. Ability 4.6
    c. Effort 4.1

18. On a scale of 1 to 6, with 1 being low and 6 being high, indicate the degree to which you like the following aspects of Rotisserie/fantasy baseball:

a.	Gambling/risk	3.1
b.	Increases interest in baseball	4.9
c.	Competition	4.9
d.	Opportunity to make money	2.5
e.	Opportunity to apply baseball knowledge	4.5
f.	Entertainment	5.3
g.	Draft/auction of players	4.9
h.	Friends in league	4.6
i.	Increases knowledge of baseball	4.4
j.	Trading players	3.9
k.	Communication with other Rotisserie/ fantasy players	3.9

19. Rank of characteristics of Rotisserie/fantasy baseball in order of preference:

	Characteristic	Number of times mentioned as one of three most important	% of total
1.	Entertainment	62	56%
2.	Increases interest in baseball	50	45%
3.	Competition	49	44%
4.	Draft/auction of players	43	39%
5.	Friends in league	39	35%
6.	Opportunity to apply baseball knowledge	30	27%
7.	Increases knowledge of baseball	25	23%
8.	Gambling/risk	9	8%
9.	Trading players	8	7%
10.	Communication with other Rotisserie/fantasy players	7	6%
11.	Opportunity to make money	4	3%

20. Number of hours per week spent on Rotisserie/fantasy baseball:

Hours/Week	Number of Respondents	Percentage
< 5	29	26%
5–10	42	38%
10–15	27	24%
15–20	7	6%
> 20	6	5%

21. How has becoming a Rotisserie owner affected your interest in your favorite major league team?

Interest +/-	Number of Respondents	Percentage
Significant increase	6	5%
Slight increase	26	23%
No change	50	45%
Slight decrease	20	18%
Significant decrease	9	8%

22. How has becoming a Rotisserie owner affected your interest in major league baseball:

Interest +/-	Number of Respondents	Percentage
Significant increase	61	55%
Slight increase	37	33%
Stay same	11	10%
Slight decrease	2	2%
Significant decrease	0	0%

23. How would you best describe your current athletic involvement:

Response	Number of Respondents	Percentage
None	1	1%
Spectator only	24	21%
Weekend athlete	37	33%
Organized rec league	26	23%
Competitive league	23	21%

24. Use of personal computer for Rotisserie/fantasy baseball: 78%

   a. Use an on-line service to obtain daily baseball information 39%
   b. Use a program to keep track of players for use during draft/auction 33%
   c. Use an on-line service to communicate with other Rotisserie/fantasy players 37%

25. Rate your use of the following publications in selecting and managing.
   1 = Never 2 = Sometimes 3 = Often 4 = Every issue/edition

	Publication	Mean
a.	USA Today	2.5
b.	Baseball Weekly	3.1
c.	The Sporting News	1.4
d.	Sports Illustrated	1.4

e.	Fantasy Baseball	1.5	
f.	Rotisserie League Baseball	1.7	
g.	Baseball America	1.5	

26. Gender:

Male	108	97%
Female	3	3%

27. Age:

Mean	30 yrs
Median	27 yrs
Range	20 yrs to 62 yrs

28. Race:

African American	2	2%
Hispanic	1	1%
Asian/Asian American	5	5%
Caucasian	101	90%
Native American	1	1%

29. Highest Level of Education Completed:

1.	Grade School	1	1%
2.	Some High School	0	0%
3.	High School Graduate	0	0%
4.	Some College	20	18%
5.	College Graduate	35	31%
6.	Some Graduate School	17	15%
7.	Graduate Degree	37	33%

30. Annual Household Income:

1.	< $15,000	3	3%
2.	$15,000–25,000	4	4%
3.	$25,000–50,000	42	38%
4.	$50,000–75,000	24	21%
5.	$75,000–100,000	20	18%
6.	$100,000–150,000	8	7%
7.	> $150,000	7	6%

DISCUSSION OF SELECTED RESULTS

The demographic information paints a relatively clear portrait of the Rotisserie/fantasy baseball owner. According to this sample, the typical Rotisserie/fantasy owner is a male, in his late 20s to early 30s, is a college graduate, in a white-collar occupation, with a household income of around $50,000 a year. The typical owner has been involved in his league for around five years and is involved in 1.4 baseball leagues. If he is involved in another fantasy sport it is most likely football.

I cannot stress enough that this profile only applies to the sample in this study. Since the sample was not randomly selected, which would be difficult for a study of this type, the characteristics of the identified may not reflect those of other Rotisserie/fantasy players. This sample was certainly a predominately Caucasian, upper-middle-class selection, potentially skewed due to the fact that this type of sample would be more likely to have access to a computer and e-mail, to receive my subject request. By comparison, for instance, Ron Shandler, who publishes the newsletter *Baseball Forecaster*, found that the average age of his subscribers in 1994 was 39 years. Consistent with my findings, Shandler also found that the most widely used sources of information are *Baseball Weekly* and *USA Today*.

In this study, two findings in particular emerge as the most significant. Both findings are related to owner motivation for involvement in Rotisserie/fantasy baseball. I hypothesized in the first portion of this chapter that certain needs—namely, perception of control and self-efficacy—were not being fulfilled in the context of traditional fandom. While some press attention has been given to the gambling aspect of Rotisserie/fantasy baseball, my feeling has been that the gambling/risk aspect has been overplayed. In fact, in this study, four of the top five reasons given for involvement in Rotisserie/fantasy baseball were items relating to perception of control and self-efficacy. Gambling/risk and the opportunity to make money were eighth and eleventh (last), respectively. Another explanation about the low rating for gambling/risk may be that the results are a function of the sample, who likely have other income sources and for whom therefore the gambling/risk aspects would be secondary.

The second significant finding lends additional credence to the theoretical explanation offered earlier. While 71% of the respondents claimed that their interest in their favorite major league baseball team has *stayed the same or decreased*, more than 88% of the respondents claimed that their interest in baseball in general has *increased* (either slightly or significantly). This finding implies that Rotisserie/fantasy owners have replaced (or at least decreased) the emotional attachment they feel for their favorite team with a deeper involvement for their Rotisserie/fantasy team as they have been empowered with the perception that their knowledge can now be tested against others and that this knowledge will ultimately affect the performance of their Rotisserie/fantasy team.

While only a preliminary study, this article offers some initial insights into the world of Rotisserie/fantasy baseball owners. At this writing, however, the baseball strike has yet to be settled and the 1995 season is still in doubt. An interesting follow-up study would be to determine the effects of the strike on Rotisserie/fantasy baseball. Maybe for next year's edition.

Comments or questions can be sent to:

Andrew Stavisky
Department of Kinesiology
College of Health and Human Performance
University of Maryland
College Park, MD 20742-2611
e-mail to: Stavman@wam.umd.edu

The Rules, Simplified

1. Rotisserie League teams are made up of real, live major league baseball players who are selected at an auction draft that takes place at the beginning of the season (typically on the first weekend following Opening Day).

2. Each team in a Rotisserie League is composed of 23 players taken from the active rosters of National or American League teams. A Rotisserie League drawn from National League or American League players should have 12 teams. You can, however, have fewer teams.

3. A team consists of five outfielders, two catchers, one second baseman, one shortstop, one middle infielder (either 2B or SS), one first baseman, one third baseman, one corner man (1B or 3B), one utility man (NL) or designated hitter (AL), and nine pitchers.

4. Players are purchased at an open auction. Spending is limited to $260 per team. (If you don't want to use money, call them units or pocorobas or whatever. The point is resource allocation.) Teams may spend less. The first bidder opens the auction with a minimum bid of $1 for any player. The bidding then proceeds around the room (at minimum increments of $1) until only one bidder is left. The process is repeated, with successive owners introducing players to be bid on, until every team has a complement of 23 players.

5. A player is eligible to be drafted for any position at which he appeared in 20 or more games the preceding year. If he did not appear in 20 games at any one position, he is eligible for the position at which he appeared the most times. Once the season starts, a player qualifies for a position by playing it once. Multiple eligibility is okay.

6. Trading is permissible from Auction Draft Day until midnight August 31. After every trade, both teams must be whole—that is, they must have the same number of active players at each position that they had before the trade.

7. If a major league player is put on the disabled list, sent to the minors, traded to the other league, or released, he may be replaced by a player from the free agent pool of unowned talent. Replacement must be made by position. The original player may either be released or placed on his Rotisserie team's reserve list. A team may not release, reserve, or waive a player without replacing him with another active player.

8. Cumulative team performance is tabulated in four offensive and four pitching categories:
   - Composite batting average (BA)
   - Total home runs (HR)

- Total runs batted in (RBI)
- Total stolen bases (SB)
- Composite earned run average (ERA)
- Total wins (W)
- Total saves (S)
- Composite ratio: walks (BB) + hits (H) ÷ innings pitched (IP)

9. Teams are ranked from first to last in each of the eight categories. For example, in a 12-team league, the first-place team receives 12 points, the second-place team 11 points, on down to one point for last place. The team with the most points wins the pennant.

10. Prize money is distributed as follows: 50% for first place, 20% for second, 15% for third, 10% for fourth, and 5% for fifth. Even more important, the owner of the winning team receives a bottle of Yoo-Hoo—poured over his/her head. (See Chapter 8, Postgame Shower, pages 315–319.)

● ● ●

"Do I have to play for money?" No. We do, but unlike the big league version, Rotisserie League Baseball can be played for very little money, or none at all. You can play for pennies, Cracker Jack prizes, or nothing at all and still have fun. Just be sure to keep the ratio of "acquisition units" to players at 260:23 for each team on Auction Draft Day.

"What do I do if it's May 15 and I've just gotten around to reading this book? Wait till next year?" Absolutely not! That's second-division thinking! You can start anytime! Put your league together, hold your auction draft, and deduct all stats that accrue prior to that glorious day. Next year, start from scratch.

The rest of your questions are dealt with in the pages that follow. We hope. If not, write us c/o **Rotisserie League Baseball Association, 370 Seventh Avenue, Suite 312, New York, NY 10001**. Or call at **212-695-3463**. We'll do our best to get you playing what we still modestly call The Greatest Game for Baseball Fans Since Baseball.

ROTI·STATS
THE BEST STATS SERVICE IN THE GAME

CALL 800-884-7684

2

Scouting Report

1995 Player Ratings

What the hell, it probably wouldn't have turned out to be much of a season anyway. Matt Williams would have ended up with just 60 homers. Frank Thomas would have lost the Triple Crown on the final day when Joe Carter knocked in 7 runs. Cal Ripken would have come down with a hangnail and missed a game. Tony Gwynn would have finished at .3994.

Ruin the summer? No way. The strike gave us plenty of time to screen all those World Cup soccer matches we taped. How about that 0–0 trouncing Brazil gave Italy in the final! Wow, what a game! Don't tell us the ball isn't juiced.

We caught up on Nancy Kerrigan's latest career moves, learned Italian, and began the countdown to the 1995 Stanley Cup playoffs. (Go, Canucks!) We read David Halberstam's new book (*October 1964*) about baseball's good old days, *i.e.,* when they played games after August 12. And we watched Beloved Founder and Former Commissioner for Life Dan Okrent do his star turn in Ken Burns's smash hit documentary, *Baseball*.

We've got lives. We don't need Jerry Reinsdorf's permission to lead them.

But that's all blood under the bridge. Now we have more important things to worry about—namely, the 1995 Rotisserie auction draft. The salary projections here are based on a zero-sum game—that is, a start-from-scratch auction draft. If yours is a continuing league and you carry over a certain number of players from year to year, your auction day prices will be skewed by the quality and quantity of available talent. If all but a handful of ace starters are being kept, for example, the starting pitchers who are in the draft will be pricey. Our salary projections will be less useful in such situations, and you should draw more heavily—as you undoubtedly already do—on the raw (and cooked) data we also provide.

Also note that players traded from one league to the other during the season appear in the league in which they finished the year. Thus, look for Wes Chamberlain among AL outfielders and Paul Quantrill among NL relief pitchers.

As veteran readers may know, the original Rotisserians are hidebound, dyed-in-the-polyester National Leaguers. So, to assist us with American League evaluations and salaries this year, we signed free agent and former

RLBA batboy John Hassan. In his capacity as ridiculously underpaid consultant, John bears full responsibility for all errors in judgment, inaccurate projections, and wildly out-of-line salaries in the American League sections. Thanks, John.

Here you get four years of major league stats (where applicable) for about 550 position players and pitchers, along with substantive (and sometimes silly) observations that, in the best of all possible worlds, will be of some small benefit as you devise your own winning auction draft strategy. Immediately after the 1995 Player Ratings, we present in Chapter 3 our newest, biggest, better-than-ever edition of Rotisserie Stat-Pak, which gives you lists of last season's best (and worst) categories in all the Rotisserie scoring categories (and then some). The Stat-Pak provides solid, objective data that can be used as an antidote to the subjective musings and off-the-wall opinions in this chapter.

Happy Yoo-Hoo!

1994—THE UNCUT VERSION

For the fifth consecutive season, STATS, Inc. is responsible for the numbers in this chapter, for the Rotisserie Stat-Pak in Chapter 3, and for the final 1994 averages at the end of the book. The STATS team, with John Dewan at the helm and Bob Mecca batting cleanup, is also responsible for a lot of the fancy number-crunching in *Sports Illustrated* and *USA Today*, and we're honored that they're playing on our side as well. Check out page 214 for a full list of their publications and services, all of which will help you solve the mysteries of life.

In years past, the last line of numbers for each position player summarized his preceding four seasons in a "Seasonal Notation," a device invented by the great Bill James to express a player's performance over several seasons in a way that is immediately comprehensible. In essence, Seasonal Notation shows what a player does every 162 games.

This year, with last season so cruelly snatched away from us two-thirds of the way through, we decided to do something a little different. We asked STATS, Inc. to work out computer projections for 1994 *as if The Strike had never happened*. We wanted to know whether Matt Williams or Junior or somebody else would have hit 62 home runs. We wanted to know whether Tony Gwynn hung in to hit .400. We wanted to know if the Big Hurt won the Triple Crown. And now we do: the STATS, Inc. *projections* for 1994 appear in the last line of stats for each player in this chapter.

Pure fantasy? Hey, that's the name of *our* game.

HITS. RUNS. NO ERRORS.
ROTI•STATS
CALL 800-884-7684

Behind the Plate

NATIONAL LEAGUE

Catchers
pp. 33–46

Corners
pp. 46–65

Infield
pp. 66–85

Outfield
pp. 85–115

DH
pp. 115–119

Starters
pp. 119–155

Relievers
pp. 155–187

BRAD AUSMUS   Age 25/R $4

The Padres like his ability to handle pitching. That's all well and good, but we prefer the quiet glimpses of power he's begun to show.

Year	Team	Lg.	Pos.	G	AB	R	H	HR	RBI	SB	BA
1993	San Diego	NL	C	49	160	18	41	5	12	2	.256
1994	San Diego	NL	C	101	327	45	82	7	24	5	.251
1994 PROJECTION				118	387	51	96	8	29	5	.248

DARREN DAULTON   Age 33/L $22

No, 1994 will not go down as Darren's favorite year. There was the nasty divorce from his pinup wife, whose scantily clad image stared at him throughout spring training from Hooter's sign on the right-center-field fence at Jack Russell Field in Clearwater. Later, a foul ball broke his collarbone. Next, a malignant skin growth was removed from his stomach. Then, during a rather heated "negotiating" session he offered to punch out owners' hit man Dick Ravitch. Finally, to cap it off, he had his seventh knee operation in the last eight years. Never has Satchell Paige's advice about never looking back made more sense. And 15 dingers in 257 AB tells us he still has plenty to look forward to.

Year	Team	Lg.	Pos.	G	AB	R	H	HR	RBI	SB	BA
1991	Philadelphia	NL	C	89	285	36	56	12	42	5	.196
1992	Philadelphia	NL	C	145	485	80	131	27	109	11	.270
1993	Philadelphia	NL	C	147	510	90	131	24	105	5	.257
1994	Philadelphia	NL	C	69	257	43	77	15	56	4	.300
1994 PROJECTION				69	257	43	77	15	56	4	.300

BRIAN DORSETT   Age 33/R $1

We've always admired a 5/1 dinger-to-dollar ratio, especially in our backup backstop.

Year	Team	Lg.	Pos.	G	AB	R	H	HR	RBI	SB	BA
1991	San Diego	NL	1B	11	12	0	1	0	1	0	.083
1993	Cincinnati	NL	C	25	63	7	16	2	12	0	.254
1994	Cincinnati	NL	C	76	216	21	53	5	26	0	.245
1994 PROJECTION				99	272	26	66	7	34	0	.243

TONY EUSEBIO   Age 27/R $4

Started last season as Houston's #3 catcher, moved to #2 when Eddie Taubensee was traded to the Reds, and should begin this year as #1. Nice career arc.

Year	Team	Lg.	Pos.	G	AB	R	H	HR	RBI	SB	BA
1991	Houston	NL	C	10	19	4	2	0	0	0	.105
1994	Houston	NL	C	55	159	18	47	5	30	0	.296
1994 PROJECTION				92	269	30	74	8	47	0	.275

DARRIN FLETCHER
Age 28/L   **$9**

Amid the flash and dash of all that young Expos talent, this guy quietly established himself as a solid, productive hitter. But any Expos contract is subject to being dumped at any time, and there are many NL scouts who think Fletcher would not be the same player away from Montreal. We are required to make this disclosure under Canada's consumer awareness regulations.

Year	Team	Lg.	Pos.	G	AB	R	H	HR	RBI	SB	BA
1991	Philadelphia	NL	C	46	136	5	31	1	12	0	.228
1992	Montreal	NL	C	83	222	13	54	2	26	0	.243
1993	Montreal	NL	C	133	396	33	101	9	60	0	.255
1994	Montreal	NL	C	94	285	28	74	10	57	0	.260
1994 PROJECTION				122	365	38	94	14	75	0	.258

JOE GIRARDI
Age 30/R   **$2**

High marks for pluck. Low marks for power.

Year	Team	Lg.	Pos.	G	AB	R	H	HR	RBI	SB	BA
1991	Chicago	NL	C	21	47	3	9	0	6	0	.191
1992	Chicago	NL	C	91	270	19	73	1	12	0	.270
1993	Colorado	NL	C	86	310	35	90	3	31	6	.290
1994	Colorado	NL	C	93	330	47	91	4	34	3	.276
1994 PROJECTION				134	473	63	134	5	43	4	.283

CARLOS HERNANDEZ
Age 27/R   **$1**

Only if you also own Mike Piazza.

Year	Team	Lg.	Pos.	G	AB	R	H	HR	RBI	SB	BA
1991	Los Angeles	NL	C	15	14	1	3	0	1	1	.214
1992	Los Angeles	NL	C	69	173	11	45	3	17	0	.260
1993	Los Angeles	NL	C	50	99	6	25	2	7	0	.253
1994	Los Angeles	NL	C	32	64	6	14	2	6	0	.219
1994 PROJECTION				47	101	9	25	3	8	0	.248

TODD HUNDLEY
Age 25/B   **$7**

As you wind your merry way through these astute observations, you will encounter occasional mention of juiced baseballs, awful pitching, a shrunken strike zone, corked bats, and other assorted explanations of why certain suspect hitters put up such gaudy offensive numbers last season. This started out to be the first such mention. Have you ever seen this guy's swing? It's a big, looping uppercut that reminds you of Bill Murray in *Caddyshack*. But two straight years of double-digit dingers from a guy who's still just 25 have to be taken seriously.

Year	Team	Lg.	Pos.	G	AB	R	H	HR	RBI	SB	BA
1991	New York	NL	C	21	60	5	8	1	7	0	.133
1992	New York	NL	C	123	358	32	75	7	32	3	.209
1993	New York	NL	C	130	417	40	95	11	53	1	.228
1994	New York	NL	C	91	291	45	69	16	42	2	.237
1994 PROJECTION				126	395	57	89	19	51	2	.225

BRIAN JOHNSON   **Age 27/R**   **$1**

Of the two players who wear the Tools of Ignorance for the Padres, Ausmus is a Dartmouth graduate and Johnson went to Stanford. Suppose this says something about standards in higher education today?

Year	Team	Lg.	Pos.	G	AB	R	H	HR	RBI	SB	BA
1994	San Diego	NL	C	36	93	7	23	3	16	0	.247
1994 PROJECTION				64	186	21	47	7	31	0	.253

CHARLES JOHNSON   **Age 23/R**   **$7**

Don't mix up your Johnsons going into the auction draft: *Charles* is the one you want. Based on the little taste of his potential he showed Miami last year—four taters in 11 AB—we calculate that if he gets just 450 AB this season that he (*Charles Johnson*) will hit, uh . . . *164* homers? Could that be right? Probably not, but he (*Charles Edward Johnson, Jr.*) is the real deal. We think he's got a chance to be the next Mike Piazza. We just don't have the guts to price him accordingly.

Year	Team	Lg.	Pos.	G	AB	R	H	HR	RBI	SB	BA
1994	Florida	NL	C	4	11	5	5	1	4	0	.455
1994 PROJECTION				28	84	9	16	2	11	1	.190

MIKE LIEBERTHAL   **Age 23/R**   **$1**

Given Daulton's medical record, Lieberthal is worth a buck or two.

Year	Team	Lg.	Pos.	G	AB	R	H	HR	RBI	SB	BA
1994	Philadelphia	NL	C	24	79	6	21	1	5	0	.266
1994 PROJECTION				59	203	16	47	3	21	0	.232

JAVY LOPEZ   **Age 24/R**   **$12**

Major league pitching overmatched him at times last season, but he's on his way to becoming one of baseball's top catchers.

Year	Team	Lg.	Pos.	G	AB	R	H	HR	RBI	SB	BA
1992	Atlanta	NL	C	9	16	3	6	0	2	0	.375
1993	Atlanta	NL	C	8	16	1	6	1	2	0	.375
1994	Atlanta	NL	C	80	277	27	68	13	35	0	.245
1994 PROJECTION				113	403	45	95	19	50	0	.236

KIRT MANWARING   **Age 29/R**   **$3**

Took a step backward at the plate last year, metaphorically speaking, to produce what may have been the quietest .250 BA in baseball.

Year	Team	Lg.	Pos.	G	AB	R	H	HR	RBI	SB	BA
1991	San Francisco	NL	C	67	178	16	40	0	19	1	.225
1992	San Francisco	NL	C	109	349	24	85	4	26	2	.244
1993	San Francisco	NL	C	130	432	48	119	5	49	1	.275
1994	San Francisco	NL	C	97	316	30	79	1	29	1	.250
1994 PROJECTION				139	460	40	98	2	41	1	.213

Catchers
pp. 33–46

Corners
pp. 46–65

Infield
pp. 66–85

Outfield
pp. 85–115

DH
pp. 115–119

Starters
pp. 119–155

Relievers
pp. 155–187

TERRY McGRIFF   Age 31/R $1

No.

Year	Team	Lg.	Pos.	G	AB	R	H	HR	RBI	SB	BA
1993	Florida	NL	C	3	7	0	0	0	0	0	0.000
1994	St. Louis	NL	C	42	114	10	25	0	13	0	.219
1994 PROJECTION				66	149	13	34	0	18	0	.228

CHARLIE O'BRIEN   Age 33/R $2

Hit as many HR last year as in three previous seasons combined, but keep in mind that the at-bats will diminish as Lopez continues to improve.

Year	Team	Lg.	Pos.	G	AB	R	H	HR	RBI	SB	BA
1991	New York	NL	C	69	168	16	31	2	14	0	.185
1992	New York	NL	C	68	156	15	33	2	13	0	.212
1993	New York	NL	C	67	188	15	48	4	23	1	.255
1994	Atlanta	NL	C	51	152	24	37	8	28	0	.243
1994 PROJECTION				71	216	32	55	10	36	0	.255

JOE OLIVER   Age 29/R $5

Mysterious ailment stopped his streak of double-digit HR seasons at three, then the Reds cut him loose. Maybe they see more in the Taubensee-Dorsett tandem than we do. If he's healthy, look for a comeback ... somewhere.

Year	Team	Lg.	Pos.	G	AB	R	H	HR	RBI	SB	BA
1991	Cincinnati	NL	C	94	269	21	58	11	41	0	.216
1992	Cincinnati	NL	C	143	485	42	131	10	57	2	.270
1993	Cincinnati	NL	C	139	482	40	115	14	75	0	.239
1994	Cincinnati	NL	C	6	19	1	4	1	5	0	.211
1994 PROJECTION				6	19	1	4	1	5	0	.211

TOM PAGNOZZI   Age 32/R $6

Finished strong after fulfilling his cutomary stint on the DL. When a player his age has back-to-back seasons shortened by injuries we get a little skittish.

Year	Team	Lg.	Pos.	G	AB	R	H	HR	RBI	SB	BA
1991	St. Louis	NL	C	140	459	38	121	2	57	9	.264
1992	St. Louis	NL	C	139	485	33	121	7	44	2	.249
1993	St. Louis	NL	C	92	330	31	85	7	41	1	.258
1994	St. Louis	NL	C	70	243	21	66	7	40	0	.272
1994 PROJECTION				89	306	27	80	8	46	0	.261

MARK PARENT   Age 33/R $1

The archetypal $1 catcher. Always has been, always will be.

Year	Team	Lg.	Pos.	G	AB	R	H	HR	RBI	SB	BA
1991	Texas	AL	C	3	1	0	0	0	0	0	0.000
1992	Baltimore	AL	C	17	34	4	8	2	4	0	.235
1993	Baltimore	AL	C	22	54	7	14	4	12	0	.259
1994	Chicago	NL	C	44	99	8	26	3	16	0	.263
1994 PROJECTION				64	144	12	39	4	19	0	.271

LANCE PARRISH   Age 38/R $1

Of the three catchers in baseball history with more lifetime home runs than Parrish, two are already in the Hall of Fame (Johnny Bench, Yogi Berra)

---

and one is a lock to be elected as soon as he is eligible (Carlton Fisk). Pretty good company Mr. Parrish has been keeping.

Catchers
pp. 33–46

Corners
pp. 46–65

Infield
pp. 66–85

Outfield
pp. 85–115

DH
pp. 115–119

Starters
pp. 119–155

Relievers
pp. 155–187

Year	Team	Lg.	Pos.	G	AB	R	H	HR	RBI	SB	BA
1991	California	AL	C	119	402	38	87	19	51	0	.216
1992	California	AL	C	24	83	7	19	4	11	0	.229
1992	Seattle	AL	C	69	192	19	45	8	21	1	.234
1993	Cleveland	AL	C	10	20	2	4	1	2	1	.200
1994	Pittsburgh	NL	C	40	126	10	34	3	16	1	.270
1994 PROJECTION				62	186	18	51	4	23	1	.274

MIKE PIAZZA   Age 26/R $30

You don't need us to tell you to get a home equity loan, sell the kids, bounce checks, do whatever it takes to grab the best offensive catcher since Johnny Bench. But you may need us to tell you the tale of his millionaire dad, Vince, whom baseball stopped from buying the Giants and moving them to St. Petersburg because of mysterious "security" reasons, whereupon Vince sued baseball for $280 million. And we can also tell you that Vince's lawyer related in court the story of how Marge Schott, upon meeting Piazza's dad for the first time, exclaimed with that girlish charm of hers, "A guy named Vince? What are you, the Mafia or something?" Chalk up another ethnic insult to baseball's league leader in that category.

Year	Team	Lg.	Pos.	G	AB	R	H	HR	RBI	SB	BA
1992	Los Angeles	NL	C	21	69	5	16	1	7	0	.232
1993	Los Angeles	NL	C	149	547	81	174	35	112	3	.318
1994	Los Angeles	NL	C	107	405	64	129	24	92	1	.319
1994 PROJECTION				149	555	85	179	32	127	1	.323

TODD PRATT   Age 28/R $1

Given Daulton's medical record, Pratt is worth a buck or two.

Year	Team	Lg.	Pos.	G	AB	R	H	HR	RBI	SB	BA
1992	Philadelphia	NL	C	16	46	6	13	2	10	0	.283
1993	Philadelphia	NL	C	33	87	8	25	5	13	0	.287
1994	Philadelphia	NL	C	28	102	10	20	2	9	0	.196
1994 PROJECTION				54	165	18	31	4	14	0	.188

JEFF REED   Age 32/L $1

Proof positive that the ball is not juiced.

Year	Team	Lg.	Pos.	G	AB	R	H	HR	RBI	SB	BA
1991	Cincinnati	NL	C	91	270	20	72	3	31	0	.267
1992	Cincinnati	NL	C	15	25	2	4	0	2	0	.160
1993	San Francisco	NL	C	66	119	10	31	6	12	0	.261
1994	San Francisco	NL	C	50	103	11	18	1	7	0	.175
1994 PROJECTION				61	118	13	23	1	10	0	.195

BENITO SANTIAGO   Age 30/R $6

Woulda-coulda-shoulda been a big hero in south Florida, but now the mercurial Sr. Santiago will pack up and move on to make room for Charles Johnson, who one scout said looked like "a man among boys" in Double-A last season. Wherever he ends up, Benito will be worth a modest investment, because his offensive production still puts most big league catchers to shame.

Year	Team	Lg.	Pos.	G	AB	R	H	HR	RBI	SB	BA
1991	San Diego	NL	C	152	580	60	155	17	87	8	.267
1992	San Diego	NL	C	106	386	37	97	10	42	2	.251
1993	Florida	NL	C	139	469	49	108	13	50	10	.230
1994	Florida	NL	C	101	337	35	92	11	41	1	.273
1994 PROJECTION				123	408	40	104	12	45	1	.255

SCOTT SERVAIS   Age 27/R $4

The trade of Eddie Taubensee to the Reds seemed to have opened the door to full-time service by Scott, but Tony Eusebio may slam it shut.

Year	Team	Lg.	Pos.	G	AB	R	H	HR	RBI	SB	BA
1991	Houston	NL	C	16	37	0	6	0	6	0	.162
1992	Houston	NL	C	77	205	12	49	0	15	0	.239
1993	Houston	NL	C	85	258	24	63	11	32	0	.244
1994	Houston	NL	C	78	251	27	49	9	41	0	.195
1994 PROJECTION				103	299	32	59	9	41	0	.197

DON SLAUGHT   Age 36/R $3

Long one of our favorites. But Sluggo managed just 9 extra-base hits last year, his RBI total almost fell off the charts, and if he were any slower getting down the line, he'd be going backwards. Maybe he was pining for Bonds, Bonilla, Drabek, Smiley, LaValliere, and all the other departed warriors from those great Pirates teams of not so long ago. We were.

Year	Team	Lg.	Pos.	G	AB	R	H	HR	RBI	SB	BA
1991	Pittsburgh	NL	C	77	220	19	65	1	29	1	.295
1992	Pittsburgh	NL	C	87	255	26	88	4	37	2	.345
1993	Pittsburgh	NL	C	116	377	34	113	10	55	2	.300
1994	Pittsburgh	NL	C	76	240	21	69	2	21	0	.287
1994 PROJECTION				114	348	37	100	5	38	0	.287

KELLY STINNETT   Age 25/R $1

Earth to Mets: Instead of trying to teach Kelly Stinnett to hit, why not teach Todd Hundley to catch?

Year	Team	Lg.	Pos.	G	AB	R	H	HR	RBI	SB	BA
1994	New York	NL	C	47	150	20	38	2	14	2	.253
1994 PROJECTION				70	223	29	56	4	21	4	.251

EDDIE TAUBENSEE | Age 26/L | $8

In Houston, he would always be The Guy We Got for Kenny Lofton. In Cincinnati, he can get on with his career. We predict a solid one, with several seasons of 12–15 HR and 50–60 RBI. And on off-days, he can drive up to Cleveland and watch The Guy They Got for Eddie Taubensee perform miracles.

Year	Team	Lg.	Pos.	G	AB	R	H	HR	RBI	SB	BA
1991	Cleveland	AL	C	26	66	5	16	0	8	0	.242
1992	Houston	NL	C	104	297	23	66	5	28	2	.222
1993	Houston	NL	C	94	288	26	72	9	42	1	.250
1994	Houston	NL	C	5	10	0	1	0	0	0	.100
1994	Cincinnati	NL	C	61	177	29	52	8	21	2	.294
1994 PROJECTION				103	304	46	88	12	38	3	.289

LENNY WEBSTER | Age 30/R | $1

Primer inter pares, which is Latin for "Better him than Dorsett, Hernandez, (Brian) Johnson, Lieberthal, McGriff, Parent, Pratt, or Reed."

Year	Team	Lg.	Pos.	G	AB	R	H	HR	RBI	SB	BA
1991	Minnesota	AL	C	18	34	7	10	3	8	0	.294
1992	Minnesota	AL	C	53	118	10	33	1	13	0	.280
1993	Minnesota	AL	C	49	106	14	21	1	8	1	.198
1994	Montreal	NL	C	57	143	13	39	5	23	0	.273
1994 PROJECTION				84	230	27	65	5	29	0	.283

RICK WILKINS | Age 27/L | $7

Ouch. We know he was a second-half hitter, and we didn't get really worried until after the All-Star break. But then we started hearing whispers from scouts that maybe 1993 was a fluke, and now we're as worried as the Cubs must be. He could be the biggest bargain in the auction draft.

Year	Team	Lg.	Pos.	G	AB	R	H	HR	RBI	SB	BA
1991	Chicago	NL	C	86	203	21	45	6	22	3	.222
1992	Chicago	NL	C	83	244	20	66	8	22	0	.270
1993	Chicago	NL	C	136	446	78	135	30	73	2	.303
1994	Chicago	NL	C	100	313	44	71	7	39	4	.227
1994 PROJECTION				141	451	58	103	10	57	4	.228

AMERICAN LEAGUE

SANDY ALOMAR, JR. | Age 28/R | $11

No jokes about him using Albert Belle's bats, no snide references to baseballs that contain helium, no sarcastic references to the awful pitching. One of these years, he's going to be healthy all season and blow past the overrated Pudge Rodriguez as the most valuable catcher in the league.

Year	Team	Lg.	Pos.	G	AB	R	H	HR	RBI	SB	BA
1991	Cleveland	AL	C	51	184	10	40	0	7	0	.217
1992	Cleveland	AL	C	89	299	22	75	2	26	3	.251
1993	Cleveland	AL	C	64	215	24	58	6	32	3	.270
1994	Cleveland	AL	C	80	292	44	84	14	43	8	.288
1994 PROJECTION				118	424	67	121	22	63	8	.285

Catchers
pp. 33–46

Corners
pp. 46–65

Infield
pp. 66–85

Outfield
pp. 85–115

DH
pp. 115–119

Starters
pp. 119–155

Relievers
pp. 155–187

DAMON BERRYHILL
Age 31/B $3

Roger Clemens liked pitching to him, which should clinch him a place in the Boston lineup, so long as the Red Sox don't go out and sign free agent Mike Macfarlane.

Year	Team	Lg.	Pos.	G	AB	R	H	HR	RBI	SB	BA
1991	Chicago	NL	C	62	159	13	30	5	14	1	.189
1991	Atlanta	NL	C	1	1	0	0	0	0	0	0.000
1992	Atlanta	NL	C	101	307	21	70	10	43	0	.228
1993	Atlanta	NL	C	115	335	24	82	8	43	0	.245
1994	Boston	AL	C	82	255	30	67	6	34	0	.263
1994 PROJECTION				123	411	50	105	10	51	0	.255

PAT BORDERS
Age 31/R $2

If you read this august journal every year, you know that Borders has been buried more times than Richard Nixon, only to come back from the grave. But this time, for both Pat and Dick alike, it's for keeps. After a Hall of Fame start, Carlos Delgado was sent back to the minors to learn how to catch and rediscover how to hit. He learned both lessons well, so Toronto watchers won't have Borders to kick around any more.

Year	Team	Lg.	Pos.	G	AB	R	H	HR	RBI	SB	BA
1991	Toronto	AL	C	105	291	22	71	5	36	0	.244
1992	Toronto	AL	C	138	480	47	116	13	53	1	.242
1993	Toronto	AL	C	138	488	38	124	9	55	2	.254
1994	Toronto	AL	C	85	295	24	73	3	26	1	.247
1994 PROJECTION				119	403	35	101	4	34	1	.251

JORGE FABREGAS
Age 25/L $1

Worth another look, even though—in a year when Eddie Gaedel would have probably hit a half-dozen homers—his utter lack of power was not awe-inspiring.

Year	Team	Lg.	Pos.	G	AB	R	H	HR	RBI	SB	BA
1994	California	AL	C	43	127	12	36	0	16	2	.283
1994 PROJECTION				43	127	12	36	0	16	2	.283

BILL HASELMAN
Age 28/R $1

The Strike obscured the amazing fact that Mariners catchers slugged a grand total of *five* home runs last year. Our advice? Avoid anyone from Seattle who wears a mask and chest protector.

Year	Team	Lg.	Pos.	G	AB	R	H	HR	RBI	SB	BA
1992	Seattle	AL	C	8	19	1	5	0	0	0	.263
1993	Seattle	AL	C	58	137	21	35	5	16	2	.255
1994	Seattle	AL	C	38	83	11	16	1	8	1	.193
1994 PROJECTION				39	85	11	17	1	8	1	.200

SCOTT HEMOND
Age 29/R $4

At times, he's a versatile and useful player. But be careful of drafting any Oakland A's if Tony LaRussa ends up managing somewhere else. Like Jim Leyland, LaRussa excels at bringing out the best in ordinary players.

Year	Team	Lg.	Pos.	G	AB	R	H	HR	RBI	SB	BA
1991	Oakland	AL	C	23	23	4	5	0	0	1	.217
1992	Oakland	AL	C	17	27	7	6	0	1	1	.222
1992	Chicago	AL	DH	8	13	1	3	0	1	0	.231
1993	Oakland	AL	C	91	215	31	55	6	26	14	.256
1994	Oakland	AL	C	91	198	23	44	3	20	7	.222
1994 PROJECTION				134	325	35	64	6	32	9	.197

Catchers
pp. 33–46

Corners
pp. 46–65

Infield
pp. 66–85

Outfield
pp. 85–115

DH
pp. 115–119

Starters
pp. 119–155

Relievers
pp. 155–187

CHRIS HOILES   Age 30/R $20

The only catcher in baseball history to receive Opening Day pitches from two different presidents (Bush in 1992, Clinton 1993). Average sagged a bit, and ribbie rate continues to lag, but he's still the best power bet among AL backstops.

Year	Team	Lg.	Pos.	G	AB	R	H	HR	RBI	SB	BA
1991	Baltimore	AL	C	107	341	36	83	11	31	0	.243
1992	Baltimore	AL	C	96	310	49	85	20	40	0	.274
1993	Baltimore	AL	C	126	419	80	130	29	82	1	.310
1994	Baltimore	AL	C	99	332	45	82	19	53	2	.247
1994 PROJECTION				144	491	75	141	31	80	2	.287

RON KARKOVICE   Age 31/R $5

Looks like 1993 was a career year rather than the beginning of a whole new ball game. White Sox must have seen it coming, because they drafted a bunch of catchers in last June's amateur draft.

Year	Team	Lg.	Pos.	G	AB	R	H	HR	RBI	SB	BA
1991	Chicago	AL	C	75	167	25	41	5	22	0	.246
1992	Chicago	AL	C	123	342	39	81	13	50	10	.237
1993	Chicago	AL	C	128	403	60	92	20	54	2	.228
1994	Chicago	AL	C	77	207	33	44	11	29	0	.213
1994 PROJECTION				95	260	38	58	12	35	1	.223

RANDY KNORR   Age 26/R $2

Delgado will almost definitely sit against most lefties, and Knorr can definitely hit them—.333 last year against portsiders. The best #2 catcher in the league, who might well be a #1 in a different uniform.

Year	Team	Lg.	Pos.	G	AB	R	H	HR	RBI	SB	BA
1991	Toronto	AL	C	3	1	0	0	0	0	0	0.000
1992	Toronto	AL	C	8	19	1	5	1	2	0	.263
1993	Toronto	AL	C	39	101	11	25	4	20	0	.248
1994	Toronto	AL	C	40	124	20	30	7	19	0	.242
1994 PROJECTION				52	162	22	39	9	23	0	.241

CHAD KREUTER   Age 30/B $1

Don't say we didn't warn you, right here, a year ago.

Year	Team	Lg.	Pos.	G	AB	R	H	HR	RBI	SB	BA
1991	Texas	AL	C	3	4	0	0	0	0	0	0.000
1992	Detroit	AL	C	67	190	22	48	2	16	0	.253
1993	Detroit	AL	C	119	374	59	107	15	51	2	.286
1994	Detroit	AL	C	65	170	17	38	1	19	0	.224
1994 PROJECTION				85	219	27	50	2	26	0	.228

MIKE LaVALLIERE   Age 34/L $2

The extra buck is for Spanky's positive effect on any clubhouse he enters, even a Rotisserie clubhouse.

Year	Team	Lg.	Pos.	G	AB	R	H	HR	RBI	SB	BA
1991	Pittsburgh	NL	C	108	336	25	97	3	41	2	.289
1992	Pittsburgh	NL	C	95	293	22	75	2	29	0	.256
1993	Pittsburgh	NL	C	1	5	0	1	0	0	0	.200
1993	Chicago	AL	C	37	97	6	25	0	8	0	.258
1994	Chicago	AL	C	59	139	6	39	1	24	0	.281
1994 PROJECTION				81	205	13	49	1	27	0	.239

JIM LEYRITZ   Age 31/R $21

One of his teammates looked at Leyritz styling around the batting cage last June and said, "He thinks he's Reggie Bleeping Jackson and Mel Bleeping Gibson rolled up into one. But the bleeper is one strong son of a bleeper." We think this probably means Leyritz won't be winning any Most Popular Bleeping Yankee awards anytime soon, at least not by a unanimous vote. No problem: he'll be welcome on our team, ego and all.

Year	Team	Lg.	Pos.	G	AB	R	H	HR	RBI	SB	BA
1991	New York	AL	3B	32	77	8	14	0	4	0	.182
1992	New York	AL	DH	63	144	17	37	7	26	0	.257
1993	New York	AL	1B	95	259	43	80	14	53	0	.309
1994	New York	AL	C	75	249	47	66	17	58	0	.265
1994 PROJECTION				103	346	64	101	25	84	0	.292

MIKE MACFARLANE   Age 30/R $13

Solid player who could be headed elsewhere. If it's Boston, as some of the rumors have it, then his power numbers will escalate significantly and make him a hero throughout New England.

Year	Team	Lg.	Pos.	G	AB	R	H	HR	RBI	SB	BA
1991	Kansas City	AL	C	84	267	34	74	13	41	1	.277
1992	Kansas City	AL	C	129	402	51	94	17	48	1	.234
1993	Kansas City	AL	C	117	388	55	106	20	67	2	.273
1994	Kansas City	AL	C	92	314	53	80	14	47	1	.255
1994 PROJECTION				133	463	69	111	20	74	1	.240

BRENT MAYNE   Age 26/L $2

And if Macfarlane does leave Kansas City, the guy with the movie star monicker will get back the job he lost to Macfarlane two years ago. This will not, however, make Mayne a hero throughout the Midwest.

Year	Team	Lg.	Pos.	G	AB	R	H	HR	RBI	SB	BA
1991	Kansas City	AL	C	85	231	22	58	3	31	2	.251
1992	Kansas City	AL	C	82	213	16	48	0	18	0	.225
1993	Kansas City	AL	C	71	205	22	52	2	22	3	.254
1994	Kansas City	AL	C	46	144	19	37	2	20	1	.257
1994 PROJECTION				55	171	21	42	2	22	1	.246

BOB MELVIN   Age 33/R $1

We're never exactly sure whose roster he is on—six teams in ten major league seasons, a different one each of the last four—but it's always somebody's. Try to make sure it's not *yours*.

Year	Team	Lg.	Pos.	G	AB	R	H	HR	RBI	SB	BA
1991	Baltimore	AL	C	79	228	11	57	1	23	0	.250
1992	Kansas City	AL	C	32	70	5	22	0	6	0	.314
1993	Boston	AL	C	77	176	13	39	3	23	0	.222
1994	New York	AL	C	9	14	2	4	1	3	0	.286
1994	Chicago	AL	C	11	19	3	3	0	1	0	.158
1994 PROJECTION				37	81	10	18	1	6	0	.222

GREG MYERS   Age 28/L $1

He's a left-handed-hitting catcher, so he'll probably play forever. Just not very well.

Year	Team	Lg.	Pos.	G	AB	R	H	HR	RBI	SB	BA
1991	Toronto	AL	C	107	309	25	81	8	36	0	.262
1992	Toronto	AL	C	22	61	4	14	1	13	0	.230
1992	California	AL	C	8	17	0	4	0	0	0	.235
1993	California	AL	C	108	290	27	74	7	40	3	.255
1994	California	AL	C	45	126	10	31	2	8	0	.246
1994 PROJECTION				79	249	19	55	5	22	0	.221

DAVE NILSSON   Age 25/L $12

We should probably cut that price back to $7, what with Milwaukee being a small-market team and all, but we think the best baseball player in Australian history is on the verge of becoming a big star here in the U.S.A.

Year	Team	Lg.	Pos.	G	AB	R	H	HR	RBI	SB	BA
1992	Milwaukee	AL	C	51	164	15	38	4	25	2	.232
1993	Milwaukee	AL	C	100	296	35	76	7	40	3	.257
1994	Milwaukee	AL	C	109	397	51	109	12	69	1	.275
1994 PROJECTION				149	544	73	159	16	93	2	.292

JUNIOR ORTIZ   Age 35/R $1

Believe us when we tell you that there is no more good-natured, unassuming, humble, straightforward, standup guy in baseball than the father of Junior Ortiz, Jr.'s. But being around all the egos and moods and personalities in the Rangers' clubhouse wore down even Junior Senior. As he said one late-July day, "I'll probably hit a home run before this place ever gets straightened out." We could all grow old waiting for either to happen.

Year	Team	Lg.	Pos.	G	AB	R	H	HR	RBI	SB	BA
1991	Minnesota	AL	C	61	134	9	28	0	11	0	.209
1992	Cleveland	AL	C	86	244	20	61	0	24	1	.250
1993	Cleveland	AL	C	95	249	19	55	0	20	1	.221
1994	Texas	AL	C	29	76	3	21	0	9	0	.276
1994 PROJECTION				40	107	5	35	0	14	0	.327

DEREK PARKS   Age 26/R $1

If Matt Walbeck is the real goods, there could be a long wait between at-bats for Parks.

Year	Team	Lg.	Pos.	G	AB	R	H	HR	RBI	SB	BA
1992	Minnesota	AL	C	7	6	1	2	0	0	0	.333
1993	Minnesota	AL	C	7	20	3	4	0	1	0	.200
1994	Minnesota	AL	C	31	89	6	17	1	9	0	.191
1994 PROJECTION				41	103	7	21	1	10	0	.204

Catchers
pp. 33–46

Corners
pp. 46–65

Infield
pp. 66–85

Outfield
pp. 85–115

DH
pp. 115–119

Starters
pp. 119–155

Relievers
pp. 155–187

TONY PENA   Age 37/R $1

One of the smaller joys of what had been a splendid season before it was cruelly snuffed out was Peña's semi-miraculous recovery of enough stick to let him hold down the backup job in Cleveland. We feel a lot better knowing he's still in baseball, if only as a fringe player.

Year	Team	Lg.	Pos.	G	AB	R	H	HR	RBI	SB	BA
1991	Boston	AL	C	141	464	45	107	5	48	8	.231
1992	Boston	AL	C	133	410	39	99	1	38	3	.241
1993	Boston	AL	C	126	304	20	55	4	19	1	.181
1994	Cleveland	AL	C	40	112	18	33	2	10	0	.295
1994 PROJECTION				55	157	22	44	2	11	0	.280

IVAN RODRIGUEZ   Age 23/R $20

Don't you just hate it when someone as selfish, arrogant, boorish, surly, and generally obnoxious as this guy turns out to be almost as good as he thinks he is?

Year	Team	Lg.	Pos.	G	AB	R	H	HR	RBI	SB	BA
1991	Texas	AL	C	88	280	24	74	3	27	0	.264
1992	Texas	AL	C	123	420	39	109	8	37	0	.260
1993	Texas	AL	C	137	473	56	129	10	66	8	.273
1994	Texas	AL	C	99	363	56	108	16	57	6	.298
1994 PROJECTION				141	536	79	153	25	89	6	.285

RICH ROWLAND   Age 28/R $1

He became an instant folk hero in Boston when it was discovered that he was actually three years older than his listed age. It was that kind of year in Fenway Park.

Year	Team	Lg.	Pos.	G	AB	R	H	HR	RBI	SB	BA
1991	Detroit	AL	C	4	4	0	1	0	1	0	.250
1992	Detroit	AL	C	6	14	2	3	0	0	0	.214
1993	Detroit	AL	C	21	46	2	10	0	4	0	.217
1994	Boston	AL	C	46	118	14	27	9	20	0	.229
1994 PROJECTION				53	139	19	34	10	23	1	.245

MIKE STANLEY   Age 31/R $22

Last year the Yanks got more HR (41), more RBI (134), and a higher BA (.285) from the catcher slot than any team in baseball. One of the reasons: a second-straight terrific season from the late-blooming Mr. Stanley. We are now, officially, believers.

Year	Team	Lg.	Pos.	G	AB	R	H	HR	RBI	SB	BA
1991	Texas	AL	C	95	181	25	45	3	25	0	.249
1992	New York	AL	C	68	173	24	43	8	27	0	.249
1993	New York	AL	C	130	423	70	129	26	84	1	.305
1994	New York	AL	C	82	290	54	87	17	57	0	.300
1994 PROJECTION				105	370	72	112	24	80	0	.303

TERRY STEINBACH   Age 33/R $10

The guts of the Oakland A's, year after year.

Year	Team	Lg.	Pos.	G	AB	R	H	HR	RBI	SB	BA
1991	Oakland	AL	C	129	456	50	125	6	67	2	.274
1992	Oakland	AL	C	128	438	48	122	12	53	2	.279
1993	Oakland	AL	C	104	389	47	111	10	43	3	.285
1994	Oakland	AL	C	103	369	51	105	11	57	2	.285
1994 PROJECTION				147	534	62	139	16	76	2	.260

JEFF TACKETT   Age 29/R $1

Made his movie debut and gave a masterful performance in the political satire *Dave*. His role was to play himself, which meant he had to portray a fringe, backup catcher trying to hang on to a major league job by his fingernails. He deserved an Oscar.

Year	Team	Lg.	Pos.	G	AB	R	H	HR	RBI	SB	BA
1991	Baltimore	AL	C	6	8	1	1	0	0	0	.125
1992	Baltimore	AL	C	65	179	21	43	5	24	0	.240
1993	Baltimore	AL	C	39	87	8	15	0	9	0	.172
1994	Baltimore	AL	C	26	53	5	12	2	9	0	.226
1994 PROJECTION				31	62	8	14	2	9	0	.226

MICKEY TETTLETON   Age 34/B $21

Home runs, strikeouts, and walks are all that ever happen when the Tigers play baseball, whether they're hitting or pitching.

Year	Team	Lg.	Pos.	G	AB	R	H	HR	RBI	SB	BA
1991	Detroit	AL	C	154	501	85	132	31	89	3	.263
1992	Detroit	AL	C	157	525	82	125	32	83	0	.238
1993	Detroit	AL	1B	152	522	79	128	32	110	3	.245
1994	Detroit	AL	C	107	339	57	84	17	51	0	.248
1994 PROJECTION				150	486	84	116	29	78	0	.239

DAVE VALLE   Age 34/R $1

A few years ago in Seattle, when he got a huge raise in salary arbitration, he was the poster child symbolizing all that was wrong with The System. Last year he was run out of Boston because none of the Red Sox pitchers wanted to throw to him. That he ended up with Bud Selig's Brewers is, we believe, a righteous example of poetic justice. Now we understand why small-market clubs have so much difficulty competing.

Year	Team	Lg.	Pos.	G	AB	R	H	HR	RBI	SB	BA
1991	Seattle	AL	C	132	324	38	63	8	32	0	.194
1992	Seattle	AL	C	124	367	39	88	9	30	0	.240
1993	Seattle	AL	C	135	423	48	109	13	63	1	.258
1994	Boston	AL	C	30	76	6	12	1	5	0	.158
1994	Milwaukee	AL	C	16	36	8	14	1	5	0	.389
1994 PROJECTION				55	133	14	29	2	13	0	.218

Catchers
pp. 33-46

Corners
pp. 46-65

Infield
pp. 66-85

Outfield
pp. 85-115

DH
pp. 115-119

Starters
pp. 119-155

Relievers
pp. 155-187

MATT WALBECK   Age 25/B $4

Tom Kelly thinks he has a chance to be a solid everyday catcher. That's good enough for us.

Year	Team	Lg.	Pos.	G	AB	R	H	HR	RBI	SB	BA
1993	Chicago	NL	C	11	30	2	6	1	6	0	.200
1994	Minnesota	AL	C	97	338	31	69	5	35	1	.204
1994 PROJECTION				140	466	41	95	7	48	1	.204

DAN WILSON   Age 26/R $1

Didn't even make Mariners fans (all seven of them) forget Dave Valle.

Year	Team	Lg.	Pos.	G	AB	R	H	HR	RBI	SB	BA
1992	Cincinnati	NL	C	12	25	2	9	0	3	0	.360
1993	Cincinnati	NL	C	36	76	6	17	0	8	0	.224
1994	Seattle	AL	C	91	282	24	61	3	27	1	.216
1994 PROJECTION				134	423	36	94	5	38	1	.222

At the Corners

NATIONAL LEAGUE

JEFF BAGWELL   Age 26/R $42

Several years ago, when Bagwell was still a Red Sox farmhand, Bill James opined that he—Bagwell, not James—would someday win an NL batting title (or several). Bill didn't say that Bagwell would also turn into a great power hitter, a run-producing machine, and a shoo-in MVP. If we'd known all *that*, we would have bid up his price long before now. We are pleased to note that Bagwell's ego has not grown proportionately with his accomplishments.

Year	Team	Lg.	Pos.	G	AB	R	H	HR	RBI	SB	BA
1991	Houston	NL	1B	156	554	79	163	15	82	7	.294
1992	Houston	NL	1B	162	586	87	160	18	96	10	.273
1993	Houston	NL	1B	142	535	76	171	20	88	13	.320
1994	Houston	NL	1B	110	400	104	147	39	116	15	.368
1994 PROJECTION				133	481	118	163	45	130	15	.339

KIM BATISTE   Age 27/R $1

Too erratic defensively to be trusted, too spotty offensively to play every day, and too old to get much better. In other words, a typical product of a Phillies farm system that is among the worst in baseball.

Year	Team	Lg.	Pos.	G	AB	R	H	HR	RBI	SB	BA
1991	Philadelphia	NL	SS	10	27	2	6	0	1	0	.222
1992	Philadelphia	NL	SS	44	136	9	28	1	10	0	.206
1993	Philadelphia	NL	3B	79	156	14	44	5	29	0	.282
1994	Philadelphia	NL	3B	64	209	17	49	1	13	1	.234
1994 PROJECTION				83	231	19	53	1	16	1	.229

TODD BENZINGER   Age 32/B $2

Released by the Giants, he'll end up somewhere. Not on your team, we hope.

Year	Team	Lg.	Pos.	G	AB	R	H	HR	RBI	SB	BA
1991	Cincinnati	NL	1B	51	123	7	23	1	11	2	.187
1991	Kansas City	AL	1B	78	293	29	86	2	40	2	.294
1992	Los Angeles	NL	OF	121	293	24	70	4	31	2	.239
1993	San Francisco	NL	1B	86	177	25	51	6	26	0	.288
1994	San Francisco	NL	1B	107	328	32	87	9	31	2	.265
1994 PROJECTION				143	402	42	105	12	37	2	.261

SEAN BERRY   Age 29/R $14

More SB than any other third baseman in the NL last year. What's more, runner-up Tony Fernandez (12) spent the summer insisting that he wasn't really a third baseman at all. No other third-sacker was in double figures. On the horizon, though, is Expos prospect Shane Andrews.

Year	Team	Lg.	Pos.	G	AB	R	H	HR	RBI	SB	BA
1991	Kansas City	AL	3B	31	60	5	8	0	1	0	.133
1992	Montreal	NL	3B	24	57	5	19	1	4	2	.333
1993	Montreal	NL	3B	122	299	50	78	14	49	12	.261
1994	Montreal	NL	3B	103	320	43	89	11	41	14	.278
1994 PROJECTION				136	440	56	121	18	63	16	.275

BOBBY BONILLA   Age 32/B $28

He lost *how much* a day during The Strike? Was it really $31,148? Wow, poor guy . . . What's that? Oh, yeah. We almost forgot. That also means he made that much each day *before* The Strike. Time for Bonilla to shelve his tough guy act with the media. Time for fans and Rotisserie owners to accept him for what he has been for much of the last decade: a very good but not great power hitter. Time to be on the lookout for signs of slipping?

Year	Team	Lg.	Pos.	G	AB	R	H	HR	RBI	SB	BA
1991	Pittsburgh	NL	OF	157	577	102	174	18	100	2	.302
1992	New York	NL	OF	128	438	62	109	19	70	4	.249
1993	New York	NL	OF	139	502	81	133	34	87	3	.265
1994	New York	NL	3B	108	403	60	117	20	67	1	.290
1994 PROJECTION				154	572	81	157	29	93	2	.274

RICO BROGNA   Age 24/L $7

Some NL insiders think he will come plummeting back to earth when pitching staffs get more familiar with the weaknesses in his big swing. Others think he's a natural born hitter who will make the necessary adjustments. We think one hot streak does not a career make. There's a lot of depth in the first-base talent pool. Be careful.

Year	Team	Lg.	Pos.	G	AB	R	H	HR	RBI	SB	BA
1992	Detroit	AL	1B	9	26	3	5	1	3	0	.192
1994	New York	NL	1B	39	131	16	46	7	20	1	.351
1994 PROJECTION				74	261	32	76	14	40	1	.291

JERRY BROWNE Age 29/B $2

Useful.

Year	Team	Lg.	Pos.	G	AB	R	H	HR	RBI	SB	BA
1991	Cleveland	AL	2B	107	290	28	66	1	29	2	.228
1992	Oakland	AL	3B	111	324	43	93	3	40	3	.287
1993	Oakland	AL	OF	76	260	27	65	2	19	4	.250
1994	Florida	NL	3B	101	329	42	97	3	30	3	.295
1994 PROJECTION				148	508	80	149	6	40	6	.293

STEVE BUECHELE Age 33/R $11

An unexciting player of modest accomplishment who stood tall one day last summer when he confronted Larry Himes, the joyless fraud who was such a disaster as Cubs GM, and told him what he could do with his Mickey Mouse rules. Unfortunately, that does not translate into Rotisserie greatness.

Year	Team	Lg.	Pos.	G	AB	R	H	HR	RBI	SB	BA
1991	Texas	AL	3B	121	416	58	111	18	66	0	.267
1991	Pittsburgh	NL	3B	31	114	16	28	4	19	0	.246
1992	Pittsburgh	NL	3B	80	285	27	71	8	43	0	.249
1992	Chicago	NL	3B	65	239	25	66	1	21	1	.276
1993	Chicago	NL	3B	133	460	53	125	15	65	1	.272
1994	Chicago	NL	3B	104	339	33	82	14	52	1	.242
1994 PROJECTION				144	480	55	129	19	74	2	.269

KEN CAMINITI Age 31/B $19

Broke out of a rut: after three straight 13-HR seasons. Maybe he got riled by all the rumors over the winter that he was going to be sent somewhere, anywhere, by an Astros front office looking to shave its payroll. Still on the block at press time—a pity, since he and Babe Bagwell make such a fine pair of infield bookends. Look for his power numbers to go up sharply if he moves to a new ballpark.

Year	Team	Lg.	Pos.	G	AB	R	H	HR	RBI	SB	BA
1991	Houston	NL	3B	152	574	65	145	13	80	4	.253
1992	Houston	NL	3B	135	506	68	149	13	62	10	.294
1993	Houston	NL	3B	143	543	75	142	13	75	8	.262
1994	Houston	NL	3B	111	406	63	115	18	75	4	.283
1994 PROJECTION				158	595	92	170	23	96	6	.286

ARCHI CIANFROCCO Age 28/R $1

Something happened on his way to becoming the valuable low-cost power source that we saw lurking in his 1993 numbers. A butcher in the field with no natural position, he has some pop, but last year he struck out 39 times while walking just twice. Maybe this native of Rome (New York, that is) ought to be a Detroit Tiger, which is what Padres teammate . . .

Year	Team	Lg.	Pos.	G	AB	R	H	HR	RBI	SB	BA
1992	Montreal	NL	1B	86	232	25	56	6	30	3	.241
1993	Montreal	NL	1B	12	17	3	4	1	1	0	.235
1993	San Diego	NL	3B	84	279	27	68	11	47	2	.244
1994	San Diego	NL	3B	59	146	9	32	4	13	2	.219
1994 PROJECTION				73	176	15	38	6	17	2	.216

PHIL CLARK   Age 26/R $2

... was before coming over to the NL in 1993 and getting us all excited with a .313 BA and nine HR in just 240 AB. But last season Clark struggled almost as much as Cianfrocco, and neither figures to be a leading candidate for your third corner slot. Consider, though, that Clark is two years younger, makes more frequent contact at the plate, and is a better fielder. He's still going to be on our "Acceptable" list when the year's auction draft reaches the end game.

Year	Team	Lg.	Pos.	G	AB	R	H	HR	RBI	SB	BA
1992	Detroit	AL	OF	23	54	3	22	1	5	1	.407
1993	San Diego	NL	OF	102	240	33	75	9	33	2	.313
1994	San Diego	NL	1B	61	149	14	32	5	20	1	.215
1994 PROJECTION				72	183	18	36	5	20	1	.197

GREG COLBRUNN   Age 25/R $6

Two years ago we tabbed him as "not a bad hunch bet." Then he got hurt. Last year, with his *tabula* still more or less *rasa*, we concluded there was no reason to conclude that he was anything other than "not a bad hunch bet." Well, as luck would have it, he was hurt again for much of last season. So, fresh with new information gleaned from our extensive network of unimpeachable sources, we are confident in saying once again that Colbrunn is "not a bad hunch bet."

Year	Team	Lg.	Pos.	G	AB	R	H	HR	RBI	SB	BA
1992	Montreal	NL	1B	52	168	12	45	2	18	3	.268
1993	Montreal	NL	1B	70	153	15	39	4	23	4	.255
1994	Florida	NL	1B	47	155	17	47	6	31	1	.303
1994 PROJECTION				81	251	27	72	9	40	1	.287

TONY FERNANDEZ   Age 32/B $8

After spurning offers in the $1 million range as gross insults to a player of his caliber, Fernandez was not only forced to accept a measly $350,000 from the Reds but also told—get this!—that he would have to play third base. Talk about your Double Indignity! He sulked his way through the first few months of the season (wouldn't anyone?) until Reds coach Ray Knight got in his face and told him to shut up and play ball. To Tony's credit, he took this friendly advice and went on to have a solid year. Yet, while there's no doubt that he's the most talented graduate of the San Pedro de Macoris Academy of Shortstops, he is precisely the kind of veteran player who could fall through the cracks in the post-Strike era.

Year	Team	Lg.	Pos.	G	AB	R	H	HR	RBI	SB	BA
1991	San Diego	NL	SS	145	558	81	152	4	38	23	.272
1992	San Diego	NL	SS	155	622	84	171	4	37	20	.275
1993	New York	NL	SS	48	173	20	39	1	14	6	.225
1993	Toronto	AL	SS	94	353	45	108	4	50	15	.306
1994	Cincinnati	NL	3B	104	366	50	102	8	50	12	.279
1994 PROJECTION				137	507	70	142	11	68	13	.280

Catchers
pp. 33–46

Corners
pp. 46–65

Infield
pp. 66–85

Outfield
pp. 85–115

DH
pp. 115–119

Starters
pp. 119–155

Relievers
pp. 155–187

CLIFF FLOYD   Age 22/L $16

At one point in his minor league career, Floyd was termed by a sun-dazed but otherwise astute NL personnel man as "a Willie McCovey with speed." That's a heckuva load to hang on a young player's shoulders, and it should have surprised no one that Floyd began his career on a solid but modest note. (The first McCovey, on the other hand, hit .354 in 192 AB with 13 HR in his first season.) But Floyd's power will eventually develop, and a few years from now we might be calling him a "Fred McGriff with speed."

Year	Team	Lg.	Pos.	G	AB	R	H	HR	RBI	SB	BA
1993	Montreal	NL	1B	10	31	3	7	1	2	0	.226
1994	Montreal	NL	1B	100	334	43	94	4	41	10	.281
1994 PROJECTION				142	485	67	138	9	64	11	.285

ANDRES GALARRAGA   Age 33/R $29

As long as Don Baylor is around to keep the Big Cat locked into that funky-looking open batting stance, National League pitchers aren't going to be able to tame him.

Year	Team	Lg.	Pos.	G	AB	R	H	HR	RBI	SB	BA
1991	Montreal	NL	1B	107	375	34	82	9	33	5	.219
1992	St. Louis	NL	1B	95	325	38	79	10	39	5	.243
1993	Colorado	NL	1B	120	470	71	174	22	98	2	.370
1994	Colorado	NL	1B	103	417	77	133	31	85	8	.319
1994 PROJECTION				103	417	77	133	31	85	8	.319

MARK GRACE   Age 30/L $14

Last year his season was reduced to writing letters to Mayor Daley The Younger, reminding that lifelong White Sox fan that there was another major league baseball team in Chicago. Given all those North Side lineups that included names like Maksudian, Parent, Zambrano, Isley, Wendell, and Otto, we're not sure to which major league team Grace might have been referring. To put Grace's power stroke in context, *Todd Benzinger* had three more homers in 75 fewer AB. So much for 1993 being a harbinger of Grace's final emergence as a productive hitter.

Year	Team	Lg.	Pos.	G	AB	R	H	HR	RBI	SB	BA
1991	Chicago	NL	1B	160	619	87	169	8	58	3	.273
1992	Chicago	NL	1B	158	603	72	185	9	79	6	.307
1993	Chicago	NL	1B	155	594	86	193	14	98	8	.325
1994	Chicago	NL	1B	106	403	55	120	6	44	0	.298
1994 PROJECTION				154	592	85	175	9	62	2	.296

CHARLIE HAYES   Age 29/R $18

A broken cheek forced him to wear a helmet that made him look like a bobsled racer, and maybe that affected his fielding. (When your third baseman makes more errors than your shortstop, you've got trouble at the hot corner.) But as long as they can afford him, the talent-thin Rockies will go to the post with Hayes because of his bat. So should you.

Year	Team	Lg.	Pos.	G	AB	R	H	HR	RBI	SB	BA
1991	Philadelphia	NL	3B	142	460	34	106	12	53	3	.230
1992	New York	AL	3B	142	509	52	131	18	66	3	.257
1993	Colorado	NL	3B	157	573	89	175	25	98	11	.305
1994	Colorado	NL	3B	113	423	46	122	10	50	3	.288
1994 PROJECTION				157	593	68	167	14	63	4	.282

DAVE HOLLINS   Age 28/B $19

There were few bigger on-field disappointments in baseball last year (although, considering how 1994 ended, "disappointment" is obviously a relative term). Injuries contributed to Hollins's freefall, but so did a hardheadedness that had some of his grizzled Phillies teammates wondering if his elevator was stopping on all floors. Now he moves to first base to replace John Kruk, after flat-out refusing to give the outfield a shot. The Phils desperately need his bat somewhere in the lineup, assuming he can find it after a lost year.

Year	Team	Lg.	Pos.	G	AB	R	H	HR	RBI	SB	BA
1991	Philadelphia	NL	3B	56	151	18	45	6	21	1	.298
1992	Philadelphia	NL	3B	156	586	104	158	27	93	9	.270
1993	Philadelphia	NL	3B	143	543	104	148	18	93	2	.273
1994	Philadelphia	NL	3B	44	162	28	36	4	26	1	.222
1994 PROJECTION				44	162	28	36	4	26	1	.222

BRIAN HUNTER   Age 27/R $15

More than a few baseball people dismiss Reds GM Jim Bowden as a smarmy little preppy who plays Rotisserie League Baseball in real life. Now, to us, of course, that is hardly criticism. But we digress. The point is that Bowden has been one GM not afraid to wheel and deal in search of better athletes. Here's one of them. Bowden, looking ahead to Kevin Mitchell's departure, got Hunter almost as cheap as you could have gotten him—last year. Now, of course, you're going to have to pay for all those dingers Hunter donged when given his shot. One nagging little question: will he get enough AB on a team that is loaded?

Year	Team	Lg.	Pos.	G	AB	R	H	HR	RBI	SB	BA
1991	Atlanta	NL	1B	97	271	32	68	12	50	0	.251
1992	Atlanta	NL	1B	102	238	34	57	14	41	1	.239
1993	Atlanta	NL	1B	37	80	4	11	0	8	0	.138
1994	Pittsburgh	NL	1B	76	233	28	53	11	47	0	.227
1994	Cincinnati	NL	OF	9	23	6	7	4	10	0	.304
1994 PROJECTION				110	299	38	69	17	67	0	.231

TIM HYERS   Age 23/L $1

So what was he, *third* on the Padres' depth chart at first base?

Year	Team	Lg.	Pos.	G	AB	R	H	HR	RBI	SB	BA
1994	San Diego	NL	1B	52	118	13	30	0	7	3	.254
1994 PROJECTION				72	142	14	40	0	12	4	.282

GREGG JEFFERIES   Age 27/B $34

The Cardinals let him go because of their organizational aversion to paying market value for quality players. Like the Phillies, you should have no such reservations.

Year	Team	Lg.	Pos.	G	AB	R	H	HR	RBI	SB	BA
1991	New York	NL	2B	136	486	59	132	9	62	26	.272
1992	Kansas City	AL	3B	152	604	66	172	10	75	19	.285
1993	St. Louis	NL	1B	142	544	89	186	16	83	46	.342
1994	St. Louis	NL	1B	103	397	52	129	12	55	12	.325
1994 PROJECTION				151	587	80	194	17	88	26	.330

RICKY JORDAN   Age 29/R $9

If someone tells Jordan to call an American League team looking for a right-handed-hitting DH, let's all sing "Rickey, don't lose that number." Bad joke, but Jordan's a good hitter. Problem is, John Kruk's a better one. Ditto Dave Hollins, should he end up with the first baseman's mitt in Philly. More than any other player that comes immediately to mind, Jordan needs a change of venue.

Year	Team	Lg.	Pos.	G	AB	R	H	HR	RBI	SB	BA
1991	Philadelphia	NL	1B	101	301	38	82	9	49	0	.272
1992	Philadelphia	NL	1B	94	276	33	84	4	34	3	.304
1993	Philadelphia	NL	1B	90	159	21	46	5	18	0	.289
1994	Philadelphia	NL	1B	72	220	29	62	8	37	0	.282
1994 PROJECTION				103	291	34	77	8	44	0	.265

ERIC KARROS   Age 27/R $19

With Karros, Piazza, Mondesi, and Wallach forming a critical power mass, no wonder the Dodgers won the pennant last year. (Oh, that's right. There was no pennant last year.) As one NL pitching coach puts it, "Like most guys, Karros can be pitched to, but he's just strong enough and good enough to hit 20 mistakes out every year." Mistakes to the coach, dingers for us.

Year	Team	Lg.	Pos.	G	AB	R	H	HR	RBI	SB	BA
1991	Los Angeles	NL	1B	14	14	0	1	0	1	0	.071
1992	Los Angeles	NL	1B	149	545	63	140	20	88	2	.257
1993	Los Angeles	NL	1B	158	619	74	153	23	80	0	.247
1994	Los Angeles	NL	1B	111	406	51	108	14	46	2	.266
1994 PROJECTION				152	574	70	155	21	68	2	.270

JEFF KING   Age 30/R $11

An average player on a team full of average players. So spend what you'd spend on an average player and not a penny more.

Year	Team	Lg.	Pos.	G	AB	R	H	HR	RBI	SB	BA
1991	Pittsburgh	NL	3B	33	109	16	26	4	18	3	.239
1992	Pittsburgh	NL	3B	130	480	56	111	14	65	4	.231
1993	Pittsburgh	NL	3B	158	611	82	180	9	98	8	.295
1994	Pittsburgh	NL	3B	94	339	36	89	5	42	3	.263
1994 PROJECTION				140	529	59	139	9	66	3	.263

JOHN KRUK
Age 34/L   **$13**

He handled the cancer thing with his usual good humor. And he battled his way back to another .300 year. But the future is cloudy for one of our all-Rotisserie heroes. His knees are shot, his power is fading, and he entered baseball's nuclear winter as a free agent.

Year	Team	Lg.	Pos.	G	AB	R	H	HR	RBI	SB	BA
1991	Philadelphia	NL	1B	152	538	84	158	21	92	7	.294
1992	Philadelphia	NL	1B	144	507	86	164	10	70	3	.323
1993	Philadelphia	NL	1B	150	535	100	169	14	85	6	.316
1994	Philadelphia	NL	1B	75	255	35	77	5	38	4	.302
1994 PROJECTION				115	379	51	113	6	55	5	.298

SCOTT LIVINGSTONE
Age 29/L   **$1**

A key element of the Padres' comprehensive rebuilding program.

Year	Team	Lg.	Pos.	G	AB	R	H	HR	RBI	SB	BA
1991	Detroit	AL	3B	44	127	19	37	2	11	2	.291
1992	Detroit	AL	3B	117	354	43	100	4	46	1	.282
1993	Detroit	AL	3B	98	304	39	89	2	39	1	.293
1994	Detroit	AL	DH	15	23	0	5	0	1	0	.217
1994	San Diego	NL	3B	57	180	11	49	2	10	2	.272
1994 PROJECTION				104	308	24	78	4	17	2	.253

DAVE MAGADAN
Age 32/L   **$3**

For three or four seasons in a row he was the most overpriced corner man in Rotisserie baseball this side of Mark Grace. Not anymore.

Year	Team	Lg.	Pos.	G	AB	R	H	HR	RBI	SB	BA
1991	New York	NL	1B	124	418	58	108	4	51	1	.258
1992	New York	NL	3B	99	321	33	91	3	28	1	.283
1993	Florida	NL	3B	66	227	22	65	4	29	0	.286
1993	Seattle	AL	1B	71	228	27	59	1	21	2	.259
1994	Florida	NL	3B	74	211	30	58	1	17	0	.275
1994 PROJECTION				82	239	32	63	1	19	0	.264

FRED McGRIFF
Age 31/L   **$36**

As The Strike date approached, there was some question about Crime Dog keeping intact his streak of 30-plus home run seasons. Thus challenged, he launched a half-dozen taters in one week and put that question to rest. Unless the labor wars keep him under wraps until Independence Day, that streak should continue into the next century.

Year	Team	Lg.	Pos.	G	AB	R	H	HR	RBI	SB	BA
1991	San Diego	NL	1B	153	528	84	147	31	106	4	.278
1992	San Diego	NL	1B	152	531	79	152	35	104	8	.286
1993	San Diego	NL	1B	83	302	52	83	18	46	4	.275
1993	Atlanta	NL	1B	68	255	59	79	19	55	1	.310
1994	Atlanta	NL	1B	113	424	81	135	34	94	7	.318
1994 PROJECTION				158	601	114	193	47	128	8	.321

RANDY MILLIGAN   Age 33/R $1

Bullwinkle has more value these days than the Moose.

Year	Team	Lg.	Pos.	G	AB	R	H	HR	RBI	SB	BA
1991	Baltimore	AL	1B	141	483	57	127	16	70	0	.263
1992	Baltimore	AL	1B	137	462	71	111	11	53	0	.240
1993	Cincinnati	NL	1B	83	234	30	64	6	29	0	.274
1993	Cleveland	AL	1B	19	47	7	20	0	7	0	.426
1994	Montreal	NL	1B	47	82	10	19	2	12	0	.232
1994 PROJECTION				61	102	13	22	2	14	0	.216

HAL MORRIS   Age 29/L $18

Do you think it was our relentless chiding in these pages that caused him to take stock in himself and finally start driving in a few runs to go with his fancy BA? We don't. We think the power surge was caused by (a) hitting in the middle of one of the most exciting lineups in baseball, (b) seeing a lot of fastballs hitting in front of Kevin Mitchell and Reggie Sanders, and (c) sitting on the bench watching Brian Hunter give a clinic in the way a first baseman ought to hit. Whatever the precise mix of reasons, his Rotissevalue has skyrocketed.

Year	Team	Lg.	Pos.	G	AB	R	H	HR	RBI	SB	BA
1991	Cincinnati	NL	1B	136	478	72	152	14	59	10	.318
1992	Cincinnati	NL	1B	115	395	41	107	6	53	6	.271
1993	Cincinnati	NL	1B	101	379	48	120	7	49	2	.317
1994	Cincinnati	NL	1B	112	436	60	146	10	78	6	.335
1994 PROJECTION				156	586	81	203	15	115	7	.346

JOSE OLIVA   Age 24/R $8

Showed a lot of pop while filling in for Terry Pendleton. Showed a lot of poise by not grousing when he was sent back to Richmond on Pendleton's return from the DL. With Pendleton gone, Oliva will be a hot ticket at the auction draft, especially if he has a good spring. Be careful.

Year	Team	Lg.	Pos.	G	AB	R	H	HR	RBI	SB	BA
1994	Atlanta	NL	3B	19	59	9	17	6	11	0	.288
1994 PROJECTION				35	108	20	26	8	18	0	.241

TERRY PENDLETON   Age 34/B $14

Like Andy Van Slyke, John Kruk, and several other veterans, Pendleton needed a strong second half to boost his market value as a free agent. But he didn't have a second half of any kind because of the You-Know-What. And while he is only 34, his knees are more like 64. Could have a few productive years left if he lands in the right place, but that won't be automatic.

Year	Team	Lg.	Pos.	G	AB	R	H	HR	RBI	SB	BA
1991	Atlanta	NL	3B	153	586	94	187	22	86	10	.319
1992	Atlanta	NL	3B	160	640	98	199	21	105	5	.311
1993	Atlanta	NL	3B	161	633	81	172	17	84	5	.272
1994	Atlanta	NL	3B	77	309	25	78	7	30	2	.252
1994 PROJECTION				123	494	52	140	17	56	6	.283

GERALD PERRY　　　　　　　　　　　　Age 34/L　　　$1

For what it's worth, he remains one of the great pinch hitters of his time. In Rotisserie baseball, unfortunately, that's not worth very much at all.

Year	Team	Lg.	Pos.	G	AB	R	H	HR	RBI	SB	BA
1991	St. Louis	NL	1B	109	242	29	58	6	36	15	.240
1992	St. Louis	NL	1B	87	143	13	34	1	18	3	.238
1993	St. Louis	NL	1B	96	98	21	33	4	16	1	.337
1994	St. Louis	NL	1B	60	77	12	25	3	18	1	.325
1994 PROJECTION				91	107	16	35	5	26	1	.327

DAVID SEGUI　　　　　　　　　　　　Age 28/B　　　$7

If Rico Brogna is for real, Segui is back to square one. Too bad. He's a terrific first baseman, and he demonstrated more pop than anyone expected last season.

Year	Team	Lg.	Pos.	G	AB	R	H	HR	RBI	SB	BA
1991	Baltimore	AL	1B	86	212	15	59	2	22	1	.278
1992	Baltimore	AL	1B	115	189	21	44	1	17	1	.233
1993	Baltimore	AL	1B	146	450	54	123	10	60	2	.273
1994	New York	NL	1B	92	336	46	81	10	43	0	.241
1994 PROJECTION				125	422	58	102	12	54	0	.242

CRAIG SHIPLEY　　　　　　　　　　　Age 32/R　　　$1

He has as much chance of doing it again as Roseanne does of being invited back to sing "The Star-Spangled Banner."

Year	Team	Lg.	Pos.	G	AB	R	H	HR	RBI	SB	BA
1991	San Diego	NL	SS	37	91	6	25	1	6	0	.275
1992	San Diego	NL	SS	52	105	7	26	0	7	1	.248
1993	San Diego	NL	SS	105	230	25	54	4	22	12	.235
1994	San Diego	NL	3B	81	240	32	80	4	30	6	.333
1994 PROJECTION				115	362	47	107	5	36	7	.296

TIM WALLACH　　　　　　　　　　　　Age 37/R　　　$18

Let's get this straight: All new Dodgers hitting coach Reggie Smith does is make a few adjustments and—presto!—the clock is turned back to the days when only Mike Schmidt was a more productive National League third baseman? Hey, if Schmidty hears that, and they expand again, maybe he'll come out of retirement.

Year	Team	Lg.	Pos.	G	AB	R	H	HR	RBI	SB	BA
1991	Montreal	NL	3B	151	577	60	130	13	73	2	.225
1992	Montreal	NL	3B	150	537	53	120	9	59	2	.223
1993	Los Angeles	NL	3B	133	477	42	106	12	62	0	.222
1994	Los Angeles	NL	3B	113	414	68	116	23	78	0	.280
1994 PROJECTION				159	596	96	159	32	105	0	.267

EDDIE WILLIAMS　　　　　　　　　　　Age 30/R　　　$12

A former number one draft pick is rediscovered playing in a twilight league, tears up Triple-A pitching, and returns to the majors where for two months he looks like the second coming of Gary Sheffield. And the *next* year, he . . . nope, better leave it at that for now. Bid with extreme caution because no one, least of all the Padres, has any idea if the Eddie Williams Story has

Catchers
pp. 33–46

Corners
pp. 46–65

Infield
pp. 66–85

Outfield
pp. 85–115

DH
pp. 115–119

Starters
pp. 119–155

Relievers
pp. 155–187

another chapter. But even if Eddie turns into a pumpkin tomorrow, last season his story was a baseball fairy tale come true.

Year	Team	Lg.	Pos.	G	AB	R	H	HR	RBI	SB	BA
1994	San Diego	NL	1B	49	175	32	58	11	42	0	.331
1994 PROJECTION				88	343	52	108	18	75	0	.315

MATT WILLIAMS   Age 29/R $39

We think he would have done It.

Year	Team	Lg.	Pos.	G	AB	R	H	HR	RBI	SB	BA
1991	San Francisco	NL	3B	157	589	72	158	34	98	5	.268
1992	San Francisco	NL	3B	146	529	58	120	20	66	7	.227
1993	San Francisco	NL	3B	145	579	105	170	38	110	1	.294
1994	San Francisco	NL	3B	112	445	74	119	43	96	1	.267
1994 PROJECTION				159	644	105	170	62	144	1	.264

TODD ZEILE   Age 29/R $22

Until The Strike hit, he was overcoming a wretched start and on the way to another big RBI year. Because big years usually translate into big raises, the beer salesmen who run the Cardinals would undoubtedly like to dump him. After mastering one role in the worst Cardinals defense at the corners since Ray Jablonski teamed with Steve Bilko, he now takes on the other.

Year	Team	Lg.	Pos.	G	AB	R	H	HR	RBI	SB	BA
1991	St. Louis	NL	3B	155	565	76	158	11	81	17	.280
1992	St. Louis	NL	3B	126	439	51	113	7	48	7	.257
1993	St. Louis	NL	3B	157	571	82	158	17	103	5	.277
1994	St. Louis	NL	3B	113	415	62	111	19	75	1	.267
1994 PROJECTION				160	598	90	158	25	98	1	.264

AMERICAN LEAGUE

MIKE BLOWERS   Age 29/R $10

If the Mariners had a few more role players like this to surround Junior, they might keep the roof from caving in every year.

Year	Team	Lg.	Pos.	G	AB	R	H	HR	RBI	SB	BA
1991	New York	AL	3B	15	35	3	7	1	1	0	.200
1992	Seattle	AL	3B	31	73	7	14	1	2	0	.192
1993	Seattle	AL	3B	127	379	55	106	15	57	1	.280
1994	Seattle	AL	3B	85	270	37	78	9	49	2	.289
1994 PROJECTION				108	314	44	90	11	55	2	.287

WADE BOGGS   Age 36/L $19

The only player we know of for whom a spring training injury might be good news, provided it involved his ribs. During a most uncharacteristic power surge last year, Boggs claimed that a rib injury was affecting his swing and making the ball go ... well, out of the park. "Home runs are a mistake for me," he said. (Funny, our mistakes never get out of the infield.) His homer total was the second highest of his career, and he was on an 80+ RBI pace.

Still, he's no spring chicken, however many of them he eats, and we don't forecast a continuation of last season's power surge.

Year	Team	Lg.	Pos.	G	AB	R	H	HR	RBI	SB	BA
1991	Boston	AL	3B	144	546	93	181	8	51	1	.332
1992	Boston	AL	3B	143	514	62	133	7	50	1	.259
1993	New York	AL	3B	143	560	83	169	2	59	0	.302
1994	New York	AL	3B	97	366	61	125	11	55	2	.342
1994 PROJECTION				145	558	112	197	18	89	3	.353

SCOTT BROSIUS   Age 28/R $9

The A's think he has only begun to show his power potential. We agree.

Year	Team	Lg.	Pos.	G	AB	R	H	HR	RBI	SB	BA
1991	Oakland	AL	2B	36	68	9	16	2	4	3	.235
1992	Oakland	AL	OF	38	87	13	19	4	13	3	.218
1993	Oakland	AL	OF	70	213	26	53	6	25	6	.249
1994	Oakland	AL	3B	96	324	31	77	14	49	2	.238
1994 PROJECTION				140	485	47	115	19	58	3	.237

WILL CLARK   Age 31/L $27

It was a late afternoon in the Rangers' new ballpark, and the Thrill was sitting in the dugout gazing at the menagerie around him. A preening José Canseco was flexing for the benefit of some teenage girls. A sulking Juan Gonzalez was being coaxed by his personal Rangers PR person to sit for a TV interview. A self-centered Pudge Rodriguez was arguing with two team-mates. What passed for a pitching staff was listlessly doing exercises. The manager was just arriving, showing the effects of a late night. The Thrill just shook his head and said to a friend, "Sometimes, this free agent stuff ain't all it's cracked up to be."

Year	Team	Lg.	Pos.	G	AB	R	H	HR	RBI	SB	BA
1991	San Francisco	NL	1B	148	565	84	170	29	116	4	.301
1992	San Francisco	NL	1B	144	513	69	154	16	73	12	.300
1993	San Francisco	NL	1B	132	491	82	139	14	73	2	.283
1994	Texas	AL	1B	110	389	73	128	13	80	5	.329
1994 PROJECTION				158	574	104	180	21	103	5	.314

SCOTT COOPER   Age 27/L $13

Since making the All-Star team is not a Rotisserie category, we'd like to remind one and all that Cooper is an oh-so-average third basemen. Fewer RBI than "Bad Ribs" Boggs last year, too.

Year	Team	Lg.	Pos.	G	AB	R	H	HR	RBI	SB	BA
1991	Boston	AL	3B	14	35	6	16	0	7	0	.457
1992	Boston	AL	1B	123	337	34	93	5	33	1	.276
1993	Boston	AL	3B	156	526	67	147	9	63	5	.279
1994	Boston	AL	3B	104	369	49	104	13	53	0	.282
1994 PROJECTION				104	369	49	104	13	53	0	.282

DAMION EASLEY   Age 25/R $2

The Angels continue to gush about his potential, a highly suspect word when applied to players from this feeble franchise. (By the way, can someone explain to us how the Angels got lumped in with the "small market" franchises last summer? Did they move to Bakersfield and not tell us?)

Year	Team	Lg.	Pos.	G	AB	R	H	HR	RBI	SB	BA
1992	California	AL	3B	47	151	14	39	1	12	9	.258
1993	California	AL	2B	73	230	33	72	2	22	6	.313
1994	California	AL	3B	88	316	41	68	6	30	4	.215
1994 PROJECTION				89	317	41	68	6	30	4	.215

CECIL FIELDER
Age 31/R $32

Come see the—*whiff!*—Tigers, the same, tired act that—*whiff!*—produces so few wins and so—*whiff!*—little actual excitement, no matter whether it's—*whiff!*—Cecil or Gibby or . . .

Year	Team	Lg.	Pos.	G	AB	R	H	HR	RBI	SB	BA
1991	Detroit	AL	1B	162	624	102	163	44	133	0	.261
1992	Detroit	AL	1B	155	594	80	145	35	124	0	.244
1993	Detroit	AL	1B	154	573	80	153	30	117	0	.267
1994	Detroit	AL	1B	109	425	67	110	28	90	0	.259
1994 PROJECTION				156	604	92	147	36	117	0	.243

TRAVIS FRYMAN
Age 26/R $21

. . . who is too good a player to—*whiff!*—keep flailing away, *whiff!* after *whiff!* after *whiff!* Sure, we love the big power numbers put up by the Detroit corners, and we always put our money where our Rotissecategories are at the auction draft. But we never have much liked Whiff Ball. Probably the Tigers have so much trouble finding players with more than one dimension to their games because Detroit is a small-market franchise.

Year	Team	Lg.	Pos.	G	AB	R	H	HR	RBI	SB	BA
1991	Detroit	AL	3B	149	557	65	144	21	91	12	.259
1992	Detroit	AL	SS	161	659	87	175	20	96	8	.266
1993	Detroit	AL	SS	151	607	98	182	22	97	9	.300
1994	Detroit	AL	3B	114	464	66	122	18	85	2	.263
1994 PROJECTION				159	650	95	175	22	108	2	.269

GARY GAETTI
Age 36/R $10

Is this the same Gary Gaetti who was all washed up, at the end of the line, stick-a-fork-in-him-he's-done just a few years back? (At least that's what we read about him here.) Whatever it is he's taking, we want some of it.

Year	Team	Lg.	Pos.	G	AB	R	H	HR	RBI	SB	BA
1991	California	AL	3B	152	586	58	144	18	66	5	.246
1992	California	AL	3B	130	456	41	103	12	48	3	.226
1993	California	AL	3B	20	50	3	9	0	4	1	.180
1993	Kansas City	AL	3B	82	281	37	72	14	46	0	.256
1994	Kansas City	AL	3B	90	327	53	94	12	57	0	.287
1994 PROJECTION				136	490	63	130	15	78	0	.265

LEO GOMEZ
Age 28/R $11

At one point, another team could have picked him up for a Dick Ravitch autographed jockstrap. At another point, the Orioles were close to releasing him. Then, when Chris Sabo went out with an injury, and he was forced into action, all Gomez did was play the best ball of his career, keep Sabo

on the bench after his injury, and prove once again that the old ball sometimes takes funny bounces.

Year	Team	Lg.	Pos.	G	AB	R	H	HR	RBI	SB	BA
1991	Baltimore	AL	3B	118	391	40	91	16	45	1	.233
1992	Baltimore	AL	3B	137	468	62	124	17	64	2	.265
1993	Baltimore	AL	3B	71	244	30	48	10	25	0	.197
1994	Baltimore	AL	3B	84	285	46	78	15	56	0	.274
1994 PROJECTION				121	408	64	102	22	76	1	.250

CHIP HALE   Age 30/L $1

This one's easy. If Chip ends up on your active roster, you won't win.

Year	Team	Lg.	Pos.	G	AB	R	H	HR	RBI	SB	BA
1993	Minnesota	AL	2B	69	186	25	62	3	27	2	.333
1994	Minnesota	AL	3B	67	118	13	31	1	11	0	.263
1994 PROJECTION				98	181	17	38	1	14	1	.210

DAVID HOWARD   Age 28/B $1

Before becoming a switch-hitter, he was Howard David. Worth no more
than 50 cents per side.

Year	Team	Lg.	Pos.	G	AB	R	H	HR	RBI	SB	BA
1991	Kansas City	AL	SS	94	236	20	51	1	17	3	.216
1992	Kansas City	AL	SS	74	219	19	49	1	18	3	.224
1993	Kansas City	AL	2B	15	24	5	8	0	2	1	.333
1994	Kansas City	AL	3B	46	83	9	19	1	13	3	.229
1994 PROJECTION				52	88	9	20	1	13	3	.227

KENT HRBEK   Age 34/L   No Price

A tip of our cap to one of our all-time favorites. May your retirement be one
endless buffet table, Hrbie. But do keep an eye on the old cholesterol, okay?

Year	Team	Lg.	Pos.	G	AB	R	H	HR	RBI	SB	BA
1991	Minnesota	AL	1B	132	462	72	131	20	89	4	.284
1992	Minnesota	AL	1B	112	394	52	96	15	58	5	.244
1993	Minnesota	AL	1B	123	392	60	95	25	83	4	.242
1994	Minnesota	AL	1B	81	274	34	74	10	53	0	.270
1994 PROJECTION				116	387	41	96	10	60	1	.248

JOHN JAHA   Age 28/R $10

Great work, Bud. Consider that this Wally Joyner-with-a-lousy-BA is one of
the Commish's team's best prospects in years. Then convince us that all this
small-market bullbleep that triggered The Strike isn't really about incompe-
tent people who have bungled the operation of their franchises and are now
looking for the players to bail them out.

Year	Team	Lg.	Pos.	G	AB	R	H	HR	RBI	SB	BA
1992	Milwaukee	AL	1B	47	133	17	30	2	10	10	.226
1993	Milwaukee	AL	1B	153	515	78	136	19	70	13	.264
1994	Milwaukee	AL	1B	84	291	45	70	12	39	3	.241
1994 PROJECTION				129	462	69	109	22	61	3	.236

WALLY JOYNER
Age 32/L $12

Has finally reached the point where he is as good as Don Mattingly. Once upon a time, that would have been a compliment.

Year	Team	Lg.	Pos.	G	AB	R	H	HR	RBI	SB	BA
1991	California	AL	1B	143	551	79	166	21	96	2	.301
1992	Kansas City	AL	1B	149	572	66	154	9	66	11	.269
1993	Kansas City	AL	1B	141	497	83	145	15	65	5	.292
1994	Kansas City	AL	1B	97	363	52	113	8	57	3	.311
1994 PROJECTION				141	524	74	160	10	78	3	.305

SCOTT LEIUS
Age 29/R $14

Terry Crowley, the Twins' fine hitting instructor, has been working with Leius to get him up in the box, to be more aggressive at the plate, and to try swinging for more power. The results are beginning to show: we say he's a sleeper candidate to crack the 20-HR barrier this year. (Shhh! Let's let that be our little secret.)

Year	Team	Lg.	Pos.	G	AB	R	H	HR	RBI	SB	BA
1991	Minnesota	AL	3B	109	199	35	57	5	20	5	.286
1992	Minnesota	AL	3B	129	409	50	102	2	35	6	.249
1993	Minnesota	AL	SS	10	18	4	3	0	2	0	.167
1994	Minnesota	AL	3B	97	350	57	86	14	49	2	.246
1994 PROJECTION				135	460	73	112	17	61	2	.243

EDGAR MARTINEZ
Age 32/R $14

Pay attention to the health bulletins, even if it means watching "ER" *and* "Chicago Hope." Could be a steal. Has plenty left.

Year	Team	Lg.	Pos.	G	AB	R	H	HR	RBI	SB	BA
1991	Seattle	AL	3B	150	544	98	167	14	52	0	.307
1992	Seattle	AL	3B	135	528	100	181	18	73	14	.343
1993	Seattle	AL	DH	42	135	20	32	4	13	0	.237
1994	Seattle	AL	3B	89	326	47	93	13	51	6	.285
1994 PROJECTION				135	510	75	153	26	79	6	.300

TINO MARTINEZ
Age 27/L $20

His 20 HR ranked him fifth among AL first basemen last year. Not bad. His 61 RBI ranked him seventh. Not great. But does anyone lie awake at night hoping to get the sixth best guy at his position? Not likely. But if last year was a stepping-stone, and this is the season he finally plays up to his potential, he could make a giant leap forward in the first base ranking. Will he? We're thinking, we're thinking.... (Whew, this crystal-balling is tough. Glad we don't have to do it for a living.)

Year	Team	Lg.	Pos.	G	AB	R	H	HR	RBI	SB	BA
1991	Seattle	AL	1B	36	112	11	23	4	9	0	.205
1992	Seattle	AL	1B	136	460	53	118	16	66	2	.257
1993	Seattle	AL	1B	109	408	48	108	17	60	0	.265
1994	Seattle	AL	1B	97	329	42	86	20	61	1	.261
1994 PROJECTION				145	509	65	142	28	91	2	.279

DON MATTINGLY
Age 33/L $14

Jonathan Schwartz is a New York disk jockey and music historian with two great passions in life: Frank Sinatra and the Boston Red Sox. Last August,

---

when everybody in Gotham was lamenting the fact that their beloved Donnie's best (and perhaps last) shot at post-season play was being threatened by The Strike, Schwartz commented to a friend, "The Red Sox are out of it, the Yankees are in first, so I hope the season does end. I don't want Don Mattingly to get into the playoffs and the World Series. Not this year, not ever." Now *that*'s the voice of a true, diehard, take-no-prisoners fan, and we applaud that sort of unwavering, uncompromising, absolute loyalty to one's team. In this particular case, though, we don't agree. We want to see Mattingly get a shot at post-season play, even as a Steinbrenner employee. Earlier this winter Mattingly was making noises that he was so disgusted with last season's turn of events that he might hang up his spikes. Come on back, Donnie. Particularly now, baseball needs gamers like you.

Year	Team	Lg.	Pos.	G	AB	R	H	HR	RBI	SB	BA
1991	New York	AL	1B	152	587	64	169	9	68	2	.288
1992	New York	AL	1B	157	640	89	184	14	86	3	.287
1993	New York	AL	1B	134	530	78	154	17	86	0	.291
1994	New York	AL	1B	97	372	62	113	6	51	0	.304
1994 PROJECTION				146	552	95	176	9	79	0	.319

DAVE McCARTY   Age 25/R $5

Make or break time. We're not bubbling with optimism.

Year	Team	Lg.	Pos.	G	AB	R	H	HR	RBI	SB	BA
1993	Minnesota	AL	OF	98	350	36	75	2	21	2	.214
1994	Minnesota	AL	1B	44	131	21	34	1	12	2	.260
1994 PROJECTION				60	168	25	45	2	18	3	.268

MARK McGWIRE   Age 31/R $29

For a big, strong, muscular hulk of a guy, he sure gets a lot of boo-boos. If he's healthy, McGwire will push Junior and the Big Hurt and Corky Belle for the league lead in homers. And when he's in the lineup, he makes the entire Oakland team better, especially . . .

Year	Team	Lg.	Pos.	G	AB	R	H	HR	RBI	SB	BA
1991	Oakland	AL	1B	154	483	62	97	22	75	2	.201
1992	Oakland	AL	1B	139	467	87	125	42	104	0	.268
1993	Oakland	AL	1B	27	84	16	28	9	24	0	.333
1994	Oakland	AL	1B	47	135	26	34	9	25	0	.252
1994 PROJECTION				47	135	26	34	9	25	0	.252

TROY NEEL   Age 29/L $19

. . . whose left-handed thump the A's want to have in the lineup *with* McGwire instead of replacing him. Now's the time to get Neel, because starting this season he becomes a 25-homer guy.

Year	Team	Lg.	Pos.	G	AB	R	H	HR	RBI	SB	BA
1992	Oakland	AL	DH	24	53	8	14	3	9	0	.264
1993	Oakland	AL	DH	123	427	59	124	19	63	3	.290
1994	Oakland	AL	1B	83	278	43	74	15	48	2	.266
1994 PROJECTION				117	402	49	99	17	60	3	.246

JOHN OLERUD
Age 26/L   **$21**

If last year's run at .300 is a little more realistic barometer of what to expect than 1993's run at .400, then maybe we were all a little, ah, premature in dubbing him the next Ted Williams. And it's not as if he sacrificed BA points for power: indeed, it's the slight power slippage that is most disturbing. What seems to have happened last season is that AL pitchers found they could jam him with hard stuff. The question this year is whether he can adjust.

Year	Team	Lg.	Pos.	G	AB	R	H	HR	RBI	SB	BA
1991	Toronto	AL	1B	139	454	64	116	17	68	0	.256
1992	Toronto	AL	1B	138	458	68	130	16	66	1	.284
1993	Toronto	AL	1B	158	551	109	200	24	107	0	.363
1994	Toronto	AL	1B	108	384	47	114	12	67	1	.297
1994 PROJECTION				155	566	72	172	21	98	1	.304

SPIKE OWEN
Age 33/B   **$2**

When an 11-year veteran hits 67 points over his lifetime average, we try to restrain our optimism that he can do it again.

Year	Team	Lg.	Pos.	G	AB	R	H	HR	RBI	SB	BA
1991	Montreal	NL	SS	139	424	39	108	3	26	2	.255
1992	Montreal	NL	SS	122	386	52	104	7	40	9	.269
1993	New York	AL	SS	103	334	41	78	2	20	3	.234
1994	California	AL	3B	82	268	30	83	3	37	2	.310
1994 PROJECTION				121	431	51	132	4	53	2	.306

RAFAEL PALMEIRO
Age 30/L   **$33**

He tailed off in late July and August, and there is a growing school of thought that says Raffy is a much better hitter when either his team is out of the race or the race hasn't started yet. All that said, he has that sweet swing, and he plays in a perfect ballpark for several more years of delightful numbers.

Year	Team	Lg.	Pos.	G	AB	R	H	HR	RBI	SB	BA
1991	Texas	AL	1B	159	631	115	203	26	88	4	.322
1992	Texas	AL	1B	159	608	84	163	22	85	2	.268
1993	Texas	AL	1B	160	597	124	176	37	105	22	.295
1994	Baltimore	AL	1B	111	436	82	139	23	76	7	.319
1994 PROJECTION				158	622	104	191	31	102	12	.307

DEAN PALMER
Age 26/R   **$27**

Big-time power, but listen to what one AL manager has to say: "Sometimes individual players symbolize their entire team, and one of them is Dean Palmer. He's an all-or-nothing hitter who can't run, is brutal in the field, and doesn't play a lick of fundamental baseball. He's the perfect Texas Ranger." Oh, well—nobody's perfect.

Year	Team	Lg.	Pos.	G	AB	R	H	HR	RBI	SB	BA
1991	Texas	AL	3B	81	268	38	50	15	37	0	.187
1992	Texas	AL	3B	152	541	74	124	26	72	10	.229
1993	Texas	AL	3B	148	519	88	127	33	96	11	.245
1994	Texas	AL	3B	93	342	50	84	19	59	3	.246
1994 PROJECTION				121	449	66	111	25	75	3	.247

EDUARDO PEREZ
Age 25/R   **$7**

We don't get it: the Angels keep saying how Eduardo is such an important part of their future, but then they jerk him around from one position to another in between intermediate stops in the minors. What's worse is that it looks like the kid may not have enough power to follow in his father's footsteps.

Year	Team	Lg.	Pos.	G	AB	R	H	HR	RBI	SB	BA
1993	California	AL	3B	52	180	16	45	4	30	5	.250
1994	California	AL	1B	38	129	10	27	5	16	3	.209
1994 PROJECTION				47	156	11	32	5	17	3	.205

CHRIS SABO
Age 33/R   **$9**

Captain Marvel moped around most of last season like a man who wanted to be somewhere else. He got his wish, but now there's a real chance that we have seen the last of this odd but intriguing character. After the Baltimore experience, not many GMs are going to risk big bucks on his bad back.

Year	Team	Lg.	Pos.	G	AB	R	H	HR	RBI	SB	BA
1991	Cincinnati	NL	3B	153	582	91	175	26	88	19	.301
1992	Cincinnati	NL	3B	96	344	42	84	12	43	4	.244
1993	Cincinnati	NL	3B	148	552	86	143	21	82	6	.259
1994	Baltimore	AL	3B	68	258	41	66	11	42	1	.256
1994 PROJECTION				89	327	48	84	13	51	1	.257

KEVIN SEITZER
Age 33/R   **$3**

Members of The Commish's baseball brain trust were dancing in the halls after getting Seitzer back, even though Roseanne Barr has more defensive range and Larry Sanders has more power. The reason for all the glee? Simple. Seitzer is exactly the kind of player a team needs to finish fourth or fifth every year and keep the old payroll down. Welcome to Bud's World.

Year	Team	Lg.	Pos.	G	AB	R	H	HR	RBI	SB	BA
1991	Kansas City	AL	3B	85	234	28	62	1	25	4	.265
1992	Milwaukee	AL	3B	148	540	74	146	5	71	13	.270
1993	Oakland	AL	3B	73	255	24	65	4	27	4	.255
1993	Milwaukee	AL	3B	47	162	21	47	7	30	3	.290
1994	Milwaukee	AL	3B	80	309	44	97	5	49	2	.314
1994 PROJECTION				127	497	77	158	6	76	4	.318

J. T. SNOW
Age 27/B   **$7**

Needs a new start somewhere else. Why not trade him to the Yankees for Jim Abbott?

Year	Team	Lg.	Pos.	G	AB	R	H	HR	RBI	SB	BA
1992	New York	AL	1B	7	14	1	2	0	2	0	.143
1993	California	AL	1B	129	419	60	101	16	57	3	.241
1994	California	AL	1B	61	223	22	49	8	30	0	.220
1994 PROJECTION				101	373	34	87	12	51	0	.233

PAUL SORRENTO Age 29/L $17

What a lineup! On any other team, Come-Back-To would get twice the attention and three times the attendant pressure. In Cleveland, easily over-looked in a galaxy of stars, he can continue to develop into a solidly produc-tive hitter without undue distraction. Slightly older heads in our scouting combine see him as the Chris Chambliss of the '90s.

Year	Team	Lg.	Pos.	G	AB	R	H	HR	RBI	SB	BA
1991	Minnesota	AL	1B	26	47	6	12	4	13	0	.255
1992	Cleveland	AL	1B	140	458	52	123	18	60	0	.269
1993	Cleveland	AL	1B	148	463	75	119	18	65	3	.257
1994	Cleveland	AL	1B	95	322	43	90	14	62	0	.280
1994 PROJECTION				129	415	56	112	16	70	1	.270

BILL SPIERS Age 28/L $1

As New York is a larger market, somebody in your league will probably bid $2.

Year	Team	Lg.	Pos.	G	AB	R	H	HR	RBI	SB	BA
1991	Milwaukee	AL	SS	133	414	71	117	8	54	14	.283
1992	Milwaukee	AL	SS	12	16	2	5	0	2	1	.313
1993	Milwaukee	AL	2B	113	340	43	81	2	36	9	.238
1994	Milwaukee	AL	3B	73	214	27	54	0	17	7	.252
1994 PROJECTION				100	300	36	78	0	22	9	.260

ED SPRAGUE Age 27/R $12

Last season, said one AL pitching coach, "Sprague was the guy you wanted up there with men on base. He was so uptight, he'd swing at anything." But he was just one among many Blue Jays to thud back to earth in 1994. Maybe they guessed they weren't going to get a chance to three-peat and decided the hell with it, wait till next year. But "next year" is now this year, and Toronto needs Sprague to take wing.

Year	Team	Lg.	Pos.	G	AB	R	H	HR	RBI	SB	BA
1991	Toronto	AL	3B	61	160	17	44	4	20	0	.275
1992	Toronto	AL	C	22	47	6	11	1	7	0	.234
1993	Toronto	AL	3B	150	546	50	142	12	73	1	.260
1994	Toronto	AL	3B	109	405	38	97	11	44	1	.240
1994 PROJECTION				148	531	50	123	11	59	2	.232

B. J. SURHOFF Age 30/L $9

Hurt most of the year and had surgery during The Strike. A mortal lock to be somewhere other than Milwaukee. Could still be a sleeper as a catcher for someone.

Year	Team	Lg.	Pos.	G	AB	R	H	HR	RBI	SB	BA
1991	Milwaukee	AL	C	143	505	57	146	5	68	5	.289
1992	Milwaukee	AL	C	139	480	63	121	4	62	14	.252
1993	Milwaukee	AL	3B	148	552	66	151	7	79	12	.274
1994	Milwaukee	AL	3B	40	134	20	35	5	22	0	.261
1994 PROJECTION				40	134	20	35	5	22	0	.261

FRANK THOMAS   Age 26/R $42

For the second straight season, his SB total has declined precipitously. We're worried.

Year	Team	Lg.	Pos.	G	AB	R	H	HR	RBI	SB	BA
1991	Chicago	AL	DH	158	559	104	178	32	109	1	.318
1992	Chicago	AL	1B	160	573	108	185	24	115	6	.323
1993	Chicago	AL	1B	153	549	106	174	41	128	4	.317
1994	Chicago	AL	1B	113	399	106	141	38	101	2	.353
1994 PROJECTION				161	561	141	188	53	140	2	.335

JIM THOME   Age 24/L $24

Nobody in the first-base box seats at Jacobs Field was killed or maimed by one of his errant rockets last year, so the Indians aren't going to lose any sleep worrying about his fielding. Neither are we. Sandwiched into the middle of that thunderous Tribe lineup and hitting in that new ballpark, Thome looks like a mortal lock to hit 30+ homers a season through the rest of the decade. He'll never be cheaper until the end of the century than he is right now. Get him.

Year	Team	Lg.	Pos.	G	AB	R	H	HR	RBI	SB	BA
1991	Cleveland	AL	3B	27	98	7	25	1	9	1	.255
1992	Cleveland	AL	3B	40	117	8	24	2	12	2	.205
1993	Cleveland	AL	3B	47	154	28	41	7	22	2	.266
1994	Cleveland	AL	3B	98	321	58	86	20	52	3	.268
1994 PROJECTION				144	480	80	124	29	75	3	.258

MO VAUGHN   Age 27/L $28

As good as Big Mo is both on and off the field, he wants to get better. We think he will. If he can cut down the strikeouts just a little and be just a little more selective as he gains experience, we're going to be seeing some Big Hurt-ish numbers beside Big Mo's name.

Year	Team	Lg.	Pos.	G	AB	R	H	HR	RBI	SB	BA
1991	Boston	AL	1B	74	219	21	57	4	32	2	.260
1992	Boston	AL	1B	113	355	42	83	13	57	3	.234
1993	Boston	AL	1B	152	539	86	160	29	101	4	.297
1994	Boston	AL	1B	111	394	65	122	26	82	4	.310
1994 PROJECTION				157	569	91	165	39	115	4	.290

ROBIN VENTURA   Age 27/L $23

The White Sox worry about his deteriorating defense. But as long as he keeps approaching 20 HR and 90 RBI, a Rotisserie owner needn't have a worry in the world.

Year	Team	Lg.	Pos.	G	AB	R	H	HR	RBI	SB	BA
1991	Chicago	AL	3B	157	606	92	172	23	100	2	.284
1992	Chicago	AL	3B	157	592	85	167	16	93	2	.282
1993	Chicago	AL	3B	157	554	85	145	22	94	1	.262
1994	Chicago	AL	3B	109	401	57	113	18	78	3	.282
1994 PROJECTION				153	564	79	158	29	104	3	.280

Catchers
pp. 33–46

Corners
pp. 46–65

Infield
pp. 66–85

Outfield
pp. 85–115

DH
pp. 115–119

Starters
pp. 119–155

Relievers
pp. 155–187

Up the Middle

NATIONAL LEAGUE

KURT ABBOTT   Age 25/R $9

You get the idea that the Marlins know what they're doing. They saved millions by allowing Walter Weiss to disappear via expensive free agency. Then they dipped into what is their organization's deepest commodity—young outfield prospects—and dealt Kerwin Moore to Oakland in exchange for Abbott, who is a better athlete than the oft-injured Weiss, has much more extra-base power, and is six years younger. While Weiss is as good as he's going to get, Abbott's best days are yet to come.

Year	Team	Lg.	Pos.	G	AB	R	H	HR	RBI	SB	BA
1993	Oakland	AL	OF	20	61	11	15	3	9	2	.246
1994	Florida	NL	SS	101	345	41	86	9	33	3	.249
1994 PROJECTION				142	480	53	120	13	45	3	.250

LUIS ALICEA   Age 29/B $3

He seems destined to be a fringe, utility type.

Year	Team	Lg.	Pos.	G	AB	R	H	HR	RBI	SB	BA
1991	St. Louis	NL	2B	56	68	5	13	0	0	0	.191
1992	St. Louis	NL	2B	85	265	26	65	2	32	2	.245
1993	St. Louis	NL	2B	115	362	50	101	3	46	11	.279
1994	St. Louis	NL	2B	88	205	32	57	5	29	4	.278
1994 PROJECTION				127	311	46	85	8	44	8	.273

ALEX ARIAS   Age 27/R $1

Florida's version of Rafael Belliard.

Year	Team	Lg.	Pos.	G	AB	R	H	HR	RBI	SB	BA
1992	Chicago	NL	SS	32	99	14	29	0	7	0	.293
1993	Florida	NL	2B	96	249	27	67	2	20	1	.269
1994	Florida	NL	SS	59	113	4	27	0	15	0	.239
1994 PROJECTION				82	148	5	33	0	16	0	.223

BRET BARBERIE   Age 27/B $6

You'll never have to fear that Barberie will coast. He's a solid, hardworking player who figures always to be around .300.

Year	Team	Lg.	Pos.	G	AB	R	H	HR	RBI	SB	BA
1991	Montreal	NL	SS	57	136	16	48	2	18	0	.353
1992	Montreal	NL	3B	111	285	26	66	1	24	9	.232
1993	Florida	NL	2B	99	375	45	104	5	33	2	.277
1994	Florida	NL	2B	107	372	40	112	5	31	2	.301
1994 PROJECTION				147	483	51	148	7	43	2	.306

JAY BELL

Age 29/R   **$11**

Rebounded from a terrible start to have a productive, Jay Bell–like season, despite distractions from active involvement—some Pirates front office people thought *hyper*-active involvement—with the Players Association. Yeah, it was one of those years.

Year	Team	Lg.	Pos.	G	AB	R	H	HR	RBI	SB	BA
1991	Pittsburgh	NL	SS	157	608	96	164	16	67	10	.270
1992	Pittsburgh	NL	SS	159	632	87	167	9	55	7	.264
1993	Pittsburgh	NL	SS	154	604	102	187	9	51	16	.310
1994	Pittsburgh	NL	SS	110	424	68	117	9	45	2	.276
1994 PROJECTION				157	621	99	170	15	64	6	.274

JUAN BELL

Age 27/B   **$1**

After his first couple of weeks, Expos coaches were saying, "Gee, we can't understand why he's had so many problems with so many other teams." After another couple more weeks, they understood. Likely to move on.

Year	Team	Lg.	Pos.	G	AB	R	H	HR	RBI	SB	BA
1991	Baltimore	AL	2B	100	209	26	36	1	15	0	.172
1992	Philadelphia	NL	SS	46	147	12	30	1	8	5	.204
1993	Philadelphia	NL	SS	24	65	5	13	0	7	0	.200
1993	Milwaukee	AL	2B	91	286	42	67	5	29	6	.234
1994	Montreal	NL	2B	38	97	12	27	2	10	4	.278
1994 PROJECTION				56	122	17	32	2	13	6	.262

CRAIG BIGGIO

Age 29/R   **$28**

Just think: if the Astros hadn't traded Kenny Lofton, we never would have found out that Biggio might be the best leadoff hitter in baseball this side of . . . Kenny Lofton. And here you thought trading Lofton was a mistake.

Year	Team	Lg.	Pos.	G	AB	R	H	HR	RBI	SB	BA
1991	Houston	NL	C	149	546	79	161	4	46	19	.295
1992	Houston	NL	2B	162	613	96	170	6	39	38	.277
1993	Houston	NL	2B	155	610	98	175	21	64	15	.287
1994	Houston	NL	2B	114	437	88	139	6	56	39	.318
1994 PROJECTION				161	629	125	198	8	74	54	.315

JEFF BLAUSER

Age 29/R   **$12**

Miserable start last season, partly because of injuries, but also because NL pitchers discovered how much easier it was to pitch to Blauser without Nixon or Deion on base ahead of him or Gant hitting behind him. Before the world as we know it screeched to a halt on August 12, the Braves sounded like they wouldn't lose sleep if they lost Blauser to free agency.

Year	Team	Lg.	Pos.	G	AB	R	H	HR	RBI	SB	BA
1991	Atlanta	NL	SS	129	352	49	91	11	54	5	.259
1992	Atlanta	NL	SS	123	343	61	90	14	46	5	.262
1993	Atlanta	NL	SS	161	597	110	182	15	73	16	.305
1994	Atlanta	NL	SS	96	380	56	98	6	45	1	.258
1994 PROJECTION				139	554	80	149	7	63	3	.269

BRET BOONE   Age 25/R $18

As usual, we were right. We predicted he would blossom once he escaped
from under Lou Piniella's thumb. We predicted that playing with Barry
Larkin would help him grow up. We predicted that having his father on the
coaching staff would keep him focused. We predicted the hapless Mariners
would live to regret trading him. Unfortunately, modesty prevents us from
telling you how we *really* feel.

Year	Team	Lg.	Pos.	G	AB	R	H	HR	RBI	SB	BA
1992	Seattle	AL	2B	33	129	15	25	4	15	1	.194
1993	Seattle	AL	2B	76	271	31	68	12	38	2	.251
1994	Cincinnati	NL	2B	108	381	59	122	12	68	3	.320
1994 PROJECTION				154	554	81	179	19	102	3	.323

RAFAEL BOURNIGAL   Age 28/R $1

LA's answer to Rafael Belliard.

Year	Team	Lg.	Pos.	G	AB	R	H	HR	RBI	SB	BA
1992	Los Angeles	NL	SS	10	20	1	3	0	0	0	.150
1993	Los Angeles	NL	2B	8	18	0	9	0	3	0	.500
1994	Los Angeles	NL	SS	40	116	2	26	0	11	0	.224
1994 PROJECTION				72	228	5	49	0	21	0	.215

JEFF BRANSON   Age 28/L $2

You don't expect to get so many dingers from your utility infielder in so few
ABs. We don't expect it to happen again.

Year	Team	Lg.	Pos.	G	AB	R	H	HR	RBI	SB	BA
1992	Cincinnati	NL	2B	72	115	12	34	0	15	0	.296
1993	Cincinnati	NL	SS	125	381	40	92	3	22	4	.241
1994	Cincinnati	NL	2B	58	109	18	31	6	16	0	.284
1994 PROJECTION				73	134	19	36	7	20	0	.269

VINNY CASTILLA   Age 27/R $2

Only a part-timer, but his offensive skills make him worth considering.

Year	Team	Lg.	Pos.	G	AB	R	H	HR	RBI	SB	BA
1991	Atlanta	NL	SS	12	5	1	1	0	0	0	.200
1992	Atlanta	NL	3B	9	16	1	4	0	1	0	.250
1993	Colorado	NL	SS	105	337	36	86	9	30	2	.255
1994	Colorado	NL	SS	52	130	16	43	3	18	2	.331
1994 PROJECTION				79	211	24	70	5	26	4	.332

ANDUJAR CEDENO   Age 25/R $12

The Astros grew tiring of him scattering the paying customers with his wild
throws, which is why they gave Orlando Miller a long look. They liked what
they saw, but Cedeno's offensive ability makes him a hard player to part
with. Also, he doesn't carry one of those big salaries that the Astros are
committed to shedding.

Year	Team	Lg.	Pos.	G	AB	R	H	HR	RBI	SB	BA
1991	Houston	NL	SS	67	251	27	61	9	36	4	.243
1992	Houston	NL	SS	71	220	15	38	2	13	2	.173
1993	Houston	NL	SS	149	505	69	143	11	56	9	.283
1994	Houston	NL	SS	98	342	38	90	9	49	1	.263
1994 PROJECTION				139	484	49	120	12	68	1	.248

ROYCE CLAYTON   Age 25/R $10

Defensively, he's as good as anyone in the game. And those stolen bases were a nice surprise. But NL pitchers found out that they can overpower Clayton with average hard stuff, and it became obvious last year that he will never be able to carry the bat of . . .

Year	Team	Lg.	Pos.	G	AB	R	H	HR	RBI	SB	BA
1991	San Francisco	NL	SS	9	26	0	3	0	2	0	.115
1992	San Francisco	NL	SS	98	321	31	72	4	24	8	.224
1993	San Francisco	NL	SS	153	549	54	155	6	70	11	.282
1994	San Francisco	NL	SS	108	385	38	91	3	30	23	.236
1994 PROJECTION				155	580	56	133	3	42	24	.229

WIL CORDERO   Age 23/R $22

. . . who under Felipe Alou's incomparable leadership has matured into a much more reliable defensive shortstop and a big-time four-category offensive player who is going to keep getting better.

Year	Team	Lg.	Pos.	G	AB	R	H	HR	RBI	SB	BA
1992	Montreal	NL	SS	45	126	17	38	2	8	0	.302
1993	Montreal	NL	SS	138	475	56	118	10	58	12	.248
1994	Montreal	NL	SS	110	415	65	122	15	63	16	.294
1994 PROJECTION				158	609	99	185	19	95	23	.304

DELINO DeSHIELDS   Age 26/L $22

Injuries and an early slump had him stumbling out of the gate, and then The Strike nipped his return to form in the bud. Bet on a big year now that he's comfortable in Southern California.

Year	Team	Lg.	Pos.	G	AB	R	H	HR	RBI	SB	BA
1991	Montreal	NL	2B	151	563	83	134	10	51	56	.238
1992	Montreal	NL	2B	135	530	82	155	7	56	46	.292
1993	Montreal	NL	2B	123	481	75	142	2	29	43	.295
1994	Los Angeles	NL	2B	89	320	51	80	2	33	27	.250
1994 PROJECTION				129	473	78	124	5	54	42	.262

MARIANO DUNCAN   Age 32/R $11

A rock-solid performer at four positions for a team in shambles, he went spinning into free agent limbo. He batted 46 points higher on the road than at home, so a new venue should not diminish his attractiveness.

Year	Team	Lg.	Pos.	G	AB	R	H	HR	RBI	SB	BA
1991	Cincinnati	NL	2B	100	333	46	86	12	40	5	.258
1992	Philadelphia	NL	OF	142	574	71	153	8	50	23	.267
1993	Philadelphia	NL	2B	124	496	68	140	11	73	6	.282
1994	Philadelphia	NL	2B	88	347	49	93	8	48	10	.268
1994 PROJECTION				134	534	70	138	12	73	12	.258

Catchers
pp. 33–46

Corners
pp. 46–65

Infield
pp. 66–85

Outfield
pp. 85–115

DH
pp. 115–119

Starters
pp. 119–155

Relievers
pp. 155–187

SHAWON DUNSTON   Age 32/R $15

Little about the Cubs is certain nowadays, what with the mess Larry Himes left for new boss Andy MacPhail. But isn't a healthy Dunston more exciting to contemplate than any of the other ho-hum players the Cubs have standing around in their infield?

Year	Team	Lg.	Pos.	G	AB	R	H	HR	RBI	SB	BA
1991	Chicago	NL	SS	142	492	59	128	12	50	21	.260
1992	Chicago	NL	SS	18	73	8	23	0	2	2	.315
1993	Chicago	NL	SS	7	10	3	4	0	2	0	.400
1994	Chicago	NL	SS	88	331	38	92	11	35	3	.278
1994 PROJECTION				130	486	57	120	18	56	3	.247

TOM FOLEY   Age 35/L $1

Not a candidate for the Rotisserie Hall of Fame.

Year	Team	Lg.	Pos.	G	AB	R	H	HR	RBI	SB	BA
1991	Montreal	NL	SS	86	168	12	35	0	15	2	.208
1992	Montreal	NL	SS	72	115	7	20	0	5	3	.174
1993	Pittsburgh	NL	2B	86	194	18	49	3	22	0	.253
1994	Pittsburgh	NL	2B	59	123	13	29	3	15	0	.236
1994 PROJECTION				85	157	15	35	3	16	0	.223

CARLOS GARCIA   Age 27/R $12

Solid sophomore season. Look for improvement as a junior.

Year	Team	Lg.	Pos.	G	AB	R	H	HR	RBI	SB	BA
1991	Pittsburgh	NL	SS	12	24	2	6	0	1	0	.250
1992	Pittsburgh	NL	2B	22	39	4	8	0	4	0	.205
1993	Pittsburgh	NL	2B	141	546	77	147	12	47	18	.269
1994	Pittsburgh	NL	2B	98	412	49	114	6	28	18	.277
1994 PROJECTION				144	612	74	167	8	45	20	.273

RICKY GUTIERREZ   Age 24/R $1

Triple-A skills, which make him a perfect choice as Padres shortstop.

Year	Team	Lg.	Pos.	G	AB	R	H	HR	RBI	SB	BA
1993	San Diego	NL	SS	133	438	76	110	5	26	4	.251
1994	San Diego	NL	SS	90	275	27	66	1	28	2	.240
1994 PROJECTION				123	362	38	91	1	36	2	.251

JOSE HERNANDEZ   Age 25/R $1

Pass.

Year	Team	Lg.	Pos.	G	AB	R	H	HR	RBI	SB	BA
1991	Texas	AL	SS	45	98	8	18	0	4	0	.184
1992	Cleveland	AL	SS	3	4	0	0	0	0	0	0.000
1994	Chicago	NL	3B	56	132	18	32	1	9	2	.242
1994 PROJECTION				87	221	27	57	1	17	6	.258

JEFF KENT   Age 27/R $18

Led NL second sackers in errors again, but there will always be room in Rotisserie baseball for defensively challenged middle infielders with as much pop as Kent.

Year	Team	Lg.	Pos.	G	AB	R	H	HR	RBI	SB	BA
1992	Toronto	AL	3B	65	192	36	46	8	35	2	.240
1992	New York	NL	2B	37	113	16	27	3	15	0	.239
1993	New York	NL	2B	140	496	65	134	21	80	4	.270
1994	New York	NL	2B	107	415	53	121	14	68	1	.292
1994 PROJECTION				154	601	73	172	20	88	1	.286

MIKE LANSING — Age 26/R — $9

The Expos want him to be Tony Phillips when he grows up.

Year	Team	Lg.	Pos.	G	AB	R	H	HR	RBI	SB	BA
1993	Montreal	NL	3B	141	491	64	141	3	45	23	.287
1994	Montreal	NL	2B	106	394	44	105	5	35	12	.266
1994 PROJECTION				151	551	66	148	5	50	19	.269

BARRY LARKIN — Age 30/R — $18

Missed only four games last year, but the back is still a problem and minor injuries still nagged him. This year he turns 30, so don't figure on any sudden increase in durability. Or offensive numbers, for that matter. Good as he has been, there has always been this expectation that Larkin would be—should be—even better. He's now entering the phase of his career when what we've seen is what we'll get: no more, maybe less. But even if he isn't the second coming of Honus Wagner, he's a heckuva player.

Year	Team	Lg.	Pos.	G	AB	R	H	HR	RBI	SB	BA
1991	Cincinnati	NL	SS	123	464	88	140	20	69	24	.302
1992	Cincinnati	NL	SS	140	533	76	162	12	78	15	.304
1993	Cincinnati	NL	SS	100	384	57	121	8	51	14	.315
1994	Cincinnati	NL	SS	110	427	78	119	9	52	26	.279
1994 PROJECTION				158	615	115	170	12	69	33	.276

MARK LEMKE — Age 29/B — $3

Scrappy, spunky, plucky, gritty, flinty, unshaven.

Year	Team	Lg.	Pos.	G	AB	R	H	HR	RBI	SB	BA
1991	Atlanta	NL	2B	136	269	36	63	2	23	1	.234
1992	Atlanta	NL	2B	155	427	38	97	6	26	0	.227
1993	Atlanta	NL	2B	151	493	52	124	7	49	1	.252
1994	Atlanta	NL	2B	104	350	40	103	3	31	0	.294
1994 PROJECTION				147	487	53	140	6	48	0	.287

NELSON LIRIANO — Age 30/B — $1

Journeyman bit-player, but he does have some stick.

Year	Team	Lg.	Pos.	G	AB	R	H	HR	RBI	SB	BA
1991	Kansas City	AL	2B	10	22	5	9	0	1	0	.409
1993	Colorado	NL	SS	48	151	28	46	2	15	6	.305
1994	Colorado	NL	2B	87	255	39	65	3	31	0	.255
1994 PROJECTION				118	358	49	91	4	46	0	.254

LUIS LOPEZ
Age 24/B   **$1**

Good bat, could blossom into a valuable offensive shortstop. Or he could be the next Ricky Gutierrez. You can't tell about those young Padres.

Year	Team	Lg.	Pos.	G	AB	R	H	HR	RBI	SB	BA
1993	San Diego	NL	2B	17	43	1	5	0	1	0	.116
1994	San Diego	NL	SS	77	235	29	65	2	20	3	.277
1994 PROJECTION				120	395	52	113	5	42	5	.286

ROBERTO MEJIA
Age 22/R   **$3**

The Rockies sent him down, but they still have high hopes. So do we.

Year	Team	Lg.	Pos.	G	AB	R	H	HR	RBI	SB	BA
1993	Colorado	NL	2B	65	229	31	53	5	20	4	.231
1994	Colorado	NL	2B	38	116	11	28	4	14	3	.241
1994 PROJECTION				48	135	14	31	6	20	3	.230

ORLANDO MILLER
Age 26/R   **$3**

The Astros like his skills, and so do we. But last season, confided a Houston official, "We were really trying to build him up just to light a fire under Andujar Cedeno's ass."

Year	Team	Lg.	Pos.	G	AB	R	H	HR	RBI	SB	BA
1994	Houston	NL	SS	16	40	3	13	2	9	1	.325
1994 PROJECTION				29	58	5	17	2	10	1	.293

MICKEY MORANDINI
Age 28/L   **$4**

Look up "overachiever" in the dictionary and you see the Mick's baseball card. So long as Mariano Duncan is around, he won't have to worry much about batting against left-handers (.235). But too much exposure to tough lefties would definitely be injurious to his Rotisserie value.

Year	Team	Lg.	Pos.	G	AB	R	H	HR	RBI	SB	BA
1991	Philadelphia	NL	2B	98	325	38	81	1	20	13	.249
1992	Philadelphia	NL	2B	127	422	47	112	3	30	8	.265
1993	Philadelphia	NL	2B	120	425	57	105	3	33	13	.247
1994	Philadelphia	NL	2B	87	274	40	80	2	26	10	.292
1994 PROJECTION				129	412	58	127	5	42	13	.308

JOSE OFFERMAN
Age 26/B   **$2**

Tommy Lasorda could live with the errors. He could even live with the erratic offensive production. But when Offerman refused to bunt when ordered and then told the Dodgers skipper to do something anatomically difficult if not impossible with his bunt, that was enough. Hello, Albuquerque. He'll get a chance for redemption this spring, because the only other legitimate shortstop in the Dodgers organization is Bill Russell.

Year	Team	Lg.	Pos.	G	AB	R	H	HR	RBI	SB	BA
1991	Los Angeles	NL	SS	52	113	10	22	0	3	3	.195
1992	Los Angeles	NL	SS	149	534	67	139	1	30	23	.260
1993	Los Angeles	NL	SS	158	590	77	159	1	62	30	.269
1994	Los Angeles	NL	SS	72	243	27	51	1	25	2	.210
1994 PROJECTION				93	308	31	68	2	37	3	.221

JOSE OQUENDO   Age 31/B $1

Could help the Dodgers. Won't do much for you.

Year	Team	Lg.	Pos.	G	AB	R	H	HR	RBI	SB	BA
1991	St. Louis	NL	2B	127	366	37	88	1	26	1	.240
1992	St. Louis	NL	2B	14	35	3	9	0	3	0	.257
1993	St. Louis	NL	SS	46	73	7	15	0	4	0	.205
1994	St. Louis	NL	SS	55	129	13	34	0	9	1	.264
1994 PROJECTION				72	151	14	37	0	11	1	.245

JOHN PATTERSON   Age 28/B $3

Quick, without looking, name the Giant who finished third behind Matt
Williams and Barry Bonds in RBI last year. We'll give you a hint: it wasn't
Todd Benzinger, Royce Clayton, Darren Lewis, Kurt Manwaring ... or
Dusty Baker.

Year	Team	Lg.	Pos.	G	AB	R	H	HR	RBI	SB	BA
1992	San Francisco	NL	2B	32	103	10	19	0	4	5	.184
1993	San Francisco	NL	2B	16	16	1	3	1	2	0	.188
1994	San Francisco	NL	2B	85	240	36	57	3	32	13	.237
1994 PROJECTION				118	354	43	84	4	49	14	.237

GERONIMO PENA   Age 28/B $9

The Cardinals have been waiting a l-o-o-o-ng time for him to harness and
direct his considerable talents. He's still a risk. Peña's problem all along has
been in sustaining a high level of play over a whole season, and last year—
as you may have noticed—we all got short-changed in the whole season
department. So maybe he will revert to the on-again, off-again pattern of his
first three seasons. Without any solid empirical evidence, we prefer to think
that he has finally arrived.

Year	Team	Lg.	Pos.	G	AB	R	H	HR	RBI	SB	BA
1991	St. Louis	NL	2B	104	185	38	45	5	17	15	.243
1992	St. Louis	NL	2B	62	203	31	62	7	31	13	.305
1993	St. Louis	NL	2B	74	254	34	65	5	30	13	.256
1994	St. Louis	NL	2B	83	213	33	54	11	34	9	.254
1994 PROJECTION				83	213	33	54	11	34	9	.254

BIP ROBERTS   Age 31/B $16

Good season, but didn't win any friends around the Padres clubhouse with
his noisy complaints about his contract. You see, Bipster, when you're making
four times as much as the five guys sitting around you *combined*, maybe you
ought to keep it down about just how underpaid you are. On the other hand,
you're not likely to be in that clubhouse this year, so who cares?

Year	Team	Lg.	Pos.	G	AB	R	H	HR	RBI	SB	BA
1991	San Diego	NL	2B	117	424	66	119	3	32	26	.281
1992	Cincinnati	NL	OF	147	532	92	172	4	45	44	.323
1993	Cincinnati	NL	2B	83	292	46	70	1	18	26	.240
1994	San Diego	NL	2B	105	403	52	129	2	31	21	.320
1994 PROJECTION				142	536	70	166	3	48	27	.310

Catchers
pp. 33–46

Corners
pp. 46–65

Infield
pp. 66–85

Outfield
pp. 85–115

DH
pp. 115–119

Starters
pp. 119–155

Relievers
pp. 155–187

REY SANCHEZ   Age 27/R $3

Shares the same initials as the guy he succeeded at second base in the
Friendly Confines. That's where any similarity ends.

Year	Team	Lg.	Pos.	G	AB	R	H	HR	RBI	SB	BA
1991	Chicago	NL	SS	13	23	1	6	0	2	0	.261
1992	Chicago	NL	SS	74	255	24	64	1	19	2	.251
1993	Chicago	NL	SS	105	344	35	97	0	28	1	.282
1994	Chicago	NL	2B	96	291	26	83	0	24	2	.285
1994 PROJECTION				136	454	45	125	1	39	2	.275

RYNE SANDBERG   Age 35/R   No Price

We can understand him walking away from the $15 million or so in Cubs
money, but how could he stiff the prominent Rotisserie owner—we can't say
who, but his picture's on the back of this book who—paid $32 for him at
last year's auction draft?

Year	Team	Lg.	Pos.	G	AB	R	H	HR	RBI	SB	BA
1991	Chicago	NL	2B	158	585	104	170	26	100	22	.291
1992	Chicago	NL	2B	158	612	100	186	26	87	17	.304
1993	Chicago	NL	2B	117	456	67	141	9	45	9	.309
1994	Chicago	NL	2B	57	223	36	53	5	24	2	.238
1994 PROJECTION				57	223	36	53	5	24	2	.238

STEVE SCARSONE   Age 28/R $1

Spare part.

Year	Team	Lg.	Pos.	G	AB	R	H	HR	RBI	SB	BA
1992	Philadelphia	NL	2B	7	13	1	2	0	0	0	.154
1992	Baltimore	AL	2B	11	17	2	3	0	0	0	.176
1993	San Francisco	NL	2B	44	103	16	26	2	15	0	.252
1994	San Francisco	NL	2B	52	103	21	28	2	13	0	.272
1994 PROJECTION				71	163	27	48	4	21	0	.294

OZZIE SMITH   Age 40/B $5

If Ozzie is 40, then that must mean *Cork* Smith is . . . we don't want to
think about it. The most remarkable thing about the Wiz is how he transformed himself into a potent offensive player. Coming over to St. Louis and
that wonderful lineup in the 1980s had something to do with it, but so did
hard work and his determination to become a complete ballplayer, not just
a glove man. Dramatic drop in SB yet another sign that all good things come
to an end.

Year	Team	Lg.	Pos.	G	AB	R	H	HR	RBI	SB	BA
1991	St. Louis	NL	SS	150	550	96	157	3	50	35	.285
1992	St. Louis	NL	SS	132	518	73	153	0	31	43	.295
1993	St. Louis	NL	SS	141	545	75	157	1	53	21	.288
1994	St. Louis	NL	SS	98	381	51	100	3	30	6	.262
1994 PROJECTION				134	503	64	132	3	37	12	.262

KEVIN STOCKER
Age 25/B **$6**

What sophomore jinx? Despite injuries, he had a solid season, the second of many to come. Stocker is that rarest of players in the City of Brotherly Love: a quality everyday player developed by an organization whose woeful farm system is the worst in baseball.

Year	Team	Lg.	Pos.	G	AB	R	H	HR	RBI	SB	BA
1993	Philadelphia	NL	SS	70	259	46	84	2	31	5	.324
1994	Philadelphia	NL	SS	82	271	38	74	2	28	2	.273
1994 PROJECTION				129	427	56	123	3	45	2	.288

ROBBY THOMPSON
Age 32/R **$16**

Pay close attention to the medical reports and to how many innings he plays in spring training. Healthy, he's one of the best.

Year	Team	Lg.	Pos.	G	AB	R	H	HR	RBI	SB	BA
1991	San Francisco	NL	2B	144	492	74	129	19	48	14	.262
1992	San Francisco	NL	2B	128	443	54	115	14	49	5	.260
1993	San Francisco	NL	2B	128	494	85	154	19	65	10	.312
1994	San Francisco	NL	2B	35	129	13	27	2	7	3	.209
1994 PROJECTION				35	129	13	27	2	7	3	.209

FERNANDO VINA
Age 25/L **$1**

He was closing on 7 RBI when The Strike hit.

Year	Team	Lg.	Pos.	G	AB	R	H	HR	RBI	SB	BA
1993	Seattle	AL	2B	24	45	5	10	0	2	6	.222
1994	New York	NL	2B	79	124	20	31	0	6	3	.250
1994 PROJECTION				79	124	20	31	0	6	3	.250

JOSE VIZCAINO
Age 27/B **$2**

He made the Mets forget Rafael Santana. But one question: how on earth could he have been caught stealing 11 times in 12 attempts? Doesn't Dallas Green have a stop sign?

Year	Team	Lg.	Pos.	G	AB	R	H	HR	RBI	SB	BA
1991	Chicago	NL	3B	93	145	7	38	0	10	2	.262
1992	Chicago	NL	SS	86	285	25	64	1	17	3	.225
1993	Chicago	NL	SS	151	551	74	158	4	54	12	.287
1994	New York	NL	SS	103	410	47	105	3	33	1	.256
1994 PROJECTION				150	591	70	164	5	48	3	.277

WALT WEISS
Age 31/B **$5**

Two solid years without breaking down.

Year	Team	Lg.	Pos.	G	AB	R	H	HR	RBI	SB	BA
1991	Oakland	AL	SS	40	133	15	30	0	13	6	.226
1992	Oakland	AL	SS	103	316	36	67	0	21	6	.212
1993	Florida	NL	SS	158	500	50	133	1	39	7	.266
1994	Colorado	NL	SS	110	423	58	106	1	32	12	.251
1994 PROJECTION				153	598	85	155	3	52	12	.259

Catchers
pp. 33-46

Corners
pp. 46-65

Infield
pp. 66-85

Outfield
pp. 85-115

DH
pp. 115-119

Starters
pp. 119-155

Relievers
pp. 155-187

AMERICAN LEAGUE

ROBERTO ALOMAR
Age 27/B $37

Like many Blue Jays, he seemed to lose interest when it was obvious that Toronto wasn't going anywhere. Expect a rebound, especially in steals, now that the Jays have a second chance to three-peat.

Year	Team	Lg.	Pos.	G	AB	R	H	HR	RBI	SB	BA
1991	Toronto	AL	2B	161	637	88	188	9	69	53	.295
1992	Toronto	AL	2B	152	571	105	177	8	76	49	.310
1993	Toronto	AL	2B	153	589	109	192	17	93	55	.326
1994	Toronto	AL	2B	107	392	78	120	8	38	19	.306
1994 PROJECTION				151	572	115	177	15	64	39	.309

RICH AMARAL
Age 33/R $1

From a Mariner insider: "For a two-month period, I don't think anyone has ever played a worse second base than Amaral did for us." Hmmm.

Year	Team	Lg.	Pos.	G	AB	R	H	HR	RBI	SB	BA
1991	Seattle	AL	2B	14	16	2	1	0	0	0	.063
1992	Seattle	AL	3B	35	100	9	24	1	7	4	.240
1993	Seattle	AL	2B	110	373	53	108	1	44	19	.290
1994	Seattle	AL	2B	77	228	37	60	4	18	5	.263
1994 PROJECTION				111	288	45	75	4	20	11	.260

CARLOS BAERGA
Age 26/B $33

Time for a little perspective. In baseball history just two second basemen have hit .300 with 200 hits, 20 home runs, and 100 RBI in a single season. Rogers Hornsby (five times) and Baerga (twice), and all that prevented Baerga from reaching those marks a third consecutive time was the stupid You-Know-What. He's no Golden Glover, and he doesn't have Roberto Alomar's speed, but he's a year younger. We're leaning toward giving the edge to Baerga.

Year	Team	Lg.	Pos.	G	AB	R	H	HR	RBI	SB	BA
1991	Cleveland	AL	3B	158	593	80	171	11	69	3	.288
1992	Cleveland	AL	2B	161	657	92	205	20	105	10	.312
1993	Cleveland	AL	2B	154	624	105	200	21	114	15	.321
1994	Cleveland	AL	2B	103	442	81	139	19	80	8	.314
1994 PROJECTION				151	643	114	202	30	116	10	.314

MIKE BORDICK
Age 29/R $2

Tony LaRussa said last year that Bordick was his favorite player. Please note he said *favorite*, not *best*. With Tony's pet we are now entering a run of several guys who play a lot but end up with offensive stats reflecting a good home stand for Frank Thomas. When reading through this list of practically interchangeable parts, think: "end of the draft; $1 or $2 or $3 bucks at the most; extremely small cog in my machine." A lot of Rotisserie owners we hear from outsmart themselves by thinking that getting Bordick or Joey Cora or Felix Fermin for pennies is the key to this game. Sorry, guys—the key is those Frank Thomas home stands.

Year	Team	Lg.	Pos.	G	AB	R	H	HR	RBI	SB	BA
1991	Oakland	AL	SS	90	235	21	56	0	21	3	.238
1992	Oakland	AL	2B	154	504	62	151	3	48	12	.300
1993	Oakland	AL	SS	159	546	60	136	3	48	10	.249
1994	Oakland	AL	SS	114	391	38	99	2	37	7	.253
1994 PROJECTION				155	531	51	126	3	42	7	.237

DOMINGO CEDENO · Age 26/B · $1

There is nothing going on here that you need to be concerned about.

Year	Team	Lg.	Pos.	G	AB	R	H	HR	RBI	SB	BA
1993	Toronto	AL	SS	15	46	5	8	0	7	1	.174
1994	Toronto	AL	2B	47	97	14	19	0	10	1	.196
1994 PROJECTION				58	118	16	22	0	10	1	.186

JOEY CORA · Age 29/B · $2

Joey is the diminutive of Joseph. Joey's stats are the diminutive of a real second baseman's. That stolen base total for 1993 must have been a typo. (See MIKE BORDICK.)

Year	Team	Lg.	Pos.	G	AB	R	H	HR	RBI	SB	BA
1991	Chicago	AL	2B	100	228	37	55	0	18	11	.241
1992	Chicago	AL	2B	68	122	27	30	0	9	10	.246
1993	Chicago	AL	2B	153	579	95	155	2	51	20	.268
1994	Chicago	AL	2B	90	312	55	86	2	30	8	.276
1994 PROJECTION				128	443	71	127	4	40	10	.287

GARY DiSARCINA · Age 27/R · $2

Aside from Chad Curtis, who runs the bases as well as he does everything else, the Angels were terrible on the base paths last year: 38 SB, 40 CS. We ran the numbers on this when we discovered that DiSarcina was out two out of every three times he tried to steal. Maybe he should start using a little restraint.

Year	Team	Lg.	Pos.	G	AB	R	H	HR	RBI	SB	BA
1991	California	AL	SS	18	57	5	12	0	3	0	.211
1992	California	AL	SS	157	518	48	128	3	42	9	.247
1993	California	AL	SS	126	416	44	99	3	45	5	.238
1994	California	AL	SS	112	389	53	101	3	33	3	.260
1994 PROJECTION				159	558	74	146	6	40	3	.262

ALVARO ESPINOZA · Age 33/R · $1

Why on earth are you reading about Alvaro Espinoza?

Year	Team	Lg.	Pos.	G	AB	R	H	HR	RBI	SB	BA
1991	New York	AL	SS	148	480	51	123	5	33	4	.256
1993	Cleveland	AL	3B	129	263	34	73	4	27	2	.278
1994	Cleveland	AL	3B	90	231	27	55	1	19	1	.238
1994 PROJECTION				107	263	28	61	1	23	1	.232

Catchers
pp. 33–46

Corners
pp. 46–65

Infield
pp. 66–85

Outfield
pp. 85–115

DH
pp. 115–119

Starters
pp. 119–155

Relievers
pp. 155–187

FELIX FERMIN   Age 31/R $3

El Gato had himself a nice little year, but somebody else in your league already has him for a buck and is keeping him. Probably thinks Fermín is the key to victory. (See MIKE BORDICK.)

Year	Team	Lg.	Pos.	G	AB	R	H	HR	RBI	SB	BA
1991	Cleveland	AL	SS	129	424	30	111	0	31	5	.262
1992	Cleveland	AL	SS	79	215	27	58	0	13	0	.270
1993	Cleveland	AL	SS	140	480	48	126	2	45	4	.262
1994	Seattle	AL	SS	101	379	52	120	1	35	4	.317
1994 PROJECTION				147	577	67	163	3	48	4	.282

SCOTT FLETCHER   Age 36/R $1

Represented by the law firm of Gutsy, Scrappy, and Jobless.

Year	Team	Lg.	Pos.	G	AB	R	H	HR	RBI	SB	BA
1991	Chicago	AL	2B	90	248	14	51	1	28	0	.206
1992	Milwaukee	AL	2B	123	386	53	106	3	51	17	.275
1993	Boston	AL	2B	121	480	81	137	5	45	16	.285
1994	Boston	AL	2B	63	185	31	42	3	11	8	.227
1994 PROJECTION				76	210	33	48	3	12	8	.229

JEFF FRYE   Age 28/R $2

His season-long battle with Doug Strange for playing time evoked no comparisons with Hector and Achilles. The BA was in 205 AB, so calm down.

Year	Team	Lg.	Pos.	G	AB	R	H	HR	RBI	SB	BA
1992	Texas	AL	2B	67	199	24	51	1	12	1	.256
1994	Texas	AL	2B	57	205	37	67	0	18	6	.327
1994 PROJECTION				100	350	55	102	0	37	10	.291

GREG GAGNE   Age 33/R $8

At the top of the second tier of AL middle infielders.

Year	Team	Lg.	Pos.	G	AB	R	H	HR	RBI	SB	BA
1991	Minnesota	AL	SS	139	408	52	108	8	42	11	.265
1992	Minnesota	AL	SS	146	439	53	108	7	39	6	.246
1993	Kansas City	AL	SS	159	540	66	151	10	57	10	.280
1994	Kansas City	AL	SS	107	375	39	97	7	51	10	.259
1994 PROJECTION				154	544	56	138	10	73	10	.254

MIKE GALLEGO   Age 34/R $3

The Yankees would still love to unload Gallego and his big contract, especially now that Derek Jeter is only a telephone call away from being ready. Away from that potent Yankee lineup Gallego's modest offensive output might well become more modest still.

Year	Team	Lg.	Pos.	G	AB	R	H	HR	RBI	SB	BA
1991	Oakland	AL	2B	159	482	67	119	12	49	6	.247
1992	New York	AL	2B	53	173	24	44	3	14	0	.254
1993	New York	AL	SS	119	403	63	114	10	54	3	.283
1994	New York	AL	SS	89	306	39	73	6	41	0	.239
1994 PROJECTION				115	382	49	87	7	52	0	.228

BRENT GATES
Age 25/B   **$9**

His season ended in mid-July with a leg injury. We're still convinced he's the real deal.

Year	Team	Lg.	Pos.	G	AB	R	H	HR	RBI	SB	BA
1993	Oakland	AL	2B	139	535	64	155	7	69	7	.290
1994	Oakland	AL	2B	64	233	29	66	2	24	3	.283
1994 PROJECTION				64	233	29	66	2	24	3	.283

CHRIS GOMEZ
Age 23/R   **$6**

Made a little noise in almost 300 AB last year. His strikeouts project to about 120 for a full season, so he'll fit right in with his Tiger teammates. Note that he hit .349 against lefties, just .219 against righties last year. The disparity could spell trouble ahead.

Year	Team	Lg.	Pos.	G	AB	R	H	HR	RBI	SB	BA
1993	Detroit	AL	SS	46	128	11	32	0	11	2	.250
1994	Detroit	AL	SS	84	296	32	76	8	53	5	.257
1994 PROJECTION				121	392	44	101	8	57	5	.258

CRAIG GREBECK
Age 30/R   **$1**

Next.

Year	Team	Lg.	Pos.	G	AB	R	H	HR	RBI	SB	BA
1991	Chicago	AL	3B	107	224	37	63	6	31	1	.281
1992	Chicago	AL	SS	88	287	24	77	3	35	0	.268
1993	Chicago	AL	SS	72	190	25	43	1	12	1	.226
1994	Chicago	AL	2B	35	97	17	30	0	5	0	.309
1994 PROJECTION				53	139	21	39	0	6	0	.281

OZZIE GUILLEN
Age 31/L   **$4**

He poked fun at Michael Jordan in spring training. He rags Frank Thomas mercilessly. He hides Julio Franco's batting gloves. He talks endlessly to umpires, opposing players, and fans, to anyone who'll listen (although that is not a prerequisite). Anytime we spot a major league baseball player who seems like he's having fun and enjoys playing the game, we take him to our bosom. C'mere, Ozzie.

Year	Team	Lg.	Pos.	G	AB	R	H	HR	RBI	SB	BA
1991	Chicago	AL	SS	154	524	52	143	3	49	21	.273
1992	Chicago	AL	SS	12	40	5	8	0	7	1	.200
1993	Chicago	AL	SS	134	457	44	128	4	50	5	.280
1994	Chicago	AL	SS	100	365	46	105	1	39	5	.288
1994 PROJECTION				142	514	69	152	1	57	5	.296

TIM HULETT
Age 35/R   **$1**

You could fill your final roster slot with a less useful player. It might take some doing, but you could.

Year	Team	Lg.	Pos.	G	AB	R	H	HR	RBI	SB	BA
1991	Baltimore	AL	3B	79	206	29	42	7	18	0	.204
1992	Baltimore	AL	3B	57	142	11	41	2	21	0	.289
1993	Baltimore	AL	3B	85	260	40	78	2	23	1	.300
1994	Baltimore	AL	2B	36	92	11	21	2	15	0	.228
1994 PROJECTION				43	107	13	24	3	18	0	.224

Catchers
pp. 33–46

Corners
pp. 46–65

Infield
pp. 66–85

Outfield
pp. 85–115

DH
pp. 115–119

Starters
pp. 119–155

Relievers
pp. 155–187

PAT KELLY   Age 27/R $6

His Rotisserie value depends on his running, but the Yankees don't need to steal bases to score runs. Consider that the next time you start thinking that this is going be the year Kelly cuts loose.

Year	Team	Lg.	Pos.	G	AB	R	H	HR	RBI	SB	BA
1991	New York	AL	3B	96	298	35	72	3	23	12	.242
1992	New York	AL	2B	106	318	38	72	7	27	8	.226
1993	New York	AL	2B	127	406	49	111	7	51	14	.273
1994	New York	AL	2B	93	286	35	80	3	41	6	.280
1994 PROJECTION				130	409	57	122	7	57	7	.298

CHUCK KNOBLAUCH   Age 26/R $18

A premier player, just entering his prime, Knoblauch was chasing Earl Webb's six-decade-old record for doubles (67, 1931) as seriously as anyone was chasing anything last year.

Year	Team	Lg.	Pos.	G	AB	R	H	HR	RBI	SB	BA
1991	Minnesota	AL	2B	151	565	78	159	1	50	25	.281
1992	Minnesota	AL	2B	155	600	104	178	2	56	34	.297
1993	Minnesota	AL	2B	153	602	82	167	2	41	29	.277
1994	Minnesota	AL	2B	109	445	85	139	5	51	35	.312
1994 PROJECTION				152	609	106	177	9	71	50	.291

MANUEL LEE   Age 29/B $1

Get him for a buck and you just might be pleasantly surprised. Pay any more and you set up unwarranted expectations.

Year	Team	Lg.	Pos.	G	AB	R	H	HR	RBI	SB	BA
1991	Toronto	AL	SS	138	445	41	104	0	29	7	.234
1992	Toronto	AL	SS	128	396	49	104	3	39	6	.263
1993	Texas	AL	SS	73	205	31	45	1	12	2	.220
1994	Texas	AL	SS	95	335	41	93	2	38	3	.278
1994 PROJECTION				136	472	57	138	2	49	6	.292

JOSE LIND   Age 30/R $3

He was headed for career highs in SB, BA, and RBI when the season ended. Before you go off the deep end, however, reflect for a moment on the fact that Chico's career highs in those categories are pretty low.

Year	Team	Lg.	Pos.	G	AB	R	H	HR	RBI	SB	BA
1991	Pittsburgh	NL	2B	150	502	53	133	3	54	7	.265
1992	Pittsburgh	NL	2B	135	468	38	110	0	39	3	.235
1993	Kansas City	AL	2B	136	431	33	107	0	37	3	.248
1994	Kansas City	AL	2B	85	290	34	78	1	31	9	.269
1994 PROJECTION				126	423	46	110	1	36	9	.260

PAT LISTACH   Age 27/B $5

Spent most of 1994 on the DL, but obviously we can't get the memory of 1992 and those 54 SB out of our minds.

Year	Team	Lg.	Pos.	G	AB	R	H	HR	RBI	SB	BA
1992	Milwaukee	AL	SS	149	579	93	168	1	47	54	.290
1993	Milwaukee	AL	SS	98	356	50	87	3	30	18	.244
1994	Milwaukee	AL	SS	16	54	8	16	0	2	2	.296
1994 PROJECTION				16	54	8	16	0	2	2	.296

MARK McLEMORE Age 30/B $5

Hit .167 against lefties. Think maybe he might want to reconsider that switch-hitting business? Played some good second base, stole a few bases, but we caution against making too much of either fact. The Rangers would be well-advised to move him back into a utility role.

Year	Team	Lg.	Pos.	G	AB	R	H	HR	RBI	SB	BA
1991	Houston	NL	2B	21	61	6	9	0	2	0	.148
1992	Baltimore	AL	2B	101	228	40	56	0	27	11	.246
1993	Baltimore	AL	OF	148	581	81	165	4	72	21	.284
1994	Baltimore	AL	2B	104	343	44	88	3	29	20	.257
1994 PROJECTION				148	501	62	135	5	45	21	.269

PAT MEARES Age 26/R $1

Rotisserie is all about trying to avoid ending up with Pat Meares as your shortstop.

Year	Team	Lg.	Pos.	G	AB	R	H	HR	RBI	SB	BA
1993	Minnesota	AL	SS	111	346	33	87	0	33	4	.251
1994	Minnesota	AL	SS	80	229	29	61	2	24	5	.266
1994 PROJECTION				116	338	41	93	2	33	6	.275

TIM NAEHRING Age 28/R $7

Anointed by the Red Sox back in 1990 as their shortstop for the next decade, Naehring has logged almost as much DL time as Mickey Klutts. (You remember him, the perpetual prospect who had more days on the DL than career at-bats. You don't? That's okay. He was hurt too often to do much of anything.) But we advise taking a shot because he—Naehring, not Klutts—could be a heck of an offensive find.

Year	Team	Lg.	Pos.	G	AB	R	H	HR	RBI	SB	BA
1991	Boston	AL	SS	20	55	1	6	0	3	0	.109
1992	Boston	AL	SS	72	186	12	43	3	14	0	.231
1993	Boston	AL	2B	39	127	14	42	1	17	1	.331
1994	Boston	AL	2B	80	297	41	82	7	42	1	.276
1994 PROJECTION				124	458	60	125	10	57	1	.273

SPIKE OWEN Age 33/B $1

Nice year, but our minds are made up.

Year	Team	Lg.	Pos.	G	AB	R	H	HR	RBI	SB	BA
1991	Montreal	NL	SS	139	424	39	108	3	26	2	.255
1992	Montreal	NL	SS	122	386	52	104	7	40	9	.269
1993	New York	AL	SS	103	334	41	78	2	20	3	.234
1994	California	AL	3B	82	268	30	83	3	37	2	.310
1994 PROJECTION				121	431	51	132	4	53	2	.306

JEFF REBOULET Age 30/R $1

Rhymes with "not today."

Year	Team	Lg.	Pos.	G	AB	R	H	HR	RBI	SB	BA
1992	Minnesota	AL	SS	73	137	15	26	1	16	3	.190
1993	Minnesota	AL	SS	109	240	33	62	1	15	5	.258
1994	Minnesota	AL	SS	74	189	28	49	3	23	0	.259
1994 PROJECTION				93	228	32	57	3	24	0	.250

Catchers
pp. 33–46

Corners
pp. 46–65

Infield
pp. 66–85

Outfield
pp. 85–115

DH
pp. 115–119

Starters
pp. 119–155

Relievers
pp. 155–187

JODY REED   Age 32/R $2

Another example of the canny way in which Bud the Commish runs his
franchise. He brings in this sprightly, power-hitting, team-oriented guy to
play second base for just one reason: he came cheap. Phil Garner, who as
a player was the antithesis of Reed, just turns away when asked to talk
about him.

Year	Team	Lg.	Pos.	G	AB	R	H	HR	RBI	SB	BA
1991	Boston	AL	2B	153	618	87	175	5	60	6	.283
1992	Boston	AL	2B	143	550	64	136	3	40	7	.247
1993	Los Angeles	NL	2B	132	445	48	123	2	31	1	.276
1994	Milwaukee	AL	2B	108	399	48	108	2	37	5	.271
1994 PROJECTION				149	566	73	151	3	54	5	.267

HAROLD REYNOLDS   Age 34/B $2

Reynolds got a little huffy when California didn't act on his demand to be
traded, but perhaps he forgot that there had to be another team interested
for California to be able to trade him.

Year	Team	Lg.	Pos.	G	AB	R	H	HR	RBI	SB	BA
1991	Seattle	AL	2B	161	631	95	160	3	57	28	.254
1992	Seattle	AL	2B	140	458	55	113	3	33	15	.247
1993	Baltimore	AL	2B	145	485	64	122	4	47	12	.252
1994	California	AL	2B	74	207	33	48	0	11	10	.232
1994 PROJECTION				111	355	67	95	2	24	15	.268

CAL RIPKEN   Age 34/R $20

Hit 40 points above his lifetime BA and was on a 125-RBI clip, so he wasn't
just punching the clock and worrying about The Streak. A chilling thought:
if the owners and the players don't reach a settlement, and if the owners
decide to open the season with scabs, then The Streak will end, courtesy of
Bud Selig, Jerry Reinsdorf, the Tribune Company, and 25 sheep.

Year	Team	Lg.	Pos.	G	AB	R	H	HR	RBI	SB	BA
1991	Baltimore	AL	SS	162	650	99	210	34	114	6	.323
1992	Baltimore	AL	SS	162	637	73	160	14	72	4	.251
1993	Baltimore	AL	SS	162	641	87	165	24	90	1	.257
1994	Baltimore	AL	SS	112	444	71	140	13	75	1	.315
1994 PROJECTION				160	638	98	187	21	111	1	.293

CARLOS RODRIGUEZ   Age 27/B $2

He is a shortstop, a rookie, and a prospect, but he is not *the* Rodriguez of
the year. That one is Alex, he's a Mariner, and you can read about him in John
Benson's 1995 Farm System Prospects (see Chapter 4). Carlos brings a fine
glove and a little offensive skill to the party, a good blend for a potential utility
guy. He incidentally had the distinction of playing in a Triple-A lineup that
included three other Rodriguezes last year.

Year	Team	Lg.	Pos.	G	AB	R	H	HR	RBI	SB	BA
1991	New York	AL	SS	15	37	1	7	0	2	0	.189
1994	Boston	AL	SS	57	174	15	50	1	13	1	.287
1994 PROJECTION				99	321	25	87	4	35	2	.271

STEVE SAX   Age 35/R $1

There is no such thing as safe Sax.

Year	Team	Lg.	Pos.	G	AB	R	H	HR	RBI	SB	BA
1991	New York	AL	2B	158	652	85	198	10	56	31	.304
1992	Chicago	AL	2B	143	567	74	134	4	47	30	.236
1993	Chicago	AL	OF	57	119	20	28	1	8	7	.235
1994	Oakland	AL	2B	7	24	2	6	0	1	0	.250
1994 PROJECTION				7	24	2	6	0	1	0	.250

DICK SCHOFIELD   Age 32/R $1

The most he will do is hold the fort, doing precious little of value, until Alex Gonzalez is ready to take over.

Year	Team	Lg.	Pos.	G	AB	R	H	HR	RBI	SB	BA
1991	California	AL	SS	134	427	44	96	0	31	8	.225
1992	California	AL	SS	1	3	0	1	0	0	0	.333
1992	New York	NL	SS	142	420	52	86	4	36	11	.205
1993	Toronto	AL	SS	36	110	11	21	0	5	3	.191
1994	Toronto	AL	SS	95	325	38	83	4	32	7	.255
1994 PROJECTION				132	439	51	105	5	40	8	.239

TERRY SHUMPERT   Age 28/R $4

When Oliver Stone starts casting his film on the Great Juiced Ball Conspiracy, Shumpert will likely land a major supporting role. Last season the Royals second baseman launched 8 dingers in 183 official trips to the plate, after hitting a total of 6 in his previous 564 AB covering parts of four seasons. If Shumpert repeats his power show this season in Boston, we promise to lock ourselves in a room and watch tapes of Dick Ravitch and Don Fehr appearances on the *Larry King* show for 18½ straight hours.

Year	Team	Lg.	Pos.	G	AB	R	H	HR	RBI	SB	BA
1991	Kansas City	AL	2B	144	369	45	80	5	34	17	.217
1992	Kansas City	AL	2B	36	94	6	14	1	11	2	.149
1993	Kansas City	AL	2B	8	10	0	1	0	0	1	.100
1994	Kansas City	AL	2B	64	183	28	44	8	24	18	.240
1994 PROJECTION				72	205	30	48	8	25	20	.234

Catchers
pp. 33–46

Corners
pp. 46–65

Infield
pp. 66–85

Outfield
pp. 85–115

DH
pp. 115–119

Starters
pp. 119–155

Relievers
pp. 155–187

DOUG STRANGE   Age 30/B $1

No.

Year	Team	Lg.	Pos.	G	AB	R	H	HR	RBI	SB	BA
1991	Chicago	NL	3B	3	9	0	4	0	1	1	.444
1992	Chicago	NL	3B	52	94	7	15	1	5	1	.160
1993	Texas	AL	2B	145	484	58	124	7	60	6	.256
1994	Texas	AL	2B	73	226	26	48	5	26	1	.212
1994 PROJECTION				110	323	33	69	5	33	2	.214

ALAN TRAMMELL   Age 37/R $5

The year he played in his first All-Star Game, 1980, was also the first year of Rotisserie League Baseball. You can imagine our emotional investment in his hanging in there for another couple of years . . . hell, for another couple of decades. But that may not be in the cards.

Year	Team	Lg.	Pos.	G	AB	R	H	HR	RBI	SB	BA
1991	Detroit	AL	SS	101	375	57	93	9	55	11	.248
1992	Detroit	AL	SS	29	102	11	28	1	11	2	.275
1993	Detroit	AL	SS	112	401	72	132	12	60	12	.329
1994	Detroit	AL	SS	76	292	38	78	8	28	3	.267
1994 PROJECTION				113	431	56	112	12	45	5	.260

JOHN VALENTIN   Age 28/R $13

The last three years have been building blocks for his emergence—this season—as one of the premier offensive shortstops in baseball. We're talking Cal Ripken–Barry Larkin numbers, or a pretty good facsimile thereof. Okay, maybe we're getting a little overheated, but we can't think of a single American League shortstop likely to post better numbers this year. Can you?

Year	Team	Lg.	Pos.	G	AB	R	H	HR	RBI	SB	BA
1992	Boston	AL	SS	58	185	21	51	5	25	1	.276
1993	Boston	AL	SS	144	468	50	130	11	66	3	.278
1994	Boston	AL	SS	84	301	53	95	9	49	3	.316
1994 PROJECTION				130	479	75	144	15	70	3	.301

JOSE VALENTIN   Age 25/B $8

Had a huge year filling in for Pat Listach, and frankly we don't quite know what to make of it. Our gut feeling is that he should do it again before we get too excited.

Year	Team	Lg.	Pos.	G	AB	R	H	HR	RBI	SB	BA
1992	Milwaukee	AL	2B	4	3	1	0	0	1	0	0.000
1993	Milwaukee	AL	SS	19	53	10	13	1	7	1	.245
1994	Milwaukee	AL	SS	97	285	47	68	11	46	12	.239
1994 PROJECTION				144	439	64	116	14	66	13	.264

RANDY VELARDE   Age 32/R $11

Buck Showalter needs to get out more, have a few laughs, not spend so many nights sleeping in the Yankee Stadium clubhouse. But one thing is certain—he's a heckuva manager. Case in point: his masterful use of Velarde, whose Rotissevalue is linked to the uniform he wears. So long as he's in pinstripes, pay up.

Year	Team	Lg.	Pos.	G	AB	R	H	HR	RBI	SB	BA
1991	New York	AL	3B	80	184	19	45	1	15	3	.245
1992	New York	AL	SS	121	412	57	112	7	46	7	.272
1993	New York	AL	OF	85	226	28	68	7	24	2	.301
1994	New York	AL	SS	77	280	47	78	9	34	4	.279
1994 PROJECTION				112	401	69	108	16	52	5	.269

Catchers
pp. 33–46

Corners
pp. 46–65

Infield
pp. 66–85

Outfield
pp. 85–115

DH
pp. 115–119

Starters
pp. 119–155

Relievers
pp. 155–187

OMAR VIZQUEL   Age 27/B $5

Provided glue for the Indians infield until Pudge Rodriguez's violent breakup slide sent him limping to the disabled list. The offensive numbers are a little suspect, although he has provided hints before that he's not a cipher at the plate or on the bases. But we'll remain a little skittish until he proves in spring training that his pins are sound.

Year	Team	Lg.	Pos.	G	AB	R	H	HR	RBI	SB	BA
1991	Seattle	AL	SS	142	426	42	98	1	41	7	.230
1992	Seattle	AL	SS	136	483	49	142	0	21	15	.294
1993	Seattle	AL	SS	158	560	68	143	2	31	12	.255
1994	Cleveland	AL	SS	69	286	39	78	1	33	13	.273
1994 PROJECTION				112	444	60	123	2	53	15	.277

LOU WHITAKER   Age 37/L $13

Obviously Sweet Lou played hooky one day during spring training last year and discovered the Fountain of Youth somewhere in the environs of greater Lakeland. Sparky sat him against the tougher lefties and made sure he got plenty of rest, so there's no reason not to expect that Whitaker's 19th big league season will be as productive as his 18th.

Year	Team	Lg.	Pos.	G	AB	R	H	HR	RBI	SB	BA
1991	Detroit	AL	2B	138	470	94	131	23	78	4	.279
1992	Detroit	AL	2B	130	453	77	126	19	71	6	.278
1993	Detroit	AL	2B	119	383	72	111	9	67	3	.290
1994	Detroit	AL	2B	92	322	67	97	12	43	2	.301
1994 PROJECTION				129	444	77	137	15	60	2	.309

In the Outfield

NATIONAL LEAGUE

MOISES ALOU   Age 28/R $32

His mangled ankle is still not 100%, and he has only two full seasons as a regular under his belt, so the best is yet to come for this budding superstar. Wow. One cautionary note: if the Expos aren't sold and moved out of Quebec, the financially strapped organization will continue to ship away its better players as they become more expensive, and Moises could quickly be left without any effective lineup protection. While we're on the subject of Montreal, will someone please show us where it is written that there has to be major league baseball in a city that obviously doesn't give a hockey puck about hardball? We find it hard to be all that sympathetic about a "small market" team's struggles to survive when the people in that small market don't support the team. The same goes for Pittsburgh, by the way. When crowds of 30,000-plus come out to root, root, root for the home team and it *still* runs in the red, well, maybe then we'll get upset.

Year	Team	Lg.	Pos.	G	AB	R	H	HR	RBI	SB	BA
1992	Montreal	NL	OF	115	341	53	96	9	56	16	.282
1993	Montreal	NL	OF	136	482	70	138	18	85	17	.286
1994	Montreal	NL	OF	107	422	81	143	22	78	7	.339
1994 PROJECTION				154	605	120	209	31	111	12	.345

KEVIN BASS   Age 35/B $2

Still around, still marginally useful.

Year	Team	Lg.	Pos.	G	AB	R	H	HR	RBI	SB	BA
1991	San Francisco	NL	OF	124	361	43	84	10	40	7	.233
1992	San Francisco	NL	OF	89	265	25	71	7	30	7	.268
1992	New York	NL	OF	46	137	15	37	2	9	7	.270
1993	Houston	NL	OF	111	229	31	65	3	37	7	.284
1994	Houston	NL	OF	82	203	37	63	6	35	2	.310
1994 PROJECTION				112	281	45	83	8	51	4	.295

BILLY BEAN   Age 30/L $1

A member of the All Foods team, a tasty group that includes Darryl Strawberry, Jose Oliva, Sammy Sosa, Sean Berry, Mike Piazza, Doug Brocail, and Greg Pirkl. Even so, Mr. Bean is not worth making a special trip to the market.

Year	Team	Lg.	Pos.	G	AB	R	H	HR	RBI	SB	BA
1993	San Diego	NL	OF	88	177	19	46	5	32	2	.260
1994	San Diego	NL	OF	84	135	7	29	0	14	0	.215
1994 PROJECTION				100	151	8	32	0	16	0	.212

DEREK BELL   Age 26/R $24

Bell has shown signs of growing up. Among other things, he has impressed the Padres with his willingness to work hard to find a defensive position. Not necessary if the Padres are demoted to a Triple-A league where the DH can be used, but a pretty good move on Bell's part so long as the Padres are permitted to "compete" in the National League.

Year	Team	Lg.	Pos.	G	AB	R	H	HR	RBI	SB	BA
1991	Toronto	AL	OF	18	28	5	4	0	1	3	.143
1992	Toronto	AL	OF	61	161	23	39	2	15	7	.242
1993	San Diego	NL	OF	150	542	73	142	21	72	26	.262
1994	San Diego	NL	OF	108	434	54	135	14	54	24	.311
1994 PROJECTION				142	558	67	168	17	65	28	.301

DANTE BICHETTE   Age 31/R $39

The 30-30-100-.300 Club takes a lot longer to say than it does to list its members. Look for Bichette to join this year. While word is that Coors Field may not be the offensive bandbox that Mile High Stadium is, Bichette's big game shouldn't suffer too much in the rarefied air. By the way, we're not ready to go out on any limbs, but take a look at Bichette's 1994 numbers next to the ones posted by the next guy. . . .

Year	Team	Lg.	Pos.	G	AB	R	H	HR	RBI	SB	BA
1991	Milwaukee	AL	OF	134	445	53	106	15	59	14	.238
1992	Milwaukee	AL	OF	112	387	37	111	5	41	18	.287
1993	Colorado	NL	OF	141	538	93	167	21	89	14	.310
1994	Colorado	NL	OF	116	484	74	147	27	95	21	.304
1994 PROJECTION				161	678	95	196	36	119	28	.289

BARRY BONDS   Age 30/L $42

You can lament his surly attitude, but Bonds has always played the game hard. What he did after the All-Star break last year makes us wonder if *he* wasn't the Giant most likely to hit 62. And when you realize he had another monster year while playing with a seriously injured elbow all season, you might want to rethink passing on the crown of "Best Player in Baseball" to Ken Griffey Jr. or Frank Thomas just yet.

Year	Team	Lg.	Pos.	G	AB	R	H	HR	RBI	SB	BA
1991	Pittsburgh	NL	OF	153	510	95	149	25	116	43	.292
1992	Pittsburgh	NL	OF	140	473	109	147	34	103	39	.311
1993	San Francisco	NL	OF	159	539	129	181	46	123	29	.336
1994	San Francisco	NL	OF	112	391	89	122	37	81	29	.312
1994 PROJECTION				159	568	139	179	55	122	37	.315

JACOB BRUMFIELD   Age 29/R $8

Gets his big chance this year in Pittsburgh. We think he could be a steal.

Year	Team	Lg.	Pos.	G	AB	R	H	HR	RBI	SB	BA
1992	Cincinnati	NL	OF	24	30	6	4	0	2	6	.133
1993	Cincinnati	NL	OF	103	272	40	73	6	23	20	.268
1994	Cincinnati	NL	OF	68	122	36	38	4	11	6	.311
1994 PROJECTION				94	173	47	57	5	13	9	.329

ELLIS BURKS   Age 30/R $19

It's easy enough for us to say that Burks will be a huge asset if he can just stay healthy. But for the past five years, it has not been easy for him to stay healthy. Not only that, but wrist injuries are especially nasty, particularly if your line of work involves swinging a baseball bat. Remember Bob Horner? We do, and we are going to be very cautious when Burks's name comes up in the auction draft.

Year	Team	Lg.	Pos.	G	AB	R	H	HR	RBI	SB	BA
1991	Boston	AL	OF	130	474	56	119	14	56	6	.251
1992	Boston	AL	OF	66	235	35	60	8	30	5	.255
1993	Chicago	AL	OF	146	499	75	137	17	74	6	.275
1994	Colorado	NL	OF	42	149	33	48	13	24	3	.322
1994 PROJECTION				65	190	43	61	17	36	3	.321

JEROMY BURNITZ   Age 25/L $2

His stock went thud as pitchers found out how vulnerable he was to breaking stuff and hard sliders. Then it went thudder when the Mets packed him off to Cleveland, where he'll be lucky to get 200 AB.

Year	Team	Lg.	Pos.	G	AB	R	H	HR	RBI	SB	BA
1993	New York	NL	OF	86	263	49	64	13	38	3	.243
1994	New York	NL	OF	45	143	26	34	3	15	1	.238
1994 PROJECTION				65	200	33	46	4	20	1	.230

Catchers
pp. 33-46

Corners
pp. 46-65

Infield
pp. 66-85

Outfield
pp. 85-115

DH
pp. 115-119

Starters
pp. 119-155

Relievers
pp. 155-187

BRETT BUTLER   Age 37/L $19

If Terry Shumpert plays a supporting role in the Great Juiced Ball Conspiracy, then The Butler will be one of the leading men. Butler hitting eight home runs in a single season is like Don Fehr telling eight jokes. We don't advise buying Butler as your main power supply, but even at his advanced years he remains a hitting, running machine.

Year	Team	Lg.	Pos.	G	AB	R	H	HR	RBI	SB	BA
1991	Los Angeles	NL	OF	161	615	112	182	2	38	38	.296
1992	Los Angeles	NL	OF	157	553	86	171	3	39	41	.309
1993	Los Angeles	NL	OF	156	607	80	181	1	42	39	.298
1994	Los Angeles	NL	OF	111	417	79	131	8	33	27	.314
1994 PROJECTION				155	597	113	188	9	38	43	.315

CHUCK CARR   Age 26/B $24

Chuck E. is fun to watch, but he can also be exasperating. One sultry Florida evening, as Carr was prancing in the dugout, manager Rene Lachemann told him, "If you keep striking out, you're going to be doing your styling on the end of that goddamn bench." Subtlety is not one Lach's strong suits, but speed and great D are Carr's, so there's little chance his running game will be stalled anytime soon.

Year	Team	Lg.	Pos.	G	AB	R	H	HR	RBI	SB	BA
1991	New York	NL	OF	12	11	1	2	0	1	1	.182
1992	St. Louis	NL	OF	22	64	8	14	0	3	10	.219
1993	Florida	NL	OF	142	551	75	147	4	41	58	.267
1994	Florida	NL	OF	106	433	61	114	2	30	32	.263
1994 PROJECTION				146	552	73	142	4	41	39	.257

MARK CARREON   Age 31/R $2

An ideal DH. Probably belongs in the American League. What about Baltimore? Phil Regan would love him.

Year	Team	Lg.	Pos.	G	AB	R	H	HR	RBI	SB	BA
1991	New York	NL	OF	106	254	18	66	4	21	2	.260
1992	Detroit	AL	OF	101	336	34	78	10	41	3	.232
1993	San Francisco	NL	OF	78	150	22	49	7	33	1	.327
1994	San Francisco	NL	OF	51	100	8	27	3	20	0	.270
1994 PROJECTION				66	129	14	37	3	23	1	.287

DAVE CLARK   Age 32/L $9

The only Pirate to reach double figures in HR last year. The whole Pirates team hit only 80 last year, a total matched by Matt Williams and Barry Bonds. Maybe it's time for the Pirates to pack up and move somewhere.

Year	Team	Lg.	Pos.	G	AB	R	H	HR	RBI	SB	BA
1991	Kansas City	AL	DH	11	10	1	2	0	1	0	.200
1992	Pittsburgh	NL	OF	23	33	3	7	2	7	0	.212
1993	Pittsburgh	NL	OF	110	277	43	75	11	46	1	.271
1994	Pittsburgh	NL	OF	86	223	37	66	10	46	2	.296
1994 PROJECTION				126	374	72	119	23	84	2	.318

JEFF CONINE

Catchers
pp. 33–46

Corners
pp. 46–65

Infield
pp. 66–85

Outfield
pp. 85–115

DH
pp. 115–119

Starters
pp. 119–155

Relievers
pp. 155–187

JEFF CONINE   **Age 28/R**   **$24**

A world-class racquetball player, but that's beside the point. A durable performer who has not missed a game in two years, but that still leaves him 12 years shy of Cal Ripken. A .300-hitting RBI machine who took a big leap forward in homers last season, but you already know that. The big news is Conine's anticipated move to third base, a position change that is an important part of the Marlins' master plan. If the move works, the Marlins will be able to promote one of their hot young outfielders, the team will be strengthened, and Conine's development as a power hitter will be accelerated. Pay close attention to those spring training box scores.

Year	Team	Lg.	Pos.	G	AB	R	H	HR	RBI	SB	BA
1992	Kansas City	AL	OF	28	91	10	23	0	9	0	.253
1993	Florida	NL	OF	162	595	75	174	12	79	2	.292
1994	Florida	NL	OF	115	451	60	144	18	82	1	.319
1994 PROJECTION				162	648	78	206	25	113	3	.318

MIDRE CUMMINGS   **Age 23/L**   **$8**

The Pirates think Cummings will develop some power as he refines his considerable skills. Right now, says one Pirates coach, "he's so raw you wonder if he knows which end of the bat to hold." No problem: Jim Leyland will show him.

Year	Team	Lg.	Pos.	G	AB	R	H	HR	RBI	SB	BA
1993	Pittsburgh	NL	OF	13	36	5	4	0	3	0	.111
1994	Pittsburgh	NL	OF	24	86	11	21	1	12	0	.244
1994 PROJECTION				72	259	31	78	6	40	1	.301

LENNY DYKSTRA   **Age 32/L**   **$28**

Throw out 1994. Nails has always been a slow starter, and once he hit his stride, he was hobbled by a series of aches and pains. Most important, he is not the kind of player who puts up huge numbers when they don't mean anything. If the Phillies are in the race, you get the Monster of 1993. If the Phillies are out of the race, you get something less, good but not great. So only draft him if you're prepared to start rooting for the Phillies.

Year	Team	Lg.	Pos.	G	AB	R	H	HR	RBI	SB	BA
1991	Philadelphia	NL	OF	63	246	48	73	3	12	24	.297
1992	Philadelphia	NL	OF	85	345	53	104	6	39	30	.301
1993	Philadelphia	NL	OF	161	637	143	194	19	66	37	.305
1994	Philadelphia	NL	OF	84	315	68	86	5	24	15	.273
1994 PROJECTION				131	502	104	146	7	41	33	.291

JIM EISENREICH   **Age 35/L**   **$4**

We think the word "Eisenreich" must mean "consummate professional" in German. We know that's what "Jim Eisenreich" means in baseball.

Year	Team	Lg.	Pos.	G	AB	R	H	HR	RBI	SB	BA
1991	Kansas City	AL	OF	135	375	47	113	2	47	5	.301
1992	Kansas City	AL	OF	113	353	31	95	2	28	11	.269
1993	Philadelphia	NL	OF	153	362	51	115	7	54	5	.318
1994	Philadelphia	NL	OF	104	290	42	87	4	43	6	.300
1994 PROJECTION				148	452	66	139	6	67	8	.308

MIKE FELDER
Age 32/B   **$1**

Will likely be swept aside by the influx of young Astros outfield prospects. Will end up somewhere. Will steal a few bases and make his Rotisserie owner feel smug for not having forgotten him.

Year	Team	Lg.	Pos.	G	AB	R	H	HR	RBI	SB	BA
1991	San Francisco	NL	OF	132	348	51	92	0	18	21	.264
1992	San Francisco	NL	OF	145	322	44	92	4	23	14	.286
1993	Seattle	AL	OF	109	342	31	72	1	20	15	.211
1994	Houston	NL	OF	58	117	10	28	0	13	3	.239
1994 PROJECTION				69	120	11	30	0	14	3	.250

STEVE FINLEY
Age 30/L   **$16**

His big contract is on Astros owner Drayton McLane's hit list. Last year's power surge makes him more interesting than ever. In another park, he might join the 15-40 Club. At least until they un-juice the ball.

Year	Team	Lg.	Pos.	G	AB	R	H	HR	RBI	SB	BA
1991	Houston	NL	OF	159	596	84	170	8	54	34	.285
1992	Houston	NL	OF	162	607	84	177	5	55	44	.292
1993	Houston	NL	OF	142	545	69	145	8	44	19	.266
1994	Houston	NL	OF	94	373	64	103	11	33	13	.276
1994 PROJECTION				140	565	85	162	14	61	20	.287

LOU FRAZIER
Age 30/B   **$11**

From the Rotisserie perspective, which is always the way we prefer to look at things, Frazier is a lot more interesting at second base than in the outfield. If he's still on second by the end of spring training, you may want to double his price.

Year	Team	Lg.	Pos.	G	AB	R	H	HR	RBI	SB	BA
1993	Montreal	NL	OF	112	189	27	54	1	16	17	.286
1994	Montreal	NL	OF	76	140	25	38	0	14	20	.271
1994 PROJECTION				108	224	39	61	0	25	25	.272

DAVE GALLAGHER
Age 34/R   **$1**

You know the line on Gallagher by now: a plus for a major league baseball team, a minus for a Rotisserie League baseball team. Hey, our standards must be a little higher.

Year	Team	Lg.	Pos.	G	AB	R	H	HR	RBI	SB	BA
1991	California	AL	OF	90	270	32	79	1	30	2	.293
1992	New York	NL	OF	98	175	20	42	1	21	4	.240
1993	New York	NL	OF	99	201	34	55	6	28	1	.274
1994	Atlanta	NL	OF	89	152	27	34	2	14	0	.224
1994 PROJECTION				107	203	33	44	3	18	0	.217

RON GANT
Age 30/R   **$25**

Who knows? Not too long ago, he was one of the best players in baseball, but you have to question whether he will be able to get back up to speed—literally—after a year's layoff and the terrible damage he did to his legs on that stupid motorbike. Some baseball people have always seen him as a "fine-line" player, that is, someone for whom a small slip means going from great to merely okay. We peg him at somewhere in the middle, at least for now.

Year	Team	Lg.	Pos.	G	AB	R	H	HR	RBI	SB	BA
1991	Atlanta	NL	OF	154	561	101	141	32	105	34	.251
1992	Atlanta	NL	OF	153	544	74	141	17	80	32	.259
1993	Atlanta	NL	OF	157	606	113	166	36	117	26	.274
1994	Did not play										

BERNARD GILKEY   Age 28/R $16

Not too long ago it looked like the Cardinals had assembled the Outfield of the '90s, and Gilkey was one of its pillars. But when a player goes from .302 and .305 to .253, you wonder if that pillar might have structural damage. We think it was just an off year (and a bad metaphor).

Year	Team	Lg.	Pos.	G	AB	R	H	HR	RBI	SB	BA
1991	St. Louis	NL	OF	81	268	28	58	5	20	14	.216
1992	St. Louis	NL	OF	131	384	56	116	7	43	18	.302
1993	St. Louis	NL	OF	137	557	99	170	16	70	15	.305
1994	St. Louis	NL	OF	105	380	52	96	6	45	15	.253
1994 PROJECTION				140	503	64	126	9	59	17	.250

LUIS GONZALEZ   Age 27/L $19

Late last summer, here's how Gonzalez explained his sluggish start in an otherwise solid season: "For a while there at the beginning I was sort of standing around watching Bags. It was like those guys who played with Michael Jordan. They would find themselves taking time off in a game just to see what Michael would do next." We assume Gonzalez was talking about Michael the *basketball* player.

Year	Team	Lg.	Pos.	G	AB	R	H	HR	RBI	SB	BA
1991	Houston	NL	OF	137	473	51	120	13	69	10	.254
1992	Houston	NL	OF	122	387	40	94	10	55	7	.243
1993	Houston	NL	OF	154	540	82	162	15	72	20	.300
1994	Houston	NL	OF	112	392	57	107	8	67	15	.273
1994 PROJECTION				159	570	88	161	14	93	19	.282

MARQUIS GRISSOM   Age 27/R $37

By necessity, he was often jerked around in the Expos batting order. But one of Grissom's many positive qualities is that he never complains. He just goes out and does just about everything well.

Year	Team	Lg.	Pos.	G	AB	R	H	HR	RBI	SB	BA
1991	Montreal	NL	OF	148	558	73	149	6	39	76	.267
1992	Montreal	NL	OF	159	653	99	180	14	66	78	.276
1993	Montreal	NL	OF	157	630	104	188	19	95	53	.298
1994	Montreal	NL	OF	110	475	96	137	11	45	36	.288
1994 PROJECTION				154	667	127	191	13	59	47	.286

Catchers
pp. 33–46

Corners
pp. 46–65

Infield
pp. 66–85

Outfield
pp. 85–115

DH
pp. 115–119

Starters
pp. 119–155

Relievers
pp. 155–187

TONY GWYNN   Age 34/L $33

We'll never know whether he would have hit .400, but we do know that of the 45 games the Padres lost to The Strike, 24 of them were against the five worst pitching staffs in the league—Chicago, Florida, Pittsburgh, St. Louis, and Colorado.

Year	Team	Lg.	Pos.	G	AB	R	H	HR	RBI	SB	BA
1991	San Diego	NL	OF	134	530	69	168	4	62	8	.317
1992	San Diego	NL	OF	128	520	77	165	6	41	3	.317
1993	San Diego	NL	OF	122	489	70	175	7	59	14	.358
1994	San Diego	NL	OF	110	419	79	165	12	64	5	.394
1994 PROJECTION				155	607	107	232	16	93	5	.382

GLENALLEN HILL   Age 30/R $18

Not well regarded within the Cubs organization, despite the good numbers. Said one club official: "Hill is one of those guys who always seems to do something when it doesn't mean anything." Don't be surprised if he's playing somewhere else this spring.

Year	Team	Lg.	Pos.	G	AB	R	H	HR	RBI	SB	BA
1991	Toronto	AL	DH	35	99	14	25	3	11	2	.253
1991	Cleveland	AL	OF	37	122	15	32	5	14	4	.262
1992	Cleveland	AL	OF	102	369	38	89	18	49	9	.241
1993	Cleveland	AL	OF	66	174	19	39	5	25	7	.224
1993	Chicago	NL	OF	31	87	14	30	10	22	1	.345
1994	Chicago	NL	OF	89	269	48	80	10	38	19	.297
1994 PROJECTION				128	424	67	119	14	59	25	.281

THOMAS HOWARD   Age 30/B $1

Once such a good prospect that he was the Padres' first pick and the 11th player taken overall in the 1986 amateur draft. Now just a spare part.

Year	Team	Lg.	Pos.	G	AB	R	H	HR	RBI	SB	BA
1991	San Diego	NL	OF	106	281	30	70	4	22	10	.249
1992	San Diego	NL	OF	5	3	1	1	0	0	0	.333
1992	Cleveland	AL	OF	117	358	36	99	2	32	15	.277
1993	Cleveland	AL	OF	74	178	26	42	3	23	5	.236
1993	Cincinnati	NL	OF	38	141	22	39	4	13	5	.277
1994	Cincinnati	NL	OF	83	178	24	47	5	24	4	.264
1994 PROJECTION				108	208	29	56	6	29	5	.269

PETE INCAVIGLIA   Age 30/R $5

Sayonara, Inky. If you can't hack it in baseball, you might want to consider sumo wrestling.

Year	Team	Lg.	Pos.	G	AB	R	H	HR	RBI	SB	BA
1991	Detroit	AL	OF	97	337	38	72	11	38	1	.214
1992	Houston	NL	OF	113	349	31	93	11	44	2	.266
1993	Philadelphia	NL	OF	116	368	60	101	24	89	1	.274
1994	Philadelphia	NL	OF	80	244	28	56	13	32	1	.230
1994 PROJECTION				114	315	40	73	19	48	1	.232

HOWARD JOHNSON

Age 34/B $5

Sic transit gloria mundi.

Year	Team	Lg.	Pos.	G	AB	R	H	HR	RBI	SB	BA
1991	New York	NL	3B	156	564	108	146	38	117	30	.259
1992	New York	NL	OF	100	350	48	78	7	43	22	.223
1993	New York	NL	3B	72	235	32	56	7	26	6	.238
1994	Colorado	NL	OF	93	227	30	48	10	40	11	.211
1994 PROJECTION				123	296	41	65	13	50	13	.220

BRIAN JORDAN

Age 28/R $8

Maybe he was a little hasty in giving up that football thing.

Year	Team	Lg.	Pos.	G	AB	R	H	HR	RBI	SB	BA
1992	St. Louis	NL	OF	55	193	17	40	5	22	7	.207
1993	St. Louis	NL	OF	67	223	33	69	10	44	6	.309
1994	St. Louis	NL	OF	53	178	14	46	5	15	4	.258
1994 PROJECTION				75	219	18	57	5	19	6	.260

DAVE JUSTICE

Age 28/L $31

The ball was juiced, everybody was hitting everything over the fence, yet Justice plonked only five more dingers than Steve Buechele. How come? Perhaps we shouldn't worry about that sort of thing, not in a year when he brought his BA up 43 points, but we figure you pay good money for us to fret about such matters. The Braves don't seem too worried, but that's maybe because they know that . . .

Year	Team	Lg.	Pos.	G	AB	R	H	HR	RBI	SB	BA
1991	Atlanta	NL	OF	109	396	67	109	21	87	8	.275
1992	Atlanta	NL	OF	144	484	78	124	21	72	2	.256
1993	Atlanta	NL	OF	157	585	90	158	40	120	3	.270
1994	Atlanta	NL	OF	104	352	61	110	19	59	2	.313
1994 PROJECTION				131	445	84	153	28	86	2	.344

MIKE KELLY

Age 24/R $9

. . . is just about ready. The scouts say he might need another few months of Triple-A, but toward the end of last year he was cutting down his swing, hitting rockets to all fields, and generally looking like he belonged.

Year	Team	Lg.	Pos.	G	AB	R	H	HR	RBI	SB	BA
1994	Atlanta	NL	OF	30	77	14	21	2	9	0	.273
1994 PROJECTION				47	119	19	34	2	12	0	.286

ROBERTO KELLY

Age 30/R $22

He's not much of a cornerback, but he fit in very nicely in Atlanta. By the way, that was a good, old-fashioned, value-for-value trade. How come we see so few of them these days? Outside of Rotisserie baseball, that is.

Year	Team	Lg.	Pos.	G	AB	R	H	HR	RBI	SB	BA
1991	New York	AL	OF	126	486	68	130	20	69	32	.267
1992	New York	AL	OF	152	580	81	158	10	66	28	.272
1993	Cincinnati	NL	OF	78	320	44	102	9	35	21	.319
1994	Cincinnati	NL	OF	47	179	29	54	3	21	9	.302
1994	Atlanta	NL	OF	63	255	44	73	6	24	10	.286
1994 PROJECTION				153	621	105	191	21	74	26	.308

Catchers pp. 33–46

Corners pp. 46–65

Infield pp. 66–85

Outfield pp. 85–115

DH pp. 115–119

Starters pp. 119–155

Relievers pp. 155–187

MIKE KINGERY   Age 34/L $8

He came to spring training as just another non-roster filler, playing for his
fifth organization, and perfectly fitting the description of a career fringe guy.
Then he got a chance to play every day when injuries hit the Rockies outfield.
Suddenly, eight seasons after his major league debut, he was an overnight
success. We like stories like that, even if there's not likely to be a sequel.

Year	Team	Lg.	Pos.	G	AB	R	H	HR	RBI	SB	BA
1991	San Francisco	NL	OF	91	110	13	20	0	8	1	.182
1992	Oakland	AL	OF	12	28	3	3	0	1	0	.107
1994	Colorado	NL	OF	105	301	56	105	4	41	5	.349
1994 PROJECTION				146	460	71	145	8	56	9	.315

RYAN KLESKO   Age 23/L $22

He was platooned last year, but one Braves executive assured us that "he's
ready to play every day. We just want him to stay mad for a while longer."

Year	Team	Lg.	Pos.	G	AB	R	H	HR	RBI	SB	BA
1992	Atlanta	NL	1B	13	14	0	0	0	1	0	0.000
1993	Atlanta	NL	1B	22	17	3	6	2	5	0	.353
1994	Atlanta	NL	OF	92	245	42	68	17	47	1	.278
1994 PROJECTION				125	380	60	98	23	62	1	.258

RAY LANKFORD   Age 27/L $27

All that turbulence in the Midwest over the summer was the Cardinals
organization breathing a collective sigh of relief as Lankford took a giant
step back to where he left off in 1992. He almost made it. This year will
tell us whether he's a superstar or just a star.

Year	Team	Lg.	Pos.	G	AB	R	H	HR	RBI	SB	BA
1991	St. Louis	NL	OF	151	566	83	142	9	69	44	.251
1992	St. Louis	NL	OF	153	598	87	175	20	86	42	.293
1993	St. Louis	NL	OF	127	407	64	97	7	45	14	.238
1994	St. Louis	NL	OF	109	416	89	111	19	57	11	.267
1994 PROJECTION				156	590	122	164	25	83	14	.278

DARREN LEWIS   Age 27/R $21

Cheer up, Darren. We know you feel bad about making your first big league
error, but we want to assure you that it will in no manner or means diminish
your Rotisserie value.

Year	Team	Lg.	Pos.	G	AB	R	H	HR	RBI	SB	BA
1991	San Francisco	NL	OF	72	222	41	55	1	15	13	.248
1992	San Francisco	NL	OF	100	320	38	74	1	18	28	.231
1993	San Francisco	NL	OF	136	522	84	132	2	48	46	.253
1994	San Francisco	NL	OF	114	451	70	116	4	29	30	.257
1994 PROJECTION				157	637	100	169	5	48	50	.265

JIM LINDEMAN   Age 33/R $3

Years of back problems prevented him from becoming the star St. Louis
once thought he could be, and he knocked around Triple-A for a couple of
years. But last season Lindeman resurfaced with the Mets as a valuable

bench player, a job for which he has all the tools (including an outfielder's glove and a first baseman's mitt).

Year	Team	Lg.	Pos.	G	AB	R	H	HR	RBI	SB	BA
1991	Philadelphia	NL	OF	65	95	13	32	0	12	0	.337
1992	Philadelphia	NL	OF	29	39	6	10	1	6	0	.256
1993	Houston	NL	1B	9	23	2	8	0	0	0	.348
1994	New York	NL	OF	52	137	18	37	7	20	0	.270
1994 PROJECTION				85	247	31	63	11	34	0	.255

TONY LONGMIRE   Age 26/L $1

Uh-uh.

Year	Team	Lg.	Pos.	G	AB	R	H	HR	RBI	SB	BA
1993	Philadelphia	NL	OF	11	13	1	3	0	1	0	.231
1994	Philadelphia	NL	OF	69	139	10	33	0	17	2	.237
1994 PROJECTION				100	199	16	49	0	20	2	.246

AL MARTIN   Age 27/L $16

Wrist injuries scare us (see ELLIS BURKS), but if Martin is healthy he has 20-20 potential.

Year	Team	Lg.	Pos.	G	AB	R	H	HR	RBI	SB	BA
1992	Pittsburgh	NL	OF	12	12	1	2	0	2	0	.167
1993	Pittsburgh	NL	OF	143	480	85	135	18	64	16	.281
1994	Pittsburgh	NL	OF	82	276	48	79	9	33	15	.286
1994 PROJECTION				82	276	48	79	9	33	15	.286

DAVE MARTINEZ   Age 30/L $3

He'll have a modest role somewhere.

Year	Team	Lg.	Pos.	G	AB	R	H	HR	RBI	SB	BA
1991	Montreal	NL	OF	124	396	47	117	7	42	16	.295
1992	Cincinnati	NL	OF	135	393	47	100	3	31	12	.254
1993	San Francisco	NL	OF	91	241	28	58	5	27	6	.241
1994	San Francisco	NL	OF	97	235	23	58	4	27	3	.247
1994 PROJECTION				138	363	40	103	6	41	7	.284

DERRICK MAY   Age 26/L $11

We thought we'd see more home runs, but he at least has established himself as a productive RBI man in a less-than-full-time role.

Year	Team	Lg.	Pos.	G	AB	R	H	HR	RBI	SB	BA
1991	Chicago	NL	OF	15	22	4	5	1	3	0	.227
1992	Chicago	NL	OF	124	351	33	96	8	45	5	.274
1993	Chicago	NL	OF	128	465	62	137	10	77	10	.295
1994	Chicago	NL	OF	100	345	43	98	8	51	3	.284
1994 PROJECTION				137	450	61	129	10	61	3	.287

LLOYD McCLENDON   Age 36/R $1

Good guy to have on your bench.

Year	Team	Lg.	Pos.	G	AB	R	H	HR	RBI	SB	BA
1991	Pittsburgh	NL	OF	85	163	24	47	7	24	2	.288
1992	Pittsburgh	NL	OF	84	190	26	48	3	20	1	.253
1993	Pittsburgh	NL	OF	88	181	21	40	2	19	0	.221
1994	Pittsburgh	NL	OF	51	92	9	22	4	12	0	.239
1994 PROJECTION				74	116	11	30	6	20	0	.259

Catchers
pp. 33–46

Corners
pp. 46–65

Infield
pp. 66–85

Outfield
pp. 85–115

DH
pp. 115–119

Starters
pp. 119–155

Relievers
pp. 155–187

WILLIE McGEE   Age 36/B $3

Could be the end of the trail for this 1985 MVP, two-time batting champion, and wonderful outfielder. We've enjoyed watching him work.

Year	Team	Lg.	Pos.	G	AB	R	H	HR	RBI	SB	BA
1991	San Francisco	NL	OF	131	497	67	155	4	43	17	.312
1992	San Francisco	NL	OF	138	474	56	141	1	36	13	.297
1993	San Francisco	NL	OF	130	475	53	143	4	46	10	.301
1994	San Francisco	NL	OF	45	156	19	44	5	23	3	.282
1994 PROJECTION				45	156	19	44	5	23	3	.282

KEVIN McREYNOLDS   Age 35/R $1

Go away.

Year	Team	Lg.	Pos.	G	AB	R	H	HR	RBI	SB	BA
1991	New York	NL	OF	143	522	65	135	16	74	6	.259
1992	Kansas City	AL	OF	109	373	45	92	13	49	7	.247
1993	Kansas City	AL	OF	110	351	44	86	11	42	2	.245
1994	New York	NL	OF	51	180	23	46	4	21	2	.256
1994 PROJECTION				71	203	25	56	4	24	2	.276

ORLANDO MERCED   Age 28/L $12

Never hit a home run off a left-hander until last year, when he had three dingers off southpaws. Never mind that the three lefties weren't exactly Spahn, Koufax, and Carlton. (They were Boucher, Plesac, and Hampton.) The Pirates now think Merced is on the verge of becoming a 15–20 HR man. We think the Pirates are growing quietly desperate for good news.

Year	Team	Lg.	Pos.	G	AB	R	H	HR	RBI	SB	BA
1991	Pittsburgh	NL	1B	120	411	83	113	10	50	8	.275
1992	Pittsburgh	NL	1B	134	405	50	100	6	60	5	.247
1993	Pittsburgh	NL	OF	137	447	68	140	8	70	3	.313
1994	Pittsburgh	NL	OF	108	386	48	105	9	51	4	.272
1994 PROJECTION				155	561	81	165	12	80	4	.294

KEVIN MITCHELL   Age 33/R $34

Look for him to return to San Francisco, where, as one of the Giants said, "We'll leave him alone, stick him between Barry and Mitch, let him play his 110 games and hit 35 to 40 home runs, and help us win the pennant." Sounds like a good plan.

Year	Team	Lg.	Pos.	G	AB	R	H	HR	RBI	SB	BA
1991	San Francisco	NL	OF	113	371	52	95	27	69	2	.256
1992	Seattle	AL	OF	99	360	48	103	9	67	0	.286
1993	Cincinnati	NL	OF	93	323	56	110	19	64	1	.341
1994	Cincinnati	NL	OF	95	310	57	101	30	77	2	.326
1994 PROJECTION				138	457	89	148	41	107	2	.324

RAUL MONDESI   Age 24/R $25

The third straight Rookie of the Year to wear Dodger blue, Mondesi has the best arm in baseball. We note that to show that we care about the whole game, not just its Rotisserie aspects. But speaking of HR, RBI, and SB, this guy is going to deliver plenty over the next several years, so consider the listed salary as a floor rather than a ceiling.

Year	Team	Lg.	Pos.	G	AB	R	H	HR	RBI	SB	BA
1993	Los Angeles	NL	OF	42	86	13	25	4	10	4	.291
1994	Los Angeles	NL	OF	112	434	63	133	16	56	11	.306
1994 PROJECTION				150	572	82	176	19	69	13	.308

JAMES MOUTON   Age 26/R $12

The Astros rolled the dice and made him their leadoff hitter and opening-day right fielder, a position he was still learning to play. A former second baseman, he was ready for neither role. They sent him back down for seasoning, and he will be back up to stay this year. With the Astros farm system loaded with outfield talent, Mouton might well evolve into a Mariano Duncan–type utility guy, only with less power and more speed. Nothing wrong with that.

Year	Team	Lg.	Pos.	G	AB	R	H	HR	RBI	SB	BA
1994	Houston	NL	OF	99	310	43	76	2	16	24	.245
1994 PROJECTION				116	315	48	77	2	17	32	.244

JOE ORSULAK   Age 32/L $5

Class act. Somebody should follow Orsulak around with a video camera for a couple of weeks and make an instructional tape for rookies. They could call it "This Is How to Play the Game."

Year	Team	Lg.	Pos.	G	AB	R	H	HR	RBI	SB	BA
1991	Baltimore	AL	OF	143	486	57	135	5	43	6	.278
1992	Baltimore	AL	OF	117	391	45	113	4	39	5	.289
1993	New York	NL	OF	134	409	59	116	8	35	5	.284
1994	New York	NL	OF	96	292	39	76	8	42	4	.260
1994 PROJECTION				133	404	50	101	10	47	5	.250

PHIL PLANTIER   Age 26/L $21

Pitching coaches around the league say he has huge holes in his swing. But those holes didn't bother him too much in 1993 when he launched those 34 taters. The bad wrist ruined 1994, but we think he'll come all the way back—possibly, according to current rumor, in Phildelphia.

Year	Team	Lg.	Pos.	G	AB	R	H	HR	RBI	SB	BA
1991	Boston	AL	OF	53	148	27	49	11	35	1	.331
1992	Boston	AL	OF	108	349	46	86	7	30	2	.246
1993	San Diego	NL	OF	138	462	67	111	34	100	4	.240
1994	San Diego	NL	OF	96	341	44	75	18	41	3	.220
1994 PROJECTION				120	392	51	90	19	47	3	.230

KARL RHODES   Age 26/L $4

If only The Strike had begun with the season's second game, Tuffy would have won MVP with his three-homer opener. Unfortunately, he hit only five more in his next 94 games, which gives you some hint why he had spent most of the preceding decade in the minors.

Year	Team	Lg.	Pos.	G	AB	R	H	HR	RBI	SB	BA
1991	Houston	NL	OF	44	136	7	29	1	12	2	.213
1992	Houston	NL	OF	5	4	0	0	0	0	0	0.000
1993	Houston	NL	OF	5	2	0	0	0	0	0	0.000
1993	Chicago	NL	OF	15	52	12	15	3	7	2	.288
1994	Chicago	NL	OF	95	269	39	63	8	19	6	.234
1994 PROJECTION				129	312	47	76	10	29	7	.244

KEVIN ROBERSON   Age 27/B $2

Talented but disappointing to Cubs brass who thought he would knock the ivy off Wrigley's walls.

Year	Team	Lg.	Pos.	G	AB	R	H	HR	RBI	SB	BA
1993	Chicago	NL	OF	62	180	23	34	9	27	0	.189
1994	Chicago	NL	OF	44	55	8	12	4	9	0	.218
1994 PROJECTION				44	55	8	12	4	9	0	.218

HENRY RODRIGUEZ   Age 27/L $8

A pleasant surprise, but the Dodgers are banking on blue-chip kids Todd Hollandsworth and Billy Ashley. If either makes it, Rodriguez pulls fourth outfielder duties.

Year	Team	Lg.	Pos.	G	AB	R	H	HR	RBI	SB	BA
1992	Los Angeles	NL	OF	53	146	11	32	3	14	0	.219
1993	Los Angeles	NL	OF	76	176	20	39	8	23	1	.222
1994	Los Angeles	NL	OF	104	306	33	82	8	49	0	.268
1994 PROJECTION				144	422	44	107	10	60	0	.254

DEION SANDERS   Age 27/L $24

We're still trying to get our mind around the picture of Neon playing for Marge. And you know what? The mind reels.

Year	Team	Lg.	Pos.	G	AB	R	H	HR	RBI	SB	BA
1991	Atlanta	NL	OF	54	110	16	21	4	13	11	.191
1992	Atlanta	NL	OF	97	303	54	92	8	28	26	.304
1993	Atlanta	NL	OF	95	272	42	75	6	28	19	.276
1994	Atlanta	NL	OF	46	191	32	55	4	21	19	.288
1994	Cincinnati	NL	OF	46	184	26	51	0	7	19	.277
1994 PROJECTION				135	552	93	162	9	47	50	.293

REGGIE SANDERS   Age 27/R $36

We don't know how he would fare at cornerback, but the best baseball-only Sanders in Cincinnati is on target for a huge, breakout season.

Year	Team	Lg.	Pos.	G	AB	R	H	HR	RBI	SB	BA
1991	Cincinnati	NL	OF	9	40	6	8	1	3	1	.200
1992	Cincinnati	NL	OF	116	385	62	104	12	36	16	.270
1993	Cincinnati	NL	OF	138	496	90	136	20	83	27	.274
1994	Cincinnati	NL	OF	107	400	66	105	17	62	21	.262
1994 PROJECTION				154	574	87	149	27	87	24	.260

GARY SHEFFIELD   Age 26/R $39

The Marlins say he grew up a lot in the past year, played heads-up ball, never sulked, and worked hard to learn how to play right field. If he hadn't been out awhile with assorted injuries, he would have been right up there with Bagwell and Williams. This could be the year he passes them.

Year	Team	Lg.	Pos.	G	AB	R	H	HR	RBI	SB	BA
1991	Milwaukee	AL	3B	50	175	25	34	2	22	5	.194
1992	San Diego	NL	3B	146	557	87	184	33	100	5	.330
1993	San Diego	NL	3B	68	258	34	76	10	36	5	.295
1993	Florida	NL	3B	72	236	33	69	10	37	12	.292
1994	Florida	NL	OF	87	322	61	89	27	78	12	.276
1994 PROJECTION				133	485	81	133	34	102	16	.274

CORY SNYDER   Age 32/R $1

No longer any place for him in a Dodger outfield brimming with young talent, but he still has the hands to play a little third and the arm to play a lot of outfield. The bat? Enough to help a lot of teams.

Year	Team	Lg.	Pos.	G	AB	R	H	HR	RBI	SB	BA
1991	Chicago	AL	OF	50	117	10	22	3	11	0	.188
1991	Toronto	AL	OF	21	49	4	7	0	6	0	.143
1992	San Francisco	NL	OF	124	390	48	105	14	57	4	.269
1993	Los Angeles	NL	OF	143	516	61	137	11	56	4	.266
1994	Los Angeles	NL	OF	73	153	18	36	6	18	1	.235
1994 PROJECTION				99	211	26	52	10	33	1	.246

SAMMY SOSA   Age 26/R $32

From what we hear, it wouldn't be too swell being his general manager, his manager, or his teammate. But being his Rotisserie owner . . . ah, that's a whole different ballgame.

Year	Team	Lg.	Pos.	G	AB	R	H	HR	RBI	SB	BA
1991	Chicago	AL	OF	116	316	39	64	10	33	13	.203
1992	Chicago	NL	OF	67	262	41	68	8	25	15	.260
1993	Chicago	NL	OF	159	598	92	156	33	93	36	.261
1994	Chicago	NL	OF	105	426	59	128	25	70	22	.300
1994 PROJECTION				148	605	86	184	36	102	32	.304

DARRYL STRAWBERRY   Age 33/L $15

Not clear how much he has left, but he started with so much that whatever it is may be enough for him to finish out a checkered career with dignity and style. There seems to be no question that his presence in the lineup was a big plus for the Giants last season, even more than the numbers he put up would indicate. Maybe it helped that, for the first time in his career, he wasn't expected to be The Man.

Year	Team	Lg.	Pos.	G	AB	R	H	HR	RBI	SB	BA
1991	Los Angeles	NL	OF	139	505	86	134	28	99	10	.265
1992	Los Angeles	NL	OF	43	156	20	37	5	25	3	.237
1993	Los Angeles	NL	OF	32	100	12	14	5	12	1	.140
1994	San Francisco	NL	OF	29	92	13	22	4	17	0	.239
1994 PROJECTION				74	243	39	62	10	42	1	.255

TONY TARASCO   Age 24/L $6

The more the Braves see of him, the more they see a fourth outfielder.

Year	Team	Lg.	Pos.	G	AB	R	H	HR	RBI	SB	BA
1993	Atlanta	NL	OF	24	35	6	8	0	2	0	.229
1994	Atlanta	NL	OF	87	132	16	36	5	19	5	.273
1994 PROJECTION				121	222	29	64	8	34	6	.288

MILT THOMPSON

Age 36/L $4

Money in the bank. Just not too much of it.

Year	Team	Lg.	Pos.	G	AB	R	H	HR	RBI	SB	BA
1991	St. Louis	NL	OF	115	326	55	100	6	34	16	.307
1992	St. Louis	NL	OF	109	208	31	61	4	17	18	.293
1993	Philadelphia	NL	OF	129	340	42	89	4	44	9	.262
1994	Philadelphia	NL	OF	87	220	29	60	3	30	7	.273
1994	Houston	NL	OF	9	21	5	6	1	3	2	.286
1994 PROJECTION				135	352	50	99	4	46	16	.281

RYAN THOMPSON

Age 27/R $16

Exasperating, but intriguing. You watch him for a stretch and he looks like the second coming of Willie Mays. You watch him for another stretch and he looks like the second coming of Willy Wonka.

Year	Team	Lg.	Pos.	G	AB	R	H	HR	RBI	SB	BA
1992	New York	NL	OF	30	108	15	24	3	10	2	.222
1993	New York	NL	OF	80	288	34	72	11	26	2	.250
1994	New York	NL	OF	98	334	39	75	18	59	1	.225
1994 PROJECTION				147	511	61	113	29	81	3	.221

ANDY VAN SLYKE

Age 34/L $15

Last season, after returning from the DL, he seemed to be playing at half-speed, odd timing for someone in his free agent season. Worse still, he seemed to prefer talking about his idol, Rush Limbaugh, to talking about hitting or fielding. He's always been one of our favorites, but last year we got the distinct impression that he is flat out bored with baseball. We hope we're wrong.

Year	Team	Lg.	Pos.	G	AB	R	H	HR	RBI	SB	BA
1991	Pittsburgh	NL	OF	138	491	87	130	17	83	10	.265
1992	Pittsburgh	NL	OF	154	614	103	199	14	89	12	.324
1993	Pittsburgh	NL	OF	83	323	42	100	8	50	11	.310
1994	Pittsburgh	NL	OF	105	374	41	92	6	30	7	.246
1994 PROJECTION				153	571	73	161	11	59	13	.282

LARRY WALKER

Age 28/L $32

Goofy enough to hand a ball to a kid in the stands when it was only the second out, stubborn enough to argue with the Expos over a fine that amounted to petty cash, talented enough to put up huge numbers without breaking a sweat, and tough enough to learn how to play first base because his shoulder was too sore to play the outfield. Probably not an Expo by the time you read this, but a star who will shine brightly somewhere.

Year	Team	Lg.	Pos.	G	AB	R	H	HR	RBI	SB	BA
1991	Montreal	NL	OF	137	487	59	141	16	64	14	.290
1992	Montreal	NL	OF	143	528	85	159	23	93	18	.301
1993	Montreal	NL	OF	138	490	85	130	22	86	29	.265
1994	Montreal	NL	OF	103	395	76	127	19	86	15	.322
1994 PROJECTION				149	553	103	174	26	123	18	.315

MITCH WEBSTER
Age 35/B $1

Dictionary definition of "role player."

Year	Team	Lg.	Pos.	G	AB	R	H	HR	RBI	SB	BA
1991	Cleveland	AL	OF	13	32	2	4	0	0	2	.125
1991	Pittsburgh	NL	OF	36	97	9	17	1	9	0	.175
1991	Los Angeles	NL	OF	58	74	12	21	1	10	0	.284
1992	Los Angeles	NL	OF	135	262	33	70	6	35	11	.267
1993	Los Angeles	NL	OF	88	172	26	42	2	14	4	.244
1994	Los Angeles	NL	OF	82	84	16	23	4	12	1	.274
1994 PROJECTION				111	115	19	29	4	14	1	.252

RONDELL WHITE
Age 23/R $13

Liked what we saw of him last year. We'll see a whole lot more this year, especially if Larry Walker departs. The Expos see him as a Marquis Grissom type with a little less speed and a little more power. We'll buy that.

Year	Team	Lg.	Pos.	G	AB	R	H	HR	RBI	SB	BA
1993	Montreal	NL	OF	23	73	9	19	2	15	1	.260
1994	Montreal	NL	OF	40	97	16	27	2	13	1	.278
1994 PROJECTION				62	143	23	36	3	24	1	.252

MARK WHITEN
Age 28/B $16

Big man, big power, big disappointment to everybody who paid big bucks for him expecting a big year last season. Big question mark this year.

Year	Team	Lg.	Pos.	G	AB	R	H	HR	RBI	SB	BA
1991	Toronto	AL	OF	46	149	12	33	2	19	0	.221
1991	Cleveland	AL	OF	70	258	34	66	7	26	4	.256
1992	Cleveland	AL	OF	148	508	73	129	9	43	16	.254
1993	St. Louis	NL	OF	152	562	81	142	25	99	15	.253
1994	St. Louis	NL	OF	92	334	57	98	14	53	10	.293
1994 PROJECTION				140	513	83	152	23	86	16	.296

ERIC YOUNG
Age 27/R $9

Respectable production, but the speed is what matters.

Year	Team	Lg.	Pos.	G	AB	R	H	HR	RBI	SB	BA
1992	Los Angeles	NL	2B	49	132	9	34	1	11	6	.258
1993	Colorado	NL	2B	144	490	82	132	3	42	42	.269
1994	Colorado	NL	OF	90	228	37	62	7	30	18	.272
1994 PROJECTION				112	302	46	80	9	37	22	.265

EDDIE ZAMBRANO
Age 29/R $2

We thought he was a kid until we found out that the Cubs were his fifth organization. We thought he might stick as a useful Cub until it became clear he can't play any position. We have dropped the thought of making him an integral part of our team.

Year	Team	Lg.	Pos.	G	AB	R	H	HR	RBI	SB	BA
1993	Chicago	NL	OF	8	17	1	5	0	2	0	.294
1994	Chicago	NL	OF	67	116	17	30	6	18	2	.259
1994 PROJECTION				97	183	36	48	10	29	2	.262

MIKE ALDRETE

Age 34/L $1

Enough Aldrete.

Year	Team	Lg.	Pos.	G	AB	R	H	HR	RBI	SB	BA
1991	San Diego	NL	OF	12	15	2	0	0	1	0	0.000
1991	Cleveland	AL	1B	85	183	22	48	1	19	1	.262
1993	Oakland	AL	1B	95	255	40	68	10	33	1	.267
1994	Oakland	AL	OF	76	178	23	43	4	18	2	.242
1994 PROJECTION				100	256	29	54	4	19	3	.211

BRADY ANDERSON

Age 31/L $20

Count on him for lots of SB, double-digit HR, lots of RBI, oodles of hustle, and long sideburns. One cautionary note: Brady booster Johnny Oates is gone, and the Orioles have a several young outfielders ready to break out. Meaning? You shouldn't be startled to see Anderson turn up in a trade.

Year	Team	Lg.	Pos.	G	AB	R	H	HR	RBI	SB	BA
1991	Baltimore	AL	OF	113	256	40	59	2	27	12	.230
1992	Baltimore	AL	OF	159	623	100	169	21	80	53	.271
1993	Baltimore	AL	OF	142	560	87	147	13	66	24	.262
1994	Baltimore	AL	OF	111	453	78	119	12	48	31	.263
1994 PROJECTION				159	649	108	161	18	64	38	.248

ERIC ANTHONY

Age 27/L $15

Five different guys saw left field duty for the Mariners last season, mainly because of Anthony's inconsistency, but he is still the one to invest in. We thought last year was going to be his breakout year. Now we're beginning to wonder if what we've seen is all we'll ever get.

Year	Team	Lg.	Pos.	G	AB	R	H	HR	RBI	SB	BA
1991	Houston	NL	OF	39	118	11	18	1	7	1	.153
1992	Houston	NL	OF	137	440	45	105	19	80	5	.239
1993	Houston	NL	OF	145	486	70	121	15	66	3	.249
1994	Seattle	AL	OF	79	262	31	62	10	30	6	.237
1994 PROJECTION				115	349	39	84	13	37	6	.241

DANNY BAUTISTA

Age 22/R $4

Look at it this way: Junior Felix stole his playing time.

Year	Team	Lg.	Pos.	G	AB	R	H	HR	RBI	SB	BA
1993	Detroit	AL	OF	17	61	6	19	1	9	3	.311
1994	Detroit	AL	OF	31	99	12	23	4	15	1	.232
1994 PROJECTION				64	169	21	43	9	33	3	.254

ALBERT BELLE

Age 28/R $42

If the Belle toils for thee, the morning box score will always be a good read. The best thing to happen to Cleveland since 1948.

Year	Team	Lg.	Pos.	G	AB	R	H	HR	RBI	SB	BA
1991	Cleveland	AL	OF	123	461	60	130	28	95	3	.282
1992	Cleveland	AL	DH	153	585	81	152	34	112	8	.260
1993	Cleveland	AL	OF	159	594	93	172	38	129	23	.290
1994	Cleveland	AL	OF	106	412	90	147	36	101	9	.357
1994 PROJECTION				153	584	129	217	52	153	13	.372

Catchers
pp. 33–46

Corners
pp. 46–65

Infield
pp. 66–85

Outfield
pp. 85–115

DH
pp. 115–119

Starters
pp. 119–155

Relievers
pp. 155–187

DARYL BOSTON   Age 32/L $1

If you are looking for big numbers from your fifth outfield slot, please don't come to Boston, at least so long as he's in New York. Too many good bats there for him to get enough playing time. Somewhere else, he could be a steal, because he still has more offensive tools than most fifth outfielders.

Year	Team	Lg.	Pos.	G	AB	R	H	HR	RBI	SB	BA
1991	New York	NL	OF	137	255	40	70	4	21	15	.275
1992	New York	NL	OF	130	289	37	72	11	35	12	.249
1993	Colorado	NL	OF	124	291	46	76	14	40	1	.261
1994	New York	AL	OF	52	77	11	14	4	14	0	.182
1994 PROJECTION				62	97	13	18	4	16	1	.186

TOM BRUNANSKY   Age 34/R $8

Dan Duquette revived Bruno's all-but-over career by duping the Commish's team into taking stiff-of-the-year Dave Valle in trade for this former Red Sox hero. Brunansky responded by hitting four more HR in half a Fenway season than the other four Boston right fielders totaled together. The Boston roster is wide open this year, however, so you can't count on Brunansky being given the chance to pick up where he left off. Pay attention to the Florida box scores to see how much playing time he gets.

Year	Team	Lg.	Pos.	G	AB	R	H	HR	RBI	SB	BA
1991	Boston	AL	OF	142	459	54	105	16	70	1	.229
1992	Boston	AL	OF	138	458	47	122	15	74	2	.266
1993	Milwaukee	AL	OF	80	224	20	41	6	29	3	.183
1994	Milwaukee	AL	OF	16	28	2	6	0	0	0	.214
1994	Boston	AL	OF	48	177	22	42	10	34	0	.237
1994 PROJECTION				92	302	38	66	15	46	0	.219

JAY BUHNER   Age 30/R $24

In the world headquarters of grunge, somebody came up with the idea for a promotion in which Mariners fans who got "Jay Buhner" haircuts would get in free. Nearly 1,000 people willing to have their heads shaved turned out, and Buhner capped the night by driving in four runs. Who said baseball doesn't market itself well?

Year	Team	Lg.	Pos.	G	AB	R	H	HR	RBI	SB	BA
1991	Seattle	AL	OF	137	406	64	99	27	77	0	.244
1992	Seattle	AL	OF	152	543	69	132	25	79	0	.243
1993	Seattle	AL	OF	158	563	91	153	27	98	2	.272
1994	Seattle	AL	OF	101	358	74	100	21	68	0	.279
1994 PROJECTION				149	550	106	156	34	107	0	.284

JOE CARTER   Age 35/R $35

Instant replay? Close your eyes and recall Carter leaping around the bases after hitting the home run that won the last World Series ever played. As vivid as if it were on *Baseball Tonight* tonight, right? If there is such a thing as a mortal lock in baseball, it is that Joe Carter will drive in at least 100 runs a season—even when a season isn't a season.

Year	Team	Lg.	Pos.	G	AB	R	H	HR	RBI	SB	BA
1991	Toronto	AL	OF	162	638	89	174	33	108	20	.273
1992	Toronto	AL	OF	158	622	97	164	34	119	12	.264
1993	Toronto	AL	OF	155	603	92	153	33	121	8	.254
1994	Toronto	AL	OF	111	435	70	118	27	103	11	.271
1994 PROJECTION				158	621	104	173	40	146	11	.279

WES CHAMBERLAIN   Age 28/R $7

Couldn't win the job Billy Hatcher left behind when they were traded for each other. He has the ability. Maybe the half season he spent with Andre Dawson will adjust his attitude.

Year	Team	Lg.	Pos.	G	AB	R	H	HR	RBI	SB	BA
1991	Philadelphia	NL	OF	101	383	51	92	13	50	9	.240
1992	Philadelphia	NL	OF	76	275	26	71	9	41	4	.258
1993	Philadelphia	NL	OF	96	284	34	80	12	45	2	.282
1994	Philadelphia	NL	OF	24	69	7	19	2	6	0	.275
1994	Boston	AL	OF	51	164	13	42	4	20	0	.256
1994 PROJECTION				90	283	28	76	10	38	0	.269

ALEX COLE   Age 29/L $15

Four teams in five years. What does that mean? It means his tools are easily replaceable. His Rotisserie appeal, of course, lies in his speed. The rest of his stats can be found on every bench on every team in baseball—for whom, sooner or later, Cole will undoubtedly play.

Year	Team	Lg.	Pos.	G	AB	R	H	HR	RBI	SB	BA
1991	Cleveland	AL	OF	122	387	58	114	0	21	27	.295
1992	Cleveland	AL	OF	41	97	11	20	0	5	9	.206
1992	Pittsburgh	NL	OF	64	205	33	57	0	10	7	.278
1993	Colorado	NL	OF	126	348	50	89	0	24	30	.256
1994	Minnesota	AL	OF	105	345	68	102	4	23	29	.296
1994 PROJECTION				134	437	82	127	5	27	38	.291

VINCE COLEMAN   Age 33/B $29

Those 50 SB in 99 games are nothing to sneeze at, and you have to applaud the way he pulled himself together and made the best of his new surroundings. But those surroundings are changing again this season. They've pulled up the carpet at Kauffman Stadium and replaced it with good old-fashioned grass: great news for baseball purists but potentially disastrous news for Coleman, who hit .300 at home last year but only .181 on the road.

Year	Team	Lg.	Pos.	G	AB	R	H	HR	RBI	SB	BA
1991	New York	NL	OF	72	278	45	71	1	17	37	.255
1992	New York	NL	OF	71	229	37	63	2	21	24	.275
1993	New York	NL	OF	92	373	64	104	2	25	38	.279
1994	Kansas City	AL	OF	104	438	61	105	2	33	50	.240
1994 PROJECTION				121	499	71	116	2	35	53	.232

DARNELL COLES
Age 32/R   **$1**

If Darnell figures in your auction draft plans, you don't figure to finish in the first division this year.

Year	Team	Lg.	Pos.	G	AB	R	H	HR	RBI	SB	BA
1991	San Francisco	NL	OF	11	14	1	3	0	0	0	.214
1992	Cincinnati	NL	3B	55	141	16	44	3	18	1	.312
1993	Toronto	AL	OF	64	194	26	49	4	26	1	.253
1994	Toronto	AL	OF	48	143	15	30	4	15	0	.210
1994 PROJECTION				72	208	19	41	7	24	0	.197

CHAD CURTIS
Age 26/R   **$24**

Just calling him the best all-around player on the hapless Angels is insufficient praise. This guy could play anywhere. And if you think of him only as a speed guy, then think again. This year he turns into a three-category offensive threat, with 40+ SB, 70+ RBI, and 15+ HR.

Year	Team	Lg.	Pos.	G	AB	R	H	HR	RBI	SB	BA
1992	California	AL	OF	139	441	59	114	10	46	43	.259
1993	California	AL	OF	152	583	94	166	6	59	48	.285
1994	California	AL	OF	114	453	67	116	11	50	25	.256
1994 PROJECTION				149	529	77	135	11	58	30	.255

MILT CUYLER
Age 26/B   **$3**

Was it only three years ago that he stole 41 bases? He hasn't helped the Tigers much since then, and he won't help you.

Year	Team	Lg.	Pos.	G	AB	R	H	HR	RBI	SB	BA
1991	Detroit	AL	OF	154	475	77	122	3	33	41	.257
1992	Detroit	AL	OF	89	291	39	70	3	28	8	.241
1993	Detroit	AL	OF	82	249	46	53	0	19	13	.213
1994	Detroit	AL	OF	48	116	20	28	1	11	5	.241
1994 PROJECTION				92	255	37	69	2	30	11	.271

ERIC DAVIS
Age 32/R   **$1**

So this is what it has come down to with Mr. Davis: we give up. After season after season of what-ifs and maybe-this-years and howlers like "we think Detroit breathed new life into Davis's career" (1994), we just flat out give up. The price is a buck, which is about 75 cents more than he was worth last year. Take him. He's yours. And if this is finally the season that he stays healthy and rolls back the clock to 1987 and does all those things that made him the most exciting player in baseball for a while, then just remember that we told you so, year after year after year.

Year	Team	Lg.	Pos.	G	AB	R	H	HR	RBI	SB	BA
1991	Cincinnati	NL	OF	89	285	39	67	11	33	14	.235
1992	Los Angeles	NL	OF	76	267	21	61	5	32	19	.228
1993	Los Angeles	NL	OF	108	376	57	88	14	53	33	.234
1993	Detroit	AL	OF	23	75	14	19	6	15	2	.253
1994	Detroit	AL	OF	37	120	19	22	3	13	5	.183
1994 PROJECTION				37	120	19	22	3	13	5	.183

MIKE DEVEREAUX   Age 31/R $8

Has nowhere to go but up after a season-long freefall. Someone will take the
risk and reap huge rewards, on the reasoning that a guy who until so recently
was so good couldn't really be as bad as he looked last season. That someone
will not, however, be the one of us who had Devereaux on his team in the
much-publicized league run by *Baseball Weekly*—a team that finished a weak
eleventh. That someone has decided to blame it all on Devereaux.

Year	Team	Lg.	Pos.	G	AB	R	H	HR	RBI	SB	BA
1991	Baltimore	AL	OF	149	608	82	158	19	59	16	.260
1992	Baltimore	AL	OF	156	653	76	180	24	107	10	.276
1993	Baltimore	AL	OF	131	527	72	132	14	75	3	.250
1994	Baltimore	AL	OF	85	301	35	61	9	33	1	.203
1994 PROJECTION				126	442	48	97	15	55	2	.219

ALEX DIAZ   Age 26/B $1

Maybe as your fifth outfielder.

Year	Team	Lg.	Pos.	G	AB	R	H	HR	RBI	SB	BA
1992	Milwaukee	AL	OF	22	9	5	1	0	1	3	.111
1993	Milwaukee	AL	OF	32	69	9	22	0	1	5	.319
1994	Milwaukee	AL	OF	79	187	17	47	1	17	5	.251
1994 PROJECTION				91	191	18	48	1	17	5	.251

JIM EDMONDS   Age 24/L $7

The Angels have high hopes. We have medium-high hopes.

Year	Team	Lg.	Pos.	G	AB	R	H	HR	RBI	SB	BA
1993	California	AL	OF	18	61	5	15	0	4	0	.246
1994	California	AL	OF	94	289	35	79	5	37	4	.273
1994 PROJECTION				133	420	45	112	8	53	4	.267

JUNIOR FELIX   Age 27/B $8

Go figure. His career went south so fast that he didn't even make the final
cut in last year's book. So all he does is come back to post some very
respectable numbers as the Tigers' regular right fielder. Now what are we
supposed to do? Count on him to do it again? What do you think we are,
nuts or something?

Year	Team	Lg.	Pos.	G	AB	R	H	HR	RBI	SB	BA
1991	California	AL	OF	66	230	32	65	2	26	7	.283
1992	California	AL	OF	139	509	63	125	9	72	8	.246
1993	Florida	NL	OF	57	214	25	51	7	22	2	.238
1994	Detroit	AL	OF	86	301	54	92	13	49	1	.306
1994 PROJECTION				118	399	65	118	14	57	1	.296

JUAN GONZALEZ   Age 25/R $40

The Rangers hope that his temperamental reaction to signing a huge new
contract will gradually wear off. The Rangers also hope that their new ballpark, with its Death Valley in left and Homer Porch in right, won't perma-
nently spook Juan. Hey, even in a troubled season, he remained at times the
most frightening hitter alive.

Year	Team	Lg.	Pos.	G	AB	R	H	HR	RBI	SB	BA
1991	Texas	AL	OF	142	545	78	144	27	102	4	.264
1992	Texas	AL	OF	155	584	77	152	43	109	0	.260
1993	Texas	AL	OF	140	536	105	166	46	118	4	.310
1994	Texas	AL	OF	107	422	57	116	19	85	6	.275
1994 PROJECTION				152	601	86	167	29	114	7	.278

Catchers
pp. 33–46

Corners
pp. 46–65

Infield
pp. 66–85

Outfield
pp. 85–115

DH
pp. 115–119

Starters
pp. 119–155

Relievers
pp. 155–187

MIKE GREENWELL   Age 31/L $14

Williams. Yastrzemski. Rice. Greenwell. Sort of peters out there at the end, doesn't it? All it means, though, is that Greenwell isn't as good as two Hall of Famers and a third Red Sox left fielder with an outside chance of joining his predecessors in Cooperstown. But he is good enough to put up solid numbers as your third outfielder. Just don't pay him a Hall of Fame salary.

Year	Team	Lg.	Pos.	G	AB	R	H	HR	RBI	SB	BA
1991	Boston	AL	OF	147	544	76	163	9	83	15	.300
1992	Boston	AL	OF	49	180	16	42	2	18	2	.233
1993	Boston	AL	OF	146	540	77	170	13	72	5	.315
1994	Boston	AL	OF	95	327	60	88	11	45	2	.269
1994 PROJECTION				95	327	60	88	11	45	2	.269

RUSTY GREER   Age 26/L $9

Even Texas people weren't sure who he was until he had a good season in the Arizona Fall League (something all Rotisserie GMs should always watch closely). That earned him a look in the spring, an early call-up from the minors, and the chance to show he has surprising power to go along with clutch hitting ability and abundant exuberance.

Year	Team	Lg.	Pos.	G	AB	R	H	HR	RBI	SB	BA
1994	Texas	AL	OF	80	277	36	87	10	46	0	.314
1994 PROJECTION				124	436	62	131	13	66	0	.300

KEN GRIFFEY, JR.   Age 25/L $44

Think how much better he would be if only he would wear his cap turned around the right way.

Year	Team	Lg.	Pos.	G	AB	R	H	HR	RBI	SB	BA
1991	Seattle	AL	OF	154	548	76	179	22	100	18	.327
1992	Seattle	AL	OF	142	565	83	174	27	103	10	.308
1993	Seattle	AL	OF	156	582	113	180	45	109	17	.309
1994	Seattle	AL	OF	111	433	94	140	40	90	11	.323
1994 PROJECTION				159	615	132	202	54	125	14	.328

DARRYL HAMILTON   Age 30/L $14

Elbow surgery wiped out his season. The two preceding years tell you what to look for when he's healthy.

Year	Team	Lg.	Pos.	G	AB	R	H	HR	RBI	SB	BA
1991	Milwaukee	AL	OF	122	405	64	126	1	57	16	.311
1992	Milwaukee	AL	OF	128	470	67	140	5	62	41	.298
1993	Milwaukee	AL	OF	135	520	74	161	9	48	21	.310
1994	Milwaukee	AL	OF	36	141	23	37	1	13	3	.262
1994 PROJECTION				36	141	23	37	1	13	3	.262

JEFFREY HAMMONDS — Age 24/R — $12

Great potential threatened by leg problems. Said one Orioles exec: "You just hope that he doesn't turn into one of those China doll types. The guy is always in the training room. He might look up one day and see Alex Ochoa going right by him." Surgery last fall. Pay close attention to how many innings he plays this spring before bidding on his substantial upside.

Year	Team	Lg.	Pos.	G	AB	R	H	HR	RBI	SB	BA
1993	Baltimore	AL	OF	33	105	10	32	3	19	4	.305
1994	Baltimore	AL	OF	68	250	45	74	8	31	5	.296
1994 PROJECTION				115	457	79	138	14	54	7	.302

DAVE HENDERSON — Age 36/R — $5

Baseball has its dark side, but Hendu has always been part of its bright side.

Year	Team	Lg.	Pos.	G	AB	R	H	HR	RBI	SB	BA
1991	Oakland	AL	OF	150	572	86	158	25	85	6	.276
1992	Oakland	AL	OF	20	63	1	9	0	2	0	.143
1993	Oakland	AL	OF	107	382	37	84	20	53	0	.220
1994	Kansas City	AL	OF	56	198	27	49	5	31	2	.247
1994 PROJECTION				63	220	28	52	5	31	2	.236

RICKEY HENDERSON — Age 36/R — $28

As your broker, we advise you to sell, not buy. The trend line is definitely down.

Year	Team	Lg.	Pos.	G	AB	R	H	HR	RBI	SB	BA
1991	Oakland	AL	OF	134	470	105	126	18	57	58	.268
1992	Oakland	AL	OF	117	396	77	112	15	46	48	.283
1993	Oakland	AL	OF	90	318	77	104	17	47	31	.327
1993	Toronto	AL	OF	44	163	37	35	4	12	22	.215
1994	Oakland	AL	OF	87	296	66	77	6	20	22	.260
1994 PROJECTION				131	454	94	113	10	33	36	.249

DAVID HULSE — Age 27/L — $12

The Rangers got so fed up with his inability to stay out of the whirlpool that they resurrected Oddibe McDowell. Hulse might be worth more if he played more, but don't pay for what he *might* do.

Year	Team	Lg.	Pos.	G	AB	R	H	HR	RBI	SB	BA
1992	Texas	AL	OF	32	92	14	28	0	2	3	.304
1993	Texas	AL	OF	114	407	71	118	1	29	29	.290
1994	Texas	AL	OF	77	310	58	79	1	19	18	.255
1994 PROJECTION				82	325	59	83	1	20	19	.255

BO JACKSON — Age 32/R — $9

Bo, Deion, and Michael have made one great collective contribution to baseball: they have proved how difficult it is to play.

Year	Team	Lg.	Pos.	G	AB	R	H	HR	RBI	SB	BA
1991	Chicago	AL	DH	23	71	8	16	3	14	0	.225
1993	Chicago	AL	OF	85	284	32	66	16	45	0	.232
1994	California	AL	OF	75	201	23	56	13	43	1	.279
1994 PROJECTION				113	334	44	97	23	69	1	.290

DARRIN JACKSON   Age 31/R $19

One of the great comebacks of the year and one of the major free agent steals. Expect more of the same.

Year	Team	Lg.	Pos.	G	AB	R	H	HR	RBI	SB	BA
1991	San Diego	NL	OF	122	359	51	94	21	49	5	.262
1992	San Diego	NL	OF	155	587	72	146	17	70	14	.249
1993	Toronto	AL	OF	46	176	15	38	5	19	0	.216
1993	New York	NL	OF	31	87	4	17	1	7	0	.195
1994	Chicago	AL	OF	104	369	43	115	10	51	7	.312
1994 PROJECTION				151	541	61	160	15	78	7	.296

CHRIS JAMES   Age 32/R $2

We don't know for sure, but we suspect that James isn't even drafted in most leagues. Makes sense—he's never slotted for more than fifth outfielder–pinch hitter duties at the beginning of the season. Then somebody gets hurt, he fills in and hits a few home runs, and Rotisserie owners start calling him to fill roster holes. He hits a few more home runs the rest of the way, but not enough to make much of a mark, and then he's forgotten again. Wouldn't it be smarter to pay a buck or two for him at the draft as your fifth outfielder, be patient the first couple of months of the season when he doesn't play much, and then benefit from all seven home runs he has averaged the last three years?

Year	Team	Lg.	Pos.	G	AB	R	H	HR	RBI	SB	BA
1991	Cleveland	AL	DH	115	437	31	104	5	41	3	.238
1992	San Francisco	NL	OF	111	248	25	60	5	32	2	.242
1993	Houston	NL	OF	65	129	19	33	6	19	2	.256
1993	Texas	AL	OF	8	31	5	11	3	7	0	.355
1994	Texas	AL	OF	52	133	28	34	7	19	0	.256
1994 PROJECTION				77	202	36	55	9	30	1	.272

STAN JAVIER   Age 31/B $17

He finally blossomed last year, and Tony LaRussa is coming back to nurture his continued growth. We don't much like the metaphor, but we do like Javier's chances of doing it again.

Year	Team	Lg.	Pos.	G	AB	R	H	HR	RBI	SB	BA
1991	Los Angeles	NL	OF	121	176	21	36	1	11	7	.205
1992	Los Angeles	NL	OF	56	58	6	11	1	5	1	.190
1992	Philadelphia	NL	OF	74	276	36	72	0	24	17	.261
1993	California	AL	OF	92	237	33	69	3	28	12	.291
1994	Oakland	AL	OF	109	419	75	114	10	44	24	.272
1994 PROJECTION				156	603	99	164	13	64	33	.272

LANCE JOHNSON   Age 31/L $19

Watch him run and you expect the SB. It's the RBI that are such a delightful surprise. He's everything you think Alex Cole is but isn't.

Year	Team	Lg.	Pos.	G	AB	R	H	HR	RBI	SB	BA
1991	Chicago	AL	OF	160	588	72	161	0	49	26	.274
1992	Chicago	AL	OF	157	567	67	158	3	47	41	.279
1993	Chicago	AL	OF	147	540	75	168	0	47	35	.311
1994	Chicago	AL	OF	106	412	56	114	3	54	26	.277
1994 PROJECTION				153	590	81	156	3	70	38	.264

Catchers
pp. 33–46

Corners
pp. 46–65

Infield
pp. 66–85

Outfield
pp. 85–115

DH
pp. 115–119

Starters
pp. 119–155

Relievers
pp. 155–187

FELIX JOSE   Age 29/B $12

No one in Rotissehistory has ever underpaid for Felix José. That should tell you something about the gap between perceived potential and performance. He *looks* like a $35 ballplayer. One of the great heartbreakers.

Year	Team	Lg.	Pos.	G	AB	R	H	HR	RBI	SB	BA
1991	St. Louis	NL	OF	154	568	69	173	8	77	20	.305
1992	St. Louis	NL	OF	131	509	62	150	14	75	28	.295
1993	Kansas City	AL	OF	149	499	64	126	6	43	31	.253
1994	Kansas City	AL	OF	99	366	56	111	11	55	10	.303
1994 PROJECTION				143	530	78	152	13	69	15	.287

WAYNE KIRBY   Age 31/L $7

In the minors nearly a decade before finally getting a chance, he is the fourth outfielder on a team where the first three could someday soon make the same All-Star squad. But Kirby seems to have the quick-start temperament needed to be a good bench player, and he has the skills to make the best of his limited chances. What with injuries, off-days for regulars, and suspensions for using corked bats, he should play enough to steal 15 bases and provide a little punch at the plate.

Year	Team	Lg.	Pos.	G	AB	R	H	HR	RBI	SB	BA
1991	Cleveland	AL	OF	21	43	4	9	0	5	1	.209
1992	Cleveland	AL	DH	21	18	9	3	1	1	0	.167
1993	Cleveland	AL	OF	131	458	71	123	6	60	17	.269
1994	Cleveland	AL	OF	78	191	33	56	5	23	11	.293
1994 PROJECTION				106	283	46	80	7	31	11	.283

KENNY LOFTON   Age 27/L $42

So all of a sudden *he's* a power hitter, too? One of the best half-dozen all-around players on earth even before he started hitting home runs.

Year	Team	Lg.	Pos.	G	AB	R	H	HR	RBI	SB	BA
1991	Houston	NL	OF	20	74	9	15	0	0	2	.203
1992	Cleveland	AL	OF	148	576	96	164	5	42	66	.285
1993	Cleveland	AL	OF	148	569	116	185	1	42	70	.325
1994	Cleveland	AL	OF	112	459	105	160	12	57	60	.349
1994 PROJECTION				159	654	147	225	17	82	81	.344

SHANE MACK   Age 31/R $19

Shane came back. Still nagged by shoulder troubles, but when he was in the lineup he was his old self.

Year	Team	Lg.	Pos.	G	AB	R	H	HR	RBI	SB	BA
1991	Minnesota	AL	OF	143	442	79	137	18	74	13	.310
1992	Minnesota	AL	OF	156	600	101	189	16	75	26	.315
1993	Minnesota	AL	OF	128	503	66	139	10	61	15	.276
1994	Minnesota	AL	OF	81	303	55	101	15	61	4	.333
1994 PROJECTION				129	486	76	152	22	81	6	.313

ODDIBE McDOWELL   Age 32/L $3

Oddibe young again. Does this mean we can expect a big comeback this year from Brad Komminsk?

Year	Team	Lg.	Pos.	G	AB	R	H	HR	RBI	SB	BA
1994	Texas	AL	OF	59	183	34	48	1	15	14	.262
1994 PROJECTION				103	325	52	88	1	31	26	.271

BRIAN McRAE   Age 27/B $17

Those who know around the Royals say that Brian will hardly sulk about his dad getting fired as KC manager. Dad really didn't like to manage, and Brian will be more relaxed without Dad around. Look for the more relaxed Brian to pay some big dividends.

Year	Team	Lg.	Pos.	G	AB	R	H	HR	RBI	SB	BA
1991	Kansas City	AL	OF	152	629	86	164	8	64	20	.261
1992	Kansas City	AL	OF	149	533	63	119	4	52	18	.223
1993	Kansas City	AL	OF	153	627	78	177	12	69	23	.282
1994	Kansas City	AL	OF	114	436	71	119	4	40	28	.273
1994 PROJECTION				161	627	99	172	7	56	31	.274

MATT MIESKE   Age 27/R $8

He still has to show he can catch up with major league hard stuff. But he has interesting power.

Year	Team	Lg.	Pos.	G	AB	R	H	HR	RBI	SB	BA
1993	Milwaukee	AL	OF	23	58	9	14	3	7	0	.241
1994	Milwaukee	AL	OF	84	259	39	67	10	38	3	.259
1994 PROJECTION				109	321	46	78	12	48	3	.243

PEDRO MUNOZ   Age 26/R $13

Has never been healthy enough to provide a true measure of what he is capable of. At one point, the Twins thought he would be a 25-homer guy who would have trouble hitting for average. Then they concluded he had the potential to be a solid .280 to .300 hitter with modest power. One of these years he might put it all together, but the Twins are growing tired of waiting for that year to happen.

Year	Team	Lg.	Pos.	G	AB	R	H	HR	RBI	SB	BA
1991	Minnesota	AL	OF	51	138	15	39	7	26	3	.283
1992	Minnesota	AL	OF	127	418	44	113	12	71	4	.270
1993	Minnesota	AL	OF	104	326	34	76	13	38	1	.233
1994	Minnesota	AL	OF	75	244	35	72	11	36	0	.295
1994 PROJECTION				111	365	50	107	16	47	0	.293

WARREN NEWSON   Age 30/L $1

No.

Year	Team	Lg.	Pos.	G	AB	R	H	HR	RBI	SB	BA
1991	Chicago	AL	OF	71	132	20	39	4	25	2	.295
1992	Chicago	AL	OF	63	136	19	30	1	11	3	.221
1993	Chicago	AL	DH	26	40	9	12	2	6	0	.300
1994	Chicago	AL	OF	63	102	16	26	2	7	1	.255
1994 PROJECTION				86	149	22	38	5	15	1	.255

OTIS NIXON   Age 36/B $29

His defining Red Sox moment came when he stole home in an early-season game with Mo Vaughn at bat. Said Mo, "I looked up, saw this blur coming at me and yelled, 'Otis, you gotta be nuts.' If I had swung, I would have killed the dude." Nixon gave Boston a dimension they haven't had in years, which is exactly what the Rangers expect of him.

Year	Team	Lg.	Pos.	G	AB	R	H	HR	RBI	SB	BA
1991	Atlanta	NL	OF	124	401	81	119	0	26	72	.297
1992	Atlanta	NL	OF	120	456	79	134	2	22	41	.294
1993	Atlanta	NL	OF	134	461	77	124	1	24	47	.269
1994	Boston	AL	OF	103	398	60	109	0	25	42	.274
1994 PROJECTION				150	592	86	162	0	32	53	.274

PAUL O'NEILL   Age 32/L $32

From the moment the trade was announced, we thought that the Yankees had made a brilliant move in bringing O'Neill to the Bronx. And though he's not going to flirt with .400 every year, he is in the perfect park and with the perfect manager, who picks the perfect spots for him to produce damn-near perfect numbers. Not only that, but his sister, Molly, writes a dead-solid perfect food column in the *New York Times Sunday Magazine*.

Year	Team	Lg.	Pos.	G	AB	R	H	HR	RBI	SB	BA
1991	Cincinnati	NL	OF	152	532	71	136	28	91	12	.256
1992	Cincinnati	NL	OF	148	496	59	122	14	66	6	.246
1993	New York	AL	OF	141	498	71	155	20	75	2	.311
1994	New York	AL	OF	103	368	68	132	21	83	5	.359
1994 PROJECTION				144	527	105	190	32	121	5	.361

TONY PHILLIPS   Age 35/B $15

Another typical year for one of the game's most overlooked players. At first glance, he doesn't quite fit the current Tigers mold, because he's versatile and plays solid defense. But a closer look at his season reveals that at the plate, at least, he is in fact the prototypical Tiger, someone who walked 95 times, struck out 105 times, and thus provided absolutely no action for roughly 40% of his plate appearances. And that pizza guy who owns the team wonders why he can't draw any customers.

Year	Team	Lg.	Pos.	G	AB	R	H	HR	RBI	SB	BA
1991	Detroit	AL	OF	146	564	87	160	17	72	10	.284
1992	Detroit	AL	OF	159	606	114	167	10	64	12	.276
1993	Detroit	AL	OF	151	566	113	177	7	57	16	.313
1994	Detroit	AL	OF	114	438	91	123	19	61	13	.281
1994 PROJECTION				159	603	122	173	25	80	19	.287

LUIS POLONIA   Age 30/L $18

The Yankees can afford his lack of punch. They can overlook the fact that he's caught stealing more than a third of the time. They can forgive his lackluster play in the outfield. So can you.

Year	Team	Lg.	Pos.	G	AB	R	H	HR	RBI	SB	BA
1991	California	AL	OF	150	604	92	179	2	50	48	.296
1992	California	AL	OF	149	577	83	165	0	35	51	.286
1993	California	AL	OF	152	576	75	156	1	32	55	.271
1994	New York	AL	OF	95	350	62	109	1	36	20	.311
1994 PROJECTION				126	483	90	152	3	48	28	.315

KIRBY PUCKETT
Age 34/R $35

He didn't confide in us, but Kirby probably hated The Strike. Not because he hit .500 with two HR and eight RBI in the last four days of the season, but because he loves playing baseball. At least that's the attitude he exudes. Worth about nine Danny Tartabulls.

Year	Team	Lg.	Pos.	G	AB	R	H	HR	RBI	SB	BA
1991	Minnesota	AL	OF	152	611	92	195	15	89	11	.319
1992	Minnesota	AL	OF	160	639	104	210	19	110	17	.329
1993	Minnesota	AL	OF	156	622	89	184	22	89	8	.296
1994	Minnesota	AL	OF	108	439	79	139	20	112	6	.317
1994 PROJECTION				157	634	101	195	28	144	7	.308

TIM RAINES
Age 35/B $17

Has settled into the role of workmanlike veteran, capable of helping with power or speed. And as one AL scout said, "Even now, when he doesn't run close to how he used to, there's no better base stealer when it absolutely matters."

Year	Team	Lg.	Pos.	G	AB	R	H	HR	RBI	SB	BA
1991	Chicago	AL	OF	155	609	102	163	5	50	51	.268
1992	Chicago	AL	OF	144	551	102	162	7	54	45	.294
1993	Chicago	AL	OF	115	415	75	127	16	54	21	.306
1994	Chicago	AL	OF	101	384	80	102	10	52	13	.266
1994 PROJECTION				142	531	103	138	14	68	16	.260

MANNY RAMIREZ
Age 22/R $20

Born in the Dominican Republic but grew up in New York City, where he had nearly 50 friends and relatives watching a couple of years ago when he launched a couple of rookie homers in the Bronx. He can be dangerous in the field, and his base-running mistakes had his fellow Indians literally covering their eyes at times. But he's still a baby, and the sky's the limit. Another year and there won't even be any debate about the Indians having the best outfield in baseball.

Year	Team	Lg.	Pos.	G	AB	R	H	HR	RBI	SB	BA
1993	Cleveland	AL	DH	22	53	5	9	2	5	0	.170
1994	Cleveland	AL	OF	91	290	51	78	17	60	4	.269
1994 PROJECTION				127	397	68	109	26	79	4	.275

TIM SALMON
Age 26/R $33

Considering the feeble lineup around him, there was not much hint of any sophomore jinx here.

Year	Team	Lg.	Pos.	G	AB	R	H	HR	RBI	SB	BA
1992	California	AL	OF	23	79	8	14	2	6	1	.177
1993	California	AL	OF	142	515	93	146	31	95	5	.283
1994	California	AL	OF	100	373	67	107	23	70	1	.287
1994 PROJECTION				147	552	108	160	38	112	2	.290

JUAN SAMUEL
Age 34/R $3

All right, so we admit a bias. He's always been a favorite, both when he was putting up stupendous numbers for the Phillies and when he was wandering aimlessly around center field for the Mets. He's just a utility guy now, but he still has some pop and he can steal a base in a pinch. Plus he's got league-leading class.

Year	Team	Lg.	Pos.	G	AB	R	H	HR	RBI	SB	BA
1991	Los Angeles	NL	2B	153	594	74	161	12	58	23	.271
1992	Los Angeles	NL	2B	47	122	7	32	0	15	2	.262
1992	Kansas City	AL	OF	29	102	15	29	0	8	6	.284
1993	Cincinnati	NL	2B	103	261	31	60	4	26	9	.230
1994	Detroit	AL	OF	59	136	32	42	5	21	5	.309
1994 PROJECTION				83	189	40	51	7	33	6	.270

RUBEN SIERRA   Age 29/B $33

He didn't go into a shell when challenged by Tony LaRussa to play hard. Instead, he stood up and had a solid season. We'd like to see what he could do with McGwire healthy and hitting behind him.

Year	Team	Lg.	Pos.	G	AB	R	H	HR	RBI	SB	BA
1991	Texas	AL	OF	161	661	110	203	25	116	16	.307
1992	Texas	AL	OF	124	500	66	139	14	70	12	.278
1992	Oakland	AL	OF	27	101	17	28	3	17	2	.277
1993	Oakland	AL	OF	158	630	77	147	22	101	25	.233
1994	Oakland	AL	OF	110	426	71	114	23	92	8	.268
1994 PROJECTION				158	609	85	163	30	122	12	.268

DWIGHT SMITH   Age 31/L $5

When the Angels dumped him to save money, California veterans saw it as a sign that the club's bizarre ownership didn't care about winning. That might be something of a reach, since the Angels weren't going to win anything anyway. But Smith is a good role player who can turn around any fastball when pitchers make the mistake of going at him with hard cheese.

Year	Team	Lg.	Pos.	G	AB	R	H	HR	RBI	SB	BA
1991	Chicago	NL	OF	90	167	16	38	3	21	2	.228
1992	Chicago	NL	OF	109	217	28	60	3	24	9	.276
1993	Chicago	NL	OF	111	310	51	93	11	35	8	.300
1994	California	AL	OF	45	122	19	32	5	18	2	.262
1994	Baltimore	AL	OF	28	74	12	23	3	12	0	.311
1994 PROJECTION				90	233	33	69	8	37	2	.296

LEE TINSLEY   Age 26/B $4

Fenway speed; no longer an oxymoron.

Year	Team	Lg.	Pos.	G	AB	R	H	HR	RBI	SB	BA
1993	Seattle	AL	OF	11	19	2	3	1	2	0	.158
1994	Boston	AL	OF	78	144	27	32	2	14	13	.222
1994 PROJECTION				113	277	44	59	6	33	13	.213

GREG VAUGHN   Age 29/R $25

Assuming he's healthy, the second best Vaughn in the majors figures to bounce back with a big year—although mostly as a DH.

Year	Team	Lg.	Pos.	G	AB	R	H	HR	RBI	SB	BA
1991	Milwaukee	AL	OF	145	542	81	132	27	98	2	.244
1992	Milwaukee	AL	OF	141	501	77	114	23	78	15	.228
1993	Milwaukee	AL	OF	154	569	97	152	30	97	10	.267
1994	Milwaukee	AL	OF	95	370	59	94	19	55	9	.254
1994 PROJECTION				142	550	85	136	28	98	11	.247

Catchers
pp. 33–46

Corners
pp. 46–65

Infield
pp. 66–85

Outfield
pp. 85–115

DH
pp. 115–119

Starters
pp. 119–155

Relievers
pp. 155–187

DEVON WHITE   Age 32/B $19

Probably streaky when he sleeps, but if you can abide the ups and downs, the peaks and valleys, the highs and lows of this startlingly inconsistent player, you will find that his season evens out at a very nice level by October . . . in years they play that long.

Year	Team	Lg.	Pos.	G	AB	R	H	HR	RBI	SB	BA
1991	Toronto	AL	OF	156	642	110	181	17	60	33	.282
1992	Toronto	AL	OF	153	641	98	159	17	60	37	.248
1993	Toronto	AL	OF	146	598	116	163	15	52	34	.273
1994	Toronto	AL	OF	100	403	67	109	13	49	11	.270
1994 PROJECTION				147	615	105	172	19	72	27	.280

BERNIE WILLIAMS   Age 26/B $22

Except for his remarks about Barry Bonds's and Ken Griffey Jr.'s conduct as unbecoming of professsional baseball players, Buck Showalter had a lot of things to be happy about last season. One of them was Bernie Williams: "If there was one thing that I enjoyed more than anything, it was the way Bernie got himself out of an awful start and came back to be one hell of a player over the last couple of months. When a young guy of his talent has the guts and the work ethic to do that, it's something that can establish him as a big-time player." We concur.

Year	Team	Lg.	Pos.	G	AB	R	H	HR	RBI	SB	BA
1991	New York	AL	OF	85	320	43	76	3	34	10	.237
1992	New York	AL	OF	62	261	39	73	5	26	7	.280
1993	New York	AL	OF	139	567	67	152	12	68	9	.268
1994	New York	AL	OF	108	408	80	118	12	57	16	.289
1994 PROJECTION				155	598	107	165	17	77	18	.276

Designated Hitters

HAROLD BAINES   Age 36/L $16

Spotted more than when he was young and had two serviceable knees, and that means his HR and RBI totals will suffer. But he will alway be around .300, drive in big runs, and add a lot of class to any team.

Year	Team	Lg.	Pos.	G	AB	R	H	HR	RBI	SB	BA
1991	Oakland	AL	DH	141	488	76	144	20	90	0	.295
1992	Oakland	AL	DH	140	478	58	121	16	76	1	.253
1993	Baltimore	AL	DH	118	416	64	130	20	78	0	.313
1994	Baltimore	AL	DH	94	326	44	96	16	54	0	.294
1994 PROJECTION				139	474	65	124	22	71	1	.262

GERONIMO BERROA   Age 30/R $12

One of our favorite stories of 1994. Some of us got excited about this guy, oh, ages ago when he was an Atlanta Braves farmhand. Some of us even drafted him into our farm systems. A lot of years he had great springs but always got sent down, and we never could figure out why. From time to time he would be called up for a cup of coffee, but he never got much of a chance. One reason, undoubtedly, was the curve ball, the primary cause of most shattered big league dreams. Another reason became evident last summer when we saw him play outfield for the first time. (There should have been a Parental Discretion Advisory before he took the field.) But the DH Rule, God bless it, finally gave Gerónimo a season in the sun. Tony LaRussa is a genius at getting the best out of players with limited skills, and Berroa is a natural-born hitter, so we are looking forward to the sequel this summer.

Year	Team	Lg.	Pos.	G	AB	R	H	HR	RBI	SB	BA
1992	Cincinnati	NL	OF	13	15	2	4	0	0	0	.267
1993	Florida	NL	OF	14	34	3	4	0	0	0	.118
1994	Oakland	AL	DH	96	340	55	104	13	65	7	.306
1994 PROJECTION				130	468	66	132	17	80	12	.282

JOSE CANSECO   Age 30/R $34

Avoided shenanigans on and off the field, stayed out of everybody's way, paid attention to the game, worked hard, and got himself back to being one of the most feared hitters in baseball. Frankly, we wouldn't have wagered a plugged pocaroba on such a dramatic turnaround. This year, hitting in front of Mo Vaughn, he's likely to launch 65 or 70 over the Green Monster.

Year	Team	Lg.	Pos.	G	AB	R	H	HR	RBI	SB	BA
1991	Oakland	AL	OF	154	572	115	152	44	122	26	.266
1992	Oakland	AL	OF	97	366	66	90	22	72	5	.246
1992	Texas	AL	OF	22	73	8	17	4	15	1	.233
1993	Texas	AL	OF	60	231	30	59	10	46	6	.255
1994	Texas	AL	DH	111	429	88	121	31	90	15	.282
1994 PROJECTION				159	623	121	169	43	117	16	.271

CHILI DAVIS   Age 35/B $27

Even the dreariness surrounding the Angels didn't dampen his enthusiasm for the game or his remarkable rejuvenation as a big-time run producer.

Year	Team	Lg.	Pos.	G	AB	R	H	HR	RBI	SB	BA
1991	Minnesota	AL	DH	153	534	84	148	29	93	5	.277
1992	Minnesota	AL	DH	138	444	63	128	12	66	4	.288
1993	California	AL	DH	153	573	74	139	27	112	4	.243
1994	California	AL	DH	108	392	72	122	26	84	3	.311
1994 PROJECTION				151	560	103	174	38	123	3	.311

ANDRE DAWSON   Age 40/R $9

The Hawk may not be back for an encore. Too bad, because he deserves an Andre Dawson Day at every Rotisserie League park in America (*and* Canada). Last July, one of us encountered him sitting alone in an almost empty Red Sox clubhouse, long after a sloppy Boston loss, an ice pack on a knee that has been subjected to nine different surgical procedures. Asked about his condition, Dawson offered a weary smile. "The doctors tell me there's no cartilage left, that if I keep tearing it up, I'll probably need knee replacement. I'm afraid I don't have much more to give to this game." Few players ever gave as much.

Year	Team	Lg.	Pos.	G	AB	R	H	HR	RBI	SB	BA
1991	Chicago	NL	OF	149	563	69	153	31	104	4	.272
1992	Chicago	NL	OF	143	542	60	150	22	90	6	.277
1993	Boston	AL	DH	121	461	44	126	13	67	2	.273
1994	Boston	AL	DH	75	292	34	70	16	48	2	.240
1994 PROJECTION				96	370	39	86	17	53	2	.232

JULIO FRANCO   Age 33/R $27

Zowie! If this is what a change of scenery does for you, we're moving to Chicago *today*.

Year	Team	Lg.	Pos.	G	AB	R	H	HR	RBI	SB	BA
1991	Texas	AL	2B	146	589	108	201	15	78	36	.341
1992	Texas	AL	DH	35	107	19	25	2	8	1	.234
1993	Texas	AL	DH	144	532	85	154	14	84	9	.289
1994	Chicago	AL	DH	112	433	72	138	20	98	8	.319
1994 PROJECTION				160	613	94	195	27	134	9	.318

KIRK GIBSON   Age 37/L $19

His remarkable second coming defies good sense, so there's no reason to doubt that he doesn't have several years left. Then he may want to commence his career in the NFL.

Year	Team	Lg.	Pos.	G	AB	R	H	HR	RBI	SB	BA
1991	Kansas City	AL	OF	132	462	81	109	16	55	18	.236
1992	Pittsburgh	NL	OF	16	56	6	11	2	5	3	.196
1993	Detroit	AL	DH	116	403	62	105	13	62	15	.261
1994	Detroit	AL	DH	98	330	71	91	23	72	4	.276
1994 PROJECTION				136	441	94	122	32	95	8	.277

BOB HAMELIN   Age 27/L $22

The Hammer has been a big-time Royals prospect for years, but back problems threatened to make him The Bust. Isn't good health a wonderful thing? Isn't it great how Congress worked so hard to give the country health care reform?

Year	Team	Lg.	Pos.	G	AB	R	H	HR	RBI	SB	BA
1993	Kansas City	AL	1B	16	49	2	11	2	5	0	.224
1994	Kansas City	AL	DH	101	312	64	88	24	65	4	.282
1994 PROJECTION				145	473	88	129	36	94	4	.273

BRIAN HARPER   Age 35/R $15

Questionable physical status needs to be cleared up. Also, Bud's Brewers may not want him back because his salary was determined in a free market.

Year	Team	Lg.	Pos.	G	AB	R	H	HR	RBI	SB	BA
1991	Minnesota	AL	C	123	441	54	137	10	69	1	.311
1992	Minnesota	AL	C	140	502	58	154	9	73	0	.307
1993	Minnesota	AL	C	147	530	52	161	12	73	1	.304
1994	Milwaukee	AL	DH	64	251	23	73	4	32	0	.291
1994 PROJECTION				64	251	23	73	4	32	0	.291

Catchers
pp. 33–46

Corners
pp. 46–65

Infield
pp. 66–85

Outfield
pp. 85–115

DH
pp. 115–119

Starters
pp. 119–155

Relievers
pp. 155–187

REGGIE JEFFERSON   Age 26/B $8

Has finally found a nice niche in Seattle after disappointing both Cincinnati and Cleveland.

Year	Team	Lg.	Pos.	G	AB	R	H	HR	RBI	SB	BA
1991	Cincinnati	NL	1B	5	7	1	1	1	1	0	.143
1991	Cleveland	AL	1B	26	101	10	20	2	12	0	.198
1992	Cleveland	AL	1B	24	89	8	30	1	6	0	.337
1993	Cleveland	AL	DH	113	366	35	91	10	34	1	.249
1994	Seattle	AL	DH	63	162	24	53	8	32	0	.327
1994 PROJECTION				107	331	51	101	14	48	0	.305

CANDY MALDONADO   Age 34/R $3

Candy is bad for your teeth. Maldonado means "bad gift" in Spanish. 'Nuf said.

Year	Team	Lg.	Pos.	G	AB	R	H	HR	RBI	SB	BA
1991	Milwaukee	AL	OF	34	111	11	23	5	20	1	.207
1991	Toronto	AL	OF	52	177	26	49	7	28	3	.277
1992	Toronto	AL	OF	137	489	64	133	20	66	2	.272
1993	Chicago	NL	OF	70	140	8	26	3	15	0	.186
1993	Cleveland	AL	OF	28	81	11	20	5	20	0	.247
1994	Cleveland	AL	DH	42	92	14	18	5	12	1	.196
1994 PROJECTION				49	105	17	21	5	12	1	.200

PAUL MOLITOR   Age 38/R $28

Wasn't affected by all those Blue Jays sinking into mediocrity all around him. A pro's pro, with plenty left.

Year	Team	Lg.	Pos.	G	AB	R	H	HR	RBI	SB	BA
1991	Milwaukee	AL	DH	158	665	133	216	17	75	19	.325
1992	Milwaukee	AL	DH	158	609	89	195	12	89	31	.320
1993	Toronto	AL	DH	160	636	121	211	22	111	22	.332
1994	Toronto	AL	DH	115	454	86	155	14	75	20	.341
1994 PROJECTION				162	647	120	212	22	110	32	.328

EDDIE MURRAY   Age 39/B $20

Gee, after all that was written and said about his sojourn in Shea Stadium, isn't it kind of funny that his presence didn't seem to disrupt the Indians clubhouse? For that matter, neither did his RBI.

Year	Team	Lg.	Pos.	G	AB	R	H	HR	RBI	SB	BA
1991	Los Angeles	NL	1B	153	576	69	150	19	96	10	.260
1992	New York	NL	1B	156	551	64	144	16	93	4	.261
1993	New York	NL	1B	154	610	77	174	27	100	2	.285
1994	Cleveland	AL	DH	108	433	57	110	17	76	8	.254
1994 PROJECTION				155	621	80	153	23	105	8	.246

DANNY TARTABULL   Age 32/R $29

Has a lot of trouble reaching 140 games played, so don't bother thinking about what he could do in a full season. He'll never play one because he's not tough enough. The softest 30 HR/90 RBI guy in baseball. Master of the two-run dinger with his team down or up by seven in the ninth. The best evidence that our little game is flawed is that Tartabull is so valuable in it.

Year	Team	Lg.	Pos.	G	AB	R	H	HR	RBI	SB	BA
1991	Kansas City	AL	OF	132	484	78	153	31	100	6	.316
1992	New York	AL	OF	123	421	72	112	25	85	2	.266
1993	New York	AL	DH	138	513	87	128	31	102	0	.250
1994	New York	AL	DH	104	399	68	102	19	67	1	.256
1994 PROJECTION				138	524	88	134	26	98	1	.256

DAVE WINFIELD   Age 43/R $11

We hope his career doesn't end on a double trivia footnote, as in "Who was not only the first player traded during a strike but also the first player traded for a dinner?" Yup, it's Winnie. Because he didn't play at all for the Indians after being dealt by the Twins for a player to be named later, the GMs agreed that the Cleveland execs would buy the Minnesota execs a dinner.

Year	Team	Lg.	Pos.	G	AB	R	H	HR	RBI	SB	BA
1991	California	AL	OF	150	568	75	149	28	86	7	.262
1992	Toronto	AL	DH	156	583	92	169	26	108	2	.290
1993	Minnesota	AL	DH	143	547	72	148	21	76	2	.271
1994	Minnesota	AL	DH	77	294	35	74	10	43	2	.252
1994 PROJECTION				105	369	43	94	12	50	2	.255

Catchers
pp. 33–46

Corners
pp. 46–65

Infield
pp. 66–85

Outfield
pp. 85–115

DH
pp. 115–119

Starters
pp. 119–155

Relievers
pp. 155–187

On the Mound

NATIONAL LEAGUE

RENE AROCHA   Age 29/R $7

First he started. Then he relieved. Then he started. Then he relieved. A guy who's still trying to cope with life in a brand-new country doesn't need such confusion. His future depends on who takes over the Cardinals baseball operation. But Arocha's makeup and pitching style suggest that his home will end up being the bullpen. Accordingly, his salary is based on his becoming chairman of the Cardinals bullpen committee. As a starter, he's one of a couple of dozen guys worth no more than $2.

Year	Team	Lg.	G	IP	H	BB	SO	W	L	ERA	SV	Ratio
1993	St. Louis	NL	32	188.0	197	31	96	11	8	3.78	0	1.213
1994	St. Louis	NL	45	83.0	94	21	62	4	4	4.01	11	1.386
1994 PROJECTION			61	105.1	130	26	78	4	6	4.53	14	1.481

FREE OPENING DAY *ROTISSERIE HOT LIST*

(See page 277)

ANDY ASHBY   Age 27/R $2

Had a six-week stretch in which he was unhittable. Showed signs of being able to pitch out of trouble. Plus he added a breaking ball to what had been an all-the-same-speed pitching assortment. True, Ashby is not going to win any Cy Young Awards pitching for the Padres. But if you're looking for a fifth starter, you could do a whole lot worse.

Year	Team	Lg.	G	IP	H	BB	SO	W	L	ERA	SV	Ratio
1991	Philadelphia	NL	8	42.0	41	19	26	1	5	6.00	0	1.429
1992	Philadelphia	NL	10	37.0	42	21	24	1	3	7.54	0	1.703
1993	Colorado	NL	20	54.0	89	32	33	0	4	8.50	1	2.241
1993	San Diego	NL	12	69.0	79	24	44	3	6	5.48	0	1.493
1994	San Diego	NL	24	164.1	145	43	121	6	11	3.40	0	1.144
1994	PROJECTION		34	227.1	218	54	163	10	14	3.68	0	1.196

PEDRO ASTACIO   Age 25/R $3

A major Dodgers letdown—and supposedly one big reason why they fired longtime pitching coach Ron Perranoski. His value is in limbo because Astacio is one of those guys who's fine when he has his good stuff but has no clue how to adjust when he doesn't have it. To a far lesser extent, the same goes for . . .

Year	Team	Lg.	G	IP	H	BB	SO	W	L	ERA	SV	Ratio
1992	Los Angeles	NL	11	82.0	80	20	43	5	5	1.98	0	1.220
1993	Los Angeles	NL	31	186.1	165	68	122	14	9	3.57	0	1.250
1994	Los Angeles	NL	23	149.0	142	47	108	6	8	4.29	0	1.268
1994	PROJECTION		33	218.2	202	66	153	12	10	3.79	0	1.225

STEVE AVERY   Age 24/L $18

. . . from whom we all have probably been expecting too much, too soon. No, he hasn't won any Cy Youngs yet. And yes, last year was considerably less than a masterpiece. But how much can be wrong with a 24-year-old left-hander who never misses a start and over his last four major league seasons is 27 games above .500? Write off 1994 as a fluke and grab him while his perceived value is at a discount.

Year	Team	Lg.	G	IP	H	BB	SO	W	L	ERA	SV	Ratio
1991	Atlanta	NL	35	210.1	189	65	137	18	8	3.38	0	1.208
1992	Atlanta	NL	35	233.2	216	71	129	11	11	3.20	0	1.228
1993	Atlanta	NL	35	223.1	216	43	125	18	6	2.94	0	1.160
1994	Atlanta	NL	24	151.2	127	55	122	8	3	4.04	0	1.200
1994	PROJECTION		34	218.0	177	69	177	11	6	3.67	0	1.128

WILLIE BANKS   Age 26/R $1

Once NL hitters caught on to his changeup, things got ugly. How ugly? Well, he was 0–6 in his last eight starts. Not exactly the pattern you want to see from a developing young pitcher.

Year	Team	Lg.	G	IP	H	BB	SO	W	L	ERA	SV	Ratio
1991	Minnesota	AL	5	17.1	21	12	16	1	1	5.71	0	1.904
1992	Minnesota	AL	16	71.0	80	37	37	4	4	5.70	0	1.648
1993	Minnesota	AL	31	171.1	186	78	138	11	12	4.04	0	1.541
1994	Chicago	NL	23	138.1	139	56	91	8	12	5.40	0	1.410
1994	PROJECTION		32	187.1	189	73	118	10	14	5.09	0	1.398

ANDY BENES   Age 27/R $17

Close your eyes to the W/L mark. The stuff is still there, as is a renewed willingness to pitch inside. If the team improves around him, so will his record. And if he ever gets traded to a *major league* team, he could win a Cy Young or two.

Year Team	Lg.	G	IP	H	BB	SO	W	L	ERA	SV	Ratio
1991 San Diego	NL	33	223.0	194	59	167	15	11	3.03	0	1.135
1992 San Diego	NL	34	231.1	230	61	169	13	14	3.35	0	1.258
1993 San Diego	NL	34	230.2	200	86	179	15	15	3.78	0	1.240
1994 San Diego	NL	25	172.1	155	51	189	6	14	3.86	0	1.195
1994 PROJECTION		34	241.2	217	69	250	8	17	3.58	0	1.183

BUD BLACK   Age 37/L $1

He's a lefty, and he's still breathing, so somebody will take a chance on him. Just hope that somebody is not you, unless your health insurance pays triple indemnity. The word was that he was throwing well after his latest extended rehab from elbow-shoulder-arm troubles, but we've heard that word before.

Year Team	Lg.	G	IP	H	BB	SO	W	L	ERA	SV	Ratio
1991 San Francisco	NL	34	214.1	201	71	104	12	16	3.99	0	1.269
1992 San Francisco	NL	28	177.0	178	59	82	10	12	3.97	0	1.339
1993 San Francisco	NL	16	93.2	89	33	45	8	2	3.56	0	1.302
1994 San Francisco	NL	10	54.1	50	16	28	4	2	4.47	0	1.215
1994 PROJECTION		22	122.2	116	35	68	6	5	3.89	0	1.231

RYAN BOWEN   Age 27/R $1

The Marlins still think he has the stuff to be a valuable big league pitcher, but to use it, he has to be healthy.

Year Team	Lg.	G	IP	H	BB	SO	W	L	ERA	SV	Ratio
1991 Houston	NL	14	71.2	73	36	49	6	4	5.15	0	1.521
1992 Houston	NL	11	33.2	48	30	22	0	7	10.96	0	2.317
1993 Florida	NL	27	156.2	156	87	98	8	12	4.42	0	1.551
1994 Florida	NL	8	47.1	50	19	32	1	5	4.94	0	1.458
1994 PROJECTION		18	100.1	115	46	65	3	10	4.84	0	1.604

TOM BROWNING   Age 34/L $1

Probably time to say good-bye to a gritty pitcher who was a much underrated commodity for many years.

Year Team	Lg.	G	IP	H	BB	SO	W	L	ERA	SV	Ratio
1991 Cincinnati	NL	36	230.1	241	56	115	14	14	4.18	0	1.289
1992 Cincinnati	NL	16	87.0	108	28	33	6	5	5.07	0	1.563
1993 Cincinnati	NL	21	114.0	159	20	53	7	7	4.74	0	1.570
1994 Cincinnati	NL	7	40.2	34	13	22	3	1	4.20	0	1.156
1994 PROJECTION		7	40.2	34	13	22	3	1	4.21	0	1.156

Catchers
pp. 33-46

Corners
pp. 46-65

Infield
pp. 66-85

Outfield
pp. 85-115

DH
pp. 115-119

Starters
pp. 119-155

Relievers
pp. 155-187

JIM BULLINGER   Age 29/R $4

Pitched solidly as a late-season starter, especially after he re-acquired his
lost, lucky ESPN T-shirt.

Year Team	Lg.	G	IP	H	BB	SO	W	L	ERA	SV	Ratio
1992 Chicago	NL	39	85.0	72	54	36	2	8	4.66	7	1.482
1993 Chicago	NL	15	16.2	18	9	10	1	0	4.32	1	1.620
1994 Chicago	NL	33	100.0	87	34	72	6	2	3.60	2	1.210
1994 PROJECTION		43	167.1	156	46	117	9	3	3.55	2	1.207

JOHN BURKETT   Age 30/R $18

He's never going to blind you with his stuff. But if the Giants of 1995 are
closer to being the Giants of 1993 than the Giants of 1994, then Burkett
should at least have as good a year as he had in 1992.

Year Team	Lg.	G	IP	H	BB	SO	W	L	ERA	SV	Ratio
1991 San Francisco	NL	36	206.2	223	60	131	12	11	4.18	0	1.369
1992 San Francisco	NL	32	189.2	194	45	107	13	9	3.84	0	1.260
1993 San Francisco	NL	34	231.2	224	40	145	22	7	3.65	0	1.140
1994 San Francisco	NL	25	159.1	176	36	85	6	8	3.62	0	1.331
1994 PROJECTION		35	225.2	249	44	121	11	11	3.63	0	1.298

TOM CANDIOTTI   Age 37/R $8

He has become the best knuckleballer in the majors. He is also the only
knuckleballer in the majors.

Year Team	Lg.	G	IP	H	BB	SO	W	L	ERA	SV	Ratio
1991 Cleveland	AL	15	108.1	88	28	86	7	6	2.24	0	1.071
1991 Toronto	AL	19	129.2	114	45	81	6	7	2.98	0	1.226
1992 Los Angeles	NL	32	203.2	177	63	152	11	15	3.00	0	1.178
1993 Los Angeles	NL	33	213.2	192	71	155	8	10	3.12	0	1.231
1994 Los Angeles	NL	23	153.0	149	54	102	7	7	4.12	0	1.327
1994 PROJECTION		30	198.0	208	69	129	9	10	4.27	0	1.399

STEVE COOKE   Age 25/L $4

A week or so before The Strike, some Pirates were talking about the issues.
The name of Marvin Miller was invoked, and Cooke asked, "Who's he, that
band leader guy?"

Year Team	Lg.	G	IP	H	BB	SO	W	L	ERA	SV	Ratio
1992 Pittsburgh	NL	11	23.0	22	4	10	2	0	3.52	1	1.130
1993 Pittsburgh	NL	32	210.2	207	59	132	10	10	3.89	0	1.263
1994 Pittsburgh	NL	25	134.1	157	46	74	4	11	5.02	0	1.511
1994 PROJECTION		36	164.1	192	51	83	5	13	4.93	0	1.479

RHEAL CORMIER   Age 27/L $4

We're not saying it was comparable to, say, Sandy Koufax retiring. But the
deplorable Cardinals pitching staff felt the loss of this competent lefty.

Year Team	Lg.	G	IP	H	BB	SO	W	L	ERA	SV	Ratio
1991 St. Louis	NL	11	67.2	74	8	38	4	5	4.12	0	1.212
1992 St. Louis	NL	31	186.0	194	33	117	10	10	3.68	0	1.220
1993 St. Louis	NL	38	145.1	163	27	75	7	6	4.33	0	1.307
1994 St. Louis	NL	7	39.2	40	7	26	3	2	5.45	0	1.185
1994 PROJECTION		16	92.0	93	28	60	5	5	4.79	0	1.315

DOUG DRABEK   Age 32/R $23

Last year we bet the farm that the real Doug Drabek would come back in 1994. He did, and this year we're betting the farm that he stays put as one of the league's toughest competitors and best pitchers.

Year Team	Lg.	G	IP	H	BB	SO	W	L	ERA	SV	Ratio
1991 Pittsburgh	NL	35	234.2	245	62	142	15	14	3.07	0	1.308
1992 Pittsburgh	NL	34	256.2	218	54	177	15	11	2.77	0	1.060
1993 Houston	NL	34	237.2	242	60	157	9	18	3.79	0	1.271
1994 Houston	NL	23	164.2	132	45	121	12	6	2.84	0	1.075
1994 PROJECTION		33	235.2	193	62	173	17	6	2.56	0	1.082

JEFF FASSERO   Age 32/L $18

A 20-game winner waiting to happen. Is there any other lefty starter in the league you'd rather have? Avery is a lot younger, so maybe him for the long run. But for right now Fassero is the portsider of preference. Last year NL batters hit just .229 against him. That's stingy.

Year Team	Lg.	G	IP	H	BB	SO	W	L	ERA	SV	Ratio
1991 Montreal	NL	51	55.1	39	17	42	2	5	2.44	8	1.012
1992 Montreal	NL	70	85.2	81	34	63	8	7	2.84	1	1.342
1993 Montreal	NL	56	149.2	119	54	140	12	5	2.29	1	1.156
1994 Montreal	NL	21	138.2	119	40	119	8	6	2.99	0	1.147
1994 PROJECTION		24	157.1	139	42	134	9	7	3.15	0	1.150

KEVIN FOSTER   Age 26/R $5

One of the few moves by the Cubs that worked out. They dealt away Shawn Boskie for this unknown and rather undersized right-hander, who showed up in Wrigley Field with one of the best changeups in baseball and a sneaky quick fastball.

Year Team	Lg.	G	IP	H	BB	SO	W	L	ERA	SV	Ratio
1993 Philadelphia	NL	2	6.2	13	7	6	0	1	14.85	0	3.000
1994 Chicago	NL	13	81.0	70	35	75	3	4	2.89	0	1.296
1994 PROJECTION		24	137.1	128	55	119	7	7	3.41	0	1.332

MARVIN FREEMAN   Age 31/R $13

What's up with Bad Marvin? Says a Rockies executive, "He finally decided to work on being a pitcher instead of a jackass." His focus thus redirected, Freeman went on to learn how to keep his mean slider down in the strike zone, and that made him downright nasty.

Year Team	Lg.	G	IP	H	BB	SO	W	L	ERA	SV	Ratio
1991 Atlanta	NL	34	48.0	37	13	34	1	0	3.00	1	1.042
1992 Atlanta	NL	58	64.1	61	29	41	7	5	3.22	3	1.399
1993 Atlanta	NL	21	23.2	24	10	25	2	0	6.08	0	1.437
1994 Colorado	NL	19	112.2	113	23	67	10	2	2.80	0	1.207
1994 PROJECTION		29	174.1	186	33	116	11	4	3.36	0	1.256

Catchers
pp. 33–46

Corners
pp. 46–65

Infield
pp. 66–85

Outfield
pp. 85–115

DH
pp. 115–119

Starters
pp. 119–155

Relievers
pp. 155–187

MARK GARDNER
Age 33/R   **$1**

Too many of his many curveballs float through the strike zone with a big "Hit Me" sign stamped on them.

Year Team	Lg.	G	IP	H	BB	SO	W	L	ERA	SV	Ratio
1991 Montreal	NL	27	168.1	139	75	107	9	11	3.85	0	1.271
1992 Montreal	NL	33	179.2	179	60	132	12	10	4.36	0	1.330
1993 Kansas City	AL	17	91.2	92	36	54	4	6	6.19	0	1.396
1994 Florida	NL	20	92.1	97	30	57	4	4	4.87	0	1.375
1994 PROJECTION		28	126.1	144	47	84	4	8	5.63	0	1.512

TOM GLAVINE
Age 29/L   **$24**

An automatic 20-game winner who still wanted to get better, Glavine went on a tough strengthening program, refined his delivery and fastball grip, and added five miles per hour to his heater. He needed some time to adjust to the added pop and its tendency to rise, which is why some of his numbers look untidy. But he'll have that fixed by the time somebody finally yells "Play ball!" this spring.

Year Team	Lg.	G	IP	H	BB	SO	W	L	ERA	SV	Ratio
1991 Atlanta	NL	34	246.2	201	69	192	20	11	2.55	0	1.095
1992 Atlanta	NL	33	225.0	197	70	129	20	8	2.76	0	1.187
1993 Atlanta	NL	36	239.1	236	90	120	22	6	3.20	0	1.362
1994 Atlanta	NL	25	165.1	173	70	140	13	9	3.97	0	1.470
1994 PROJECTION		34	225.2	232	94	187	18	10	4.07	0	1.444

DWIGHT GOODEN
Age 30/R   **No Price**

Get well, Doc.

Year Team	Lg.	G	IP	H	BB	SO	W	L	ERA	SV	Ratio
1991 New York	NL	27	190.0	185	56	150	13	7	3.60	0	1.268
1992 New York	NL	31	206.0	197	70	145	10	13	3.67	0	1.296
1993 New York	NL	29	208.2	188	61	149	12	15	3.45	0	1.193
1994 New York	NL	7	41.1	46	15	40	3	4	6.31	0	1.476
1994 PROJECTION		7	41.1	46	15	40	3	4	6.31	0	1.476

TOMMY GREENE
Age 27/R   **$8**

He seems to combine generally good health and a relatively mature approach to his craft in alternate years, so this figures to be one of his solid seasons. But the Phillies are losing their patience, and so are we.

Year Team	Lg.	G	IP	H	BB	SO	W	L	ERA	SV	Ratio
1991 Philadelphia	NL	36	207.2	177	66	154	13	7	3.38	0	1.170
1992 Philadelphia	NL	13	64.1	75	34	39	3	3	5.32	0	1.694
1993 Philadelphia	NL	31	200.0	175	62	167	16	4	3.42	0	1.185
1994 Philadelphia	NL	7	35.2	37	22	28	2	0	4.54	0	1.654
1994 PROJECTION		12	67.0	71	32	51	2	3	3.90	0	1.537

KEVIN GROSS
Age 33/R   **$6**

You can count on him. Not to win any ERA titles or lead the league in strikeouts or make any All-Star teams. But what he does is almost as rare these days. He takes the ball, piles up the innings, and wins 10–13 games a season. No, it's not pretty, but it's at least comforting to know what you're going to get. Could be key to a Rangers pennant.

Year Team	Lg.	G	IP	H	BB	SO	W	L	ERA	SV	Ratio
1991 Los Angeles	NL	46	115.2	123	50	95	10	11	3.58	3	1.496
1992 Los Angeles	NL	34	204.2	182	77	158	8	13	3.17	0	1.265
1993 Los Angeles	NL	33	202.1	224	74	150	13	13	4.14	0	1.473
1994 Los Angeles	NL	25	157.1	162	43	124	9	7	3.60	1	1.303
1994 PROJECTION		34	222.1	223	59	175	14	9	3.16	1	1.268

Catchers
pp. 33–46

Corners
pp. 46–65

Infield
pp. 66–85

Outfield
pp. 85–115

DH
pp. 115–119

Starters
pp. 119–155

Relievers
pp. 155–187

JOEY HAMILTON   Age 24/R $12

Good control, polished delivery, command of four pitches, guts enough to pitch inside, tenacious makeup, doesn't rattle under pressure. Yep, he's the full package.

Year Team	Lg.	G	IP	H	BB	SO	W	L	ERA	SV	Ratio
1994 San Diego	NL	16	108.2	98	29	61	9	6	2.98	0	1.169
1994 PROJECTION		23	150.0	142	34	86	9	8	3.36	0	1.173

CHRIS HAMMOND   Age 29/L $3

If he had a Rotisserie team, it would be the Hammond Eggs. Wonder how much would he pay for the fifth starter on a mediocre team.

Year Team	Lg.	G	IP	H	BB	SO	W	L	ERA	SV	Ratio
1991 Cincinnati	NL	20	99.2	92	48	50	7	7	4.06	0	1.405
1992 Cincinnati	NL	28	147.1	149	55	79	7	10	4.21	0	1.385
1993 Florida	NL	32	191.0	207	66	108	11	12	4.66	0	1.429
1994 Florida	NL	13	73.1	79	23	40	4	4	3.07	0	1.391
1994 PROJECTION		19	85.1	94	29	48	5	4	3.16	0	1.441

ERIK HANSON   Age 29/R $6

Declared he'd be willing to take a cut in pay in order to stay in Cincinnati. That's big of him. After his last few years, he should be happy to have a job. Maybe playing for Marge has been an inspiration for him. Maybe he likes dogs. Anyway, his kissing up to the boss didn't help. The Reds cut him loose. Could be valuable, depending on where he lands.

Year Team	Lg.	G	IP	H	BB	SO	W	L	ERA	SV	Ratio
1991 Seattle	AL	27	174.2	182	56	143	8	8	3.81	0	1.363
1992 Seattle	AL	31	186.2	209	57	112	8	17	4.82	0	1.425
1993 Seattle	AL	31	215.0	215	60	163	11	12	3.47	0	1.279
1994 Cincinnati	NL	22	122.2	137	23	101	5	5	4.11	0	1.304
1994 PROJECTION		22	122.2	137	23	101	5	5	4.11	0	1.304

MIKE HARKEY   Age 28/R $1

Harkey's own assessment on his performance last year: "I stunk." He's too easy on himself. Is it really that long ago that he was a can't-miss phenom who was going to win 30 games in Wrigley, sweep the Rookie of the Year and Cy Young votes, and then run for mayor of Chicago? Yes, we suppose it is. What with the shortage of pitching in the post-expansion era, somebody will give him another shot.

Year Team	Lg.	G	IP	H	BB	SO	W	L	ERA	SV	Ratio
1991 Chicago	NL	4	18.2	21	6	15	0	2	5.30	0	1.446
1992 Chicago	NL	7	38.0	34	15	21	4	0	1.89	0	1.289
1993 Chicago	NL	28	157.1	187	43	67	10	10	5.26	0	1.462
1994 Colorado	NL	24	91.2	125	35	39	1	6	5.79	0	1.745
1994 PROJECTION		28	111.1	150	39	46	2	8	5.90	0	1.697

PETE HARNISCH

Age 28/R   **$12**

One of our personal favorites has been bugged by injuries large and small for the past year and a half. Healthy again, he should come back strong. Good move by the Mets.

Year Team	Lg.	G	IP	H	BB	SO	W	L	ERA	SV	Ratio
1991 Houston	NL	33	216.2	169	83	172	12	9	2.70	0	1.163
1992 Houston	NL	34	206.2	182	64	164	9	10	3.70	0	1.190
1993 Houston	NL	33	217.2	171	79	185	16	9	2.98	0	1.149
1994 Houston	NL	17	95.0	100	39	62	8	5	5.40	0	1.463
1994 PROJECTION		27	156.0	158	57	110	12	7	5.13	0	1.378

GREG W. HARRIS

Age 31/R   **$1**

Horrible season, but there was *somebody* who had an even worse one. It was . . . whatshizname, you know. Wait a minute, it's on the tip of our tongue. Oh, hell, you know who we mean. Don't rush us, we'll think of the guy's name in a minute. . . .

Year Team	Lg.	G	IP	H	BB	SO	W	L	ERA	SV	Ratio
1991 San Diego	NL	20	133.0	116	27	95	9	5	2.23	0	1.075
1992 San Diego	NL	20	118.0	113	35	66	4	8	4.12	0	1.254
1993 San Diego	NL	22	152.0	151	39	83	10	9	3.67	0	1.250
1993 Colorado	NL	13	73.1	88	30	40	1	8	6.50	0	1.609
1994 Colorado	NL	29	130.0	154	52	82	3	12	6.65	1	1.585
1994 PROJECTION		37	175.0	196	72	106	6	14	6.02	1	1.531

BUTCH HENRY

Age 26/L   **$8**

Coaches at the major league level sometimes make a real difference. Case in point: Montreal pitching coach Joe Kerrigan's work with Butch Henry last year. Throughout his career, Henry has been just another fringe pitcher, and nothing appeared different when he landed in Montreal to work middle relief. Then, when he was needed as a fifth starter, Kerrigan convinced Henry to junk his curveball, spot his slider, and concentrate on adding oomph to his sinking fastball. The result: Henry became the best fifth starter in the National League.

Year Team	Ig.	G	IP	H	BB	SO	W	L	ERA	SV	Ratio
1992 Houston	NL	28	165.2	185	41	96	6	9	4.02	0	1.364
1993 Colorado	NL	20	84.2	117	24	39	2	8	6.59	0	1.665
1993 Montreal	NL	10	18.1	18	4	8	1	1	3.93	0	1.200
1994 Montreal	NL	24	107.1	97	20	70	8	3	2.43	1	1.090
1994 PROJECTION		33	175.0	149	33	106	13	4	2.01	1	1.040

OREL HERSHISER

Age 36/R   **$5**

The Bulldog has lost most of his teeth, and he can only go so far on heart.

Year Team	Lg.	G	IP	H	BB	SO	W	L	ERA	SV	Ratio
1991 Los Angeles	NL	21	112.0	112	32	73	7	2	3.46	0	1.286
1992 Los Angeles	NL	33	210.2	209	69	130	10	15	3.67	0	1.320
1993 Los Angeles	NL	33	215.2	201	72	141	12	14	3.59	0	1.266
1994 Los Angeles	NL	21	135.1	146	42	72	6	6	3.79	0	1.389
1994 PROJECTION		31	198.2	223	56	106	9	11	3.90	0	1.404

BRYAN HICKERSON

Age 31/L   **$1**

The Giants media guide reveals that he is an avid reader. He gave up 20 home runs in less than 100 innings pitched. Read on.

Year Team	Lg.	G	IP	H	BB	SO	W	L	ERA	SV	Ratio
1991 San Francisco	NL	17	50.0	53	17	43	2	2	3.60	0	1.400
1992 San Francisco	NL	61	87.1	74	21	68	5	3	3.09	0	1.088
1993 San Francisco	NL	47	120.1	137	39	69	7	5	4.26	0	1.463
1994 San Francisco	NL	28	98.1	118	38	59	4	8	5.40	1	1.586
1994 PROJECTION		35	122.2	150	51	74	6	9	5.58	1	1.638

KEN HILL   Age 29/R $24

In a world that did not include Greg Maddux, he would have been the best pitcher in the National League.

Year Team	Lg.	G	IP	H	BB	SO	W	L	ERA	SV	Ratio
1991 St. Louis	NL	30	181.1	147	67	121	11	10	3.57	0	1.180
1992 Montreal	NL	33	218.0	187	75	150	16	9	2.68	0	1.202
1993 Montreal	NL	28	183.2	163	74	90	9	7	3.23	0	1.290
1994 Montreal	NL	23	154.2	145	44	85	16	5	3.32	0	1.222
1994 PROJECTION		33	227.0	217	61	128	21	7	3.25	0	1.224

CHARLIE HOUGH   Age 47/R   No Price

How tough was his floater to hit? Over 25 seasons NL and AL hitters batted just .231 against him. We were sort of hoping he would go on forever.

Year Team	Lg.	G	IP	H	BB	SO	W	L	ERA	SV	Ratio
1991 Chicago	AL	31	199.1	167	94	107	9	10	4.02	0	1.309
1992 Chicago	AL	27	176.1	160	66	76	7	12	3.93	0	1.282
1993 Florida	NL	34	204.1	202	71	126	9	16	4.27	0	1.336
1994 Florida	NL	21	113.2	118	52	65	5	9	5.15	0	1.496
1994 PROJECTION		21	113.2	118	52	65	5	9	5.15	0	1.495

DANNY JACKSON   Age 33/L $19

Back-to-back healthy, productive seasons from *Danny Jackson?* Or are we having another flashback? Cardinals desperately need him to three-peat.

Year Team	Lg.	G	IP	H	BB	SO	W	L	ERA	SV	Ratio
1991 Chicago	NL	17	70.2	89	48	31	1	5	6.75	0	1.939
1992 Chicago	NL	19	113.0	117	48	51	4	9	4.22	0	1.460
1992 Pittsburgh	NL	15	88.1	94	29	46	4	4	3.36	0	1.392
1993 Philadelphia	NL	32	210.1	214	80	120	12	11	3.77	0	1.398
1994 Philadelphia	NL	25	179.1	183	46	129	14	6	3.26	0	1.277
1994 PROJECTION		35	246.2	245	67	179	20	9	3.43	0	1.265

JASON JACOME   Age 24/L $4

Okay, the first reader to present us with documented evidence that he or she had even heard of Jason Jacome a year ago this time, much less predicted Jacome would come up and do what he did, will receive an autographed photo of Harry Stein. (All other contestants receive two photos.) Now, about young Mr. Jacome. We were pretty impressed, but we're reserving judgment until league hitters get to see him another couple of times.

Year Team	Lg.	G	IP	H	BB	SO	W	L	ERA	SV	Ratio
1994 New York	NL	8	54.0	54	17	30	4	3	2.67	0	1.315
1994 PROJECTION		17	102.0	102	24	53	6	5	3.18	0	1.235

BOBBY JONES   Age 25/R $9

In a Mets farm system brimming with a new generation of pitching prospects, he is by no means the most impressive looking on the mound. All he does better than the others is win.

Year Team	Lg.	G	IP	H	BB	SO	W	L	ERA	SV	Ratio
1993 New York	NL	9	61.2	61	22	35	2	4	3.65	0	1.346
1994 New York	NL	24	160.0	157	56	80	12	7	3.15	0	1.331
1994 PROJECTION		34	230.1	224	74	119	16	10	3.09	0	1.294

DARRYL KILE   Age 26/R $11

Said one Astro: "Kile should never lose with the stuff he has. The trouble is that they call balls and strikes." If he gets his control back, and most Astro watchers are convinced he will, Kile may lose, but not very much.

Year Team	Lg.	G	IP	H	BB	SO	W	L	ERA	SV	Ratio
1991 Houston	NL	37	153.2	144	84	100	7	11	3.69	0	1.484
1992 Houston	NL	22	125.1	124	63	90	5	10	3.95	0	1.492
1993 Houston	NL	32	171.2	152	69	141	15	8	3.51	0	1.287
1994 Houston	NL	24	147.2	153	82	105	9	6	4.57	0	1.591
1994 PROJECTION		33	189.1	207	110	131	11	10	5.28	0	1.674

JON LIEBER   Age 25/R $5

Marginal stuff, good changeup, excellent control. That's all you need these days to get people talking Cooperstown.

Year Team	Lg.	G	IP	H	BB	SO	W	L	ERA	SV	Ratio
1994 Pittsburgh	NL	17	108.2	116	25	71	6	7	3.73	0	1.298
1994 PROJECTION		27	177.0	178	40	111	9	8	3.46	0	1.231

GREG MADDUX   Age 28/R $27

King of the Hill.

Year Team	Lg.	G	IP	H	BB	SO	W	L	ERA	SV	Ratio
1991 Chicago	NL	37	263.0	232	66	198	15	11	3.35	0	1.133
1992 Chicago	NL	35	268.0	201	70	199	20	11	2.18	0	1.011
1993 Atlanta	NL	36	267.0	228	52	197	20	10	2.36	0	1.049
1994 Atlanta	NL	25	202.0	150	31	156	16	6	1.56	0	0.896
1994 PROJECTION		34	274.0	214	45	198	20	8	1.74	0	0.945

PEDRO J. MARTINEZ   Age 23/R $18

Made a lot star appearances on "Baseball Tonight" early in the season when it seemed like he was triggering a bench-clearing brawl every other outing. But the reason he deserves a "Most Wanted" logo on his mug shot . . . uh, baseball card is that in his first year as a starter he established himself as one of the most promising pitchers in the league. Not to mention the toughest.

Year Team	Lg.	G	IP	H	BB	SO	W	L	ERA	SV	Ratio
1992 Los Angeles	NL	2	8.0	6	1	8	0	1	2.25	0	0.875
1993 Los Angeles	NL	65	107.0	76	57	119	10	5	2.61	2	1.243
1994 Montreal	NL	24	144.2	115	45	142	11	5	3.42	1	1.106
1994 PROJECTION		34	214.0	179	68	223	15	10	3.79	1	1.154

RAMON MARTINEZ   Age 27/R $13

Maybe older brother Ramón started reading those Montreal box scores and figured, hey, no way that little punk is going to show me up. Whatever it was, sibling rivalry or maybe fewer innings pitched in winter ball, Martinez the Elder had more velocity on his fastball and breathed life into his shaky career.

Year	Team	Lg.	G	IP	H	BB	SO	W	L	ERA	SV	Ratio
1991	Los Angeles	NL	33	220.1	190	69	150	17	13	3.27	0	1.175
1992	Los Angeles	NL	25	150.2	141	69	101	8	11	4.00	0	1.394
1993	Los Angeles	NL	32	211.2	202	104	127	10	12	3.44	0	1.446
1994	Los Angeles	NL	24	170.0	160	56	119	12	7	3.97	0	1.271
1994	PROJECTION		33	236.0	227	78	153	14	12	3.62	0	1.292

KENT MERCKER   Age 27/L $11

We have a hunch that this is the year he moves up a notch in the rotation (probably bumping John Smoltz). Those extra starts will make him worth some extra bucks.

Year	Team	Lg.	G	IP	H	BB	SO	W	L	ERA	SV	Ratio
1991	Atlanta	NL	50	73.1	56	35	62	5	3	2.58	6	1.241
1992	Atlanta	NL	53	68.1	51	35	49	3	2	3.42	6	1.259
1993	Atlanta	NL	43	66.0	52	36	59	3	1	2.86	0	1.333
1994	Atlanta	NL	20	112.1	90	45	111	9	4	3.45	0	1.202
1994	PROJECTION		30	187.1	138	77	181	13	7	2.93	0	1.147

MIKE MORGAN   Age 35/R $1

We just remembered the name of the guy who had a worse season than Greg Harris.

Year	Team	Lg.	G	IP	H	BB	SO	W	L	ERA	SV	Ratio
1991	Los Angeles	NL	34	236.1	197	61	140	14	10	2.78	1	1.092
1992	Chicago	NL	34	240.0	203	79	123	16	8	2.55	0	1.175
1993	Chicago	NL	32	207.2	206	74	111	10	15	4.03	0	1.348
1994	Chicago	NL	15	80.2	111	35	57	2	10	6.69	0	1.810
1994	PROJECTION		15	80.2	111	35	57	2	10	6.69	0	1.810

BOBBY MUNOZ   Age 27/R $11

There was early speculation that Muñoz would end up in the bullpen, which is where he did his best work as a Yankees farmhand. And well he might have, if Doug Jones hadn't come back from the dead. The Phillies are mighty pleased that Big Bobby (6'7", 237) stayed in the rotation, because they now have a terrific-looking number two man to follow a rejuvenated Danny Jackson. If Schilling and Greene return to form, the Phillies have an outside chance at their second-straight pennant.

Year	Team	Lg.	G	IP	H	BB	SO	W	L	ERA	SV	Ratio
1993	New York	AL	38	45.2	48	26	33	3	3	5.32	0	1.620
1994	Philadelphia	NL	21	104.1	101	35	59	7	5	2.67	1	1.304
1994	PROJECTION		31	156.2	162	49	89	9	10	3.27	2	1.347

Catchers
pp. 33–46

Corners
pp. 46–65

Infield
pp. 66–85

Outfield
pp. 85–115

DH
pp. 115–119

Starters
pp. 119–155

Relievers
pp. 155–187

DENNY NEAGLE   Age 26/L $1

Doesn't rhyme with beagle, but he pitched like one about half the time.

Year Team	Lg.	G	IP	H	BB	SO	W	L	ERA	SV	Ratio
1991 Minnesota	AL	7	20.0	28	7	14	0	1	4.05	0	1.750
1992 Pittsburgh	NL	55	86.1	81	43	77	4	6	4.48	2	1.436
1993 Pittsburgh	NL	50	81.1	82	37	73	3	5	5.31	1	1.463
1994 Pittsburgh	NL	24	137.0	135	49	122	9	10	5.12	0	1.343
1994 PROJECTION		35	191.2	203	69	174	12	14	5.40	0	1.419

DAVE NIED   Age 26/R $8

Started pitching like everyone thought he would, then labored under a cloud created by the premature birth and lengthy illness of his first child. The baby is now healthy, and so is Dad. This could be his breakout year.

Year Team	Lg.	G	IP	H	BB	SO	W	L	ERA	SV	Ratio
1992 Atlanta	NL	6	23.0	10	5	19	3	0	1.17	0	0.652
1993 Colorado	NL	16	87.0	99	42	46	5	9	5.17	0	1.621
1994 Colorado	NL	22	122.0	137	47	74	9	7	4.80	0	1.508
1994 PROJECTION		31	173.0	194	66	89	13	9	4.53	0	1.503

LANCE PAINTER   Age 27/L $1

Has enough stuff to remain a plausible prospect, but Colorado is a tough proving ground.

Year Team	Lg.	G	IP	H	BB	SO	W	L	ERA	SV	Ratio
1993 Colorado	NL	10	39.0	52	9	16	2	2	6.00	0	1.564
1994 Colorado	NL	15	73.2	91	26	41	4	6	6.11	0	1.588
1994 PROJECTION		23	95.0	123	32	52	5	9	6.35	0	1.631

MARK PORTUGAL   Age 32/R $9

Pitched through some pain but finished the year on the DL. Not noted for his commitment to training and fitness, Portugal might turn out to be a very costly mistake for the Giants.

Year Team	Lg.	G	IP	H	BB	SO	W	L	ERA	SV	Ratio
1991 Houston	NL	32	168.1	163	59	120	10	12	4.49	1	1.319
1992 Houston	NL	18	101.1	76	41	62	6	3	2.66	0	1.155
1993 Houston	NL	33	208.0	194	77	131	18	4	2.77	0	1.303
1994 San Francisco	NL	21	137.1	135	45	87	10	8	3.93	0	1.311
1994 PROJECTION		21	137.1	135	45	87	10	8	3.93	0	1.310

PAT RAPP   Age 27/R $4

Selected in the expansion draft from the Giants organization, which probably didn't protect him because he has no history of arm trouble. (Heck, he just wouldn't have fit in.) The rap on Pat pertains to his control, or lack thereof. Until he learns to find the plate with more regularity, his live fastball and good stuff aren't going to be enough to get us too excited.

Year Team	Lg.	G	IP	H	BB	SO	W	L	ERA	SV	Ratio
1992 San Francisco	NL	3	10.0	8	6	3	0	2	7.20	0	1.400
1993 Florida	NL	16	94.0	101	39	57	4	6	4.02	0	1.489
1994 Florida	NL	24	133.1	132	69	75	7	8	3.85	0	1.508
1994 PROJECTION		33	180.0	205	97	102	8	14	4.90	0	1.678

SHANE REYNOLDS

Age 27/R   **$9**

Excellent control, exciting stuff. Before last season Astros brass had been thinking of him as a potential closer, but the emergence of John Hudek and Reynolds's excellent work as a starter put the kibosh on that notion. He will likely bump Brian Williams if Greg Swindell isn't traded. This could be the last year to get him relatively cheap.

Year Team	Lg.	G	IP	H	BB	SO	W	L	ERA	SV	Ratio
1992 Houston	NL	8	25.1	42	6	10	1	3	7.11	0	1.895
1993 Houston	NL	5	11.0	11	6	10	0	0	0.82	0	1.545
1994 Houston	NL	33	124.0	128	21	110	8	5	3.05	0	1.202
1994 PROJECTION		43	189.0	208	28	166	12	8	3.10	0	1.248

ARMANDO REYNOSO

Age 28/R   **$2**

One good year under his belt, but he finished last season on the DL. High risk, modest reward.

Year Team	Lg.	G	IP	H	BB	SO	W	L	ERA	SV	Ratio
1991 Atlanta	NL	6	23.1	26	10	10	2	1	6.17	0	1.543
1992 Atlanta	NL	3	7.2	11	2	2	1	0	4.70	1	1.696
1993 Colorado	NL	30	189.0	206	63	117	12	11	4.00	0	1.423
1994 Colorado	NL	9	52.1	54	22	25	3	4	4.82	0	1.452
1994 PROJECTION		9	52.1	54	22	25	3	4	4.82	0	1.452

JOSE RIJO

Age 29/R   **$21**

As a good-luck gesture before each new season, Rijo sacrifices some goats from his herd in the Dominican Republic. He then has the goats barbecued for a great preseason feast. So a reporter asked him last spring: "What does goat taste like?" His response: "Hey, you know, man, it tastes like *cabrito*." Thanks, José.

Year Team	Lg.	G	IP	H	BB	SO	W	L	ERA	SV	Ratio
1991 Cincinnati	NL	30	204.1	165	55	172	15	6	2.51	0	1.077
1992 Cincinnati	NL	33	211.0	185	44	171	15	10	2.56	0	1.085
1993 Cincinnati	NL	36	257.1	218	62	227	14	9	2.48	0	1.088
1994 Cincinnati	NL	26	172.1	177	52	171	9	6	3.08	0	1.329
1994 PROJECTION		33	217.1	227	67	210	12	8	3.40	0	1.353

BEN RIVERA

Age 27/R   **$1**

Spearheaded by Rivera (6'6"), Bobby Muñoz (6'7"), Jeff Juden (6'8"), and David West (6'6"), the Phillies are just one point guard away from being able to kick some 76ers butt. And if home plate were as big as a backboard, Big Ben would be a Cy Young candidate. Eye-popping stuff, no clue how to control it.

Year Team	Lg.	G	IP	H	BB	SO	W	L	ERA	SV	Ratio
1992 Atlanta	NL	8	15.1	21	13	11	0	1	4.70	0	2.217
1992 Philadelphia	NL	20	102.0	78	32	66	7	3	2.82	0	1.078
1993 Philadelphia	NL	30	163.0	175	85	123	13	9	5.02	0	1.595
1994 Philadelphia	NL	9	38.0	40	22	19	3	4	6.87	0	1.632
1994 PROJECTION		22	63.2	80	34	35	4	7	7.49	0	1.790

Catchers
pp. 33–46

Corners
pp. 46–65

Infield
pp. 66–85

Outfield
pp. 85–115

DH
pp. 115–119

Starters
pp. 119–155

Relievers
pp. 155–187

JOHN ROPER   Age 23/R $2

How can a pitcher give up four and half runs a game and still win three-fourths of his decisions? By pitching for a team that scores nearly six and a half runs behind him. Therein lies a nugget of Rotisserie wisdom, but we'll let you dig it out for yourself.

Year Team	Lg.	G	IP	H	BB	SO	W	L	ERA	SV	Ratio
1993 Cincinnati	NL	16	80.0	92	36	54	2	5	5.63	0	1.600
1994 Cincinnati	NL	16	92.0	90	30	51	6	2	4.50	0	1.304
1994 PROJECTION		26	160.1	153	49	95	10	5	3.93	0	1.260

KIRK RUETER   Age 24/L $4

Last year we misspelled his name, and we promptly heard from his cousin, an attorney. We settled out of court by promising to get it right this year. In between editions, Rueter had a rough sophomore season. Hitters found out that if they waited him out, he would eventually have to come over the middle of the plate with his less-than-world-beating stuff. And when he did, they took batting practice at a .294 clip. If the Expos hadn't scored over six runs a game behind Rueter, he might not still be around, and we wouldn't have had the opportunity to correct the spelling of his name. The good news is that he's making progress in developing a better breaking ball. With his already excellent control, that should be enough to get him back a little closer to 1993 form.

Year Team	Lg.	G	IP	H	BB	SO	W	L	ERA	SV	Ratio
1993 Montreal	NL	14	85.2	85	18	31	8	0	2.73	0	1.202
1994 Montreal	NL	20	92.1	106	23	50	7	3	5.17	0	1.397
1994 PROJECTION		29	152.2	150	31	76	13	4	4.01	0	1.185

BRET SABERHAGEN   Age 30/R $24

He shoved aside all the controversies, unfunny practical jokes, petulant behavior, contract squabbles, questions about his future, and problems with Dallas Green. Then he reared back, threw gas to every hitter he faced, and went back to being one of the half-dozen best pitchers in the game. (P.S.: Check out that walk-to-strikeout ratio. Zowie!)

Year Team	Lg.	G	IP	H	BB	SO	W	L	ERA	SV	Ratio
1991 Kansas City	AL	28	196.1	165	45	136	13	8	3.07	0	1.070
1992 New York	NL	17	97.2	84	27	81	3	5	3.50	0	1.137
1993 New York	NL	19	139.1	131	17	93	7	7	3.29	0	1.062
1994 New York	NL	24	177.1	169	13	143	14	4	2.74	0	1.026
1994 PROJECTION		34	250.0	239	24	193	17	8	2.77	0	1.052

SCOTT SANDERS   Age 26/R $3

The 109 Ks in 111 IP tell you he has big league stuff, but the 48 BB tell you he is not always in command of it. On a better team—and show us one this side of tee-ball that isn't better than the Padres—he could be an effective pitcher.

Year Team	Lg.	G	IP	H	BB	SO	W	L	ERA	SV	Ratio
1993 San Diego	NL	9	52.1	54	23	37	3	3	4.13	0	1.471
1994 San Diego	NL	23	111.0	103	48	109	4	8	4.78	1	1.360
1994 PROJECTION		32	171.1	157	69	164	9	11	4.46	1	1.319

CURT SCHILLING   Age 28/R $7

After the 1993 World Series he irritated teammates by becoming a media darling who showed up on more talk shows than Alan Dershowitz. Then he started the 1994 season 0–7, went on the DL, and had teammates sneering openly that he was jaking it. The arm injury was real enough, though, and when he recovered he showed tentative signs that all might be well again— if not with his teammates, at least with those of us who employ him.

Year	Team	Lg.	G	IP	H	BB	SO	W	L	ERA	SV	Ratio
1991	Houston	NL	56	75.2	79	39	71	3	5	3.81	8	1.559
1992	Philadelphia	NL	42	226.1	165	59	147	14	11	2.35	2	0.990
1993	Philadelphia	NL	34	235.1	234	57	186	16	7	4.02	0	1.237
1994	Philadelphia	NL	13	82.1	87	28	58	2	8	4.48	0	1.397
1994	PROJECTION		23	140.0	145	48	98	2	12	4.37	0	1.378

PETE SCHOUREK   Age 25/L $4

"I always liked the guy more than people in New York," said Davey Johnson last season of Schourek. That was easy enough for Davey to say, considering the bang-up job Schourek did after escaping from Dallas Green's doghouse to become Schottzie II's teammate.

Year	Team	Lg.	G	IP	H	BB	SO	W	L	ERA	SV	Ratio
1991	New York	NL	35	86.1	82	43	67	5	4	4.27	2	1.448
1992	New York	NL	22	136.0	137	44	60	6	8	3.64	0	1.331
1993	New York	NL	41	128.1	168	45	72	5	12	5.96	0	1.660
1994	Cincinnati	NL	22	81.1	90	29	69	7	2	4.09	0	1.463
1994	PROJECTION		27	100.2	127	35	83	7	6	5.54	0	1.609

JOHN SMILEY   Age 30/L $14

Came more than halfway back from the elbow trouble that ruined 1993. Our team of medical experts down at the local HMO tells us that it usually takes a full year for an elbow to heal completely. If that's so, then put on your Smiley face and go get him.

Year	Team	Lg.	G	IP	H	BB	SO	W	L	ERA	SV	Ratio
1991	Pittsburgh	NL	33	207.2	194	44	129	20	8	3.08	0	1.146
1992	Minnesota	AL	34	241.0	205	65	163	16	9	3.21	0	1.120
1993	Cincinnati	NL	18	105.2	117	31	60	3	9	5.62	0	1.401
1994	Cincinnati	NL	24	158.2	169	37	112	11	10	3.86	0	1.298
1994	PROJECTION		34	223.2	243	52	159	17	12	4.23	0	1.319

PETE SMITH   Age 29/R $1

Running out of chances.

Year	Team	Lg.	G	IP	H	BB	SO	W	L	ERA	SV	Ratio
1991	Atlanta	NL	14	48.0	48	22	29	1	3	5.06	0	1.458
1992	Atlanta	NL	12	79.0	63	28	43	7	0	2.05	0	1.152
1993	Atlanta	NL	20	90.2	92	36	53	4	8	4.37	0	1.412
1994	New York	NL	21	131.1	145	42	62	4	10	5.55	0	1.424
1994	PROJECTION		29	184.1	200	49	82	6	12	5.47	0	1.351

Catchers
pp. 33–46

Corners
pp. 46–65

Infield
pp. 66–85

Outfield
pp. 85–115

DH
pp. 115–119

Starters
pp. 119–155

Relievers
pp. 155–187

ZANE SMITH
Age 34/L   **$16**

Makes too much money to stay in Pittsburgh. If he's dealt to a contender, he will win big—provided, of course, that his oft-injured arm holds up.

Year	Team	Lg.	G	IP	H	BB	SO	W	L	ERA	SV	Ratio
1991	Pittsburgh	NL	35	228.0	234	29	120	16	10	3.20	0	1.154
1992	Pittsburgh	NL	23	141.0	138	19	56	8	8	3.06	0	1.113
1993	Pittsburgh	NL	14	83.0	97	22	32	3	7	4.55	0	1.434
1994	Pittsburgh	NL	25	157.0	162	34	57	10	8	3.27	0	1.248
1994	PROJECTION		35	223.0	228	44	85	15	12	3.63	0	1.220

JOHN SMOLTZ
Age 27/R   **$14**

The Braves were perplexed by Smoltz's ineffectiveness and troubled by his subsequent knee problems. There were whispers of turning him into a closer. There were rumors of trade. Our crystal ball tells us he will come back strong, but it still may not be good enough to keep Kent Mercker from pushing him out of the number four slot. Does that help?

Year	Team	Lg.	G	IP	H	BB	SO	W	L	ERA	SV	Ratio
1991	Atlanta	NL	36	229.2	206	77	148	14	13	3.80	0	1.232
1992	Atlanta	NL	35	246.2	206	80	215	15	12	2.85	0	1.159
1993	Atlanta	NL	35	243.2	208	100	208	15	11	3.62	0	1.264
1994	Atlanta	NL	21	134.2	120	48	113	6	10	4.14	0	1.248
1994	PROJECTION		26	167.0	142	55	138	9	10	3.88	0	1.179

RICK SUTCLIFFE
Age 38/R   **$1**

Whoever first used the word "gamer" must have had him in mind. But it's time to say good-bye, Rick. Past time, in fact.

Year	Team	Lg.	G	IP	H	BB	SO	W	L	ERA	SV	Ratio
1991	Chicago	NL	19	96.2	96	45	52	6	5	4.10	0	1.459
1992	Baltimore	AL	36	237.1	251	74	109	16	15	4.47	0	1.369
1993	Baltimore	AL	29	166.0	212	74	80	10	10	5.75	0	1.723
1994	St. Louis	NL	16	67.2	93	32	26	6	4	6.52	0	1.847
1994	PROJECTION		16	67.2	93	32	26	6	4	6.52	0	1.847

BILL SWIFT
Age 33/R   **$18**

Swift missed some starts last year with assorted arm troubles, but he did not finish the year on the DL, in a hospital, or scheduled for surgery. Does that suggest an injury-free 1995? You've got to be kidding. But unless he is laid low by having his arm laid open, Swift is strictly blue chip. (And we're not talking about his elbow.)

Year	Team	Lg.	G	IP	H	BB	SO	W	L	ERA	SV	Ratio
1991	Seattle	AL	71	90.1	74	26	48	1	2	1.99	17	1.107
1992	San Francisco	NL	30	164.2	144	43	77	10	4	2.08	1	1.136
1993	San Francisco	NL	34	232.2	195	55	157	21	8	2.82	0	1.074
1994	San Francisco	NL	17	109.1	109	31	62	8	7	3.38	0	1.280
1994	PROJECTION		28	178.0	184	47	101	13	11	3.29	0	1.298

GREG SWINDELL
Age 30/L   **$4**

Judging from his silhouette, one of the reasons for Swindell's two straight stinko years since signing his big, fat, four-year contract might be that he spends too much time grazing in Astros owner Drayton McLane's wholesale grocery warehouse. With Swindell utterly untradable, the Astros are between a rock and a hard place, because McLane will not eat his contract. Why not cover it with tomato sauce, cheese, and pepperoni and see if Swindell will?

Year	Team	Lg.	G	IP	H	BB	SO	W	L	ERA	SV	Ratio
1991	Cleveland	AL	33	238.0	241	31	169	9	16	3.48	0	1.143
1992	Cincinnati	NL	31	213.2	210	41	138	12	8	2.70	0	1.175
1993	Houston	NL	31	190.1	215	40	124	12	13	4.16	0	1.340
1994	Houston	NL	24	148.1	175	26	74	8	9	4.37	0	1.355
1994	PROJECTION		31	193.1	215	35	98	11	11	3.96	0	1.293

BOB TEWKSBURY   Age 34/R $6

For a control artist like Tewks, who makes up for a lack of overpowering stuff with precision work in the paint, the Incredible Shrinking Strike Zone of the past few years has been a tough row to hoe. Compounding his troubles are a bad back, a worse bullpen, and a rotten infield defense. Yet even though the numbers are hideous to behold, he still grinds out the wins.

Year	Team	Lg.	G	IP	H	BB	SO	W	L	ERA	SV	Ratio
1991	St. Louis	NL	30	191.0	206	38	75	11	12	3.25	0	1.277
1992	St. Louis	NL	33	233.0	217	20	91	16	5	2.16	0	1.017
1993	St. Louis	NL	32	213.2	258	20	97	17	10	3.83	0	1.301
1994	St. Louis	NL	24	155.2	190	22	79	12	10	5.32	0	1.362
1994	PROJECTION		32	210.1	251	33	98	16	14	4.96	0	1.350

SALOMON TORRES   Age 23/R $1

On the last day of the 1993 season Torres, then a 21-year-old rookie, was sent out to win a game that would put the Giants in a playoff for the division title. He was hammered mercilessly in a 12–1 loss to the Dodgers. The defeat was emotionally devastating to the fragile young man from San Pedro de Macorís: in the off-season, he talked of quitting baseball. Last season, he pitched as if he *had* quit. While the Giants are publicly hopeful that time will heal his wounds, they are privately worried that Torres may not recover the confidence needed to survive on a major league pitching mound.

Year	Team	Lg.	G	IP	H	BB	SO	W	L	ERA	SV	Ratio
1993	San Francisco	NL	8	44.2	37	27	23	3	5	4.03	0	1.433
1994	San Francisco	NL	16	84.1	95	34	42	2	8	5.44	0	1.530
1994	PROJECTION		20	103.1	120	41	58	2	10	5.84	0	1.558

STEVE TRACHSEL   Age 24/R $14

Tough, focused rookie with the makeup of a veteran. Give him the ball and get out of the way. Impressed scouts with his ability to keep the team in the game on days he didn't have his quality stuff.

Year	Team	Lg.	G	IP	H	BB	SO	W	L	ERA	SV	Ratio
1993	Chicago	NL	3	19.2	16	3	14	0	2	4.58	0	0.966
1994	Chicago	NL	22	146.0	133	54	108	9	7	3.21	0	1.281
1994	PROJECTION		32	214.1	198	78	163	12	12	3.36	0	1.288

Catchers
pp. 33–46

Corners
pp. 46–65

Infield
pp. 66–85

Outfield
pp. 85–115

DH
pp. 115–119

Starters
pp. 119–155

Relievers
pp. 155–187

TOM URBANI   Age 27/L $1

If you're looking for a spot starter on the team with the worst starting rotation in the National League, he's your man.

Year Team	Lg.	G	IP	H	BB	SO	W	L	ERA	SV	Ratio
1993 St. Louis	NL	18	62.0	73	26	33	1	3	4.65	0	1.597
1994 St. Louis	NL	20	80.1	98	21	43	3	7	5.15	0	1.481
1994 PROJECTION		29	130.2	142	38	64	5	7	4.82	0	1.377

FERNANDO VALENZUELA   Age 34/L $1

For the first time in his career he was not the portliest guy in uniform. He celebrated with a Philly cheese steak from Pat's.

Year Team	Lg.	G	IP	H	BB	SO	W	L	ERA	SV	Ratio
1991 California	AL	2	6.2	14	3	5	0	2	12.15	0	2.550
1993 Baltimore	AL	32	178.2	179	79	78	8	10	4.94	0	1.444
1994 Philadelphia	NL	8	45.0	42	7	19	1	2	3.00	0	1.089
1994 PROJECTION		17	93.0	88	24	44	3	3	3.39	0	1.204

WILLIAM VAN LANDINGHAM   Age 24/R $8

With a name like that, you'd think he'd be off playing polo or racing yachts somewhere. But he's a big, strapping right-hander with a good moving fast-ball and an improving breaking ball. Scary wild, but the Giants think that condition will decrease with experience and more work on mechanics.

Year Team	Lg.	G	IP	H	BB	SO	W	L	ERA	SV	Ratio
1994 San Francisco	NL	16	84.0	70	43	56	8	2	3.54	0	1.345
1994 PROJECTION		24	124.0	118	66	78	10	5	4.72	0	1.484

PAUL WAGNER   Age 27/R $2

Will he end up being a starter or a reliever? We don't know, and we're beginning to suspect that it doesn't matter.

Year Team	Lg.	G	IP	H	BB	SO	W	L	ERA	SV	Ratio
1992 Pittsburgh	NL	6	13.0	9	5	5	2	0	0.69	0	1.077
1993 Pittsburgh	NL	44	141.1	143	42	114	8	8	4.27	2	1.309
1994 Pittsburgh	NL	29	119.2	136	50	86	7	8	4.59	0	1.554
1994 PROJECTION		50	146.0	169	58	107	7	10	4.99	0	1.555

ALLEN WATSON   Age 24/L $1

He was lit up, injured, and otherwise brought firmly back to earth. The word is that his fastball is just too short for him to be anything special.

Year Team	Lg.	G	IP	H	BB	SO	W	L	ERA	SV	Ratio
1993 St. Louis	NL	16	86.0	90	28	49	6	7	4.60	0	1.372
1994 St. Louis	NL	22	115.2	130	53	74	6	5	5.52	0	1.582
1994 PROJECTION		31	166.0	189	73	104	8	10	5.53	0	1.578

DAVE WEATHERS   Age 25/R $1

The extended forecast calls for five months of overcast skies and intermittent rain if he finds his way onto your staff.

Year Team	Lg.	G	IP	H	BB	SO	W	L	ERA	SV	Ratio
1991 Toronto	AL	15	14.2	15	17	13	1	0	4.91	0	2.182
1992 Toronto	AL	2	3.1	5	2	3	0	0	8.10	0	2.100
1993 Florida	NL	14	45.2	57	13	34	2	3	5.12	0	1.533
1994 Florida	NL	24	135.0	166	59	72	8	12	5.27	0	1.667
1994 PROJECTION		33	181.1	239	83	95	9	17	5.76	0	1.776

DAVID WEST
Age 30/L $3

Startled everyone in the Philadelphia organization with his success as a starting pitcher. (It was a grasping-at-straws kind of year in the City of Brotherly Love.) He will get every opportnity to remain in the rotation, but be ye forewarned of his uncanny resemblance to Sid Fernandez: left-hander, slinging motion, nasty stuff, body of Jell-O, never completes games, susceptible to injury.

Year Team	Lg.	G	IP	H	BB	SO	W	L	ERA	SV	Ratio
1991 Minnesota	AL	15	71.1	66	28	52	4	4	4.54	0	1.318
1992 Minnesota	AL	9	28.1	32	20	19	1	3	6.99	0	1.835
1993 Philadelphia	NL	76	86.1	60	51	87	6	4	2.92	3	1.286
1994 Philadelphia	NL	31	99.0	74	61	83	4	10	3.55	0	1.364
1994 PROJECTION		48	132.0	101	85	112	5	12	3.61	0	1.409

WALLY WHITEHURST
Age 30/R $1

Not unless you're looking for someone to throw BP.

Year Team	Lg.	G	IP	H	BB	SO	W	L	ERA	SV	Ratio
1991 New York	NL	36	133.1	142	25	87	7	12	4.18	1	1.253
1992 New York	NL	44	97.0	99	33	70	3	9	3.62	0	1.361
1993 San Diego	NL	21	105.2	109	30	57	4	7	3.83	0	1.315
1994 San Diego	NL	13	64.0	84	26	43	4	7	4.92	0	1.719
1994 PROJECTION		13	64.0	84	26	43	4	7	4.92	0	1.719

BRIAN WILLIAMS
Age 26/R $1

Originally drafted as a shortstop out of high school. The Astros thought he'd be a much better pitcher by now. They also thought Andujar Cedeño would be a better shortstop. There isn't much chance of Cedeño losing his spot in the infield to Orlando Miller, but we do think Williams will lose his spot in the rotation to Shane Reynolds.

Year Team	Lg.	G	IP	H	BB	SO	W	L	ERA	SV	Ratio
1991 Houston	NL	2	12.0	11	4	4	0	1	3.75	0	1.250
1992 Houston	NL	16	96.1	92	42	54	7	6	3.92	0	1.391
1993 Houston	NL	42	82.0	76	38	56	4	4	4.83	3	1.390
1994 Houston	NL	20	78.1	112	41	49	6	5	5.74	0	1.953
1994 PROJECTION		22	83.1	121	47	52	6	5	6.26	0	2.016

ANTHONY YOUNG
Age 29/R $1

Blew out his shoulder, pretty much assuring that he will only be remembered for the Losing Streak.

Year Team	Lg.	G	IP	H	BB	SO	W	L	ERA	SV	Ratio
1991 New York	NL	10	49.1	48	12	20	2	5	3.10	0	1.216
1992 New York	NL	52	121.0	134	31	64	2	14	4.17	15	1.364
1993 New York	NL	39	100.1	103	42	62	1	16	3.77	3	1.445
1994 Chicago	NL	20	114.2	103	46	65	4	6	3.92	0	1.299
1994 PROJECTION		20	114.2	103	46	65	4	6	3.92	0	1.299

Catchers
pp. 33–46

Corners
pp. 46–65

Infield
pp. 66–85

Outfield
pp. 85–115

DH
pp. 115–119

Starters
pp. 119–155

Relievers
pp. 155–187

AMERICAN LEAGUE

JIM ABBOTT   Age 27/L $8

A mystery. Two up and down years in Yankee Stadium, where lefty pitchers supposedly start off with a built-in advantage. Looked overweight last season. Scouts said he had lost a couple of feet off his fastball. George ragged him in spring training for doing too much charity work. Come to think of it, that had to be it. Nothing ruins a pitcher's arm faster than signing too many autographs, making too many appearances before youth groups, and visiting too many kids in hospitals. The Yankees would love to trade him. Maybe they could get J. T. Snow back.

Year Team	Lg.	G	IP	H	BB	SO	W	L	ERA	SV	Ratio
1991 California	AL	34	243.0	222	73	158	18	11	2.89	0	1.214
1992 California	AL	29	211.0	208	68	130	7	15	2.77	0	1.308
1993 New York	AL	32	214.0	221	73	95	11	14	4.37	0	1.374
1994 New York	AL	24	160.1	167	64	90	9	8	4.55	0	1.441
1994 PROJECTION		32	212.0	225	74	111	13	11	4.50	0	1.410

WILSON ALVAREZ   Age 25/L $19

Says one AL manager: "Let's just hope that the White Sox can't find the pitching coach who can get through to Alvarez. Once someone is able to turn on his light bulb so he doesn't lose his concentration every few innings or so, the only way you're going to beat him is by getting lucky and hitting a line drive off his knee."

Year Team	Lg.	G	IP	H	BB	SO	W	L	ERA	SV	Ratio
1991 Chicago	AL	10	56.1	47	29	32	3	2	3.51	0	1.349
1992 Chicago	AL	34	100.1	103	65	66	5	3	5.20	1	1.674
1993 Chicago	AL	31	207.2	168	122	155	15	8	2.95	0	1.396
1994 Chicago	AL	24	161.2	147	62	108	12	8	3.45	0	1.293
1994 PROJECTION		34	223.2	205	82	147	16	10	3.38	0	1.283

BRIAN ANDERSON   Age 22/L $7

A baseball baby who was rushed to the majors by the mindless Angels organization, Anderson escaped unscathed from his rugged initiation and could pay big dividends down the road.

Year Team	Lg.	G	IP	H	BB	SO	W	L	ERA	SV	Ratio
1993 California	AL	4	11.1	11	2	4	0	0	3.97	0	1.147
1994 California	AL	18	101.2	120	27	47	7	5	5.22	0	1.446
1994 PROJECTION		27	161.0	180	35	76	12	8	4.70	0	1.335

KEVIN APPIER   Age 27/R $18

Back and shoulder troubles, which he and the Royals kept quiet, supposedly cost him some velocity. That would explain why he gave up a run more per game than in 1993. If you own him and were counting on keeping him, the arm and shoulder news can't be too comforting, but we calls 'em like we sees 'em, and let the bone chips fall where they may.

Catchers
pp. 33–46

Corners
pp. 46–65

Infield
pp. 66–85

Outfield
pp. 85–115

DH
pp. 115–119

Starters
pp. 119–155

Relievers
pp. 155–187

Year	Team	Lg.	G	IP	H	BB	SO	W	L	ERA	SV	Ratio
1991	Kansas City	AL	34	207.2	205	61	158	13	10	3.42	0	1.281
1992	Kansas City	AL	30	208.1	167	68	150	15	8	2.46	0	1.128
1993	Kansas City	AL	34	238.2	183	81	186	18	8	2.56	0	1.106
1994	Kansas City	AL	23	155.0	137	63	145	7	6	3.83	0	1.290
1994	PROJECTION		33	224.0	200	89	206	13	8	4.14	0	1.290

TIM BELCHER Age 33/R $1

The Strike cost him a chance to lose 20.

Year	Team	Lg.	G	IP	H	BB	SO	W	L	ERA	SV	Ratio
1991	Los Angeles	NL	33	209.1	189	75	156	10	9	2.62	0	1.261
1992	Cincinnati	NL	35	227.2	201	80	149	15	14	3.91	0	1.234
1993	Cincinnati	NL	22	137.0	134	47	101	9	6	4.47	0	1.321
1993	Chicago	AL	12	71.2	64	27	34	3	5	4.40	0	1.270
1994	Detroit	AL	25	162.0	192	78	76	7	15	5.89	0	1.667
1994	PROJECTION		34	204.2	249	103	99	8	19	6.55	0	1.720

JASON BERE Age 23/R $23

Says a veteran scout: "McDowell is the toughest competitor, Alvarez has the best stuff, and Fernandez has the best mechanics. Bere? A close second best in all three." Sounds like the makeup of 20-game winner to us.

Year	Team	Lg.	G	IP	H	BB	SO	W	L	ERA	SV	Ratio
1993	Chicago	AL	24	142.2	109	81	129	12	5	3.47	0	1.332
1994	Chicago	AL	24	141.2	119	80	127	12	2	3.81	0	1.405
1994	PROJECTION		34	210.1	163	110	189	17	7	3.51	0	1.298

RICKY BONES Age 25/R $12

Maybe we're nuts, but we don't think the fact that Bones made the All-Star team will have Milwaukee fans cheering the Gary Sheffield trade as a great deal for the Brew Crew. There's an old Rotisserie axiom about the perils of owning good starting pitchers on lousy teams, but we forget exactly how it goes. It has something to do with ending up with five fewer wins than you rightfully deserve.

Year	Team	Lg.	G	IP	H	BB	SO	W	L	ERA	SV	Ratio
1991	San Diego	NL	11	54.0	57	18	31	4	6	4.83	0	1.389
1992	Milwaukee	AL	31	163.1	169	48	65	9	10	4.57	0	1.329
1993	Milwaukee	AL	32	203.2	222	63	63	11	11	4.86	0	1.399
1994	Milwaukee	AL	24	170.2	166	45	57	10	9	3.43	0	1.236
1994	PROJECTION		33	229.2	236	58	70	11	13	3.45	0	1.280

CHRIS BOSIO Age 31/R $5

An off-season rumor in the Pacific Northwest had the Nintendo guys who bought the Mariners turning loose the Mario Brothers on whoever decided to give all that money to the fragile Boz.

Year	Team	Lg.	G	IP	H	BB	SO	W	L	ERA	SV	Ratio
1991	Milwaukee	AL	32	204.2	187	58	117	14	10	3.25	0	1.197
1992	Milwaukee	AL	33	231.1	223	44	120	16	6	3.62	0	1.154
1993	Seattle	AL	29	164.1	138	59	119	9	9	3.45	1	1.199
1994	Seattle	AL	19	125.0	137	40	67	4	10	4.32	0	1.416
1994	PROJECTION		21	137.2	147	46	74	5	11	4.31	0	1.402

KEVIN BROWN

Age 30/R   **$9**

Kevin Kennedy called him "the most self-destructive player I've ever seen"—and most observers say Kennedy was being kind. Brown's strident, overbearing attempt to become baseball's answer to Jimmy Hoffa in last summer's non-talks had both sides of the table united on at least one thing: they wanted to throttle him. If he focuses as much energy on pitching, maybe he can rediscover the stuff that made him the Rangers' ace-apparent two summers back.

Year Team	Lg.	G	IP	H	BB	SO	W	L	ERA	SV	Ratio
1991 Texas	AL	33	210.2	233	90	96	9	12	4.40	0	1.533
1992 Texas	AL	35	265.2	262	76	173	21	11	3.32	0	1.272
1993 Texas	AL	34	233.0	228	74	142	15	12	3.59	0	1.296
1994 Texas	AL	26	170.0	218	50	123	7	9	4.82	0	1.576
1994 PROJECTION		36	229.2	299	70	161	10	14	5.09	0	1.607

MARK CLARK

Age 26/R   **$14**

Ever wonder just why baseball people always speak of new Orioles manager Phil "The Vulture" Regan in such reverential tones? The main reason is that he's such a good teacher. Early last year, Regan—then Cleveland's pitching coach—suggested to Clark that he change the point at which he began his delivery. The move was only a matter of inches, but it allowed Clark to drive off his back foot at a slightly different angle, which in turn produced an increase in velocity. The change also made it more difficult for batters to pick up the spin of his pitches. You know the result.

Year Team	Lg.	G	IP	H	BB	SO	W	L	ERA	SV	Ratio
1991 St. Louis	NL	7	22.1	17	11	13	1	1	4.03	0	1.254
1992 St. Louis	NL	20	113.1	117	36	44	3	10	4.45	0	1.350
1993 Cleveland	AL	26	109.1	119	25	57	7	5	4.28	0	1.317
1994 Cleveland	AL	20	127.1	133	40	60	11	3	3.82	0	1.359
1994 PROJECTION		20	127.1	133	40	60	11	3	3.82	0	1.358

ROGER CLEMENS

Age 32/R   **$24**

We talked to a respected AL hitter about whether the Rocket might be slowing down: "Slowing down? Are you nuts? He can still throw cheese by anybody. His trouble is that he's pitching for a horsebleep team."

Year Team	Lg.	G	IP	H	BB	SO	W	L	ERA	SV	Ratio
1991 Boston	AL	35	271.1	219	65	241	18	10	2.62	0	1.047
1992 Boston	AL	32	246.2	203	62	208	18	11	2.41	0	1.074
1993 Boston	AL	29	191.2	175	67	160	11	14	4.46	0	1.263
1994 Boston	AL	24	170.2	124	71	168	9	7	2.85	0	1.143
1994 PROJECTION		34	249.1	195	101	244	14	11	3.25	0	1.187

DAVID CONE

Age 32/R   **$25**

A remarkable transformation. Throughout his career he has behaved like he didn't believe an out counted unless it was caused by three strikes. Last season he decided to become a pitcher.

Year	Team	Lg.	G	IP	H	BB	SO	W	L	ERA	SV	Ratio
1991	New York	NL	34	232.2	204	73	241	14	14	3.29	0	1.191
1992	New York	NL	27	196.2	162	82	214	13	7	2.88	0	1.241
1992	Toronto	AL	8	53.0	39	29	47	4	3	2.55	0	1.283
1993	Kansas City	AL	34	254.0	205	114	191	11	14	3.33	0	1.256
1994	Kansas City	AL	23	171.2	130	54	132	16	5	2.94	0	1.072
1994	PROJECTION		33	244.2	187	75	197	19	12	3.16	0	1.071

JIM CONVERSE   Age 23/R $1

Not likely to be an All-Star.

Year	Team	Lg.	G	IP	H	BB	SO	W	L	ERA	SV	Ratio
1993	Seattle	AL	4	20.1	23	14	10	1	3	5.31	0	1.820
1994	Seattle	AL	13	48.2	73	40	39	0	5	8.69	0	2.322
1994	PROJECTION		23	94.2	130	64	67	1	7	7.13	0	2.049

JOHN CUMMINGS   Age 25/L $1

Those Mariners can really run out some arms, can't they?

Year	Team	Lg.	G	IP	H	BB	SO	W	L	ERA	SV	Ratio
1993	Seattle	AL	10	46.1	59	16	19	0	6	6.02	0	1.619
1994	Seattle	AL	17	64.0	66	37	33	2	4	5.63	0	1.609
1994	PROJECTION		27	118.2	118	65	58	5	8	4.85	0	1.542

RON DARLING   Age 34/R $4

When he was with the Mets, he was the only player on either New York team who was a regular reader of the *Village Voice*. What, you may well ask, does that have to do with his ability to hang on tenaciously to a starting job in the major leagues and combine power and finesse to be reasonably effective about half the time he gets the ball? We're not sure.

Year	Team	Lg.	G	IP	H	BB	SO	W	L	ERA	SV	Ratio
1991	New York	NL	17	102.1	96	28	58	5	6	3.87	0	1.212
1991	Montreal	NL	3	17.0	25	5	11	0	2	7.41	0	1.765
1991	Oakland	AL	12	75.0	64	38	60	3	7	4.08	0	1.360
1992	Oakland	AL	33	206.1	198	72	99	15	10	3.66	0	1.309
1993	Oakland	AL	31	178.0	198	72	95	5	9	5.16	0	1.517
1994	Oakland	AL	25	160.0	162	59	108	10	11	4.50	0	1.381
1994	PROJECTION		34	218.0	220	70	143	12	15	4.29	0	1.330

DANNY DARWIN   Age 39/R $3

Took the ball when he was hurting, moved back and forth between the bullpen and the rotation without complaining, and pitched tough for some defensively challenged Boston teams. Now it's probably all over. On the right team, he might have enough left for a small payback on a modest investment.

Year	Team	Lg.	G	IP	H	BB	SO	W	L	ERA	SV	Ratio
1991	Boston	AL	12	68.0	71	15	42	3	6	5.16	0	1.265
1992	Boston	AL	51	161.1	159	53	124	9	9	3.96	3	1.314
1993	Boston	AL	34	229.1	196	49	130	15	11	3.26	0	1.068
1994	Boston	AL	13	75.2	101	24	54	7	5	6.30	0	1.652
1994	PROJECTION		13	75.2	101	24	54	7	5	6.30	0	1.652

JIM DESHAIES   Age 34/L $1

The Strike cost him a chance at allowing 40 homers.

Year Team	Lg.	G	IP	H	BB	SO	W	L	ERA	SV	Ratio
1991 Houston	NL	28	161.0	156	72	98	5	12	4.98	0	1.416
1992 San Diego	NL	15	96.0	92	33	46	4	7	3.28	0	1.302
1993 Minnesota	AL	27	167.1	159	51	80	11	13	4.41	0	1.255
1993 San Francisco	NL	5	17.0	24	6	5	2	2	4.24	0	1.765
1994 Minnesota	AL	25	130.1	170	54	78	6	12	7.39	0	1.719
1994 PROJECTION		31	153.0	200	62	89	6	15	7.12	0	1.712

JOHN DOHERTY   Age 27/R $1

"What's the matter with Doherty?" we asked a Tigers executive. The executive replied, "We kept him in the rotation too long to trade him." Hey, that happens.

Year Team	Lg.	G	IP	H	BB	SO	W	L	ERA	SV	Ratio
1992 Detroit	AL	47	116.0	131	25	37	7	4	3.88	3	1.345
1993 Detroit	AL	32	184.2	205	48	63	14	11	4.44	0	1.370
1994 Detroit	AL	18	101.1	139	26	28	6	7	6.48	0	1.628
1994 PROJECTION		18	101.1	139	26	28	6	7	6.48	0	1.628

CAL ELDRED   Age 27/R $13

Among the league leaders in innings pitched again. Opposing batters hit just .236 against him. Suffered from lack of support—offensively and defensively—from the atrocious team behind him. But he's a trooper, one of our favorites, and we're counting the days until the Commish lets him walk rather than pay him what he's worth. On a good team, he could be great.

Year Team	Lg.	G	IP	H	BB	SO	W	L	ERA	SV	Ratio
1991 Milwaukee	AL	3	16.0	20	6	10	2	0	4.50	0	1.625
1992 Milwaukee	AL	14	100.1	76	23	62	11	2	1.79	0	0.987
1993 Milwaukee	AL	36	258.0	232	91	180	16	16	4.01	0	1.252
1994 Milwaukee	AL	25	179.0	158	84	98	11	11	4.68	0	1.352
1994 PROJECTION		33	235.0	208	103	133	15	14	4.52	0	1.323

SCOTT ERICKSON   Age 27/R $1

His manager has given up on him. So should we all.

Year Team	Lg.	G	IP	H	BB	SO	W	L	ERA	SV	Ratio
1991 Minnesota	AL	32	204.0	189	71	108	20	8	3.18	0	1.275
1992 Minnesota	AL	32	212.0	197	83	101	13	12	3.40	0	1.321
1993 Minnesota	AL	34	218.2	266	71	116	8	19	5.19	0	1.541
1994 Minnesota	AL	23	144.0	173	59	104	8	11	5.44	0	1.611
1994 PROJECTION		33	204.1	243	79	136	10	15	5.24	0	1.576

HECTOR FAJARDO   Age 24/R $2

When assessing Rangers pitchers, you have to close your eyes to certain things and look for rays of hopes. So forget about last year's ERA and the 15 home runs allowed in only 83 innings and cling to the hope that, as he moves farther away from his serious arm problems, he might still live up to his flickering potential. Yes, we know it's a lot to ask.

Year Team	Lg.	G	IP	H	BB	SO	W	L	ERA	SV	Ratio
1991 Pittsburgh	NL	2	6.1	10	7	8	0	0	9.95	0	2.684
1991 Texas	AL	4	19.0	25	4	15	0	2	5.68	0	1.526
1993 Texas	AL	1	0.2	0	0	1	0	0	0.00	0	0.000
1994 Texas	AL	18	83.1	95	26	45	5	7	6.91	0	1.452
1994 PROJECTION		18	83.1	95	26	45	5	7	6.91	0	1.452

ALEX FERNANDEZ   Age 25/R $20

Says a scout: "You get by McDowell, you survive Alvarez, and you don't get it shoved completely up your butt by Bere, and you start feeling good. Then Fernandez comes along with that shot-put fastball of his and you break about a dozen bats." Bad news for other AL teams: the White Sox have more terrific young pitchers on the way, led by hot prospect James Baldwin.

Year Team	Lg.	G	IP	H	BB	SO	W	L	ERA	SV	Ratio
1991 Chicago	AL	34	191.2	186	88	145	9	13	4.51	0	1.430
1992 Chicago	AL	29	187.2	199	50	95	8	11	4.27	0	1.327
1993 Chicago	AL	34	247.1	221	67	169	18	9	3.13	0	1.164
1994 Chicago	AL	24	170.1	163	50	122	11	7	3.86	0	1.250
1994 PROJECTION		34	231.1	225	71	164	13	11	4.08	0	1.279

SID FERNANDEZ   Age 32/L $4

When mouthy Orioles owner Peter Angelos starts lecturing other owners on how to run their businesses, several of the leagues, ah, more experienced owners supposedly start chanting, "Sid . . . Sid . . . Sid." And they don't mean Sid Bream. As he did for so many years in the NL, so El Sid can be expected to do in the AL: dazzle and disappoint in equal measure. When El Rotundo is not on the DL, his stuff can be nasty as a rattlesnake for five, six innings. But if there's a new way to lose a 2–1 game, he will find it.

Year Team	Lg.	G	IP	H	BB	SO	W	L	ERA	SV	Ratio
1991 New York	NL	8	44.0	36	9	31	1	3	2.86	0	1.023
1992 New York	NL	32	214.2	162	67	193	14	11	2.73	0	1.067
1993 New York	NL	18	119.2	82	36	81	5	6	2.93	0	0.986
1994 Baltimore	AL	19	115.1	109	46	95	6	6	5.15	0	1.344
1994 PROJECTION		28	172.1	166	67	133	8	11	5.33	0	1.352

CHUCK FINLEY   Age 32/L $12

We would love to see him with a good team just once. Bet he would, too.

Year Team	Lg.	G	IP	H	BB	SO	W	L	ERA	SV	Ratio
1991 California	AL	34	227.1	205	101	171	18	9	3.80	0	1.346
1992 California	AL	31	204.1	212	98	124	7	12	3.96	0	1.517
1993 California	AL	35	251.1	243	82	187	16	14	3.15	0	1.293
1994 California	AL	25	183.1	178	71	148	10	10	4.32	0	1.358
1994 PROJECTION		34	235.1	237	85	187	14	14	4.09	0	1.368

DAVE FLEMING   Age 25/L $2

What symmetry. Fleming had an equal number of walks and strikeouts. He allowed exactly 100 more base runners than innings pitched. No wonder the Mariners fired their pitching coach after the season.

Year Team	Lg.	G	IP	H	BB	SO	W	L	ERA	SV	Ratio
1991 Seattle	AL	9	17.2	19	3	11	1	0	6.62	0	1.245
1992 Seattle	AL	33	228.1	225	60	112	17	10	3.39	0	1.248
1993 Seattle	AL	26	167.1	189	67	75	12	5	4.36	0	1.530
1994 Seattle	AL	23	117.0	152	65	65	7	11	6.46	0	1.855
1994 PROJECTION		33	177.0	213	79	97	12	13	5.54	0	1.650

TOM GORDON   Age 27/R $12

Some surprising things happened in Kansas City last season—or didn't happen, to be more precise. Not only did David Cone not try to strike out every batter, but Tom Gordon didn't spend the summer bouncing from the rotation to the bullpen, from the pen to somebody's doghouse, from the doghouse to being the star attraction on the trade rumor mill—and back again. The Royals just put Flash in the rotation and let him pitch. What a concept! Now, if he can just cut down on the walks, he might finally turn into a pitcher worthy of his curve.

Year Team	Lg.	G	IP	H	BB	SO	W	L	ERA	SV	Ratio
1991 Kansas City	AL	45	158.0	129	87	167	9	14	3.87	1	1.367
1992 Kansas City	AL	40	117.2	116	55	98	6	10	4.59	0	1.453
1993 Kansas City	AL	48	155.2	125	77	143	12	6	3.58	1	1.298
1994 Kansas City	AL	24	155.1	136	87	126	11	7	4.35	0	1.436
1994 PROJECTION		34	224.2	186	113	181	16	11	4.01	0	1.331

JASON GRIMSLEY   Age 27/R $1

After considering everybody but Don Mossi as their fifth starter in spring training, the Indians gave the job to Grimsley who, despite a lackluster background as yet another phailed Phillies prospect, gave them some solid starts. But Cleveland has several legit phenoms pushing for a chance, so don't get too excited.

Year Team	Lg.	G	IP	H	BB	SO	W	L	ERA	SV	Ratio
1991 Philadelphia	NL	12	61.0	54	41	42	1	7	4.87	0	1.557
1993 Cleveland	AL	10	42.1	52	20	27	3	4	5.31	0	1.701
1994 Cleveland	AL	14	82.2	91	34	59	5	2	4.57	0	1.512
1994 PROJECTION		23	137.0	155	56	90	9	5	4.86	0	1.540

MARK GUBICZA   Age 32/R $1

Running on empty.

Year Team	Lg.	G	IP	H	BB	SO	W	L	ERA	SV	Ratio
1991 Kansas City	AL	26	133.0	168	42	89	9	12	5.68	0	1.579
1992 Kansas City	AL	18	111.1	110	36	81	7	6	3.72	0	1.311
1993 Kansas City	AL	49	104.1	128	43	80	5	8	4.66	2	1.639
1994 Kansas City	AL	22	130.0	158	26	59	7	9	4.50	0	1.415
1994 PROJECTION		31	181.1	211	33	76	9	12	4.27	0	1.345

BILL GULLICKSON   Age 36/R $1

Never gives up many walks. Can you imagine what his ERA would be if he did?

Year Team	Lg.	G	IP	H	BB	SO	W	L	ERA	SV	Ratio
1991 Detroit	AL	35	226.1	256	44	91	20	9	3.90	0	1.325
1992 Detroit	AL	34	221.2	228	50	64	14	13	4.34	0	1.254
1993 Detroit	AL	28	159.1	186	44	70	13	9	5.37	0	1.444
1994 Detroit	AL	21	115.1	156	25	65	4	5	5.93	0	1.569
1994 PROJECTION		27	150.0	198	27	83	5	6	5.76	0	1.500

JUAN GUZMAN   Age 28/R $15

Gave up more hits than innings pitched for the first time in his major league career—without any decrease in walks. Throw in 20 home run balls and 13 wild pitches (tied for league lead), and you begin to get a picture of Guzman's year. Not very pretty, was it? We say don't look at it. Look at the three preceding seasons as indicators of what to expect this year. Other say that his pitching motion, which puts a heavy strain on his shoulder and makes him a five-inning pitcher, may finally be taking its toll on his stuff. You takes your choice, and you pays your money.

Year Team	Lg.	G	IP	H	BB	SO	W	L	ERA	SV	Ratio
1991 Toronto	AL	23	138.2	98	66	123	10	3	2.99	0	1.183
1992 Toronto	AL	28	180.2	135	72	165	16	5	2.64	0	1.146
1993 Toronto	AL	33	221.0	211	110	194	14	3	3.99	0	1.452
1994 Toronto	AL	25	147.1	165	76	124	12	11	5.68	0	1.636
1994 PROJECTION		34	206.2	219	111	177	16	14	5.23	0	1.597

PAT HENTGEN   Age 26/R $15

While the other members of the Toronto rotation stumbled, scrambled, and fell, Hentgen was steady as a rock. Nothing fancy, just a lot of hard stuff and a lot of determination. An ace by force of will.

Year Team	Lg.	G	IP	H	BB	SO	W	L	ERA	SV	Ratio
1991 Toronto	AL	3	7.1	5	3	3	0	0	2.45	0	1.091
1992 Toronto	AL	28	50.1	49	32	39	5	2	5.36	0	1.609
1993 Toronto	AL	34	216.1	215	74	122	19	9	3.87	0	1.336
1994 Toronto	AL	24	174.2	158	59	147	13	8	3.40	0	1.242
1994 PROJECTION		33	245.0	217	71	214	19	10	3.34	0	1.175

JOE HESKETH   Age 36/L $3

Going 8–5 with an ERA under 4.50 is practically Hall of Fame quality by today's standards, but it would be a big mistake to believe last season was a portent of future immortality.

Year Team	Lg.	G	IP	H	BB	SO	W	L	ERA	SV	Ratio
1991 Boston	AL	39	153.1	142	53	104	12	4	3.29	0	1.272
1992 Boston	AL	30	148.2	162	58	104	8	9	4.36	1	1.480
1993 Boston	AL	28	53.1	62	29	34	3	4	5.06	1	1.706
1994 Boston	AL	25	114.0	117	46	83	8	5	4.26	0	1.430
1994 PROJECTION		32	147.1	153	57	105	9	6	4.52	0	1.425

GREG HIBBARD Age 30/L $1

The Tigers should trade for Hibbard. He would fit right in on that staff.

Year Team	Lg.	G	IP	H	BB	SO	W	L	ERA	SV	Ratio
1991 Chicago	AL	32	194.0	196	57	71	11	11	4.31	0	1.304
1992 Chicago	AL	31	176.0	187	57	69	10	7	4.40	1	1.386
1993 Chicago	NL	31	191.0	209	47	82	15	11	3.96	0	1.340
1994 Seattle	AL	15	80.2	115	31	39	1	5	6.69	0	1.810
1994 PROJECTION		15	80.2	115	31	39	1	5	6.69	0	1.810

TED HIGUERA Age 36/L $1

We've already talked about The Strike way too much, but there is one last moral lesson to be learned, and we would be remiss if we did not ascend into our pulpit and deliver it. Our tale today involves two men. One is the leader of a faction of major league owners who insist that the game's economic structure must be radically altered if small-market teams are to compete with large-market teams. The other man is the turkey-brained owner who gave this pitcher with the hummingbird arm a four-year, $18 million contract (net yield: five wins). And who are these men? Ha! They're one and the same, himself, The Commish, Allan H. "Bud" Selig. And the moral? *The problem ain't market size, baby. It's bad baseball management.*

Year Team	Lg.	G	IP	H	BB	SO	W	L	ERA	SV	Ratio
1991 Milwaukee	AL	7	36.1	37	10	33	3	2	4.46	0	1.294
1993 Milwaukee	AL	8	30.0	43	16	27	1	3	7.20	0	1.967
1994 Milwaukee	AL	17	58.2	74	36	35	1	5	7.06	0	1.875
1994 PROJECTION		19	66.2	82	38	40	1	5	6.48	0	1.800

STERLING HITCHCOCK Age 23/L $3

Wasn't that the name of a character in *The Age of Innocence?* Or was it *Dynasty?* There was also a Yankee rookie by that name last season, a left-hander who showed some promise. Could step into the rotation if the Yankees succeed in moving Jim Abbott.

Year Team	Lg.	G	IP	H	BB	SO	W	L	ERA	SV	Ratio
1992 New York	AL	3	13.0	23	6	6	0	2	8.31	0	2.231
1993 New York	AL	6	31.0	32	14	26	1	2	4.65	0	1.484
1994 New York	AL	23	49.1	48	29	37	4	1	4.20	2	1.561
1994 PROJECTION		32	105.1	107	50	74	8	3	4.27	2	1.490

BRUCE HURST Age 37/L $1

He had the class to leave the party without having to be told it was over.

Year Team	Lg.	G	IP	H	BB	SO	W	L	ERA	SV	Ratio
1991 San Diego	NL	31	221.2	201	59	141	15	8	3.29	0	1.173
1992 San Diego	NL	32	217.1	223	51	131	14	9	3.85	0	1.261
1993 San Diego	NL	2	4.1	9	3	3	0	1	12.46	0	2.769
1993 Colorado	NL	3	8.2	6	3	6	0	1	5.19	0	1.038
1994 Texas	AL	8	38.0	53	16	24	2	1	7.11	0	1.816
1994 PROJECTION		8	38.0	53	16	24	2	1	7.11	0	1.816

RANDY JOHNSON   Age 31/L $24

Threw the very last pitch of the 1994 season. It was a strike.

Year	Team	Lg.	G	IP	H	BB	SO	W	L	ERA	SV	Ratio
1991	Seattle	AL	33	201.1	151	152	228	13	10	3.98	0	1.505
1992	Seattle	AL	31	210.1	154	144	241	12	14	3.77	0	1.417
1993	Seattle	AL	35	255.1	185	99	308	19	8	3.24	1	1.112
1994	Seattle	AL	23	172.0	132	72	204	13	6	3.19	0	1.186
1994	PROJECTION		32	235.0	191	94	273	17	9	3.56	0	1.213

SCOTT KAMIENIECKI   Age 30/R $10

A grinder, nothing fancy, but the Yankees like his grit. Anybody in that rotation is a good bet in 1995.

Year	Team	Lg.	G	IP	H	BB	SO	W	L	ERA	SV	Ratio
1991	New York	AL	9	55.1	54	22	34	4	4	3.90	0	1.373
1992	New York	AL	28	188.0	193	74	88	6	14	4.36	0	1.420
1993	New York	AL	30	154.1	163	59	72	10	7	4.08	1	1.438
1994	New York	AL	22	117.1	115	59	71	8	6	3.76	0	1.483
1994	PROJECTION		32	193.2	180	95	110	15	8	3.35	0	1.420

STEVE KARSAY   Age 23/R $9

This is the phenom Oakland got for loaning Rickey Henderson to the Blue Jays for a couple of months in 1993. Good thing Pat Gillick retired, because that deal would have come back to haunt him. (To be fair, it was the only bad deal he made in Toronto, and at the time it seemed to make a lot of sense.) Karsay only made four starts last year, and he spent some time on the DL. But if he is healthy, he could win 15 games this year. And that's just the beginning.

Year	Team	Lg.	G	IP	H	BB	SO	W	L	ERA	SV	Ratio
1993	Oakland	AL	8	49.0	49	16	33	3	3	4.04	0	1.327
1994	Oakland	AL	4	28.0	26	8	15	1	1	2.57	0	1.214
1994	PROJECTION		4	28.0	26	8	15	1	1	2.57	0	1.214

JIMMY KEY   Age 33/L $23

The best free agent signing by the Yankees since Reggie Jackson, but shoulder surgery last October casts a shadow over his future.

Year	Team	Lg.	G	IP	H	BB	SO	W	L	ERA	SV	Ratio
1991	Toronto	AL	33	209.1	207	44	125	16	12	3.05	0	1.199
1992	Toronto	AL	33	216.2	205	59	117	13	13	3.53	0	1.218
1993	New York	AL	34	236.2	219	43	173	18	6	3.00	0	1.107
1994	New York	AL	25	168.0	177	52	97	17	4	3.27	0	1.363
1994	PROJECTION		34	229.2	248	72	137	23	6	3.80	0	1.393

MARK LANGSTON   Age 34/L $17

We would love to see him with a good team just once. Bet he would, too.

Year	Team	Lg.	G	IP	H	BB	SO	W	L	ERA	SV	Ratio
1991	California	AL	34	246.1	190	96	183	19	8	3.00	0	1.161
1992	California	AL	32	229.0	206	74	174	13	14	3.66	0	1.223
1993	California	AL	35	256.1	220	85	196	16	11	3.20	0	1.190
1994	California	AL	18	119.1	121	54	109	7	8	4.68	0	1.466
1994	PROJECTION		27	178.2	183	82	160	10	12	5.14	0	1.483

Catchers
pp. 33–46

Corners
pp. 46–65

Infield
pp. 66–85

Outfield
pp. 85–115

DH
pp. 115–119

Starters
pp. 119–155

Relievers
pp. 155–187

PHIL LEFTWICH
Age 25/R   **$1**

Being on a good team wouldn't make much difference in his case. In fact, if he were on it, it couldn't possibly be all that good.

Year Team	Lg.	G	IP	H	BB	SO	W	L	ERA	SV	Ratio
1993 California	AL	12	80.2	81	27	31	4	6	3.79	0	1.339
1994 California	AL	20	114.0	127	42	67	5	10	5.68	0	1.482
1994 PROJECTION		30	173.0	201	54	96	9	11	5.88	0	1.474

AL LEITER
Age 29/L   **$3**

If you're counting on the whole Toronto team to bounce back, and we are, then he's worth a look this year.

Year Team	Lg.	G	IP	H	BB	SO	W	L	ERA	SV	Ratio
1991 Toronto	AL	3	1.2	3	5	1	0	0	27.00	0	4.800
1992 Toronto	AL	1	1.0	1	2	0	0	0	9.00	0	3.000
1993 Toronto	AL	34	105.0	93	56	66	9	6	4.11	2	1.419
1994 Toronto	AL	20	111.2	125	65	100	6	7	5.08	0	1.701
1994 PROJECTION		29	158.2	185	107	130	8	12	5.96	0	1.840

JOE MAGRANE
Age 30/L   **$1**

There is no known cure for a Magrane headache.

Year Team	Lg.	G	IP	H	BB	SO	W	L	ERA	SV	Ratio
1992 St. Louis	NL	5	31.1	34	15	20	1	2	4.02	0	1.564
1993 St. Louis	NL	22	116.0	127	37	38	8	10	4.97	0	1.414
1993 California	AL	8	48.0	48	21	24	3	2	3.94	0	1.438
1994 California	AL	20	74.0	89	51	33	2	6	7.30	0	1.892
1994 PROJECTION		25	89.1	101	55	38	2	7	6.85	0	1.746

PAT MAHOMES
Age 24/R   **$5**

Slow start, but in his last several outings he began to pitch the way the scouting reports said he could. A good sleeper candidate to make a big splash this season.

Year Team	Lg.	G	IP	H	BB	SO	W	L	ERA	SV	Ratio
1992 Minnesota	AL	14	69.2	73	37	44	3	4	5.04	0	1.579
1993 Minnesota	AL	12	37.1	47	16	23	1	5	7.71	0	1.688
1994 Minnesota	AL	21	120.0	121	62	53	9	5	4.72	0	1.525
1994 PROJECTION		22	124.2	127	63	53	9	6	4.84	0	1.524

DENNIS MARTINEZ
Age 39/R   **$19**

On Opening Day, he drilled Edgar Martinez with his fifth pitch of the season. That sort of set the tone for the whole Indians staff, which became a tough, aggressive, inside-corner-is-mine crew. El Presidente might not be the most popular pitcher around, but he is absolutely one of the most competitive. One opposing manager expressed a common feeling: "I hate his guts, and I wish we had him."

Year Team	Lg.	G	IP	H	BB	SO	W	L	ERA	SV	Ratio
1991 Montreal	NL	31	222.0	187	62	123	14	11	2.39	0	1.122
1992 Montreal	NL	32	226.1	172	60	147	16	11	2.47	0	1.025
1993 Montreal	NL	35	224.2	211	64	138	15	9	3.85	1	1.224
1994 Cleveland	AL	24	176.2	166	44	92	11	6	3.52	0	1.189
1994 PROJECTION		32	225.2	216	56	113	14	8	3.59	0	1.205

BEN McDONALD   Age 27/R $22

Made great strides last season. We liked the way he pitched through some injuries, cut his gopher balls way down, sliced his walk total nearly in half, and learned how to change speeds. He is ready to ascend into the league's elite, and he has the perfect manager to help him along the way.

Year Team	Lg.	G	IP	H	BB	SO	W	L	ERA	SV	Ratio
1991 Baltimore	AL	21	126.1	126	43	85	6	8	4.84	0	1.338
1992 Baltimore	AL	35	227.0	213	74	158	13	13	4.24	0	1.264
1993 Baltimore	AL	34	220.1	185	86	171	13	14	3.39	0	1.230
1994 Baltimore	AL	24	157.1	151	54	94	14	7	4.06	0	1.303
1994 PROJECTION		33	219.1	226	70	127	19	10	4.23	0	1.349

JACK McDOWELL   Age 29/R $24

The financial hatchet man who does the White Sox contracts said last winter during an ugly pre-arbitration outburst that "McDowell is probably the fourth-best starter on our staff. Why should we pay him all that money?" And wouldn't you know it, that's the way McDowell began the 1994 season— only maybe he was just fifth-best, behind Scott Sanderson as well as Alvarez-Bere-Fernandez. But then he adjusted his mechanics, regained mastery over his splitter, and established once and for all that he is The Man. The Yankees now expect The Man to get them a pennant. Can you blame them?

Year Team	Lg.	G	IP	H	BB	SO	W	L	ERA	SV	Ratio
1991 Chicago	AL	35	253.2	212	82	191	17	10	3.41	0	1.159
1992 Chicago	AL	34	260.2	247	75	178	20	10	3.18	0	1.235
1993 Chicago	AL	34	256.2	261	69	158	22	10	3.37	0	1.286
1994 Chicago	AL	25	181.0	186	42	127	10	9	3.73	0	1.260
1994 PROJECTION		35	255.1	271	57	177	15	11	3.91	0	1.284

ANGEL MIRANDA   Age 25/L $2

Blew out his knee in winter ball, came back late in what was a washed-out year, and never got the chance to prove whether he's the real thing. We'll find out this year.

Year Team	Lg.	G	IP	H	BB	SO	W	L	ERA	SV	Ratio
1993 Milwaukee	AL	22	120.0	100	52	88	4	5	3.30	0	1.267
1994 Milwaukee	AL	8	46.0	39	27	24	2	5	5.28	0	1.435
1994 PROJECTION		15	89.1	86	47	40	4	6	5.04	0	1.489

MIKE MOORE   Age 35/R $2

Detroit's Mr. Dependable. That's sort of like being a Chef of the Year at McDonald's.

Year Team	Lg.	G	IP	H	BB	SO	W	L	ERA	SV	Ratio
1991 Oakland	AL	33	210.0	176	105	153	17	8	2.96	0	1.338
1992 Oakland	AL	36	223.0	229	103	117	17	12	4.12	0	1.489
1993 Detroit	AL	36	213.2	227	89	89	13	9	5.22	0	1.479
1994 Detroit	AL	25	154.1	152	89	62	11	10	5.42	0	1.562
1994 PROJECTION		34	201.2	204	109	83	12	13	5.76	0	1.552

JACK MORRIS   Age 39/R $1

Leaving the team every week to perform at his own Farm Aid benefit didn't sit well with anybody, and when he was released in August, none of his teammates complained. Morris has never won pretty: last year's 10 victories came the way most of his other 244 career wins have come, on guts and guile. And he will never win any Mr. Nice Guy contests. But some team may figure there's a little left in the tank. If that team is a contender, put him on your list. And hope that farm prices rise.

Year Team	Lg.	G	IP	H	BB	SO	W	L	ERA	SV	Ratio
1991 Minnesota	AL	35	246.2	226	92	163	18	12	3.43	0	1.289
1992 Toronto	AL	34	240.2	222	80	132	21	6	4.04	0	1.255
1993 Toronto	AL	27	152.2	189	65	103	7	12	6.19	0	1.664
1994 Cleveland	AL	23	141.1	163	67	100	10	6	5.60	0	1.627
1994 PROJECTION		23	141.1	163	67	100	10	6	5.60	0	1.627

JAMIE MOYER   Age 32/L $1

Less.

Year Team	Lg.	G	IP	H	BB	SO	W	L	ERA	SV	Ratio
1991 St. Louis	NL	8	31.1	38	16	20	0	5	5.74	0	1.723
1993 Baltimore	AL	25	152.0	154	38	90	12	9	3.43	0	1.263
1994 Baltimore	AL	23	149.0	158	38	87	5	7	4.77	0	1.315
1994 PROJECTION		32	212.2	217	47	108	10	9	4.49	0	1.241

TERRY MULHOLLAND   Age 32/L $7

On the whole, he'd rather have been in Philadelphia.

Year Team	Lg.	G	IP	H	BB	SO	W	L	ERA	SV	Ratio
1991 Philadelphia	NL	34	232.0	231	49	142	16	13	3.61	0	1.207
1992 Philadelphia	NL	32	229.0	227	46	125	13	11	3.81	0	1.192
1993 Philadelphia	NL	29	191.0	177	40	116	12	9	3.25	0	1.136
1994 New York	AL	24	120.2	150	37	72	6	7	6.49	0	1.550
1994 PROJECTION		32	149.1	180	51	95	8	8	6.27	1	1.547

MIKE MUSSINA   Age 26/R $26

His stuff, his articulate demeanor, and his sometimes imperious manner, all remind us a little of Jim Palmer. And just like Underwear Boy, he also has a detached way of talking about the home runs he allows. "I don't mind the really long ones. In fact I secretly admire the majestic nature of some of the ones I've served up," he says. "But they're building these new ballparks like Camden Yards where you can almost touch left-center field from second base, and where the wall is so low that you can almost hit a grounder out of the park. Oh well, the fans love home runs, and I still win, so what the hell."

Year Team	Lg.	G	IP	H	BB	SO	W	L	ERA	SV	Ratio
1991 Baltimore	AL	12	87.2	77	21	52	4	5	2.87	0	1.118
1992 Baltimore	AL	32	241.0	212	48	130	18	5	2.54	0	1.079
1993 Baltimore	AL	25	167.2	163	44	117	14	6	4.46	0	1.235
1994 Baltimore	AL	24	176.1	163	42	99	16	5	3.06	0	1.163
1994 PROJECTION		34	256.2	232	52	143	20	8	2.98	0	1.106

CHRIS NABHOLZ   Age 28/L $1

Pitched like a poor man's Joe Hesketh last year. We think he's better than that, but we're not willing to bet on it.

Year Team	Lg.	G	IP	H	BB	SO	W	L	ERA	SV	Ratio
1991 Montreal	NL	24	153.2	134	57	99	8	7	3.63	0	1.243
1992 Montreal	NL	32	195.0	176	74	130	11	12	3.32	0	1.282
1993 Montreal	NL	26	116.2	100	63	74	9	8	4.09	0	1.397
1994 Cleveland	AL	6	11.0	23	9	5	0	1	11.45	0	2.909
1994 Boston	AL	8	42.0	44	29	23	3	4	6.64	0	1.738
1994 PROJECTION		23	104.1	131	59	57	5	9	6.04	0	1.821

CHARLES NAGY   Age 27/R $16

Came back strong after a year of shoulder troubles. Look for even bigger and better things this season.

Year Team	Lg.	G	IP	H	BB	SO	W	L	ERA	SV	Ratio
1991 Cleveland	AL	33	211.1	228	66	109	10	15	4.13	0	1.391
1992 Cleveland	AL	33	252.0	245	57	169	17	10	2.96	0	1.198
1993 Cleveland	AL	9	48.2	66	13	30	2	6	6.29	0	1.623
1994 Cleveland	AL	23	169.1	175	48	108	10	8	3.45	0	1.317
1994 PROJECTION		33	245.2	243	61	163	16	9	3.37	0	1.237

JAIME NAVARRO   Age 27/R $1

Second big step backward in two years. Isn't he a little young to be heading in that direction, especially after showing so much promise in 1991 and 1992? (That was a rhetorical question, but if you know the answer, please let us know.)

Year Team	Lg.	G	IP	H	BB	SO	W	L	ERA	SV	Ratio
1991 Milwaukee	AL	34	234.0	237	73	114	15	12	3.92	0	1.325
1992 Milwaukee	AL	34	246.0	224	64	100	17	11	3.33	0	1.171
1993 Milwaukee	AL	35	214.1	254	73	114	11	12	5.33	0	1.526
1994 Milwaukee	AL	29	89.2	115	35	65	4	9	6.62	0	1.673
1994 PROJECTION		40	118.2	141	43	82	5	10	5.46	0	1.550

STEVE ONTIVEROS   Age 34/R $4

You would have figured that Lazarus had a better chance of coming back to lead the big leagues in ERA. "The Steve Ontiveros Story" is definitely a TV movie script waiting to be made. Thing is, no producer is going to touch it until Ontiveros provides the sequel.

Year Team	Lg.	G	IP	H	BB	SO	W	L	ERA	SV	Ratio
1993 Seattle	AL	14	18.0	18	6	13	0	2	1.00	0	1.333
1994 Oakland	AL	27	115.1	93	26	56	6	4	2.65	0	1.032
1994 PROJECTION		36	171.2	136	38	86	8	7	2.52	0	1.013

ROGER PAVLIK   Age 27/R $1

Paging Dr. Jobe.

Year Team	Lg.	G	IP	H	BB	SO	W	L	ERA	SV	Ratio
1992 Texas	AL	13	62.0	66	34	45	4	4	4.21	0	1.613
1993 Texas	AL	26	166.1	151	80	131	12	6	3.41	0	1.389
1994 Texas	AL	11	50.1	61	30	31	2	5	7.69	0	1.808
1994 PROJECTION		19	80.1	108	43	47	3	8	8.29	0	1.879

Catchers
pp. 33–46

Corners
pp. 46–65

Infield
pp. 66–85

Outfield
pp. 85–115

DH
pp. 115–119

Starters
pp. 119–155

Relievers
pp. 155–187

MELIDO PEREZ
Age 29/R   **$9**

Healthy again, he should win 12–15 games, what with all the firepower the Yankees have to support their pitchers. They may not be things of beauty, however, so exercise some restraint.

Year Team	Lg.	G	IP	H	BB	SO	W	L	ERA	SV	Ratio
1991 Chicago	AL	49	135.2	111	52	128	8	7	3.12	1	1.201
1992 New York	AL	33	247.2	212	93	218	13	16	2.87	0	1.231
1993 New York	AL	25	163.0	173	64	148	6	14	5.19	0	1.454
1994 New York	AL	22	151.1	134	58	109	9	4	4.10	0	1.269
1994 PROJECTION		31	218.1	190	77	166	18	4	3.92	0	1.223

CARLOS PULIDO
Age 23/L   **$1**

We'd rather have dinner with the guy from the Zima commercials than have this guy in our rotation.

Year Team	Lg.	G	IP	H	BB	SO	W	L	ERA	SV	Ratio
1994 Minnesota	AL	19	84.1	87	40	32	3	7	5.98	0	1.506
1994 PROJECTION		30	133.1	133	60	52	5	13	5.54	0	1.447

ARTHUR RHODES
Age 25/L   **$6**

On his way to being traded, Rhodes was taken on as a project by Orioles minor league coaches Steve Luebbers and Mike Flanagan. They expounded the apparently novel notion—novel to Rhodes, at least—that one doesn't have to throw every pitch as if one were trying to throw it through a wall to be successful in the major leagues. They further allowed that when one is a left-hander with 90 mph gas, delivering the ball to the immediate vicinity of the strike zone is generally sufficient, and that nature will take its course. Thus inspired, Rhodes returned to the majors and pitched consecutive gems before the season was killed. Provided Rhodes the Scholar doesn't forget the lessons he learned in summer school last year, he could make the Dean's List this season, particularly now that Dr. Regan is around to be his mentor. (Excuse me, will someone call us when this metaphor is over?)

Year Team	Lg.	G	IP	H	BB	SO	W	L	ERA	SV	Ratio
1991 Baltimore	AL	8	36.0	47	23	23	0	3	8.00	0	1.944
1992 Baltimore	AL	15	94.1	87	38	77	7	5	3.63	0	1.325
1993 Baltimore	AL	17	85.2	91	49	49	5	6	6.51	0	1.634
1994 Baltimore	AL	10	52.2	51	30	47	3	5	5.81	0	1.538
1994 PROJECTION		19	109.1	107	58	87	6	7	5.19	0	1.509

KENNY ROGERS
Age 30/L   **$14**

If he had pitched half a dozen more very good games instead of the one perfect one, we would be talking about him as one of the premier pitchers in the league. As is, he's near the top of the second tier.

Year Team	Lg.	G	IP	H	BB	SO	W	L	ERA	SV	Ratio
1991 Texas	AL	63	109.2	121	61	73	10	10	5.42	5	1.660
1992 Texas	AL	81	78.2	80	26	70	3	6	3.09	6	1.347
1993 Texas	AL	35	208.1	210	71	140	16	10	4.10	0	1.349
1994 Texas	AL	24	167.1	169	52	120	11	8	4.46	0	1.321
1994 PROJECTION		34	247.2	232	67	177	18	11	3.71	0	1.207

SCOTT SANDERSON   Age 38/R $2

Two years ago he won four big games for the Giants down the stretch. Last year he won seven straight without a loss for the White Sox while Jack McDowell was trying get his ERA under 6.00. This year he will hook up somewhere as a fifth starter. If that somewhere has a team that can provide him some support, at the plate and in the field, he will win some more important games. All he has going for him these days is 17 seasons of savvy, but that's plenty.

Year	Team	Lg.	G	IP	H	BB	SO	W	L	ERA	SV	Ratio
1991	New York	AL	34	208.0	200	29	130	16	10	3.81	0	1.101
1992	New York	AL	33	193.1	220	64	104	12	11	4.93	0	1.469
1993	California	AL	21	135.1	153	27	66	7	11	4.46	0	1.330
1993	San Francisco	NL	11	48.2	48	7	36	4	2	3.51	0	1.130
1994	Chicago	AL	18	92.0	110	12	36	8	4	5.09	0	1.326
1994	PROJECTION		25	130.0	154	18	55	11	6	5.19	0	1.323

AARON SELE   Age 24/R $15

After he beaned Dick Schofield, Sele became reluctant to throw inside and lost the aggressiveness he needs to be a successful pitcher. The Red Sox hope time will heal his bruised psyche—soon.

Year	Team	Lg.	G	IP	H	BB	SO	W	L	ERA	SV	Ratio
1993	Boston	AL	18	111.2	100	48	93	7	2	2.74	0	1.325
1994	Boston	AL	22	143.1	140	60	105	8	7	3.83	0	1.395
1994	PROJECTION		31	202.1	194	84	139	11	10	4.05	0	1.374

DAVE STEWART   Age 38/R $1

Thanks for the memories. Nobody since Bob Gibson gave better glare.

Year	Team	Lg.	G	IP	H	BB	SO	W	L	ERA	SV	Ratio
1991	Oakland	AL	35	226.0	245	105	144	11	11	5.18	0	1.549
1992	Oakland	AL	31	199.1	175	79	130	12	10	3.66	0	1.274
1993	Toronto	AL	26	162.0	146	72	96	12	8	4.44	0	1.346
1994	Toronto	AL	22	133.1	151	62	111	7	8	5.87	0	1.597
1994	PROJECTION		32	209.0	218	95	174	11	10	5.38	0	1.497

TODD STOTTLEMYRE   Age 29/R $4

If Duane Ward doesn't come back, Stottlemyre might still wind up in the bullpen as half of a R/L tandem with Darren Hall. We'd be a lot more interested in him in that role.

Year	Team	Lg.	G	IP	H	BB	SO	W	L	ERA	SV	Ratio
1991	Toronto	AL	34	219.0	194	75	116	15	8	3.78	0	1.228
1992	Toronto	AL	28	174.0	175	63	98	12	11	4.50	0	1.368
1993	Toronto	AL	30	176.2	204	69	98	11	12	4.84	0	1.545
1994	Toronto	AL	26	140.2	149	48	105	7	7	4.22	1	1.400
1994	PROJECTION		36	214.2	222	73	169	12	11	4.15	1	1.374

Catchers
pp. 33–46

Corners
pp. 46–65

Infield
pp. 66–85

Outfield
pp. 85–115

DH
pp. 115–119

Starters
pp. 119–155

Relievers
pp. 155–187

KEVIN TAPANI
Age 31/R $7

The final numbers suggest that his slide continued last season. But factor out a brutal first month and there is some reason to believe that he may have fixed whatever was broke.

Year Team	Lg.	G	IP	H	BB	SO	W	L	ERA	SV	Ratio
1991 Minnesota	AL	34	244.0	225	40	135	16	9	2.99	0	1.086
1992 Minnesota	AL	34	220.0	226	48	138	16	11	3.97	0	1.245
1993 Minnesota	AL	36	225.2	243	57	150	12	15	4.43	0	1.329
1994 Minnesota	AL	24	156.0	181	39	91	11	7	4.62	0	1.410
1994 PROJECTION		34	217.2	250	53	127	12	12	4.92	0	1.392

TODD VAN POPPEL
Age 23/R $6

Oakland coach Dave Duncan is a wise man when it comes to the black arts of pitching, so we listen to him: "People forget that Todd is so young. They forget he lost nearly a year because of injuries. They forget he's a big kid and it takes time for big kids to get their mechanics together. And they don't know that he never threw 95 the way we were all led to believe. But I tell you, he's going to put things together one of these years and be a damned good pitcher." This is the year.

Year Team	Lg.	G	IP	H	BB	SO	W	L	ERA	SV	Ratio
1991 Oakland	AL	1	4.2	7	2	6	0	0	9.64	0	1.929
1993 Oakland	AL	16	84.0	76	62	47	6	6	5.04	0	1.643
1994 Oakland	AL	23	116.2	108	89	83	7	10	6.09	0	1.689
1994 PROJECTION		33	178.1	161	127	118	8	17	5.65	0	1.615

FRANK VIOLA
Age 34/L $1

Bet you thought you were going to read about Sweet Music being silenced, about Viola breaking a string, about his career hitting a sour note, about the chances of an encore, ta-dah, ta-dah. Nope. Not our style. None of that cheap wordplay for us. But we do believe we hear the Fat Lady singing. . . .

Year Team	Lg.	G	IP	H	BB	SO	W	L	ERA	SV	Ratio
1991 New York	NL	35	231.1	259	54	132	13	15	3.97	0	1.353
1992 Boston	AL	35	238.0	214	89	121	13	12	3.44	0	1.273
1993 Boston	AL	29	183.2	180	72	91	11	8	3.14	0	1.372
1994 Boston	AL	6	31.0	34	17	9	1	1	4.65	0	1.645
1994 PROJECTION		6	31.0	34	17	9	1	1	4.65	0	1.645

BILL WEGMAN
Age 32/R $4

Steady.

Year Team	Lg.	G	IP	H	BB	SO	W	L	ERA	SV	Ratio
1991 Milwaukee	AL	28	193.1	176	40	89	15	7	2.84	0	1.117
1992 Milwaukee	AL	35	261.2	251	55	127	13	14	3.20	0	1.169
1993 Milwaukee	AL	20	120.2	135	34	50	4	14	4.48	0	1.401
1994 Milwaukee	AL	19	115.2	140	26	59	8	4	4.51	0	1.435
1994 PROJECTION		28	171.0	214	36	85	10	7	4.79	0	1.462

BOB WELCH

Age 38/R **$1**

If he's still around, it will be in somebody's bullpen.

Year Team	Lg.	G	IP	H	BB	SO	W	L	ERA	SV	Ratio
1991 Oakland	AL	35	220.0	220	91	101	12	13	4.58	0	1.414
1992 Oakland	AL	20	123.2	114	43	47	11	7	3.27	0	1.270
1993 Oakland	AL	30	166.2	208	56	63	9	11	5.29	0	1.584
1994 Oakland	AL	25	68.2	79	43	44	3	6	7.08	0	1.777
1994 PROJECTION		31	88.2	104	53	57	4	7	7.31	0	1.770

DAVID WELLS

Age 31/L **$2**

If he's still around, it won't be on our team.

Year Team	Lg.	G	IP	H	BB	SO	W	L	ERA	SV	Ratio
1991 Toronto	AL	40	198.1	188	49	106	15	10	3.72	1	1.195
1992 Toronto	AL	41	120.0	138	36	62	7	9	5.40	2	1.450
1993 Detroit	AL	32	187.0	183	42	139	11	9	4.19	0	1.203
1994 Detroit	AL	16	111.1	113	24	71	5	7	3.96	0	1.231
1994 PROJECTION		25	178.2	164	41	108	11	9	3.68	0	1.147

BOBBY WITT

Age 30/R **$3**

And if he's still around, he better hope it's with Oakland, where Dave Duncan and Tony LaRussa represent Witt's last, best hope for major league success.

Year Team	Lg.	G	IP	H	BB	SO	W	L	ERA	SV	Ratio
1991 Texas	AL	17	88.2	84	74	82	3	7	6.09	0	1.782
1992 Texas	AL	25	161.1	152	95	100	9	13	4.46	0	1.531
1992 Oakland	AL	6	31.2	31	19	25	1	1	3.41	0	1.579
1993 Oakland	AL	35	220.0	226	91	131	14	13	4.21	0	1.441
1994 Oakland	AL	24	135.2	151	70	111	8	10	5.04	0	1.629
1994 PROJECTION		34	191.2	226	100	154	10	16	5.26	0	1.701

Out of the Bullpen

NATIONAL LEAGUE

LARRY ANDERSEN

Age 41/R **$1**

"I sent Jake [John Kruk] one of those fruit and nut baskets when he was in the hospital. I don't know if he'll eat the fruit, but I know he'll appreciate the nuts." One of these springs, Mr. Andersen won't be able to find work, and baseball will be the poorer for it.

Year Team	Lg.	G	IP	H	BB	SO	W	L	ERA	SV	Ratio
1991 San Diego	NL	38	47.0	39	13	40	3	4	2.30	13	1.106
1992 San Diego	NL	34	35.0	26	8	35	1	1	3.34	2	0.971
1993 Philadelphia	NL	64	61.2	54	21	67	3	2	2.92	0	1.216
1994 Philadelphia	NL	29	32.2	33	15	27	1	2	4.41	0	1.469
1994 PROJECTION		44	50.1	59	21	40	1	4	4.65	1	1.589

Catchers
pp. 33–46

Corners
pp. 46–65

Infield
pp. 66–85

Outfield
pp. 85–115

DH
pp. 115–119

Starters
pp. 119–155

Relievers
pp. 155–187

LUIS AQUINO

Age 29/R **$1**

A productive middle man. Will deliver okay numbers and pick up some vulture wins. Logged some DL time the last two years.

Year Team	Lg.	G	IP	H	BB	SO	W	L	ERA	SV	Ratio
1991 Kansas City	AL	38	157.0	152	47	80	8	4	3.44	3	1.268
1992 Kansas City	AL	15	67.2	81	20	11	3	6	4.52	0	1.493
1993 Florida	NL	38	110.2	115	40	67	6	8	3.42	0	1.401
1994 Florida	NL	29	50.2	39	22	22	2	1	3.73	0	1.204
1994 PROJECTION		48	82.1	66	35	35	5	2	3.28	2	1.227

JOSE BAUTISTA

Age 30/R **$3**

The Energizer Reliever—116 appearances in two years and still going strong.

Year Team	Lg.	G	IP	H	BB	SO	W	L	ERA	SV	Ratio
1991 Baltimore	AL	5	5.1	13	5	3	0	1	16.88	0	3.375
1993 Chicago	NL	58	111.2	105	27	63	10	3	2.82	2	1.182
1994 Chicago	NL	58	69.1	75	17	45	4	5	3.89	1	1.327
1994 PROJECTION		73	89.2	95	21	61	9	6	3.51	1	1.293

ROD BECK

Age 26/R **$40**

A little problem with gopher balls (10) and another with allowing inherited runners to score (7 of 18, not a good ratio), but we prefer to focus on the number of blown saves last year: 0.

Year Team	Lg.	G	IP	H	BB	SO	W	L	ERA	SV	Ratio
1991 San Francisco	NL	31	52.1	53	13	38	1	1	3.78	1	1.261
1992 San Francisco	NL	65	92.0	62	15	87	3	3	1.76	17	0.837
1993 San Francisco	NL	76	79.1	57	13	86	3	1	2.16	48	0.882
1994 San Francisco	NL	48	48.2	49	13	39	2	4	2.77	28	1.274
1994 PROJECTION		58	58.1	59	13	41	2	5	2.78	36	1.234

STEVE BEDROSIAN

Age 37/R **$1**

Solid for the Braves as a situational reliever, but not much value to a Rotisserie bullpen.

Year Team	Lg.	G	IP	H	BB	SO	W	L	ERA	SV	Ratio
1991 Minnesota	AL	56	77.1	70	35	44	5	3	4.42	6	1.358
1993 Atlanta	NL	49	49.2	34	14	33	5	2	1.63	0	0.966
1994 Atlanta	NL	46	46.0	41	18	43	0	2	3.33	0	1.283
1994 PROJECTION		66	67.0	60	22	60	1	5	3.63	1	1.224

WILLIE BLAIR

Age 29/R **$1**

We're looking for something nice to say, something positive and encouraging. We'll let you know if we find anything.

Year Team	Lg.	G	IP	H	BB	SO	W	L	ERA	SV	Ratio
1991 Cleveland	AL	11	36.0	58	10	13	2	3	6.75	0	1.889
1992 Houston	NL	29	78.2	74	25	48	5	7	4.00	0	1.258
1993 Colorado	NL	46	146.0	184	42	84	6	10	4.75	0	1.548
1994 Colorado	NL	47	77.2	98	39	68	0	5	5.79	3	1.764
1994 PROJECTION		63	102.2	147	50	96	0	6	6.49	3	1.919

JEFF BRANTLEY

Age 31/R **$28**

Last year he was Committee Chairman; this year he could be The Man. Strikes out a man an inning, doesn't walk a lot of guys, gave up only six home runs, and opposing hitters batted just .202 against him. Frankly, we are at a loss to explain his six blown saves.

Year Team	Lg.	G	IP	H	BB	SO	W	L	ERA	SV	Ratio
1991 San Francisco	NL	67	95.1	78	52	81	5	2	2.45	15	1.364
1992 San Francisco	NL	56	91.2	67	45	86	7	7	2.95	7	1.222
1993 San Francisco	NL	53	113.2	112	46	76	5	6	4.28	0	1.390
1994 Cincinnati	NL	50	65.1	46	28	63	6	6	2.48	15	1.133
1994 PROJECTION		68	83.0	67	35	77	8	7	2.82	21	1.229

DAVE BURBA   Age 28/R $2

A good pitcher in a bullpen where only one man gets all the save opportunities. Burba's value is directly proportional to the Giants' success. If they win a lot of games, and we think they will, a fair number will appear on his record. Heck, he could even be a candidate for Vulture of the Year.

Year Team	Lg.	G	IP	H	BB	SO	W	L	ERA	SV	Ratio
1991 Seattle	AL	22	36.2	34	14	16	2	2	3.68	1	1.309
1992 San Francisco	NL	23	70.2	80	31	47	2	7	4.97	0	1.571
1993 San Francisco	NL	54	95.1	95	37	88	10	3	4.25	0	1.385
1994 San Francisco	NL	57	74.0	59	45	84	3	6	4.38	0	1.405
1994 PROJECTION		79	102.0	82	60	108	4	9	4.59	1	1.392

HECTOR CARRASCO   Age 25/R $9

Former Reds coach Bob Boone was high on him last season, although he admitted Carrasco "doesn't have a clue about how to pitch." What Boonie meant is that Carrasco has plenty of stuff but little idea how best to use it. We think he'll learn.

Year Team	Lg.	G	IP	H	BB	SO	W	L	ERA	SV	Ratio
1994 Cincinnati	NL	45	56.1	42	30	41	5	6	2.24	6	1.278
1994 PROJECTION		66	76.2	55	42	57	7	6	2.00	9	1.265

ANDY CARTER   Age 26/L $1

For what it's worth, he was the only lefty left in the Phillies bullpen last year when David West was turned into a starter. We don't think that's worth very much, and we suspect the Phils will do something about that situation before Opening Day, but some of us are invariably attracted to the much-discredited Only Lefty in the Bullpen Theory.

Year Team	Lg.	G	IP	H	BB	SO	W	L	ERA	SV	Ratio
1994 Philadelphia	NL	20	34.1	34	12	18	0	2	4.46	0	1.340
1994 PROJECTION		20	34.1	34	12	18	0	2	4.46	0	1.340

CHUCK CRIM
Age 33/R   **$2**

Here you have one of the reasons why former Cubs GM Larry Himes is now responsible for making sure that the pinto beans in the press room cafeteria at Ho-Ho-Kam Park in Mesa are hot and spicy.

Year Team	Lg.	G	IP	H	BB	SO	W	L	ERA	SV	Ratio
1991 Milwaukee	AL	66	91.1	115	25	39	8	5	4.63	3	1.533
1992 California	AL	57	87.0	100	29	30	7	6	5.17	1	1.483
1993 California	AL	11	15.1	17	5	10	2	2	5.87	0	1.435
1994 Chicago	NL	49	64.1	69	24	43	5	4	4.48	2	1.446
1994 PROJECTION		68	88.0	91	29	59	8	4	4.40	2	1.363

OMAR DAAL
Age 23/L   **$1**

One of those pitchers who is rarely allowed to face more than one or two batters. Often that's one or two too many.

Year Team	Lg.	G	IP	H	BB	SO	W	L	ERA	SV	Ratio
1993 Los Angeles	NL	47	35.1	36	21	19	2	3	5.09	0	1.613
1994 Los Angeles	NL	24	13.2	12	5	9	0	0	3.29	0	1.244
1994 PROJECTION		41	22.0	20	8	15	1	0	3.68	0	1.270

MARK DAVIS
Age 34/L   **$1**

One of the great conundrums of the modern era, but probably not a major league pitcher in 1995.

Year Team	Lg.	G	IP	H	BB	SO	W	L	ERA	SV	Ratio
1991 Kansas City	AL	29	62.2	55	39	47	6	3	4.45	1	1.500
1992 Kansas City	AL	13	36.1	42	28	19	1	3	7.18	0	1.927
1992 Atlanta	NL	14	16.2	22	13	15	1	0	7.02	0	2.100
1993 Philadelphia	NL	25	31.1	35	24	28	1	2	5.17	0	1.883
1993 San Diego	NL	35	38.1	44	20	42	0	3	3.52	4	1.670
1994 San Diego	NL	20	16.1	20	13	15	0	1	8.82	0	2.020
1994 PROJECTION		20	16.1	20	13	15	0	1	8.82	0	2.020

DARREN DREIFORT
Age 22/R   **$15**

The Dodgers rolled the dice that their first-round pick in the 1993 amateur draft could step right into the big leagues without spending a day in the minors. They came up snake eyes, but that was last year. Dreifort has a big-time heater, a nasty splitter, a year in the minors under his belt, and no trace of shell shock from last seasons' harrowing debut. Plus, they cleared out the bullpen to give him a clear shot this year. We should all have so much going for us.

Year Team	Lg.	G	IP	H	BB	SO	W	L	ERA	SV	Ratio
1994 Los Angeles	NL	27	29.0	45	15	22	0	5	6.21	6	2.069
1994 PROJECTION		31	32.2	49	21	24	0	5	7.16	6	2.143

TOM EDENS
Age 33/R   **$1**

More wins than all but two of the 11 pitchers who started games for the Phillies last year. That tells you a little something about the serendipity of middle-relief success—and a lot about Philadelphia's starting pitching.

Year Team	Lg.	G	IP	H	BB	SO	W	L	ERA	SV	Ratio
1991 Minnesota	AL	8	33.0	34	10	19	2	2	4.09	0	1.333
1992 Minnesota	AL	52	76.1	65	36	57	6	3	2.83	3	1.323
1993 Houston	NL	38	49.0	47	19	21	1	1	3.12	0	1.347
1994 Houston	NL	39	50.0	55	17	38	4	1	4.50	1	1.440
1994 Philadelphia	NL	3	4.0	4	1	1	1	0	2.25	0	1.250
1994 PROJECTION		56	76.1	73	25	60	5	1	3.54	1	1.284

DONNIE ELLIOTT
Age 26/R $1

He's gone from being a Phillies prospect to a Braves maybe to a Padres middle reliever. And he may have found his niche on a San Diego staff that has been quietly stocked with some seriously hard-throwing young arms.

Year Team	Lg.	G	IP	H	BB	SO	W	L	ERA	SV	Ratio
1994 San Diego	NL	30	33.0	31	21	24	0	1	3.27	0	1.576
1994 PROJECTION		30	33.0	31	21	24	0	1	3.27	0	1.576

BRYAN EVERSGERD
Age 26/L $1

If your kid says he wants to be a major league player, don't step on his dream, especially if he throws left-handed. Eversgerd, who went to school at that noted baseball factory, Kaskaskia College, was spotted at a tryout camp held by the Cardinals in southern Illinois. Last year, he cranked it up 40 times in the bigs. Never mind that the numbers weren't pretty. And never mind that the Cardinals had one of the worst pitching staffs in the major leagues. The guy made it to The Show.

Year Team	Lg.	G	IP	H	BB	SO	W	L	ERA	SV	Ratio
1994 St. Louis	NL	40	67.2	75	20	47	2	3	4.52	0	1.404
1994 PROJECTION		60	87.2	94	22	60	2	5	4.31	0	1.323

BRYCE FLORIE
Age 24/R $1

A few token appearances late last season have the Padres thinking he can play a key role in their much-improved bullpen. With Trevor Hoffman around, we'll have to see what that role is before we open the vault.

Year Team	Lg.	G	IP	H	BB	SO	W	L	ERA	SV	Ratio
1994 San Diego	NL	9	9.1	8	3	8	0	0	0.96	0	1.179
1994 PROJECTION		14	14.2	17	5	14	0	0	4.91	0	1.500

TIM FORTUGNO
Age 32/L $1

The Reds thought so much of this much-traveled vagabond that they sent him to the minors just prior to The Strike so he could stay sharp and be ready to help out when The Strike ended. "Middle relievers will be important after a long layoff because the starters won't be going many innings," said GM Jim Bowden. Plausible theory.

Year Team	Lg.	G	IP	H	BB	SO	W	L	ERA	SV	Ratio
1992 California	AL	14	41.2	37	19	31	1	1	5.18	1	1.344
1994 Cincinnati	NL	25	30.0	32	14	29	1	0	4.20	0	1.533
1994 PROJECTION		37	42.2	45	17	43	1	0	3.80	1	1.453

Catchers
pp. 33–46

Corners
pp. 46–65

Infield
pp. 66–85

Outfield
pp. 85–115

DH
pp. 115–119

Starters
pp. 119–155

Relievers
pp. 155–187

JOHN FRANCO
Age 34/L   **$24**

Who says there was no happy news in 1994? His sinker came back, along with his old bravado, and so did a big payoff for all those Rotisserie loyalists who stayed with one of their old reliables through think and thin. Attention, Francophiles: thin is coming back.

Year Team	Lg.	G	IP	H	BB	SO	W	L	ERA	SV	Ratio
1991 New York	NL	52	55.1	61	18	45	5	9	2.93	30	1.428
1992 New York	NL	31	33.0	24	11	20	6	2	1.64	15	1.061
1993 New York	NL	35	36.1	46	19	29	4	3	5.20	10	1.789
1994 New York	NL	47	50.0	47	19	42	1	4	2.70	30	1.320
1994 PROJECTION		61	63.2	57	21	57	1	5	2.54	42	1.225

STEVE FREY
Age 31/L   **$1**

Nope.

Year Team	Lg.	G	IP	H	BB	SO	W	L	ERA	SV	Ratio
1991 Montreal	NL	31	39.2	43	23	21	0	1	4.99	1	1.664
1992 California	AL	51	45.1	39	22	24	4	2	3.57	4	1.346
1993 California	AL	55	48.1	41	26	22	2	3	2.98	13	1.386
1994 San Francisco	NL	44	31.0	37	15	20	1	0	4.94	0	1.677
1994 PROJECTION		60	39.1	52	19	22	1	0	6.64	0	1.805

PAT GOMEZ
Age 27/L   **$1**

More nope.

Year Team	Lg.	G	IP	H	BB	SO	W	L	ERA	SV	Ratio
1993 San Diego	NL	27	31.2	35	19	26	1	2	5.12	0	1.705
1994 San Francisco	NL	26	33.1	23	20	14	0	1	3.78	0	1.290
1994 PROJECTION		39	44.2	33	27	21	2	2	3.63	0	1.343

JIM GOTT
Age 35/R   **$1**

May have trouble finding work.

Year Team	Lg.	G	IP	H	BB	SO	W	L	ERA	SV	Ratio
1991 Los Angeles	NL	55	76.0	63	32	73	4	3	2.96	2	1.250
1992 Los Angeles	NL	68	88.0	72	41	75	3	3	2.45	6	1.284
1993 Los Angeles	NL	62	77.2	71	17	67	4	8	2.32	25	1.133
1994 Los Angeles	NL	37	36.1	46	20	29	5	3	5.94	2	1.817
1994 PROJECTION		54	55.2	70	29	45	5	5	5.66	2	1.778

ERIC GUNDERSON
Age 29/L   **$1**

A left-handed reliever who got some left-handed hitters out. Should we alert the media?

Year Team	Lg.	G	IP	H	BB	SO	W	L	ERA	SV	Ratio
1991 San Francisco	NL	2	3.1	6	1	2	0	0	5.40	1	2.100
1992 Seattle	AL	9	9.1	12	5	2	2	1	8.68	0	1.821
1994 New York	NL	14	9.0	5	4	4	0	0	0.00	0	1.000
1994 PROJECTION		30	23.0	21	13	14	2	0	4.30	0	1.478

JOHN HABYAN
Age 31/R   **$2**

Once a Baltimore Orioles phenom, Habyan is a hard thrower with decent control who has developed into a solid middle-innings man. Could be his year to be kissed by the vulture. (That's not a reference to the new Baltimore manager, but Rotissespeak for piling up garbage wins.)

Year	Team	Lg.	G	IP	H	BB	SO	W	L	ERA	SV	Ratio
1991	New York	AL	66	90.0	73	20	70	4	2	2.30	2	1.033
1992	New York	AL	56	72.2	84	21	44	5	6	3.84	7	1.445
1993	New York	AL	36	42.1	45	16	29	2	1	4.04	1	1.441
1993	Kansas City	AL	12	14.0	14	4	10	0	0	4.50	0	1.286
1994	St. Louis	NL	52	47.1	50	20	46	1	0	3.23	1	1.479
1994	PROJECTION		68	64.2	68	27	60	1	1	3.34	1	1.469

MIKE HAMPTON   Age 22/L $1

The best darned pitcher to come out of Homasassa, Florida, since Hall of Famer Dazzy Vance.

Year	Team	Lg.	G	IP	H	BB	SO	W	L	ERA	SV	Ratio
1993	Seattle	AL	13	17.0	28	17	8	1	3	9.53	1	2.647
1994	Houston	NL	44	41.1	46	16	24	2	1	3.70	0	1.500
1994	PROJECTION		53	52.2	63	20	28	2	2	3.42	0	1.576

BRYAN HARVEY   Age 31/R $36/1

First the Marlins gambled on him in the expansion draft, and they won. Then the Marlins gambled that offers for him from other teams would continue to grow if he stayed healthy and had another year like 1993, and they lost. You know the drill: healthy, he's The Man; unhealthy, he's just another guy.

Year	Team	Lg.	G	IP	H	BB	SO	W	L	ERA	SV	Ratio
1991	California	AL	67	78.2	51	17	101	2	4	1.60	46	0.864
1992	California	AL	25	28.2	22	11	34	0	4	2.83	13	1.151
1993	Florida	NL	59	69.0	45	13	73	1	5	1.70	45	0.841
1994	Florida	NL	12	10.1	12	4	10	0	0	5.23	6	1.548
1994	PROJECTION		12	10.1	12	4	10	0	0	5.23	6	1.550

GIL HEREDIA   Age 29/R $3

Another one of those largely unknown Expos hard throwers who perform well as a spot starter and a middle reliever.

Year	Team	Lg.	G	IP	H	BB	SO	W	L	ERA	SV	Ratio
1991	San Francisco	NL	7	33.0	27	7	13	0	2	3.82	0	1.030
1992	San Francisco	NL	13	30.0	32	16	15	2	3	5.40	0	1.600
1992	Montreal	NL	7	14.2	12	4	7	0	0	1.84	0	1.091
1993	Montreal	NL	20	57.1	66	14	40	4	2	3.92	2	1.395
1994	Montreal	NL	39	75.1	85	13	62	6	3	3.46	0	1.301
1994	PROJECTION		47	125.2	132	19	107	9	5	3.37	0	1.201

JEREMY HERNANDEZ   Age 28/R $7

Bagged a few saves while filling in for Bryan Harvey before he, too, went on the DL for the duration, but he's much better suited for the set-up role. Good thing, because with the emergence of Robb Nen, the closer's role is spoken for—even if Harvey doesn't come back.

Year	Team	Lg.	G	IP	H	BB	SO	W	L	ERA	SV	Ratio
1991	San Diego	NL	9	14.1	8	5	9	0	0	0.00	2	0.907
1992	San Diego	NL	26	36.2	39	11	25	1	4	4.17	1	1.364
1993	San Diego	NL	21	34.1	41	7	26	0	2	4.72	0	1.398
1993	Cleveland	AL	49	77.1	75	27	44	6	5	3.14	8	1.319
1994	Florida	NL	21	23.1	16	14	13	3	3	2.70	9	1.286
1994	PROJECTION		21	23.1	16	14	13	3	3	2.70	9	1.280

Catchers
pp. 33-46

Corners
pp. 46-65

Infield
pp. 66-85

Outfield
pp. 85-115

DH
pp. 115-119

Starters
pp. 119-155

Relievers
pp. 155-187

TREVOR HOFFMAN   Age 27/R $36

The Sheffield deal looks better and better each time Hoffman comes on in the ninth.

Year Team	Lg.	G	IP	H	BB	SO	W	L	ERA	SV	Ratio
1993 Florida	NL	28	35.2	24	19	26	2	2	3.28	2	1.206
1993 San Diego	NL	39	54.1	56	20	53	2	4	4.31	3	1.399
1994 San Diego	NL	47	56.0	39	20	68	4	4	2.57	20	1.054
1994 PROJECTION		61	70.0	54	29	80	7	5	3.34	27	1.186

DARREN HOLMES   Age 28/R $1

An even bigger disappointment in Colorado than that new airport.

Year Team	Lg.	G	IP	H	BB	SO	W	L	ERA	SV	Ratio
1991 Milwaukee	AL	40	76.1	90	27	59	1	4	4.72	3	1.533
1992 Milwaukee	AL	41	42.1	35	11	31	4	4	2.55	6	1.087
1993 Colorado	NL	62	66.2	56	20	60	3	3	4.05	25	1.140
1994 Colorado	NL	29	28.1	35	24	33	0	3	6.35	3	2.082
1994 PROJECTION		39	37.0	52	28	41	0	5	7.05	3	2.162

JOHN HUDEK   Age 28/R $24

Let's see if we have this right. The Tigers recognized his potential and snatched him out of the White Sox organization, but then allowed him to walk away to Houston for absolutely nothing via the waiver wire? Not surprising, since they act like Joe Boever is the second coming of Dick Radatz. How could they let an arm like Hudek's just disappear? All we know is Hudek looks awfully good in the Astros bullpen, would have looked just as good in the Tigers', and will look even better in yours. But be warned: if he falters, the Astros have plenty of other young arms to replace him.

Year Team	Lg.	G	IP	H	BB	SO	W	L	ERA	SV	Ratio
1994 Houston	NL	42	39.1	24	18	39	0	2	2.97	16	1.068
1994 PROJECTION		59	62.2	39	28	65	3	2	2.44	25	1.069

MIKE JACKSON   Age 30/R $9

Knee problems and a shoulder injury shut him down last season, but he is one nasty pitcher when he's healthy. Just don't expect him to step forward and be the closer should something happen to Beck. Many a Rotisserie heart has been broken by Jackson, because he's always worked best as a set-up man and stumbled when given a shot at the closer's role.

Year Team	Lg.	G	IP	H	BB	SO	W	L	ERA	SV	Ratio
1991 Seattle	AL	72	88.2	64	34	74	7	7	3.25	14	1.105
1992 San Francisco	NL	67	82.0	76	33	80	6	6	3.73	2	1.329
1993 San Francisco	NL	81	77.1	58	24	70	6	6	3.03	1	1.060
1994 San Francisco	NL	36	42.1	23	11	51	3	2	1.49	4	0.803
1994 PROJECTION		50	66.0	38	13	72	3	2	1.50	4	0.773

DOUG JONES   Age 37/R $28

Replacing Wild Thing with this junk-throwing craftsman was like having Perry Como fill in for Axl Rose. Jones did an amazing job last season, but he was the highest-paid Phillie, and he may have to take a pay cut to stay. Fiscal responsibility is a drag.

Year Team	Lg.	G	IP	H	BB	SO	W	L	ERA	SV	Ratio
1991 Cleveland	AL	36	63.1	87	17	48	4	8	5.54	7	1.642
1992 Houston	NL	80	111.2	96	17	93	11	8	1.85	36	1.012
1993 Houston	NL	71	85.1	102	21	66	4	10	4.54	26	1.441
1994 Philadelphia	NL	47	54.0	55	6	38	2	4	2.17	27	1.130
1994 PROJECTION		60	69.1	75	9	46	2	6	2.86	32	1.211

Catchers
pp. 33–46

Corners
pp. 46–65

Infield
pp. 66–85

Outfield
pp. 85–115

DH
pp. 115–119

Starters
pp. 119–155

Relievers
pp. 155–187

TODD JONES
Age 26/R $6

If Hudek wavers, Jones will be The Man in Houston. In fact, he might end up being The Man anyhow. You can't go wrong betting on the upside.

Year Team	Lg.	G	IP	H	BB	SO	W	L	ERA	SV	Ratio
1993 Houston	NL	27	37.1	28	15	25	1	2	3.13	2	1.152
1994 Houston	NL	48	72.2	52	26	63	5	2	2.72	5	1.073
1994 PROJECTION		72	112.2	75	39	98	10	6	2.48	9	1.012

DOUG LINTON
Age 29/R $1

A former Blue Jay hot prospect, Linton once went 14–2 in A ball. But that was one torn rotator cuff and many innings ago. Now throws BP too many times out.

Year Team	Lg.	G	IP	H	BB	SO	W	L	ERA	SV	Ratio
1992 Toronto	AL	8	24.0	31	17	16	1	3	8.63	0	2.000
1993 Toronto	AL	4	11.0	11	9	4	0	1	6.55	0	1.818
1993 California	AL	19	25.2	35	14	19	2	0	7.71	0	1.909
1994 New York	NL	32	50.1	74	20	29	6	2	4.47	0	1.868
1994 PROJECTION		40	81.2	109	34	47	6	5	4.52	0	1.751

MIKE MADDUX
Age 33/R $1

Once a solid major league pitcher, but that was a team ago.

Year Team	Lg.	G	IP	H	BB	SO	W	L	ERA	SV	Ratio
1991 San Diego	NL	64	98.2	78	27	57	7	2	2.46	5	1.064
1992 San Diego	NL	50	79.2	71	24	60	2	2	2.37	5	1.192
1993 New York	NL	58	75.0	67	27	57	3	8	3.60	5	1.253
1994 New York	NL	27	44.0	45	13	32	2	1	5.11	2	1.318
1994 PROJECTION		38	60.0	62	19	44	2	3	5.40	2	1.350

JOSIAS MANZANILLO
Age 27/R $5

He is right-handed, lives in Boston, has good control, throws beebees, can be helpful if kept away from powerful left-handed hitters, and is believed to be only 27 years old. On the other hand, his brother . . .

Year Team	Lg.	G	IP	H	BB	SO	W	L	ERA	SV	Ratio
1991 Boston	AL	1	1.0	2	3	1	0	0	18.00	0	5.000
1993 Milwaukee	AL	10	17.0	22	10	10	1	1	9.53	1	1.882
1993 New York	NL	6	12.0	8	9	11	0	0	3.00	0	1.417
1994 New York	NL	37	47.1	34	13	48	3	2	2.66	2	0.993
1994 PROJECTION		46	60.0	42	16	63	7	3	2.40	2	0.967

RAVELO MANZANILLO
Age 31/L $1

. . . is left-handed, still lives in the Dominican Republic, walks almost a batter an inning, gets beaten up by right-handers, and is of indeterminate age. "He

---

says he's 31," says Pirates coach Tommy Sandt, "but all I know is that he was supposedly 25 when I was 28 and now I'm 43."

Year Team	Lg.	G	IP	H	BB	SO	W	L	ERA	SV	Ratio
1994 Pittsburgh	NL	46	50.0	45	42	39	4	2	4.14	1	1.740
1994 PROJECTION		69	70.0	54	59	49	6	3	3.99	7	1.614

PEDRO A. MARTINEZ   Age 26/L $4

Another excellent arm in a Padres bullpen that will soon cease being one of baseball's best-kept secrets. In the aftermath of their dismantling, the Padres can point with pride to the flock of young pitchers they have assembled.

Year Team	Lg.	G	IP	H	BB	SO	W	L	ERA	SV	Ratio
1993 San Diego	NL	32	37.0	23	13	32	3	1	2.43	0	0.973
1994 San Diego	NL	48	68.1	52	49	52	3	2	2.90	3	1.478
1994 PROJECTION		68	98.2	73	64	75	3	4	2.65	6	1.388

ROGER MASON   Age 36/R $1

He'll take the ball. Unfortunately, he'll also throw it.

Year Team	Lg.	G	IP	H	BB	SO	W	L	ERA	SV	Ratio
1991 Pittsburgh	NL	24	29.2	21	6	21	3	2	3.03	3	0.910
1992 Pittsburgh	NL	65	88.0	80	33	56	5	7	4.09	8	1.284
1993 San Diego	NL	34	50.0	43	18	39	0	7	3.24	0	1.220
1993 Philadelphia	NL	34	49.2	47	16	32	5	5	4.89	0	1.268
1994 Philadelphia	NL	6	8.2	11	5	7	1	1	5.19	0	1.846
1994 New York	NL	41	51.1	44	20	26	2	4	3.51	1	1.247
1994 PROJECTION		63	75.0	79	34	40	4	8	5.04	2	1.506

TIM MAUSER   Age 28/R $1

Has developed good split-finger fastball, but might be the odd man out among all those up-and-coming relievers in San Diego.

Year Team	Lg.	G	IP	H	BB	SO	W	L	ERA	SV	Ratio
1991 Philadelphia	NL	3	10.2	18	3	6	0	0	7.59	0	1.969
1993 Philadelphia	NL	8	16.1	15	7	14	0	0	4.96	0	1.347
1993 San Diego	NL	28	37.2	36	17	32	0	1	3.58	0	1.407
1994 San Diego	NL	35	49.0	50	19	32	2	4	3.49	2	1.408
1994 PROJECTION		53	72.2	86	28	50	4	7	4.58	2	1.569

ROGER McDOWELL   Age 34/R $1

The merry prankster may have trouble finding work.

Year Team	Lg.	G	IP	H	BB	SO	W	L	ERA	SV	Ratio
1991 Philadelphia	NL	38	59.0	61	32	28	3	6	3.20	3	1.576
1991 Los Angeles	NL	33	42.1	39	16	22	6	3	2.55	7	1.299
1992 Los Angeles	NL	65	83.2	103	42	50	6	10	4.09	14	1.733
1993 Los Angeles	NL	54	68.0	76	30	27	5	3	2.25	2	1.559
1994 Los Angeles	NL	32	41.1	50	22	29	0	3	5.23	0	1.742
1994 PROJECTION		46	58.2	71	32	38	2	3	4.76	0	1.755

CHUCK McELROY   Age 27/L $7

It was team picture day and his Cincinnati teammates were complaining about having to wait until Schottzie 2 arrived with his keeper, Marge. But the little left-hander just smiled: "Man, these guys don't know what miserable is until they play on a team where Larry Himes is GM."

Year Team	Lg.	G	IP	H	BB	SO	W	L	ERA	SV	Ratio
1991 Chicago	NL	71	101.1	73	57	92	6	2	1.95	3	1.283
1992 Chicago	NL	72	83.2	73	51	83	4	7	3.55	6	1.482
1993 Chicago	NL	49	47.1	51	25	31	2	2	4.56	0	1.606
1994 Cincinnati	NL	52	57.2	52	15	38	1	2	2.34	5	1.162
1994 PROJECTION		77	77.1	69	20	51	2	2	2.44	6	1.151

GREG McMICHAEL   Age 28/R $12

He gets the job done, so why is it that no one—including the Braves—is willing to say, yeah, he's the closer in Atlanta?

Year Team	Lg.	G	IP	H	BB	SO	W	L	ERA	SV	Ratio
1993 Atlanta	NL	74	91.2	68	29	89	2	3	2.06	19	1.058
1994 Atlanta	NL	51	58.2	66	19	47	4	6	3.84	21	1.449
1994 PROJECTION		65	70.1	87	20	60	4	8	4.48	28	1.521

DANNY MICELI   Age 24/R $1

Jim Leyland has always gone with bullpens by committee, but we think he should consider cutting down on its size. Starting here.

Year Team	Lg.	G	IP	H	BB	SO	W	L	ERA	SV	Ratio
1993 Pittsburgh	NL	9	5.1	6	3	4	0	0	5.06	0	1.688
1994 Pittsburgh	NL	28	27.1	28	11	27	2	1	5.93	2	1.427
1994 PROJECTION		51	55.0	51	16	56	8	2	4.75	6	1.218

BLAS MINOR   Age 29/R $1

Not of major interest.

Year Team	Lg.	G	IP	H	BB	SO	W	L	ERA	SV	Ratio
1992 Pittsburgh	NL	1	2.0	3	0	0	0	0	4.50	0	1.500
1993 Pittsburgh	NL	65	94.1	94	26	84	8	6	4.10	2	1.272
1994 Pittsburgh	NL	17	19.0	27	9	17	0	1	8.05	1	1.895
1994 PROJECTION		17	19.0	27	9	17	0	1	8.05	1	1.895

RICH MONTELEONE   Age 32/R $1

Won't hurt you, which is a lot more than can be said for many in this price range.

Year Team	Lg.	G	IP	H	BB	SO	W	L	ERA	SV	Ratio
1991 New York	AL	26	47.0	42	19	34	3	1	3.64	0	1.298
1992 New York	AL	47	92.2	82	27	62	7	3	3.30	0	1.176
1993 New York	AL	42	85.2	85	35	50	7	4	4.94	0	1.401
1994 San Francisco	NL	39	45.1	43	13	16	4	3	3.18	0	1.235
1994 PROJECTION		64	67.2	73	16	25	5	7	3.72	0	1.315

MARCUS MOORE   Age 24/R $1

Hard thrower. Jury's still out. Nice symmetry with his IP, H, and K. Moore's big problem is that he came so close to going four for four with his BB.

Year Team	Lg.	G	IP	H	BB	SO	W	L	ERA	SV	Ratio
1993 Colorado	NL	27	26.1	30	20	13	3	1	6.84	0	1.899
1994 Colorado	NL	29	33.2	33	21	33	1	1	6.15	0	1.604
1994 PROJECTION		31	43.2	43	28	42	1	2	5.56	0	1.626

Catchers
pp. 33–46

Corners
pp. 46–65

Infield
pp. 66–85

Outfield
pp. 85–115

DH
pp. 115–119

Starters
pp. 119–155

Relievers
pp. 155–187

MIKE MUNOZ   Age 29/L $2

A Dodgers phenom from days gone by, Muñoz has always had good stuff. Indeed, many Rotisserie owners have left the auction draft gloating to themselves that Muñoz was their secret weapon. The secret was well kept until last year, when he did yeoman's work for the Rockies, stranding 75% of the runners he inherited. Unless Bruce Ruffin turns into a pumpkin, though, Muñoz won't get too many save opportunities.

Year	Team	Lg.	G	IP	H	BB	SO	W	L	ERA	SV	Ratio
1991	Detroit	AL	6	9.1	14	5	3	0	0	9.64	0	2.036
1992	Detroit	AL	65	48.0	44	25	23	1	2	3.00	2	1.438
1993	Detroit	AL	8	3.0	4	6	1	0	1	6.00	0	3.333
1993	Colorado	NL	21	18.0	21	9	16	2	1	4.50	0	1.667
1994	Colorado	NL	57	45.2	37	31	32	4	2	3.74	1	1.489
1994	PROJECTION		86	72.1	58	45	53	5	3	3.24	1	1.424

JEFF MUTIS   Age 28/L $1

Ain't expansion grand?

Year	Team	Lg.	G	IP	H	BB	SO	W	L	ERA	SV	Ratio
1991	Cleveland	AL	3	12.1	23	7	6	0	3	11.68	0	2.432
1992	Cleveland	AL	3	11.1	24	6	8	0	2	9.53	0	2.647
1993	Cleveland	AL	17	81.0	93	33	29	3	6	5.78	0	1.556
1994	Florida	NL	35	38.1	51	15	30	1	0	5.40	0	1.722
1994	PROJECTION		35	38.1	51	15	30	1	0	5.40	0	1.722

RANDY MYERS   Age 32/L $34

Still a Nasty Boy after all these years.

Year	Team	Lg.	G	IP	H	BB	SO	W	L	ERA	SV	Ratio
1991	Cincinnati	NL	58	132.0	116	80	108	6	13	3.55	6	1.485
1992	San Diego	NL	66	79.2	84	34	66	3	6	4.29	38	1.481
1993	Chicago	NL	73	75.1	65	26	86	2	4	3.11	53	1.208
1994	Chicago	NL	38	40.1	40	16	32	1	5	3.79	21	1.388
1994	PROJECTION		56	61.2	61	23	51	4	6	3.21	32	1.362

ROBB NEN   Age 25/R $29

World-class gas from the hardest-throwing palindrome in baseball history. A legit star in the making.

Year	Team	Lg.	G	IP	H	BB	SO	W	L	ERA	SV	Ratio
1993	Texas	AL	9	22.2	28	26	12	1	1	6.35	0	2.382
1993	Florida	NL	15	33.1	35	20	27	1	0	7.02	0	1.650
1994	Florida	NL	44	58.0	46	17	60	5	5	2.95	15	1.086
1994	PROJECTION		58	72.2	62	26	71	7	5	2.97	20	1.211

GREGG OLSON   Age 28/R $1

They kept him under wraps for most of the year, but by the end of the summer Braves people felt that Otter was finally getting the juice back on his fastball and a little snap back on his curve. If they re-sign him, take a flyer.

Year Team	Lg.	G	IP	H	BB	SO	W	L	ERA	SV	Ratio
1991 Baltimore	AL	72	73.2	74	29	72	4	6	3.18	31	1.398
1992 Baltimore	AL	60	61.1	46	24	58	1	5	2.05	36	1.141
1993 Baltimore	AL	50	45.0	37	18	44	0	2	1.60	29	1.222
1994 Atlanta	NL	16	14.2	19	13	10	0	2	9.20	1	2.182
1994 PROJECTION		28	30.2	39	26	20	2	4	8.22	1	2.119

ALEJANDRO PENA   Age 35/R $1

Stick a fork in him.

Year Team	Lg.	G	IP	H	BB	SO	W	L	ERA	SV	Ratio
1991 New York	NL	44	63.0	63	19	49	6	1	2.71	4	1.302
1991 Atlanta	NL	15	19.1	11	3	13	2	0	1.40	11	0.724
1992 Atlanta	NL	41	42.0	40	13	34	1	6	4.07	15	1.262
1994 Pittsburgh	NL	22	28.2	22	10	27	3	2	5.02	7	1.116
1994 PROJECTION		22	28.2	22	10	27	3	2	5.02	7	1.110

MIKE PEREZ   Age 30/R $3

How do you know you have bullpen problems? When the BA of opposing hitters against your putative closer is .391.

Year Team	Lg.	G	IP	H	BB	SO	W	L	ERA	SV	Ratio
1991 St. Louis	NL	14	17.0	19	7	7	0	2	5.82	0	1.529
1992 St. Louis	NL	77	93.0	70	32	46	9	3	1.84	0	1.097
1993 St. Louis	NL	65	72.2	65	20	58	7	2	2.48	7	1.170
1994 St. Louis	NL	36	31.0	52	10	20	2	3	8.71	12	2.000
1994 PROJECTION		36	31.0	52	10	20	2	3	8.71	12	2.000

YORKIS PEREZ   Age 27/L $2

A great name, a great yakker, a good future.

Year Team	Lg.	G	IP	H	BB	SO	W	L	ERA	SV	Ratio
1991 Chicago	NL	3	4.1	2	2	3	1	0	2.08	0	0.923
1994 Florida	NL	44	40.2	33	14	41	3	0	3.54	0	1.156
1994 PROJECTION		67	56.0	47	20	52	3	1	4.02	0	1.196

DAN PLESAC   Age 33/L $1

Still death against left-handers (.186 BA), but from the look of that ERA, he must have been kept in to pitch to a few righties last year as well. Big mistake.

Year Team	Lg.	G	IP	H	BB	SO	W	L	ERA	SV	Ratio
1991 Milwaukee	AL	45	92.1	92	39	61	2	7	4.29	8	1.419
1992 Milwaukee	AL	44	79.0	64	35	54	5	4	2.96	1	1.253
1993 Chicago	NL	57	62.2	74	21	47	2	1	4.74	0	1.516
1994 Chicago	NL	54	54.2	61	13	53	2	3	4.61	1	1.354
1994 PROJECTION		72	75.1	83	15	72	3	4	4.30	2	1.301

ROSS POWELL   Age 27/L $1

The Astros liked what they saw last year. They'll take an even longer look this year. So will we.

Year Team	Lg.	G	IP	H	BB	SO	W	L	ERA	SV	Ratio
1993 Cincinnati	NL	9	16.1	13	6	17	0	3	4.41	0	1.163
1994 Houston	NL	12	7.1	6	5	5	0	0	1.23	0	1.500
1994 PROJECTION		25	17.0	14	11	8	0	1	2.65	0	1.470

Catchers
pp. 33–46

Corners
pp. 46–65

Infield
pp. 66–85

Outfield
pp. 85–115

DH
pp. 115–119

Starters
pp. 119–155

Relievers
pp. 155–187

STEVE REED   Age 29/R $2

Counting the games that he warmed up but wasn't called in to pitch, you have to figure Reed spent more time on the mound last year than a resin bag.

Year Team	Lg.	G	IP	H	BB	SO	W	L	ERA	SV	Ratio
1992 San Francisco	NL	18	15.2	13	3	11	1	0	2.30	0	1.021
1993 Colorado	NL	64	84.1	80	30	51	9	5	4.48	3	1.304
1994 Colorado	NL	61	64.0	79	26	51	3	2	3.94	3	1.641
1994 PROJECTION		89	95.2	111	39	75	5	5	3.86	5	1.568

RICH RODRIGUEZ   Age 32/L $1

Led all Cards relievers in appearances last season. Wonder if that will fit on his Hall of Fame plaque?

Year Team	Lg.	G	IP	H	BB	SO	W	L	ERA	SV	Ratio
1991 San Diego	NL	64	80.0	66	44	40	3	1	3.26	0	1.375
1992 San Diego	NL	61	91.0	77	29	64	6	3	2.37	0	1.165
1993 San Diego	NL	34	30.0	34	9	22	2	3	3.30	2	1.433
1993 Florida	NL	36	46.0	39	24	21	0	1	4.11	1	1.370
1994 St. Louis	NL	56	60.1	62	26	43	3	5	4.03	0	1.459
1994 PROJECTION		70	74.0	75	34	47	4	6	4.50	2	1.473

KEVIN ROGERS   Age 26/L $6

Late last July, in the clubhouse at Candlestick before a game, Dusty Baker was talking about his team: "People say that we miss Will Clark, or that we miss Robby Thompson, and of course it's true—how could we not miss guys like that? But losing Rogers was the single worst thing that happened to us this year. With him and Beck, I had the best left-right combination of any bullpen around." If Beck is still around, he will get the lion's share of the saves. But if Beck goes, Rogers has the stuff and the makeup to be Dusty's go-to guy—and is worth about five times the salary we're giving him here.

Year Team	Lg.	G	IP	H	BB	SO	W	L	ERA	SV	Ratio
1992 San Francisco	NL	6	34.0	37	13	26	0	2	4.24	0	1.471
1993 San Francisco	NL	64	80.2	71	28	62	2	2	2.68	0	1.227
1994 San Francisco	NL	9	10.1	10	6	7	0	0	3.48	0	1.548
1994 PROJECTION		15	15.2	12	9	9	0	0	2.87	1	1.340

MEL ROJAS   Age 28/R $12

"Even though he is my nephew, sometimes I would like to take this bat and pound it on his thick skull," said Felipe Alou last season when asked about Rojas stepping in when Wetteland was on the DL. "But he is a boy who is still not fully a man, so I must be patient." Just as long as Felipe doesn't hit Rojas's arm, we don't care about that other stuff. Triple his salary if the Expos deal Wetteland.

Year Team	Lg.	G	IP	H	BB	SO	W	L	ERA	SV	Ratio
1991 Montreal	NL	37	48.0	42	13	37	3	3	3.75	6	1.146
1992 Montreal	NL	68	100.2	71	34	70	7	1	1.43	10	1.043
1993 Montreal	NL	66	88.1	80	30	48	5	8	2.95	10	1.245
1994 Montreal	NL	58	84.0	71	21	84	3	2	3.32	16	1.095
1994 PROJECTION		76	106.1	99	28	106	4	3	3.64	16	1.194

BRUCE RUFFIN   Age 31/L $21

Look, miracles *do* happen. This one occurred, say the scouts, when he altered his pitching mechanics and begin to throw a 92 mph sinker for strikes. Certain Rotisserie owners remain skeptical, but their number is shrinking.

Year	Team	Lg.	G	IP	H	BB	SO	W	L	ERA	SV	Ratio
1991	Philadelphia	NL	31	119.0	125	38	85	4	7	3.78	0	1.370
1992	Milwaukee	AL	25	58.0	66	41	45	1	6	6.67	0	1.845
1993	Colorado	NL	59	139.2	145	69	126	6	5	3.87	2	1.532
1994	Colorado	NL	56	55.2	55	30	65	4	5	4.04	16	1.527
1994	PROJECTION		76	73.1	76	38	79	6	7	4.42	23	1.554

JOHNNY RUFFIN   Age 23/R $3

Good middle-innings reliever on a good team. We like that combination.

Year	Team	Lg.	G	IP	H	BB	SO	W	L	ERA	SV	Ratio
1993	Cincinnati	NL	21	37.2	36	11	30	2	1	3.58	2	1.248
1994	Cincinnati	NL	51	70.0	57	27	44	7	2	3.09	1	1.200
1994	PROJECTION		69	104.1	94	35	71	8	4	3.11	1	1.236

TIM SCOTT   Age 28/R $3

Not many people south of the border know that he throws 90-plus gas and mixes in a mean splitter on occasion. For that matter, not many people south of the border know that . . .

Year	Team	Lg.	G	IP	H	BB	SO	W	L	ERA	SV	Ratio
1991	San Diego	NL	2	1.0	2	0	1	0	0	9.00	0	2.000
1992	San Diego	NL	34	37.2	39	21	30	4	1	5.26	0	1.593
1993	San Diego	NL	24	37.2	38	15	30	2	0	2.39	0	1.407
1993	Montreal	NL	32	34.0	31	19	35	5	2	3.71	1	1.471
1994	Montreal	NL	40	53.1	51	18	37	5	2	2.70	1	1.294
1994	PROJECTION		56	75.0	77	24	50	6	4	2.52	2	1.346

JEFF SHAW   Age 28/R $2

. . . throws 90-plus gas and mixes in a mean splitter on occasion. That's what happens to players on a team laboring in bilingual anonymity in a town that couldn't care less about it, even though it was the best team in baseball last season.

Year	Team	Lg.	G	IP	H	BB	SO	W	L	ERA	SV	Ratio
1991	Cleveland	AL	29	72.1	72	27	31	0	5	3.36	1	1.369
1992	Cleveland	AL	2	7.2	7	4	3	0	1	8.22	0	1.435
1993	Montreal	NL	55	95.2	91	32	50	2	7	4.14	0	1.286
1994	Montreal	NL	46	67.1	67	15	47	5	2	3.88	1	1.218
1994	PROJECTION		59	80.1	86	18	56	6	3	4.37	1	1.294

HEATHCLIFF SLOCUMB   Age 28/R $4

Eye-popping numbers from the Phillies' bullpen workhorse last season. But don't get too caught up in the fantasy that Slocumb might step into the closer's role anytime soon: he blew all five save opportunities he had last year.

Year Team	Lg.	G	IP	H	BB	SO	W	L	ERA	SV	Ratio
1991 Chicago	NL	52	62.2	53	30	34	2	1	3.45	1	1.324
1992 Chicago	NL	30	36.0	52	21	27	0	3	6.50	1	2.028
1993 Chicago	NL	10	10.2	7	4	4	1	0	3.38	0	1.031
1993 Cleveland	AL	20	27.1	28	16	18	3	1	4.28	0	1.610
1994 Philadelphia	NL	52	72.1	75	28	58	5	1	2.86	0	1.424
1994 PROJECTION		67	94.1	104	33	72	7	2	3.05	1	1.452

MIKE STANTON   Age 27/L $7

Virtually to a man, Braves executives view Stanton as the biggest disappointment in the organization. But none of them is ready to throw in the towel: Stanton still has the stuff, and he's only 27.

Year Team	Lg.	G	IP	H	BB	SO	W	L	ERA	SV	Ratio
1991 Atlanta	NL	74	78.0	62	21	54	5	5	2.88	7	1.064
1992 Atlanta	NL	65	63.2	59	20	44	5	4	4.10	8	1.241
1993 Atlanta	NL	63	52.0	51	29	43	4	6	4.67	27	1.538
1994 Atlanta	NL	49	45.2	41	26	35	3	1	3.55	3	1.467
1994 PROJECTION		72	68.2	66	36	47	6	1	3.15	6	1.485

ISMAEL VALDES   Age 21/R $5

Call him Ismael if you want, but with his gas you ought to call him Exxon Valdés. The Dodgers love his Hershiser-like mechanics and poise. We love the 1.118 ratio in three minor league seasons coming into last year. We love the fact that his *highest* minor league ERA was 2.42. Do we love him as a starter, which is what he's always been before last season? Yeah. A little less than as a closer-in-training. But yeah, we still love him. And we especially love the idea of getting him cheap, at least this once.

Year Team ·	Lg.	G	IP	H	BB	SO	W	L	ERA	SV	Ratio
1994 Los Angeles	NL	21	28.1	21	10	28	3	1	3.18	0	1.094
1994 PROJECTION		30	53.0	48	20	47	5	3	3.40	0	1.283

DAVE VERES   Age 28/R $2

With his third organization, he has developed an excellent changeup and may have found a permanent home in Houston.

Year Team	Lg.	G	IP	H	BB	SO	W	L	ERA	SV	Ratio
1994 Houston	NL	32	41.0	39	7	28	3	3	2.41	1	1.122
1994 PROJECTION		49	75.1	67	16	49	5	4	2.51	1	1.102

GARY WAYNE   Age 32/L $1

No.

Year Team	Lg.	G	IP	H	BB	SO	W	L	ERA	SV	Ratio
1991 Minnesota	AL	8	12.1	11	4	7	1	0	5.11	1	1.216
1992 Minnesota	AL	41	48.0	46	19	29	3	3	2.63	0	1.354
1993 Colorado	NL	65	62.1	68	26	49	5	3	5.05	1	1.508
1994 Los Angeles	NL	19	17.1	19	6	10	1	3	4.67	0	1.442
1994 PROJECTION		19	17.1	19	6	10	1	3	4.67	0	1.440

JOHN WETTELAND   Age 28/R $41

Some will take Beck. Others might opt for a healthy Harvey or Nasty Boy Myers. But Wetteland has the best stuff in the National League. He's *our* number one pick.

Year	Team	Lg.	G	IP	H	BB	SO	W	L	ERA	SV	Ratio
1991	Los Angeles	NL	6	9.0	5	3	9	1	0	0.00	0	0.889
1992	Montreal	NL	67	83.1	64	36	99	4	4	2.92	37	1.200
1993	Montreal	NL	70	85.1	58	28	113	9	3	1.37	43	1.008
1994	Montreal	NL	52	63.2	46	21	68	4	6	2.83	25	1.052
1994	PROJECTION		68	80.0	62	23	79	5	8	2.70	34	1.062

RICK WHITE   Age 26/R $9

The Pirates like his potential. But last season he let 10 of 18 inherited runners score, he blew a third of his save opportunities, and opposing batters hit .280 against him. We're reserving judgment until we've had a second look.

Year	Team	Lg.	G	IP	H	BB	SO	W	L	ERA	SV	Ratio
1994	Pittsburgh	NL	43	75.1	79	17	38	4	5	3.82	6	1.274
1994	PROJECTION		54	140.1	160	27	66	10	6	3.72	6	1.332

MITCH WILLIAMS   Age 30/L $5

An Angel from Hell.

Year	Team	Lg.	G	IP	H	BB	SO	W	L	ERA	SV	Ratio
1991	Philadelphia	NL	69	88.1	56	62	84	12	5	2.34	30	1.336
1992	Philadelphia	NL	66	81.0	69	64	74	5	8	3.78	29	1.642
1993	Philadelphia	NL	65	62.0	56	44	60	3	7	3.34	43	1.613
1994	Houston	NL	25	20.0	21	24	21	1	4	7.65	6	2.250
1994	PROJECTION		25	20.0	21	24	21	1	4	7.65	6	2.250

MARK WOHLERS   Age 25/R $4

The small minority of Braves executives who don't view Stanton as the biggest disappointment in the organization give the nod to Wohlers. But none of them is ready to throw in the towel: the 95 mph man still has the stuff, and he's only 25.

Year	Team	Lg.	G	IP	H	BB	SO	W	L	ERA	SV	Ratio
1991	Atlanta	NL	17	19.2	17	13	13	3	1	3.20	2	1.525
1992	Atlanta	NL	32	35.1	28	14	17	1	2	2.55	4	1.189
1993	Atlanta	NL	46	48.0	37	22	45	6	2	4.50	0	1.229
1994	Atlanta	NL	51	51.0	51	33	58	7	2	4.59	1	1.647
1994	PROJECTION		69	65.2	68	40	70	9	3	4.93	2	1.644

TODD WORRELL   Age 35/R $8

Still not all the way back, and this year the competition gets tough with a lot of new, young arms in the Dodgers bullpen. Plus, Tommy Lasorda has always been disposed to the committee approach. After last season's unpleasantness between the two of them, you can also figure that Tommy will be looking for excuses to replace Worrell as chairman.

Year	Team	Lg.	G	IP	H	BB	SO	W	L	ERA	SV	Ratio
1992	St. Louis	NL	67	64.0	45	25	64	5	3	2.11	3	1.094
1993	Los Angeles	NL	35	38.2	46	11	31	1	1	6.05	5	1.474
1994	Los Angeles	NL	38	42.0	37	12	44	6	5	4.29	11	1.167
1994	PROJECTION		57	64.0	53	15	61	6	6	3.23	22	1.062

Catchers
pp. 33–46

Corners
pp. 46–65

Infield
pp. 66–85

Outfield
pp. 85–115

DH
pp. 115–119

Starters
pp. 119–155

Relievers
pp. 155–187

AMERICAN LEAGUE

MARK ACRE   Age 26/R $10

At 6'8", 240 pounds, Acre has a head start on becoming the whole nine yards. He promises big value down the road, initially as a set-up man and then maybe as Eck's successor. And if the Raiders move back to Oakland, he can always play a little tight end.

Year Team	Lg.	G	IP	H	BB	SO	W	L	ERA	SV	Ratio
1994 Oakland	AL	34	34.1	24	23	21	5	1	3.41	0	1.369
1994 PROJECTION		56	60.0	40	49	32	5	1	3.60	1	1.483

RICK AGUILERA   Age 33/R $30

Many times last season he went more than a week without a save opportunity. We'd prefer to see him dealt to a contender. So would he.

Year Team	Lg.	G	IP	H	BB	SO	W	L	ERA	SV	Ratio
1991 Minnesota	AL	63	69.0	44	30	61	4	5	2.35	42	1.072
1992 Minnesota	AL	64	66.2	60	17	52	2	6	2.84	41	1.155
1993 Minnesota	AL	65	72.1	60	14	59	4	3	3.11	34	1.023
1994 Minnesota	AL	44	44.2	57	10	46	1	4	3.63	23	1.500
1994 PROJECTION		61	58.0	74	13	64	1	7	4.03	31	1.500

PAUL ASSENMACHER   Age 34/L $1

Has left arm, will travel.

Year Team	Lg.	G	IP	H	BB	SO	W	L	ERA	SV	Ratio
1991 Chicago	NL	75	102.2	85	31	117	7	8	3.24	15	1.130
1992 Chicago	NL	70	68.0	72	26	67	4	4	4.10	8	1.441
1993 Chicago	NL	46	38.2	44	13	34	2	1	3.49	0	1.474
1993 New York	AL	26	17.1	10	9	11	2	2	3.12	0	1.096
1994 Chicago	AL	44	33.0	26	13	29	1	2	3.55	1	1.182
1994 PROJECTION		63	46.1	40	14	39	2	3	3.50	3	1.165

JOE AUSANIO   Age 29/R $1

Has right arm, will travel.

Year Team	Lg.	G	IP	H	BB	SO	W	L	ERA	SV	Ratio
1994 New York	AL	13	15.2	16	6	15	2	1	5.17	0	1.404
1994 PROJECTION		31	36.2	39	13	33	4	1	3.44	0	1.418

BOBBY AYALA   Age 25/R $23

Considering that he was learning how to be a closer for what was one of the worst pitching staffs on earth under a manager whose idea of patience is punching out windows in a McDonald's drive-thru lane when the Big Mac isn't ready, Ayala made outstanding progress. He has the stuff to be a genuine save machine, assuming Seattle enters the ninth inning with a lead often enough.

Year Team	Lg.	G	IP	H	BB	SO	W	L	ERA	SV	Ratio
1992 Cincinnati	NL	5	29.0	33	13	23	2	1	4.34	0	1.586
1993 Cincinnati	NL	43	98.0	106	45	65	7	10	5.60	3	1.541
1994 Seattle	AL	46	56.2	42	26	76	4	3	2.86	18	1.200
1994 PROJECTION		68	80.2	55	29	106	4	4	2.57	35	1.041

SCOTT BANKHEAD   Age 31/R $1

Account overdrawn, but he could make a few deposits as a middle man in Yankee Stadium.

Year	Team	Lg.	G	IP	H	BB	SO	W	L	ERA	SV	Ratio
1991	Seattle	AL	17	60.2	73	21	28	3	6	4.90	0	1.549
1992	Cincinnati	NL	54	70.2	57	29	53	10	4	2.93	1	1.217
1993	Boston	AL	40	64.1	59	29	47	2	1	3.50	0	1.368
1994	Boston	AL	27	37.2	34	12	25	3	2	4.54	0	1.221
1994	PROJECTION		42	57.0	56	20	40	4	5	4.74	1	1.333

STAN BELINDA   Age 28/R $2

Now just a journeyman, but don't expect to go anywhere with him on your staff.

Year	Team	Lg.	G	IP	H	BB	SO	W	L	ERA	SV	Ratio
1991	Pittsburgh	NL	60	78.1	50	35	71	7	5	3.45	16	1.085
1992	Pittsburgh	NL	59	71.1	58	29	57	6	4	3.15	18	1.220
1993	Pittsburgh	NL	40	42.1	35	11	30	3	1	3.61	19	1.087
1993	Kansas City	AL	23	27.1	30	6	25	1	1	4.28	0	1.317
1994	Kansas City	AL	37	49.0	47	24	37	2	2	5.14	1	1.449
1994	PROJECTION		53	67.1	68	28	53	2	2	4.28	1	1.426

JOE BOEVER   Age 34/R $7

A season that middle relievers dream about—Boever's nine wins last year were the second highest total on the Detroit staff. Seasons like that are generally unpredictable: a vulture doesn't have regular mealtimes. But given the combination of awful starting pitching and tremendous offensive firepower in Detroit, Boever is a better than even bet to enjoy another win feast this summer.

Year	Team	Lg.	G	IP	H	BB	SO	W	L	ERA	SV	Ratio
1991	Philadelphia	NL	68	98.1	90	54	89	3	5	3.84	0	1.464
1992	Houston	NL	81	111.1	103	45	67	3	6	2.51	2	1.329
1993	Oakland	AL	42	79.1	87	33	49	4	2	3.86	0	1.513
1993	Detroit	AL	19	23.0	14	11	14	2	1	2.74	3	1.087
1994	Detroit	AL	46	81.1	80	37	49	9	2	3.98	3	1.439
1994	PROJECTION		69	111.0	105	48	69	13	5	4.14	4	1.378

BILLY BREWER   Age 26/L $5

Milwaukee should trade for him. Not only would he instantly become the best pitcher in the Brewers bullpen, but he could double in brass as the franchise's mascot. Think of the money this would save the Commish! In Kansas City, all Brewer can look forward to is setting up saves for Jeff Montgomery and picking up an S or two in his own right when Montgomery can't work. Last year he handled that job reasonably well, and not just by nailing left-handed hitters: lefties hit .246 off him, righties only .179.

Year	Team	Lg.	G	IP	H	BB	SO	W	L	ERA	SV	Ratio
1993	Kansas City	AL	46	39.0	31	20	28	2	2	3.46	0	1.308
1994	Kansas City	AL	50	38.2	28	16	25	4	1	2.56	3	1.138
1994	PROJECTION		65	47.1	38	20	30	4	3	3.23	3	1.225

JOHN BRISCOE　　　　　　　　　　　　　Age 27/R　　　$6

After Dave Duncan, the A's pitching doctor, tinkered with his delivery and changed the grip on his fastball, Briscoe became much more difficult to hit. Next he needs to learn to throw more strikes.

Year Team	Lg.	G	IP	H	BB	SO	W	L	ERA	SV	Ratio
1991 Oakland	AL	11	14.0	12	10	9	0	0	7.07	0	1.571
1992 Oakland	AL	2	7.0	12	9	4	0	1	6.43	0	3.000
1993 Oakland	AL	17	24.2	26	26	24	1	0	8.03	0	2.108
1994 Oakland	AL	37	49.1	31	39	45	4	2	4.01	1	1.419
1994 PROJECTION		65	90.2	46	58	85	5	4	3.47	2	1.147

SCOTT BROW　　　　　　　　　　　　　Age 26/R　　　$2

There remains some hope he can emerge as a closer candidate, but as one member of the Toronto brain trust put it last summer, "Until his aggressiveness catches up to his stuff, and until he stops giving the hitters too much credit, he's never going to be the guy you look to in late innings."

Year Team	Lg.	G	IP	H	BB	SO	W	L	ERA	SV	Ratio
1993 Toronto	AL	6	18.0	19	10	7	1	1	6.00	0	1.611
1994 Toronto	AL	18	29.0	34	19	15	0	3	5.90	2	1.828
1994 PROJECTION		19	30.1	37	20	16	0	4	5.93	2	1.879

MIKE BUTCHER　　　　　　　　　　　　Age 28/R　　　$2

The Angels thought he had a chance to be a solid part of their rebuilt bullpen. Think again.

Year Team	Lg.	G	IP	H	BB	SO	W	L	ERA	SV	Ratio
1992 California	AL	19	27.2	29	13	24	2	2	3.25	0	1.518
1993 California	AL	23	28.1	21	15	24	1	0	2.86	8	1.271
1994 California	AL	33	29.2	31	23	19	2	1	6.67	1	1.820
1994 PROJECTION		42	39.2	41	26	24	4	2	5.67	1	1.689

GREG CADARET　　　　　　　　　　　　Age 33/L　　　$1

As one of those left-handers with nine lives who keeps getting dumped from team to team, it was only a matter of time before he wound up in Tiger Stadium.

Year Team	Lg.	G	IP	H	BB	SO	W	L	ERA	SV	Ratio
1991 New York	AL	68	121.2	110	59	105	8	6	3.62	3	1.389
1992 New York	AL	46	103.2	104	74	73	4	8	4.25	1	1.717
1993 Cincinnati	NL	34	32.2	40	23	23	2	1	4.96	1	1.929
1993 Kansas City	AL	13	15.1	14	7	2	1	1	2.93	0	1.370
1994 Toronto	AL	21	20.0	24	17	15	0	1	5.85	0	2.050
1994 Detroit	AL	17	20.0	17	16	14	1	0	3.60	2	1.650
1994 PROJECTION		55	47.2	55	40	34	1	1	5.29	2	1.993

CRIS CARPENTER　　　　　　　　　　　Age 29/R　　　$3

We still think he is a better pitcher than he has shown. It's just hard to tell amid the wreckage of that Texas pitching staff.

Year Team	Lg.	G	IP	H	BB	SO	W	L	ERA	SV	Ratio
1991 St. Louis	NL	59	66.0	53	20	47	10	4	4.23	0	1.106
1992 St. Louis	NL	73	88.0	69	27	46	5	4	2.97	1	1.091
1993 Florida	NL	29	37.1	29	13	26	0	1	2.89	0	1.125
1993 Texas	AL	27	32.0	35	12	27	4	1	4.22	1	1.469
1994 Texas	AL	47	59.0	69	20	39	2	5	5.03	5	1.508
1994 PROJECTION		66	79.0	82	22	47	5	6	4.22	5	1.316

LARRY CASIAN   Age 29/L $1

Here's a possible exception to the rule that any left-hander with a pulse will always have a job in major league baseball.

Year Team	Lg.	G	IP	H	BB	SO	W	L	ERA	SV	Ratio
1991 Minnesota	AL	15	18.1	28	7	6	0	0	7.36	0	1.909
1992 Minnesota	AL	6	6.2	7	1	2	1	0	2.70	0	1.200
1993 Minnesota	AL	54	56.2	59	14	31	5	3	3.02	1	1.288
1994 Minnesota	AL	33	40.2	57	12	18	1	3	7.08	1	1.697
1994 Cleveland	AL	7	8.1	16	4	2	0	2	8.64	0	2.400
1994 PROJECTION		56	63.2	91	19	23	1	6	6.50	1	1.728

TONY CASTILLO   Age 32/L $3

Solid year, but not someone you want to build your pennant dreams around.

Year Team	Lg.	G	IP	H	BB	SO	W	L	ERA	SV	Ratio
1991 Atlanta	NL	7	8.2	13	5	8	1	1	7.27	0	2.077
1991 New York	NL	10	23.2	27	6	10	1	0	1.90	0	1.394
1993 Toronto	AL	51	50.2	44	22	28	3	2	3.38	0	1.303
1994 Toronto	AL	41	68.0	66	28	43	5	2	2.51	1	1.382
1994 PROJECTION		57	80.2	87	32	50	5	3	3.12	1	1.475

DENNIS COOK   Age 32/L $1

Solid year, but not someone you want to build your pennant dreams around.

Year Team	Lg.	G	IP	H	BB	SO	W	L	ERA	SV	Ratio
1991 Los Angeles	NL	20	17.2	12	7	8	1	0	0.51	0	1.075
1992 Cleveland	AL	32	158.0	156	50	96	5	7	3.82	0	1.304
1993 Cleveland	AL	25	54.0	62	16	34	5	5	5.67	0	1.444
1994 Chicago	AL	38	33.0	29	14	26	3	1	3.55	0	1.303
1994 PROJECTION		54	53.0	40	20	45	4	1	3.06	0	1.132

DANNY COX   Age 35/R $9

He came back from elbow injury late in the season and threw as well as ever. Bet you never thought you'd hear a major league manager, much less the manager of the reigning World Champions, say, "We just couldn't make up for the loss of Cox."

Year Team	Lg.	G	IP	H	BB	SO	W	L	ERA	SV	Ratio
1991 Philadelphia	NL	23	102.1	98	39	46	4	6	4.57	0	1.339
1992 Philadelphia	NL	9	38.1	46	19	30	2	2	5.40	0	1.696
1992 Pittsburgh	NL	16	24.1	20	8	18	3	1	3.33	3	1.151
1993 Toronto	AL	44	83.2	73	29	84	7	6	3.12	2	1.219
1994 Toronto	AL	10	18.2	7	7	14	1	1	1.45	3	0.750
1994 PROJECTION		23	38.2	28	17	27	2	3	3.03	4	1.164

Catchers
pp. 33–46

Corners
pp. 46–65

Infield
pp. 66–85

Outfield
pp. 85–115

DH
pp. 115–119

Starters
pp. 119–155

Relievers
pp. 155–187

STORM DAVIS   Age 33/R $1

Let the storm pass.

Year	Team	Lg.	G	IP	H	BB	SO	W	L	ERA	SV	Ratio
1991	Kansas City	AL	51	114.1	140	46	53	3	9	4.96	2	1.627
1992	Baltimore	AL	48	89.1	79	36	53	7	3	3.43	4	1.287
1993	Oakland	AL	19	62.2	68	33	37	2	6	6.18	0	1.612
1993	Detroit	AL	24	35.1	25	15	36	0	2	3.06	4	1.132
1994	Detroit	AL	35	48.0	36	34	38	2	4	3.56	0	1.458
1994	PROJECTION		50	73.1	49	50	56	4	5	2.95	0	1.350

TIM DAVIS   Age 24/L $2

Had never pitched above Class A when he showed up on the Mariners' Opening Day roster. Performed well, all things considered. Look for some improvement.

Year	Team	Lg.	G	IP	H	BB	SO	W	L	ERA	SV	Ratio
1994	Seattle	AL	42	49.1	57	25	28	2	2	4.01	2	1.662
1994	PROJECTION		51	70.2	86	33	41	2	4	4.71	2	1.684

JOSE DELEON   Age 34/R $5

Someone you bring in when your starter gets knocked out early. He throws gas for a couple of innings and gives your team a chance to catch up. The downside is that he does this for the White Sox, whose starters rarely get knocked out early. Still has dazzling stuff: opposing hitters batted just .200 against him last tear.

Year	Team	Lg.	G	IP	H	BB	SO	W	L	ERA	SV	Ratio
1991	St. Louis	NL	28	162.2	144	61	118	5	9	2.71	0	1.260
1992	St. Louis	NL	29	102.1	95	43	72	2	7	4.57	0	1.349
1992	Philadelphia	NL	3	15.0	16	5	7	0	1	3.00	0	1.400
1993	Philadelphia	NL	24	47.0	39	27	34	3	0	3.26	0	1.404
1993	Chicago	AL	11	10.1	5	3	6	0	0	1.74	0	0.774
1994	Chicago	AL	42	67.0	48	31	67	3	2	3.36	2	1.179
1994	PROJECTION		62	98.0	63	47	99	5	3	2.94	3	1.122

DENNIS ECKERSLEY   Age 40/R $25

The Eck at 39. *Tony LaRussa:* "We never gave Eck a chance to find a groove. We didn't work him enough in spring training, and then we stunk for the first six weeks." *An AL advance scout:* "He still looks like Eck, and he still thinks like Eck, and he still competes like Eck. He just doesn't throw like Eck anymore." *An established AL hitter:* "You used to be 0 and 2 against him when you were still in the on-deck circle. Now, you feel like you're starting out even. That's a big difference." *Us:* "It ain't over 'till it's over."

Year	Team	Lg.	G	IP	H	BB	SO	W	L	ERA	SV	Ratio
1991	Oakland	AL	67	76.0	60	9	87	5	4	2.96	43	0.908
1992	Oakland	AL	69	80.0	62	11	93	7	1	1.91	51	0.913
1993	Oakland	AL	64	67.0	67	13	80	2	4	4.16	36	1.194
1994	Oakland	AL	45	44.1	49	13	47	5	4	4.26	19	1.398
1994	PROJECTION		57	57.2	61	16	61	6	6	4.21	24	1.335

MARK EICHHORN
Age 34/R   **$7**

He proved to be a staff-saver for Baltimore, leading all Orioles relievers in innings. Stranded 76% of the runners he inherited. Gave up just one home run. New skipper Phil Regan will surely take note.

Year Team	Lg.	G	IP	H	BB	SO	W	L	ERA	SV	Ratio
1991 California	AL	70	81.2	63	13	49	3	3	1.98	1	0.931
1992 California	AL	42	56.2	51	18	42	2	4	2.38	2	1.218
1992 Toronto	AL	23	31.0	35	7	19	2	0	4.35	0	1.355
1993 Toronto	AL	54	72.2	76	22	47	3	1	2.72	0	1.349
1994 Baltimore	AL	43	71.0	62	19	35	6	5	2.15	1	1.141
1994 PROJECTION		57	91.2	80	22	44	8	6	1.96	1	1.113

STEVE FARR
Age 38/R   **$1**

Not even close.

Year Team	Lg.	G	IP	H	BB	SO	W	L	ERA	SV	Ratio
1991 New York	AL	60	70.0	57	20	60	5	5	2.19	23	1.100
1992 New York	AL	50	52.0	34	19	37	2	2	1.56	30	1.019
1993 New York	AL	49	47.0	44	28	39	2	2	4.21	25	1.532
1994 Cleveland	AL	19	15.1	17	15	12	1	1	5.28	4	2.087
1994 Boston	AL	11	13.0	24	3	8	1	0	6.23	0	2.077
1994 PROJECTION		46	44.0	67	28	33	3	5	6.14	4	2.159

MIKE FETTERS
Age 30/R   **$29**

Quietly blossomed as a top-notch closer on a bottom-notch team.

Year Team	Lg.	G	IP	H	BB	SO	W	L	ERA	SV	Ratio
1991 California	AL	19	44.2	53	28	24	2	5	4.84	0	1.813
1992 Milwaukee	AL	50	62.2	38	24	43	5	1	1.87	2	0.989
1993 Milwaukee	AL	45	59.1	59	22	23	3	3	3.34	0	1.365
1994 Milwaukee	AL	42	46.0	41	27	31	1	4	2.54	17	1.478
1994 PROJECTION		55	57.1	55	37	40	2	6	3.30	23	1.604

TONY FOSSAS
Age 37/L   **$1**

Another one of those vampire lefties who won't die.

Year Team	Lg.	G	IP	H	BB	SO	W	L	ERA	SV	Ratio
1991 Boston	AL	64	57.0	49	28	29	3	2	3.47	1	1.351
1992 Boston	AL	60	29.2	31	14	19	1	2	2.43	2	1.517
1993 Boston	AL	71	40.0	38	15	39	1	1	5.18	0	1.325
1994 Boston	AL	44	34.0	35	15	31	2	0	4.76	1	1.471
1994 PROJECTION		57	42.2	47	26	39	2	2	6.12	1	1.711

MIKE GARDINER
Age 29/R   **$3**

The Tigers might try starting him this year. Good news for Gardiner, because when it comes to middle relief, the Tigers had rather leave it to Boever.

Year Team	Lg.	G	IP	H	BB	SO	W	L	ERA	SV	Ratio
1991 Boston	AL	22	130.0	140	47	91	9	10	4.85	0	1.438
1992 Boston	AL	28	130.2	126	58	79	4	10	4.75	0	1.408
1993 Montreal	NL	24	38.0	40	19	21	2	3	5.21	0	1.553
1993 Detroit	AL	10	11.1	12	7	4	0	0	3.97	0	1.676
1994 Detroit	AL	38	58.2	53	23	31	2	2	4.14	5	1.295
1994 PROJECTION		53	73.0	80	29	36	2	2	5.67	5	1.493

Catchers
pp. 33–46

Corners
pp. 46–65

Infield
pp. 66–85

Outfield
pp. 85–115

DH
pp. 115–119

Starters
pp. 119–155

Relievers
pp. 155–187

PAUL GIBSON

Age 35/L $1

Will land somewhere. Not on your team, we hope.

Year Team	Lg.	G	IP	H	BB	SO	W	L	ERA	SV	Ratio
1991 Detroit	AL	68	96.0	112	48	52	5	7	4.59	8	1.667
1992 New York	NL	43	62.0	70	25	49	0	1	5.23	0	1.532
1993 New York	NL	8	8.2	14	2	12	1	1	5.19	0	1.846
1993 New York	AL	20	35.1	31	9	25	2	0	3.06	0	1.132
1994 New York	AL	30	29.0	26	17	21	1	1	4.97	0	1.483
1994 PROJECTION		41	35.2	36	21	26	1	2	5.80	0	1.598

GOOSE GOSSAGE

Age 43/R $1

According to every player who's ever been a teammate, no one loved what he did more than the Goose. We hope someone gives him a chance to keep on doing it. If not, then here's one final tip of the Rotisserie cap to one of our all-time favorites.

Year Team	Lg.	G	IP	H	BB	SO	W	L	ERA	SV	Ratio
1991 Texas	AL	44	40.1	33	16	28	4	2	3.57	1	1.215
1992 Oakland	AL	30	38.0	32	19	26	0	2	2.84	0	1.342
1993 Oakland	AL	39	47.2	49	26	40	4	5	4.53	1	1.573
1994 Seattle	AL	36	47.1	44	15	29	3	0	4.18	1	1.246
1994 PROJECTION		55	72.1	68	23	61	4	0	3.73	1	1.258

JOE GRAHE

Age 27/R $9

Opposing batters hit .362 off him. He gave up 68 hits in 43 innings. You'd need Robert Stack and his friends at "Unsolved Mysteries" to account for the 13 saves. There are less damaging ways to get 13 saves, but if the Angels keep giving him the ball in the ninth inning, you'd be crazy not to grab him for anything under ten bucks. You'll just need about 200 healthy Jimmy Key innings to offset his numbers.

Year Team	Lg.	G	IP	H	BB	SO	W	L	ERA	SV	Ratio
1991 California	AL	18	73.0	84	33	40	3	7	4.81	0	1.603
1992 California	AL	46	94.2	85	39	39	5	6	3.52	21	1.310
1993 California	AL	45	56.2	54	25	31	4	1	2.86	11	1.394
1994 California	AL	40	43.1	68	18	26	2	5	6.65	13	1.985
1994 PROJECTION		59	65.0	94	25	37	4	7	6.37	15	1.831

BUDDY GROOM

Age 29/L $1

You have to be intrigued by the prospect of owning the guy who has made the most career appearances without a victory of any active pitcher. Wouldn't the odds suggest that this might be the year for Groom to chalk up a W? Wouldn't you love to be the one who benefits from that cosmic happening?

Year Team	Lg.	G	IP	H	BB	SO	W	L	ERA	SV	Ratio
1992 Detroit	AL	12	38.2	48	22	15	0	5	5.82	1	1.810
1993 Detroit	AL	19	36.2	48	13	15	0	2	6.14	0	1.664
1994 Detroit	AL	40	32.0	31	13	27	0	1	3.94	1	1.375
1994 PROJECTION		54	50.2	50	21	40	2	2	4.26	1	1.401

MARK GUTHRIE

Age 29/L $1

On the one hand, we're inclined to write off last year as a freak slump by a solid pitcher. On the other hand, the trend line of his ERA the last three seasons suggests a second interpretation.

Year Team	Lg.	G	IP	H	BB	SO	W	L	ERA	SV	Ratio
1991 Minnesota	AL	41	98.0	116	41	72	7	5	4.32	2	1.602
1992 Minnesota	AL	54	75.0	59	23	76	2	3	2.88	5	1.093
1993 Minnesota	AL	22	21.0	20	16	15	2	1	4.71	0	1.714
1994 Minnesota	AL	50	51.1	65	18	38	4	2	6.14	1	1.617
1994 PROJECTION		73	68.0	83	27	42	4	5	5.96	1	1.617

DARREN HALL   Age 30/R $22

Hall throws strikes and gets batters to hit grounders. Not sexy, but it works. If Duane Ward hasn't mended by Opening Day, Hall gets the ball.

Year Team	Lg.	G	IP	H	BB	SO	W	L	ERA	SV	Ratio
1994 Toronto	AL	30	31.2	26	14	28	2	3	3.41	17	1.263
1994 PROJECTION		45	43.1	36	18	38	2	4	2.91	24	1.246

GENE HARRIS   Age 30/R $2

It was Leo Durocher (or maybe it was John McGraw) who coined the phrase, "A million-dollar arm and 10-cent head." It applies for this much-traveled, often-injured, still-talented hard thrower.

Year Team	Lg.	G	IP	H	BB	SO	W	L	ERA	SV	Ratio
1991 Seattle	AL	8	13.1	15	10	6	0	0	4.05	1	1.875
1992 Seattle	AL	8	9.0	8	6	6	0	0	7.00	0	1.556
1992 San Diego	NL	14	21.1	15	9	19	0	2	2.95	0	1.125
1993 San Diego	NL	59	59.1	57	37	39	6	6	3.03	23	1.584
1994 San Diego	NL	13	12.1	21	8	9	1	1	8.03	0	2.351
1994 Detroit	AL	11	11.1	13	4	10	0	0	7.15	1	1.500
1994 PROJECTION		33	40.0	49	18	27	1	1	5.63	1	1.675

GREG HARRIS   Age 39/R $1

It's now time for Harris to wave good-bye, with either hand.

Year Team	Lg.	G	IP	H	BB	SO	W	L	ERA	SV	Ratio
1991 Boston	AL	53	173.0	157	69	127	11	12	3.85	2	1.306
1992 Boston	AL	70	107.2	82	60	73	4	9	2.51	4	1.319
1993 Boston	AL	80	112.1	95	60	103	6	7	3.77	8	1.380
1994 Boston	AL	35	45.2	60	23	44	3	4	8.28	2	1.818
1994 New York	AL	3	5.0	4	3	4	0	1	5.40	0	1.400
1994 PROJECTION		38	50.2	64	26	48	3	5	7.99	2	1.776

TOM HENKE   Age 37/R $25

As the season died, with his forkball not forking and his back aching, he was strongly considering retirement. But then a phone call from St. Louis chased away his blues.

Year Team	Lg.	G	IP	H	BB	SO	W	L	ERA	SV	Ratio
1991 Toronto	AL	49	50.1	33	11	53	0	2	2.32	32	0.874
1992 Toronto	AL	57	55.2	40	22	46	3	2	2.26	34	1.114
1993 Texas	AL	66	74.1	55	27	79	5	5	2.91	40	1.103
1994 Texas	AL	37	38.0	33	12	39	3	6	3.79	15	1.184
1994 PROJECTION		53	54.0	43	19	55	4	8	3.33	26	1.148

MIKE HENNEMAN   Age 33/R $12

Henneman also declared he was going to retire because he was sick of being booed, sick of not doing the job, sick of not being 100% healthy. Anyway, Sparky laughed at the whole idea, saying, "He ain't gonna retire, he's a guy who loves to pitch and hates to lose. He's also a guy who loves money, and he ain't going to run away from all that cash."

Year Team	Lg.	G	IP	H	BB	SO	W	L	ERA	SV	Ratio
1991 Detroit	AL	60	84.1	81	34	61	10	2	2.88	21	1.364
1992 Detroit	AL	60	77.1	75	20	58	2	6	3.96	24	1.228
1993 Detroit	AL	63	71.2	69	32	58	5	3	2.64	24	1.409
1994 Detroit	AL	30	34.2	43	17	27	1	3	5.19	8	1.731
1994 PROJECTION		45	49.0	56	21	41	1	4	4.41	18	1.571

DOUG HENRY   Age 31/R $1

We'd rather not.

Year Team	Lg.	G	IP	H	BB	SO	W	L	ERA	SV	Ratio
1991 Milwaukee	AL	32	36.0	16	14	28	2	1	1.00	15	0.833
1992 Milwaukee	AL	68	65.0	64	24	52	1	4	4.02	29	1.354
1993 Milwaukee	AL	54	55.0	67	25	38	4	4	5.56	17	1.673
1994 Milwaukee	AL	25	31.1	32	23	20	2	3	4.60	0	1.755
1994 PROJECTION		36	44.0	45	27	27	3	5	4.50	0	1.636

ROBERTO HERNANDEZ   Age 30/R $37

When he was kicking away saves and his ERA was soaring, did the White Sox panic? Did they shop for another closer? Did they exile him to long relief? Nah, they just fired the bullpen coach, whereupon the big guy regained the killer slider and sinking fastball that let the Hawk scream "Grab some bench!" every time he Ks another hitter.

Year Team	Lg.	G	IP	H	BB	SO	W	L	ERA	SV	Ratio
1991 Chicago	AL	9	15.0	18	7	6	1	0	7.80	0	1.667
1992 Chicago	AL	43	71.0	45	20	68	7	3	1.65	12	0.915
1993 Chicago	AL	70	78.2	66	20	71	3	4	2.29	38	1.093
1994 Chicago	AL	45	47.2	44	19	50	4	4	4.91	14	1.322
1994 PROJECTION		59	62.1	52	19	64	5	4	3.90	26	1.139

XAVIER HERNANDEZ   Age 29/R $6

The Yankees have made a lot of smart moves the last few years, thanks mostly to Gene Michael. This was not one of them.

Year Team	Lg.	G	IP	H	BB	SO	W	L	ERA	SV	Ratio
1991 Houston	NL	32	63.0	66	32	55	2	7	4.71	3	1.556
1992 Houston	NL	77	111.0	81	42	96	9	1	2.11	7	1.108
1993 Houston	NL	72	96.2	75	28	101	4	5	2.61	9	1.066
1994 New York	AL	31	40.0	48	21	37	4	4	5.85	6	1.725
1994 PROJECTION		40	50.2	58	27	44	5	4	5.68	6	1.677

RICK HONEYCUTT   Age 40/L $1

A good warrior who might have pitched his last season. For his longevity and ability to adapt to a specialized relief role, he will remain the idol of fringe lefties like . . .

Year Team	Lg.	G	IP	H	BB	SO	W	L	ERA	SV	Ratio
1991 Oakland	AL	43	37.2	37	20	26	2	4	3.58	0	1.513
1992 Oakland	AL	54	39.0	41	10	32	1	4	3.69	3	1.308
1993 Oakland	AL	52	41.2	30	20	21	1	4	2.81	1	1.200
1994 Texas	AL	42	25.0	37	9	18	1	2	7.20	1	1.840
1994 PROJECTION		47	32.1	45	13	27	1	2	6.40	1	1.794

VINCE HORSMAN   Age 28/L $1

... and ...

Year Team	Lg.	G	IP	H	BB	SO	W	L	ERA	SV	Ratio
1991 Toronto	AL	4	4.0	2	3	2	0	0	0.00	0	1.250
1992 Oakland	AL	58	43.1	39	21	18	2	1	2.49	1	1.385
1993 Oakland	AL	40	25.0	25	15	17	2	0	5.40	0	1.600
1994 Oakland	AL	33	29.1	29	11	20	0	1	4.91	0	1.364
1994 PROJECTION		46	42.2	44	16	23	0	2	4.85	0	1.406

CHRIS HOWARD   Age 29/L $1

..., who had a better year than the other two, but not good enough to come in from the fringe.

Year Team	Lg.	G	IP	H	BB	SO	W	L	ERA	SV	Ratio
1993 Chicago	AL	3	2.1	2	3	1	1	0	0.00	0	2.143
1994 Boston	AL	37	39.2	35	12	22	1	0	3.63	1	1.185
1994 PROJECTION		54	59.1	53	16	32	2	0	3.34	1	1.163

STEVE HOWE   Age 37/L $19

Showed up at one of the negotiating sessions and yelled at the owners about "lacking integrity" and "not being straight with the public." He should know.

Year Team	Lg.	G	IP	H	BB	SO	W	L	ERA	SV	Ratio
1991 New York	AL	37	48.1	39	7	34	3	1	1.68	3	0.952
1992 New York	AL	20	22.0	9	3	12	3	0	2.45	6	0.545
1993 New York	AL	51	50.2	58	10	19	3	5	4.97	4	1.342
1994 New York	AL	40	40.0	28	7	18	3	0	1.80	15	0.875
1994 PROJECTION		55	53.1	34	8	27	3	0	1.52	28	0.788

JAY HOWELL   Age 39/R $1

A great competitor, but he may have thrown his last heater.

Year Team	Lg.	G	IP	H	BB	SO	W	L	ERA	SV	Ratio
1991 Los Angeles	NL	44	51.0	39	11	40	6	5	3.18	16	0.980
1992 Los Angeles	NL	41	46.2	41	18	36	1	3	1.54	4	1.264
1993 Atlanta	NL	54	58.1	48	16	37	3	3	2.31	0	1.097
1994 Texas	AL	40	43.0	44	16	22	4	1	5.44	2	1.395
1994 PROJECTION		53	57.2	59	26	30	4	1	5.46	2	1.474

DAVE LEIPER   Age 32/L $3

On a staff that included the Ontiveros Miracle and the Billy Taylor Saga, here's another amazing story of a lefty who came back from heart problems to be as nasty a specialty reliever as there was in the league.

Year Team	Lg.	G	IP	H	BB	SO	W	L	ERA	SV	Ratio
1994 Oakland	AL	26	18.2	13	6	14	0	0	1.93	1	1.018
1994 PROJECTION		42	34.2	26	11	19	1	2	1.82	2	1.067

Catchers
pp. 33-46

Corners
pp. 46-65

Infield
pp. 66-85

Outfield
pp. 85-115

DH
pp. 115-119

Starters
pp. 119-155

Relievers
pp. 155-187

DEREK LILLIQUIST Age 29/L $5

One of the Indians' few big disappointments in their best season since 1954. Write it off as a bad year. And if he has another one, the Braves can always use him as a pinch hitter.

Year Team	Lg.	G	IP	H	BB	SO	W	L	ERA	SV	Ratio
1991 San Diego	NL	6	14.1	25	4	7	0	2	8.79	0	2.023
1992 Cleveland	AL	71	61.2	39	18	47	5	3	1.75	6	0.924
1993 Cleveland	AL	56	64.0	64	19	40	4	4	2.25	10	1.297
1994 Cleveland	AL	36	29.1	34	8	15	1	3	4.91	1	1.432
1994 PROJECTION		51	49.2	52	12	26	3	3	4.17	1	1.288

GRAEME LLOYD Age 27/L $5

If you think it was a sophomore slump, pick him up cheap. We think the emergence of Fetters means Lloyd will be nothing more than a bullpen bit player.

Year Team	Lg.	G	IP	H	BB	SO	W	L	ERA	SV	Ratio
1993 Milwaukee	AL	55	63.2	64	13	31	3	4	2.83	0	1.209
1994 Milwaukee	AL	43	47.0	49	15	31	2	3	5.17	3	1.362
1994 PROJECTION		60	61.0	67	18	42	2	4	4.72	3	1.393

KIRK McCASKILL Age 33/R $2

Has added three feet to his fastball and found a second career as a middle reliever. Unfortunately, that translates into precious little Rotisserie value.

Year Team	Lg.	G	IP	H	BB	SO	W	L	ERA	SV	Ratio
1991 California	AL	30	177.2	193	66	71	10	19	4.26	0	1.458
1992 Chicago	AL	34	209.0	193	95	109	12	13	4.18	0	1.378
1993 Chicago	AL	30	113.2	144	36	65	4	8	5.23	2	1.584
1994 Chicago	AL	40	52.2	51	22	37	1	4	3.42	3	1.386
1994 PROJECTION		62	75.1	73	30	53	6	4	3.58	3	1.367

RUSTY MEACHAM Age 27/R $1

Middling good middle man.

Year Team	Lg.	G	IP	H	BB	SO	W	L	ERA	SV	Ratio
1991 Detroit	AL	10	27.2	35	11	14	2	1	5.20	0	1.663
1992 Kansas City	AL	64	101.2	88	21	64	10	4	2.74	2	1.072
1993 Kansas City	AL	15	21.0	31	5	13	2	2	5.57	0	1.714
1994 Kansas City	AL	36	50.2	51	12	36	3	3	3.73	4	1.243
1994 PROJECTION		55	67.2	65	17	50	6	5	3.59	4	1.212

JOSE MERCEDES Age 24/R $4

Plucked out of the Orioles organization, Mercedes had moments when he looked like a luxury model. He'd be worth more on a better team.

Year Team	Lg.	G	IP	H	BB	SO	W	L	ERA	SV	Ratio
1994 Milwaukee	AL	19	31.0	22	16	11	2	0	2.32	0	1.226
1994 PROJECTION		36	49.2	44	27	20	7	2	3.08	0	1.429

JOSE MESA Age 28/R $9

Mesa has always had nasty stuff, and last year he finally used it to full advantage in his first full season as a reliever. Considering how the Indians score runs, he should dine more often than your average middle-inning vulture. He might even get a shot at the closer role if Jeff Russell's elbow acts up.

Catchers
pp. 33–46

Corners
pp. 46–65

Infield
pp. 66–85

Outfield
pp. 85–115

DH
pp. 115–119

Starters
pp. 119–155

Relievers
pp. 155–187

Year Team	Lg.	G	IP	H	BB	SO	W	L	ERA	SV	Ratio
1991 Baltimore	AL	23	123.2	151	62	64	6	11	5.97	0	1.722
1992 Baltimore	AL	13	67.2	77	27	22	3	8	5.19	0	1.537
1992 Cleveland	AL	15	93.0	92	43	40	4	4	4.16	0	1.452
1993 Cleveland	AL	34	208.2	232	62	118	10	12	4.92	0	1.409
1994 Cleveland	AL	51	73.0	71	26	63	7	5	3.82	2	1.329
1994 PROJECTION		70	97.2	99	33	88	7	7	3.96	4	1.351

ALAN MILLS   Age 28/R $3

"His stuff is as good as anyone's in the league, but he just has this knack for serving up bombs," said his ex-manager Johnny Oates. Says Mills, "He ain't lying. I give up some awesome shots. I remember one I served up to Tettleton. I mean, this ball was so high that it was above the light towers and it still went over that back right-field fence at Camden Yards. If he didn't get under it so much, that sucker would have smashed the warehouse." It's nice that he appreciates what hitters do to his pitches, because he has yet to do much with all his stuff.

Year Team	Lg.	G	IP	H	BB	SO	W	L	ERA	SV	Ratio
1991 New York	AL	6	16.1	16	8	11	1	1	4.41	0	1.469
1992 Baltimore	AL	35	103.1	78	54	60	10	4	2.61	2	1.277
1993 Baltimore	AL	45	100.1	80	51	68	5	4	3.23	4	1.306
1994 Baltimore	AL	47	45.1	43	24	44	3	3	5.16	2	1.478
1994 PROJECTION		57	58.2	52	30	51	3	3	4.91	2	1.398

JEFF MONTGOMERY   Age 33/R $35

We are second to none in our admiration of Montgomery's achievements over the last six years. Yet, there are signs the tide is turning. His ERA nearly doubled last year. The walks and hits were up. The same sort of indicators popped up in Eckersley's 1993 numbers. Montgomery is 33, and he's probably good for that many saves, but don't say you weren't warned about the slippage.

Year Team	Lg.	G	IP	H	BB	SO	W	L	ERA	SV	Ratio
1991 Kansas City	AL	67	90.0	83	28	77	4	4	2.90	33	1.233
1992 Kansas City	AL	65	82.2	61	27	69	1	6	2.18	39	1.065
1993 Kansas City	AL	69	87.1	65	23	66	7	5	2.27	45	1.008
1994 Kansas City	AL	42	44.2	48	15	50	2	3	4.03	27	1.410
1994 PROJECTION		57	59.0	59	17	58	3	3	3.20	39	1.288

JEFF NELSON   Age 28/R $1

The Mariners found the key to his success. They never let him pitch when the game was close. Effective strategy, but hardly the ticket to Rotisserie happiness. No wins, no saves, no value.

Year Team	Lg.	G	IP	H	BB	SO	W	L	ERA	SV	Ratio
1992 Seattle	AL	66	81.0	71	44	46	1	7	3.44	6	1.420
1993 Seattle	AL	71	60.0	57	34	61	5	3	4.35	1	1.517
1994 Seattle	AL	28	42.1	35	20	44	0	0	2.76	0	1.299
1994 PROJECTION		47	68.1	54	30	69	2	3	2.50	0	1.229

DARREN OLIVER   Age 24/L $10

Bleary-eyed and soon-to-be-fired Rangers pitching coach Claude Osteen said in late summer, "It seems like every pitcher we've thrown out there has been terrible. Everyone we started the year with, everyone we brought up, everyone we traded for, every darned one—except for Oliver. He was the only one who exceeded expectations." If Henke retires, pencil in Oliver as the Rangers' closer this year.

Year Team	Lg.	G	IP	H	BB	SO	W	L	ERA	SV	Ratio
1993 Texas	AL	2	3.1	2	1	4	0	0	2.70	0	0.900
1994 Texas	AL	43	50.0	40	35	50	4	0	3.42	2	1.500
1994 PROJECTION		61	66.1	59	43	64	5	1	3.12	2	1.537

JESSE OROSCO   Age 37/L $1

No thanks.

Year Team	Lg.	G	IP	H	BB	SO	W	L	ERA	SV	Ratio
1991 Cleveland	AL	47	45.2	52	15	36	2	0	3.74	0	1.467
1992 Milwaukee	AL	59	39.0	33	13	40	3	1	3.23	1	1.179
1993 Milwaukee	AL	57	56.2	47	17	67	3	5	3.18	8	1.129
1994 Milwaukee	AL	40	39.0	32	26	36	3	1	5.08	0	1.487
1994 PROJECTION		57	49.2	44	30	46	4	1	4.35	0	1.490

BOB PATTERSON   Age 35/L $1

He's a lefty. You may have heard this can extend the career of an otherwise washed-up pitcher.

Year Team	Lg.	G	IP	H	BB	SO	W	L	ERA	SV	Ratio
1991 Pittsburgh	NL	54	65.2	67	15	57	4	3	4.11	2	1.249
1992 Pittsburgh	NL	60	64.2	59	23	43	6	3	2.92	9	1.268
1993 Texas	AL	52	52.2	59	11	46	2	4	4.78	1	1.329
1994 California	AL	47	42.0	35	15	30	2	3	4.07	1	1.190
1994 PROJECTION		61	57.1	56	19	35	2	5	4.24	7	1.308

ERIC PLUNK   Age 31/R $9

With Mesa, Plunk gives the Indians a strong one-two punch when a starter falters. And like Mesa, Plunk could become the Indians' closer—or more likely the chairman of the bullpen committee—if Russell stumbles.

Year Team	Lg.	G	IP	H	BB	SO	W	L	ERA	SV	Ratio
1991 New York	AL	43	111.2	128	62	103	2	5	4.76	0	1.701
1992 Cleveland	AL	58	71.2	61	38	50	9	6	3.64	4	1.381
1993 Cleveland	AL	70	71.0	61	30	77	4	5	2.79	15	1.282
1994 Cleveland	AL	41	71.0	61	37	73	7	2	2.54	3	1.380
1994 PROJECTION		59	97.0	87	47	96	10	2	3.06	5	1.381

JIM POOLE   Age 28/L $1

The league seems to have caught up with him.

Year Team	Lg.	G	IP	H	BB	SO	W	L	ERA	SV	Ratio
1991 Texas	AL	5	6.0	10	3	4	0	0	4.50	1	2.167
1991 Baltimore	AL	24	36.0	19	9	34	3	2	2.00	0	0.778
1992 Baltimore	AL	6	3.1	3	1	3	0	0	0.00	0	1.200
1993 Baltimore	AL	55	50.1	30	21	29	2	1	2.15	2	1.013
1994 Baltimore	AL	38	20.1	32	11	18	1	0	6.64	0	2.115
1994 PROJECTION		47	26.0	42	11	25	2	0	5.88	0	2.038

CARLOS REYES
Age 26/R   **$3**

A product of the Braves organization, Reyes threw one of the best changeups in the American League until he was hurt. If he improves his control, he could move out of the bullpen and into the Oakland rotation.

Year Team	Lg.	G	IP	H	BB	SO	W	L	ERA	SV	Ratio
1991 Oakland	AL	27	78.0	71	44	57	0	3	4.15	1	1.474
1994 PROJECTION		38	90.0	81	51	65	1	4	4.17	2	1.467

BILL RISLEY
Age 27/R   **$9**

A hard thrower whom Lou Piniella stole out of the Reds organization. Big-time stuff: opponents batted just .170 against him. A rare positive development on the Mariners staff, Risley should be a major force alongside Ayala in the Seattle bullpen.

Year Team	Lg.	G	IP	H	BB	SO	W	L	ERA	SV	Ratio
1992 Montreal	NL	1	5.0	4	1	2	1	0	1.80	0	1.000
1993 Montreal	NL	2	3.0	2	2	2	0	0	6.00	0	1.333
1994 Seattle	AL	37	52.1	31	19	61	9	6	3.44	0	0.955
1994 PROJECTION		58	76.1	51	23	89	13	7	2.71	0	0.969

JEFF RUSSELL
Age 33/R   **$14**

After Red Sox GM Dan Duquette traded Paul Quantrill and Billy Hatcher, Russell whined that "he ruined our chemistry." Duquette replied: "He's crazy. I always did well in chemistry." A few weeks later, Duquette improved the Red Sox' chemistry by trading Russell to the Indians, who tired of him quickly. The six *blown* saves are a more significant indicator than the 17 saves. Cleveland went shopping for a closer over the winter.

Year Team	Lg.	G	IP	H	BB	SO	W	L	ERA	SV	Ratio
1991 Texas	AL	68	79.1	71	26	52	6	4	3.29	30	1.223
1992 Texas	AL	51	56.2	51	22	43	2	3	1.91	28	1.288
1992 Oakland	AL	8	9.2	4	3	5	2	0	0.00	2	0.724
1993 Boston	AL	51	46.2	39	14	45	1	4	2.70	33	1.136
1994 Boston	AL	29	28.0	30	13	18	0	5	5.14	12	1.536
1994 Cleveland	AL	13	12.2	13	3	10	1	1	4.97	5	1.263
1994 PROJECTION		59	55.2	65	19	40	4	7	4.85	21	1.509

KEN RYAN
Age 26/R   **$28**

Boston's closer job is Ryan's to lose this spring, barring any major Red Sox deals. We say he keeps it.

Year Team	Lg.	G	IP	H	BB	SO	W	L	ERA	SV	Ratio
1992 Boston	AL	7	7.0	4	5	5	0	0	6.43	1	1.286
1993 Boston	AL	47	50.0	43	29	49	7	2	3.60	1	1.440
1994 Boston	AL	42	48.0	46	17	32	2	3	2.44	13	1.313
1994 PROJECTION		53	57.2	60	20	38	2	4	2.81	19	1.387

LEE SMITH
Age 37/R   **$25**

We know Mr. Smith gets a little testy about suggestions that he is getting a little—how to put this delicately?—*old*. He also demurs at speculation that his days as a premier closer are coming to an end. He correctly points out that idiots like us have been saying that sort of thing for five years. And the

Catchers
pp. 33–46

Corners
pp. 46–65

Infield
pp. 66–85

Outfield
pp. 85–115

DH
pp. 115–119

Starters
pp. 119–155

Relievers
pp. 155–187

33 saves last year do seem to bear him out. But without intending any disrespect whatsoever, and in full cognizance of how wrong we have been in the past in prematurely forecasting Mr. Smith's professional decline, and with all due respect to the Angels, we wish to point out the number of saves that Mr. Smith recorded after the All-Star break last year: zero.

Year Team	Lg.	G	IP	H	BB	SO	W	L	ERA	SV	Ratio
1991 St. Louis	NL	67	73.0	70	13	67	6	3	2.34	47	1.137
1992 St. Louis	NL	70	75.0	62	26	60	4	9	3.12	43	1.173
1993 St. Louis	NL	55	50.0	49	9	49	2	4	4.50	43	1.160
1993 New York	AL	8	8.0	4	5	11	0	0	0.00	3	1.125
1994 Baltimore	AL	41	38.1	34	11	42	1	4	3.29	33	1.174
1994 PROJECTION		53	50.1	42	15	53	1	5	3.04	43	1.132

DAVE STEVENS   Age 25/R $4

Forget those ghastly numbers. The Twins think this hard thrower has a chance.

Year Team	Lg.	G	IP	H	BB	SO	W	L	ERA	SV	Ratio
1994 Minnesota	AL	24	45.0	55	23	24	5	2	6.80	0	1.733
1994 PROJECTION		44	72.1	80	32	41	6	2	5.60	0	1.548

BILLY TAYLOR   Age 33/R $2

Let's hear it one more time for last year's Thirtysomething Rookie of the Year. Bil-ly! Bil-ly! Bil-ly!

Year Team	Lg.	G	IP	H	BB	SO	W	L	ERA	SV	Ratio
1994 Oakland	AL	41	46.1	38	18	48	1	3	3.50	1	1.209
1994 PROJECTION		41	46.1	38	18	48	1	3	3.50	1	1.208

MIKE TIMLIN   Age 29/R $7

You have to have good stuff to average almost a strikeout an inning in the major leagues, so Blue Jays brass know that Timlin's failure to step up to the next level as a pitcher is not a question of his arm. The body part that worries them is the one that sits on top of his shoulders. If Duane Ward can't come back, this could be a make-or-break year for Timlin. We vote make.

Year Team	Lg.	G	IP	H	BB	SO	W	L	ERA	SV	Ratio
1991 Toronto	AL	63	108.1	94	50	85	11	6	3.16	3	1.329
1992 Toronto	AL	26	43.2	45	20	35	0	2	4.12	1	1.489
1993 Toronto	AL	54	55.2	63	27	49	4	2	4.69	1	1.617
1994 Toronto	AL	34	40.0	41	20	38	0	1	5.18	2	1.525
1994 PROJECTION		49	55.1	57	27	54	3	1	4.55	3	1.518

DUANE WARD   Age 30/R $37

The Blue Jays are hopeful. Ward is optimistic. All that's well and good, but make sure he shows up regularly in spring training box scores before taking out your wallet. But if he *is* back, he's the best in the league. Period.

Year Team	Lg.	G	IP	H	BB	SO	W	L	ERA	SV	Ratio
1991 Toronto	AL	81	107.1	80	33	132	7	6	2.77	23	1.053
1992 Toronto	AL	79	101.1	76	39	103	7	4	1.95	12	1.135
1993 Toronto	AL	71	71.2	49	25	97	2	3	2.13	45	1.033
1994 Did not play											

MATT WHITESIDE

Age 27/R   **$1**

The word is that he was buried by Kevin Kennedy and lost his confidence. A new Texas manager could get his once-promising career back on track.

Year Team	Lg.	G	IP	H	BB	SO	W	L	ERA	SV	Ratio
1992 Texas	AL	20	28.0	26	11	13	1	1	1.93	4	1.321
1993 Texas	AL	60	73.0	78	23	39	2	1	4.32	1	1.384
1994 Texas	AL	47	61.0	68	28	37	2	2	5.02	1	1.574
1994 PROJECTION		64	82.0	96	35	48	2	3	4.83	1	1.597

BOB WICKMAN

Age 26/R   **$10**

The Yankees love his durability, his sinker, and his competitiveness. So do we.

Year Team	Lg.	G	IP	H	BB	SO	W	L	ERA	SV	Ratio
1992 New York	AL	8	50.1	51	20	21	6	1	4.11	0	1.411
1993 New York	AL	41	140.0	156	69	70	14	4	4.63	4	1.607
1994 New York	AL	53	70.0	54	27	56	5	4	3.09	6	1.157
1994 PROJECTION		73	97.2	75	40	77	7	4	2.58	8	1.177

CARL WILLIS

Age 34/R   **$1**

The Twins had the highest team ERA in baseball last summer: 5.68. Willis was one of Minnesota's team leaders.

Year Team	Lg.	G	IP	H	BB	SO	W	L	ERA	SV	Ratio
1991 Minnesota	AL	40	89.0	76	19	53	8	3	2.63	2	1.067
1992 Minnesota	AL	59	79.1	73	11	45	7	3	2.72	1	1.059
1993 Minnesota	AL	53	58.0	56	17	44	3	0	3.10	5	1.259
1994 Minnesota	AL	49	59.1	89	12	37	2	4	5.92	3	1.702
1994 PROJECTION		67	79.0	117	14	51	3	4	4.90	3	1.658

AUCTION DRAFT UPDATE? YOU BETCHA!

See page 277 to find out how to get your free _Rotisserie Hot List_

Catchers
pp. 33–46

Corners
pp. 46–65

Infield
pp. 66–85

Outfield
pp. 85–115

DH
pp. 115–119

Starters
pp. 119–155

Relievers
pp. 155–187

3

By the Numbers

1995 Rotisserie Stat-Pak: Never Leave for the Auction Draft Without It

A certain kind of Rotisserie owner breezes into the auction draft without so much as pencil or notepad. The night before, he went to the movies. The week before, he went snorkeling in the Caribbean and didn't see a single newspaper for six days. The month before, he re-read all of Raymond Chandler and the new James Lee Burke. Preparation? Well, he rented *Major League* on Super Bowl Sunday and watched it instead of the game. While other owners at the table are frantically rearranging their lists, agonizing over which of seven alternative strategies to pursue, and trying to remember their own names, he leans back, folds his arms over his chest, and, with a dreamy look in his eyes, asks of no one in particular, "I wonder how much Bobby Bonds will go for?" Six months later, *he*'s the one taking the Yoo-Hoo shower.

We hate that guy.

But we have to admit he may be on to something. Maybe you really don't need to show up at the auction draft with the *Baseball Register,* all the spring training box scores from *USA Today,* Bill James, the last six months of *Baseball America* and *Baseball Weekly,* a stack of computer printouts, all of John Benson's newsletters for the past year, a well-thumbed copy of *Nine Innings,* and your original 1948 Cleveland Indians cap. Maybe all you need is the Rotisserie Stat-Pak.

The Rotisserie Stat-Pak is the nearest thing in this book to a grand-slam homer. Here you get the top peformers in all the Rotissecategories (plus Runs Scored for batters and Strikeouts and Net Wins for pitchers). You also get the *worst* performers in ERA, Ratio, and BA so you can find out in an instant who might hurt you. And for batters, you get the top performers in each category by position. The Stat-Pak provides the data. *You* provide the analysis.

So forget all that other stuff. Just tear out this chapter and travel light. You can wear your lucky Indians cap. But remember to take it off just before they pour the Yoo-Hoo.

LEAGUE LEADERS, 1994

NATIONAL LEAGUE PITCHERS

RATIO
(Minimum 75 Innings Pitched)

1. Maddux, G.	0.896	11. Avery, S.	1.200	21. Martinez, R.	1.271
2. Saberhagen, B.	1.026	12. Reynolds, S.	1.202	22. White, R.	1.274
3. Drabek, D.	1.075	13. Mercker, K.	1.202	23. Jackson, D.	1.277
4. Henry, B.	1.090	14. Freeman, M.	1.207	24. Swift, B.	1.280
5. Rojas, M.	1.095	15. Bullinger, J.	1.210	25. Trachsel, S.	1.281
6. Martinez, P.	1.106	16. Hill, K.	1.222	26. Foster, K.	1.296
7. Ashby, A.	1.144	17. Smoltz, J.	1.248	27. Lieber, J.	1.298
8. Fassero, J.	1.147	18. Smith, Z.	1.248	28. Smiley, J.	1.298
9. Hamilton, J.	1.169	19. Palacios, V.	1.249	29. Young, A.	1.299
10. Benes, A.	1.195	20. Astacio, P.	1.268	30. Heredia, G.	1.301

WORST RATIOS
(Minimum 75 Innings Pitched)

1. Williams, B.	1.953	11. Torres, S.	1.530	21. Banks, W.	1.410
2. Morgan, M.	1.810	12. Cooke, S.	1.511	22. Rueter, K.	1.397
3. Blair, W.	1.764	13. Nied, D.	1.508	23. Schilling, C.	1.397
4. Harkey, M.	1.745	14. Rapp, P.	1.508	24. Hershiser, O.	1.389
5. Weathers, D.	1.667	15. Hough, C.	1.496	25. Arocha, R.	1.386
6. Kile, D.	1.591	16. Urbani, T.	1.481	26. Gardner, M.	1.375
7. Hickerson, B.	1.586	17. Glavine, T.	1.470	27. West, D.	1.364
8. Harris, G.	1.585	18. Harnisch, P.	1.463	28. Tewksbury, B.	1.362
9. Watson, A.	1.582	19. Schourek, P.	1.463	29. Sanders, S.	1.360
10. Wagner, P.	1.554	20. Smith, P.	1.424	30. Swindell, G.	1.355

EARNED RUN AVERAGE
(Minimum 75 Innings Pitched)

1. Maddux, G.	1.56	11. Rijo, J.	3.08	21. Mercker, K.	3.45
2. Henry, B.	2.43	12. Jones, B.	3.15	22. Heredia, G.	3.46
3. Munoz, B.	2.67	13. Trachsel, S.	3.21	23. Van Landingham	3.54
4. Saberhagen, B.	2.74	14. Jackson, D.	3.26	24. West, D.	3.55
5. Freeman, M.	2.80	15. Smith, Z.	3.27	25. Bullinger, J.	3.60
6. Drabek, D.	2.84	16. Hill, K.	3.32	26. Gross, K.	3.60
7. Foster, K.	2.89	17. Rojas, M.	3.32	27. Burkett, J.	3.62
8. Hamilton, J.	2.98	18. Swift, B.	3.38	28. Lieber, J.	3.73
9. Fassero, J.	2.99	19. Ashby, A.	3.40	29. Hershiser, O.	3.79
10. Reynolds, S.	3.05	20. Martinez, P.	3.42	30. White, R.	3.82

WORST EARNED RUN AVERAGES
(Minimum 75 Innings Pitched)

1. Morgan, M.	6.69	11. Banks, W.	5.40	21. Nied, D.	4.80		
2. Harris, G.	6.65	12. Tewksbury, B.	5.32	22. Sanders, S.	4.78		
3. Blair, W.	5.79	13. Weathers, D.	5.27	23. Wagner, P.	4.59		
4. Harkey, M.	5.79	14. Rueter, K.	5.17	24. Kile, D.	4.57		
5. Williams, B.	5.74	15. Urbani, T.	5.15	25. Roper, J.	4.50		
6. Smith, P.	5.55	16. Hough, C.	5.15	26. Schilling, C.	4.48		
7. Watson, A.	5.52	17. Neagle, D.	5.12	27. Palacios, V.	4.44		
8. Torres, S.	5.44	18. Cooke, S.	5.02	28. Swindell, G.	4.37		
9. Harnisch, P.	5.40	19. Boskie, S.	5.01	29. Astacio, P.	4.29		
10. Hickerson, B.	5.40	20. Gardner, M.	4.87	30. Smoltz, J.	4.14		

WINS

1. Maddux, G.	16	12. Smith, Z.	10	23. Swift, B.	8
2. Hill, K.	16	13. Portugal, M.	10	24. Swindell, G.	8
3. Saberhagen, B.	14	14. Freeman, M.	10	25. Harnisch, P.	8
4. Jackson, D.	14	15. Gross, K.	9	26. Avery, S.	8
5. Glavine, T.	13	16. Rijo, J.	9	27. Fassero, J.	8
6. Tewksbury, B.	12	17. Mercker, K.	9	28. Banks, W.	8
7. Drabek, D.	12	18. Kile, D.	9	29. Weathers, D.	8
8. Martinez, R.	12	19. Neagle, D.	9	30. Henry, B.	8
9. Jones, B.	12	20. Nied, D.	9	31. Reynolds, S.	8
10. Smiley, J.	11	21. Trachsel, S.	9	32. Van Landingham, W.	8
11. Martinez, P.	11	22. Hamilton, J.	9		

SAVES

1. Franco, J.	30	12. Nen, R.	15	23. McElroy, C.	5
2. Beck, R.	28	13. Perez, M.	12	24. Jones, T.	5
3. Jones, D.	27	14. Worrell, T.	11	25. Jackson, M.	4
4. Wetteland, J.	25	15. Arocha, R.	11	26. Dyer, M.	4
5. Myers, R.	21	16. Hernandez, J.	9	27. Stanton, M.	3
6. McMichael, G.	21	17. Pena, A.	7	28. Blair, W.	3
7. Hoffman, T.	20	18. Williams, M.	6	29. Holmes, D.	3
8. Ruffin, B.	16	19. Harvey, B.	6	30. Reed, S.	3
9. Rojas, M.	16	20. Carrasco, H.	6	31. Martinez, P.	3
10. Hudek, J.	16	21. White, R.	6		
11. Brantley, J.	15	22. Dreifort, D.	6		

STRIKEOUTS

1. Benes, A.	189	11. Drabek, D.	121	21. Trachsel, S.	108
2. Rijo, J.	171	12. Ashby, A.	121	22. Kile, D.	105
3. Maddux, G.	156	13. Martinez, R.	119	23. Candiotti, T.	102
4. Saberhagen, B.	143	14. Fassero, J.	119	24. Hanson, E.	101
5. Martinez, P.	142	15. Smoltz, J.	113	25. Palacios, V.	95
6. Glavine, T.	140	16. Smiley, J.	112	26. Banks, W.	91
7. Jackson, D.	129	17. Mercker, K.	111	27. Portugal, M.	87
8. Gross, K.	124	18. Reynolds, S.	110	28. Wagner, P.	86
9. Avery, S.	122	19. Sanders, S.	109	29. Burkett, J.	85
10. Neagle, D.	122	20. Astacio, P.	108	30. Hill, K.	85

Catchers
pp. 33–46

Corners
pp. 46–65

Infield
pp. 66–85

Outfield
pp. 85–115

DH
pp. 115–119

Starters
pp. 119–155

Relievers
pp. 155–187

NET WINS

1. Hill, K.	11	12. Schourek, P.	5	23. Rueter, K.	4
2. Saberhagen, B.	10	13. Wohlers, M.	5	24. Rijo, J.	3
3. Maddux, G.	10	14. Henry, B.	5	25. Harnisch, P.	3
4. Jackson, D.	8	15. Ruffin, J.	5	26. Shaw, J.	3
5. Freeman, M.	8	16. Jones, B.	5	27. Heredia, G.	3
6. Drabek, D.	6	17. Edens, T.	4	28. Kile, D.	3
7. Martinez, P.	6	18. Glavine, T.	4	29. Scott, T.	3
8. Van Landingham, W.	6	19. Slocumb, H.	4	30. Perez, Y.	3
9. Martinez, R.	5	20. Bullinger, J.	4	31. Reynolds, S.	3
10. Mercker, K.	5	21. Linton, D.	4	32. Jones, T.	3
11. Avery, S.	5	22. Roper, J.	4	33. Hamilton, J.	3

NATIONAL LEAGUE POSITION PLAYERS

HOME RUNS

1. Williams, M.	43	12. Alou, M.	22	23. Klesko, R.	17
2. Bagwell, J.	39	13. Bonilla, B.	20	24. Hundley, T.	16
3. Bonds, B.	37	14. Walker, L.	19	25. Mondesi, R.	16
4. McGriff, F.	34	15. Justice, D.	19	26. Daulton, D.	15
5. Galarraga, A.	31	16. Zeile, T.	19	27. Hunter, B.	15
6. Mitchell, K.	30	17. Lankford, R.	19	28. Cordero, W.	15
7. Bichette, D.	27	18. Caminiti, K.	18	29. Buechele, S.	14
8. Sheffield, G.	27	19. Plantier, P.	18	30. Whiten, M.	14
9. Sosa, S.	25	20. Conine, J.	18	31. Bell, D.	14
10. Piazza, M.	24	21. Thompson, R.	18	32. Karros, E.	14
11. Wallach, T.	23	22. Sanders, R.	17	33. Kent, J.	14

RUNS BATTED IN

1. Bagwell, J.	116	12. Sheffield, G.	78	23. Cordero, W.	63
2. Williams, M.	96	13. Alou, M.	78	24. Sanders, R.	62
3. Bichette, D.	95	14. Mitchell, K.	77	25. Justice, D.	59
4. McGriff, F	94	15. Caminiti, K.	75	26. Thompson, R.	59
5. Piazza, M.	92	16. Zeile, T.	75	27. Fletcher, D.	57
6. Walker, L.	86	17. Sosa, S.	70	28. Lankford, R.	57
7. Galarraga, A.	85	18. Kent, J.	68	29. Hunter, B.	57
8. Conine, J.	82	19. Boone, B.	68	30. Daulton, D.	56
9. Bonds, B.	81	20. Bonilla, B.	67	31. Biggio, C.	56
10. Wallach, T.	78	21. Gonzalez, L.	67	32. Mondesi, R.	56
11. Morris, H.	78	22. Gwynn, T.	64		

STOLEN BASES

1. Biggio, C.	39	12. Clayton, R.	23	23. Dykstra, L.	15
2. Sanders, D.	38	13. Sosa, S.	22	24. Walker, L.	15
3. Grissom, M.	36	14. Roberts, B.	21	25. Gilkey, B.	15
4. Carr, C.	32	15. Bichette, D.	21	26. Gonzalez, L.	15
5. Lewis, D.	30	16. Sanders, R.	21	27. Bagwell, J.	15
6. Bonds, B.	29	17. Frazier, L.	20	28. Martin, A.	15
7. Butler, B.	27	18. Hill, G.	19	29. Berry, S.	14
8. DeShields, D	27	19. Kelly, R.	19	30. Finley, S.	13
9. Larkin, B.	26	20. Garcia, C.	18	31. Patterson, J.	13
10. Bell, D.	24	21. Young, E.	18		
11. Mouton, J.	24	22. Cordero, W.	16		

RUNS SCORED

1. Bagwell, J.	104	12. Walker, L.	76	23. Piazza, M.	64				
2. Grissom, M.	96	13. Williams, M.	74	24. Caminiti, K.	63				
3. Bonds, B.	89	14. Bichette, D.	74	25. Mondesi, R.	63				
4. Lankford, R.	89	15. Kelly, R.	73	26. Zeile, T.	62				
5. Biggio, C.	88	16. Lewis, D.	70	27. Sheffield, G.	61				
6. McGriff, F	81	17. Wallach, T.	68	28. Justice, D.	61				
7. Alou, M.	81	18. Dykstra, L.	68	29. Carr, C.	61				
8. Butler, B.	79	19. Bell, J.	68	30. Bonilla, B.	60				
9. Gwynn, T.	79	20. Sanders, R.	66	31. Morris, H.	60				
10. Larkin, B.	78	21. Cordero, W.	65	32. Conine, J.	60				
11. Galarraga, A.	77	22. Finley, S.	64						

BATTING AVERAGE
(Minimum 225 At Bats)

1. Gwynn, T.	.394	11. Roberts, B.	.320	21. Mondesi, R.	.306
2. Bagwell, J.	.368	12. Conine, J.	.319	22. Bichette, D.	.304
3. Kingery, M.	.349	13. Galarraga, A.	.319	23. Kruk, J.	.302
4. Alou, M.	.339	14. Piazza, M.	.319	24. Barberie, B.	.301
5. Morris, H.	.335	15. McGriff, F	.318	25. Sosa, S.	.300
6. Shipley, C.	.333	16. Biggio, C.	.318	26. Eisenreich, J.	.300
7. Mitchell, K.	.326	17. Butler, B.	.314	27. Daulton, D.	.300
8. Jefferies, G.	.325	18. Justice, D.	.313	28. Grace, M.	.298
9. Walker, L.	.322	19. Bonds, B.	.312	29. Hill, G.	.297
10. Boone, B.	.320	20. Bell, D.	.311	30. Browne, J.	.295

WORST BATTING AVERAGES
(Minimum 225 At Bats)

1. Servais, S.	.195	11. Hundley, T.	.237	21. Manwaring, K.	.250
2. Offerman, J.	.210	12. Patterson, J.	.237	22. DeShields, D.	.250
3. Johnson, H.	.211	13. Gutierrez, R.	.240	23. Weiss, W.	.251
4. Plantier, P.	.220	14. Segui, D.	.241	24. Ausmus, B.	.251
5. Thompson, R.	.225	15. Buechele, S.	.242	25. Pendleton, T.	.252
6. Wilkins, R.	.227	16. Mouton, J.	.245	26. Gilkey, B.	.253
7. Incaviglia, P.	.230	17. Lopez, J.	.245	27. Liriano, N.	.255
8. Rhodes, K.	.234	18. Van Slyke, A.	.246	28. Vizcaino, J.	.256
9. Hunter, B.	.234	19. Martinez, D.	.247	29. Lewis, D.	.257
10. Clayton, R.	.236	20. Abbott, K.	.249	30. Blauser, J.	.258

AMERICAN LEAGUE PITCHERS

RATIO
(Minimum 75 Innings Pitched)

1. Ontiveros, S.	1.032	11. McDowell, J	1.260	21. Eldred, C.	1.352
2. Cone, D.	1.072	12. Perez, M.	1.269	22. Finley, C.	1.358
3. Clemens, R.	1.143	13. Appier, K.	1.290	23. Clark, M.	1.359
4. Mussina, M.	1.163	14. Alvarez, W.	1.293	24. Key, J.	1.363
5. Johnson, R.	1.186	15. McDonald, B	1.303	25. Darling, R.	1.381
6. Martinez, D.	1.189	16. Moyer, J.	1.315	26. Sele, A.	1.395
7. Wells, D.	1.231	17. Nagy, C.	1.317	27. Stottlemyre, T.	1.400
8. Bones, R.	1.236	18. Rogers, K.	1.321	28. Bere, J.	1.405
9. Hentgen, P.	1.242	19. Sanderson, S.	1.326	29. Leiter, M.	1.406
10. Fernandez, A.	1.250	20. Fernandez, S.	1.344	30. Scanlan, B.	1.408

Catchers
pp. 33–46

Corners
pp. 46–65

Infield
pp. 66–85

Outfield
pp. 85–115

DH
pp. 115–119

Starters
pp. 119–155

Relievers
pp. 155–187

WORST RATIOS
(Minimum 75 Innings Pitched)

1. Fleming, D.	1.855	11. Doherty, J.	1.628	21. Pulido, C.	1.506
2. Hibbard, G.	1.810	12. Morris, J.	1.627	22. Kamieniecki, S.	1.483
3. Deshaies, J.	1.719	13. Erickson, S.	1.611	23. Leftwich, P.	1.482
4. Leiter, A.	1.701	14. Stewart, D.	1.597	24. Reyes, C.	1.474
5. Van Poppel, T.	1.689	15. Brown, K.	1.576	25. Langston, M.	1.466
6. Navarro, J.	1.673	16. Gullickson, B.	1.569	26. Fajardo, H.	1.452
7. Belcher, T.	1.667	17. Moore, M.	1.562	27. Anderson, B.	1.446
8. Darwin, D.	1.652	18. Mulholland, T.	1.550	28. Abbott, J.	1.441
9. Guzman, J.	1.636	19. Mahomes, P.	1.525	29. Boever, J.	1.439
10. Witt, B.	1.629	20. Grimsley, J.	1.512	30. Gordon, T.	1.436

EARNED RUN AVERAGE
(Minimum 75 Innings Pitched)

1. Ontiveros, S.	2.65	11. Martinez, D.	3.52	21. McDonald, B.	4.06
2. Clemens, R.	2.85	12. McDowell, J	3.73	22. Perez, M.	4.10
3. Cone, D.	2.94	13. Kamieniecki, S.	3.76	23. Scanlan, B.	4.11
4. Mussina, M.	3.06	14. Bere, J.	3.81	24. Reyes, C.	4.15
5. Johnson, R.	3.19	15. Clark, M.	3.82	25. Stottlemyre, T.	4.22
6. Key, J.	3.27	16. Sele, A.	3.83	26. Hesketh, J.	4.26
7. Hentgen, P.	3.40	17. Appier, K.	3.83	27. Bosio, C.	4.32
8. Bones, R.	3.43	18. Fernandez, A.	3.86	28. Finley, C.	4.32
9. Alvarez, W.	3.45	19. Wells, D.	3.96	29. Gordon, T.	4.35
10. Nagy, C.	3.45	20. Boever, J.	3.98	30. Rogers, K.	4.46

WORST EARNED RUN AVERAGES
(Minimum 75 Innings Pitched)

1. Deshaies, J.	7.39	11. Gullickson, B.	5.93	21. Sanderson, S.	5.09
2. Fajardo, H.	6.91	12. Belcher, T.	5.89	22. Leiter, A.	5.08
3. Hibbard, G.	6.69	13. Stewart, D.	5.87	23. Witt, B.	5.04
4. Navarro, J.	6.62	14. Leftwich, P.	5.68	24. Brown, K.	4.82
5. Mulholland, T.	6.49	15. Guzman, J.	5.68	25. Moyer, J.	4.77
6. Doherty, J.	6.48	16. Morris, J.	5.60	26. Mahomes, P.	4.72
7. Fleming, D.	6.46	17. Erickson, S.	5.44	27. Leiter, M.	4.72
8. Darwin, D.	6.30	18. Moore, M.	5.42	28. Langston, M.	4.68
9. Van Poppel, T.	6.09	19. Anderson, B.	5.22	29. Eldred, C.	4.68
10. Pulido, C.	5.98	20. Fernandez, S.	5.15	30. Tapani, K.	4.62

WINS

1. Key, J.	17	13. Gordon, T.	11	25. Boever, J.	9
2. Cone, D.	16	14. Tapani, K.	11	26. Perez, M.	9
3. Mussina, M.	16	15. Fernandez, A.	11	27. Abbott, J.	9
4. McDonald, B	14	16. Clark, M.	11	28. Mahomes, P.	9
5. Johnson, R.	13	17. Eldred, C.	11	29. Risley, B.	9
6. Hentgen, P.	13	18. Darling, R.	10	30. Sanderson, S.	8
7. Alvarez, W.	12	19. Morris, J.	10	31. Hesketh, J.	8
8. Guzman, J.	12	20. Finley, C.	10	32. Wegman, B.	8
9. Bere, J.	12	21. McDowell, J	10	33. Witt, B.	8
10. Martinez, D.	11	22. Nagy, C.	10	34. Erickson, S.	8
11. Moore, M.	11	23. Bones, R.	10	35. Kamieniecki, S.	8
12. Rogers, K.	11	24. Clemens, R.	9	36. Sele, A.	8

SAVES

1. Smith, L.	33	11. Hernandez, R.	14	21. Meacham, R.	4		
2. Montgomery, J.	27	12. Grahe, J.	13	22. Cox, D.	3		
3. Aguilera, R.	23	13. Ryan, K.	13	23. Willis, C.	3		
4. Eckersley, D.	19	14. Henneman, M.	8	24. McCaskill, K	3		
5. Ayala, B.	18	15. Hernandez, X.	6	25. Boever, J.	3		
6. Russell, J.	17	16. Wickman, B.	6	26. Plunk, E.	3		
7. Fetters, M.	17	17. Carpenter, C.	5	27. Pichardo, H.	3		
8. Hall, D.	17	18. Gardiner, M.	5	28. Brewer, B.	3		
9. Howe, S.	15	19. Shuey, P.	5	29. Lloyd, G.	3		
10. Henke, T.	15	20. Farr, S.	4				

STRIKEOUTS

1. Johnson, R.	204	11. Brown, K.	123	21. Stottlemyre, T.	105
2. Clemens, R.	168	12. Fernandez, A.	122	22. Sele, A.	105
3. Finley, C.	148	13. Rogers, K.	120	23. Erickson, S.	104
4. Hentgen, P.	147	14. Stewart, D.	111	24. Morris, J.	100
5. Appier, K.	145	15. Witt, B.	111	25. Leiter, A.	100
6. Cone, D.	132	16. Langston, M.	109	26. Mussina, M.	99
7. McDowell, J	127	17. Perez, M.	109	27. Eldred, C.	98
8. Bere, J.	127	18. Darling, R.	108	28. Key, J.	97
9. Gordon, T.	126	19. Alvarez, W.	108	29. Fernandez, S.	95
10. Guzman, J.	124	20. Nagy, C.	108	30. McDonald, B.	94

NET WINS

1. Key, J.	13	12. Hentgen, P.	5	23. Howe, S.	3
2. Cone, D.	11	13. Sanderson, S.	4	24. Howell, J.	3
3. Mussina, M.	11	14. Morris, J.	4	25. Hesketh, J.	3
4. Bere, J.	10	15. Wegman, B.	4	26. Gossage, G.	3
5. Clark, M.	8	16. Gordon, T.	4	27. Rogers, K.	3
6. Boever, J.	7	17. Tapani, K.	4	28. Castillo, T.	3
7. Johnson, R.	7	18. Alvarez, W.	4	29. Grimsley, J.	3
8. McDonald, B	7	19. Fernandez, A.	4	30. Risley, B.	3
9. Martinez, D.	5	20. Mahomes, P.	4	31. Hitchcock, S.	3
10. Plunk, E.	5	21. Oliver, D.	4	32. Brewer, B.	3
11. Perez, M.	5	22. Acre, M.	4	33. Stevens, D.	3

AMERICAN LEAGUE POSITION PLAYERS

HOME RUNS

1. Griffey Jr., K.	40	12. Palmeiro, R.	23	23. Vaughn, G.	19
2. Thomas, F.	38	13. Salmon, T.	23	24. Gonzalez, J.	19
3. Belle, A.	36	14. O'Neill, P	21	25. Palmer, D.	19
4. Canseco, J.	31	15. Buhner, J.	21	26. Baerga, C.	19
5. Fielder, C.	28	16. Franco, J.	20	27. Ventura, R.	18
6. Carter, J.	27	17. Puckett, K.	20	28. Fryman, T.	18
7. Davis, C.	26	18. Martinez, T.	20	29. Tettleton, M.	17
8. Vaughn, M.	26	19. Thome, J.	20	30. Murray, E.	17
9. Hamelin, B.	24	20. Phillips, T.	19	31. Stanley, M.	17
10. Gibson, K.	23	21. Tartabull, D.	19	32. Leyritz, J.	17
11. Sierra, R.	23	22. Hoiles, C.	19	33. Ramirez, M.	17

Catchers
pp. 33–46

Corners
pp. 46–65

Infield
pp. 66–85

Outfield
pp. 85–115

DH
pp. 115–119

Starters
pp. 119–155

Relievers
pp. 155–187

RUNS BATTED IN

1. Puckett, K.	112	11. Fryman, T.	85	21. Ripken, C.	75
2. Carter, J.	103	12. Davis, C.	84	22. Gibson, K.	72
3. Belle, A.	101	13. O'Neill, P	83	23. Salmon, T.	70
4. Thomas, F.	101	14. Vaughn, M.	82	24. Nilsson, D.	69
5. Franco, J.	98	15. Clark, W.	80	25. Buhner, J.	68
6. Sierra, R.	92	16. Baerga, C.	80	26. Tartabull, D.	67
7. Fielder, C.	90	17. Ventura, R.	78	27. Olerud, J.	67
8. Canseco, J.	90	18. Palmeiro, R.	76	28. Berroa, G.	65
9. Griffey Jr., K	90	19. Murray, E.	76	29. Hamelin, B.	65
10. Gonzalez, J.	85	20. Molitor, P.	75	30. Sorrento, P.	62

STOLEN BASES

1. Lofton, K.	60	12. Molitor, P.	20	23. Vizquel, O.	13
2. Coleman, V.	50	13. McLemore, M	20	24. Tinsley, L.	13
3. Nixon, O.	42	14. Polonia, L.	20	25. Valentin, J.	12
4. Knoblauch, C.	35	15. Alomar, R.	19	26. Carter, J.	11
5. Anderson, B.	31	16. Shumpert, T.	18	27. White, D.	11
6. Cole, A.	29	17. Hulse, D.	18	28. Griffey Jr., K	11
7. McRae, B	28	18. Williams, B.	16	29. Kirby, W.	11
8. Johnson, L.	26	19. Canseco, J.	15	30. Gagne, G.	10
9. Curtis, C.	25	20. McDowell, O.	14	31. Reynolds, H.	10
10. Javier, S.	24	21. Raines, T.	13	32. Jose, F.	10
11. Henderson, R.	22	22. Phillips, T.	13		

RUNS SCORED

1. Thomas, F.	106	12. Williams, B.	80	23. Sierra, R.	71
2. Lofton, K.	105	13. Puckett, K.	79	24. McRae, B	71
3. Griffey Jr., K.	94	14. Anderson, B.	78	25. Carter, J.	70
4. Phillips, T.	91	15. Alomar, R.	78	26. Tartabull, D.	68
5. Belle, A.	90	16. Javier, S.	75	27. O'Neill, P	68
6. Canseco, J.	88	17. Buhner, J.	74	28. Cole, A.	68
7. Molitor, P.	86	18. Clark, W.	73	29. Whitaker, L.	67
8. Knoblauch, C.	85	19. Davis, C.	72	30. White, D.	67
9. Palmeiro, R.	82	20. Franco, J.	72	31. Fielder, C.	67
10. Baerga, C.	81	21. Gibson, K.	71	32. Curtis, C.	67
11. Raines, T.	80	22. Ripken, C.	71	33. Salmon, T.	67

BATTING AVERAGE
(Minimum 225 At Bats)

1. O'Neill, P.	.359	11. Franco, J.	.319	21. Polonia, L.	.311
2. Belle, A.	.357	12. Puckett, K.	.317	22. Joyner, W.	.311
3. Thomas, F.	.353	13. Fermin, F.	.317	23. Davis, C.	.311
4. Lofton, K.	.349	14. Valentin, J.	.316	24. Owen, S.	.310
5. Boggs, W.	.342	15. Ripken, C.	.315	25. Vaughn, M.	.310
6. Molitor, P.	.341	16. Baerga, C.	.314	26. Alomar, R.	.306
7. Mack, S.	.333	17. Greer, R.	.314	27. Berroa, G.	.306
8. Clark, W.	.329	18. Seitzer, K.	.314	28. Felix, J.	.306
9. Griffey Jr, K	.323	19. Knoblauch, C.	.312	29. Mattingly, D.	.304
10. Palmeiro, R.	.319	20. Jackson, D.	.312	30. Jose, F.	.303

WORST BATTING AVERAGES
(Minimum 225 At Bats)

1. Devereaux, M.	.203	11. Valentin, J.	.239	21. Winfield, D.	.252
2. Walbeck, M.	.204	12. Sprague, E.	.240	22. Bordick, M.	.253
3. Strange, D.	.212	13. Dawson, A.	.240	23. Murray, E.	.254
4. Easley, D.	.215	14. Coleman, V.	.240	24. Vaughn, G.	.254
5. Wilson, D.	.216	15. Jaha, J.	.241	25. Macfarlane, M.	.255
6. Ward, T.	.232	16. Palmer, D.	.246	26. Hulse, D.	.255
7. Anthony, E.	.237	17. Leius, S.	.246	27. Schofield, D.	.255
8. Brosius, S.	.238	18. Hoiles, C.	.247	28. Tartabull, D.	.256
9. Espinoza, A.	.238	19. Borders, P.	.247	29. Sabo, C.	.256
10. Gallego, M.	.239	20. Tettleton, M.	.248	30. Curtis, C.	.256

PRE-SEASON CHECKLIST

✓ 1. Call Roti•Stats for info about stats service: 800-884-7684.

✓ 2. Join the RLBA (see page 274).

✓ 3. Send in for Free Opening Day Update (see page 277).

✓ 4. Fill out Rotiserrie Owners Survey (see page 267).

✓ 5. Outfit entire neighborhood in Rotisserie Caps and T-shirts (see page 279).

✓ 6. Sign up to Beat the Founding Fathers at Their Own Game (see page 276)

✓ 7. Cancel all business and social plans for two weeks prior to auction draft.

TOP POSITION PLAYERS, 1994

NL CATCHERS
(20 Games or More)

HOME RUNS

1. Piazza, M.	24	9. Taubensee, E.	8	17. Parrish, L.	3
2. Hundley, T.	16	10. Pagnozzi, T.	7	18. Parent, M.	3
3. Daulton, D.	15	11. Wilkins, R.	7	19. Johnson, B.	3
4. Lopez, J.	13	12. Ausmus, B.	7	20. Slaught, D.	2
5. Santiago, B.	11	13. Dorsett, B.	5	21. Hernandez, C.	2
6. Fletcher, D.	10	14. Webster, L.	5	22. Pratt, T.	2
7. Servais, S.	9	15. Eusebio, T.	5	23. Stinnett, K.	2
8. O'Brien, C.	8	16. Girardi, J.	4		

BATTING AVERAGE

1. Piazza, M.	.318	8. Webster, L.	.273	15. Ausmus, B.	.251
2. Daulton, D.	.300	9. Pagnozzi, T.	.271	16. Manwaring, K.	.250
3. Eusebio, T.	.295	10. Parrish, L.	.270	17. Spehr, T.	.250
4. Slaught, D.	.288	11. Lieberthal, M.	.266	18. Johnson, B.	.247
5. Taubensee, E.	.283	12. Parent, M.	.263	19. Lopez, J.	.246
6. Girardi, J.	.276	13. Fletcher, D.	.260	20. Dorsett, B.	.245
7. Santiago, B.	.273	14. Stinnett, K.	.253		

RUNS BATTED IN

1. Piazza, M.	92	8. Wilkins, R.	39	15. Ausmus, B.	24
2. Fletcher, D.	57	9. Lopez, J.	35	16. Webster, L.	23
3. Daulton, D.	56	10. Girardi, J.	34	17. Slaught, D.	21
4. Hundley, T.	42	11. Eusebio, T.	30	18. Taubensee, E.	21
5. Santiago, B.	41	12. Manwaring, K.	29	19. Parrish, L.	16
6. Servais, S.	41	13. O'Brien, C.	28	20. Parent, M.	16
7. Pagnozzi, T.	40	14. Dorsett, B.	26	21. Johnson, B.	16

STOLEN BASES

1. Ausmus, B.	5	5. Hundley, T.	2	9. Parrish, L.	1
2. Daulton, D.	4	6. Taubensee, E.	2	10. Santiago, B.	1
3. Wilkins, R.	4	7. Spehr, T.	2	11. Manwaring, K.	1
4. Girardi, J.	3	8. Stinnett, K.	2	12. Piazza, M.	1

RUNS SCORED

1. Piazza, M.	64	8. Manwaring, K.	30	15. Dorsett, B.	21
2. Girardi, J.	47	9. Taubensee, E.	29	16. Pagnozzi, T.	21
3. Hundley, T.	45	10. Fletcher, D.	28	17. Stinnett, K.	20
4. Ausmus, B.	45	11. Servais, S.	27	18. Eusebio, T.	18
5. Wilkins, R.	44	12. Lopez, J.	27	19. Webster, L.	13
6. Daulton, D.	43	13. O'Brien, C.	24	20. Reed, J.	11
7. Santiago, B.	35	14. Slaught, D.	21	21. Sheaffer, D.	11

AL CATCHERS
(20 Games or More)

HOME RUNS

1. Hoiles, C.	19	9. Karkovice, R.	11	17. Hemond, S.	3
2. Tettleton, M.	17	10. Steinbach, T.	11	18. Wilson, D.	3
3. Stanley, M.	17	11. Rowland, R.	9	19. Pena, T.	2
4. Leyritz, J.	17	12. Knorr, R.	7	20. Valle, D.	2
5. Rodriguez, I.	16	13. Berryhill, D.	6	21. Myers, G.	2
6. Macfarlane, M.	14	14. Walbeck, M.	5	22. Mayne, B.	2
7. Alomar Jr, S.	14	15. Harper, B.	4	23. Tackett, J.	2
8. Nilsson, D.	12	16. Borders, P.	3		

BATTING AVERAGE

1. Stanley, M.	.300	8. LaValliere, M.	.281	15. Tettleton, M.	.248
2. Rodriguez, I.	.297	9. Ortiz, J.	.276	16. Borders, P.	.248
3. Pena, T.	.294	10. Nilsson, D.	.274	17. Hoiles, C.	.247
4. Harper, B.	.291	11. Leyritz, J.	.265	18. Myers, G.	.246
5. Alomar Jr, S.	.288	12. Berryhill, D.	.263	19. Knorr, R.	.242
6. Steinbach, T.	.285	13. Mayne, B.	.257	20. Turner, C.	.242
7. Fabregas, J.	.284	14. Macfarlane, M.	.255		

RUNS BATTED IN

1. Nilsson, D.	69	8. Macfarlane, M.	47	15. Borders, P.	26
2. Leyritz, J.	58	9. Alomar Jr, S.	43	16. LaValliere, M.	24
3. Steinbach, T.	57	10. Walbeck, M.	35	17. Hemond, S.	20
4. Stanley, M.	57	11. Berryhill, D.	34	18. Rowland, R.	20
5. Rodriguez, I.	57	12. Harper, B.	32	19. Mayne, B.	20
6. Hoiles, C.	53	13. Karkovice, R.	29	20. Kreuter, C.	19
7. Tettleton, M.	51	14. Wilson, D.	27	21. Knorr, R.	19

STOLEN BASES

1. Alomar Jr, S.	8	6. Hoiles, C.	2	11. Mayne, B.	1
2. Hemond, S.	7	7. Fabregas, J.	2	12. Nilsson, D.	1
3. Rodriguez, I.	6	8. Macfarlane, M.	1	13. Wilson, D.	1
4. Turner, C.	3	9. Borders, P.	1	14. Walbeck, M.	1
5. Steinbach, T.	2	10. Haselman, B.	1		

RUNS SCORED

1. Tettleton, M.	57	8. Hoiles, C.	45	15. Harper, B.	23
2. Rodriguez, I.	56	9. Alomar Jr, S.	44	16. Hemond, S.	23
3. Stanley, M.	54	10. Karkovice, R.	33	17. Turner, C.	23
4. Macfarlane, M.	53	11. Walbeck, M.	31	18. Knorr, R.	20
5. Steinbach, T.	51	12. Berryhill, D.	30	19. Mayne, B.	19
6. Nilsson, D.	51	13. Borders, P.	24	20. Pena, T.	18
7. Leyritz, J.	47	14. Wilson, D.	24		

Catchers
pp. 33–46

Corners
pp. 46–65

Infield
pp. 66–85

Outfield
pp. 85–115

DH
pp. 115–119

Starters
pp. 119–155

Relievers
pp. 155–187

NL CORNERS
(20 Games or More)

HOME RUNS

1. Williams, M.	43	15. Williams, E.	11	29. Colbrunn, G.	6
2. Bagwell, J.	39	16. Berry, S.	11	30. Kruk, J.	5
3. McGriff, F.	34	17. Morris, H.	10	31. Destrade, O.	5
4. Galarraga, A.	31	18. Hayes, C.	10	32. King, J.	5
5. Wallach, T.	23	19. Segui, D.	10	33. Clark, P.	5
6. Bonilla, B.	20	20. Benzinger, T.	9	34. Lansing, M.	5
7. Walker, L.	19	21. Merced, O.	9	35. Martinez, D.	4
8. Zeile, T.	19	22. Fernandez, T.	8	36. Shipley, C.	4
9. Caminiti, K.	18	23. Duncan, M.	8	37. Hollins, D.	4
10. Conine, J.	18	24. Jordan, R.	8	38. Cianfrocco, A.	4
11. Hunter, B.	15	25. Pendleton, T.	7	39. Staton, D.	4
12. Buechele, S.	14	26. Brogna, R.	7	40. Floyd, C.	4
13. Karros, E.	14	27. Grace, M.	6		
14. Jefferies, G.	12	28. Branson, J.	6		

BATTING AVERAGE

1. Bagwell, J.	.368	15. Bonilla, B.	.291	29. Lansing, M.	.267
2. Brogna, R.	.351	16. Hayes, C.	.289	30. Livingstone, S.	.266
3. Morris, H.	.335	17. Branson, J.	.284	31. Karros, E.	.266
4. Shipley, C.	.333	18. Caminiti, K.	.283	32. Benzinger, T.	.265
5. Williams, E.	.332	19. Jordan, R.	.282	33. King, J.	.263
6. Jefferies, G.	.325	20. Floyd, C.	.281	34. Hyers, T.	.254
7. Walker, L.	.321	21. Wallach, T.	.280	35. Pendleton, T.	.252
8. Conine, J.	.319	22. Fernandez, T.	.279	36. Martinez, D.	.247
9. Galarraga, A.	.319	23. Berry, S.	.278	37. Hernandez, J.	.242
10. McGriff, F.	.318	24. Magadan, D.	.275	38. Buechele, S.	.242
11. Colbrunn, G.	.303	25. Merced, O.	.272	39. Segui, D.	.241
12. Kruk, J.	.302	26. Duncan, M.	.268	40. Hunter, B.	.234
13. Grace, M.	.298	27. Williams, M.	.268	41. Batiste, K.	.234
14. Browne, J.	.295	28. Zeile, T.	.268		

RUNS BATTED IN

1. Bagwell, J.	116	15. Merced, O.	51	29. Benzinger, T.	31
2. Williams, M.	96	16. Fernandez, T.	50	30. Colbrunn, G.	31
3. McGriff, F.	94	17. Hayes, C.	50	31. Pendleton, T.	30
4. Walker, L.	86	18. Duncan, M.	48	32. Browne, J.	30
5. Galarraga, A.	85	19. Karros, E.	46	33. Shipley, C.	30
6. Conine, J.	82	20. Grace, M.	44	34. Martinez, D.	27
7. Wallach, T.	78	21. Segui, D.	43	35. Hollins, D.	26
8. Morris, H.	78	22. Williams, E.	42	36. Clark, P.	20
9. Caminiti, K.	75	23. King, J.	42	37. Brogna, R.	20
10. Zeile, T.	75	24. Berry, S.	41	38. Magadan, D.	17
11. Bonilla, B.	67	25. Floyd, C.	41	39. Pecota, B.	16
12. Hunter, B.	57	26. Kruk, J.	38	40. Branson, J.	16
13. Jefferies, G.	55	27. Jordan, R.	37		
14. Buechele, S.	52	28. Lansing, M.	35		

STOLEN BASES

1. Walker, L.	15	14. Caminiti, K.	4	27. Buechele, S.	1
2. Bagwell, J.	15	15. Merced, O.	4	28. Bonilla, B.	1
3. Berry, S.	14	16. Browne, J.	3	29. Destrade, O.	1
4. Fernandez, T.	12	17. Martinez, D.	3	30. Pecota, B.	1
5. Jefferies, G.	12	18. Hayes, C.	3	31. Williams, M.	1
6. Lansing, M.	12	19. King, J.	3	32. Zeile, T.	1
7. Duncan, M.	10	20. Hyers, T.	3	33. Hollins, D.	1
8. Floyd, C.	10	21. Pendleton, T.	2	34. Conine, J.	1
9. Galarraga, A.	8	22. Benzinger, T.	2	35. Batiste, K.	1
10. McGriff, F.	7	23. Livingstone, S.	2	36. Clark, P.	1
11. Shipley, C.	6	24. Hernandez, J.	2	37. Colbrunn, G.	1
12. Morris, H.	6	25. Karros, E.	2	38. Brogna, R.	1
13. Kruk, J.	4	26. Cianfrocco, A.	2	39. Bogar, T.	1

RUNS SCORED

1. Bagwell, J.	104	15. Fernandez, T.	50	29. Shipley, C.	32
2. McGriff, F.	81	16. Duncan, M.	49	30. Benzinger, T.	32
3. Galarraga, A.	77	17. Merced, O.	48	31. Magadan, D.	30
4. Walker, L.	76	18. Hayes, C.	46	32. Jordan, R.	29
5. Williams, M.	74	19. Segui, D.	46	33. Hollins, D.	28
6. Wallach, T.	68	20. Lansing, M.	44	34. Pendleton, T.	25
7. Caminiti, K.	63	21. Berry, S.	43	35. Martinez, D.	23
8. Zeile, T.	62	22. Floyd, C.	43	36. Hernandez, J.	18
9. Bonilla, B.	60	23. Browne, J.	42	37. Branson, J.	18
10. Morris, H.	60	24. King, J.	36	38. Batiste, K.	17
11. Conine, J.	60	25. Kruk, J.	35	39. Colbrunn, G.	17
12. Grace, M.	55	26. Hunter, B.	34	40. Brogna, R.	16
13. Jefferies, G.	2	27. Buechele, S.	33		
14. Karros, E.	51	28. Williams, E.	32		

AL CORNERS
(20 Games or More)

HOME RUNS

1. Thomas, F.	38	15. Sorrento, P.	14	29. Velarde, R.	9
2. Fielder, C.	28	16. Leius, S.	14	30. Blowers, M.	9
3. Vaughn, M.	26	17. Brosius, S.	14	31. Joyner, W.	8
4. Hamelin, B.	24	18. Clark, W.	13	32. Shumpert, T.	8
5. Palmeiro, R.	23	19. Martinez, E.	13	33. Snow, J.	8
6. Martinez, T.	20	20. Cooper, S.	13	34. Mattingly, D.	6
7. Thome, J.	20	21. Gaetti, G.	12	35. Easley, D.	6
8. Palmer, D.	19	22. Olerud, J.	12	36. Seitzer, K.	5
9. Ventura, R.	18	23. Jaha, J.	12	37. Surhoff, B.	5
10. Fryman, T.	18	24. Boggs, W.	11	38. Perez, E.	5
11. Murray, E.	17	25. Sabo, C.	11	39. Edmonds, J.	5
12. Tettleton, M.	17	26. Sprague, E.	11	40. Aldrete, M.	4
13. Gomez, L.	15	27. Hrbek, K.	10		
14. Neel, T.	15	28. McGwire, M.	9		

Catchers
pp. 33–46

Corners
pp. 46–65

Infield
pp. 66–85

Outfield
pp. 85–115

DH
pp. 115–119

Starters
pp. 119–155

Relievers
pp. 155–187

BATTING AVERAGE

1.	Thomas, F.	.354	15.	Ventura, R.	.282	29.	Fielder, C.	.259
2.	Boggs, W.	.341	16.	Cooper, S.	.282	30.	Sabo, C.	.256
3.	Clark, W.	.329	17.	Sorrento, P.	.279	31.	Murray, E.	.254
4.	Palmeiro, R.	.319	18.	Velarde, R.	.279	32.	Spiers, B.	.252
5.	Seitzer, K.	.314	19.	Gomez, L.	.274	33.	McGwire, M.	.252
6.	Joyner, W.	.312	20.	Edmonds, J.	.273	34.	Tettleton, M.	.248
7.	Owen, S.	.310	21.	Hrbek, K.	.270	35.	Palmer, D.	.246
8.	Vaughn, M.	.310	22.	Thome, J.	.268	36.	Leius, S.	.246
9.	Mattingly, D.	.304	23.	Neel, T.	.266	37.	Aldrete, M.	.241
10.	Olerud, J.	.297	24.	Hale, C.	.263	38.	Shumpert, T.	.240
11.	Blowers, M.	.289	25.	Fryman, T.	.263	39.	Jaha, J.	.240
12.	Gaetti, G.	.288	26.	Surhoff, B.	.261	40.	Sprague, E.	.240
13.	Martinez, E.	.285	27.	Martinez, T.	.261			
14.	Hamelin, B.	.282	28.	McCarty, D.	.260			

RUNS BATTED IN

1.	Thomas, F.	101	15.	Joyner, W.	57	29.	Sprague, E.	44
2.	Fielder, C.	90	16.	Gomez, L.	56	30.	Sabo, C.	42
3.	Fryman, T.	85	17.	Boggs, W.	55	31.	Jaha, J.	39
4.	Vaughn, M.	82	18.	Hrbek, K.	53	32.	Owen, S.	37
5.	Clark, W.	80	19.	Cooper, S.	53	33.	Edmonds, J.	37
6.	Ventura, R.	78	20.	Thome, J.	52	34.	Velarde, R.	34
7.	Murray, E.	76	21.	Mattingly, D.	51	35.	Easley, D.	30
8.	Palmeiro, R.	76	22.	Tettleton, M.	51	36.	Snow, J.	30
9.	Olerud, J.	67	23.	Martinez, E.	51	37.	McGwire, M.	25
10.	Hamelin, B.	65	24.	Seitzer, K.	49	38.	Shumpert, T.	24
11.	Sorrento, P.	62	25.	Blowers, M.	49	39.	Surhoff, B.	22
12.	Martinez, T.	61	26.	Leius, S.	49	40.	Espinoza, A.	19
13.	Palmer, D.	59	27.	Brosius, S.	49			
14.	Gaetti, G.	57	28.	Neel, T.	48			

STOLEN BASES

1.	Shumpert, T.	18	13.	Palmer, D.	3	25.	Thomas, F.	2
2.	Murray, E.	8	14.	Ventura, R.	3	26.	Leius, S.	2
3.	Palmeiro, R.	7	15.	Howard, D.	3	27.	Brosius, S.	2
4.	Spiers, B.	7	16.	Thome, J.	3	28.	Neel, T.	2
5.	Martinez, E.	6	17.	Jaha, J.	3	29.	McCarty, D.	2
6.	Clark, W.	5	18.	Perez, E.	3	30.	Espinoza, A.	1
7.	Velarde, R.	4	19.	Boggs, W.	2	31.	Sabo, C.	1
8.	Vaughn, M.	4	20.	Owen, S.	2	32.	Olerud, J.	1
9.	Easley, D.	4	21.	Seitzer, K.	2	33.	Martinez, T.	1
10.	Edmonds, J.	4	22.	Aldrete, M.	2	34.	Sprague, E.	1
11.	Hamelin, B.	4	23.	Blowers, M.	2			
12.	Joyner, W.	3	24.	Fryman, T.	2			

PLAY BALL—AGAINST THE
FOUNDING FATHERS
(See page 276)

RUNS SCORED

1. Thomas, F.	106	15. Gaetti, G.	53	29. Easley, D.	41
2. Palmeiro, R.	82	16. Joyner, W.	52	30. Sprague, E.	38
3. Clark, W.	73	17. Palmer, D.	50	31. Blowers, M.	37
4. Fielder, C.	67	18. Cooper, S.	49	32. Edmonds, J.	35
5. Fryman, T.	66	19. Velarde, R.	47	33. Hrbek, K.	34
6. Vaughn, M.	65	20. Martinez, E.	47	34. Brosius, S.	31
7. Hamelin, B.	64	21. Olerud, J.	47	35. Owen, S.	30
8. Mattingly, D.	62	22. Gomez, L.	46	36. Shumpert, T.	28
9. Boggs, W.	61	23. Jaha, J.	45	37. Espinoza, A.	27
10. Thome, J.	58	24. Seitzer, K.	44	38. Spiers, B.	27
11. Murray, E.	57	25. Sorrento, P.	43	39. McGwire, M.	26
12. Tettleton, M.	57	26. Neel, T.	43	40. Aldrete, M.	23
13. Ventura, R.	57	27. Martinez, T.	42		
14. Leius, S.	57	28. Sabo, C.	41		

NL MIDDLE INFIELDERS
(20 Games or More)

HOME RUNS

1. Cordero, W.	15	16. Alicea, L.	5	31. Thompson, R.	2
2. Kent, J.	14	17. Barberie, B.	5	32. Bell, J.	2
3. Boone, B.	12	18. Lansing, M.	5	33. DeShields, D.	2
4. Dunston, S.	11	19. Shipley, C.	4	34. Morandini, M.	2
5. Pena, G.	11	20. Mejia, R.	4	35. Scarsone, S.	2
6. Larkin, B.	9	21. Smith, O.	3	36. Stocker, K.	2
7. Bell, J.	9	22. Foley, T.	3	37. Lopez, L.	2
8. Cedeno, A.	9	23. Liriano, N.	3	38. Weiss, W.	1
9. Abbott, K.	9	24. Lemke, M.	3	39. Benjamin, M.	1
10. Duncan, M.	8	25. Vizcaino, J.	3	40. Offerman, J.	1
11. Blauser, J.	6	26. Castilla, V.	3	41. Hernandez, J.	1
12. Biggio, C.	6	27. Clayton, R.	3	42. Stankiewicz, A.	1
13. Garcia, C.	6	28. Patterson, J.	3	43. Gutierrez, R.	1
14. Branson, J.	6	29. Ingram, G.	3		
15. Sandberg, R.	5	30. Roberts, B.	2		

BATTING AVERAGE

1. Shipley, C.	.333	15. Larkin, B.	.279	29. Stankiewicz, A.	259
2. Castilla, V.	.331	16. Bell, J.	.278	30. Benjamin, M.	.258
3. Roberts, B.	.320	17. Dunston, S.	.278	31. Blauser, J.	.258
4. Boone, B.	.320	18. Alicea, L.	.278	32. Vizcaino, J.	.256
5. Biggio, C.	.318	19. Garcia, C.	.277	33. Liriano, N.	.255
6. Barberie, B.	.301	20. Lopez, L.	.276	34. Pena, G.	.253
7. Treadway, J.	.298	21. Bell, J.	.276	35. Weiss, W.	.250
8. Lemke, M.	.294	22. Stocker, K.	.273	36. DeShields, D.	.250
9. Cordero, W.	.294	23. Scarsone, S.	.272	37. Vina, F.	.250
10. Morandini, M.	.292	24. Duncan, M.	.268	38. Abbott, K.	.249
11. Kent, J.	.292	25. Lansing, M.	.267	39. Hernandez, J.	.242
12. Sanchez, R.	.285	26. Oquendo, J.	.264	40. Belliard, R.	.242
13. Branson, J.	.284	27. Cedeno, A.	.263		
14. Ingram, G.	.282	28. Smith, O.	.263		

RUNS BATTED IN

1. Kent, J.	68	15. Abbott, K.	33	29. Morandini, M.	26
2. Boone, B.	68	16. Weiss, W.	32	30. Offerman, J.	25
3. Cordero, W.	63	17. Patterson, J.	32	31. Sandberg, R.	24
4. Biggio, C.	56	18. Roberts, B.	31	32. Sanchez, R.	24
5. Larkin, B.	52	19. Liriano, N.	31	33. Lopez, L.	20
6. Cedeno, A.	49	20. Lemke, M.	31	34. Castilla, V.	18
7. Duncan, M.	48	21. Barberie, B.	31	35. Branson, J.	16
8. Bell, J.	45	22. Smith, O.	30	36. Foley, T.	15
9. Blauser, J.	45	23. Shipley, C.	30	37. Arias, A.	15
10. Dunston, S.	35	24. Clayton, R.	30	38. Mejia, R.	14
11. Lansing, M.	35	25. Alicea, L.	29	39. Scarsone, S.	13
12. Pena, G.	34	26. Garcia, C.	28	40. Bournigal, R.	11
13. Vizcaino, J.	33	27. Gutierrez, R.	28		
14. DeShields, D.	33	28. Stocker, K.	28		

STOLEN BASES

1. Biggio, C.	39	15. Shipley, C.	6	29. Barberie, B.	2
2. DeShields, D.	27	16. Benjamin, M.	5	30. Hernandez, J.	2
3. Larkin, B.	26	17. Bell, J.	4	31. Castilla, V.	2
4. Clayton, R.	23	18. Alicea, L.	4	32. Sanchez, R.	2
5. Roberts, B.	21	19. Dunston, S.	3	33. Gutierrez, R.	2
6. Garcia, C.	18	20. Thompson, R.	3	34. Stocker, K.	2
7. Cordero, W.	16	21. Boone, B.	3	35. Oquendo, J.	1
8. Patterson, J.	13	22. Vina, F.	3	36. Blauser, J.	1
9. Weiss, W.	12	23. Mejia, R.	3	37. Treadway, J.	1
10. Lansing, M.	12	24. Abbott, K.	3	38. Vizcaino, J.	1
11. Duncan, M.	10	25. Lopez, L.	3	39. Cedeno, A.	1
12. Morandini, M.	10	26. Sandberg, R.	2	40. Stankiewicz, A.	1
13. Pena, G.	9	27. Bell, J.	2	41. Kent, J.	1
14. Smith, O.	6	28. Offerman, J.	2		

RUNS SCORED

1. Biggio, C.	88	15. Lansing, M.	44	29. Alicea, L.	32
2. Larkin, B.	78	16. Abbott, K.	41	30. Lopez, L.	29
3. Bell, J.	68	17. Lemke, M.	40	31. Offerman, J.	27
4. Cordero, W.	65	18. Morandini, M.	40	32. Gutierrez, R.	27
5. Boone, B.	59	19. Barberie, B.	40	33. Sanchez, R.	26
6. Weiss, W.	58	20. Liriano, N.	39	34. Scarsone, S.	21
7. Blauser, J.	56	21. Dunston, S.	38	35. Vina, F.	20
8. Kent, J.	53	22. Cedeno, A.	38	36. Hernandez, J.	18
9. Roberts, B.	52	23. Clayton, R.	38	37. Branson, J.	18
10. Smith, O.	51	24. Stocker, K.	38	38. Castilla, V.	16
11. DeShields, D.	51	25. Sandberg, R.	36	39. Treadway, J.	14
12. Duncan, M.	49	26. Patterson, J.	36	40. Foley, T.	13
13. Garcia, C.	49	27. Pena, G.	33	41. Oquendo, J.	13
14. Vizcaino, J.	47	28. Shipley, C.	32	42. Thompson, R.	13

AL MIDDLE INFIELDERS
(20 Games or More)

HOME RUNS

1. Baerga, C.	19	15. Sojo, L.	6	29. Cora, J.	2
2. Ripken, C.	13	16. Easley, D.	6	30. Reed, J.	2
3. Whitaker, L.	12	17. Strange, D.	5	31. Lovullo, T.	2
4. Valentin, J.	11	18. Knoblauch, C.	5	32. Bordick, M.	2
5. Velarde, R.	9	19. Schofield, D.	4	33. Meares, P.	2
6. Valentin, J.	9	20. Amaral, R.	4	34. Gates, B.	2
7. Trammell, A.	8	21. Fletcher, S.	3	35. Espinoza, A.	1
8. Hudler, R.	8	22. McLemore, M.	3	36. Guillen, O.	1
9. Alomar, R.	8	23. Hemond, S.	3	37. Fermin, F.	1
10. Shumpert, T.	8	24. DiSarcina, G.	3	38. Lind, J.	1
11. Gomez, C.	8	25. Kelly, P.	3	39. Vizquel, O.	1
12. Gagne, G.	7	26. Reboulet, J.	3	40. Rodriguez, C.	1
13. Naehring, T.	7	27. Hulett, T.	2	41. Martin, N.	1
14. Gallego, M.	6	28. Lee, M.	2		

BATTING AVERAGE

1. Frye, J.	.327	15. Kelly, P.	.280	29. Reboulet, J.	.259
2. Fermin, F.	.316	16. Velarde, R.	.279	30. Gagne, G.	.259
3. Ripken, C.	.315	17. Lee, M.	.278	31. Gomez, C.	.257
4. Valentin, J.	.315	18. Sojo, L.	.277	32. McLemore, M.	.256
5. Baerga, C.	.314	19. Cora, J.	.276	33. Schofield, D.	.255
6. Knoblauch, C.	.313	20. Naehring, T.	.276	34. Bordick, M.	.253
7. Grebeck, C.	.309	21. Martin, N.	.275	35. Spiers, B.	.252
8. Alomar, R.	.306	22. Vizquel, O.	.273	36. Shumpert, T.	.240
9. Whitaker, L.	.301	23. Reed, J.	.271	37. Gallego, M.	.239
10. Hudler, R.	.298	24. Lind, J.	.269	38. Valentin, J.	.239
11. Guillen, O.	.288	25. Trammell, A.	.267	39. Espinoza, A.	.238
12. Rodriguez, C.	.288	26. Meares, P.	.267	40. Reynolds, H.	.232
13. Gates, B.	.283	27. Amaral, R.	.263		
14. Beltre, E.	.282	28. DiSarcina, G.	.260		

RUNS BATTED IN

1. Baerga, C.	80	15. Reed, J.	37	29. Meares, P.	24
2. Ripken, C.	75	16. Bordick, M.	37	30. Gates, B.	24
3. Gomez, C.	53	17. Fermin, F.	35	31. Reboulet, J.	23
4. Gagne, G.	51	18. Velarde, R.	34	32. Sojo, L.	22
5. Knoblauch, C.	51	19. Vizquel, O.	33	33. Hudler, R.	20
6. Valentin, J.	49	20. DiSarcina, G.	33	34. Hemond, S.	20
7. Valentin, J.	46	21. Schofield, D.	32	35. Espinoza, A.	19
8. Whitaker, L.	43	22. Lind, J.	31	36. Amaral, R.	18
9. Naehring, T.	42	23. Cora, J.	30	37. Frye, J.	18
10. Gallego, M.	41	24. Easley, D.	30	38. Spiers, B.	17
11. Kelly, P.	41	25. McLemore, M.	29	39. Martin, N.	16
12. Guillen, O.	39	26. Trammell, A.	28	40. Hulett, T.	15
13. Lee, M.	38	27. Strange, D.	26		
14. Alomar, R.	38	28. Shumpert, T.	24		

STOLEN BASES

1. Knoblauch, C.	35	16. Bordick, M.	7	31. Valentin, J.	3
2. McLemore, M.	20	17. Kelly, P.	6	32. Gates, B.	3
3. Alomar, R.	19	18. Frye, J.	6	33. Whitaker, L.	2
4. Shumpert, T.	18	19. Guillen, O.	5	34. Hudler, R.	2
5. Vizquel, O.	13	20. Reed, J.	5	35. Sojo, L.	2
6. Valentin, J.	12	21. Amaral, R.	5	36. Beltre, E.	2
7. Gagne, G.	10	22. Meares, P.	5	37. Ripken, C.	1
8. Reynolds, H.	10	23. Gomez, C.	5	38. Espinoza, A.	1
9. Lind, J.	9	24. Fermin, F.	4	39. Lovullo, T.	1
10. Fletcher, S.	8	25. Velarde, R.	4	40. Strange, D.	1
11. Cora, J.	8	26. Easley, D.	4	41. Naehring, T.	1
12. Baerga, C.	8	27. Martin, N.	4	42. Rodriguez, C.	1
13. Schofield, D.	7	28. Trammell, A.	3	43. Cedeno, D.	1
14. Spiers, B.	7	29. Lee, M.	3		
15. Hemond, S.	7	30. DiSarcina, G.	3		

RUNS SCORED

1. Knoblauch, C.	85	15. Lee, M.	41	29. Sojo, L.	32
2. Baerga, C.	81	16. Naehring, T.	41	30. Gomez, C.	32
3. Alomar, R.	78	17. Easley, D.	41	31. Fletcher, S.	31
4. Ripken, C.	71	18. Gagne, G.	39	32. Meares, P.	29
5. Whitaker, L.	67	19. Gallego, M.	39	33. Gates, B.	29
6. Cora, J.	55	20. Vizquel, O.	39	34. Shumpert, T.	28
7. DiSarcina, G.	53	21. Trammell, A.	38	35. Reboulet, J.	28
8. Valentin, J.	53	22. Schofield, D.	38	36. Espinoza, A.	27
9. Fermin, F.	52	23. Bordick, M.	38	37. Spiers, B.	27
10. Reed, J.	48	24. Amaral, R.	37	38. Strange, D.	26
11. Velarde, R.	47	25. Frye, J.	37	39. Hemond, S.	23
12. Valentin, J.	47	26. Kelly, P.	35	40. Martin, N.	19
13. Guillen, O.	46	27. Lind, J.	34		
14. McLemore, M.	44	28. Reynolds, H.	33		

NL OUTFIELDERS
(20 Games or More)

HOME RUNS

1. Bonds, B.	37	23. Johnson, H.	10	45. Howard, T.	5
2. Mitchell, K.	30	24. Clark, D.	10	46. Jordan, B.	5
3. Bichette, D.	27	25. Hill, G.	10	47. Tarasco, T.	5
4. Sheffield, G.	27	26. Segui, D.	10	48. Eisenreich, J.	4
5. Sosa, S.	25	27. Kelly, R.	9	49. Webster, M.	4
6. Alou, M.	22	28. Merced, O.	9	50. Strawberry, D.	4
7. Walker, L.	19	29. Martin, A.	9	51. McReynolds, K.	4
8. Justice, D.	19	30. Butler, B.	8	52. Thompson, M.	4
9. Lankford, R.	19	31. Orsulak, J.	8	53. Kingery, M.	4
10. Plantier, P.	18	32. Rhodes, K.	8	54. Martinez, D.	4
11. Conine, J.	18	33. May, D.	8	55. McClendon, L.	4
12. Thompson, R.	18	34. Gonzalez, L.	8	56. Sanders, D.	4
13. Sanders, R.	17	35. Rodriguez, H.	8	57. Lewis, D.	4
14. Klesko, R.	17	36. Lindeman, J.	7	58. Brumfield, J.	4
15. Mondesi, R.	16	37. Young, E.	7	59. Floyd, C.	4
16. Whiten, M.	14	38. Bass, K.	6	60. Hatcher, B.	3
17. Bell, D.	14	39. Van Slyke, A.	6	61. Browne, J.	3
18. Incaviglia, P.	13	40. Snyder, C.	6	62. Gwynn, C.	3
19. Burks, E.	13	41. Gilkey, B.	6	63. Carreon, M.	3
20. Gwynn, T.	12	42. Zambrano, E.	6	64. Burnitz, J.	3
21. Finley, S.	11	43. McGee, W.	5		
22. Grissom, M.	11	44. Dykstra, L.	5		

BATTING AVERAGE

1. Gwynn, T.	.394	21. Clark, D.	.296	41. Merced, O.	.272
2. Kingery, M.	.349	22. Browne, J.	.295	42. Young, E.	.272
3. Alou, M.	.339	23. Whiten, M.	.293	43. Frazier, L.	.271
4. Mitchell, K.	.326	24. Kelly, R.	.292	44. Lindeman, J.	.270
5. Burks, E.	.322	25. Grissom, M.	.289	45. Carreon, M.	.270
6. Walker, L.	.321	26. Martin, A.	.286	46. Rodriguez, H.	.268
7. Roberts, B.	.320	27. May, D.	.284	47. Gwynn, C.	.268
8. Conine, J.	.319	28. Sanders, D.	.283	48. Lankford, R.	.267
9. Butler, B.	.314	29. McGee, W.	.282	49. Howard, T.	.264
10. Justice, D.	.313	30. Floyd, C.	.281	50. Carr, C.	.263
11. Bonds, B.	.312	31. White, R.	.278	51. Sanders, R.	.263
12. Brumfield, J.	.312	32. Klesko, R.	.277	52. Orsulak, J.	.260
13. Bell, D.	.311	33. Sheffield, G.	.276	53. Zambrano, E.	.259
14. Bass, K.	.311	34. Finley, S.	.276	54. Jordan, B.	.258
15. Walton, J.	.309	35. Webster, M.	.274	55. Lewis, D.	.257
16. Mondesi, R.	.307	36. Thompson, M.	.274	56. Varsho, G.	.256
17. Bichette, D.	.304	37. Dykstra, L.	.273	57. McReynolds, K.	.255
18. Sosa, S.	.300	38. Gonzalez, L.	.273	58. Cangelosi, J.	.252
19. Eisenreich, J.	.300	39. Tarasco, T.	.273	59. Gilkey, B.	.252
20. Hill, G.	.297	40. Kelly, M.	.273	60. Carrillo, M.	.250

RUNS BATTED IN

1. Bichette, D.	95	22. Clark, D.	46	42. Van Slyke, A.	30
2. Walker, L.	86	23. Kelly, R.	45	43. Browne, J.	30
3. Conine, J.	82	24. Grissom, M.	45	44. Carr, C.	30
4. Bonds, B.	81	25. Gilkey, B.	45	45. Young, E.	30
5. Sheffield, G.	78	26. Eisenreich, J.	43	46. Lewis, D.	29
6. Alou, M.	78	27. Segui, D.	43	47. Sanders, D.	28
7. Mitchell, K.	77	28. Orsulak, J.	42	48. Martinez, D.	27
8. Sosa, S.	70	29. Kingery, M.	41	49. Dykstra, L.	24
9. Gonzalez, L.	67	30. Plantier, P.	41	50. Burks, E.	24
10. Gwynn, T.	64	31. Floyd, C.	41	51. Howard, T.	24
11. Sanders, R.	62	32. Johnson, H.	40	52. McGee, W.	23
12. Justice, D.	59	33. Hill, G.	38	53. McReynolds, K.	21
13. Thompson, R.	59	34. Bass, K.	35	54. Lindeman, J.	20
14. Lankford, R.	57	35. Butler, B.	33	55. Carreon, M.	20
15. Mondesi, R.	56	36. Thompson, M.	33	56. Rhodes, K.	19
16. Bell, D.	54	37. Finley, S.	33	57. Tarasco, T.	19
17. Whiten, M.	53	38. Martin, A.	33	58. Snyder, C.	18
18. Merced, O.	51	39. Incaviglia, P.	32	59. Zambrano, E.	18
19. May, D.	51	40. Hatcher, B.	31	60. Strawberry, D.	17
20. Rodriguez, H.	49	41. Roberts, B.	31	61. Longmire, T.	17
21. Klesko, R.	47				

OFFICIAL ROTISSERIE LEAGUE
T-SHIRTS AND CAPS
(See page 278)

STOLEN BASES

1. Sanders, D.	38	24. Johnson, H.	11	47. Martinez, D.	3
2. Grissom, M.	36	25. Lankford, R.	11	48. Burks, E.	3
3. Carr, C.	32	26. Mondesi, R.	11	49. Plantier, P.	3
4. Lewis, D.	30	27. Whiten, M.	10	50. May, D.	3
5. Bonds, B.	29	28. Floyd, C.	10	51. Carrillo, M.	3
6. Butler, B.	27	29. Thompson, M.	9	52. Bass, K.	2
7. Bell, D.	24	30. Hatcher, B.	8	53. McReynolds, K.	2
8. Mouton, J.	24	31. Van Slyke, A.	7	54. Mitchell, K.	2
9. Sosa, S.	22	32. Alou, M.	7	55. Clark, D.	2
10. Roberts, B.	21	33. Eisenreich, J.	6	56. Justice, D.	2
11. Bichette, D.	21	34. Rhodes, K.	6	57. Longmire, T.	2
12. Sanders, R.	21	35. Brumfield, J.	6	58. Zambrano, E.	2
13. Frazier, L.	20	36. Gwynn, T.	5	59. Webster, M.	1
14. Hill, G.	19	37. Cangelosi, J.	5	60. Incaviglia, P.	1
15. Kelly, R.	19	38. Kingery, M.	5	61. Snyder, C.	1
16. Young, E.	18	39. Tarasco, T.	5	62. Walton, J.	1
17. Dykstra, L.	15	40. Orsulak, J.	4	63. Conine, J.	1
18. Walker, L.	15	41. Merced, O.	4	64. Thompson, R.	1
19. Gilkey, B.	15	42. Howard, T.	4	65. Klesko, R.	1
20. Gonzalez, L.	15	43. Jordan, B.	4	66. Burnitz, J.	1
21. Martin, A.	15	44. McGee, W.	3	67. White, R.	1
22. Finley, S.	13	45. Felder, M.	3		
23. Sheffield, G.	12	46. Browne, J.	3		

RUNS SCORED

1. Grissom, M.	96	22. Whiten, M.	57	43. Thompson, R.	39
2. Bonds, B.	89	23. Gonzalez, L.	57	44. Bass, K.	37
3. Lankford, R.	89	24. Kingery, M.	56	45. Clark, D.	37
4. Alou, M.	81	25. Bell, D.	54	46. Young, E.	37
5. Butler, B.	79	26. Roberts, B.	52	47. Brumfield, J.	36
6. Gwynn, T.	79	27. Gilkey, B.	52	48. Thompson, M.	34
7. Walker, L.	76	28. Hill, G.	48	49. Burks, E.	33
8. Bichette, D.	74	29. Merced, O.	48	50. Rodriguez, H.	33
9. Kelly, R.	73	30. Martin, A.	48	51. Johnson, H.	30
10. Lewis, D.	70	31. Segui, D.	46	52. Incaviglia, P.	28
11. Dykstra, L.	68	32. Plantier, P.	44	53. Gallagher, D.	27
12. Sanders, R.	66	33. May, D.	43	54. Burnitz, J.	26
13. Finley, S.	64	34. Floyd, C.	43	55. Frazier, L.	25
14. Mondesi, R.	63	35. Mouton, J.	43	56. Howard, T.	24
15. Sheffield, G.	61	36. Eisenreich, J.	42	57. McReynolds, K.	23
16. Justice, D.	61	37. Browne, J.	42	58. Martinez, D.	23
17. Carr, C.	61	38. Klesko, R.	42	59. McGee, W.	19
18. Conine, J.	60	39. Van Slyke, A.	41	60. Snyder, C.	18
19. Sosa, S.	59	40. Orsulak, J.	39	61. Lindeman, J.	18
20. Sanders, D.	58	41. Hatcher, B.	39		
21. Mitchell, K.	57	42. Rhodes, K.	39		

AL OUTFIELDERS
(20 Games or More)

HOME RUNS

1. Griffey Jr., K.	40	22. Lofton, K.	12	43. Henderson, D.	5
2. Belle, A.	36	23. Greenwell, M.	11	44. Samuel, J.	5
3. Carter, J.	27	24. Jose, F.	11	45. Mitchell, K.	5
4. Gibson, K.	23	25. Sabo, C.	11	46. Kirby, W.	5
5. Sierra, R.	23	26. Munoz, P.	11	47. Edmonds, J.	5
6. Salmon, T.	23	27. Curtis, C.	11	48. Coles, D.	4
7. O'Neill, P.	21	28. Raines, T.	10	49. Aldrete, M.	4
8. Buhner, J.	21	29. Brunansky, T.	10	50. Cole, A.	4
9. Puckett, K.	20	30. Javier, S.	10	51. McRae, B.	4
10. Phillips, T.	19	31. Jackson, D.	10	52. Williams, G.	4
11. Tartabull, D.	19	32. Anthony, E.	10	53. Bautista, D.	4
12. Vaughn, G.	19	33. Mieske, M.	10	54. Davis, E.	3
13. Gonzalez, J.	19	34. Greer, R.	10	55. Johnson, L.	3
14. Ramirez, M.	17	35. Devereaux, M.	9	56. Huff, M.	3
15. Mack, S.	15	36. Ward, T.	9	57. Voigt, J.	3
16. White, D.	13	37. Delgado, C.	9	58. Coleman, V.	2
17. Jackson, B.	13	38. Smith, D.	8	59. Newson, W.	2
18. Berroa, G.	13	39. Hammonds, J.	8	60. Tinsley, L.	2
19. Felix, J.	13	40. James, C.	7	61. O'Leary, T.	2
20. Anderson, B.	12	41. Henderson, R.	6		
21. Williams, B.	12	42. Chamberlain, W.	6		

BATTING AVERAGE

1. O'Neill, P.	.359	21. Salmon, T.	.287	41. Anderson, B.	.263
2. Belle, A.	.357	22. Phillips, T.	.281	42. McDowell, O.	.262
3. Lofton, K.	.349	23. Smith, D.	.281	43. Hamilton, D.	.262
4. Mack, S.	.333	24. Buhner, J.	.279	44. Chamberlain, W.	.262
5. Griffey Jr., K.	.323	25. Jackson, B.	.279	45. Henderson, R.	.260
6. Puckett, K.	.316	26. Johnson, L.	.277	46. Mieske, M.	.259
7. Greer, R.	.314	27. Gibson, K.	.276	47. Tartabull, D.	.256
8. Jackson, D.	.312	28. Gonzalez, J.	.275	48. James, C.	.256
9. Polonia, L.	.312	29. Nixon, O.	.274	49. Sabo, C.	.256
10. Samuel, J.	.309	30. Edmonds, J.	.273	50. Curtis, C.	.256
11. Berroa, G.	.306	31. McRae, B.	.273	51. Newson, W.	.255
12. Felix, J.	.306	32. O'Leary, T.	.273	52. Hulse, D.	.255
13. Huff, M.	.304	33. Javier, S.	.272	53. Vaughn, G.	.254
14. Jose, F.	.303	34. Carter, J.	.271	54. Diaz, A.	.251
15. Hammonds, J.	.296	35. White, D.	.271	55. Henderson, D.	.248
16. Cole, A.	.295	36. Greenwell, M.	.269	56. Aldrete, M.	.241
17. Munoz, P.	.295	37. Ramirez, M.	.269	57. Cuyler, M.	.241
18. Kirby, W.	.293	38. Sierra, R.	.268	58. Voigt, J.	.241
19. Williams, G.	.291	39. Raines, T.	.266	59. Coleman, V.	.240
20. Williams, B.	.289	40. Becker, R.	.265	60. Anthony, E.	.237

RUNS BATTED IN

1. Puckett, K.	112	22. Jackson, D.	51	42. Hammonds, J.	31
2. Carter, J.	103	23. Curtis, C.	50	43. Smith, D.	30
3. Belle, A.	101	24. White, D.	49	44. Anthony, E.	30
4. Sierra, R.	92	25. Felix, J.	49	45. Chamberlain, W.	26
5. Griffey Jr., K.	90	26. Anderson, B.	48	46. Nixon, O.	25
6. Gonzalez, J.	85	27. Greer, R.	46	47. Huff, M.	25
7. O'Neill, P.	83	28. Greenwell, M.	45	48. Delgado, C.	24
8. Gibson, K.	72	29. Ward, T.	45	49. Cole, A.	23
9. Salmon, T.	70	30. Javier, S.	44	50. Kirby, W.	23
10. Buhner, J.	68	31. Jackson, B.	43	51. Samuel, J.	21
11. Tartabull, D.	67	32. Sabo, C.	42	52. Henderson, R.	20
12. Berroa, G.	65	33. McRae, B.	40	53. Voigt, J.	20
13. Phillips, T.	61	34. Mieske, M.	38	54. James, C.	19
14. Mack, S.	61	35. Edmonds, J.	37	55. Hulse, D.	19
15. Ramirez, M.	60	36. Polonia, L.	36	56. Aldrete, M.	18
16. Williams, B.	57	37. Munoz, P.	36	57. Diaz, A.	17
17. Lofton, K.	57	38. Brunansky, T.	34	58. Coles, D.	15
18. Jose, F.	55	39. Coleman, V.	33	59. McDowell, O.	15
19. Vaughn, G.	55	40. Devereaux, M.	33	60. Mitchell, K.	15
20. Johnson, L.	54	41. Henderson, D.	31	61. Bautista, D.	15
21. Raines, T.	52				

STOLEN BASES

1. Lofton, K.	60	22. Jose, F.	10	43. Hamilton, D.	3
2. Coleman, V.	50	23. Belle, A.	9	44. Mieske, M.	3
3. Nixon, O.	42	24. Vaughn, G.	9	45. Turang, B.	3
4. Anderson, B.	31	25. Sierra, R.	8	46. Henderson, D.	2
5. Cole, A.	29	26. Jackson, D.	7	47. Greenwell, M.	2
6. McRae, B.	28	27. Berroa, G.	7	48. Aldrete, M.	2
7. Johnson, L.	26	28. Puckett, K.	6	49. Smith, D.	2
8. Curtis, C.	25	29. Anthony, E.	6	50. Huff, M.	2
9. Javier, S.	24	30. Gonzalez, J.	6	51. Fox, E.	2
10. Henderson, R.	22	31. Ward, T.	6	52. Tartabull, D.	1
11. Polonia, L.	20	32. Becker, R.	6	53. Jackson, B.	1
12. Hulse, D.	18	33. Samuel, J.	5	54. Devereaux, M.	1
13. Williams, B.	16	34. Davis, E.	5	55. Sabo, C.	1
14. McDowell, O.	14	35. O'Neill, P.	5	56. Felix, J.	1
15. Raines, T.	13	36. Cuyler, M.	5	57. Newson, W.	1
16. Phillips, T.	13	37. Diaz, A.	5	58. Salmon, T.	1
17. Tinsley, L.	13	38. Hammonds, J.	5	59. Williams, G.	1
18. Carter, J.	11	39. Gibson, K.	4	60. O'Leary, T.	1
19. White, D.	11	40. Mack, S.	4	61. Bautista, D.	1
20. Griffey Jr., K.	11	41. Ramirez, M.	4	62. Delgado, C.	1
21. Kirby, W.	11	42. Edmonds, J.	4		

JOIN THE RLBA!
212-695-3463

RUNS SCORED

1. Lofton, K.	105	22. Polonia, L.	62	43. Edmonds, J.	35
2. Griffey Jr, K.	94	23. Coleman, V.	61	44. McDowell, O.	34
3. Phillips, T.	91	24. Nixon, O.	60	45. Kirby, W.	33
4. Belle, A.	90	25. Greenwell, M.	60	46. Samuel, J.	32
5. Raines, T.	80	26. Vaughn, G.	59	47. Smith, D.	31
6. Williams, B.	80	27. Hulse, D.	58	48. Anthony, E.	31
7. Puckett, K.	79	28. Gonzalez, J.	57	49. Huff, M.	31
8. Anderson, B.	78	29. Jose, F.	56	50. James, C.	28
9. Javier, S.	75	30. Johnson, L.	56	51. Henderson, D.	27
10. Buhner, J.	74	31. Mack, S.	55	52. Tinsley, L.	27
11. Gibson, K.	71	32. Berroa, G.	55	53. Brunansky, T.	24
12. Sierra, R.	71	33. Ward, T.	55	54. Jackson, B.	23
13. McRae, B.	71	34. Felix, J.	54	55. Aldrete, M.	23
14. Carter, J.	70	35. Ramirez, M.	51	56. Hamilton, D.	23
15. Tartabull, D.	68	36. Hammonds, J.	45	57. Mitchell, K.	21
16. O'Neill, P.	68	37. Jackson, D.	43	58. Chamberlain, W.	20
17. Cole, A.	68	38. Sabo, C.	41	59. Cuyler, M.	20
18. White, D.	67	39. Mieske, M.	39	60. Davis, E.	19
19. Curtis, C.	67	40. Greer, R.	36	61. Williams, G.	19
20. Salmon, T.	67	41. Devereaux, M.	35		
21. Henderson, R.	66	42. Munoz, P.	35		

Catchers
pp. 33–46

Corners
pp. 46–65

Infield
pp. 66–85

Outfield
pp. 85–115

DH
pp. 115–119

Starters
pp. 119–155

Relievers
pp. 155–187

AL DESIGNATED HITTERS
(20 Games or More)

HOME RUNS

1. Canseco, J.	31	8. Tettleton, M.	17	15. Martinez, E.	13
2. Davis, C.	26	9. Leyritz, J.	17	16. Nilsson, D.	12
3. Hamelin, B.	24	10. Dawson, A.	16	17. Winfield, D.	10
4. Gibson, K.	23	11. Baines, H.	16	18. Jefferson, R.	8
5. Franco, J.	20	12. Neel, T.	15	19. Maldonado, C.	5
6. Tartabull, D.	19	13. Molitor, P.	14	20. Harper, B.	4
7. Murray, E.	17	14. Berroa, G.	13		

BATTING AVERAGE

1. Molitor, P.	.341	8. Martinez, E.	.285	15. Tartabull, D.	.256
2. Jefferson, R.	.327	9. Canseco, J.	.282	16. Murray, E.	.254
3. Franco, J.	.319	10. Hamelin, B.	.282	17. Winfield, D.	.251
4. Davis, C.	.311	11. Gibson, K.	.276	18. Tettleton, M.	.248
5. Berroa, G.	.306	12. Nilsson, D.	.274	19. Dawson, A.	.240
6. Baines, H.	.294	13. Neel, T.	.266	20. Smith, L.	.203
7. Harper, B.	.291	14. Leyritz, J.	.265		

RUNS BATTED IN

1. Franco, J.	98	8. Tartabull, D.	67	15. Dawson, A.	48
2. Canseco, J.	90	9. Berroa, G.	65	16. Neel, T.	48
3. Davis, C.	84	10. Hamelin, B.	65	17. Winfield, D.	43
4. Murray, E.	76	11. Leyritz, J.	58	18. Harper, B.	32
5. Molitor, P.	75	12. Baines, H.	54	19. Jefferson, R.	32
6. Gibson, K.	72	13. Tettleton, M.	51	20. Maldonado, C.	12
7. Nilsson, D.	69	14. Martinez, E.	51		

STOLEN BASES

1. Molitor, P.	20	7. Gibson, K.	4	13. Smith, L.	1		
2. Canseco, J.	15	8. Hamelin, B.	4	14. Maldonado, C.	1		
3. Murray, E.	8	9. Davis, C.	3	15. Tartabull, D.	1		
4. Franco, J.	8	10. Dawson, A.	2	16. Nilsson, D.	1		
5. Berroa, G.	7	11. Winfield, D.	2				
6. Martinez, E.	6	12. Neel, T.	2				

RUNS SCORED

1. Canseco, J.	88	8. Murray, E.	57	15. Neel, T.	43
2. Molitor, P.	86	9. Tettleton, M.	57	16. Winfield, D.	35
3. Davis, C.	72	10. Berroa, G.	55	17. Dawson, A.	34
4. Franco, J.	72	11. Nilsson, D.	51	18. Jefferson, R.	24
5. Gibson, K.	71	12. Martinez, E.	47	19. Harper, B.	23
6. Tartabull, D.	68	13. Leyritz, J.	47	20. Maldonado, C.	14
7. Hamelin, B.	64	14. Baines, H.	44		

STATS INK

All the stats in the Scouting Report (Chapter 2) plus all the stats in the Rotisserie Stat-Pak (Chapter 3) that you've just finished memorizing come from STATS, Inc., a band of merry number noodlers whose client list reads like a Who's Who of baseball publications: *Sports Illustrated*, *The Sporting News*, ESPN, *USA Today*, and, yours truly, *Rotisserie League Baseball*.

STATS, Inc. also publishes several books that belong in every Rotisserie owner's library. Among them:

- *Major League Handbook*. The first baseball annual to hit the bookstores every year (November 1), with player stats for the year just ended plus projections by Bill James for the year coming up.
- *Minor League Handbook*. An essential tool for building your farm system. Year-by-year data for AAA and AA players, plus Bill James's "Major League Equivalencies."
- *Player Profiles*. Detailed situational analyses, including month-by-month performance breakdowns.
- *Matchups!* A compendium of batter vs. pitcher matchups that gives you the lowdown on the game within the game.
- *The Scouting Report*. A mix of stats and analysis, this hardy annual includes "Stars, Bums, and Sleepers," a look at who's on the way up and who's on the way down.

And that's only for starters! For a complete catalog of STATS, Inc. publications and fantasy games (including something called "football"), call the STATS inksters at 800-63-STATS.

4

Down on the Farm

Back to the Future
(or, Lessons of the Great Strike of 1994)

The 1995 Minor League Report
by John Benson

Editor's Note: *Farming is hard, grinding, backbreaking work. Frankly, that's why we depend so much on John Benson's farm report every year. For the last four seasons John has been our chief agronomist, and every year he has brought in a bumper crop. This will come as no surprise to Rotisserians who know him as the founder, general manager, star pitcher, and bullpen catcher of Diamond Library, a bona fide Rotisserie think tank that could end up taking over the universe any day now. Among Diamond Library's publications are John's* Rotisserie Baseball Annual *($22.95), the* Benson A to Z Player Guide *($15.95), and* Benson Baseball Monthly *($59/year), a newsletter worth at least half a dozen points in the standings. For information on how to order and an irresistible sales pitch, call John at 800-707-9090.*

As has become customary, before attempting to separate this year's wheat from the chaff, I wish to say a few words about our farming methods.

Over the years, I have used this space to illuminate such esoteric subjects as the validity of age as a signifier in player development, the calibration of statistics from the various minor leagues for comparative purposes, the various ways to read managers' minds, and the reasons why there are more prospects at Double-A than at Triple-A.

Last year's introductory essay was devoted to self-examination, and specifically to answering the question "Just how good are these predictions that annually take up so much valuable space?" In that report, I took full credit for alerting everyone to expect big rookie seasons from Mike Piazza, Tim Salmon, Juan Gonzalez, and Kenny Lofton (to name just a few of our obvious past successes). I further patted myself on the back for correctly tabbing many of the darker horses like Brent Gates and Mike Lansing. When it came to the failures, my progress report admitted that "we" were wrong to expect big things from the likes of Lee Stevens and Johnny Guzman, and we were also wrong to have overlooked Pat Listach.

(As I confer with many authorities and experts, both in-house and out-house, when compiling each year's Farm Report, the "we" is technically correct for good and bad results alike.)

So what is our introductory topic this year? I propose another retrospective examination leading to an appraisal of our predictive methods and how they can be improved. No, it's not déjà vu all over again, and it's not senile redundancy, although the latter is always a clear and present danger. I want to look back at 1994 because it was such an unusual year on so many levels. Being in the business of news analysis, I have learned that every change has a ripple effect, and the more unusual the change, the bigger the ripples. No one can dispute that the surprising events of last season made a lot of waves.

The baseball farm crop of 1994 was uniquely affected by three powerful external forces. First, the specter of a strike shut off the trade route as a way for minor league prospects to move into major league job openings. Second, the effects of expansion continued to have a profound impact on major league needs and the talent pool, giving deeper meaning to the phrase "rushing 'em." Third, the strike itself robbed us all of a chance to see how prospects would respond when called up to the big time.

No general manager in 1994 wanted to give up a genuine prospect to get some veteran help for a pennant stretch that might never arrive. Just among the third-base prospects, for example, this phenomenon prevented the Yankees from trading Russ Davis to a team like the Twins, where he would have had a legitimate shot under ideal circumstances (i.e., without the pressure of a pennant race). And the Reds never found a taker for Tony Fernandez, so Willie Greene had to cool his heels another year in the minors.

The second of these external forces also severely distorted traditional player development patterns. The most pronounced shift was a new, liberal attitude toward giving unproven pitching talent a major league look-see, as GMs and field managers showed increased willingness to promote farmhands directly into starting rotations and prominent bullpen roles, rather than trade for known quantities.

One reason was that among those known quantities, the pickings were slim. As Lou Piniella told me during spring training, "There aren't 28 dominant closers to go around, so we have to develop new ones. Young pitching always comes out of nowhere." Thus, Bobby Ayala was handed the ball in Seattle before Opening Day, and John Hudek (who had flopped in spring training after being waived by the Tigers) was able to rise from the Tucson Toros to the top of the Houston pen in just 12 days. Hudek at least had a good fastball, which placed him clearly among the top, ah, 200 or so minor league pitchers of 1993.

(If you think this is easy, find me anyone who predicted at the end of spring training that John Hudek would go from bull bleep to blue chip by the All-Star break.)

Part of this new open-door policy in the pitching department last year was a willingness to employ untested soft tossers, something that most major league front offices seem constitutionally unable (or at least unwilling) to do.

The Mets, for example, called up Jason Jacome, who had about the lowest velocity in their organization, when they needed midseason help for their starting rotation. Upon his arrival in New York, Jacome told the beat writers that he threw a fastball in the low- to mid-80s and turned perpetually skeptical countenances into some downright dubious frowns. It was, of course, the batters for the Padres, Dodgers, Giants, and Braves who soon had the longest faces, as Jacome promptly gave them all lessons in how a lefty with decent control and a good changeup should pitch in the National League.

With hindsight, we can see such player development in 1994 as simply a consequence of Expansion–Phase Two, with a prestrike moratorium on trades catalyzing more movement within each organization. In Expansion–Phase One (1993), the major leagues started recycling marginal veterans like Mike Aldrete and Fernando Valenzuela. In 1994, with the supply of used parts fully depleted, the rush for new, untested talent finally became frantic. (In last year's book, we remarked how the 1993 expansion had not produced opportunities for as many 22-to-25-year-olds as we had expected. Those opportunities finally arrived, big-time, in 1994.)

One effect of all these changes was to throw a monkey wrench into our precisely calibrated (almost), unerringly accurate forecasting machinery. (Yes, we have heard that it is the poor craftsman who blames his tools. But we have to blame *something*, don't we?) Even so, in last year's book, we still managed to give you some obvious and some not-so-obvious picks that clicked: Raul Mondesi, Javy Lopez, Jim Thome, Cliff Floyd, Jeffrey Hammonds, Manny Ramirez, Ryan Klesko, and James Mouton have become household names, at least in Rotisserie households. And there was our favorite 1994 long shot, Bobby Jones, another Mets soft thrower who turned into a big winner with a mediocre team. We were also delighted to see a two-time pick in these pages, Rico Brogna, finally emerge with a big bang.

Some of our top picks didn't make it because they were injured: Chipper Jones, Tim Costo, Steve Karsay, and Brien Taylor. Others among our top choices from a year ago appear again on this year's list. We're confident that we weren't wrong about them, merely premature.

Last year's most glaring omission was Bob Hamelin, who turned in a Rookie of the Year performance. In Hamelin's case, we have a lengthy excuse and a brief lesson for the future. The excuse is that we *had* considered Hamelin as a candidate for our list every year for three years, and we kept cutting him for solid reasons, like his being overshadowed by Jeff Conine and being unlikely to displace George Brett. When it came time for the 1994 list, we were all under the impression that the 26-year-old Hamelin had been touted here enough times already, which he hadn't. So that's how he slid through our radar. (Also, the dog ate our homework.)

Matt Walbeck was excluded because he didn't project as a starter for the Cubs, certainly not as a rookie stuck behind Rick Wilkins, who seemed to one and all to be the second coming of Gabby Hartnett. Walbeck's career curve swooped up dramatically after a trade to the budget-conscious Twins, who had just said good-bye to Brian Harper. Other players who left us wishing we could have a do-over: Kurt Abbott, who also benefited from a trade; Jim Edmonds, who benefited from an injury to Eddie Perez; and Chris Gomez, who benefited from Sparky Anderson's annual April optimism. The lesson to be learned concerns the importance of following all the news right up until Draft Day.

Among starting pitchers last year, and in addition to Jacome, we missed Steve Trachsel, Joey Hamilton, and Jon Lieber. Among relievers, Hector Carrasco, Darren Hall, and Rick White ranked right up there with Hudek as conspicuous absences from our 1994 list. What can we say? One consolation is that *Benson Baseball Monthly* had covered all those relievers (and more) before the end of spring training. And the starters? Well, my standard advice is not to draft any rookies, unless you can store them safely on a reserve list. The black art of choosing reliable rookie starters has long eluded me. Recalling how Mark Twain's Connecticut Yankee kept good old Merlin on the Camelot payroll and gave him the menial chore of working the weather, I often wish I could delegate the job of doing starting pitcher prognostications. That way I would have someone to fire.

To put all these misses into context, however, consider that there were 128 active rookies in the majors a week before the 1994 strike, not counting those who had already come up and gone back down and, of course, not counting any September call-ups. Our 1994 Farm Report was limited to 88 names. With a list only 68% the size of the actual rookie population, we still got most of those who mattered—not a great year, but it could have been a lot worse.

We emerge from the ordeal of 1994 much humbler and a little wiser, with useful lessons learned. Specifically:

1. ***The Hector Carrasco Rule.*** When a smart GM takes all summer to decide on a player to be named later, as Jim Bowden did after trading away Chris Hammond, pay careful attention to the prospect he eventually selects. And if it's a hard-throwing Class-A pitcher who jumps to the majors, grab him.

2. ***The Darren Hall Rule.*** When an ace reliever like Duane Ward is disabled, with no clear successor on the major league roster, take any rookie who had 13 saves at Triple-A the year before and who recorded at least five games finished during spring training. (Don't worry if the pitcher is nearly 30 years old without a single day of major league experience, and ignore it if his Triple-A ERA was 5.33. He can still get saves.)

3. ***The Rick White Rule.*** Always draft relief pitchers who lead their winter league in strikeouts while working out of the pen, especially if they're going to pitch for Jim Leyland. Then dump them before June.

4. ***The Jason Jacome Rule.*** If you have nothing to lose in ERA and ratio anyway, take a flyer on any National League lefty starter with a pulse.

Not all of the strange events of 1994 were disruptive for us forecasters. Some of what happened was actually helpful for providing clues, especially for those who looked a little deeper than customary. For example, by July 31 of last year, most GMs had figured out that the September call-up process might not be business as usual. Accordingly, some of the more promising players at Double-A got August promotions to Triple-A, to test their skills further, when in a "normal" year they might have been left to finish out the season at Double-A. That's one of the reasons why Tony Clark, Brad Clontz, Terrell Wade, Alan Benes, Pork Chop Pough, Derek Jeter, and Terry Bradshaw caught our attention last summer.

Another strike-related phenomenon with portents for 1995 was the demotion of talented youngsters just before August 12 so that they could continue developing. When you take a player who is already good enough to be in the major leagues, and add the fact that his organization believes he will show further improvement with more work, then you might very well be looking at a future star. Here is a list of 1994 rookies who fit that description:

Baltimore: Arthur Rhodes, Armando Benitez
California: Andrew Lorraine
Cleveland: Albie Lopez, Chad Ogea
Detroit: Sean Bergman, Greg Gohr
Kansas City: Dwayne Hosey
Minnesota: Dave Stevens
New York Yankees: Joe Ausanio, Sterling Hitchcock
Oakland: Mark Acre, Ernie Young
Seattle: Jim Converse, Tim Davis, Roger Salkeld
Texas: John Dettmer, Hector Fajardo, James Hurst
Atlanta: Mike Kelly
Chicago Cubs: Steve Trachsel
Houston: Roberto Petagine, Orlando Miller, James Mouton
Los Angeles: Ismail Valdes
New York Mets: Jason Jacome, Jeromy Burnitz
Philadelphia: Ricky Bottalico, Mike Lieberthal
San Diego: Bryce Florie
San Francisco: William Van Landingham

One final benefit of the strike—with due acknowledgment that the words "benefit" and "strike" don't look right in the same sentence after last year—was that we all got more opportunities to watch more minor leaguers live, to see them on television, and to read about them in print. Personally, I favored the Eastern League games, where I found a seat among the radar gun–armed scouts behind home plate and listened as carefully as I watched. And regular TV access to the Norfolk Tides and Richmond Braves and all their opponents was priceless. My knowledge of the minor leagues is now deeper than ever, thanks to the strike of 1994.

Does that make me sound like a cockeyed optimist who insists on finding a silver lining in every cloud? Guilty as charged. Baseball *will* be back, and when it returns, you will especially enjoy keeping an eye on the players listed below.

1995 Farm System Prospects

Most members of the Class of 1995 will make it to the majors sooner or later. Your job is to figure out which ones will get there sooner—and which will have a major impact once they arrive. Owners in leagues with sizable farm systems that can be carried forward from year to year will want to pay close attention to the players with one-star ratings. Each player's age is as of April 1, 1995. Profiles do not include 1994 major league stats (if any), which appear on pages 321–342.

RATING GUIDE

* * * Ready to be a productive regular now.
* * Fine talent, should make it to the majors in 1995.
* Good idea for 1996–97.

CATCHERS

CARLOS DELGADO   BLUE JAYS   Age 22/L   * * *

On his way to Cooperstown in April, Delgado took a wrong turn and ended up in Syracuse. He'll find his way back to the main road. We were right in giving him two stars a year ago; we're almost certain three stars is the correct rating now. A major power source, Delgado finished his 1994 minor league season with a home run binge.

Team	Level		AB	HR	RBI	SB	BA
Syracuse	AAA		307	19	58	1	.319

CHARLES JOHNSON   MARLINS   Age 23/R   * *

Benito Santiago has been holding a spot for Florida's first-ever draft choice. Strong arm, good defensive skills, and solid power potential.

Team	Level		AB	HR	RBI	SB	BA
Portland	AA		443	28	80	4	.264

TIM LAKER   EXPOS   Age 25/R   * *

Been in the major leagues before, and he'll be back again. Laker just had his best year ever at the plate and became an International League All-Star.

Team	Level		AB	HR	RBI	SB	BA
Ottawa	AAA		424	12	71	11	.309

MIKE LIEBERTHAL   PHILLIES   Age 23/R   * *

When he was growing up in California, Lieberthal was a neighbor of Steve Yeager. Lieberthal's a similar type of catcher—long on defense, a bit short on offense. If Darren Daulton moves to first base, Lieberthal becomes the starting catcher immediately.

Team	Level		AB	HR	RBI	SB	BA
Scranton	AAA		296	1	32	1	.233

EDDIE PEREZ   **BRAVES**   **Age 26/R**   * *

A less expensive alternative to Charlie O'Brien, so he could step into the backup role this year. Perez has a better throwing arm than Javy Lopez, and some pop in his bat.

Team	Level	AB	HR	RBI	SB	BA
Richmond	AAA	388	9	49	1	.260

FIRST BASEMEN

RICH AUDE   **PIRATES**   **Age 23/R**   * *

After he started to pull the ball and hit with power in 1993, scouts expected a great season from Aude in 1994, but—even though he was playing in a park that favors righty hitters—he turned in one that was merely good. Aude was rated the best defensive first baseman in the American Association, which tells you the league was full of wooden hands.

Team	Level	AB	HR	RBI	SB	BA
Buffalo	AAA	520	15	79	9	.281

RICO BROGNA   **METS**   **Age 24/L**   * * *

Brogna's good-year, bad-year history has been reflected in this book. We gave him one star in 1991 and three in 1993, skipping him in 1992 and 1994. After one of the Mets' best trades of the '90s (straight up for Alan Zinter), Brogna has become a minor cult hero in New York.

Team	Level	AB	HR	RBI	SB	BA
Norfolk	AAA	258	12	37	1	.244

TONY CLARK   **TIGERS**   **Age 22/B**   * *

With Brogna gone from Detroit, Clark is now the candidate to push Cecil Fielder from first base to DH. Last year was the first Clark played full-time, after finishing another career hustling his 6'7" frame up and down a basketball court.

Team	Level	AB	HR	RBI	SB	BA
Trenton	AA	394	21	86	0	.279
Toledo	AAA	92	2	13	2	.261

1995 ROOKIE ALL-STAR TEAM—AMERICAN LEAGUE

C	Carlos Delgado (Blue Jays)	OF	Shawn Green (Blue Jays)
1B	Steve Dunn (Twins)	OF	Marc Newfield (Mariners)
2B	Ray Durham (White Sox)	OF	Sherman Obando (Orioles)
3B	Russ Davis (Yankees)	P	Armando Benitez (Orioles)
SS	Alex Gonzalez (Blue Jays)	P	Paul Shuey (Indians)

STEVE DUNN   TWINS   Age 24/L   * *

It took him five years to get past A-ball, but Dunn has made steady progress the last three seasons. He has now moved ahead of David McCarty in Minnesota's depth chart. With Kent Hrbek hanging up his spikes, there is a vacancy.

Team	Level	AB	HR	RBI	SB	BA
Salt Lake	AAA	330	15	73	0	.309

MATT FRANCO   CUBS   Age 25/L   * *

Why does a team with a great home run park keep bringing up slick-fielding first basemen who spray line drives? Franco's immediate future obviously depends on Mark Grace moving along.

Team	Level	AB	HR	RBI	SB	BA
Iowa	AAA	437	11	71	3	.277

HERBERT PERRY   INDIANS   Age 25/R   * * *

Perry's magnificent season, which included a lengthy successful experiment hitting everything the other way, ended with a broken wrist. He'll be back.

Team	Level	AB	HR	RBI	SB	BA
Charlotte	AAA	376	13	70	9	.327

ROBERTO PETAGINE   ASTROS   Age 23/L   * *

While no one was noticing, Houston has filled its farm system with a horde of top talents. Petagine's 1994 season would have been bigger if not for time on the DL. Of course he won't beat out Jeff Bagwell, but he might get an outfielder's glove, or get traded.

Team	Level	AB	HR	RBI	SB	BA
Tucson	AAA	247	10	44	3	.316

J. R. PHILLIPS   GIANTS   Age 24/L   * *

With Will Clark's departure, Phillips was in line to become San Francisco's regular first baseman. A year later, he's still in line. Given a decent chance, he simply failed to make contact at the plate. But when he does hit the ball, it travels a long way. And his defense is really better than reputed.

Team	Level	AB	HR	RBI	SB	BA
Phoenix	AAA	360	27	79	4	.300

LUIS RAVEN   ANGELS   Age 26/R   * *

Before last season, Raven's scouting label was "nevermore." But then he developed into one of the minors' best power hitters. Despite graduating from the Texas League in June, he still ranked second in the league in home runs.

Team	Level	AB	HR	RBI	SB	BA
Midland	AA	191	18	57	4	.304
Vancouver	AAA	326	23	59	7	.297

GENE SCHALL   **PHILLIES**   **Age 24/R**   * *

Schall became one of the International League's leading run producers with one of its lowest-scoring teams. His arrival should hasten John Kruk's departure.

Team	Level	AB	HR	RBI	SB	BA
Scranton	AAA	463	16	89	9	.285

TATE SEEFRIED   **YANKEES**   **Age 22/L**   *

Last season he set the franchise home run record at Albany. Seefried swings and misses a lot, but when he connects, the result is often awesome.

Team	Level	AB	HR	RBI	SB	BA
Albany	AA	444	27	83	1	.225

JASON THOMPSON   **PADRES**   **Age 23/L**   *

A slick fielder who last year had the sixth highest RBI total in the minors. And every year we give at least one spot to a player from Rancho Cucamonga for the sound baseball reason that we like the name.

Team	Level	AB	HR	RBI	SB	BA
R. Cucamonga	A	253	13	63	1	.360
Wichita	AA	215	8	46	0	.260

JOE VITIELLO   **ROYALS**   **Age 24/R**   * *

A very sharp batting eye placed Vitiello among the minor league leaders in both OBP and batting average. He could share some time with Bob Hamelin as a first baseman/DH in 1995. Vitiello has played some outfield, but not very well.

Team	Level	AB	HR	RBI	SB	BA
Omaha	AAA	352	10	61	3	.344

SECOND BASEMEN

EDGARDO ALFONZO   **METS**   **Age 21/R**   * *

A very strong hitter for a middle infielder, Alfonzo moved to second base so that the next Ozzie Smith, Rey Ordonez, could play short for Binghamton. Not to be confused with Edgar Alfonzo, the 27-year-old career minor leaguer.

Team	Level	AB	HR	RBI	SB	BA
Binghamton	AA	498	15	75	14	.293

RAY DURHAM   **WHITE SOX**   **Age 23/B**   * * *

Joey Cora and Norberto Martin both have reason to worry about their jobs for 1995. They simply can't do all the things that Durham can.

Team	Level	AB	HR	RBI	SB	BA
Nashville	AAA	527	16	66	34	.296

TONY GRAFFANINO   BRAVES   Age 22/R   ★ ★

Changing the spelling of his last name didn't change his prospect status, which is still spelled "very good." He has blown past Ramon Caraballo on Atlanta's farm ladder. Next wrung: Mark Lemke.

Team	Level	AB	HR	RBI	SB	BA
Greenville	AA	440	7	52	29	.300

SHANNON PENN   TIGERS   Age 25/B   ★ ★

Penn's game is based on speed, which is not often prominent in Detroit's offense. Still, the front office likes him enough that a good spring training should lead to bigger opportunities in 1995.

Team	Level	AB	HR	RBI	SB	BA
Toledo	AAA	444	2	33	45	.284

ARQUIMEDEZ POZO   MARINERS   Age 21/R   ★

Eureka! The Mariners have found the second baseman they have been looking for since Harold Reynolds got past his prime. Pozo took a while making the adjustment from the California League to the Southern, but he's AL-bound for sure.

Team	Level	AB	HR	RBI	SB	BA
Jacksonville	AA	447	14	54	11	.289

CHRIS STYNES   BLUE JAYS   Age 22/R   ★

One of the younger players in the Double-A All-Star Game, Stynes is a converted third baseman whose defense still needs refining. He can hit, but so can that other guy at second in Toronto—what's his name—oh, yeah, Alomar.

Team	Level	AB	HR	RBI	SB	BA
Knoxville	AA	545	8	79	28	.317

QUILVIO VERAS   METS   Age 23/B   ★

With great speed, and marvelous range in the field, he would be a three-star player if the Mets moved Jeff Kent to third base. Veras has started slowly at each level, and will improve with more time at Triple-A.

Team	Level	AB	HR	RBI	SB	BA
Norfolk	AAA	457	0	43	40	.249

THIRD BASEMEN

SHANE ANDREWS   EXPOS   Age 23/R   ★ ★

The former first-round draft pick was much improved in 1994. He made better contact and sharpened his defense. Andrews's power numbers were down last year, but he will be a strong power hitter in the big leagues.

Team	Level	AB	HR	RBI	SB	BA
Ottawa	AAA	460	16	85	6	.254

HOWARD BATTLE   BLUE JAYS   Age 23/R   * *

The big battle last season was with defense. If he gets to Toronto, Howard will hit even more home runs than he did in Syracuse.

Team	Level		AB	HR	RBI	SB	BA
Syracuse	AAA		517	14	75	26	.277

DAVID BELL   INDIANS   Age 22/R   * *

Progress toward joining his father (Indians coach Buddy Bell) last year didn't pan out, but he finished strong, hitting .340 after July 1.

Team	Level		AB	HR	RBI	SB	BA
Charlotte	AAA		481	18	88	2	.293

RUSS DAVIS   YANKEES   Age 25/R   * * *

Davis had hit nine home runs in the three weeks before a pitch broke his wrist in late August. Before that, Yankee trade talks with just about every team included inquiries about Davis, reflecting the current shortage of major league third basemen who can hit. Because Wade Boggs is one of those few, Davis still needs that long-delayed change of scenery.

Team	Level		AB	HR	RBI	SB	BA
Columbus	AAA		415	25	69	3	.277

WILLIE GREENE   REDS   Age 23/L   * * *

When the Reds acquired Tony Fernandez for trade bait, their GM called Greene and told him not to worry. Then when the strike ruined the trade market, and Fernandez couldn't be moved, it was the front office that had worries. But no one need worry in 1995. Even if Fernandez is still around, Greene will displace him.

Team	Level		AB	HR	RBI	SB	BA
Indianapolis	AAA		435	23	80	8	.285

BUTCH HUSKEY   METS   Age 23/R   * *

Will never be another sultan of swat unless he stops trying to be burger king. Showed up at spring training 1994 about half a person overweight, but then trimmed down during the summer. The less-husky version is becoming a good glove man, and you've got to love his home run swing.

Team	Level		AB	HR	RBI	SB	BA
Norfolk	AAA		474	10	57	16	.228

1995 ROOKIE ALL-STAR TEAM—NATIONAL LEAGUE

C	Mike Lieberthal (Phillies)		OF	Carl Everett (Marlins)
1B	J. R. Phillips (Giants)		OF	Brian Hunter (Astros)
2B	Tony Graffanino (Braves)		OF	Midre Cummings (Pirates)
3B	Willie Greene (Reds)		P	Alan Benes (Cardinals)
SS	Chipper Jones (Braves)		P	Brad Clontz (Braves)

PHIL NEVIN   ASTROS   Age 24/R   * *

The first pick overall in 1992 draft. His performance last year was hampered by migraines. Meanwhile Ken Caminiti's big season gave Houston's opponents headaches. Nevin's turn is coming soon.

Team	Level	AB	HR	RBI	SB	BA
Tucson	AAA	445	12	79	3	.263

JOSE OLIVA   BRAVES   Age 24/R   * * *

Showed increased maturity by not sulking when Terry Pendleton's return from injury pushed Oliva back down to Richmond. He was hitting major league pitching with authority then, and he will do so again.

Team	Level	AB	HR	RBI	SB	BA
Richmond	AAA	371	24	64	2	.253

LUIS ORTIZ   RED SOX   Age 24/R   * * *

When Ortíz hit a line drive off Brad Pennington's noggin, Pawtucket manager Buddy Bailey worried, "I'm afraid he's going to kill someone; he hits the ball that hard." A little higher trajectory and even the Green Monster won't be safe.

Team	Level	AB	HR	RBI	SB	BA
Pawtucket	AAA	317	6	36	1	.312

TIM UNROE   BREWERS   Age 24/R   * *

Has come a long way from his .251 average in the hitting-rich California League in 1993. Unroe was the Texas League MVP and also MVP of the Double-A All-Star Game. He has a good arm to go with his bat. If he needs another vowel for his last name, when he signs that first big league contract, he can buy one.

Team	Level	AB	HR	RBI	SB	BA
El Paso	AA	469	15	103	13	.313

SHORTSTOPS

MANNY ALEXANDER   ORIOLES   Age 24/R   * *

Fine defense. Also good speed. But he's from the Luis Mercedes School of Baserunning—which teaches you to put your head down and keep running until someone tags you out. Perpetually stuck behind Cal Ripken, Alexander is now being tried as a utility infielder.

Team	Level	AB	HR	RBI	SB	BA
Rochester	AAA	426	6	39	30	.249

BENJI GIL   RANGERS   Age 22/R   * *

It wasn't a big deal when Gil was rushed to the majors and didn't hit in 1993, but there was genuine concern when he didn't hit much at Triple-A last year. Hope renewed, though, when Gil hit .300 after August 1.

Team	Level	AB	HR	RBI	SB	BA
Oklahoma City	AAA	487	10	55	14	.248

ALEX GONZALEZ   BLUE JAYS   Age 21/R   * * *

Gonzalez was voted the International League's best defensive shortstop in the *Baseball America* poll, even while he was making over 30 errors. With improved concentration, he'll become a major league All-Star.

Team	Level	AB	HR	RBI	SB	BA
Syracuse	AAA	437	12	57	23	.284

DENNY HOCKING   TWINS   Age 24/B   * * *

Not superlative in any aspect of offense or defense, but all-around solid in every way—and thus better than all the other Twins shortstop options. Hocking is the type of player who will help your Rotisserie roster more than he helps Minnesota's, so we love him.

Team	Level	AB	HR	RBI	SB	BA
Salt Lake	AAA	394	5	57	13	.279

DEREK JETER   YANKEES   Age 20/R   * * *

No player came farther in 1994. This former first-round pick will force Yankees management to be unusually open-minded about easing rookies into the starting lineup.

Team	Level	AB	HR	RBI	SB	BA
Tampa	A	292	0	39	28	.329
Albany	AA	122	2	13	12	.377
Columbus	AAA	126	3	16	10	.349

CHIPPER JONES   BRAVES   Age 22/B   * * *

The best natural player in the minors in the early 1990s. The Braves needed a left fielder last spring, and Jones was adjusting to the new position beautifully when he tore up his knee and missed the season. Smart owners who grabbed him for $5 or so last year will be delighted this year.

Team	Level	AB	HR	RBI	SB	BA
Did not play						

POKEY REESE   REDS   Age 21/R   * *

Flashy number one pick out of high school. Reese finally learned how to hit in his second season in the Southern League. More speed than his name might suggest.

Team	Level	AB	HR	RBI	SB	BA
Chattanooga	AA	484	12	49	21	.269

ALEX RODRIGUEZ   MARINERS   Age 19/R   * * *

The first pick overall in the 1993 draft. Because of extended contract negotiations, he didn't play pro ball until 1994. But how he played!

Team	Level	AB	HR	RBI	SB	BA
Appleton	A	295	15	63	17	.315
Jacksonville	AA	59	1	8	2	.288
Calgary	AAA	119	6	21	2	.311

OUTFIELDERS

GARRET ANDERSON   ANGELS   Age 22/L   * * *

Those who viewed Jim Edmonds's arrival as meteoric will be even more impressed with Anderson, who is two years younger than Edmonds.

Team	Level		AB	HR	RBI	SB	BA
Vancouver	AAA		505	12	102	3	.321

BILLY ASHLEY   DODGERS   Age 24/R   * * *

Watching Ashley take batting practice is more exciting than watching a week of highlight films. The only problem is that you must eventually come out of the BP cage and take the field if you want to play in the National League. Ashley will get some benefit from the Dodgers' relative indifference to defense.

Team	Level		AB	HR	RBI	SB	BA
Albuquerque	AAA		388	37	105	6	.345

ALLEN BATTLE   CARDINALS   Age 26/R   * *

Necessarily compared with Terry Bradshaw. They're about the same age, but Battle remained one step ahead of Bradshaw coming up through the farm system until Bradshaw arrived in Louisville late last summer.

Team	Level		AB	HR	RBI	SB	BA
Louisville	AAA		520	6	69	23	.313

TREY BEAMON   PIRATES   Age 21/L   * *

The youngest player in the Double-A All-Star Game wasn't nervous. He tripled and singled in his first two at-bats. A hitting machine, his price will be right for Pittsburgh's budget, at least for a while.

Team	Level		AB	HR	RBI	SB	BA
Carolina	AA		434	5	47	24	.323

RICH BECKER   TWINS   Age 23/B   * *

Serious candidate to be Minnesota's center fielder in 1995. He was a serious candidate last year, too, but got hurt. The injury bugaboo is just one of his many similarities to Lenny Dykstra. The minor league ban on chewing tobacco at least helped to keep one type of stain off Becker's uniforms.

Team	Level		AB	HR	RBI	SB	BA
Salt Lake	AAA		282	2	38	7	.316

GREG BLOSSER   RED SOX   Age 23/L   * *

A much improved, more disciplined hitter last season, Blosser started the year in Boston, then became one of the few everyday players for the IL East Division champions.

Team	Level		AB	HR	RBI	SB	BA
Pawtucket	AAA		350	17	54	11	.260

TERRY BRADSHAW CARDINALS Age 26/L * *

In the classic mold of those speedy, defense-oriented St. Louis outfielders of the 1980s. Played 110 consecutive errorless games in 1994.

Team	Level		AB	HR	RBI	SB	BA
Arkansas	AA		424	10	52	13	.281
Louisville	AAA		80	4	8	5	.250

SCOTT BULLETT CUBS Age 26/L * *

A resurrected Pirates prospect, finally showing some power and better overall maturity. If you think the Cubs could use a speedy center fielder with good defensive skills, you're right—you'll take a long look at Bullett. So should the Cubs.

Team	Level		AB	HR	RBI	SB	BA
Iowa	AAA		530	13	69	27	.308

ROGER CEDENO DODGERS Age 20/B * *

Will move into center field at Dodger Stadium as soon as Brett Butler is ready to vacate the position. The only question is whether Cedeno will still be a young man when that happens.

Team	Level		AB	HR	RBI	SB	BA
Albuquerque	AAA		383	4	49	30	.321

MARTY CORDOVA TWINS Age 25/R * *

His numbers from 1994 would be even bigger if he hadn't started the season on the DL with a broken arm. Cordova can't play defense with Rich Becker, but he can hit with anyone.

Team	Level		AB	HR	RBI	SB	BA
Salt Lake	AAA		385	19	66	17	.358

MIDRE CUMMINGS PIRATES Age 23/L * * *

More than any other player, Cummings is in the right place at the right time for 1995. With Andy Van Slyke and his big salary gone, there is an obvious opening, and Cummings is definitely ready. His future is so assured that he lost some of his intensity late last year.

Team	Level		AB	HR	RBI	SB	BA
Buffalo	AAA		182	2	22	5	.313

BEST LONG-TERM PICKS—AMERICAN LEAGUE

C	Carlos Delgado (Blue Jays)	OF	Johnny Damon (Royals)
1B	Tony Clark (Tigers)	OF	Michael Tucker (Royals)
2B	Arquimedez Pozo (Mariners)	OF	Ruben Rivera (Yankees)
3B	Luis Ortíz (Red Sox)	P	Julian Tavarez (Indians)
SS	Alex Rodriguez (Mariners)	P	Andrew Lorraine (Angels)

JOHNNY DAMON   ROYALS   Age 21/L   *

For the long term, you won't find a better prospect. Damon hits for average, draws walks, steals bases, scores runs, and plays good center field. And he'll develop more power as he matures.

Team	Level	AB	HR	RBI	SB	BA
Wilmington	A	472	6	75	44	.316

CARL EVERETT   MARLINS   Age 24/B   * * *

Chuck Carr can run fast, maybe right out of Miami. Everett already plays center field like a major leaguer, and his offensive upside is much higher than Carr's. The Marlins have been careful not to rush this former first-round draft pick, plucked from the Yankees during expansion.

Team	Level	AB	HR	RBI	SB	BA
Edmonton	AAA	321	11	47	16	.336

CURTIS GOODWIN   ORIOLES   Age 22/L   * *

Speed is Goodwin's greatest asset. He handled Double-A easily and finished on a high note: 15 consecutive steals and a .347 average for the month of August. We love speed.

Team	Level	AB	HR	RBI	SB	BA
Bowie	AA	597	2	37	59	.286

SHAWN GREEN   BLUE JAYS   Age 22/L   * * *

His smooth swing has drawn comparisons to John Olerud. But Green, with the best outfield arm in the International League last year, is a more complete all-around player. Pay no attention to his brief major league struggle in 1994; he'll be fine in 1995.

Team	Level	AB	HR	RBI	SB	BA
Syracuse	AAA	433	13	61	19	.344

TODD HOLLANDSWORTH   DODGERS   Age 21/L   * *

A darling of those who saw him in the Arizona Fall League in 1993, one of a large group of precocious Dodgers prospects, Hollandsworth didn't disappoint in the PCL. His aggressive outfield play reminds us of a young Kevin McReynolds, and we mean that as a compliment.

Team	Level	AB	HR	RBI	SB	BA
Albuquerque	AAA	505	19	91	15	.285

BRIAN HUNTER   ASTROS   Age 24/R   * * *

Hunter has always been wonderful on the bases and in the field, but, amazingly, at spring training a year ago his organization was cautious about his future as a hitter. Now that he's spent a summer flirting with .400, those questions are gone, and the only one remaining is: what will the Astros do with Steve Finley?

Team	Level	AB	HR	RBI	SB	BA
Tucson	AAA	513	10	51	49	.372

MIKE KELLY   **BRAVES**   **Age 24/R**   * *

A top draft pick with raw power and speed, Kelly is sometimes regarded as a bust for developing slower than expected. Nonetheless, he's become a solid outfielder, and his strike zone judgment has improved steadily. He's still young enough to have a fine major league career, with several seasons of double digits in home runs and stolen bases.

Team	Level	AB	HR	RBI	SB	BA
Richmond	AAA	313	15	45	9	.262

JOSE MALAVE   **RED SOX**   **Age 23/R**   * *

Playing his 1994 home games at one of the toughest parks for hitters (Beehive Field) in the pitching-dominated Eastern League, Malave nonetheless placed near the top of all minor leaguers in total bases and extra-base hits. Fenway Park equivalents stagger the imagination.

Team	Level	AB	HR	RBI	SB	BA
New Britain	AA	465	24	92	4	.299

RAY McDAVID   **PADRES**   **Age 23/L**   * *

Had a cup of coffee in San Diego last summer when Derek Bell got suspended. Now McDavid's ready to consume the whole pot. His walks, doubles, and stolen bases make him more valuable than his batting average alone would suggest.

Team	Level	AB	HR	RBI	SB	BA
Las Vegas	AAA	476	13	62	24	.271

KERWIN MOORE   **ATHLETICS**   **Age 24/B**   * *

Until we finally saw the movie, we thought *Speed* was a biopic about Moore. Briefly a candidate for the A's center field job in 1994, but cooler heads tabbed Stan Javier for Oakland and put Moore in the Southern League. The additional year of experience was necessary. He's already a heckuva lot better actor than Keanu Reeves. (But then, who isn't?)

Team	Level	AB	HR	RBI	SB	BA
Huntsville	AA	494	5	33	54	.243

LYLE MOUTON   **YANKEES**   **Age 25/R**   *

Nobody hits the ball any harder, although some hit it more often. A late bloomer, but a student of the game, Mouton is working hard to make better contact. Don't bet he won't learn how.

Team	Level	AB	HR	RBI	SB	BA
Albany	AA	325	14	50	8	.295
Columbus	AAA	204	4	32	5	.314

GLENN MURRAY   **RED SOX**   **Age 24/R**   * *

Another all-or-nothing type of hitter, but a good outfielder in left or center. Dan Duquette brought Murray over from Montreal, a point favoring his advancement.

Team	Level	AB	HR	RBI	SB	BA
Pawtucket	AAA	465	25	64	9	.224

MARC NEWFIELD   MARINERS   Age 22/R   * * *

At a spring training "B" game last year, one wide-eyed scout asked the rhetorical question "How did anyone ever get this guy out when he was in high school?" Newfield has an awesome ability to cover the whole strike zone while generating power wherever the ball is pitched. Big numbers coming. Trust us on this one.

Team	Level	AB	HR	RBI	SB	BA
Calgary	AAA	430	19	83	0	.349

MELVIN NIEVES   PADRES   Age 23/B   * *

Hasn't exactly made San Diego fans—and we interviewed all of them—forget Fred McGriff, for whom Nieves was partial payment. Scouts have compared Nieves to Ruben Sierra, but at age 22 Sierra had accumulated 46 major league home runs.

Team	Level	AB	HR	RBI	SB	BA
Las Vegas	AAA	406	25	90	1	.308

SHERMAN OBANDO   ORIOLES   Age 25/R   * *

A good enough hitter to step directly into a major league DH role, and it's a good thing. For Obando, catching a fly ball is not just a job; it's an adventure.

Team	Level	AB	HR	RBI	SB	BA
Rochester	AAA	403	20	69	1	.330

RUBEN RIVERA   YANKEES   Age 21/R   *

Won the Sally League MVP award and then moved up to Tampa, where The Boss could get a closer look at his prize talent.

Team	Level	AB	HR	RBI	SB	BA
Greensboro	A	398	27	78	36	.286
Tampa	A	134	5	20	12	.261

MICHAEL TUCKER   ROYALS   Age 23/L   * *

Drafted in 1992's first round as an infielder, Tucker was one of four Omaha players to reach 20 homers last year, and he's the best of that quartet.

Team	Level	AB	HR	RBI	SB	BA
Omaha	AAA	485	21	77	11	.276

BEST LONG-TERM PICKS—NATIONAL LEAGUE

C	Charles Johnson (Marlins)	OF	Ray McDavid (Padres)
1B	Roberto Petagine (Astros)	OF	Trey Beamon (Pirates)
2B	Edgardo Alfonzo (Mets)	OF	Roger Cedeno (Dodgers)
3B	Jose Oliva (Braves)	P	Brian Barber (Cardinals)
SS	Chipper Jones (Braves)	P	Darren Dreifort (Dodgers)

PAT WATKINS   REDS   Age 22/R   *

Among the top ten in total bases among minor leaguers last year, Watkins was a first-round pick in 1992. Still at least a year away, he can play center field or right.

Team	Level	AB	HR	RBI	SB	BA
Winston-Salem	A	524	27	83	31	.290

RONDELL WHITE   EXPOS   Age 23/R   * * *

Cliff Floyd was the rookie getting the most playing time early last season, but White was frequently in the lineup after Larry Walker moved to first base. The strike came just when Rondell was hitting his stride.

Team	Level	AB	HR	RBI	SB	BA
Ottawa	AAA	169	7	18	9	.272

DARRELL WHITMORE   MARLINS   Age 26/L   * *

Whitmore's stock dropped when a late-summer tantrum got him a two-game suspension from the PCL—and eight more games from his own team for "insubordination."

Team	Level	AB	HR	RBI	SB	BA
Edmonton	AAA	421	20	61	14	.283

NIGEL WILSON   MARLINS   Age 25/L   * *

The first player taken in the expansion draft hasn't exactly blossomed. He was 0-for-September in a 1993 call-up, and in 1994 he slipped below Carl Everett among Florida's outfield prospects. Pay close attention to his spring: he could be on the way from prospect to suspect.

Team	Level	AB	HR	RBI	SB	BA
Edmonton	AAA	314	12	62	2	.309

ERNIE YOUNG   ATHLETICS   Age 25/R   * *

Injuries have held back this power prospect, who had a fine 1994 season while being shuttled up and down the Oakland organizational ladder.

Team	Level	AB	HR	RBI	SB	BA
Huntsville	AA	257	14	55	5	.346
Tacoma	AAA	102	6	16	0	.284

PITCHERS

JUAN ACEVEDO   ROCKIES   Age 24/R   * *

With a 93 mph fastball, a deceptive changeup, and an improving splitter, Acevedo was good enough to share the Eastern League's Rookie of the Year Award.

Team	Level	W	L	ERA	IP	H	BB	K
New Haven	AA	17	6	2.37	174	142	38	161

JAMES BALDWIN   WHITE SOX   Age 23/R   * *

With sunny-tempered Jack McDowell apparently headed out of the Windy City, the Sox penciled Baldwin's name into the 1995 rotation. He's a power pitcher seeking steadier control.

Team	Level	W	L	ERA	IP	H	BB	K
Nashville	AAA	12	6	3.72	162	144	83	156

BRIAN BARBER   CARDINALS   Age 22/R   * *

Looked like a hot prospect in spring training, way back in 1992. Last year was not so great on paper, but the talent is still there. And the Cards have new, liberalized criteria for breaking into their starting rotation: you have to be breathing.

Team	Level	W	L	ERA	IP	H	BB	K
Arkansas	AA	1	3	3.25	36	31	16	54
Louisville	AAA	4	7	5.38	85	79	46	95

MARC BARCELO   TWINS   Age 23/R   *

A 1993 first-round draft pick who had an excellent year in his first full pro season. With a hot start, Barcelo could arrive in mid-1995.

Team	Level	W	L	ERA	IP	H	BB	K
Nashville	AA	11	5	2.77	175	161	43	146

ALAN BENES   CARDINALS   Age 23/R   * * *

A 1993 first-rounder on the fast track. He was among the top five minor leaguers in several stats categories, and a clear first in number of promotions. The smaller of the Benes brothers (6'5" to Andy's 6'6") is clearly the Cards' top pitching prospect.

Team	Level	W	L	ERA	IP	H	BB	K
Savannah	A	2	0	1.48	24	21	7	24
St. Petersburg	A	7	1	1.61	78	55	15	69
Arkansas	AA	7	2	2.98	87	58	26	75
Louisville	AAA	1	0	2.93	15	10	4	16

ARMANDO BENITEZ   ORIOLES   Age 23/R   * * *

Last year's stats reflect a slow start. Benitez has as good a chance as anyone this year to join Todd Worrell and Gregg Olson as rare exceptions to the rule that minor league savers don't step directly into major league closer roles.

Team	Level	W	L	ERA	IP	H	BB	K
Bowie	AA	8	4	3.14	71	41	39	106

SEAN BERGMAN   TIGERS   Age 24/R   * *

Bergman will get a chance to live every young pitcher's dream: an opportunity to pitch regularly at Tiger Stadium. Hope he fares better than most Tiger pitchers, for whom pitching in the Motown bandbox is a three-scream nightmare. Bergman's 1994 record would have been better, but he couldn't beat Rochester. Fortunately, Rochester is not in the American League. Yet.

Team	Level	W	L	ERA	IP	H	BB	K
Toledo	AAA	11	8	3.72	154	147	53	145

RICKY BOTTALICO   PHILLIES   Age 25/R   * *

A hot commodity after some strong work in the 1993 Arizona Fall League, Bottalico subsequently fell back to the stature of Toby Borland. Still, success in Double-A earned him his major league debut.

Team	Level	W	L	ERA	IP	H	BB	K
Scranton	AAA	4	2	6.64	39	44	28	43
Reading	AA	2	2	2.53	42	29	10	51

BRAD CLONTZ   BRAVES   Age 23/R   * * *

The Braves wanted to see if this sidearmer could get out left-handed hitters at a higher level. After the promotion, he actually increased his pace of recording saves, finishing with 38.

Team	Level	W	L	ERA	IP	H	BB	K
Greenville	AA	1	2	1.29	48	33	14	53
Richmond	AAA	0	0	2.10	25	19	9	21

DARREN DREIFORT   DODGERS   Age 22/R   * *

Last year's best candidate to become a Worrell-Olson Exception (see Armando Benitez comment, above), Dreifort fell flat on his face. But he still has a bright future. He was the first pitcher drafted in 1993, and could well turn out to be one of the best.

Team	Level	W	L	ERA	IP	H	BB	K
San Antonio	AA	3	1	2.80	35	36	13	32
Albuquerque	AAA	1	0	5.68	6	8	3	3

JEFF GRANGER   ROYALS   Age 23/L   * *

The best possible profile for a rookie pitcher: a tall, hard-throwing lefty in a large park . . . and in 1995, with real grass on the field, to boot!

Team	Level	W	L	ERA	IP	H	BB	K
Memphis	AA	7	7	3.87	139	155	61	112

LaTROY HAWKINS   TWINS   Age 22/R   *

He shot through Minnesota's farm system in 1994, amassing as many wins as any minor league pitcher. With the Twins' rotation full of holes, Hawkins has a solid chance to get the ball every fifth day. Some caution, though: in the Humpdome, a rookie with a ball could be hazardous for your ERA.

Team	Level	W	L	ERA	IP	H	BB	K
Ft. Wayne	A	4	0	2.33	38	32	6	36
Nashville	AA	9	2	2.33	73	50	28	53
Salt Lake	AAA	5	4	4.08	81	92	33	37

JASON JACOME   METS   Age 24/L   * * *

Don't expect more stats like those he had in 1994, because this off-speed artist is the type of pitcher who is less successful once hitters have a second look at him. Still, so long as the Mets don't put him and Bobby Jones back-to-back in the rotation, both can be successful.

Team	Level	W	L	ERA	IP	H	BB	K
Norfolk	AAA	8	6	2.84	126	138	42	80

SCOTT KLINGENBECK   ORIOLES   Age 24/R   * *

His 1994 cup of coffee lasted just long enough for one victory, in a midseason emergency start. Klingenbeck will start the year at Rochester, but his curve is good enough to warrant another midseason call-up—and a longer stay— in 1995.

Team	Level	W	L	ERA	IP	H	BB	K
Bowie	AA	7	5	3.63	143	151	37	120

JOSE LIMA   TIGERS   Age 22/R   * *

When he was good, he was very, very good—including a no-hitter. When he was bad, he was a typical Tigers pitching prospect.

Team	Level	W	L	ERA	IP	H	BB	K
Toledo	AAA	7	9	3.53	135	115	48	112

ALBIE LOPEZ   INDIANS   Age 23/R   * * *

It happens every spring: management gets excited about a championship and loses patience with younger players. If the Tribe just lets Lopez pitch—and if he visits the salad bar instead of the dessert cart occasionally—he'll be just fine. He throws the hardest among Cleveland's talented starting pitching prospects.

Team	Level	W	L	ERA	IP	H	BB	K
Charlotte	AAA	13	3	3.94	144	136	42	105

ANDREW LORRAINE   ANGELS   Age 22/L   * *

It took him barely a year to grow from a draft pick into a major leaguer. The Angels have a way of acquiring fine lefties.

Team	Level	W	L	ERA	IP	H	BB	K
Vancouver	AAA	12	4	3.42	142	156	34	90

CHAD OGEA   INDIANS   Age 24/R   * *

Ditto the Albie Lopez comments, except that Ogea doesn't throw as hard and wears a smaller uniform.

Team	Level	W	L	ERA	IP	H	BB	K
Charlotte	AAA	9	10	3.85	163	146	34	113

CHAN HO PARK   DODGERS   Age 21/R   * *

The Dodgers would dearly love to see him become a big box office draw in L.A., so they will give him every opportunity. The only big question is whether Park can throw enough strikes.

Team	Level	W	L	ERA	IP	H	BB	K
San Antonio	AA	5	7	3.55	101	91	57	100

TROY PERCIVAL   ANGELS   Age 25/R   *

If there were a Comeback Player of the Year Award in the minor leagues, Percival would have won it last year. Of course, the idea is not to stay in the minors long enough to stage a comeback.

Team	Level	W	L	ERA	IP	H	BB	K
Vancouver	AAA	2	6	4.13	61	63	29	73

BILL PULSIPHER   METS   Age 21/L   * *

Confident to the point of being cocky. But hey, it ain't braggin' if you can do it, and Pulsipher has been doing it. He features a fastball that rides in on right-handers and keeps the bat factories working overtime.

Team	Level	W	L	ERA	IP	H	BB	K
Binghamton	AA	14	8	3.14	195	175	85	162

FRANK RODRIGUEZ   RED SOX   Age 22/R   * * *

Pawtucket's pennant-winning team in 1994 proved the value of keeping a core of good-guy veterans around to help the prospects mature. Rodriguez came a long way as a pro, and set a franchise record for strikeouts.

Team	Level	W	L	ERA	IP	H	BB	K
Pawtucket	AAA	8	12	3.87	179	174	59	158

SCOTT RUFFCORN   WHITE SOX   Age 25/R   * *

Hasn't been impressive in two major league chances, but the scouts and the minor league results tell the same story: Ruffcorn will make it in the bigs, and soon.

Team	Level	W	L	ERA	IP	H	BB	K
Nashville	AAA	15	3	2.72	165	139	40	144

PAUL SHUEY   INDIANS   Age 24/R   * *

If you liked Charley Kerfeld, you will love this guy, who's right up there with Armando Benitez bidding to be the next Worrell-Olson Exception. Shuey's biggest negative is a high leg kick that, although it's gotten better, once prompted Mike Hargrove to conclude, "I could steal a base off him."

Team	Level	W	L	ERA	IP	H	BB	K
Kinston	A	1	0	2.87	15	13	5	18
Charlotte	AAA	2	1	1.93	23	15	10	25

RUSS SPRINGER   ANGELS   Age 26/R   * *

In 1992 the Yankees discovered that Springer's 93 mph fastball and direct style made a good short reliever. But the Angels, who acquired him in a trade, gave Springer two more years of work as a starter, without much success. In 1995, finally back in the pen where he belongs, Springer is ready for prime time.

Team	Level	W	L	ERA	IP	H	BB	K
Vancouver	AAA	7	4	3.04	83	77	19	58

JULIAN TAVAREZ   INDIANS   Age 21/R   * * *

A long, live arm allows Tavarez to generate some real heat. And he knows how to pitch, too. Arguably the best of the Tribe Trio, with Lopez and Ogea.

Team	Level	W	L	ERA	IP	H	BB	K
Charlotte	AAA	15	6	3.48	176	167	43	102

BRIEN TAYLOR   YANKEES   Age 22/L   * *

If he comes back with the same fastball and curve he had before his late-night altercation a year ago, Taylor can quickly start paying dividends (rather than just drawing interest) on his $1.55 million signing bonus.

Team	Level	W	L	ERA	IP	H	BB	K
Did not play								

SALOMON TORRES   GIANTS   Age 23/R   * *

It's not too late for Torres to bounce back from 1994 problems that stemmed mainly from a lack of self-confidence. Worth a shot if he's traded. A change of scenery could spin that success/confidence cycle the other way.

Team	Level	W	L	ERA	IP	H	BB	K
Phoenix	AAA	5	6	4.22	79	85	31	64

TERRELL WADE   BRAVES   Age 22/L   * *

With any other organization, he'd be a spring training front-runner for a rotation spot. With the Braves, he'll be allowed to mature gradually.

Team	Level	W	L	ERA	IP	H	BB	K
Greenville	AA	9	3	3.83	105	87	58	105
Richmond	AAA	1	2	3.18	17	15	11	18

BILLY WAGNER   ASTROS   Age 23/L   *

The college scouts missed him, but the major league scouts found their way to Division III Ferrum College. Houston's 1993 first-round draft pick led all minor league pitchers in strikeouts, strikeouts per innings pitched, and opponents' batting average.

Team	Level	W	L	ERA	IP	H	BB	K
Quad City	A	8	9	3.29	153	99	91	204

GABE WHITE   EXPOS   Age 23/L   * *

Last year, White worked as both a starter and a reliever, going back and forth between the majors and Triple-A, and just kept performing steadily. Good talent, good attitude, good work habits make for a good chance to do well.

Team	Level	W	L	ERA	IP	H	BB	K
Ottawa	AAA	8	3	5.05	73	77	28	63

BRAD WOODALL   BRAVES   Age 25/L   * *

Woodall attracted little attention with his finesse pitching at the U. of North Carolina. But in 1994 he was voted the International League's most valuable pitcher. Lefties with good changeups often succeed in the NL—ask Jason Jacome.

Team	Level	W	L	ERA	IP	H	BB	K
Richmond	AAA	15	6	2.38	185	159	49	137

5

Around the Horn

Rookie of the Year
by Jay Lovinger

Fame ... Wealth Untold ... Life Everlasting ... Babes.

Those were the Four Horsemen I saw outlined against the gray November sky on the fateful day Dan Okrent asked me if I wanted to join the original Rotisserie League for the 1994 season. Yeah, *that* Dan Okrent, dude.

"Well, kid, we're on our way," I told my wife that evening, my proud little chest all puffed out like a peacock on nitrous oxide.

"How so?" my wife asked warily, giving me the look Alice used to give Ralph just after he had announced his latest harebrained get-rich-quick scheme.

"I was invited to join the original Rotisserie League."

"Another Rotisserie League?" said wife. "Be still, my heart. What's that make, four?"

"You don't understand," I protested patiently. "This isn't just another Rotisserie League. It's *the* league, the first one, the big time, the Holy Grail. The Show."

"So how much is this one gonna set us back?"

"Well, Dan says you can spend up to a thousand bucks, maybe more. But ..." and here I'm thinking to myself, *Can you ever sell it, boy!* "... it'll only cost me about $700."

"How come?"

"Because I'm inheriting such a bad team—maybe the worst in league history—that I've got no shot to cash. So I won't be throwing money at players late in the year trying to finish in the first division."

"Lucky you. I bet the other guys wish they were fortunate enough to have no shot so they could get a bargain, too."

"Geez," I cleverly rejoined, thinking maybe Mickey Spillane had the right idea about women after all, "try to contain your enthusiasm, willya? Anyway, I might not get in. Dan's the Beloved Founder and Former Commissioner for Life and all, but all he can do is recommend. I have to get approved by a majority of the other owners."

"On what basis?"

"On whether I know enough about the National League to put up a respectable fight, Dan says. They don't want any suckers."

"You mean like the kind of guy who would pay 700 bucks for a team that has no chance to win?" She got up and headed for the kitchen, chuckling to herself. And I think I heard her exclaim as she passed out of sight, "My guess is, if the check doesn't bounce, you're in."

By the time the 1993 awards banquet rolled around a few weeks later, I was a full-fledged member of the fraternity, having proved to my fellow owners that I could differentiate between Darrin Fletcher ($7 salary) and Darrin on *Bewitched*. In fact, Darrin Fletcher was the most useful player on my team, the Lovin' Spoonfuls, one of the feeblest collections of flotsam ever assembled. *How feeble were they?* This feeble: I offered to trade all 40 of them to the Fleder Mice for Mark Whiten ($1). Crafty Rob Fleder, peerless pilot of the Mice, took one look at my roster and, after he finally stopped laughing, said, "No, thanks."

More disappointment lay in store. In my little boy's heart of hearts, I had imagined the other owners would take pity on me—if for no other reason than out of overwhelming shame for robbing me of the $700 I would soon put in their pockets—but I was quickly disabused of this sentimental notion. Whenever I complained, I would constantly be instructed to gaze upon the crafty but dour Steve Wulf, who once, back in the league's Paleolithic Era, inherited a last-place team and turned it into a first-place squad *the very next season*. Lee Eisenberg, crafty taskmaster of the powerful Furriers club, a man whose reserved demeanor belies his fiercely predatory nature, offered to trade me two albatrosses, Tony Tarasco ($10) and Ozzie Smith ($19), for my only players of value, Danny Jackson and Jeromy Burnitz (only $3 and $2, respectively, but both in the last year of their contracts and therefore useless to a rebuilding team, like mine). When I politely declined, he bared his teeth and hissed at me, like the semen-tossing serial murderer Miggs in *Silence of the Lambs*, that I had just passed up the best chance I would ever have to climb into 11th place.

My wife and I left soon after the Yoo-Hoo ceremony. For me, it was something like the first time I had seen the Vietnam Wall—more moving than most men are comfortable with. My wife wondered if the integrity of the ceremony had been compromised when 1993 pennant winner Wulf took off his shirt to receive the ritual Yoo-Hoo shower in his undershirt.

As per my usual custom, I magnanimously agreed to buy my wife a fur coat if I won the 1994 championship. She requested—and was refused—a five-year option on the offer. After I had chattered on continuously for a good 45 minutes about my fellow owners' strengths, weaknesses, and psychological tics, I paused to give my wife a chance to compliment me on my keen analytical mind. "They seemed kind of functional," she said. "I'm surprised."

I made a few small pre-draft trades, just to get my feet wet, and one meaningful one—Jose Vizcaino ($5), Walt Weiss ($4), Steve Buechele ($13), Burnitz ($2), Jackson ($3), and a minor league pitcher named Bryan Barber for Phil Plantier ($21). I had formulated an aggressive strategy, which involved acquiring as many high-priced superstars as I could—through the draft and trades—then trading them *after* the draft for undervalued talents, like Chuck Carr ($10), Darryl Kile ($2), Andres Gallaraga ($11), Rod Beck

($10), and Mike Piazza ($10), who themselves had been purchased at bargain prices in previous years by rebuilding teams. With whatever I had left, I would draft the halt, the crippled, and the lame—as long as they came cheap enough—hoping they would recover their health and ability by the time I was ready to make a serious run in 1995. Prime candidates in this category were Rob Dibble, Darryl Strawberry, Norm Charlton, Chipper Jones, and Greg Olsen.

Immediately after acquiring Plantier from Eisenberg (that boa constrictor!), I asked Okrent to analyze the deal. As was to prove his custom, he made me feel like the illegitimate mutant child of Lou Gorman. He also offered a prediction: Within hours, if not minutes, Eisenberg would call back and either try to cancel the deal or upgrade his end. Sure enough, by the time I got back to my office, there was a phone message from the First Furrier, in full wheedle, wondering if I'd consider substituting for the ham-footed and aging Steve Buechele the young and quantumly improving Orlando Merced (also $13), whom he'd unaccountably failed to notice when scrutinizing my roster. He didn't want to cancel the deal; in fact, he hoped it wouldn't come to that. "Why not just come right out and threaten litigation, you terrorist?" I thought.

As it happened, I had already traded Merced to the Mice for Luis Alicea. I can't remember why, exactly; I guess I was blinded by his bargain-basement price tag, a measly $1. But as it also happened, Eisenberg was hitting me right where I lived. Joining a new league is a little like entering a new school when you're a kid, a school where everyone else has already known one another for years. You become obsessed with one question: will they like me?

Okrent did his best to calm me down before the draft, telling amusing anecdotes of drafts past and predicting how the various participants would behave: "Peter Gethers [Peter's Famous Smoked Fish] will get anxious, and no matter what happens he will be depressed about his team. Michael Pollet [the Pollet Burros] will draft a lot of Mets and lose interest toward the end of the draft. Fleder will try to rush everybody through the endgame and the rotation draft. And Bob Sklar [the Sklar Gazers] will save his money and wait for a bargain because back about 14 years ago he got Mike Schmidt for 26 dollars." Okrent also foretold that he himself had no chance to win, because everyone was freezing their starting pitching—he had none of note—thanks to my aggressive trading, which had correctly convinced the other owners that I would also be bidding aggressively in the draft, thereby driving prices up across-the-board.

As I digested this briefing, Okrent casually mentioned the Neutron Bomb Option. Apparently, out of sheer boredom, several owners were pushing to eliminate roster freezes after the 1994 season, effectively starting the league all over in 1995. When I pointed out that this rendered the rotation draft of (primarily) minor leaguers meaningless, not to mention that second-division teams would have no motivation to trade or do anything else as soon as they dropped out of contention, Okrent shrugged. When I also mentioned that this would render my rebuilding strategy pointless, meaning I would have paid $700 for absolutely nothing, he didn t even bother to shrug. *Caveat emptor,* sucker.

I'm looking at my diary notes of the night before the draft: *Can't sleep. Will they hate me when I draft, no matter what the cost, Barry Bonds and Marquis Grissom, the two best players available? At 3 A.M., compose long speech justifying my apparent callousness and greed.*

On that great and terrible day, in my anxiety not to be late, I arrived more than an hour early at the apartment building of commissioner and draftmeister Cork Smith—and suddenly realized I had to pee. Another dilemma for the novice Rotisserian: What would be more of a *faux pas*—knocking on the door of the stern but crafty Smith, perhaps awakening him and causing him to be cross with me, or relieving myself in the street in front of his building, perhaps risking arrest? Trying to attract as little attention as possible in the elegantly appointed lobby of Smith's Park Avenue residence, I hopped from one foot to the other as long as I could, then threw myself on his mercy. He was rather civilized about the whole thing.

Finally, the others arrived, except for defending champion Wulf, leader of the Wulfgang. While we waited for him, talk turned to tasteless jokes and procedural considerations big (the Neutron Bomb Option, which was defeated by a narrow margin) and small (why Willie Greene qualified to be drafted only at shortstop, despite having played only third during spring training and being slated to play only third during the year). Inevitably, the historians present felt compelled to indulge in fond remembrances of the time Steve Wulf took over a last-place team and won the pennant *the very next season.* Apparently, resentment had overwhelmed my kindly nature because, gasping and squeaking, I launched into a shrill and rambling diatribe about how the league had changed since then, making Wulf's accomplishment about as relevant as an ethics course taught by Bill Clinton, da-dum da-dum da-dum, at which point the dyspeptic yet crafty Michael Pollet turned to Okrent and drawled, "Why, Dan, you didn't tell us you were bringing a whiner into the league."

For me, the draft was over in five minutes—or as long as it took me to buy Grissom ($45) and Bonds ($52). When not indulging in penny stocks (Jesse Hollins, David Weathers, A. J. Sager, Greg Harris, and Ben Rivera for $1 each) and medical futures (Charlton for $17, Ron Gant for $15, Dibble for $5, Chipper Jones for $7), I whiled away the long hours observing the ploys, strategies, and acting techniques of my fellow owners—the latter consisting primarily of subtle modulations in facial expression or voice levels to signal to the others that, this time, they were by-God serious about a player. So the dour but crafty Wulf might drop his already barely audible voice down a few registers, forcing competing bidders to endlessly shout, "What?" or risk looking foolish when they would bid several dollars less than Wulf's last offering. Or cuddly but crafty Glen Waggoner (the Glenwag Goners) might suddenly sit up straight and start ripping off bids as if he were a human Uzi, one such display inspiring Fleder to interject, "I just love it when the Iron Horse gets hot for pitching." Or Eisenberg might rattle his pile of computer printouts, lean over, and whisper to the anxious but crafty Gethers, then feign careful consideration, thereby implicitly threatening the Rotisserie equivalent of a job action if he didn't soon get his way.

Merrily, without a care for the 1994 season, I began the dumping process before Week Two was over, trading Bonds and Larry Walker (whom I had frozen for $41) to the Okrent Fenokees for Kile, Galarraga, and Rick Wilkins ($8). This raised a few eyebrows, since Okrent is my real-life boss—and not just any boss at that, but a boss who has never won a Rotisserie championship despite the fact that he invented the game. Then I traded Grissom to the Smoked Fish for Carr. After a little more tinkering, I soon had a team that promised to provide me with as many as 14 freezes for 1995—Kile, Weathers, Dibble, Paul Wagner ($4), Tommy Greene ($11), Fletcher, Andujar Cedeño ($7), Jones, Galarraga, Plantier, Carr, Wilkins, Gant, and Rico Brogna ($10). At least it seemed that way until Plantier and Wilkins reverted to pre-1993 form, Dibble and Greene failed to come back on schedule, Galarraga broke his hand, Wagner went to the bullpen, and Carr, Cedeño, and Kile went into the toilet.

"At least I was right about Fletcher," I told my wife. She bit her hand, vainly trying to suppress a giggling fit.

Oh, well. It's always darkest before the real shitstorm hits. In July came The Trade, a fine moment of madness that made the sale of Babe Ruth to the Yankees look visionary. Surrendering unconditionally to a heretofore unsuspected Mets jones, the wan and overstressed but putatively crafty Gethers presented a pricey all-star team—Sammy Sosa ($32), Grissom, Fred McGriff ($34), Todd Zeile ($18), Lenny Dykstra ($32)—and a few role players to the terminally persistent but crafty Eisenberg for Todd Hundley ($3), Ryan Thompson ($10), Jose Vizcaino ($5), and assorted detritus.

"Why bother putting a team together piece by laborious piece, year by tedious year, when one insane trade can render the whole pennant race meaningless?" I asked Okrent. ("Cried" or perhaps even "whined" might be more accurate.)

"Good question," said Okrent, surprisingly placid considering his chances for his first pennant ever had just evaporated.

I called the oily but crafty Eisenberg in his dark and dank Knoxville office to register a philosophical complaint. "I understand that there's nothing technically illegal about this trade," I said, "but surely this is not the way you want to win the pennant."

"Of course not," he assured me. "I'm totally against this kind of thing." But, he explained, this was the only way he could see to demonstrate how flawed the rules were. He was doing it for the good of the game—and thus for the good of Rotisserie owners everywhere—and if there were those who did not understand, well, he was man enough to take the heat.

"Could this possibly be true?" I asked Okrent, wanting to give a fellow owner the benefit of the doubt.

"Pshaw," said Okrent, or something to that effect.

Then, in August came The Strike, a double blow to my ever frailer hopes for 1995. Not only would players like Gant, Jones, and Dibble be unable to return in the September that now would never be—thus denying me the opportunity to judge their kinetic usefulness—but I would have to spend the next endless months pondering the possibility that there might not even be a next year. This was like a double neutron bomb. And they say, *What you don't know can't hurt you.*

Still, I decided not to mention it to my wife.

Rotisserie League Media Guide
The 1994 Season

For most of the world, 1994 will forevermore be remembered as The Year of the Strike. For members of the original Rotisserie League, however, it will be recalled as The Year of the Trade—or, because of one Rotisserie owner, Peter "No Clue" Gethers, as The Year of Living Stupidly.

Early June. The great, glorious baseball summer bursts with promise. Storm clouds lurk like the chorus in a Greek tragedy, but all of us baseball fans are in full denial. They can't, they wouldn't, they won't muck up a season as great as this one. (*Could they? Would they? Will they?*) Junior is ahead of the Babe's pace. Joe Carter has just set a new RBI record for May. Tony Gwynn's BA is climbing toward .400. Frank Thomas and Jeff Bagwell are sparking speculation about double triple crowns. And the Rotisserie League pennant race is heating up.

Early June. Four teams in the hunt: the Abel Bakers, the Okrent Fenokees, the Wulfgang, and the Eisenberg Furriers. Taps have sounded for the rest of the league, but for the four teams at the top, the race is way too close to call. None is overpowering; each has as many weaknesses as strengths.

Early June. The seventh day of the sixth month, to be precise. The day in 1918 that the United States Supreme Court upheld the 18th Amendment, permitting Prohibition to descend across the land like a shroud. The day in 1939 that Estonia and Latvia signed a non-aggression pact with Germany. The day in 1966 that Ronald Reagan won the Republican Party's nomination for governor of California. And the day in 1994 that will live in Rotisserie infamy.

The day of The Trade.

It happens every summer, usually in early June. Team owners whose dreams of a first-division finish have turned to ashes in their mouth begin to engage in that unseemly but all-too-familiar midsummer ritual known, in genteel circles, as Building for Next Year—or, as we refer to it around here, Dumping. You know what we mean: half a dozen owners scrambling frantically to disgorge their high-priced stars and players in the final year of long-term contracts in exchange for cheap and/or young talent likely to pay rich dividends in the future.

Dumping deals are always egregiously unbalanced in terms of the current year, but the balance is usually righted in the succeeding season—unless, of course, the owner doing the dumping is utterly, absolutely unable to distinguish between blue chips and cow chips. Did someone mention No Clue Gethers?

The Sturgeon General of Peter's Famous Smoked Fish, No Clue detected a foul odor emanating from the team's clubhouse and concluded that his beloved Fish had gone rotten in the summer heat. There was only one thing to do—cut bait.

Normally, when a Rotisserie owner decides to throw in the towel and start rebuilding for next year, he calls all the teams in contention, announces his intentions, lists the players he's willing to trade, and counts on his colleagues' inherent fear of missing out on a bargain to generate trade offers. Even a bad team—and the Smoked Fish was certainly that—has a few good players with big salaries or expiring contracts. The trick is to work the phones, threaten each owner that you will give the pennant to a close rival unless he ups his offer, and dole out your valuable assets among all the contenders, thereby extracting the maximum return for next year.

Or you can do what No Clue did—make a single call, to the Eisenberg Furriers, and swap gold for dross. Here are the terms of The Trade, as reported in agate type in newspapers around the country:

PETER'S FAMOUS SMOKED FISH trade Fred McGriff, Marquis Grissom, Sammy Sosa, Lenny Dykstra, Todd Zeile, and Mike Kingery to the EISENBERG FURRIERS for Mel Rojas ($10), Jeremy Burnitz ($6), Jose Vizcaino ($4), Ryan Thompson ($15), Walt Weiss ($5), and Todd Hundley ($6).

What did The Trade mean for the Furriers? Only an additional 36 HR, 119 RBI, and 31 SB. That translates into 14 points in the standings. The Furriers' margin of victory was eight points.

And for No Clue and the Fish? Well, with Hundley, Weiss, Vizcaino, and Thompson coming back this year, they might be a smidgeon better than average up the middle.

READERS SURVEY

See page 267

ROTISSERIE LEAGUE, 1994

FINAL STANDINGS

1. EISENBERG FURRIERS	84.0		7. CARY NATIONS	51.0
2. WULFGANG	76.0		8. POLLET BURROS	45.5
3. OKRENT FENOKEES	67.5		9. FLEDER MICE	45.0
4. ABEL BAKERS	64.0		10. GLENWAG GONERS	31.5
5. STEIN BRENNERS	61.5		11. SMOKED FISH	29.0
6. SKLAR GAZERS	55.0		12. LOVIN' SPOONFULS	14.0

PITCHING RECORDS

EARNED RUN AVERAGE			RATIO		
EISENBERG FURRIERS	3.52	12.0	EISENBERG FURRIERS	1.235	12.0
STEIN BRENNERS	3.75	11.0	WULFGANG	1.270	11.0
SKLAR GAZERS	3.80	10.0	STEIN BRENNERS	1.312	10.0
POLLET BURROS	3.82	9.0	ABEL BAKERS	1.318	9.0
WULFGANG	3.83	8.0	OKRENT FENOKEES	1.334	8.0
OKRENT FENOKEES	4.03	7.0	SKLAR GAZERS	1.334	7.0
CARY NATIONS	4.24	6.0	CARY NATIONS	1.336	6.0
GLENWAG GONERS	4.26	5.0	GLENWAG GONERS	1.346	5.0
ABEL BAKERS	4.32	4.0	POLLET BURROS	1.396	4.0
FLEDER MICE	4.35	3.0	SMOKED FISH	1.453	2.0
SMOKED FISH	4.59	2.0	FELDER MICE	1.453	2.0
LOVIN' SPOONFULS	4.82	1.0	LOVIN' SPOONFULS	1.560	1.0

SAVES			WINS		
EISENBERG FURRIERS	55	12.0	STEIN BRENNERS	67	12.0
CARY NATIONS	51	11.0	CARY NATIONS	66	11.0
ABEL BAKERS	49	10.0	EISENBERG FURRIERS	64	10.0
OKRENT FENOKEES	45	9.0	SKLAR GAZERS	60	9.0
WULFGANG	44	8.0	WULFGANG	58	8.0
POLLET BURROS	35	7.0	SMOKED FISH	52	7.0
SKLAR GAZERS	25	6.0	FLEDER MICE	51	6.0
FLEDER MICE	24	5.0	ABEL BAKERS	50	5.0
SMOKED FISH	20	4.0	GLENWAG GONERS	48	4.0
GLENWAG GONERS	16	3.0	OKRENT FENOKEES	44	3.0
STEIN BRENNERS	10	2.0	POLLET BURROS	34	2.0
LOVIN' SPOONFULS	1	1.0	LOVIN' SPOONFULS	31	1.0

(Continued)

BATTING RECORDS

RUNS BATTED IN			STOLEN BASES		
WULFGANG	635	12.0	OKRENT FENOKEES	136	12.0
EISENBERG FURRIERS	634	11.0	EISENBERG FURRIERS	128	11.0
ABEL BAKERS	594	10.0	CARY NATIONS	117	10.0
SKLAR GAZERS	577	9.0	WULFGANG	114	9.0
OKRENT FENOKEES	557	8.0	FLEDER MICE	107	8.0
FLEDER MICE	532	7.0	ABEL BAKERS	106	7.0
POLLET BURROS	522	6.0	SMOKED FISH	72	6.0
STEIN BRENNERS	496	5.0	GLENWAG GONERS	68	5.0
CARY NATIONS	441	4.0	LOVIN' SPOONFULS	60	3.5
GLENWAG GONERS	405	3.0	STEIN BRENNERS	60	3.5
SMOKED FISH	387	2.0	POLLET BURROS	55	2.0
LOVIN' SPOONFULS	352	1.0	SKLAR GAZERS	45	1.0

HOME RUNS			BATTING AVERAGE		
WULFGANG	160	12.0	STEIN BRENNERS	.293	12.0
OKRENT FENOKEES	142	10.5	ABEL BAKERS	.285	11.0
POLLET BURROS	142	10.5	OKRENT FENOKEES	.284	10.0
EISENBERG FURRIERS	138	9.0	FLEDER MICE	.284	9.0
ABEL BAKERS	135	8.0	WULFGANG	.282	8.0
SKLAR GAZERS	133	7.0	EISENBERG FURRIERS	.280	7.0
STEIN BRENNERS	113	6.0	SKLAR GAZERS	.277	6.0
FLEDER MICE	108	5.0	POLLET BURROS	.274	5.0
SMOKED FISH	86	4.0	GLENWAG GONERS	.266	4.0
LOVIN' SPOONFULS	84	2.5	LOVIN' SPOONFULS	.260	3.0
GLENWAG GONERS	84	2.5	CARY NATIONS	.259	2.0
CARY NATIONS	77	1.0	SMOKED FISH	.252	1.0

1994 Rotisserie League Rosters

In the team rosters that follow, an asterisk (°) by a player's name indicates that he finished the season on the reserve list, while a pound sign (#) signifies that the player was traded, waived, or released earlier in the season. Two asterisks (°°) identify a group of players whose 1994 contributions to their Rotisserie team were lumped together to keep this chapter shorter than the collected works of Tom Clancy.

You will note several additional stats beyond the "Original Eight" Rotisserie categories that we employ in keeping score. We put them there to show the range of **Roti·Stats**, the officially authorized stat service of the Rotisserie League Baseball Association. **Roti·Stats (800-884-7684)** can add these and other extra categories for leagues that want them.

Fine-tooth combers will note that some teams finished last season with fewer than 23 active players: that is perfectly legal and relatively common-place in leagues playing Rotisserie Ultra.

#1

Eisenburg Furriers
Owner: Lee Eisenberg

The First Furrier pleads innocent on all counts of extortion, fraud, and grand larceny "Just because I spent the last 15 years of my life haggling, wheedling, scheming, and slick-dealing to make the Furriers the greatest franchise in Rotissehistory, people automatically blame me for The Trade, but not even I could come up with a deal this one-sided," he explains. "Here I am, sitting in the war room of my Tennessee mansion when the Smoked Fish call to offer me several dozen stars for a few of my cheap bums. Put yourself in my position. A sheep comes along and begs to be fleeced. What am I supposed to do, send him along to the Wulfgang so he can be eaten too?"

FINAL ROSTER

BATTERS	AB	H	BB	HR	RBI	SB	R	OBA	BA
AUSMUS, BRAD	42	15	2	1	5	0	8	.386	.357
BICHETTE, DANTE	484	147	19	27	95	21	74	.330	.304
BUECHELE, STEVE	53	15	3	3	12	0	8	.321	.283
DESHIELDS, DELINO	316	80	54	2	33	27	51	.362	.253
GILKEY, BERNARD	64	16	9	1	8	3	13	.342	.250
GONZALES, LUIS	10	3	3	0	3	0	2	.462	.300
GRACE, MARK	403	120	48	6	44	0	55	.373	.298
GRISSOM, MARQUIS	254	80	21	7	21	19	57	.367	.315
KINGERY, MIKE	206	76	19	2	29	3	42	.422	.369
LOPEZ, LUIS	11	1	1	0	1	0	0	.167	.091
MCGRIFF, FRED	221	78	23	18	57	4	43	.414	.353
O'BRIEN, CHARLIE	127	28	15	6	20	0	20	.303	.220
SNYDER, COREY	27	6	3	0	0	0	2	.300	.222
SOSA, SAMMIE	221	75	12	12	38	13	31	.373	.339
*MARTINEZ, DAVE	171	40	18	2	20	2	19	.307	.234
#HOLLINS, DAVE	159	36	23	4	26	1	28	.324	.226
#MOUTON, JAMIE	300	74	26	2	16	23	41	.307	.247
#THOMPSON, RYAN	159	40	12	12	43	0	22	.304	.252
#VIZCAINO, JOSE	204	59	20	2	17	1	26	.353	.289
#WEISS, WALT	226	64	24	1	17	7	31	.352	.283
#ZEILE, TODD	210	60	23	10	45	1	33	.356	.286
**OTHERS (18)	742	176	64	20	84	3	89	.298	.237
TOTALS	**4610**	**1289**	**442**	**138**	**634**	**128**	**695**	**.343**	**.280**

PITCHERS	W	L	S	IP	H	ER	BB	K	ERA	RATIO
CANDIOTTI, TOM	7	6	0	149.33	143	65	53	101	3.92	1.313
HARNISCH, PETE	0	0	0	.00	0	0	0	0	.00	.000
MADDUX, GREG	16	6	0	202.00	150	35	31	156	1.56	.896
MICELI, DANNY	0	0	0	1.00	3	1	1	1	9.00	4.000
ROPER, JOHN	6	2	0	86.00	85	45	27	47	4.71	1.302
RUFFIN, BRUCE	3	5	16	41.00	46	21	21	48	4.61	1.634
SMILEY, JOHN	5	2	0	58.00	62	31	16	36	4.81	1.345
TRACHSEL, STEVE	9	6	0	140.00	128	51	49	104	3.28	1.264
WETTELAND, JOHN	4	6	25	63.66	46	20	21	68	2.83	1.052
*DEWEY, MARK	1	0	0	2.66	23	8	9	8	3.48	1.549
*SMOLTZ, JOHN	6	10	0	134.66	120	62	48	113	4.14	1.248
*STANTON, MIKE	3	1	3	41.33	39	16	25	33	3.48	1.549
#ROJAS, MEL	2	1	10	42.66	29	12	10	36	2.53	.914
**OTHERS (15)	2	4	1	62.66	71	41	32	41	5.89	1.644
TOTALS	**64**	**49**	**55**	**1043.00**	**945**	**408**	**343**	**792**	**3.52**	**1.235**

Wulfgang
Owner: Steve Wulf

If you read the Introduction, you have already heard the Wulfman's howl. For a while, the Gang looked like it might win back-to-back pennants, a feat hitherto accomplished only by the Glenwag Goners. Then came The Trade. But the Leader of the Pack did not retreat back into his cave to lick his wounds. He spent the winter nurturing a new double-play combination, Elizabeth Jeanne and Eve Sandra. This year he will rebuild the Gang around Jacob Brumfield.

FINAL ROSTER

BATTERS	AB	H	BB	HR	RBI	SB	R	OBA	BA
ALICEA, LUIS	38	17	6	1	9	1	3	.523	.447
BAGWELL, JEFF	400	147	65	39	116	15	104	.456	.368
BENZINGER, TODD	328	87	17	9	31	2	32	.301	.265
BRUMFIELD, JACOB	23	5	1	0	1	0	1	.250	.217
DYKSTRA, LENNY	54	10	16	0	4	3	7	.371	.185
GARCIA, CARLOS	412	114	16	6	28	18	49	.304	.277
GWYNN, TONY	419	165	48	12	64	5	79	.456	.394
JUSTICE, DAVE	154	45	31	8	30	0	28	.411	.292
LEWIS, DARREN	451	116	53	4	29	30	70	.335	.257
MANWARING, KURT	316	79	25	1	29	1	30	.305	.250
MAY, DERRICK	226	55	17	5	25	2	24	.296	.243
REED, JEFF	13	5	2	1	5	0	3	.467	.385
SANDERS, REGGIE	400	105	41	17	62	21	66	.331	.263
WILLIAMS, EDDIE	167	53	15	10	39	0	30	.374	.317
*VAN SLYKE, ANDY	125	31	13	2	11	2	14	.319	.248
#BROWNE, JERRY	273	77	43	2	26	3	32	.380	.282
#CEDENO, ANDUJAR	94	25	8	6	17	0	10	.324	.266
#PENDLETON, TERRY	221	50	8	5	20	2	20	.253	.226
#WILLIAMS, MATT	264	64	21	23	50	0	42	.298	.242
**OTHERS (9)	248	54	25	5	15	9	19	.289	.218
TOTALS	**4755**	**1342**	**478**	**160**	**635**	**114**	**679**	**.348**	**.282**

PITCHERS	W	L	S	IP	H	ER	BB	K	ERA	RATIO
DYER, MIKE	0	1	2	7.66	12	8	8	8	9.40	2.611
FREEMAN, MORGAN	7	2	0	86.66	88	26	13	47	2.70	1.165
HOFFMAN, TREVOR	4	4	20	56.00	39	16	20	68	2.57	1.054
JACKSON, DANNY	10	6	0	128.66	138	49	29	85	3.43	1.298
MARTINEZ, PEDRO	0	1	0	7.00	6	6	11	6	7.71	2.429
MYERS, RANDY	1	5	21	4.33	40	17	16	32	3.79	1.389
SABERHAGEN, BRETT	14	4	0	177.33	169	54	13	143	2.74	1.026
VALDEZ, ISMAIL	2	1	0	16.00	15	5	7	14	2.81	1.375
WORRELL, TODD	0	0	1	1.00	1	0	0	0	.00	1.000
*HARRIS, GREG W.	2	6	0	5.66	61	38	19	33	6.75	1.579
#ASHBY, ANDY	4 ·	8	0	118.00	101	44	29	87	3.36	1.102
#BROWNING, TOM	2	1	0	23.33	21	10	4	11	3.86	1.072
#PLESAC, DAN	1	1	0	23.66	31	18	5	23	6.85	1.522
#SMITH, ZANE	9	8	0	148.00	157	57	32	57	3.47	1.277
**OTHERS (10)	2	5	0	65.33	94	56	27	55	7.71	1.853
TOTALS	**58**	**53**	**44**	**949.66**	**973**	**404**	**233**	**669**	**3.83**	**1.270**

Okrent Fenokees
Owner: Daniel Okrent

It could have been the Year of the Fenokee: the Swampmen had speed, power, and a strong bullpen, not to mention the Law of Averages working in their favor. (It stands to readon that the guy who invented the game will win the pennant one of these years, doesn't it? *Doesn't it?*) But the Fenokees also had a starting rotation of Greg Swindell, Charlie Hough, Pat Rapp, Orel Hershiser, and Andy Benes. That crew produced a tenth-place finish in wins and middle-of-the-pack performances in ERA and ratio. Then of course, there was The Trade. Coming back this season at low salaires: Cliff Floyd, John Hudek, Jeff Brantley.

FINAL ROSTER

BATTERS	AB	H	BB	HR	RBI	SB	R	OBA	BA
BASS, KEVIN	108	34	17	4	19	0	23	.408	.315
BONDS, BARRY	372	118	70	35	79	29	86	.425	.317
DORSETT, BRIAN	212	51	21	4	23	0	20	.309	.241
DUNSTON, SHAWON	331	92	16	11	35	3	38	.311	.278
FERNANDEZ, TONY	366	102	44	8	50	12	50	.356	.279
FLOYD, CLIFF	229	67	17	3	31	7	30	.341	.293
HILL, GLENALLEN	269	80	29	10	38	19	48	.366	.297
INCAVIGLIA, PETE	244	56	16	13	32	1	28	.277	.230
LARKIN, BARRY	427	119	64	9	52	26	78	.373	.279
OLIVA, JOSE	31	6	4	2	4	0	5	.286	.194
PRATT, TODD	102	20	12	2	9	0	10	.281	.196
ROBERTS, BIP	403	129	39	2	31	21	52	.380	.320
WALKER, LARRY	366	116	43	18	80	14	70	.389	.317
*CARREON, MARK	45	13	2	1	6	0	3	.319	.289
*GREENE, WILLIE	37	8	6	0	3	0	5	.326	.216
*PHILLIPS, JR	29	4	1	1	2	1	1	.167	.138
*STATON, DAVE	48	8	4	3	5	0	4	.231	.167
#BONILLA, BOBBY	252	77	42	12	42	1	38	.405	.306
#GALARRAGA, ANDRES	27	11	1	4	11	0	7	.429	.407
#MAY, DERRICK	25	6	1	0	4	0	1	.269	.240
#WILKINS, RICK	24	6	3	0	0	2	5	.333	.250
**OTHERS (3)	31	6	4	0	1	0	1	.286	.194
TOTALS	**3978**	**1129**	**456**	**142**	**557**	**136**	**603**	**.357**	**.284**

PITCHERS	W	L	S	IP	H	ER	BB	K	ERA	RATIO
BENES, ANDY	6	14	0	172.33	155	74	51	189	3.86	1.195
BRANTLEY, JEFF	6	6	15	65.33	46	18	28	63	2.48	1.133
GARDNER, MARK	1	2	0	38.66	40	25	13	18	5.82	1.371
HERSHISER, OREL	6	6	0	135.33	146	57	42	72	3.79	1.389
HUDEK, JOHN	0	2	16	35.00	23	13	17	33	3.34	1.143
JONES, DOUG	0	3	8	16.66	19	6	1	12	3.24	1.200
MCELROY, CHUCK	1	2	5	57.66	52	15	15	38	2.34	1.162
PALACIOS, VICENTE	2	7	1	10.00	98	55	39	80	4.95	1.370
RAPP, PAT	7	8	0	133.33	132	57	69	75	3.85	1.508
SWINDELL, GREG	8	9	0	148.33	175	72	26	74	4.37	1.355
*HOUGH, CHARLIE	4	9	0	1.66	99	56	48	58	5.01	1.460
#KILE, DARRYL	0	1	0	5.00	6	4	3	6	7.20	1.800
#WAGNER, PAUL	3	3	0	46.33	44	20	20	39	3.89	1.381
TOTALS	**44**	**72**	**45**	**1054.66**	**1035**	**472**	**372**	**757**	**4.03**	**1.334**

#4

Abel Bakers
Owner: Dominick Abel

The Bakery put together a solid, steady, efficient team that stayed comfortably in the upper middle of the pack all year. Hoping to move up a notch, the Bakers swapped Raul Mondesi, Jeff Kent, and Doug Jones—all at attractively low salaries—to rebuilding teams for short-term help. Bad move. The Bakers would have finished in the first division without making any deals, but they never had any realistic hope of rising in the standings, primarily because of The Trade.

FINAL ROSTER

BATTERS	AB	H	BB	HR	RBI	SB	R	OBA	BA
BELL, JAY	424	117	49	9	45	2	68	.351	.276
BIGGIO, CRAIG	437	139	62	6	56	39	88	.403	.318
BLAUSER, JEFF	194	54	21	5	22	1	35	.349	.278
BONILLA, BOBBY	151	40	13	8	25	0	22	.323	.265
BURKS, ELLIS	19	2	1	1	2	0	3	.150	.105
CONINE, JEFF	451	144	40	18	82	1	60	.375	.319
HARRIS, LENNY	65	21	4	0	8	6	11	.362	.323
LIRIANO, NELSON	124	32	22	2	15	0	21	.370	.258
LIVINGSTONE,SCOTT	129	36	5	2	9	0	8	.306	.279
LOPEZ, JAVY	277	68	17	13	35	0	27	.289	.245
MARTIN, AL	276	79	34	9	33	15	48	.365	.286
SHEFFIELD, GARY	316	89	48	27	78	12	60	.376	.282
SMITH, OZZIE	321	84	36	3	24	5	44	.336	.262
STINNETT, KELLY	59	13	4	1	4	2	7	.270	.220
#GIRARDI, JOE	164	39	15	1	11	2	24	.302	.238
#KENT, JEFF	246	73	16	11	41	1	34	.340	.297
#MONDESI, RAUL	239	79	6	9	37	8	37	.347	.331
#RODRIGUEZ, HENRY	227	69	16	6	39	0	27	.350	.304
#YOUNG, ERIC	106	27	17	4	13	10	19	.358	.255
**OTHERS (6)	135	37	12	0	15	2	13	.333	.274
TOTALS	**4360**	**1242**	**438**	**135**	**594**	**106**	**656**	**.350**	**.285**

PITCHERS	W	L	S	IP	H	ER	BB	K	ERA	RATIO
AROCHA, RENE	4	4	11	83.00	94	37	21	62	4.01	1.386
AVERY, STEVE	3	2	0	68.33	62	32	22	54	4.21	1.229
BLACK, BUD	4	2	0	54.33	50	27	16	28	4.47	1.215
GROSS, KEVIN	3	3	1	61.33	62	23	17	37	3.38	1.288
MARTINEZ, RAMON	12	7	0	17.00	160	75	56	119	3.97	1.271
SCOTT, TIM	3	2	1	4.33	36	13	16	29	2.90	1.289
TEWKSBURY, BOB	3	3	0	39.00	48	23	3	17	5.31	1.308
VALENZUELA, F.	1	2	0	45.00	42	15	7	19	3.00	1.089
WHITE, RICK	2	5	6	47.00	54	26	13	23	4.98	1.426
*JACKSON, MIKE	3	2	4	4.00	20	5	10	50	1.13	.750
*SMITH, PETE	1	3	0	34.00	42	30	14	24	7.94	1.647
#JONES, DOUG	2	1	19	37.33	36	7	5	26	1.69	1.098
#MORGAN, MIKE	0	6	0	.36	50	27	16	27	6.75	1.833
#NIED, DAVID	5	4	0	65.33	70	37	27	43	5.10	1.485
#PENA, ALEJANDRO	3	2	7	28.66	22	16	10	27	5.02	1.117
**OTHERS (4)	1	4	0	21.00	28	25	19	13	10.72	2.239
TOTALS	**50**	**52**	**49**	**87.66**	**876**	**418**	**272**	**598**	**4.32**	**1.319**

Stein Brenners
Owner: Harry Stein

The Brenners had other things on their minds last season. You may have heard about the new medical thriller written by Harry Stein that just hit the bookstores. No? It's called *The Magic Bullet* (Delacorte, $22.95), and the Brenners GM spent so much time cramming it with sex, violence, and car chases that he only had time to finish fifth. Stein said through his publicist that he was not aware of The Trade. All the other owners in the league hope he will get started on the sequel well before this year's auction draft.

FINAL ROSTER

BATTERS	AB	H	BB	HR	RBI	SB	R	OBA	BA
ABBOTT, KURT	345	86	16	9	33	3	41	.283	.249
ALOU, MOISES	422	143	42	22	78	7	81	.399	.339
BARBERIE, BRETT	372	112	23	5	31	2	40	.342	.301
BERRY, SEAN	320	89	32	11	41	14	43	.344	.278
CASTILLA, VINNY	130	43	7	3	18	2	16	.365	.331
MAGADAN, DAVE	188	54	35	1	15	0	26	.399	.287
MCGEE, WILLIE	156	44	15	5	23	3	19	.345	.282
MORRIS, HAL	436	146	34	10	78	6	60	.383	.335
PATTERSON, JEFF	240	57	16	3	32	13	36	.285	.238
PIAZZA, MIKE	405	129	33	24	92	1	64	.370	.319
RHODES, KARL	269	63	33	8	19	6	39	.318	.234
TAUBENSEE, EDDIE	187	53	15	8	21	2	29	.337	.283
WHITE, RONDELL	97	27	9	2	13	1	16	.340	.278
*DONNELS, CHRIS	10	4	1	2	2	0	3	.455	.400
**OTHERS (2)	3	0	0	0	0	0	0	.000	.000
TOTALS	3580	1050	311	113	496	60	513	.350	.293

PITCHERS	W	L	S	IP	H	ER	BB	K	ERA	RATIO
CASTILLO, JUAN	0	0	0	.00	0	0	0	0	.00	.000
DRABEK, DOUG	12	6	0	164.66	132	52	45	121	2.84	1.075
HARVEY, BRYAN	0	0	6	1.33	12	6	4	10	5.23	1.549
HICKERSON, BRIAN	4	8	1	84.66	104	57	34	50	6.06	1.630
HILL, KEN	16	5	0	154.66	145	57	44	85	3.32	1.222
HOLMES, DARREN	0	3	3	28.33	35	20	24	33	6.35	2.083
JONES, BOBBY	12	7	0	16.00	157	56	56	80	3.15	1.331
MERCKER, KENT	9	4	0	112.33	90	43	45	111	3.45	1.202
PORTUGAL, MARK	10	8	0	137.33	135	60	45	87	3.93	1.311
WEST, DOUG	4	10	0	99.00	74	39	61	83	3.55	1.364
#BOUCHER, DENNIS	0	1	0	18.66	24	14	7	17	6.75	1.661
TOTALS	67	52	10	97.00	908	404	365	677	3.75	1.312

Sklar Gazers
Owner: Robert Sklar

The Gazers by training have their heads in the clouds, but last season they kept their feet firmly rooted on the ground. Or was it concrete? By finishing dead last in stolen bases, the Gazers forfeited any hope of the first division. Even a respectable showing in the speed department would have catapaulted them past the Brenners. A mid-season trade for Roberto Kelly was too little, too late. Explained head astronomer and GM Bob Sklar: "My boys were too depressed by The Trade to run."

FINAL ROSTER

BATTERS	AB	H	BB	HR	RBI	SB	R	OBA	BA
BOONE, BRETT	381	122	24	12	68	3	59	.360	.320
CLARK, DAVE	223	66	22	10	46	2	37	.359	.296
FINLEY, STEVE	363	101	27	11	33	13	61	.328	.278
GUTIERREZ, RICKY	275	66	32	1	28	2	27	.319	.240
HAYES, CHARLIE	423	122	36	10	50	3	46	.344	.288
HUNTER, BRIAN	256	60	17	15	57	0	34	.282	.234
KELLY, ROBERTO	146	36	14	3	16	4	20	.313	.247
KRUK, JOHN	240	71	42	5	36	4	34	.401	.296
LEMKE, MARK	350	103	38	3	31	0	40	.363	.294
MITCHELL, KEVIN	310	101	59	30	77	2	57	.434	.326
SANTIAGO, BENITO	337	92	25	11	41	1	35	.323	.273
SERVAIS, SCOTT	251	49	10	9	41	0	27	.226	.195
SHIPLEY, CRAIG	141	47	6	2	13	4	20	.361	.333
ZAMBRANO, EDDIE	116	30	16	6	18	2	17	.348	.259
*CARRILLO, MATIAS	93	25	7	0	5	3	11	.320	.269
*CIANFROCCO, ARCI	139	30	2	4	13	2	9	.227	.216
#CHAMBERLAIN, WES	55	15	3	1	4	0	4	.310	.273
TOTALS	**4099**	**1136**	**380**	**133**	**577**	**45**	**538**	**.338**	**.277**

PITCHERS	W	L	S	IP	H	ER	BB	K	ERA	RATIO
EDENS, TOM	5	1	1	54.00	59	26	18	39	4.33	1.426
FASSERO, JEFF	8	6	0	138.66	119	46	40	119	2.99	1.147
GLAVINE, TOM	13	9	0	165.33	173	73	70	140	3.97	1.470
MARTINEZ, PEDRO	11	5	1	144.66	115	55	45	142	3.42	1.106
MCMICHAEL, GREG	4	6	21	58.66	66	25	19	47	3.84	1.449
MUNOZ, BOBBY	7	5	1	101.66	98	31	35	59	2.74	1.308
PEREZ, YSIDRO	1	0	0	14.00	11	6	6	18	3.86	1.214
SANDERS, SCOTT	4	7	1	103.33	94	51	41	103	4.44	1.306
SLOCUMB, HEATHCLIFF	5	1	0	72.33	75	23	28	58	2.86	1.424
*BURBA, DAVE	0	2	0	13.66	8	8	9	21	5.27	1.245
*PUGH, TIM	2	2	0	28.66	38	23	16	10	7.22	1.884
*SHAW, JEFF	0	0	0	1.00	12	5	1	6	4.50	1.300
*WILLIAMS, MIKE	0	4	0	31.66	45	23	9	20	6.54	1.706
TOTALS	**60**	**48**	**25**	**936.66**	**913**	**395**	**337**	**782**	**3.80**	**1.335**

Cary Nations
Owner: Cary Schneider

NATIONS

Plenty of pitching, paucity of poke—that pretty much sums up the Nations' disappointing performance in 1994. HoJo was NoJo until the season was dead and buried, while Bernard Gilkey seemed to be on strike six weeks before everyone else hit the picket line. "Even so," insists the abstemious Nations president, "we would have made a strong run at sixth place if it hadn't been for The Trade." Looking ahead, Rod Beck comes back for the final year of his contract at $15, and there are a lot worse ways to go into a new season than with an ace closer at that price.

FINAL ROSTER

BATTERS	AB	H	BB	HR	RBI	SB	R	OBA	BA
BUTLER, BRETT	417	131	68	8	33	27	79	.410	.314
JOHNSON, HOWARD	227	48	39	10	40	11	30	.327	.211
KARROS, ERIC	406	108	29	14	46	2	51	.315	.266
MCGRIFF, TERRY	98	21	9	0	11	0	6	.280	.214
MOUTON, JAIMIE	1	0	1	0	0	0	1	.500	.000
ORSULAK, JOE	8	2	0	0	1	0	1	.250	.250
PAGNOZZI, TOM	50	11	7	3	10	0	5	.316	.220
PEGUES, SCOTT	8	3	0	0	0	0	0	.375	.375
RODRIGUEZ, HENRY	79	13	1	2	10	0	6	.175	.165
SANCHEZ, REY	291	83	20	0	24	2	26	.331	.285
SANDERS, DEION	375	106	32	4	28	38	58	.339	.283
SCARSONE, STEVE	13	3	3	1	2	0	3	.375	.231
ZEILE, TODD	9	2	4	0	1	0	2	.462	.222
#AUSMUS, BRAD	285	67	28	6	19	5	37	.304	.235
#BUECHELE, STEVE	286	67	36	11	40	1	25	.320	.234
#GILKEY, BERNARD	316	80	30	5	37	12	39	.318	.253
#GONZALES, LUIS	382	104	46	8	64	15	55	.350	.272
#LOPEZ, LUIS	173	48	10	1	13	3	21	.317	.277
**OTHERS (10)	455	107	34	4	62	1	41	.288	.235
TOTALS	**3879**	**1004**	**397**	**77**	**441**	**117**	**486**	**.328**	**.259**

PITCHERS	W	L	S	IP	H	ER	BB	K	ERA	RATIO
BECK, ROD	2	4	28	48.66	49	15	13	39	2.77	1.274
BULLINGER, JEFF	1	0	0	8.00	5	0	2	4	.00	.875
GOTT, JIM	5	2	1	24.66	25	13	12	19	4.74	1.500
HENRY, BUTCH	1	1	0	23.33	22	6	4	15	2.31	1.114
HEREDIA, GIL	0	0	0	7.00	7	0	0	4	.00	1.000
JACOME, JASON	3	2	0	39.00	40	14	15	20	3.23	1.410
LIEBER, JON	6	6	0	102.66	111	44	23	67	3.86	1.305
REYNOLDS, SHANE	7	4	0	93.00	95	28	13	72	2.71	1.161
RUETER, KIRK	4	3	0	75.33	92	48	18	41	5.73	1.460
SMITH, ZANE	1	0	0	9.00	5	0	2	0	.00	.778
VERES, DAVE	2	2	0	28.33	23	7	4	17	2.22	.953
*PEREZ, MIKE	2	1	11	28.00	43	22	7	19	7.07	1.786
*TORRES, SALOMON	2	4	0	66.00	62	30	24	35	4.09	1.303
*WHITEHURST, WALLY	3	3	0	43.00	50	18	15	28	3.77	1.512
#HARNISCH, PETE	7	4	0	8.00	82	46	34	51	5.18	1.450
#TEWKSBURY, BOB	9	7	0	116.66	142	69	19	62	5.32	1.380
#WORRELL, TODD	6	5	10	41.00	36	20	12	44	4.39	1.171
**OTHERS (10)	5	9	1	90.00	93	55	35	52	5.50	1.423
TOTALS	**66**	**57**	**51**	**923.66**	**982**	**435**	**252**	**589**	**4.24**	**1.336**

#8

Pollet Burros
Owner: Michael Pollet

The Politburo is in the ash can of history. Does this mean that the Pollet Burros will change their name? No way. Might as well ask a donkey to stop being a jackass. . . . A shrewd late-season trade for Matt Williams ($30) gave them a leg up on 1995, at least in the power department, plus they have John Burkett, Billy Swift, and John Franco coming back at reasonable prices. That's something to bray about. When queried about the effect of The Trade, Burros GM Michael Pollet ressponded, "Huh?"

FINAL ROSTER

BATTERS	AB	H	BB	HR	RBI	SB	R	OBA	BA
CAMINITI, KEN	406	115	43	18	75	4	63	.352	.283
CANGELOSI, JOHN	12	4	2	0	1	1	4	.429	.333
CORDERO, WIL	415	122	41	15	63	16	65	.357	.294
GALLAGHER, DAVE	86	20	13	0	4	0	15	.333	.233
HERNANDEZ, CARLOS	64	14	1	2	6	0	6	.231	.219
HOWARD, THOMAS	178	47	10	5	24	4	24	.303	.264
KLESKO, RYAN	245	68	26	17	47	1	42	.347	.278
LANSING, MIKE	394	105	30	5	35	12	44	.318	.266
SLAUGHT, DON	240	69	34	2	21	0	21	.376	.288
STANKIEWICZ, ANDY	3	0	2	0	0	0	1	.400	.000
STRAWBERRY, DARRYL	92	22	19	4	17	0	13	.369	.239
TARASCO, TONY	132	36	9	5	19	5	16	.319	.273
WALLACH, TIM	414	116	46	23	78	0	68	.352	.280
WILLIAMS, MATT	181	55	12	20	46	1	32	.347	.304
*DESTRADE, ORESTES	130	27	19	5	15	1	12	.309	.208
*MEJIA, ROBERTO	116	28	15	4	14	3	11	.328	.241
*WEBSTER, MITCH	57	16	5	2	10	1	9	.339	.281
#JUSTICE, DAVE	198	65	38	11	29	2	33	.436	.328
#VAN SLYKE, ANDY	241	57	39	4	18	4	27	.343	.237
TOTALS	**3604**	**986**	**404**	**142**	**522**	**55**	**506**	**.347**	**.274**

PITCHERS	W	L	S	IP	H	ER	BB	K	ERA	RATIO
BEDROSIAN, STEVE	0	2	0	46.00	41	17	18	43	3.33	1.283
BURKETT, JOHN	6	8	0	159.33	176	64	36	85	3.62	1.331
FRANCO, JOHN	1	4	30	5.00	47	15	19	42	2.70	1.320
HAMMOND, CHRIS	4	4	0	73.33	79	25	23	40	3.07	1.391
OLSON, GREG	0	2	1	12.66	17	15	9	10	1.66	2.054
REED, STEVE	3	2	3	64.00	79	28	26	51	3.94	1.641
SWIFT, BILLY	8	7	0	109.33	109	41	31	62	3.38	1.281
WOHLERS, MARK	7	2	1	51.00	51	26	33	58	4.59	1.647
YOUNG, ANTHONY	4	6	0	114.66	103	50	46	65	3.92	1.299
*FREY, STEVE	1	0	0	15.33	20	14	8	8	8.22	1.826
TOTALS	**34**	**37**	**35**	**695.66**	**722**	**295**	**249**	**464**	**3.82**	**1.396**

Fleder Mice
Owner: Rob Fleder

Two more base hits and the Mice would have slipped past the Burros into eighth place. Whoopie! Any team that starts the season with Mitch Williams as their closer is in for tough sledding. Even more damaging were big investments in Robby Thompson and Curt Schilling. The Mice are too cheesy to deal, so there was never any question about them being party to The Trade. Bright lights for 1995: Robb Nen ($2) and Joe Hamilton ($5).

FINAL ROSTER

BATTERS	AB	H	BB	HR	RBI	SB	R	OBA	BA
BELL, DEREK	434	135	29	14	54	24	54	.354	.311
DAULTON, DARREN	257	77	33	15	56	4	43	.379	.300
EISENREICH, JIM	290	87	33	4	43	6	42	.372	.300
FRAZIER, LOU	123	35	14	0	13	17	21	.358	.285
JEFFERIES, GREG	397	129	45	12	55	12	52	.394	.325
JORDAN, RICKY	220	62	6	8	37	0	29	.301	.282
LANKFORD, RAY	416	111	58	19	57	11	89	.357	.267
MERCED, ORLANDO	386	105	42	9	51	4	48	.343	.272
MORANDINI, MICKEY	251	73	33	2	25	9	39	.373	.291
SHEAFFER, DANNY	110	24	10	1	12	0	11	.283	.218
STOCKER, KEVIN	263	71	44	2	28	1	37	.375	.270
THOMPSON, MILT	201	56	18	4	30	6	28	.338	.279
WHITEN, MARK	317	93	35	13	51	9	55	.364	.293
*LOCKHART, KEVIN	43	9	4	2	6	1	4	.277	.209
*OQUENDO, JOSE	38	8	10	0	3	0	3	.375	.211
*THOMPSON, ROBBY	122	24	13	2	7	3	10	.274	.197
#MORMAN, RUSS	29	6	1	1	2	0	2	.233	.207
**OTHERS (2)	20	6	1	0	2	0	2	.333	.300
TOTALS	**3917**	**1111**	**429**	**108**	**532**	**107**	**569**	**.354**	**.284**

PITCHERS	W	L	S	IP	H	ER	BB	K	ERA	RATIO
CRIM, CHUCK	3	4	2	45.33	50	28	17	28	5.56	1.478
FOSTER, KEVIN	1	3	0	49.66	51	18	21	54	3.26	1.450
HAMILTON, JOEY	9	6	0	108.66	98	36	29	61	2.98	1.169
NEN, ROB	5	4	15	5.00	37	13	13	52	2.34	1.000
RIJO, JOSE	9	6	0	172.33	177	59	52	171	3.08	1.329
RITZ, KEVIN	5	6	0	73.66	88	46	35	53	5.62	1.670
SCHEID, RICH	1	2	0	19.00	25	9	4	9	4.26	1.526
SCHILLING, CURT	1	8	0	77.33	82	41	26	51	4.77	1.397
VAN LANDINGHAM, W.	7	2	0	69.00	57	29	33	47	3.78	1.304
*COOKE, STEVE	4	8	0	122.33	138	65	41	69	4.78	1.463
*JUDEN, JEFF	1	4	0	27.66	29	19	12	22	6.18	1.482
*MOORE, MARCUS	0	1	0	2.66	16	9	12	19	3.92	1.355
*WILLIAMS, BRIAN	3	5	0	6.00	90	41	36	39	6.15	2.100
*WILLIAMS, MITCH	1	4	6	2.00	21	17	24	21	7.65	2.250
#BAUTISTA, JOSE	1	3	0	42.00	46	18	9	26	3.86	1.310
**OTHERS (8)	0	1	1	33.66	50	31	21	30	8.29	2.109
TOTALS	**51**	**67**	**24**	**991.33**	**1055**	**479**	**385**	**752**	**4.35**	**1.453**

• AROUND THE HORN

Glenwag Goners
Owner: Glen Waggoner

Sum up the Goners' season in two words: Ryne Sandberg. The Iron Horse was counting on a Ryno resurgence to lead them to the top of the standings (or at least as far as eighth place) when—blap!—Sandberg up and quits. "Forget the $15 million he walked away from," groaned the Iron Horse, explaining that his star's retirement coupled with The Trade meant a rare losing season for the Goners. "What about the $28 I paid him?" As this book went to press, the Goners were readying a lawsuit against Sandberg for breach of contract.

FINAL ROSTER

BATTERS	AB	H	BB	HR	RBI	SB	R	OBA	BA
BROWNE, JERRY	47	17	7	1	4	0	9	.444	.362
CLAYTON, ROYCE	385	91	30	3	30	23	38	.292	.236
CUMMINGS, MIDRE	77	19	4	1	11	0	11	.284	.247
DUNCAN, MARIANO	347	93	17	8	48	10	49	.302	.268
EUSEBIO, TONY	24	9	1	1	6	0	2	.400	.375
GIRARDI, JOE	143	42	5	3	20	1	20	.318	.294
HANSEN, DAVE	23	11	2	0	4	0	2	.520	.478
HUNTER, BRIAN	19	5	1	0	0	1	1	.300	.263
JORDAN, BRIAN	71	21	2	3	7	1	7	.315	.296
MCDAVID, RAY	17	6	1	0	1	1	2	.389	.353
MONDESI, RAUL	195	54	10	7	19	3	26	.312	.277
ROYER, STAN	0	0	0	0	0	0	0	.000	.000
SEGUI, DAVID	336	81	33	10	43	0	46	.309	.241
#BLAUSER, JEFF	186	44	17	1	23	0	21	.300	.237
#BURKS, ELLIS	130	46	15	12	22	3	30	.421	.354
#KELLY, ROBERTO	288	91	21	6	29	15	53	.362	.316
#MCREYNOLDS, KEVIN	149	37	16	4	18	2	19	.321	.248
#ORSULAK, JOE	207	56	12	7	35	3	33	.311	.271
#PAGNOZZI, TOM	135	39	10	4	26	0	9	.338	.289
#SANDBERG, RYNE	223	53	23	5	24	2	36	.309	.238
**OTHERS (7)	284	60	18	83	5	3	29	.258	.211
TOTALS	**3286**	**875**	**245**	**84**	**405**	**68**	**443**	**.317**	**.266**

PITCHERS	W	L	S	IP	H	ER	BB	K	ERA	RATIO
ASHBY, ANDY	2	1	0	22.00	20	7	5	21	2.86	1.136
ASTACIO, PEDRO	6	8	0	149.00	142	71	47	108	4.29	1.268
CASTILLO, FRANK	2	0	0	18.00	18	9	4	13	4.50	1.222
JONES, TODD	3	1	4	41.33	31	13	13	36	2.83	1.065
NEAGLE, DENNY	9	10	0	137.00	135	78	49	122	5.12	1.343
ROBERTSON, RICH	0	0	0	15.66	20	12	10	8	6.90	1.916
RODRIGUEZ, RICH	2	5	0	36.33	39	23	18	28	5.70	1.569
SAGER, A.J.	0	0	0	.00	0	0	0	0	.00	.000
SEANEZ, RUDY	1	1	0	23.66	24	7	9	18	2.66	1.395
*HERNANDEZ, JEREMY	3	3	9	23.33	16	7	14	13	2.70	1.286
#GREENE, TOMMY	2	0	0	35.66	37	18	22	28	4.54	1.655
#HANSON, ERIC	4	5	0	85.00	101	46	16	63	4.87	1.376
#MARTINEZ, PEDRO	3	1	3	57.33	44	15	34	44	2.35	1.361
#SMILEY, JOHN	6	8	0	1.66	107	37	21	76	3.31	1.272
#SMITH, PETE	3	6	0	89.33	98	50	28	32	5.04	1.411
**OTHERS (3)	2	1	0	39.33	37	21	17	29	4.81	1.373
TOTALS	**48**	**50**	**16**	**873.66**	**869**	**414**	**307**	**639**	**4.26**	**1.346**

Smoked Fish
Owner: Peter Gethers

"Boy, did I skin the Furrriers!" So says the Sturgeon General of the Smoked Fish, Peter "No Clue" Gethers, in assessing The Trade. "Look, I got a quality guy in Jose Vizcaino plus a few throw-ins and all I had to give up was Fred McGriff, Sammy Sosa, Lenny Dykstra, Marquis Grissom, Todd Zeile, and Mike Kingery. What a steal! I'd do it again in a New York minute."

FINAL ROSTER

BATTERS	AB	H	BB	HR	RBI	SB	R	OBA	BA
BURNITZ, JEROMY	65	19	11	0	8	1	11	.395	.292
EVERETT, CARL	32	7	2	2	4	2	5	.265	.219
HUNDLEY, TODD	158	37	15	6	16	2	21	.301	.234
KENT, JEFF	169	48	7	3	27	0	19	.313	.284
KING, JEFF	339	89	30	5	42	3	36	.322	.263
OFFERMAN, JOSE	243	51	38	1	25	2	27	.317	.210
PARENT, MARK	87	22	8	3	15	0	7	.316	.253
PENDLETON, TERRY	88	28	4	2	10	0	5	.348	.318
THOMPSON, RYAN	175	35	16	6	16	1	17	.267	.200
VANDERWAL, JOHN	110	27	16	5	15	2	12	.341	.245
VINA, FERNANDO	91	26	10	0	6	3	16	.356	.286
VIZCAINO, JOSE	206	46	13	1	16	0	21	.269	.223
WEISS, WALT	197	42	32	0	15	5	27	.323	.213
YOUNG, ERIC	122	35	21	3	17	8	18	.392	.287
#DYKSTRA, LENNY	214	65	48	5	17	11	54	.431	.304
#GRISSOM, MARQUIS	190	50	17	4	18	17	35	.324	.263
#KINGERY, MIKE	72	19	6	2	10	2	8	.321	.264
#MCGRIFF, FRED	203	57	27	16	37	3	38	.365	.281
#SOSA, SAMMY	205	53	13	13	32	9	28	.303	.259
#ZEILE, TODD	196	49	25	9	29	0	27	.335	.250
**OTHERS (6)	139	26	9	0	12	1	13	.236	.187
TOTALS	**3301**	**831**	**368**	**86**	**387**	**72**	**445**	**.327**	**.252**

PITCHERS	W	L	S	IP	H	ER	BB	K	ERA	RATIO
BANKS, WILLIE	8	12	0	138.33	139	83	56	91	5.40	1.410
BIELECKI, MIKE	1	0	0	13.00	13	7	10	7	4.85	1.769
CARRASCO, HECTOR	5	6	6	56.33	42	14	30	41	2.24	1.278
DREIFORT, DARREN	0	5	6	29.00	45	20	15	22	6.21	2.069
MORGAN, MIKE	2	3	0	42.33	56	27	15	27	5.74	1.677
NIED, DAVID	4	3	0	56.66	67	28	20	31	4.45	1.535
ROJAS, MEL	1	1	6	41.33	42	19	11	48	4.14	1.282
RUFFIN, JOHNNY	7	2	1	7.00	57	24	27	44	3.09	1.200
WATSON, ALLEN	6	5	0	115.66	130	71	53	74	5.52	1.582
*MADDUX, MIKE	1	0	1	21.33	24	14	7	16	5.91	1.453
*REYNOSO, ARMANDO	3	4	0	52.33	54	28	22	25	4.82	1.452
#AVERY, STEVE	5	1	0	83.33	65	36	33	68	3.89	1.176
#GOODEN, DWIGHT	3	3	0	36.00	39	21	11	33	5.25	1.389
#GROSS, KEVIN	6	4	0	96.00	100	40	26	87	3.75	1.313
**OTHERS (2)	0	0	0	17.66	22	11	7	15	5.60	1.642
TOTALS	**52**	**49**	**20**	**869.33**	**895**	**443**	**343**	**629**	**4.59**	**1.424**

Lovin' Spoonfuls
Owner: Jay Lovinger

GM Jay (formerly of Jay and the Americans) Lovinger made all the right moves, as he is quick to tell you in the introduction to this chapter. Even if he didn't make The Trade, he did make a number of smart next-year deals. And with Chuck Carr, Andujar Cedeño, Darren Fletcher, Andres Galarraga, Chipper Jones, Phil Plantier, and Rick Wilkins coming back at a cost of less than one Barry Bonds, the Spoonfuls have a giant head start on an offense. The odds-on favorite to win the 1995 pennant? Only if the four pitching categories are eliminated.

FINAL ROSTER

BATTERS	AB	H	BB	HR	RBI	SB	R	OBA	BA
CARR, CHUCK	411	107	20	2	27	31	58	.295	.260
CEDENO, ANDUJAR	248	65	21	3	32	1	28	.320	.262
FLETCHER, DARREN	285	74	25	10	57	0	28	.319	.260
GALARRAGA, ANDRES	390	122	18	27	74	8	70	.343	.313
JONES, CHIPPER	0	0	0	0	0	0	0	.000	.000
OLIVER, JOE	0	0	0	0	0	0	0	.000	.000
PENA, GERONIMO	174	48	18	9	30	7	29	.344	.276
PLANTIER, PHIL	341	75	36	18	41	3	44	.294	.220
WILKINS, RICK	289	65	37	7	39	2	39	.313	.225
#ALICEA, LUIS	76	13	12	1	5	2	13	.284	.171
#BONDS, BARRY	19	4	4	2	2	0	3	.348	.211
#BRUMFIELD, JACOB	13	3	0	0	0	1	2	.231	.231
#FLOYD, CLIFF	105	27	7	1	10	3	13	.304	.257
#GRISSOM, MARQUIS	31	7	3	0	6	0	4	.294	.226
#HANSEN, DAVE	15	4	1	0	1	0	0	.313	.267
#JORDAN, BRIEN	45	11	7	0	2	1	3	.346	.244
#MAY, DERRICK	47	19	7	1	13	0	7	.481	.404
#STATON, DAVE	16	4	5	1	1	0	2	.429	.250
#STINNETT, KELLY	73	20	5	1	6	0	10	.321	.274
#WALKER, LARRY	29	11	4	1	6	1	6	.455	.379
**OTHERS (2)	6	0	0	0	0	0	1	.000	.000
TOTALS	**2613**	**679**	**230**	**84**	**352**	**60**	**360**	**.320**	**.260**

PITCHERS	W	L	S	IP	H	ER	BB	K	ERA	RATIO
CHARLTON, NORM	0	0	0	.00	0	0	0	0	.00	.000
DIBBLE, ROB	0	0	0	.00	0	0	0	0	.00	.000
GREENE, TOMMY	0	0	0	.00	0	0	0	0	.00	.000
HOLLINS, JESSIE	0	0	0	.00	0	0	0	0	.00	.000
KILE, DARRYL	9	5	0	142.66	147	71	79	99	4.48	1.584
RIVERA, BEN	3	4	0	38.00	40	29	22	19	6.87	1.632
WAGNER, PAUL	4	5	0	73.33	92	41	30	47	5.03	1.664
WEATHERS, DAVE	8	12	0	135.00	166	79	59	72	5.27	1.667
#HARRIS, GREG W	1	1	0	42.33	38	24	21	28	5.10	1.394
#HOUGH, CHARLIE	1	0	0	12.66	15	4	3	6	2.84	1.422
#JACKSON, DANNY	4	0	0	38.66	33	11	13	30	2.56	1.190
#MADDUX, MIKE	0	0	1	5.00	2	0	1	4	.00	.600
#SAGER, A.J.	1	4	0	4.66	50	24	13	24	5.31	1.549
TOTALS	**31**	**31**	**1**	**528.33**	**583**	**283**	**241**	**329**	**4.82**	**1.560**

ROTI·STATS TOP TEAMS OF 1994

Here are some of the top 1994 Rotisserie teams around the country as tracked by Roti-Stats. These teams managed to capture the highest percentage of their leagues' possible points. Is your team here? It could be next year!

NATIONAL LEAGUES

#	% Pts.	TEAM	LEAGUE	TEAMS	CAT	HR	RBI	SB	AVG	W	SV	ERA	RTO
1.	95.3	The Dwellers	Garvey's Kids	8	8	190	683	128	.304	72	63	3.64	1.274
2.	94.4	Auto-Maddux Pilot	Spanntastic Rotball League	9	8	166	672	129	.286	60	50	3.58	1.210
3.	93.8	Max's Misfits	Tri-Valley League	8	8	196	770	136	.290	76	58	3.68	1.244
4.	93.8	Bo Pick's Peckers	Orange County Rotisserie	12	8	144	638	130	.282	71	45	3.65	1.200
5.	92.0	Bradford Bradicals	Trans-America All-Stars	10	10	205	764	177	.280	68	57	3.60	1.233
6.	91.3	Stegalls Hard Caseys	Irrational League	10	8	191	680	161	.279	74	45	3.84	1.237
7.	91.3	Nekkids on Block	Lost Gonzo League	10	8	136	646	117	.285	67	70	3.52	1.296
8.	91.0	Double Schneids	Senior Sircuit	9	8	160	665	166	.286	54	63	3.38	1.212
9.	90.6	Ashbins	Urban League	10	8	189	814	109	.297	64	69	3.66	1.265
10.	90.1	Nasty Stats	Laguna National League	12	8	148	615	119	.288	54	48	3.92	1.280

AMERICAN LEAGUES

#	% Pts.	TEAM	LEAGUE	TEAMS	CAT	HR	RBI	SB	AVG	W	SV	ERA	RTO
1.	93.2	Caesars Pallis	Steals & Deals League	12	8	157	675	104	.282	64	40	3.60	1.336
2.	91.7	Tin Men	Laguna American League	12	8	172	735	110	.287	66	48	3.99	1.394
3.	91.7	Stengels	Southern California Follies	9	8	196	747	147	.287	56	62	3.96	1.323
4.	91.5	Daff Attack	Worcester Suds League	10	10	184	822	115	.295	74	33	4.23	1.362
5.	90.9	Lee Der Hose	Barrister's Trust League	11	10	165	708	152	.285	76	43	3.99	1.324
6.	90.3	Be-Lo-Me	ProBowlers A.L. Rotball	11	8	186	782	164	.294	66	39	4.61	1.411
7.	89.6	Benderovers	Cahners Rotisserie Baseball	12	8	182	704	114	.288	70	37	4.07	1.285
8.	89.6	Let's Make A Deal	Ultimate-AL League	12	8	155	659	135	.285	69	37	4.73	1.513
9.	89.2	Ross-Cohen Tanners	Long Island Couch Potato	11	8	165	714	104	.275	70	49	4.22	1.356
10.	88.8	Toros	Terrific Coast League	10	10	185	756	81	.281	72	9	4.22	1.389

MIXED LEAGUES

#	% Pts.	TEAM	LEAGUE	TEAMS	CAT	HR	RBI	SB	AVG	W	SV	ERA	RTO
1.	95.4	Spinapair	Taxter Baseball Association	13	10	211	791	172	.294	94	43	3.58	1.223
2.	91.7	Naked Apes	Wicked Baseball League	12	10	250	912	196	.291	78	48	3.69	1.266
3.	90.7	Rawhydes	Eight Men Out	9	9	266	1057	129	.295	70	56	3.40	1.226
4.	88.8	New London Sharks	Coast To Coast	12	10	229	891	140	.282	77	67	3.46	1.257
5.	88.2	Mojo Mushers	Mystic Penguin League	9	8	231	887	178	.296	81	65	3.66	1.273
6.	88.1	Rotodogs	Appalachian Armchair	8	10	180	651	145	.307	44	44	3.63	1.248
7.	87.5	Grand Slam	Mr. Baseball League	16	12	181	738	135	.284	71	76	3.63	1.241
8.	87.5	Jacobs Fielders	GECC CTO League	11	8	237	850	189	.283	76	55	3.25	1.215
9.	87.0	Armed/Not Dangerous	Head First	8	12	264	1061	132	.311	94	0	3.73	1.300
10.	86.9	The Magic Bats	League To Be Named Later	11	8	237	968	178	.296	67	49	3.88	1.296

ROTI·STATS MOST COMPETITIVE LEAGUES 1994

Talk about close pennant races! Here are some of the most competitive leagues around the country as tracked by Roti·Stats. The "RATING" figure refers to the average point difference among the top five teams in a league.

NATIONAL LEAGUES

#	RATING	LEAGUE	LEADER	TEAMS	CAT	1ST	2ND	3RD	4TH	5TH
1.	0.75	Patrick Division League	BeHards	10	8	55.0	53.0	52.5	52.5	52.0
2.	1.00	Bankrupts	Long Balls	10	8	56.0	55.0	54.5	53.0	52.0
3.	1.25	Oly League	Yellow Tangos	11	8	65.5	64.0	62.0	61.5	60.5
4.	1.38	National Sou Cakalaki	Stray Cats	10	8	58.0	55.0	54.0	53.5	52.5
5.	1.38	Sports Arena Ultra	Steeling Home	11	8	58.0	55.0	54.0	53.0	52.5
6.	1.50	Concho Cactus League	Gallawangers	10	8	55.0	50.5	50.0	49.0	49.0
7.	1.50	Organic Rotisserie League	Mono-Men	9	8	47.0	47.0	46.0	45.0	41.0
8.	1.75	NOP Rotisserie League	Fanatics	10	8	53.5	52.0	51.0	47.0	46.5
9.	1.75	Busch League	North Coast	10	8	55.0	53.0	51.0	50.0	48.0
10.	1.88	BOA Fantasy League AT&T	Elfin Tragic	9	8	50.0	46.0	44.5	43.5	42.5

AMERICAN LEAGUES

#	RATING	LEAGUE	LEADER	TEAMS	CAT	1ST	2ND	3RD	4TH	5TH
1.	0.50	Orange Coast	J.R.'s Sloczars	8	8	39.0	38.0	38.0	37.0	37.0
2.	1.38	Super Freak RBL	Guns N Deroses	10	8	55.5	54.5	52.0	51.0	50.0
3.	1.38	Sporting Chance	Kool Klubbers	10	8	56.5	56.0	54.5	54.0	51.0
4.	1.75	Lou Skizas League	Double Trouble	12	8	63.0	63.0	60.0	58.0	56.0
5.	2.00	Advantage International	Cooperstown Cowboys	10	8	56.0	54.0	50.0	49.0	48.0
6.	2.00	Mudder of All	Money Pit	12	8	74.0	70.5	68.0	66.5	66.0
7.	2.00	Rey Quinones Memorial League	Matt Peterricks	8	8	44.0	43.0	42.5	36.5	36.0
8.	2.13	Staten Island Bud-Men	Chic Magnets	10	8	57.0	55.0	50.5	50.5	48.5
9.	2.13	Hot And Sour League	NJ Highlanders	10	8	57.0	55.5	51.5	51.5	48.5
10.	2.25	TBC Rotisserie League	Repete	10	8	60.0	56.0	54.0	53.5	51.0

MIXED LEAGUES

#	RATING	LEAGUE	LEADER	TEAMS	CAT	1ST	2ND	3RD	4TH	5TH
1.	1.50	Surgical Psychos	The Tribe	10	10	65.0	64.5	64.0	62.5	59.0
2.	1.63	Greater Westside League	Gamblers	12	8	70.5	69.5	69.0	66.5	64.0
3.	1.88	Master Batters	Kruk's Last Nut	10	10	64.0	59.5	58.0	57.0	56.5
4.	2.38	Post Office Mixed	D & G Wolves	10	10	65.0	65.0	61.5	57.5	55.5
5.	2.50	Lindsay's Rotisserie League	Field of Dreams	12	8	70.5	67.0	62.5	62.0	60.5
6.	2.50	"Yet To Be Named" League II	Flatulent Furrskins	10	8	59.0	53.0	53.0	50.5	49.0
7.	2.50	Moe Berg	Mike Berardino	18	12	157.5	157.5	151.5	148.0	147.5
8.	2.63	Love That Howie!	Corn Bunnies	11	10	77.0	74.5	73.0	70.5	66.5
9.	2.75	Viva! El Rauncho	Hollywood Stars	12	12	107.5	105.0	99.0	97.0	96.5
10.	2.88	Big 10	Pitchers of Tang	10	10	64.0	62.0	59.5	57.0	52.5

900-268-8888

Introducing the Official
Rotisserie League Statphone!
No more waiting for tomorrow's boxscores!
All the stats you want—NOW!

That's right. Just dial **900-268-8888** and get all the
numbers you need for a good night's sleep—or, as the
case may be, for some particularly vivid nightmares.
(Sorry. We *can* promise up-to-the-minute Rotissestats, but
how good they are is up to your players.)

Home Runs! RBI! Stolen Bases! Wins! Saves!
Earned Runs! Walks! Hits! Innings Pitched!
Injury Reports! Game Results!

Only 99 cents a minute!

900-268-8888

Pennant Winners!
They Beat the Founding Fathers at Their Own Game in 1994!

1. Andy Bauman (Hudson, New York)
2. Jerry Burns (Ardmore, Pennsylvania)
3. Stephen Malara (Bradley Beach, New Jersey)
4. John Stepal (Buffalo Grove, Illinois)
5. Richard Trevino (Woodlands, California)
6. Jim Williamson (Massapequa Park, New York)

(See page 276 for How to Beat the Founding Fathers in 1995!)

⚾ Who Are You Guys, Anyway? ⚾

A Readers Survey

Who plays Rotisserie baseball? We hear from other Rotisserie owners now and then: "How could you possibly..." or "You guys must be crazy..." the letters usually begin. We bump into fellow Rotisserians in the strangest places, including ballparks. And we get a lot of obscene phone calls. But we'd like to know a little more about other players of The Greatest Game for Baseball Fans Since Baseball, so we decided to conduct a little survey, the results of which we will publish in the 1996 edition of this book.

FREE ISSUES OF BASEBALL AMERICA!

To show our gratitude for helping with the survey, we have arranged with the editors of *Baseball America* to send you three free issues of the best baseball periodical in the game. *Baseball America* covers baseball the way Ozzie Smith covers short, with comprehensive reports on the major leagues and on emerging prospects in baseball. It's an essential tool for every Rotisserie owner, and it can be yours—*free*. Plus, if you send us the names and addresses of the other members of your league, we'll extend this special *Baseball America* offer to them as well. The total cost to you? Five minutes and one 29-cent stamp.

Your Name_____ Phone # (_____)_____

Address_____ City_____ State_____ Zip_____

1. How did you first become aware of this book?
   newspaper [ ]   sports publication [ ]   word of mouth [ ]   bookstore [ ]
2. How many years have you played Rotisserie baseball? [   ]
3. Do you play in other fantasy baseball leagues? Yes [ ]   No [ ]
   If Yes, which one(s)?_____
4. Would you be interested in a Rotisserie fantasy camp staged during spring training next year? Yes [ ]   No [ ] In a regional/local camp? Yes [ ]   No [ ]
5. Would it enhance your league's Rotisserie experience if we offered the following:
   a) Auction draft, record-keeping, and operational forms? Yes [ ]   No [ ]
   b) Trophies and/or certificates for special league achievements, such as record number of points, 5 years in league, etc.? Yes [ ]   No [ ]
   c) Other items of apparel, in addition to our famous T-shirts and caps, to identify you as a Rotisserie player? Yes [ ]   No [ ] Such as _____
6. Male [ ] or Female [ ]?   7. Age [   ]
8. How would you best describe your work (check as many as apply)?
   Full-time [ ]   Part-time [ ]   Student [ ]   Retired [ ]
9. Which range best reflects your total yearly household income?
   Less than $25,000 [ ] $25–50,000 [ ] $50–75,000 [ ] $75–100,000 [ ]
   Over $100,000 [ ]
10. What is your favorite major league baseball team?_____

6

Front Office

How to Keep Score

Once upon a time, the entire front office complex of Rotisserie League Baseball consisted of Beloved Founder and Former Commissioner-for-Life Daniel Okrent. There is a fading daguerreotype of Marse Dan, one hand clinching an unfiltered Camel, the other slowly stroking his abacus, sitting alone in his Berkshire woodshed, from which post he spewed out—we use the word advisedly—our fledgling league's biweekly standings every third fortnight or so. We were having too much fun to know any better that first season, but eventually we got smart and figured that the BFFCL would never compile and distribute the standings in a timely fashion until his team, the hapless Fenokees, got themselves in a pennant race and gave him something to crow about. Not willing to wait 'til the end of time or hell froze over, whichever came first, we fired him.

That single, surgical act marked the yawning of a new Rotisserie Era.

You can still do your league's stats by hand, of course—if the task required a mathematical genius, we'd still be waiting for our first standings report for the 1980 season. All you need is a calculator and about four hours of free time a week, every week of the season. (You're going to want weekly standings, whether you know it now or not.) But it's tiresome, tedious work, the only thing about Rotisserie League Baseball that isn't a whole gang of fun. We don't recommend keeping score by hand, but if you want to give it a shot, we'll be happy to send you a simple "Keeping Score" pamphlet for free; just write **Rotisserie League Baseball Association, 370 Seventh Avenue, Suite 312, New York, NY 10001.**

You can hire someone to do the stats by hand for you. We did that from 1981 through 1983, and our first (and only) Director of Statistical Services, Sandra Krempasky, was immortalized by election to the Rotisserie Hall of Fame on the first ballot in recognition of her yeowoman's effort. Problem is, Sandra retired (actually, she was phased out by a computer), and you're never going to find anyone as good as she was.

You can develop your own computer program for crunching Rotisserie stats and put the family computer to better use than prepping for the SATs, keeping track of the family fortune, or playing "Jeopardy." At least we think you can. When it comes to computers, the Founding Fathers are still trying to figure out why the light in the refrigerator comes on when you open the door. Other people say it can be done, though—something to do with spreading sheets, we think.

The *best* thing you can do, of course, is to have **Roti•Stats** compile and compute your league's stats. **Roti•Stats** is now the exclusive, officially authorized stats service for Rotisserie League Baseball—the *only* stats service sanctioned by the Founding Fathers of the game. Most important, it's the *best* stats service in the business.

We know. Last year, after a decade of running our own stats service, we decided to hang up our spikes. We went looking for a new stats service. We examined them all, and we liked what we saw in **Roti•Stats**. They've been in business just about as long as Rotisserie League Baseball, and they have an unparalleled record for accuracy and timeliness. We were delighted with their performance. We think you will be, too. Find out for yourself what they can do for your league. Call **Roti•Stats** toll-free at **800-884-7684.**

Roti•Stats!
(You Play. Let Roti•Stats Do the Hard Stuff.)

Each week **Roti•Stats** records your transactions, computes your standings, and rushes a report via first-class mail to your league secretary. (Fax, overnight express, and modem service available for the terminally anxious.) Each weekly report contains the standings, up-to-the-minute rosters for all teams, a list of free agents, and a transactions update. Your league can make free, unlimited transactions that may be made retroactively at any time. Player salaries, contract status, and positions are tracked at no additional cost. No hidden charges. Just one flat fee at the beginning of the season.

- *Quick Turnaround of Opening Day Rosters!* Reports are available after the *first* week of play. Most services make you wait two to three weeks for your first standings report. **Roti•Stats** knows how anxious your owners are to find out where they stand from the first crack of the bat.
- *Free Agent List!* Each weekly report includes a list of unowned players in your league, complete with weekly and year-to-date stats for *every* player in the league.
- *Free Custom Comment Page!* You may add an extra page to your weekly report containing important information for your league members. Many leagues use this page to reflect up-to-the-minute waiver information or to conduct general business among league members.
- *How Your Team Stacks Up Nationwide!* Periodically you'll receive special reports such as "Top Teams" in the country, "Tightest Pennant Races," and much more (see pages 264–265). You'll see how well

your team and league stack up against other **Roti•Stats** leagues nationwide.

- *Additional Stat Categories!* Want more than the original eight scoring categories? No problem. Their state-of-the art software lets you include any alternative scoring categories you want—at no extra charge.
- *Same Day & Overnight Fax Service!* Reduced fax charges permit your owners to receive their standings reports the fastest and most efficient way possible—the same day they are generated. (Monday for AL and Mixed; Tuesday for NL).
- *Player Value and Position Eligibility Reports!* Player values are generated by **Roti•Stats'** own proven formulas based on stats for the last two years for each player (by position). An invaluable tool on Auction Draft Day. Also free: a Position Eligibility Report that shows all positions for which each player is eligible to be drafted.
- *League-at-a-Glance Report!* Includes all team rosters with position, salary, and contract information. Great when you're pondering trades.
- *Free League Administration Software!* You can use this program to submit moves to **Roti•Stats** each week or just use it to track your league fees. The fee reports alone make this a tremendous aid for your secretary.
- *The Roti•Tiller Newsletter!* Dig the latest dirt in Rotisserie baseball with **Roti•Stats'** highly unofficial, semi-irregular, not-always-polite newsletter called **The Roti•Tiller.** Designed to keep the Rotissespirit alive in your league, **The Roti•Tiller** spreads gossip, stirs up rumors, and occasionally even dispenses nuggets of useful information. Don't be surprised to see your name in headlines!
- *Multiple League Discounts!* Play in more than one league? The RLBA will discreetly provide you with a list of counselors in your region who might be able to help. Better still, **Roti•Stats** will provide significant discounts when all your leagues sign up for the best service in the game.
- *Championship Hat & Certificate!* The winning owner(s) in your league will receive the coveted Roti•Stats Championship Hat, as well as a Championship Certificate suitable for framing.
- *800 Number for Transactions!* Call in your transactions toll-free.

For complete information about **Roti•Stats**, the only stats service officially authorized by the Founding Fathers of Rotisserie League Baseball, call toll-free: **800-884-7684.** You'll get a sign-up kit, sample standings and special reports, and a lot more reasons why **Roti•Stats** should be *your* stats service. Did you get that number? It's still **800-884-7684.**

The RLBA Wants You!

You've collared a roomful of other baseball fanatics, memorized this book, subscribed to *Baseball America*, made *USA Today* a daily habit, found a newsstand that carries *USA Today Baseball Weekly*, bought every baseball mag on the racks, and appointed someone else to bring chow for your first Auction Draft Day. What's next? Membership in the **Rotisserie League Baseball Association**. Join now and beat the Christmas rush. Here's what your league gets with membership in the **RLBA**:

1. ***Commissioner's Services.*** No need for your league to be rent asunder by rules disputes and internecine fighting: one Civil War was quite enough, thank you. For member leagues of the **RLBA,** we adjudicate disputes, interpret rules, issue Solomonic judgments, and otherwise maintain law and order so you can concentrate on playing the game.

2. ***Position Eligibility List.*** Complete and up-to-date. Updated every month during the season.

3. ***Quarterly Updates.*** Information on rules changes, news from other leagues, baseball gossip, and happenings around the Rotisseworld.

4. ***Opening Day Rosters.*** Official 25-man rosters, complete with last-minute disabled list moves and minor league promotions and demotions. Mailed to you Opening Day.

5. ***Monthly Farm System Updates.*** Progress reports and stat updates on the top 50 minor leaguers so you'll always know who's hot and who's not.

6. ***Championship Certificate.*** Signed by Beloved Founder and Former Commissioner-for-Life Daniel Okrent, this suitable-for-framing certificate is the perfect grace note for your pennant winner's rec room wall.

7. ***Company Store.*** The right to purchase an astonishing range of Rotisserie products at full retail price. (See the following pages.)

8. ***Yoo-Hoo.*** If you live outside the Yoo-Hoo belt, we'll send you a bottle of the precious nectar to pour over your pennant winner's head, in solemn observance of that most sacred of Rotisserituals.

How does your league join? Easy. Just fill out the form on page 279 and send it with your league's check or money order for $50 (only $25 for renewals) to the **Rotisserie League Baseball Association, 370 Seventh Avenue, Suite 312, New York, NY 10001.**

⚾ ⚾ ⚾

Rotisserie Baseball—The Video!
"Great!"—Siskel   "Terrible!"—Ebert

That's right. We made a video. Go ahead and laugh. But hey—it works for Madonna, why not us?

Hosted by Reggie Jackson (yeah, *that* Reggie Jackson), **Rotisserie Baseball—The Video** is 30 minutes of rollicking, swashbuckling, gut-wrenching excitement, with enough car chases, frontal nudity, and violence to satisfy even Peter "Sudden Pete" Gethers ("Two thumbs!"). It features Glen "Iron Horse" Waggoner ("Two cheeseburgers!"), Harry Stein ("Not since *Gone with the Wind* . . ."), BFFCL Daniel Okrent ("Not since *Deep Throat* . . ."), and all the fun-loving Rotissegang, talking about the game they love so well.

For people new to The Greatest Game etc., **Rotisserie Baseball—The Video** is an informative, vaguely useful overview of the obsession that will soon take over their lives. For veteran Rotisserie players, it's a handy way to explain what the game is all about to people who don't know a baseball from a bass fiddle. (Just invite them over, cook up a tubful of popcorn, and pop The Video into the old VCR. They'll never be able to thank you enough, so they probably won't even try.) It's also a perfect gift idea for weddings, anniversaries, divorces, bar mitzvahs, and M-O-T-H-E-R on *Her* Day!

Just $15 plus postage and handling. See order form on page 279.

⚾ ⚾ ⚾

Rotisserie Ready-to-Wear!

Even if you draft like a Pollet Burro, there's no reason you can't dress like a pennant winner. Just order a few dozen official **Rotisserie T-shirts**. Available in a variety of designer colors, all of them white, this top-quality 100% cotton shirt has the famous Rotisserie coat-of-arms emblazoned across the chest in four dazzling colors. Perfect for any social occasion, but especially suitable for Auction Draft Day. A trifling $15 (plus postage and handling). Get a couple in case you slop mustard on yourself at the ballpark.

And what's an official Rotisserie T-shirt without an official **Rotisserie Cap**? Only half a uniform, that's what. The Rotisserie Cap is a top-quality number in breathtaking white with the famous four-color Rotisserie logo. Only $18 (plus postage and handling)—and get this: One size fits all! See page 279 for information on how to order.

⚾ ⚾ ⚾

Beat the Founding Fathers
at Their Own Game!

That's right—play head-to-head against one of the Founding Fathers of Rotisserie League Baseball. Believe you can snap the Wulfgang's baton? Want a chance at draining the Okrent Fenokees' swamp? Think you're just the cat to catch the Fleder Mice? Here's your chance.

1. Pick a 23-man Rotisserie roster based on player salaries in Chapter 3, and submit it on an official Founding Fathers League registration form along with your entry fee of $50 by May 1.

2. Play National League, American League, or Mixed League—your call. Your club will be placed in a 12-team league that includes a team owned by one of the Founding Fathers (*e.g.,* the Pollet Burro League, the Stein Brenner League, *etc.*).

3. You may spend a maximum total of 260 Rotissedollars (*i.e.,* NOT real dollars) to assemble your team, using the salaries indicated in the Scouting Report, Chapter 3. You must have the customary Rotisserie alignment: 2 catchers, 3 corners, 3 middle infielders, 5 outfielders, and 1 utility/DH; and 9 pitchers.

4. Scoring will be according to the standard Rotisserie categories: Home Runs, Runs Batted In, Stolen Bases, and Batting Average for batters; Wins, Saves, Earned Run Average, and Ratio for pitchers.

5. You will receive a complete standings report every month so that you can track your team's progress in the Founding Fathers pennant race. Each report will contain a complete performance report on every player on every team in your league, as well as standings in each of the eight statistical categories.

6. At the All-Star Break, you get a chance to ditch any bums who have been dragging your team down. Each owner will be sent an updated salary list for all the eligible players in both leagues. You can release up to seven players that you currently own and use their salaries (based on their original book prices) to acquire seven new players (based on the updated salary list). After this All-Star Break transaction period, your team must still have a full 23-man Rotisserie team and your payroll may not exceed 260 Rotissedollars.

7. Pennant-winners receive a free pass to play in the Founding Fathers League in 1995, a free copy of the next edition of this book, an official Rotisserie League T-shirt, and a wall plaque testifying to your victory.

Plus you will be listed right here in next year's book as a Rotisserie owner who beat the Founding Fathers at their own game!

For your official entry registration form for the Founding Fathers League, contact the **Rotisserie League Baseball Association.** The address is **370 Seventh Avenue, Suite 312, New York, NY 10001.** The telephone number is **212-695-3463.** The fax number is **212-643-8083.** Write, call, or fax—NOW!

Free Opening Day *Rotisserie Hot List!*

Get all the lowdown on late spring training cuts, last-minute deals, nagging injuries, rising and falling stars, rookies who are going to make the club, and much, much more—all just in time for your auction draft!

We'll tell you who's going to be in every rotation (plus the guys in line to step in if somebody falters or gets hurt). We'll tell you which middle-innings relievers have the best shot at picking up 8–10 garbage wins. We'll tab the fourth and fifth outfielders who will pick up 10–15 SB. We'll identify the second-string catchers most likely to deliver five homers for your one-buck investment. We'll go through every bullpen and tell you who's going to get the saves. Trade talk! Rumors! Buzz!

What you get is a news-packed, eight-page newsletter filled with all the up-to-the-minute inside stuff you need to put the finishing touches on your auction draft strategy—*free!* All you have to do is send us your name, your address, and $1.95 to cover postage and handling. We'll ship your official *Rotisserie Hot List* by first-class mail on Thursday, March 30. After that, same-day service on all *Rotisserie Hot List* requests.

Order your *Rotisserie Hot List* now. Send your name, address, and $1.95 to cover postage and handling to **Rotisserie Hot List, 370 Seventh Avenue, Suite 312, New York, NY 10001.**

TEAR OUT THIS PAGE!

YES! Enroll our league immediately in the **Rotisserie League Baseball Associa-tion** and send us the official **1995 Position Eligibility List** by return mail! Enclosed is our check or money order for $50 payable to **RLBA.** (Renewal leagues, send $25.)

HOLD ON! We're not sure yet, we haven't had our organizational meeting, and all we want right now is information about **Roti•Stats**, the **RLBA's** officially authorized stats service.

(Please Print)

Name of League _____

c/o Commissioner _____

Address _____

City _____ State _____ Zip _____

Telephone _____ AL/NL _____

ROTISSERIE T-SHIRTS

Size	Quantity	Price
Small	_____	$15 each
Medium	_____	2 for $28
Large	_____	3 for $39
X-Large	_____	4 for $48
XX-Large	_____	5+ $10 each

ROTISSERIE CAPS

Size	Quantity	Price
One size fits all	_____	$18 each

ROTISSERIE VIDEOS

	Quantity	Price
	_____	$15 each

Guarantee
If not completely satisfied with any Official Rotisserie product, send it back. We'll replace it or refund your money.

Shirts	$_____
Caps	$_____
Videos	$_____
Postage/Hdlg.	$ 3.50
Total	$_____ *

($US only; Check or M/O)
*NY residents add sales tax.

Name _____

Address_____

City _____ State _____ Zip _____

Mail to:
Rotisserie League Baseball Association
370 Seventh Avenue, Suite 312
New York, NY 10001

7

Ground Rules

OFFICIAL CONSTITUTION OF ROTISSERIE LEAGUE BASEBALL

Preamble

We,

the People of the Rotisserie League, in order to spin a more perfect Game, drive Justice home, kiss domestic Tranquility good-bye, promote the general Welfare in Tidewater—where it's been tearing up the International League—and secure the Blessings of Puberty to ourselves and those we've left on Base, do ordain and establish this Constitution for Rotisserie League Baseball, and also finish this run-on sentence.

ARTICLE I. OBJECT

To assemble a lineup of 23 National League or American League baseball players whose cumulative statistics during the regular season, compiled and measured by the methods described in these rules, exceed those of all other teams in the League.

ARTICLE II. TEAMS

There are 12 teams in a duly constituted Rotisserie League composed of either National League or American League players.

> **NOTE:** If you choose to play with fewer teams, be sure to make necessary adjustments so that you acquire approximately 80% of all available players at your auction draft. You could have a six-team league using American League players, for example, and draft only from among your seven favorite AL teams. Unless you reduce the available player pool proportionately to reflect a reduced number of teams, you'll never learn to appreciate the value of a good bench.

> **NOTE:** Do *not* mix the two leagues. It's unrealistic and silly, it's not the way the big leagues do it, it means you end up using only All-Stars and established regulars, and it's fattening. (On the other hand, if you *do* mix leagues, we're not going to call out the Rotisserie National Guard or anything.)

ARTICLE III. ROSTER

A team's active roster consists of the following players:

1. **NATIONAL LEAGUE PLAYERS**
   Five outfielders, two catchers, one second baseman, one shortstop, one middle infielder (either second baseman or shortstop), one first baseman, one third baseman, one corner man (either first baseman or third baseman), one utility player (who may play any nonpitching position), and nine pitchers.

2. **AMERICAN LEAGUE PLAYERS**
   The same, except that the utility player is called a designated hitter, consistent with the AL's insistence on perpetuating that perversion of the game.

ARTICLE IV. AUCTION DRAFT DAY

A **Major League Player Auction** is conducted on the first weekend after Opening Day of the baseball season. Each team must acquire 23 players at a total cost not to exceed $260. A team need not spend the maximum. The League by general agreement determines the order in which teams may nominate players for acquisition. The team bidding first opens with a minimum salary bid of $1 for any eligible player, and the bidding proceeds around the room at minimum increments of $1 until only one bidder is left. That team acquires the player for that amount and announces the roster position the player will fill. The process is repeated, with successive team owners introducing players to be bid on, until every team has a squad of 23 players, by requisite position.

- Don't get hung up on the bidding order; it's irrelevant. Do allow plenty of time; your first draft will take all day.
- Players eligible at more than one position may be shifted during the course of the draft.
- No team may make a bid for a player it cannot afford. For example, a team with $3 left and two openings on its roster is limited to a maximum bid of $2 for one player.
- No team may bid for a player who qualifies only at a position that the team has already filled. For example, a team that has acquired two catchers, and whose utility or DH slot is occupied, may not enter the bidding for any player who qualifies *only* at catcher.
- Players who commence the season on a major league team's disabled list *are* eligible to be drafted. If selected, they may be reserved and replaced upon completion of the auction draft. (See **Article XII**, page 291.)

NOTE: Final Opening Day rosters for all National League or American League teams will be needed on Auction Draft Day. Because some teams don't make their final roster moves until the last minute, even *USA Today*'s rosters, published on Opening Day, have holes. The best way to get the most complete, updated rosters is with membership in the **Rotisserie League Baseball Association**. (See page 274 for information on how to join.)

A **Minor League Player Draft** is conducted immediately following the major league auction, in which each Rotisserie League team may acquire players (a) who are not on any National/American League team's active roster; and (b) who still have official rookie status, as defined by major league baseball.

NOTE: The major league rule reads: "A player shall be considered a rookie unless, during a previous season or seasons, he has (a) exceeded 130 at-bats or 50 innings pitched in the major leagues; or (b) accumulated more than 45 days on the active roster of a major league club or clubs during the period of a 25-player limit (excluding time in the military service)."

- Selection takes place in two rounds of a simple draft, not an auction.
- In the first season, the selection order shall be determined by drawing paired numbers from a hat (that is, positions 1 and 24, 2 and 23, and so on in a 12-team league).
- In subsequent years, the selection order in each of the two rounds is determined by the order in which the teams finished in the previous

season. In leagues with 12 teams, the 6th place team selects first, proceeding in descending order to the 12th place team, which is in turn followed by the 5th, 4th, 3rd, 2nd, and 1st place teams.

- The price and subsequent salary upon activation of each farm system player drafted is $10.
- See **Article XIII**, page 293, for rules governing farm systems.

NOTE: The order of selection stated above represents a change from early years of Rotisserie baseball, when teams selected in reverse order of the final standings of the preceding season's pennant race. By awarding the first selection to the highest finisher among second-division teams instead of the last-place team, we seek to offer an incentive to teams to keep plugging and a disincentive to finish last (i.e., in the past, a last place finish would be "rewarded" with the first farm system draft pick).

ARTICLE V. POSITION ELIGIBILITY

A player may be assigned to any position at which he appeared in 20 or more games in the preceding season. If a player did not appear in 20 games at a single position, he may be drafted only at the position at which he appeared most frequently. The 20 games/most games measure is used only to determine the position(s) at which a player may be drafted. Once the season is under way (but after Auction Draft Day), a player becomes eligible for assignment to any position at which he has appeared at least once. In American League versions, players selected as DHs may qualify at any position (i.e., they need not have appeared in 20 games as DH the preceding season). In National League versions, players selected for the utility slot may qualify at any position.

NOTE: Two official major league sources for determining player eligibility are the National League's *Green Book* and the American League's *Red Book*. Both list appearances by position under fielding averages. The *Red Book* lists all players who appeared as designated hitters the preceding season. Circulating an eligibility list by position before Auction Draft Day saves a lot of time. Prepare one yourself in March, when the *Green Book* and *Red Book* are published. Or obtain it with membership in the **Rotisserie League Baseball Association**—our list is available at least five months earlier, so you'll be able to spend the winter doing something worthwhile (see page 274 for details). Spend a few minutes before your auction to settle eligibility questions and assign eligibility to rookies. When in doubt, use common sense (instead of knives) to resolve disputes.

ARTICLE VI. FEES

The Rotisserie League has a schedule of fees covering all player personnel moves. No money passes directly from team to team. No bets are made on the outcome of any game. All fees are payable into the prize pool and are subsequently distributed to the top four teams in the final standings. (See **Articles VIII** and **IX**, page 288.)

1. **BASIC:** The cumulative total of salaries paid for acquisition of a 23-man roster on Auction Draft Day may not exceed $260.

2. **TRANSACTIONS:** $10 per trade (no matter how many players are involved) or player activation (from reserve list or farm system). In a trade, the team that pays the fee is subject to negotiation.

3. **CALL-UP FROM FREE AGENT POOL:** $25 for each player called up from the free agent pool.

4. **RESERVE:** $10 for each player placed on a team's reserve list (see **Article XII**, page 291).

5. **FARM SYSTEM:** $10 for each player in a team's farm system (see **Article XIII**, page 293).

6. **ACTIVATION:** $10 for each player activated from the reserve list or farm system.

7. **WAIVERS:** $10 for each player claimed on waivers (see **Article XV**, page 295).

8. **SEPTEMBER ROSTER EXPANSION:** $50 (see **Article XVI**, page 296).

ARTICLE VII. PLAYER SALARIES

The salary of a player is determined by the time and means of his acquisition and does not change unless the player becomes a free agent or is signed to a guaranteed long-term contract. (See **Article XVII**, page 297.)

- The salary of a player acquired in the major league draft is his auction price.
- The salary of a player called up from the free agent pool during the season is $10.
- The salary of a player activated from a team's farm system during the season is $10.
- The salary of a player claimed on waivers is $10.
- The salary of a player called up during September Roster Expansion to supplement the 23-man roster is $25 if he is drawn from the free agent pool. (See **Article XVI**, page 296.)

NOTE: Because you can commit only $260 for salaries on Auction Draft Day, and because you will keep some of your players from one season to the next, salaries are *extremely* important, particularly after the first season ends and winter trading begins. Would you trade Juan Gonzalez for Paul O'Neill? The Rangers wouldn't, not even if Blowhard George threw in Yankee Stadium (which he would be only too happy to do, outfield monuments and all). But a smart Rotisserie League owner just might make such a deal *in the off-season*, because the $20-plus difference between Gonzalez's and O'Neill's auction price is enough to buy a front-line starter.

Maintaining accurate, centralized player-personnel records of salary and contract status is *the most important* task of the League Secretary, who deserves hosannas from the other owners for all the work he does.

NOTE: The $260 salary limit pertains to Auction Draft Day *only*. After Auction Draft Day, free agent signings and acquisition of high-priced players in trades may well drive a team's payroll above $260.

ARTICLE VIII. PRIZE MONEY

All fees shall be promptly collected by the League Treasurer, who is empowered to subject owners to public humiliation and assess fines as needed to ensure that payments are made to the League in a timely fashion. The interest income from this investment can be used to defray the cost of a gala postseason awards ceremony and banquet. The principal shall be divided among the first four teams in the final standings as follows:

- 1st place—50%
- 2nd place—20%
- 3rd place—15%
- 4th place—10%
- 5th place—5%

ARTICLE IX. STANDINGS

The following criteria are used to determine team performance:

- Composite batting average (BA)
- Total home runs (HR)
- Total runs batted in (RBI)
- Total stolen bases (SB)
- Composite earned run average (ERA)
- Total wins (W)
- Total saves (S)
- Composite ratio: walks (BB) + hits (H) ÷ innings pitched (IP)

Teams are ranked from first to last in each of the eight categories and given points for each place. For example, in a 12-team league, the first-place team in a category receives 12 points, the second-place team 11, and so on down to 1 point for last place. The team with the most total points wins the pennant.

THE FENOKEE IP REQUIREMENT. A team must pitch a total of 900 innings to receive points in ERA and ratio. A team that does not pitch 900 innings maintains its place in ERA and ratio ranking but receives zero points in both of these categories. (Thus, a team that finished third in ERA but did not have 900 IP would receive no points in that category. The fourth-place team in ERA would still receive 9 points.) This rule was passed in 1988 in response to an "all-relief" strategy attempted by the Okrent Fenokees in the 1987 season. The strategy was not successful because Swampmaster Dan Okrent abandoned it after six weeks or so. But it might have worked, in more disciplined hands. Hence the new rule.

THE FENOKEE AB REQUIREMENT. A team must have 4250 at bats in the season. A team that does not have 4250 at bats maintains its place in the batting average ranking but receives zero points in that category. This rule was passed in 1991 in response to an "all-pitching" strategy attempted by the Okrent Fenokees in 1990. This time, the Beloved Founder and Former Commissioner-for-Life assembled an all-star pitching staff, Tony Gwynn, and 13 Ken Oberkfells (i.e., guys who didn't play enough to bring down Gwynn's "team" BA). The BFFCL hoped to amass 40 pitching points, 10 BA points, and 3 points in the other offensive categories to squeeze into the first division. The strategy was not successful because the Swampmaster abandoned it after six weeks or so. But it might have worked, in more disciplined hands. Hence the new rule.

- Pitchers' offensive stats are *not* counted, mainly because they don't appear weekly in *USA Today*. Nor are the pitching stats of the occasional position player called in to pitch when the score is 16–1 after five innings and the relief corps is hiding under the stands.
- In cases of ties in an individual category, the tied teams are assigned points by totaling points for the rankings at issue and dividing the total by the number of teams tied.
- In cases of ties in total points, final places in the standings are determined by comparing placement of teams in individual categories. Respective performances are calculated and a point given to each team for bettering the other. Should one team total more points than the other, that team is declared the winner.
- Should the point totals still be equal, the tie is broken by adding each team's *total at-bats* at season's end, plus *triple the number of its innings pitched.* The team that scores a higher total by this measure wins the pennant.

ARTICLE X. STATS

The weekly player-performance summaries published in *USA Today* beginning in late April constitute the official data base for the computation of standings in Rotisserie League Baseball.

NOTE: When we first started out, we used *The Sporting News.* That was when *TSN* cared more about baseball than about all the Stanley

Cup skate-offs, NBA playoffs, and NFL summer camping rolled into one (which, by the way, is what the Rotisserie League's Founding Fathers believe should be done with them). Not for nothing was the Holy Bible known to baseball people as *The Sporting News* of religion. But that was then, and this is now. *The Sporting News* has passed from the last Spink to new owners who seem intent on taking the "Sporting" part seriously—that is, covering other sports at the expense of baseball. A pity.

- The effective date of any transaction for purposes of statistical calculation is the Monday (AL) or Tuesday (NL) *before* the commencement of play on those days. This is because weekly stats appear in *USA Today* on Tuesday for AL games through the preceding Sunday and on Wednesday for NL games through the preceding Monday.
- Reporting deadlines should be established as close to these breaks as possible but not later than the start of any game at the beginning of a new reporting period. Noon on Monday (AL) or Tuesday (NL) makes sense.
- Transactions recorded *on* Auction Draft Day, including trades and call-ups to replace disabled players, are effective retroactive to Opening Day. Transactions occurring *after* Auction Draft Day but *before* the closing date of the first cumulative summaries to appear in *USA Today* in April are effective the Monday (AL) or Tuesday (NL) immediately after the first closing date.
- Performance stats of a player shall be assigned to a Rotisserie League team *only* when he is on the active 23-man roster of that team. It is common for a player to appear on the roster of more than one Rotisserie League team during the season because of trades and waiver-list moves. Even a player who is not traded may spend time on a team's reserve list, during which period any numbers he might compile for his major league team do not count for his Rotisserie League team.
- Standings shall be tabulated and issued in a regular and timely fashion, as determined by the League owners.

NOTE: Keeping score (see pages 271–272) is the only part of Rotisserie League Baseball that isn't any fun. Unless you're computerized, it's tedious and time-consuming. And even if your league does have a computer wonk on board, it still means he or she can't take a vacation between Opening Day and early October. (God forbid your league should go a week without standings!) The best solution: Let the official stat service authorized by the Founding Fathers do all the heavy lifting for you (see page 272).

ARTICLE XI. TRADES

From the completion of the auction draft until August 31, Rotisserie League teams are free to make trades of any kind without limit, except as stipulated below, *so long as the active rosters of both teams involved in a trade reflect the required position distribution upon completion of the transaction.* No trades are permitted from September 1 through the end of the season. Trades made from the day after the season ends until rosters are frozen on April 2 prior to Auction Draft Day are *not* bound by the position distribution requirement.

> **NOTE:** This means that if Team A wants to swap David Justice to Team B for José Rijo anytime between Auction Draft Day and the trade deadline, Team A will have to throw in a bum pitcher and Team B a duff outfielder to make the deal. During the off-season, the two could be dealt even-up.

- Trades do not affect the salaries or contract status of players.
- Each trade is subject to the $10 transaction fee. The fee is not affected by the number of players involved in the trade.
- Unless you want knife fights to break out among owners, prohibit all trades involving cash, "players to be named later," or "future considerations." Trust us.

NOTE ON DUMPING: "Dumping" is the inelegant but scientifically precise term used to describe what happens when a team out of contention gives up on the season and trades to a contending team its most expensive talent and its players who will be lost to free agency at the end of the year, typically for inexpensive players who can be kept the following season. A "dumping" trade is always unbalanced, sometimes egregiously so, with the contending team giving up far less than it gets, and the noncontending team giving up much more in order to acquire a nucleus for the following season. While this strategy makes sense for both clubs, extreme cases can potentially undermine the results of the auction draft, which should always be the primary indicator of an owner's ability to put together a successful team.

To guard against this, we have in the past employed rigid and restrictive Anti-Dumping measures to control trades between contenders and noncontenders. But in light of major shifts in international politics and economics in recent years, we decided in 1993 that these restrictive measures tended to inhibit rather than enhance the playing of the game.

Accordingly, we swept away all Anti-Dumping legislation in 1993. We did so with some trepidation, but we felt the benefits of a free market would outweigh the potential for abuses. We were right. Let freedom ring.

ARTICLE XII. THE RESERVE LIST

A team may replace any player on its 23-man roster who is:

- placed on the **disabled list,**
- **released,**
- **traded** to the other league, or
- **sent down** to the minors by his major league team.

To replace such a player, a Rotisserie League team must first release him outright or place him on its reserve list. A team reserves a player by notifying the League Secretary and paying the $10 transaction fee. A reserved player is removed from a team's active roster at the end of the stat week (on Monday or Tuesday)—when formal notification is given—and placed on the team's reserve list. There is no limit to the number of players a team may have on its reserve list. Reserving a player protects a team's rights to that player.

A team has two weeks to take action once a player is placed on the disabled list, released, traded to the other league, or sent to the minors by his major league team. If no action is taken, the position is frozen open until the original player's return, and no replacement may be made.

- *A suspended player may not be reserved, released, or replaced.*

NOTE: When we first wrote that, we were thinking about the old-fashioned things players might do to get themselves suspended—Bill Madlock hitting an umpire (1980), say, or Gaylord Perry throwing a spitter (1962 to 1983), although he was suspended for doing it only once (1982). Then came the drug suspensions of 1984 and afterward. We have decided to consider players suspended for substance abuse as if they were on the disabled list, and allow teams to replace them.

- Once a specific action has been taken to remove a player from its 23-man roster (via release or placing him on the reserve list), a team is then free to select any eligible player from the free agent pool of players not already owned by another Rotisserie League team. The salary assigned to a player so selected from the free agent pool is $10; the call-up fee is $25 (see **Article VI**, page 287).
- If the same player is claimed by more than one team in a given week, he goes to the team ranking lowest in the most recent standings.
- Every reserve move must be accompanied by a concomitant replacement move (i.e., a team may not reserve a player without replacing him).
- Placing a player *on* the reserve list and activating a player *from* the reserve list are *each* subject to a $10 transaction fee.
- The call-up takes effect as soon as it is recorded by the League Secretary, although the player's stats do not begin to accrue to his new team until Monday (AL) or Tuesday (NL) of the week the League Secretary records the call-up.
- A player on a Rotisserie League reserve list may not be traded *unless* the replacement player linked to him is also traded. Thus, a team might trade Andy Van Slyke (on reserve) and Henry Cotto (called up to replace him) for Derrick May.
- A replacement player may be traded or otherwise replaced (e.g., in case of injury, he could be reserved and a free agent called up to fill his slot). In such a case, the newly acquired player becomes linked to the original reserved player.
- When a player on a reserve list returns to active major league duty, he must be **reinstated** to the active 23-man roster of his Rotisserie League team *two weeks* after his activation or be **waived**. Failure to

notify the League Secretary shall be considered a waiver of the player on the reserve list. A player may not be **reinstated** or **waived** until he has been activated by his major league team.

NOTE: Intended to prevent stockpiling of players, this rule is tricky to monitor. Daily newspaper transaction columns and telephone sports-information lines don't always catch every single major league roster move. The clock starts ticking when the League Secretary *is made aware of* a player being reactivated. By the way, "two weeks" means two full reporting periods and may actually be as much as two weeks plus six days (as in the case of a player being reactivated the day after a reporting deadline). In fairness, and because this is not full-contact karate but a game played among friends, an owner should be given warning by the League Secretary that time is up and he will lose a player if he doesn't make a move. Especially if there are extenuating circumstances (i.e., anything from retracing Livingston's steps in Africa to just plain laziness).

- When a player is reinstated to the active 23-man Rotisserie League roster from a team's reserve list, the player originally called up to replace him must be waived, unless the replacement player *or* the original player can be shifted to another natural opening on the roster for which he qualifies.
- If the replacement player is replaced (e.g., he is injured, put on reserve, and a free agent is called up), then *his* replacement becomes linked to the original player on the reserve list.
- A player reinstated from the reserve list may not displace any active player on the Rotisserie League team's 23-man roster *other than* his original replacement (or his successor).

NOTE: The intent of all this is to minimize the benefit a team might derive from an injury. Say Andres Galarraga is injured (again!) and you call up the inevitable Gerald Perry to replace him. Galarraga comes back. What you'd like to do is activate Galarraga, keep Perry, and waive your other corner man, Frank Bolick, who hasn't had a hit in six weeks. Our rules say you can't, on the premise that *a team is not ordinarily helped by an injury to a key player.* We know the big leagues don't handle it this way, but art doesn't always imitate life. Without some restriction, an owner might never have to pay the price for his bad judgment in drafting Frank Bolick in the first place.

ARTICLE XIII. FARM SYSTEM

If a farm system player is promoted to the active roster of a major league team at any time during the regular season *prior to* September 1 (when major league rosters may expand to 40), his Rotisserie League team has *two weeks* after his promotion to **activate** him (at any position for which he qualifies) or **waive** him.

- The fee for activating a player from a team's farm system is $10.
- If a farm system player is activated, the player displaced from the 23-

man roster to make room for him must be placed on waivers, *unless* the farm system player can be activated into a natural opening, in which case no waiver is required. **Example:** One of your pitchers is placed on a major league disabled list; you reserve him and activate a pitcher from your farm system who has been called up by his major league team.

- Once brought up from its farm system by a Rotisserie League team, a player may not be returned to it, although he may be placed on a team's reserve list in the event he is returned to the minor leagues by his major league club.
- A farm system player not brought up to a team's 23-man roster during the season of his initial selection may be kept within the farm system in subsequent seasons upon payment of an additional $10 per year, so long as he retains official rookie status and the League Secretary is duly notified on April 1 each year, when rosters are frozen. (See also **Article XVIII**, page 298.)
- A team may have no more than three players in its farm system.
- A farm system player may be traded during authorized trading periods, subject to prevailing rules governing transactions, as may a team's selection rights in the minor league draft.

NOTE: This means that a team could acquire and exercise as many as three farm system draft picks, providing that it does not exceed the maximum of three players in its farm system at a given time.

ARTICLE XIV. SIGNING FREE AGENTS

Active major league players not on any Rotisserie League team's roster at the conclusion of the auction draft become free agents. During the course of the season the pool of free agents may also include minor league players not in any Rotisserie League's farm system (see **Article XIII**, page 293) who are promoted to an active major league roster; waived players who are not claimed; and players traded from the "other" major league. Such players may be signed in the following manner.

From Opening Day Until the All-Star Game. Free agents may be called up to replace players placed on a Rotisserie League team's reserve list as outlined in **Article XII** (see page 291). The only exception to **Article XII**'s provisions for signing free agents during this period is that players traded into the league from the "other" major league may be signed by a Rotisserie League team with its **Free Agent Acquisition Budget (FAAB)**, as described below.

After the All-Star Game. From the All-Star Game until the last weekly transaction deadline before September 1, free agents may be signed, without limit in number, but within the limitations of a Rotisserie League team's **Free Agent Acquisition Budget:**

- Each team shall have, for the purpose of acquiring free agents during the course of the season, a supplementary budget of $100.
- At the deadline established by each league for recording weekly transactions, a team may submit a *sealed* bid for one or more free agents.

- The minimum bid shall be $5; the maximum shall be the amount remaining in a team's **FAAB**.
- A free agent so selected goes to the highest bidder. If more than one team bids the same amount on a player, and if that amount is the highest bid, the player goes to the team that is lowest in the most recently compiled standings.
- The salary of a free agent signed in this manner is his acquisition price. His contract status is that of a first-year player.
- In addition to the player's acquisition price, a team signing a free agent must pay the $25 transaction fee for calling up free agents as set forth in **Article VI** (page 287).
- For each free agent that it signs, a team *must* at the same time waive or release a player at the same position from its *active* roster. (See page 0. If on a major league team's *active* roster, such a player is *waived*. If he has been placed on a major league team's disabled list, released, traded to the "other" league, or demoted to the minors, such a player is *released* and may not be acquired by a Rotisserie League team until he is once again on a major league roster.)
- A free agent signed for a salary in excess of $10 (i.e., more than the customary call-up fee for replacement players) is deemed to have a guaranteed two-year contract. If such a player is not protected the following season (i.e., if he is released into the free agent pool at the time rosters are frozen on April 1), then a contract buyout fee in the amount of twice his salary or $100, whichever is greater, shall be paid by the team owning his contract at the time.
- If a Rotisserie League team loses a player to the "other" league in an interleague trade, then the team's available **FAAB** dollars are increased by an amount equal to the lost player's salary.

NOTE: The provision regarding players acquired for a sum in excess of the customary $10 call-up fee is intended to discourage frivolous bidding for free agents. It is also intended to make teams who are most likely to benefit from signing costly free agents—that is, teams still in the race for the first division—pay for it dearly, by making such players expensive to dump the following spring.

NOTE: Set up a simple, common-sense mechanism for handling the "sealed bid" part of the **FAAB** process. Nothing elaborate is needed. Price, Waterhouse need not be called in. Don't permit bidders to make contingency bids (e.g., "If I don't get Ruth at $29, then I'll bid $25 for Gehrig, and if I don't get Gehrig . . .") unless your League Secretary doesn't have a day job.

ARTICLE XV. WAIVERS

Under certain conditions, a Rotisserie League player may be waived.

- When a player on a Rotisserie League team's reserve list is activated by his major league team, either he or the player called up earlier to replace him *must* be placed on waivers (see **Article XII**, page 291).

- When a team activates a player from its farm system, except into a natural opening (see **Article XIII**, page 293), the player dropped from the 23-man roster to make room for him *must* be placed on waivers.
- A player no longer on the active roster of his major league team and whose Rotisserie League position is taken by a player activated from the reserve list or farm system may not be placed on waivers but *must* be released outright.

NOTE: This is to prevent a team from picking up a disabled list player on waivers merely for the purpose of releasing him and replacing him with a player of higher quality from the free agent pool.

- The waiver period begins at noon on the Monday (AL) or Tuesday (NL) after the League Secretary has been notified that a player has been waived and lasts one week, at the end of which time the player shall become the property of the lowest-ranked team to have claimed him. To make room on its roster, the team acquiring a player on waivers must assign the player to a natural opening or waive a player at the same position played by the newly acquired player.
- Waiver claims take precedence over the replacement of an injured, released, or demoted player who has been put on reserve. That is, a player on waivers may be signed by a team with a roster opening at his position only if no other team lower in the standings claims the player on waivers.
- A team may acquire on waivers *no more* than one player in a given week, but there is no limit to the number of players a team may acquire on waivers during the season.
- A player who clears waivers—that is, is not claimed by any team—returns to the free agent pool.
- The fee for acquiring a player on waivers is $10. The salary of a player acquired on waivers shall be $10 or his current salary, whichever is greater. His contract status shall remain the same.
- A player with a guaranteed long-term contract may *not* be waived during the season. He may, however, be released and replaced if he is traded to the "other" league.
- A player may be given his outright release *only* if he is
    (a) unconditionally released,
    (b) placed on the "designated for assignment" list,
    (c) sent to the minors,
    (d) placed on the "disqualified" list,
    (e) traded to the "other" major league, or
    (f) placed on the disabled list.

ARTICLE XVI. SEPTEMBER ROSTER EXPANSION

If it chooses, a team may expand its roster for the pennant drive by calling up additional players after September 1 from the free agent pool, its own reserve list, or its own farm system. A team may call up as many players as it wishes, subject to payment of appropriate fees as outlined below, except that at no time may the number of active players on its roster exceed 40.

- The order of selection for September Roster Expansion is determined by the most recent standings, with the last-place team having first selection, and so on. During this 24-hour period, September Roster Expansion claims take precedence over waiver claims and routine call-ups to replace players who are disabled, released, or traded to the other league by their major league teams. This selection order pertains until midnight, September 2, *only,* after which time a team forfeits its order in the selection process, though *not* its right to make a selection. Selection after midnight, September 2, is on a first-come, first-served basis. Also, after midnight, September 2, waiver claims and routine call-ups to fill natural openings take precedence over September Roster Expansion claims.
- The performance stats of players called up during September Roster Expansion start to accrue on the Monday (AL) or Tuesday (NL) after the League Secretary has been notified of the player's selection.
- The fee for expanding the roster in September is $50.
- The salary assigned to a September call-up from the free agent pool is $25. The salary of a September call-up from a team's reserve list or farm system is the salary established at the time he was previously acquired (on Auction Draft Day, or subsequently from the free agent pool, or via waivers).

NOTE: A device for heightening the excitement for contending teams and for sweetening the kitty at their expense, September Roster Expansion will generally not appeal to second-division clubs (who should, however, continue to watch the waiver wire in the hope of acquiring "keepers" for next season at a $10 salary).

ARTICLE XVII. THE OPTION YEAR AND GUARANTEED LONG-TERM CONTRACTS

A player who has been under contract at the same salary during two consecutive seasons and whose service has been uninterrupted (that is, he has not been waived or released, although he may have been traded) must, prior to the freezing of rosters in his third season, be released; signed at the same salary for his option year; or signed to a guaranteed long-term contract.

If **released**, the player returns to the free agent pool and becomes available to the highest bidder at the next auction draft. If signed at the same salary for an **option year**, the player must be released back into the free agent pool at the end of that season. If signed to a **guaranteed long-term contract**, the player's salary in each year covered by the new contract (which commences with the option year) shall be the sum of his current salary plus $5 for each additional year beyond the option year. In addition, a signing bonus, equal to one half the total value of the long-term contract, but not less than $5, shall also be paid.

NOTE: This rule is intended to prevent blue-chippers, low-priced rookies who blossom into superstars, and undervalued players from being

---

tied up for the duration of their careers by the teams who originally drafted them. It guarantees periodic transfusions of top-flight talent for Auction Draft Day and provides rebuilding teams something to rebuild with. And it makes for some interesting decisions at roster-freeze time two years down the pike.

Here's how it works. Let's say you drafted Neon Deion Sanders of the Atlanta Braves for $2 in 1993, a fair price then for a football player with a strikeout swing, a questionable attitude, and too much jewelry. It's now the spring of 1995 and Sanders, whose maturity has caught up with his raw talent, has become a power threat and a team player. You could let Sanders play one more season for you and get a tremendous return on your two bucks, but that would be almost as foolish as Sanders risking his knees in the NFL. Taking a longer view, you daydream about Sanders's power and speed numbers, assess your needs, project what's likely to be available in the upcoming draft, cross your fingers against football injury—and sign him to a three-year guaranteed contract. Sanders's salary zooms to $12 ($2 + $5 + $5), but he's yours through the 1996 season. His signing bonus, which does not count against your $260 Auction Draft Day limit, is $18 (one half of 3 × $12). If he continues to mature as a ballplayer, you've got a bargain.

- In determining a player's status, "season" is understood to be a full season or any fraction thereof. Thus, a player called up from the free agent pool in the middle of the 1992 season and subsequently retained at the same salary without being released in 1993 (even though he may have been traded) enters his option year in 1994 and must be released, signed at the same salary for an option year, or signed to a long-term contract.
- A team may sign a player to only one long-term contract, at the end of which he becomes a free agent.
- Option-year and long-term contracts are entirely transferable, both in rights and obligations; the trade of a player in no way affects his contract status.
- If, during the course of a long-term contract, a player is traded from the National League to the American League (or vice versa), the contract is rendered null and void. The team that loses the player's services shall be under no further financial obligations.
- In all other cases—specifically *including* sudden loss of effectiveness— a team must honor the terms of a long-term contract, as follows: A player with such a contract *may* be released back into the free agent pool (that is, not protected on a team's roster prior to Auction Draft Day), but a team that chooses to do so must pay into the prize pool, above the $260 Auction Draft Day limit, a sum equal to *twice* the remaining value of the player's contract or $100, whichever is greater.

NOTE: This is an escape hatch for the owner who buys a dog but can't stand fleas. It's costly, but it's fair.

ARTICLE XVIII. ROSTER PROTECTION

For the first three seasons of the League's existence, each team must retain, from one season to the next, *no fewer than* **7** but *no more than* **15** of the players on its 23-man roster. After three seasons, this minimum requirement is eliminated, the maximum retained. The minimum is removed because, after three seasons, a team might find it impossible to retain a specific minimum because too many players have played out their option.

- The names of players being retained must be recorded with the League Secretary by midnight, April 1. Specific notice must also be made at that time of any guaranteed long-term contract signings and farm system renewals.
- The cumulative salaries of players protected prior to Auction Draft Day are deducted from a team's $260 expenditure limit, and the balance is available for acquisition of the remaining players needed to complete the team's 23-man roster.
- The League Secretary should promptly notify all teams in the League of each team's protected roster, including player salaries, contract status, and amount available to spend on Auction Draft Day.
- Failure to give notice of a guaranteed long-term contract for a player in his option year will result in his being continued for one season at his prior year's salary and then released into the free agent pool. Failure to renew a farm system player's minor league contract will result in his becoming available to all other teams in the subsequent minor league draft.
- A farm system player whose minor league contract is renewed on April 1 and who subsequently makes his major league team's active roster may, at his Rotisserie League owner's option, be added to the protected list of players on Auction Draft Day (and another player dropped, if necessary, to meet the 15-player limit), or he may be dropped and made available in the auction draft. He may not be retained in his Rotisserie League team's farm system.

NOTE: The April 1 roster-protection deadline was originally set to correspond with the end of the major leagues' spring interleague trading period, a rite of spring that no longer exists. We've stuck to April 1 anyway, because it gives us a week or so to fine-tune draft strategies. Until you know who the other teams are going to keep, you won't know for sure who's going to be available. And until you know how much they will have to spend on Auction Draft Day, you won't be able to complete your own pre-draft budget. So April 1 it is; don't fool with it.

ARTICLE XIX. GOVERNANCE

The Rotisserie League is governed by a Committee of the Whole consisting of all team owners. The Committee of the Whole may designate as many League officials as from time to time it deems appropriate, although only two—the League Secretary and the League Treasurer—ever do any work. The Committee of the Whole also designates annually an Executive Committee composed of three team owners in good standing. The Executive Committee has the authority to interpret playing rules and to handle all necessary and routine League business. All decisions, rulings, and interpretations by the Executive Committee are subject to veto by the Committee of the Whole. Rule changes, pronouncements, and acts of whimsy are determined by majority vote of the Committee of the Whole. Member leagues of the **Rotisserie League Baseball Association** (see page 274) may appeal to the RLBA for adjudication of disputes and interpretation of rules. The Rotisserie League has three official meetings each year: Auction Draft Day (the first weekend after Opening Day), the Midsummer Trade Meeting (at the All-Star break), and the Gala Postseason Banquet and Awards Ceremony. Failure to attend at least two official meetings is punishable by trade to the San Diego Padres.

ARTICLE XX. YOO-HOO

To consecrate the bond of friendship that unites all Rotisserie League owners in their pursuit of the pennant, to symbolize the eternal verities and values of the Greatest Game for Baseball Fans Since Baseball, and to soak the head of the League champion with a sticky brown substance before colleagues and friends duly assembled, the **Yoo-Hoo Ceremony** is hereby ordained as the culminating event of the baseball season. Each year, at the awards ceremony and banquet, the owner of the championship team shall have a bottle of Yoo-Hoo poured over his or her head by the preceding year's pennant winner. The Yoo-Hoo Ceremony shall be performed with the dignity and solemnity appropriate to the occasion.

> **NOTE:** If Yoo-Hoo, the chocolate-flavored beverage once endorsed by soft-drink connoisseur Yogi Berra, is not available in your part of the country, you have two options: (a) send up an alternative beverage, one chosen in the Yoo-Hoo spirit, as a pinch-hitter, or (b) move.

STILL CONFUSED?

Call Roti·Stats, the best Rotisserie stats service in the business, for clarifications, explanations, salutations, a current weather report, and a hard sell.

800-884-7684

ROTISSERIE ULTRA
The Rules of Play

Turn Up the Volume

Rotisserie Ultra requires more scouting, more planning, more wheeling, and more dealing. You move players off and onto your active roster as often as you want to. You ride guys on hot streaks, then ditch them when they go cold. You buy free agents. You bring along youngsters all the way from the low minors. You swing complicated, multiplayer deals. You build a strong bench with waiver moves to carry you through injuries and slumps.

Does playing Rotisserie Ultra mean giving up all pretense of having a normal life? No, you should keep up that pretense as long as you can. It does mean that you're not going to have a lot of time for scuba diving the Great Barrier Reef, reading Proust, learning to play the saxophone, paneling the rec room, or having a catch with your kid this summer. You're going to be busy, Bucky—or you're going to be in the second division.

Remember that the Sturgeon General himself—Peter Gethers, owner of Peter's Famous Smoked Fish—has warned that playing Rotisserie Ultra *before you're ready* can lead to "sensory overload, stress-related insomnia, pattern baldness, hot flashes, and premature ejaculation."

We recommend that fledgling leagues play the regular version of the game, become acclimated to its demands and pressures, and shake out owners who can't stand the heat of a pennant race before moving on to Ultra. Stay within yourselves, walk before you run, take it one game at a time, and floss regularly. Only then should you consider Ultra. After all, we can't have everybody in America having too much fun all at once.

Editor's Note: *Many of the rules in the Official Constitution of Rotisserie League Baseball also apply to Rotisserie Ultra, so we decided not to repeat every line of fine print that applies to both, except as needed for clarity. That means that the "Rules of Play" that follow for Rotisserie Ultra should be read together with the original Constitution. If you can't handle that assignment, you're going to have* real *trouble with Rotisserie Ultra.*

ULTRA I. THE ROTATION DRAFT

After the conclusion of the auction draft, in which teams acquire their 23-man active rosters for a sum not to exceed $260, owners successively draft up to 17 additional players in 17 separate rounds of selection. Initially, players acquired in this fashion comprise a team's reserve roster.

 • Any baseball player is eligible for this draft. *Exception:* In National

League versions, no player on the roster or in the minor league organization of an American League team may be selected; and, in American League versions, the opposite is true. Eligible players include (in the NL version, by way of example) previously undrafted NL players, NL-owned minor leaguers, unsigned players, Japanese players, high-school or college players, and the kid down the block with the great arm.

- In the rotation draft, owners are not required to select players by position. They may select all pitchers, all position players, or a mix.
- The order of selection for each of the 17 rounds is determined by the order of finish in the previous season. In leagues with 12 teams, the 6th place team selects first, proceeding in descending order to the 12th place team, followed by the 5th, 4th, 3rd, 2nd, and 1st place teams.

NOTE: For leagues switching over from Rotisserie League rules to Rotisserie League Ultra rules, the first two rounds of the rotation draft follow the order of the former farm system draft. Only players who have rookie status and are not on a major league 25-man roster or disabled list may be selected in these two rounds. This protects the property rights of teams that may have acquired additional farm system draft picks or improved their draft position via trades prior to the shift to Rotisserie League Ultra.

ULTRA II. THE RESERVE ROSTER

A team's reserve roster consists of those players acquired through the rotation draft, through trades, through demotions from the active roster, or through waiver claims. Any transaction (e.g., trade, demotion, waiver claim) that increases the size of the reserve roster beyond 17 players must be accompanied by a concomitant transaction (e.g., trade, promotion, waiver) that simultaneously returns the reserve roster to its maximum 17.

ULTRA III. FEES

1. **Basic:** The cumulative total of salaries paid for acquisition of a 23-man active roster on Auction Draft Day may not exceed $260.

2. **Reserve Roster:** There are no fees payable for the acquisition of players for the 17-man reserve roster.

3. **Transactions:** $10 per trade (no matter how many players are involved), $10 per player activation or demotion.

4. **Waivers:** $10 for each player claimed on waivers.

5. **September Roster Expansion:** $50 for each player added to a team's active roster after September 1.

ULTRA IV. PLAYER SALARIES

The salary of a player is determined by the time and means of his acquisition and does not change unless the player becomes a free agent by means of release or is signed to a guaranteed long-term contract.

THE TENTH PITCHER OPTION

As everybody in the baseball world knows, a Rotisserie team is composed of 9 pitchers and 14 position players (see **Article III,** page 284). Except, of course, when it's not.

A couple of years back we experimented with a slight variation on the traditional roster configuration and permitted a team to carry 10 pitchers and 13 position players.

Most major league teams carry 10 pitchers and 15 position players. But some (e.g., the Detroit Tigers in April and May in recent years) carry only 9 pitchers, while others (e.g., the Oakland A's) carry 11. It comes down to a GM's assessment of the team's needs, its personnel, and the schedule.

If this flexibility is good for the American and National leagues, why not for the third major league—the Rotisserie League? So a couple of years back we decided to let teams fill the utility slot with a position player *or* a pitcher. The result? An unqualified success.

The Tenth Pitcher Option allows a GM to realize the full potential of Ultra. Let's say you have the usual 9 pitchers and 14 position players on your active roster, and your team starts slipping in wins. Presto! You send down the outfielder hitting .227 in your utility slot and promote a good middle innings guy from your reserve roster. In AL leagues, you must still have a DH, two catchers, and three middle infielders, so the 10th pitcher must come at the expense of a corner or an outfielder.

The Tenth Pitcher Option provides more action, sweetens the pot through additional transaction fees, and is simple to administer and monitor. You can change the mix back and forth as frequently as you wish, provided only that the total number of active players does not exceed 23, and that at no time do you have more than 14 active position players or more than 10 active pitchers.

After hearing from leagues around the country regarding their experience with the Tenth Pitcher Option, we decided to leave it as just that—an option. Some leagues, particularly those using AL players, found it awkward to implement because of the DH. Others thought it was okay for Ultra but not regular Rotisserie. Still others simply didn't like it. Many made the transition smoothly.

Hey, that's why we call it an *Option.*

- The salary of a player acquired in the auction draft is his auction price.
- The salary of a player acquired in the rotation draft is determined as follows: If the player was selected in the first round, $15; rounds 2–6, $10; rounds 7–12, $5; rounds 13–17, $2.
- The salary of a player claimed on waivers is $10 or his previous salary, whichever is greater. His contract status remains the same.

ULTRA V. TRADES

From the completion of the rotation draft until noon on the Monday (AL) or Tuesday (NL) on or following August 31, teams are free to make trades of any kind without limit (except as indicated in **Ultra VI**, below). However, at no time can any team have on its active roster more players at a particular position than allowed under the rules of the auction draft (see **Article III**, page 0 of the Official Constitution of Rotisserie League Baseball). A team may, however, be underrepresented at a position. So long as these strictures are adhered to in the immediate wake of a trade, teams may trade any number of players, at any position, irrespective of the number or position of players being received in such trade (except, again, as indicated below in **Ultra VI**).

- At no point may a team have more than 17 players on its reserve roster or more than 40 players on its active and reserve rosters combined.
- At no point may a team have more than 23 players on its active roster, except during the September Roster Expansion period (see **Ultra X**, page 306).
- No trades of any kind may be made between September 1 and October 15, nor between April 2 (Roster Freeze Day) and the conclusion of the rotation draft on Auction Draft Day.

ULTRA VI. ANTI-DUMPING

Players in the last year of a guaranteed contract or playing out their option year and players with a salary of $25 or more are considered "asterisk" players. Such players may be traded only under the following conditions:

- One team may trade asterisk players to another team provided that for each asterisk player traded, one is received in the same deal.
- The above notwithstanding, a team may trade *one* asterisk player to another team without an asterisk player coming in return or receive *one* asterisk player without giving one up, but may make only *one* such unbalanced trade in the course of the season.
- Between October 15 and Roster Freeze Day, asterisk players on winter rosters may be traded without restrictions whatsoever.

ULTRA VI-A. ANTI-DUMPING REPEALED

Effective Opening Day, 1993, Article **Ultra VI** (above) was repealed. The text of **Ultra VI** is left in place so that newcomers to **Ultra** will know just what is being done away with.

ULTRA VII. MOVEMENT BETWEEN ACTIVE ROSTER
AND RESERVE ROSTER

An owner may demote a player from the active roster to the reserve roster, or promote a player in the reverse direction, at any time and for any reason, such promotions to take effect with the subsequent stat deadline (Monday noon for AL leagues, Tuesday noon for NL leagues). However, no player may be demoted without being replaced on the active roster by an eligible player—that is, a player who fulfills position eligibility requirements (which may include shifting another active player into the demoted player's position and the promoted player into the shifted player's position) *and* who is currently on a major league roster and not on a major league disabled list.

- **Exception:** If the acquisition of an active player in a trade places the acquiring team's active roster above the positional limit (e.g., more than two catchers), a player at that position may be sent down without the need for the recall of another player.
- A player acquired by trade from another team's active roster is considered active with the acquiring team on the effective date of the trade, unless the acquiring team chooses (or is compelled by roster restrictions) to demote him. Similarly, a player acquired in a trade from another team's reserve roster is considered to be reserved with the acquiring team, unless the acquiring team promotes him.

ULTRA VIII. SIGNING FREE AGENTS

Active major league players not on any Rotisserie League team's active roster or reserve roster at the conclusion of the auction draft become free agents. During the course of the season the pool of free agents may also include minor league players not on any Rotisserie League team's reserve roster who are promoted to an active major league roster; players traded from the "other" major league; and waived players who are not claimed. Beginning one week after the first standings report, and continuing through the season until the last weekly transaction deadline before September 1, such free agents may be signed, without limit, in the following manner:

- Each team shall have, for the purpose of acquiring free agents during the course of the season, a supplementary budget of $100, known as its **Free Agent Acquisition Budget (FAAB).**
- At the deadline established by each Rotisserie League for recording weekly transactions, a Rotisserie League team may submit a *sealed* bid for one or more free agents.
- The minimum bid shall be $5; the maximum shall be the amount remaining in a team's **FAAB.**
- A free agent so selected goes to the highest bidder. If more than one team bids the same amount on a player, and if that amount is the highest bid, the player goes to the team that is lowest in the most recently compiled standings.
- The salary of a free agent signed in this manner is his acquisition price. His contract status is that of a first-year player.
- For each free agent that it signs, a team *must* at the same time waive or release a player from its *active* roster.
- If a free agent signed for a salary of $25 or more is not protected on the subsequent April 1 Roster Freeze, then the owner of his contract at the time must pay into the prize pool a buyout fee of twice his salary or $100, whichever is greater.

NOTE: The reason for the pre–September 1 deadline is to prevent a Rotisserie League team from completely restocking with $5 players when the major leagues expand their rosters to 40 in September.

NOTE: The mechanics of the "sealed bid" process will vary from league to league. Where practicable, as in leagues that have weekly meetings, the sealed bid should be just that—a bid sealed in an envelope that is opened at the meeting. In other cases, it may be more efficient to recruit a disinterested party to record all bids and report them to the League Secretary for action. Whatever mechanism you devise, keep matters in perspective. These aren't the secrets to nuclear fusion, for Einstein's sake! So try to balance the gee of security with the haw of mutual trust.

ULTRA IX. WAIVERS

Players are placed on waivers (a) when they cannot be accommodated on a team's active or reserve roster, because of space and/or positional limitations; and (b) under the rules governing the winter roster (see **Ultra XI**, page 307).

- The waiver period commences at noon on the Monday (AL) or Tuesday (NL) immediately following the team's notification of waiver to the League Secretary and extends for one full reporting period (i.e., one week). At the conclusion of that week, if the player is unclaimed, he goes into the free agent pool, and may be acquired by a team only as outlined in **Ultra VIII**, above.
- Waiver claims are honored according to the inverse order of the standings effective the week before the close of the waiver period.
- A team may reclaim a player it has waived only if all other teams in the league decline to claim him.
- The fee for acquiring a player on waivers is $10. The salary of a player acquired on waivers shall be $10 or his current salary, whichever is greater; and his contract status shall remain the same.
- Only a player currently on a 25-man major league roster (i.e., not on a disabled list) may be claimed on waivers.
- A player traded to the "other" league may not be placed on waivers.
- A player on a guaranteed long-term contract may not be placed on waivers, even in the final year of his contract.

ULTRA X. SEPTEMBER ROSTER EXPANSION

If it chooses, a team may expand its roster for the pennant drive by promoting from its reserve roster an *unlimited* number of players, as the post–September 1 active-roster size expands to a maximum of 40 players. Such players may play any position.

- September expansions can be effective no earlier than noon on the Monday (AL) or Tuesday (NL) immediately following August 31.

Expansions made later in September become effective the subsequent Monday or Tuesday at noon.

- A fee of $50 must be paid for every promotion that increases the active-roster size beyond 23. Player salaries are not affected by such promotions.

ULTRA XI. WINTER ROSTER

Effective October 15, each owner is required to submit to the League Secretary a list of 23 players, irrespective of position, taken from its combined active and reserve rosters, but one not including any players who have concluded their option year or the last year of a guaranteed long-term contract. This group of players becomes the winter roster.

- Immediately after the submission of winter rosters, a waiver period concluding at noon, November 1, begins. By inverse order of the final standings in the season just ended, teams may select no more than one player from that group of players not protected on a winter roster, again with the exception of players who have concluded their option year or the final year of a guaranteed long-term contract. On claiming such a player, the claiming team must, in turn, waive a player from its own winter roster. Players thus waived become eligible for a second round of waiver claims, for a period of one week, that are conducted in the same fashion. (Unclaimed players from the first waiver period are no longer eligible.) The process continues until there is a week in which no one is claimed.
- All winter-waiver claims cost the claiming team $10, to be paid into the league treasury for the coming season.
- The salary of a player claimed on winter waivers is $10 (or his current salary, whichever is greater), and he shall be deemed to be commencing the first year of a new contract with the coming season.
- After October 23, winter rosters may exceed or fall below 23 players through trading action. Whatever size the roster, however, any successful claim of a player on waivers must be accompanied by the placing of another player from the claiming team on waivers.

ULTRA XII. ROSTER PROTECTION

Roster protection in Rotisserie League and Rotisserie League Ultra is identical (see **Article XVIII**, page 298), except as follows:

- The cumulative salaries of frozen players are deducted from a team's $260 expenditure limit in the auction draft, and the balance is available for the acquisition of the remainder of a team's active roster. However, salaries of players frozen on April 1 who are not on 25-man major league rosters on Auction Draft Day do not count against the $260 limit.
- Frozen players not on 25-man major league rosters count against the limit of 17 players on draft day reserve rosters, and the salaries they carry must be paid into the league treasury on draft day.

- In addition to the 15 players that a team may protect from its winter roster of active and reserve roster players, a team may also protect an additional 3 players on its reserve roster, provided that such players have rookie status and have never been active on a Rotisserie League team.
- Players frozen may include players who have spent the entire previous season on a reserve roster—typically because they played only in the minor leagues. Even so, such players who are subsequently frozen are deemed to be in the *second* year of their contract with their Rotisserie League Ultra team.
- Assignment of frozen players to a reserve roster position is at the owner's discretion. That is, an owner with a $10 minor leaguer carried over from the preceding year might, for strategic reasons, assign that player to the 17th position in the rotation draft, thus forgoing a $2 pick. Or the owner might assign the player to the first round and forgo a $15 pick. The assignment of frozen players by all teams will be made before the rotation draft commences.

NOTE: Some Ultra Leagues believe that the clock on minor leaguers should not start ticking until they are promoted to the majors, as in Rotisserie Regular. We feel this would tie up too many players and eventually undermine the auction draft. Effective in 1991, we increased the number of $2 and $5 players in the rotation draft (see **Ultra IV**, page 00). That should facilitate building a farm system and encourage protection of key players without providing the blanket protection of freezing the clock. This is called a compromise.

Let There Be Lite!

Great ideas often have implausibly pedestrian beginnings.

Isaac Newton was sitting under an apple tree, thinking he would like something sweet but tart and loaded with vitamin A, when the principle of gravity fell in his lap. A man who loved martinis a bit too well, Eli Whitney got his big inspiration when his wife yelled from the kitchen, "Keep your cotton-picking hands off that gin!" And because somebody else was picking up the tab, Daniel Okrent, down from his rustic estate in western Massachusetts to join Manhattan friends for lunch, found himself eating snails and making history over a decade ago in the then-fashionable East Side bistro La Rôtisserie Française, instead of wolfing down a grease-on-white-with-mayo at his favorite New York restaurant—and thus the world was deprived of Blimpie League Baseball.

Maybe there's something in the water up there in the Berkshire Mountains, or maybe there's just nothing else to do, but a few years back yet another bucolic Edison stumbled out of the backwoods with a new widget. Fortunately, BFFCL Okrent recognized his nearby neighbor's creation as an inspired variation on a great theme, an ingenious mechanism for filling an important sociocultural need, a cleverly constructed design with possible commercial potential.

So we stole it.

That's how we are able to bring you the newest version of The Greatest Game for Baseball Fans Since Youknowwhat, Rotisserie Lite! But before we do, common courtesy requires us to say a few words about the country bumpk . . . ah, *squire* who we city-slickered into giving away his invention for a handful of T-shirts and the promise to spell his name right.

Tony Lake (that's L-A-K-E) is a man for all seasons, though he definitely prefers summer. A hardscrabble farmer then biding his time between crops as a circuit-riding professor of international politics at several pricey New England colleges, Farmer-Professor Lake is currently President Clinton's National Security Adviser and the highest-ranking Rotisserian in the world. He is a terminal Boston Red Sox fan who started playing Rotisserie League Baseball almost a decade ago, when BFFCL Okrent sold him a copy of the rules for 40 acres and a mule. Farmer-Professor Lake says the idea for Rotisserie Lite came to him one day near the end of the 1989 season when he was sitting on his tractor thinking about the Middle East situation.

"Late that season I suddenly found myself going sane," the tiller-scholar recalls. "I caught myself reading boxscores to find out who won, not just to see how my players had done. Some days I even read the front page first. Clearly, I was in trouble."

The academic-agrarian attacked the problem by identifying what he liked best and least about Rotisserie Ultra play in the League of Nations, where his team—the Smuts Peddlers—had always been a strong contender. "I like boxscores, and I like listening to games on the radio," he says. "I don't like the lure of trading, because it appeals to extreme type-A personalities like Okrent. I was spending too much time thinking about trades instead of about foreign policy or that funny sound my tractor was making."

While unwilling to go cold turkey (he still plays in the League of Nations), Farmer-Professor Lake did go looking for a halfway house. He found it when he founded the Washington Slo-Pitch League, a six-team outfit whose owners hail mostly from the nation's capital. (The mayor of the founder's hometown was awarded a one-third ownership in a franchise as a hedge against local tax increases. So far it's worked.)

"I see the game we play in Slo-Pitch as a halfway house in either direction," Farmer-Professor Lake says. "If you've never played Rotisserie before, it's a great way to learn what it's all about. And if you've been playing it too hard or too long, it helps you recapture the whimsy, and whimsy is the whole point of Rotisserie in the first place."

Thanks, Tony. We needed that.

WHO WILL PLAY ROTISSERIE LITE?

- Current owners of Rotisserie Regular and Rotisserie Ultra franchises who want to learn about the "other" league (i.e., AL or NL) without giving up sleep altogether . . .
- Parent-Kid partnerships (with Kids bringing Parents along slowly until they're ready for the next threshold of Rotisseplay).
- Diagnosed sufferers from Rotisserie Burnout (plus anyone in the high-risk group) . . .
- Casual baseball fans who want to find out what this Rotisserie business is all about . . .*
- Hundreds of millions of citizens of former Iron Curtain countries who are only now discovering baseball and have the mistaken belief that "Rotisserie" is a method for cooking meat in France.

*WARNING: The Sturgeon General of Peter's Famous Smoked Fish, Peter "Sudden Pete" Gethers, has determined that Rotisserie *anything* can be injurious to your mental health.

ROTISSERIE LITE
The Rules of Play

Same Auction Draft!	**No Farm System!**
Same Stat Categories!	**No Reserve List!**
Same Yoo-Hoo!	**No Money!**

Editor's Note: *The following rules were lifted from the unwritten constitution of the Washington Slo-Pitch League, with several embellishments and alterations of our own to give them a bogus air of originality. Please note that we were too lazy to repeat all the pertinent rules of Rotisserie Regular that also apply in Rotisserie Lite. That means you'll have to go back and read the* **Official Constitution of Rotisserie League Baseball** *(pages 283–300) to figure out what we're talking about.*

LITE I. FEWER TEAMS

A Rotisserie Lite League using National League or American League players is composed of six teams.

- With only six teams, Rotisserie Lite Leagues have shorter (and probably more orderly) auction drafts, fewer friendships to wreck, and less trouble squeezing into a telephone booth.

LITE II. ONE DIVISION ONLY

A Rotisserie Lite League uses players from only *one* NL or AL division.

- Resist the temptation to draw players from an entire league or—worse still—to mix the two leagues. "Lite" doesn't mean "soft." By restricting the talent pool to players of one division, Lite owners will need to scout as diligently as do Rotisserie Regular and Rotisserie Ultra owners. You'll have to learn which middle innings relievers can be counted on for the greatest number of quality innings, which non-regular corner men will get the most at-bats, and which fourth outfielders will deliver 40 or more RBI. In other words, you'll have to become a better, more knowledgeable fan. And isn't that the Rotisserie Way?
- Using players from only one division helps an owner new to the world of Rotisserie to draw on his or her strength. After all, we all start out as fans of a particular team, which means that we enter the Rotisserie

world knowing and liking one team—and one division—better than others. What better place to start?

LITE III. NO MONEY

Each team has 23 Lite Dollars (L$) to spend at the auction draft to acquire a full roster of 23 active major league players, with a minimum salary and minimum bidding increments of 10 cents. But real money is not used.

- "The intensity of feeling in Rotisserie is unrelated to money anyhow," sez Farmer-Professor Lake. "If you play for traditional Rotissestakes—260 real dollars for 23 real players—it's enough to be irritating if you lose, but not enough to buy a new car if you win. So what's the point?"
- Using L$ still requires an owner to manage the team budget and cope with the exigencies of free market competition for the services of Barry Bonds, Cecil Fielder, and other superstars at the auction draft. Farmer-Professor Lake promises that your throat goes dry and your heart palpitates when the bidding hits L$2.70 for Jack McDowell, the same as when it crosses $30 for baseball's number-one Rock 'n' Roller in Regular and Ultra. This means that a kid owner can have just as much Rotissefun as a parent owner without having to beg for an advance against the next six months of allowances.
- Playing for L$ also makes a team owner feel a little less hysterical when the *Baseball America* and *Baseball Weekly* subs come due.

LITE IV. MONTHLY TRANSACTIONS

Transaction Day occurs once a month, on the Monday (AL) or Tuesday (NL) before stats appear in *USA Today*. The first Transaction Day falls on the first Monday or Tuesday in May. Except for the All-Star Break Trading Period described below, all Rotisserie Lite roster moves are restricted to Transaction Day.

- On Transaction Day, a Rotisserie Lite team may release players (a) placed on a major league disabled list; (b) demoted to the minor leagues; (c) traded to the other division or to the other major league; or (d) released by their major league team, *without limit* from its current roster and replace them with players from the free agent pool who qualify at the same position. Players may not be reserved. Even players on major league disabled lists must be released if their Rotisserie Lite owner chooses to replace them. Released players go into the free agent pool and may be claimed on the *next* Transaction Day.
- Player moves on Transaction Day shall take place in reverse order of the most recent standings, with the lowest team in the standings having the right of first claim on a player from the free agent pool. While there is no limit on the number of players a team may release and replace, a team may make only one transaction at a time. That is, the last-place team in a six-team league may not make a second

transaction until all other teams in the league have had an opportunity to make a transaction.

- As there is no reserve list in Rotisserie Lite, an owner whose star player is on his major league team's disabled list and isn't scheduled to come off for another two weeks will have to make a strategic call: Ride out the injury and retain the player under contract; or release him into the free agent pool and call up a replacement immediately.
- The salary of a player claimed from the free agent pool on Transaction Day is L$1.

LITE V. TRADE RESTRICTIONS

Except for a two-week trading period ending with the last out of the All-Star Game, no trades are permitted in Rotisserie Lite.

- All trades during the trading period take effect on the first pitch of the first regular season game after the All-Star Game.
- A Rotisserie Lite team may trade only one player with a salary of L$2 or more to any one team.

LITE VI. SAME SCORING CATEGORIES

Standings shall be determined on the same basis as in Rotisserie Regular and Rotisserie Ultra—that is, according to each team's cumulative performance over the course of a full season in eight statistical categories: home runs, RBI, stolen bases, and batting average for batters; wins, saves, ERA, and ratio (hits plus walks divided by innings pitched) for pitchers.

- A team receives points in each category according to its relative position. In a six-team league, the leader in home runs would receive six points, the second-place team five points, and so on. The team with the highest point total wins the Rotisserie Lite pennant.
- Standings should be compiled and distributed weekly. As keeping score is no more fun in Lite than in Regular or Ultra, new Lite leagues should consider the special deal offered by **Roti·Stats**. As transactions only take place monthly, **Roti·Stats** is able to provide timely, accurate weekly stat reports for Rotisserie Lite Leagues at a deep discount from its regular low rates. (See pages 272–273 for details.)

LITE VII. LONG-TERM CONTRACTS

The same rules governing the option year and long-term contracts that complicate an owner's life in Rotisserie Regular and Rotisserie Ultra shall also pertain in Rotisserie Lite. (See **Article XVII** of the Official Constitution, page 00.)

- **Exception:** A player under a long-term contract in Rotisserie Lite may be released and replaced at any time without penalty, subject only to the restrictions regarding player transactions.

LITE VIII. ROSTER PROTECTION

On April 1, each team may protect a certain number of players according to the following schedule: The team that finished first the preceding year may protect a maximum of seven players; all other teams, a maximum of ten players. There is no minimum requirement.

- Yes, this makes it a lot harder to build a dynasty. But trust us: One Harry Stein loose on the land is more than enough.
- Trading is not permitted over the winter on the grounds that Rotisserie Lite owners have better things to do with their time. Particularly those who also play Rotisserie Regular or Rotisserie Ultra.

LITE IX. YOO-HOO

As there is no prize pool to divvy up in Rotisserie Lite, the Yoo-Hoo running down a Rotisserie Lite pennant winner's face and trickling into the corners of his or her mouth will taste all the sweeter, if you can imagine such a thing.

Editor's Postscript: *As you play Rotisserie Lite, let us know what you think. It takes a long time to turn a piece of coal into a diamond, and it may take us a couple of seasons to get Lite exactly rite. We particularly want to hear from you about new wrinkles, adaptations, and changes that we might scarf up for next year's book. Just remember:* Keep it Lite!

8

Postgame Shower

A Yoo-Hoo to Arms

Editor's Note: *We ended our first book ten years ago with the following dispatch from Maestro Steve Wulf of the Wulfgang. We ended all our other books the same way. It's how we're ending this book. And it's the way we'll end our next book. That's because tradition is everything in Rotisserie League Baseball . . . unless you have to throw it into a deal for a stud power hitter.*

Unseen hands hold you, force your head down, and pour water, dairy whey, corn sweetener, nonfat milk, sugar, coconut oil, cocoa, sodium caseinate, salt, sodium bicarbonate, dipotassium phosphates, calcium phosphates, guar gum, natural flavors, xanthan gum, vanillin (an artificial flavor), sodium ascorbate, ferric orthophosphate, palmitate, niacinamide, vitamin D, and, yes, *riboflavin* all over your hair. The bizarre ritual is a Yoo-Hoo shampoo, and it is what you get for winning the Rotisserie League pennant.

The chocolate-flavored rinse will not leave your locks radiant and soft to the touch, and squirrels will probably follow you around for a day or two. All in all, the ritual is pretty distasteful. But there's not a member of the Rotisserie League who wouldn't gladly suffer the rite so long as it came at the end of a championship season.

Since we traditionally end each Rotisseseason with an outpouring of the chocolate drink of our youth, we figured we may as well end the book the same way. Besides, as the beverage company's former executive vice president for promotions, Lawrence Peter Berra, once noted, or at least we think he noted, "Yoo-Hoo tastes good. And it's good for you, too."

Yoo-Hoo does taste good if your taste buds also happen to be impressed with the nose on strawberry fizzies. To sophisticated palates, Yoo-Hoo tastes a little like the runoff in the gutter outside a Carvel store.

As for Yoo-Hoo being good for you, well, Yogi says he let his kids drink it, and one of them grew up to be the .255-hitting shortstop for the Pittsburgh Pirates. But then, maybe if Dale *hadn't* touched the stuff, he might actually be worth more than the $7 the Fleder Mice paid for him in 1983.

Yoo-Hoo is not unlike the Rotisserie League. Both of them taste good, and both of them are good for you. Just don't tell anybody that. Whenever one of us tries to explain just what the Rotisserie League is, we all get the same kind of look. It's the look one might get from a bartender if one ordered, say, a Kahlua and Yoo-Hoo. The look says, "Aren't you a little too old to be partaking of that stuff?" Our look invariably replies, "But it tastes good, and it's good for you."

Yoo-Hoo's current slogan is "Yoo-Hoo's Got Life." Catchy, isn't it? But then, Yogi Berra used to be a catchy. The Rotisserie League's got life, too. It enlivens not only boxscores, but "Kiner's Korner," as well. Why, the game adds color to every fiber of your being, it gives you a sense of purpose in this crazy, cockeyed world, it puts a spring in your step and a song in your heart, and it makes you care, deeply care, for your fellow man, especially if your fellow man's name is Biff Pocoroba. So the Rotisserie League is childish, is it? Yoo-Hoo and a bottle of rum, barkeep.

In case you're wondering where Yoo-Hoo comes from, we thought we'd tell you. It comes from Carlstadt, N.J. Yoo-Hoo also goes back to the days of Ruth and Gehrig. It first arrived on the American scene as a fruit drink named after a popular greeting of that day. Founder Natale Olivieri was obsessed with making a stable chocolate drink, and after years of experimentation, he hit upon the idea of heating the chocolate. The rest is soft-drink history.

In the '50s, Yoo-Hoo's Golden Age, the product came to be associated with Yogi. A billboard of Yogi and a bottle of Yoo-Hoo greeted fans in Yankee Stadium. And Yogi wasn't the only Yankee who endorsed Yoo-Hoo— Whitey, Mickey, and the Moose could all be seen on the insides of Yoo-Hoo bottle caps. Nowadays, nobody inhabits the inside of the bottle cap. However, if you turn the cap upside down, it reads, "ooh-ooy," which is Yiddish for Rod Scurry's ERA.

Yoo-Hoo is also like baseball: You don't want to know too much about it. In the interests of this chapter, we sent an envoy out to Yankee Stadium to talk to Yogi. Yes, you've read all those funny Berra quotes over the years, about how it's not over until it's over, and about how nobody goes to that restaurant anymore because it's too crowded. To tell you the truth, Yogi is not the man that people suppose him to be. He is actually two different people, depending on his mood. When he is on guard, he is full of monosyllables, and when he is relaxed, he can be genuinely engaging. But the star of "The Hathaways"* he is not.

We—actually, it was only one of us, who shall remain nameless, and if the *New Yorker* can do it, why can't we—asked Yogi if he would mind talking about Yoo-Hoo. He said, "Sorry, I can't." This caught us by surprise, but being quick on our tongue, we asked, "You can't?" Yogi said, "Nope. Ask Cerone."

At which point, we approached Rick Cerone, the catcher who took Yogi's place as executive vice president for promotions. For all their sterling qualities, Berra and Cerone do not strike us as being pillars of the corporate structure, but Yoo-Hoo obviously saw through to their executive talents. We asked Cerone if he would mind talking about Yoo-Hoo. He said, "I can't." This time, we asked, "Why?" and Cerone said, "Because I'm suing them, that's why."

*Does anybody remember who "The Hathaways" were? We've forgotten.

As it turns out, the company has changed hands, and Cerone claims that Yoo-Hoo never paid him for certain appearances. Yogi ran into similar problems, but he settled out of court. So that's why Yoo-Hoo is just like baseball: if you look too closely, it can get ugly on you.

We went back to Yogi and pleaded with him. All we cared about, we said, were the old days of Yoo-Hoo. He warmed to the subject in much the same way Natale Olivieri warmed Yoo-Hoo—slowly. Through his grunts and moans, we determined that Yogi thought Yoo-Hoo tasted good, that his kids drank it, that he wishes he had some money invested in it, and that people still link him with Yoo-Hoo, and vice versa. Then he said, "What's this for, anyway?"

We explained to him about the Rotisserie League and the book. When we said, "Then, at the end of the year, we pour Yoo-Hoo over the head of the winner," Yogi—dripping tobacco juice out of the left side of his mouth—gave us a look of partial disgust and said something like "ooh-ooy."

So, if you decide to take up baseball as played by the Rotisserie League, be warned. People will look at you funny. Pay them no mind. Just pay the Treasurer.

We hate long good-byes. When we meet again, perhaps at a theater near you showing *The Rotisserie League Goes to Japan,* let's just say, "Yoo-Hoo."

APPENDIX

Final 1994 Averages

Editor's Note: *These stats have been selected and arranged to reflect the variety of stat categories used in different Rotisserie leagues. Traditional Rotisserie stat category order can be found in Chapter 2, Scouting Report.*

NATIONAL LEAGUE: BATTERS

NL Batter	Team	BA	HR	RBI	SB	CS	G	AB	R	BB	OBP
Abbott, K.	Fla	.249	9	33	3	0	101	345	41	16	.291
Alicea, L.	StL	.278	5	29	4	5	88	205	32	30	.373
Alou, M.	Mon	.339	22	78	7	6	107	422	81	42	.397
Arias, A.	Fla	.239	0	15	0	1	59	113	4	9	.298
Ashley, B.	LA	.333	0	0	0	0	2	6	0	0	.333
Ausmus, B.	SD	.251	7	24	5	1	101	327	45	30	.314
Bagwell, J.	Hou	.368	39	116	15	4	110	400	104	65	.451
Barberie, B.	Fla	.301	5	31	2	0	107	372	40	23	.356
Bass, K.	Hou	.310	6	35	2	3	82	203	37	28	.393
Batiste, K.	Phi	.234	1	13	1	1	64	209	17	1	.239
Bean, B.	SD	.215	0	14	0	1	84	135	7	7	.248
Bell, D.	SD	.311	14	54	24	8	108	434	54	29	.354
Bell, J.	Pit	.276	9	45	2	0	110	424	68	49	.353
Bell, J.	Mon	.278	2	10	4	0	38	97	12	15	.372
Belliard, R.	Atl	.242	0	9	0	2	46	120	9	2	.264
Benavides, F.	Mon	.188	0	6	0	0	47	85	8	3	.222
Benjamin, M.	SF	.258	1	9	5	0	38	62	9	5	.343
Benzinger, T.	SF	.265	9	31	2	1	107	328	32	17	.304
Berry, S.	Mon	.278	11	41	14	0	103	320	43	32	.347
Bichette, D.	Col	.304	27	95	21	8	116	484	74	19	.334
Biggio, C.	Hou	.318	6	56	39	4	114	437	88	62	.411
Blauser, J.	Atl	.258	6	45	1	3	96	380	56	38	.329
Bogar, T.	NYN	.154	2	5	1	0	50	52	5	4	.211
Bonds, B.	SF	.312	37	81	29	9	112	391	89	74	.426
Bonilla, B.	NYN	.290	20	67	1	3	108	403	60	55	.374
Boone, B.	Cin	.320	12	68	3	4	108	381	59	24	.368
Bournigal, R.	LA	.224	0	11	0	0	40	116	2	9	.291
Branson, J.	Cin	.284	6	16	0	0	58	109	18	5	.316
Bream, S.	Hou	.344	0	7	0	1	46	61	7	9	.429
Brogna, R.	NYN	.351	7	20	1	0	39	131	16	6	.380
Brown, J.	Atl	.133	1	1	0	0	17	15	3	0	.133
Browne, J.	Fla	.295	3	30	3	0	101	329	42	52	.392
Brumfield, J.	Cin	.311	4	11	6	3	68	122	36	15	.381
Buechele, S.	ChN	.242	14	52	1	0	104	339	33	39	.325
Burks, E.	Col	.322	13	24	3	1	42	149	33	16	.388
Burnitz, J.	NYN	.238	3	15	1	1	45	143	26	23	.347
Butler, B.	LA	.314	8	33	27	8	111	417	79	68	.411
Caminiti, K.	Hou	.283	18	75	4	3	111	406	63	43	.352
Cangelosi, J.	NYN	.252	0	4	5	1	62	111	14	19	.371
Carr, C.	Fla	.263	2	30	32	8	106	433	61	22	.305
Carreon, M.	SF	.270	3	20	0	0	51	100	8	7	.324
Carrillo, M.	Fla	.250	0	9	3	3	80	136	13	9	.295
Castilla, V.	Col	.331	3	18	2	1	52	130	16	7	.357
Cedeno, A.	Hou	.263	9	49	1	1	98	342	38	29	.334
Chamberlain, W.	Phi	.275	2	6	0	0	24	69	7	3	.306
Cianfrocco, A.	SD	.219	4	13	2	0	59	146	9	3	.252
Clark, D.	Pit	.296	10	46	2	2	86	223	37	22	.355
Clark, P.	SD	.215	5	20	1	2	61	149	14	5	.250

NL Batter	Team	BA	HR	RBI	SB	CS	G	AB	R	BB	OBP
Clayton, R.	SF	.236	3	30	23	3	108	385	38	30	.295
Colbrunn, G.	Fla	.303	6	31	1	1	47	155	17	9	.345
Conine, J.	Fla	.319	18	82	1	2	115	451	60	40	.373
Coolbaugh, S.	StL	.190	2	6	0	0	15	21	4	1	.217
Cordero, W.	Mon	.294	15	63	16	3	110	415	65	41	.363
Cromer, T.	StL	.000	0	0	0	0	2	0	1	0	.000
Cummings, M.	Pit	.244	1	12	0	0	24	86	11	4	.283
Daulton, D.	Phi	.300	15	56	4	1	69	257	43	33	.380
DeShields, D.	LA	.250	2	33	27	7	89	320	51	54	.357
Destrade, O.	Fla	.208	5	15	1	0	39	130	12	19	.316
Diaz, M.	Fla	.325	0	11	0	0	32	77	10	6	.376
Donnels, C.	Hou	.267	3	5	1	0	54	86	12	13	.364
Dorsett, B.	Cin	.245	5	26	0	0	76	216	21	21	.313
Duncan, M.	Phi	.268	8	48	10	2	88	347	49	17	.306
Dunston, S.	ChN	.278	11	35	3	8	88	331	38	16	.313
Dykstra, L.	Phi	.273	5	24	15	4	84	315	68	68	.404
Eisenreich, J.	Phi	.300	4	43	6	2	104	290	42	33	.371
Eusebio, T.	Hou	.296	5	30	0	1	55	159	18	8	.320
Everett, C.	Fla	.216	2	6	4	0	16	51	7	3	.259
Faneyte, R.	SF	.115	0	4	0	0	19	26	1	3	.207
Felder, M.	Hou	.239	0	13	3	0	58	117	10	4	.264
Fernandez, T.	Cin	.279	8	50	12	7	104	366	50	44	.361
Finley, S.	Hou	.276	11	33	13	7	94	373	64	28	.329
Fletcher, D.	Mon	.260	10	57	0	0	94	285	28	25	.314
Floyd, C.	Mon	.281	4	41	10	3	100	334	43	24	.332
Foley, T.	Pit	.236	3	15	0	0	59	123	13	13	.307
Frazier, L.	Mon	.271	0	14	20	4	76	140	25	18	.358
Galarraga, A.	Col	.319	31	85	8	3	103	417	77	19	.356
Gallagher, D.	Atl	.224	2	14	0	2	89	152	27	22	.326
Garcia, C.	Pit	.277	6	28	18	9	98	412	49	16	.309
Gardner, J.	Mon	.219	0	1	0	0	18	32	4	3	.286
Gilkey, B.	StL	.253	6	45	15	8	105	380	52	39	.336
Girardi, J.	Col	.276	4	34	3	3	93	330	47	21	.321
Goff, J.	Pit	.080	0	1	0	0	8	25	0	0	.080
Gonzalez, L.	Hou	.273	8	67	15	13	112	392	57	49	.353
Grace, M.	ChN	.298	6	44	0	1	106	403	55	48	.370
Greene, W.	Cin	.216	0	3	0	0	16	37	5	6	.318
Grissom, M.	Mon	.288	11	45	36	6	110	475	96	41	.344
Gutierrez, R.	SD	.240	1	28	2	6	90	275	27	32	.321
Gwynn, C.	LA	.268	3	13	0	2	58	71	9	7	.333
Gwynn, T.	SD	.394	12	64	5	0	110	419	79	48	.454
Haney, T.	ChN	.162	1	2	2	1	17	37	6	3	.238
Hansen, D.	LA	.341	0	5	0	0	40	44	3	5	.408
Hare, S.	NYN	.225	0	2	0	0	22	40	7	4	.295
Harris, L.	Cin	.310	0	14	7	2	66	100	13	5	.340
Hatcher, B.	Phi	.246	2	13	4	1	43	134	15	6	.271
Hayes, C.	Col	.288	10	50	3	6	113	423	46	36	.348
Hernandez, C.	LA	.219	2	6	0	0	32	64	6	1	.231
Hernandez, J.	ChN	.242	1	9	2	2	56	132	18	8	.291
Hill, G.	ChN	.297	10	38	19	6	89	269	48	29	.365
Holbert, R.	SD	.200	0	0	0	0	5	5	1	0	.200
Hollins, D.	Phi	.222	4	26	1	0	44	162	28	23	.328
Howard, T.	Cin	.264	5	24	4	2	83	178	24	10	.302

NL Batter	Team	BA	HR	RBI	SB	CS	G	AB	R	BB	OBP
Hubbard, T.	Col	.280	1	3	0	0	18	25	3	3	.357
Hundley, T.	NYN	.237	16	42	2	1	91	291	45	25	.303
Hunter, B.	Cin	.304	4	10	0	0	9	23	6	2	.346
Hunter, B.	Pit	.227	11	47	0	0	76	233	28	15	.270
Hunter, B.	Hou	.250	0	0	2	1	6	24	2	1	.280
Hyers, T.	SD	.254	0	7	3	0	52	118	13	9	.307
Incaviglia, P.	Phi	.230	13	32	1	0	80	244	28	16	.278
Ingram, G.	LA	.282	3	8	0	0	26	78	10	7	.341
Jefferies, G.	StL	.325	12	55	12	5	103	397	52	45	.391
Johnson, B.	SD	.247	3	16	0	0	36	93	7	5	.283
Johnson, C.	Fla	.455	1	4	0	0	4	11	5	1	.462
Johnson, E.	SF	.154	0	0	0	0	5	13	0	0	.154
Johnson, H.	Col	.211	10	40	11	3	93	227	30	39	.323
Jones, C.	Col	.300	0	2	0	1	21	40	6	2	.333
Jordan, B.	StL	.258	5	15	4	3	53	178	14	16	.320
Jordan, R.	Phi	.282	8	37	0	0	72	220	29	6	.303
Justice, D.	Atl	.313	19	59	2	4	104	352	61	69	.427
Karros, E.	LA	.266	14	46	2	0	111	406	51	29	.310
Kelly, M.	Atl	.273	2	9	0	1	30	77	14	2	.300
Kelly, R.	Atl	.286	6	24	10	3	63	255	44	24	.345
Kelly, R.	Cin	.302	3	21	9	8	47	179	29	11	.351
Kent, J.	NYN	.292	14	68	1	4	107	415	53	23	.341
King, J.	Pit	.263	5	42	3	2	94	339	36	30	.316
Kingery, M.	Col	.349	4	41	5	7	105	301	56	30	.402
Klesko, R.	Atl	.278	17	47	1	0	92	245	42	26	.344
Kruk, J.	Phi	.302	5	38	4	1	75	255	35	42	.395
Lankford, R.	StL	.267	19	57	11	10	109	416	89	58	.359
Lansing, M.	Mon	.266	5	35	12	8	106	394	44	30	.328
Larkin, B.	Cin	.279	9	52	26	2	110	427	78	64	.369
Lemke, M.	Atl	.294	3	31	0	3	104	350	40	38	.363
Leonard, M.	SF	.364	0	2	0	0	14	11	2	3	.500
Lewis, D.	SF	.257	4	29	30	13	114	451	70	53	.340
Lieberthal, M.	Phi	.266	1	5	0	0	24	79	6	3	.301
Lindeman, J.	NYN	.270	7	20	0	0	52	137	18	6	.303
Liriano, N.	Col	.255	3	31	0	2	87	255	39	42	.357
Livingstone, S.	SD	.272	2	10	2	2	57	180	11	6	.294
Lockhart, K.	SD	.209	2	6	1	0	27	43	4	4	.286
Longmire, T.	Phi	.237	0	17	2	1	69	139	10	10	.289
Lopez, J.	Atl	.245	13	35	0	2	80	277	27	17	.299
Lopez, L.	SD	.277	2	20	3	2	77	235	29	15	.325
Mabry, J.	StL	.304	0	3	0	0	6	23	2	2	.360
Magadan, D.	Fla	.275	1	17	0	0	74	211	30	39	.386
Maksudian, M.	ChN	.269	0	4	0	1	26	26	6	10	.472
Manwaring, K.	SF	.250	1	29	1	1	97	316	30	25	.308
Marsh, T.	Phi	.278	0	3	0	0	8	18	3	1	.316
Martin, A.	Pit	.286	9	33	15	6	82	276	48	34	.367
Martinez, D.	SF	.247	4	27	3	4	97	235	23	21	.314
May, D.	ChN	.284	8	51	3	2	100	345	43	30	.340
McClendon, L.	Pit	.239	4	12	0	1	51	92	9	4	.278
McDavid, R.	SD	.250	0	2	1	0	9	28	2	1	.276
McGee, W.	SF	.282	5	23	3	0	45	156	19	15	.337
McGriff, F.	Atl	.318	34	94	7	3	113	424	81	50	.389
McGriff, T.	StL	.219	0	13	0	0	42	114	10	13	.308

NL Batter	Team	BA	HR	RBI	SB	CS	G	AB	R	BB	OBP
McKnight, J.	NYN	.148	0	2	0	0	31	27	1	4	.250
McReynolds, K.	NYN	.256	4	21	2	0	51	180	23	20	.328
Mejia, R.	Col	.241	4	14	3	1	38	116	11	15	.326
Merced, O.	Pit	.272	9	51	4	1	108	386	48	42	.343
Miller, O.	Hou	.325	2	9	1	0	16	40	3	2	.386
Milligan, R.	Mon	.232	2	12	0	0	47	82	10	14	.337
Mitchell, K.	Cin	.326	30	77	2	0	95	310	57	59	.429
Mondesi, R.	LA	.306	16	56	11	8	112	434	63	16	.333
Morandini, M.	Phi	.292	2	26	10	5	87	274	40	34	.378
Mordecai, M.	Atl	.250	1	3	0	0	4	4	1	1	.400
Morman, R.	Fla	.212	1	2	0	0	13	33	2	2	.278
Morris, H.	Cin	.335	10	78	6	2	112	436	60	34	.385
Mouton, J.	Hou	.245	2	16	24	5	99	310	43	27	.315
Natal, B.	Fla	.276	0	2	1	0	10	29	2	5	.382
Nieves, M.	SD	.263	1	4	0	0	10	19	2	3	.364
Noboa, J.	Pit	.000	0	0	0	0	2	2	0	0	.000
O'Brien, C.	Atl	.243	8	28	0	0	51	152	24	15	.322
O'Halloran, G.	Fla	.182	0	1	0	0	12	11	1	0	.167
Offerman, J.	LA	.210	1	25	2	1	72	243	27	38	314
Oliva, J.	Atl	.288	6	11	0	1	19	59	9	7	.364
Oliver, J.	Cin	.211	1	5	0	0	6	19	1	2	.286
Oquendo, J.	StL	.264	0	9	1	1	55	129	13	21	.364
Orsulak, J.	NYN	.260	8	42	4	2	96	292	39	16	.299
Owens, J.	Col	.250	0	1	0	0	6	12	4	3	.400
Pagnozzi, T.	StL	.272	7	40	0	0	70	243	21	21	.327
Pappas, E.	StL	.091	0	5	0	0	15	44	8	10	.259
Parent, M.	ChN	.263	3	16	0	1	44	99	8	13	.348
Parker, R.	NYN	.063	0	0	0	0	8	16	1	0	.063
Parrish, L.	Pit	.270	3	16	1	1	40	126	10	18	.363
Patterson, J.	SF	.237	3	32	13	3	85	240	36	16	.315
Pecota, B.	Atl	.214	2	16	1	0	64	112	11	16	.310
Pegues, S.	Cin	.300	0	0	0	0	11	10	1	1	.364
Pegues, S.	Pit	.385	0	2	1	0	7	26	1	1	.407
Pena, G.	StL	.254	11	34	9	1	83	213	33	24	.344
Pendleton, T.	Atl	.252	7	30	2	0	77	309	25	12	.280
Pennyfeather, W.	Pit	.000	0	0	0	0	4	3	0	0	.000
Perry, G.	StL	.325	3	18	1	1	60	77	12	15	.435
Petagine, R.	Hou	.000	0	0	0	0	8	7	0	1	.000
Phillips, J.	SF	.132	1	3	1	0	15	38	1	1	.150
Piazza, M.	LA	.319	24	92	1	3	107	405	64	33	.370
Plantier, P.	SD	.220	18	41	3	1	96	341	44	36	.302
Pratt, T.	Phi	.196	2	9	0	1	28	102	10	12	.281
Prince, T.	LA	.333	0	1	0	0	3	6	2	1	.429
Pye, E.	LA	.100	0	0	0	0	7	10	2	1	.182
Quinlan, T.	Phi	.200	1	3	0	0	24	35	6	3	.263
Ready, R.	Phi	.381	1	3	0	1	17	42	5	8	.480
Reed, J.	SF	.175	1	7	0	0	50	103	11	11	.254
Renteria, R.	Fla	.224	2	4	0	1	28	49	5	1	.269
Rhodes, K.	ChN	.234	8	19	6	4	95	269	39	33	.318
Rivera, L.	NYN	.279	3	5	0	1	32	43	11	4	.367
Roberson, K.	ChN	.218	4	9	0	0	44	55	8	2	.271

NL Batter	Team	BA	HR	RBI	SB	CS	G	AB	R	BB	OBP
Roberts, B.	SD	.320	2	31	21	7	105	403	52	39	.383
Rodriguez, H.	LA	.268	8	49	0	1	104	306	33	17	.307
Royer, S.	StL	.175	1	2	0	0	39	57	3	0	.175
Sanchez, R.	ChN	.285	0	24	2	5	96	291	26	20	.345
Sandberg, R.	ChN	.238	5	24	2	3	57	223	36	23	.312
Sanders, D.	Atl	.288	4	21	19	7	46	191	32	16	.343
Sanders, D.	Cin	.277	0	7	19	9	46	184	26	16	.342
Sanders, R.	Cin	.262	17	62	21	9	107	400	66	41	.332
Santiago, B.	Fla	.273	11	41	1	2	101	337	35	25	.322
Scarsone, S.	SF	.272	2	13	0	2	52	103	21	10	.330
Segui, D.	NYN	.241	10	43	0	0	92	336	46	33	.308
Servais, S.	Hou	.195	9	41	0	0	78	251	27	10	.235
Sheaffer, D.	Col	.218	1	12	0	2	44	110	11	10	.283
Sheffield, G.	Fla	.276	27	78	12	6	87	322	61	51	.380
Shipley, C.	SD	.333	4	30	6	6	81	240	32	9	.362
Simms, M.	Hou	.083	0	0	1	0	6	12	1	0	.083
Slaught, D.	Pit	.287	2	21	0	0	76	240	21	34	.381
Smith, O.	StL	.262	3	30	6	3	98	381	51	38	.326
Snyder, C.	LA	.235	6	18	1	0	73	153	18	14	.300
Sosa, S.	ChN	.300	25	70	22	13	105	426	59	25	.339
Spehr, T.	Mon	.250	0	5	2	0	52	36	8	4	.325
Stankiewicz, A.	Hou	.259	1	5	1	1	37	54	10	12	.403
Staton, D.	SD	.182	4	6	0	0	29	66	6	10	.289
Stinnett, K.	NYN	.253	2	14	2	0	47	150	20	11	.323
Stocker, K.	Phi	.273	2	28	2	2	82	271	38	44	.383
Strawberry, D.	SF	.239	4	17	0	3	29	92	13	19	.363
Tarasco, T.	Atl	.273	5	19	5	0	87	132	16	9	.313
Taubensee, E.	Cin	.294	8	21	2	0	61	177	29	15	.345
Taubensee, E.	Hou	.100	0	0	0	0	5	10	0	0	.100
Tavarez, J.	Fla	.179	0	4	1	1	17	39	4	1	.200
Thompson, M.	Hou	.286	1	3	2	0	9	21	5	1	.318
Thompson, M.	Phi	.273	3	30	7	2	87	220	29	23	.348
Thompson, R.	SF	.209	2	7	3	1	35	129	13	15	.290
Thompson, R.	NYN	.225	18	59	1	1	98	334	39	28	.301
Tingley, R.	Fla	.173	1	2	0	0	19	52	4	5	.246
Treadway, J.	LA	.299	0	5	1	1	52	67	14	5	.351
Van Burkleo, T.	Col	.000	0	0	0	0	2	5	0	0	.000
Van Slyke, A.	Pit	.246	6	30	7	0	105	374	41	52	.340
VanderWal, J.	Col	.245	5	15	2	1	91	110	12	16	.339
Varsho, G.	Pit	.256	0	5	0	1	67	82	15	4	.307
Vina, F.	NYN	.250	0	6	3	1	79	124	20	12	.372
Vizcaino, J.	NYN	.256	3	33	1	11	103	410	47	33	.310
Walker, L.	Mon	.322	19	86	15	5	103	395	76	47	.394
Wallach, T.	LA	.280	23	78	0	2	113	414	68	46	.356
Walton, J.	Cin	.309	1	9	1	3	46	68	10	4	.347
Webster, L.	Mon	.273	5	23	0	0	57	143	13	16	.370
Webster, M.	LA	.274	4	12	1	2	82	84	16	8	.344
Wehner, J.	Pit	.250	0	3	0	0	2	4	1	0	.250
Weiss, W.	Col	.251	1	32	12	7	110	423	58	56	.336
White, R.	Mon	.278	2	13	1	1	40	97	16	9	.358
Whiten, M.	StL	.293	14	53	10	5	92	334	57	37	.364
Whitmore, D.	Fla	.227	0	0	0	1	9	22	1	3	.320
Wilkins, R.	ChN	.227	7	39	4	3	100	313	44	40	.317
Williams, E.	SD	.331	11	42	0	1	49	175	32	15	.392

NL Batter	Team	BA	HR	RBI	SB	CS	G	AB	R	BB	OBP
Williams, M.	SF	.267	43	96	1	0	112	445	74	33	.319
Wilson, W.	ChN	.238	0	0	1	0	17	21	4	1	.273
Womack, T.	Pit	.333	0	1	0	0	5	12	4	2	.429
Young, E.	Col	.272	7	30	18	7	90	228	37	38	.378
Young, G.	StL	.317	0	3	2	1	16	41	5	3	.364
Young, K.	Pit	.205	1	11	0	2	59	122	15	8	.258
Zambrano, E.	ChN	.259	6	18	2	1	67	116	17	16	.353
Zeile, T.	StL	.267	19	75	1	3	113	415	62	52	.348

NATIONAL LEAGUE: PITCHERS

NL Pitcher	Team	W	L	SV	ERA	Ratio	GS	IP	H	BB	K
Andersen, L.	Phi	1	2	0	4.41	1.469	0	32.2	33	15	27
Aquino, L.	Fla	2	1	0	3.73	1.263	1	50.2	39	22	22
Arocha, R.	StL	4	4	11	4.01	1.434	7	83.0	94	21	62
Ashby, A.	SD	6	11	0	3.40	1.162	24	164.1	145	43	121
Astacio, P.	LA	6	8	0	4.29	1.295	23	149.0	142	47	108
Avery, S.	Atl	8	3	0	4.04	1.226	24	151.2	127	55	122
Ballard, J.	Pit	1	1	2	6.66	1.767	0	24.1	32	10	11
Banks, W.	ChN	8	12	0	5.40	1.424	23	138.1	139	56	91
Barnes, B.	LA	0	0	0	7.20	2.800	0	5.0	10	4	5
Bautista, J.	ChN	4	5	1	3.89	1.370	0	69.1	75	17	45
Beck, R.	SF	2	4	28	2.77	1.274	0	48.2	49	13	39
Bedrosian, S.	Atl	0	2	0	3.33	1.326	0	46.0	41	18	43
Benes, A.	SD	6	14	0	3.86	1.201	25	172.1	155	51	189
Bielecki, M.	Atl	2	0	0	4.00	1.519	1	27.0	28	12	18
Black, B.	SF	4	2	0	4.47	1.270	10	54.1	50	16	28
Blair, W.	Col	0	5	3	5.79	1.815	1	77.2	98	39	68
Borland, T.	Phi	1	0	1	2.36	1.427	0	34.1	31	14	26
Boskie, S.	ChN	0	0	0	0.00	0.818	0	3.2	3	0	2
Boskie, S.	Phi	4	6	0	5.23	1.387	14	84.1	85	29	59
Bottalico, R.	Phi	0	0	0	0.00	1.333	0	3.0	3	1	3
Bottenfield, K.	SF	0	0	0	10.80	3.000	0	1.2	5	0	0
Bottenfield, K.	Col	3	1	1	5.84	1.622	1	24.2	28	10	15
Boucher, D.	Mon	0	1	0	6.75	1.661	2	18.2	24	7	17
Bowen, R.	Fla	1	5	0	4.94	1.500	8	47.1	50	19	32
Brantley, J.	Cin	6	6	15	2.48	1.133	0	65.1	46	28	63
Brink, B.	SF	0	0	0	1.08	0.960	0	8.1	4	4	3
Brocail, D.	SD	0	0	0	5.82	1.647	0	17.0	21	5	11
Browning, T.	Cin	3	1	0	4.20	1.180	7	40.2	34	13	22
Buckels, G.	StL	0	1	0	2.25	1.250	0	12.0	8	7	9
Bullinger, J.	ChN	6	2	2	3.60	1.220	10	100.0	87	34	72
Burba, D.	SF	3	6	0	4.38	1.486	0	74.0	59	45	84
Burkett, J.	SF	6	8	0	3.62	1.374	25	159.1	176	36	85
Campbell, M.	SD	1	1	0	12.96	2.160	2	8.1	13	5	10
Candiotti, T.	LA	7	7	0	4.12	1.359	22	153.0	149	54	102
Carrasco, H.	Cin	5	6	6	2.24	1.314	0	56.1	42	30	41
Carter, A.	Phi	0	2	0	4.46	1.515	0	34.1	34	12	18
Castillo, F.	ChN	2	1	0	4.30	1.304	4	23.0	25	5	19
Castillo, J.	NYN	0	0	0	6.94	1.886	2	11.2	17	5	1
Cimorelli, F.	StL	0	0	1	8.77	2.400	0	13.1	20	10	1
Cooke, S.	Pit	4	11	0	5.02	1.548	23	134.1	157	46	74
Cormier, R.	StL	3	2	0	5.45	1.261	7	39.2	40	7	26

NL Pitcher	Team	W	L	SV	ERA	Ratio	GS	IP	H	BB	K
Crim, C.	ChN	5	4	2	4.48	1.461	1	64.1	69	24	43
Czajkowski, J.	Col	0	0	0	4.15	2.077	0	8.2	9	6	2
Daal, O.	LA	0	0	0	3.29	1.244	0	13.2	12	5	9
Davis, M.	SD	0	1	0	8.82	2.020	0	16.1	20	13	15
DeLucia, R.	Cin	0	0	0	4.22	1.313	0	10.2	9	5	15
Dewey, M.	Pit	2	1	1	3.68	1.617	0	51.1	61	19	30
Dixon, S.	StL	0	0	0	23.14	4.714	0	2.1	3	8	1
Drabek, D.	Hou	12	6	0	2.84	1.087	23	164.2	132	45	121
Drahman, B.	Fla	0	0	0	6.23	1.615	0	13.0	15	6	7
Dreifort, D.	LA	0	5	6	6.21	2.207	0	29.0	45	15	22
Dyer, M.	Pit	1	1	4	5.87	1.957	0	15.1	15	12	13
Edens, T.	Hou	4	1	1	4.50	1.480	0	50.0	55	17	38
Edens, T.	Phi	1	0	0	2.25	1.250	0	4.0	4	1	1
Eischen, J.	Mon	0	0	0	54.00	7.500	0	0.2	4	0	1
Elliott, D.	SD	0	1	0	3.27	1.606	1	33.0	31	21	24
Eversgerd, B.	StL	2	3	0	4.52	1.433	1	67.2	75	20	47
Fassero, J.	Mon	8	6	0	2.99	1.154	21	138.2	119	40	119
Florie, B.	SD	0	0	0	0.96	1.179	0	9.1	8	3	8
Fortugno, T.	Cin	1	0	0	4.20	1.633	0	30.0	32	14	29
Foster, K.	ChN	3	4	0	2.89	1.309	13	81.0	70	35	75
Franco, J.	NYN	1	4	30	2.70	1.340	0	50.0	47	19	42
Frascatore, J.	StL	0	1	0	16.20	2.700	1	3.1	7	2	2
Fraser, W.	Fla	2	0	0	5.84	2.108	0	12.1	20	6	7
Freeman, M.	Col	10	2	0	2.80	1.251	18	112.2	113	23	67
Frey, S.	SF	1	0	0	4.94	1.742	0	31.0	37	15	20
Gardner, M.	Fla	4	4	0	4.87	1.386	14	92.1	97	30	57
Glavine, T.	Atl	13	9	0	3.97	1.476	25	165.1	173	70	140
Gomez, P.	SF	0	1	0	3.78	1.290	0	33.1	23	20	14
Gooden, D.	NYN	3	4	0	6.31	1.500	7	41.1	46	15	40
Gott, J.	LA	5	3	2	5.94	1.899	0	36.1	46	20	29
Gozzo, M.	NYN	3	5	0	4.83	1.667	8	69.0	86	28	33
Greene, T.	Phi	2	0	0	4.54	1.654	7	35.2	37	22	28
Gross, K.	LA	9	7	1	3.60	1.316	23	157.1	162	43	124
Gunderson, E.	NYN	0	0	0	0.00	1.000	0	9.0	5	4	4
Guzman, J.	ChN	2	2	0	9.15	1.831	4	19.2	22	13	11
Habyan, J.	StL	1	0	1	3.23	1.479	0	47.1	50	20	46
Hamilton, J.	SD	9	6	0	2.98	1.224	16	108.2	98	29	61
Hammond, C.	Fla	4	4	0	3.07	1.405	13	73.1	79	23	40
Hampton, M.	Hou	2	1	0	3.70	1.548	0	41.1	46	16	24
Hanson, E.	Cin	5	5	0	4.11	1.329	21	122.2	137	23	101
Harkey, M.	Col	1	6	0	5.79	1.756	13	91.2	125	35	39
Harnisch, P.	Hou	8	5	0	5.40	1.495	17	95.0	100	39	62
Harris, G.	SD	1	1	0	8.03	2.351	0	12.1	21	8	9
Harris, G.	Col	3	12	1	6.65	1.623	19	130.0	154	52	82
Harvey, B.	Fla	0	0	6	5.23	1.548	0	10.1	12	4	10
Haynes, H.	Mon	0	0	0	0.00	1.636	0	3.2	3	3	1
Henderson, R.	Mon	0	1	0	9.45	2.400	2	6.2	9	7	3
Henry, B.	Mon	8	3	1	2.43	1.109	15	107.1	97	20	70
Heredia, G.	Mon	6	3	0	3.46	1.327	3	75.1	85	13	62
Hernandez, J.	Fla	3	3	9	2.70	1.371	0	23.1	16	14	13
Hershiser, O.	LA	6	6	0	3.79	1.404	21	135.1	146	42	72
Hickerson, B.	SF	4	8	1	5.40	1.597	14	98.1	118	38	59
Hill, K.	Mon	16	5	0	3.32	1.261	23	154.2	145	44	85

NL Pitcher	Team	W	L	SV	ERA	Ratio	GS	IP	H	BB	K
Hill, M.	Atl	0	0	0	7.94	2.118	0	11.1	18	6	10
Hillman, E.	NYN	0	3	0	7.79	1.673	6	34.2	45	11	20
Hoffman, T.	SD	4	4	20	2.57	1.054	0	56.0	39	20	68
Holmes, D.	Col	0	3	3	6.35	2.118	0	28.1	35	24	33
Hope, J.	Pit	0	0	0	5.79	1.714	0	14.0	18	4	6
Hough, C.	Fla	5	9	0	5.15	1.584	21	113.2	118	52	65
Hudek, J.	Hou	0	2	16	2.97	1.093	0	39.1	24	18	39
Hurst, J.	NYN	0	1	0	12.60	2.000	0	10.0	15	5	6
Ilsley, B.	ChN	0	0	0	7.80	2.267	0	15.0	25	9	9
Jackson, D.	Phi	14	6	0	3.26	1.288	25	179.1	183	46	129
Jackson, M.	SF	3	2	4	1.49	0.850	0	42.1	23	11	51
Jacome, J.	NYN	4	3	0	2.67	1.315	8	54.0	54	17	30
Jarvis, K.	Cin	1	1	0	7.13	1.528	3	17.2	22	5	10
Jeffcoat, M.	Fla	0	0	0	10.13	1.500	0	2.2	4	0	1
Johnston, J.	Pit	0	0	0	29.70	6.000	0	3.1	14	4	5
Johnstone, J.	Fla	1	2	0	5.91	1.875	0	21.1	23	16	23
Jones, B.	NYN	12	7	0	3.15	1.356	24	160.0	157	56	80
Jones, D.	Phi	2	4	27	2.17	1.130	0	54.0	55	6	38
Jones, T.	Hou	5	2	5	2.72	1.087	0	72.2	52	26	63
Juden, J.	Phi	1	4	0	6.18	1.518	5	27.2	29	12	22
Kile, D.	Hou	9	6	0	4.57	1.652	24	147.2	153	82	105
Krueger, B.	SD	3	2	0	4.83	1.220	7	41.0	42	7	30
Leskanic, C.	Col	1	1	0	5.64	1.657	3	22.1	27	10	17
Lewis, R.	Fla	1	4	0	5.67	1.870	0	54.0	62	38	45
Lieber, J.	Pit	6	7	0	3.73	1.307	17	108.2	116	25	71
Linton, D.	NYN	6	2	0	4.47	1.868	3	50.1	74	20	29
Looney, B.	Mon	0	0	0	22.50	2.500	0	2.0	4	0	2
Maddux, G.	Atl	16	6	0	1.56	0.926	25	202.0	150	31	156
Maddux, M.	NYN	2	1	2	5.11	1.318	0	44.0	45	13	32
Manzanillo, J.	NYN	3	2	2	2.66	1.056	0	47.1	34	13	48
Manzanillo, R.	Pit	4	2	1	4.14	1.800	0	50.0	45	42	39
Martinez, J.	SD	0	2	0	6.75	1.917	1	12.0	18	5	7
Martinez, P.	Mon	11	5	1	3.42	1.182	23	144.2	115	45	142
Martinez, P.	SD	3	2	3	2.90	1.493	1	68.1	52	49	52
Martinez, R.	LA	12	7	0	3.97	1.306	24	170.0	160	56	119
Mason, R.	NYN	2	4	1	3.51	1.286	0	51.1	44	20	26
Mason, R.	Phi	1	1	0	5.19	1.846	0	8.2	11	5	7
Mathews, T.	Fla	2	1	0	3.35	1.279	2	43.0	45	9	21
Mauser, T.	SD	2	4	2	3.49	1.429	0	49.0	50	19	32
McDowell, R.	LA	0	3	0	5.23	1.766	0	41.1	50	22	29
McElroy, C.	Cin	1	2	5	2.34	1.162	0	57.2	52	15	38
McMichael, G.	Atl	4	6	21	3.84	1.449	0	58.2	66	19	47
Menendez, T.	SF	0	1	0	21.60	3.000	0	3.1	8	2	2
Mercker, K.	Atl	9	4	0	3.45	1.202	17	112.1	90	45	111
Miceli, D.	Pit	2	1	2	5.93	1.500	0	27.1	28	11	27
Miller, K.	Fla	1	3	0	8.10	1.750	4	20.0	26	7	11
Minor, B.	Pit	0	1	1	8.05	1.947	0	19.0	27	9	17
Monteleone, R.	SF	4	3	0	3.18	1.235	0	45.1	43	13	16
Moore, M.	Col	1	1	0	6.15	1.752	0	33.2	33	21	33
Morgan, M.	ChN	2	10	0	6.69	1.860	15	80.2	111	35	57
Munoz, B.	Phi	7	5	1	2.67	1.313	14	104.1	101	35	59
Munoz, M.	Col	4	2	1	3.74	1.489	0	45.2	37	31	32
Murphy, R.	StL	4	3	2	3.79	1.190	0	40.1	35	13	25

• FINAL 1994 AVERAGES

NL Pitcher	Team	W	L	SV	ERA	Ratio	GS	IP	H	BB	K
Mutis, J.	Fla	1	0	0	5.40	1.748	0	38.1	51	15	30
Myers, R.	ChN	1	5	21	3.79	1.388	0	40.1	40	16	32
Neagle, D.	Pit	9	10	0	5.12	1.365	24	137.0	135	49	122
Nen, R.	Fla	5	5	15	2.95	1.086	0	58.0	46	17	60
Nied, D.	Col	9	7	0	4.80	1.541	22	122.0	137	47	74
Olivares, O.	StL	3	4	1	5.74	1.697	12	73.2	84	37	26
Olson, G.	Atl	0	2	1	9.20	2.250	0	14.2	19	13	10
Osuna, A.	LA	2	0	0	6.23	1.962	0	8.2	13	4	7
Otto, D.	ChN	0	1	0	3.80	1.600	0	45.0	49	22	19
Painter, L.	Col	4	6	0	6.11	1.602	14	73.2	91	26	41
Palacios, V.	StL	3	8	1	4.44	1.275	17	117.2	104	43	95
Pall, D.	ChN	0	0	0	4.50	2.250	0	4.0	8	1	2
Park, C.	LA	0	0	0	11.25	2.750	0	4.0	5	5	6
Pena, A.	Pit	3	2	7	5.02	1.151	0	28.2	22	10	27
Perez, M.	StL	2	3	12	8.71	2.097	0	31.0	52	10	20
Perez, Y.	Fla	3	0	0	3.54	1.180	0	40.2	33	14	41
Plesac, D.	ChN	2	3	1	4.61	1.372	0	54.2	61	13	53
Portugal, M.	SF	10	8	0	3.93	1.354	21	137.1	135	45	87
Powell, R.	Hou	0	0	0	1.23	1.636	0	7.1	6	5	5
Pugh, T.	Cin	3	3	0	6.04	1.867	9	47.2	60	26	24
Quantrill, P.	Phi	2	2	1	6.00	1.733	1	30.0	39	10	13
Rapp, P.	Fla	7	8	0	3.85	1.560	23	133.1	132	69	75
Reed, S.	Col	3	2	3	3.94	1.734	0	64.0	79	26	51
Remlinger, M.	NYN	1	5	0	4.61	1.665	9	54.2	55	35	33
Reynolds, S.	Hou	8	5	0	3.05	1.250	14	124.0	128	21	110
Reynoso, A.	Col	3	4	0	4.82	1.567	9	52.1	54	22	25
Rijo, J.	Cin	9	6	0	3.08	1.352	26	172.1	177	52	171
Ritz, K.	Col	5	6	0	5.62	1.724	15	73.2	88	35	53
Rivera, B.	Phi	3	4	0	6.87	1.658	7	38.0	40	22	19
Robertson, R.	Pit	0	0	0	6.89	1.915	0	15.2	20	10	8
Rodriguez, R.	StL	3	5	0	4.03	1.475	0	60.1	62	26	43
Rogers, K.	SF	0	0	0	3.48	1.548	0	10.1	10	6	7
Rojas, M.	Mon	3	2	16	3.32	1.143	0	84.0	71	21	84
Roper, J.	Cin	6	2	0	4.50	1.348	15	92.0	90	30	51
Rueter, K.	Mon	7	3	0	5.17	1.419	20	92.1	106	23	50
Ruffin, B.	Col	4	5	16	4.04	1.545	0	55.2	55	30	65
Ruffin, J.	Cin	7	2	1	3.09	1.200	0	70.0	57	27	44
Saberhagen, B.	NYN	14	4	0	2.74	1.049	24	177.1	169	13	143
Sager, A.	SD	1	4	0	5.98	1.714	3	46.2	62	16	26
Sanders, S.	SD	4	8	1	4.78	1.405	20	111.0	103	48	109
Scheid, R.	Fla	1	3	0	3.34	1.392	5	32.1	35	8	17
Schilling, C.	Phi	2	8	0	4.48	1.433	13	82.1	87	28	58
Schourek, P.	Cin	7	2	0	4.09	1.500	10	81.1	90	29	69
Scott, T.	Mon	5	2	1	2.70	1.331	0	53.1	51	18	37
Seanez, R.	LA	1	1	0	2.66	1.437	0	23.2	24	9	18
Seminara, F.	NYN	0	2	0	5.82	1.647	1	17.0	20	8	7
Service, S.	Cin	1	2	0	7.36	1.500	0	7.1	8	3	5
Shaw, J.	Mon	5	2	1	3.88	1.248	0	67.1	67	15	47
Slocumb, H.	Phi	5	1	0	2.86	1.452	0	72.1	75	28	58
Smiley, J.	Cin	11	10	0	3.86	1.324	24	158.2	169	37	112
Smith, P.	NYN	4	10	0	5.55	1.439	21	131.1	145	42	62
Smith, W.	StL	1	1	0	9.00	1.714	0	7.0	9	3	7

FINAL 1994 AVERAGES •

NL Pitcher	Team	W	L	SV	ERA	Ratio	GS	IP	H	BB	K
Smith, Z.	Pit	10	8	0	3.27	1.248	24	157.0	162	34	57
Smoltz, J.	Atl	6	10	0	4.14	1.277	21	134.2	120	48	113
Spradlin, J.	Cin	0	0	0	10.13	1.750	0	8.0	12	2	4
Stanton, M.	Atl	3	1	3	3.55	1.533	0	45.2	41	26	35
Sutcliffe, R.	StL	6	4	0	6.52	1.877	14	67.2	93	32	26
Swift, B.	SF	8	7	0	3.38	1.290	17	109.1	109	31	62
Swindell, G.	Hou	8	9	0	4.37	1.362	24	148.1	175	26	74
Tabaka, J.	Pit	0	0	0	18.00	3.000	0	4.0	4	8	2
Tabaka, J.	SD	3	1	1	3.89	1.270	0	37.0	28	19	30
Taylor, K.	SD	0	0	0	8.31	2.538	1	4.1	9	1	3
Telgheder, D.	NYN	0	1	0	7.20	1.900	0	10.0	11	8	4
Tewksbury, B.	StL	12	10	0	5.32	1.381	24	155.2	190	22	79
Thompson, M.	Col	1	1	0	9.00	2.778	2	9.0	16	8	5
Tomlin, R.	Pit	0	3	0	3.92	1.597	4	20.2	23	10	17
Torres, S.	SF	2	8	0	5.44	1.613	14	84.1	95	34	42
Trachsel, S.	ChN	9	7	0	3.21	1.301	22	146.0	133	54	108
Urbani, T.	StL	3	7	0	5.15	1.519	10	80.1	98	21	43
Valdes, I.	LA	3	1	0	3.18	1.094	1	28.1	21	10	28
Valenzuela, F.	Phi	1	2	0	3.00	1.089	7	45.0	42	7	19
Van Landingham	SF	8	2	0	3.54	1.369	14	84.0	70	43	56
Veres, D.	Hou	3	3	1	2.41	1.146	0	41.0	39	7	28
Veres, R.	ChN	1	1	0	5.59	1.552	0	9.2	12	2	5
Wagner, P.	Pit	7	8	0	4.59	1.621	17	119.2	136	50	86
Walton, B.	Col	1	0	0	8.44	1.688	0	5.1	6	3	1
Watson, A.	StL	6	5	0	5.52	1.651	22	115.2	130	53	74
Wayne, G.	LA	1	3	0	4.67	1.615	0	17.1	19	6	10
Weathers, D.	Fla	8	12	0	5.27	1.696	24	135.0	166	59	72
Wells, B.	Phi	1	0	0	1.80	1.600	0	5.0	4	3	3
Wendell, T.	ChN	0	1	0	11.93	2.233	2	14.1	22	10	9
West, D.	Phi	4	10	0	3.55	1.374	14	99.0	74	61	83
Wetteland, J.	Mon	4	6	25	2.83	1.099	0	63.2	46	21	68
White, G.	Mon	1	1	1	6.08	1.521	5	23.2	24	11	17
White, R.	Pit	4	5	6	3.82	1.354	5	75.1	79	17	38
Whitehurst, W.	SD	4	7	0	4.92	1.734	13	64.0	84	26	43
Williams, B.	Hou	6	5	0	5.74	2.004	13	78.1	112	41	49
Williams, M.	Phi	2	4	0	5.01	1.609	8	50.1	61	20	29
Williams, M.	Hou	1	4	6	7.65	2.300	0	20.0	21	24	21
Wohlers, M.	Atl	7	2	1	4.59	1.647	0	51.0	51	33	58
Woodall, B.	Atl	0	1	0	4.50	1.167	1	6.0	5	2	2
Worrell, T.	SD	0	1	0	3.68	0.955	3	14.2	9	5	14
Worrell, T.	LA	6	5	11	4.29	1.190	0	42.0	37	12	44
Young, A.	ChN	4	6	0	3.92	1.299	19	114.2	103	46	65

AMERICAN LEAGUE: BATTERS

AL Batter	Team	BA	HR	RBI	SB	CS	G	AB	R	BB	OBP
Aldrete, M.	Oak	.242	4	18	2	0	76	178	23	20	.313
Alomar, R.	Tor	.306	8	38	19	8	107	392	78	51	.386
Alomar Jr, S.	Cle	.288	14	43	8	4	80	292	44	25	.347
Amaral, R.	Sea	.263	4	18	5	1	77	228	37	24	.333
Amaro, R.	Cle	.217	2	5	2	1	26	23	5	2	.280

AL Batter	Team	BA	HR	RBI	SB	CS	G	AB	R	BB	OBP
Anderson, B.	Bal	.263	12	48	31	1	111	453	78	57	.356
Anderson, G.	Cal	.385	0	1	0	0	5	13	0	0	.385
Anthony, E.	Sea	.237	10	30	6	2	79	262	31	23	.297
Baerga, C.	Cle	.314	19	80	8	2	103	442	81	10	.333
Baines, H.	Bal	.294	16	54	0	0	94	326	44	30	.356
Barnes, S.	Det	.286	1	4	0	1	24	21	4	0	.286
Bautista, D.	Det	.232	4	15	1	2	31	99	12	3	.255
Becker, R.	Min	.265	1	8	6	1	28	98	12	13	.351
Belle, A.	Cle	.357	36	101	9	6	106	412	90	58	.438
Beltre, E.	Tex	.282	0	12	2	5	48	131	12	16	.358
Berroa, G.	Oak	.306	13	65	7	2	96	340	55	41	.379
Berryhill, D.	Bos	.263	6	34	0	1	82	255	30	19	.312
Blosser, G.	Bos	.091	0	1	0	0	5	11	2	4	.333
Blowers, M.	Sea	.289	9	49	2	2	85	270	37	25	.348
Boggs, W.	NYA	.342	11	55	2	1	97	366	61	61	.433
Borders, P.	Tor	.247	3	26	1	1	85	295	24	15	.284
Bordick, M.	Oak	.253	2	37	7	2	114	391	38	38	.320
Boston, D.	NYA	.182	4	14	0	1	52	77	11	6	.250
Bowie, J.	Oak	.214	0	0	0	0	6	14	0	0	.214
Bragg, D.	Sea	.158	0	2	0	0	8	19	4	2	.238
Brooks, H.	KC	.230	1	14	1	0	34	61	5	2	.239
Brosius, S.	Oak	.238	14	49	2	6	96	324	31	24	.289
Brumley, M.	Oak	.240	0	2	0	0	11	25	0	1	.269
Brunansky, T.	Bos	.237	10	34	0	2	48	177	22	23	.319
Brunansky, T.	Mil	.214	0	0	0	0	16	28	2	1	.241
Buford, D.	Bal	.500	0	0	0	0	4	2	2	0	.500
Buhner, J.	Sea	.279	21	68	0	1	101	358	74	66	.394
Butler, R.	Tor	.176	0	5	0	1	41	74	13	7	.250
Canseco, J.	Tex	.282	31	90	15	8	111	429	88	69	.386
Carter, J.	Tor	.271	27	103	11	0	111	435	70	33	.317
Cedeno, D.	Tor	.196	0	10	1	2	47	97	14	10	.261
Chamberlain, W.	Bos	.256	4	20	0	2	51	164	13	12	.307
Cirillo, J.	Mil	.238	3	12	0	1	39	126	17	11	.309
Clark, W.	Tex	.329	13	80	5	1	110	389	73	71	.431
Cole, A.	Min	.296	4	23	29	8	105	345	68	44	.375
Coleman, V.	KC	.240	2	33	50	8	104	438	61	29	.285
Coles, D.	Tor	.210	4	15	0	0	48	143	15	10	.263
Cooper, S.	Bos	.282	13	53	0	3	104	369	49	30	.333
Cora, J.	ChA	.276	2	30	8	4	90	312	55	38	.353
Correia, R.	Cal	.235	0	0	0	0	6	17	4	0	.316
Cruz, F.	Oak	.107	0	0	0	0	17	28	2	4	.219
Curtis, C.	Cal	.256	11	50	25	11	114	453	67	37	.317
Cuyler, M.	Det	.241	1	11	5	3	48	116	20	13	.318
Dalesandro, M.	Cal	.200	1	2	0	0	19	25	5	2	.259
Davis, B.	Tex	.235	0	0	1	0	4	17	2	0	.235
Davis, C.	Cal	.311	26	84	3	2	108	392	72	69	.410
Davis, E.	Det	.183	3	13	5	0	37	120	19	18	.290
Davis, R.	NYA	.143	0	1	0	0	4	14	0	0	.143
Dawson, A.	Bos	.240	16	48	2	2	75	292	34	9	.271
Delgado, C.	Tor	.215	9	24	1	1	43	130	17	25	.352
Devereaux, M.	Bal	.203	9	33	1	2	85	301	35	22	.256
Diaz, A.	Mil	.251	1	17	5	5	79	187	17	10	.285
DiSarcina, G.	Cal	.260	3	33	3	7	112	389	53	18	.294
Ducey, R.	Tex	.172	0	1	0	0	11	29	1	2	.226
Dunn, S.	Min	.229	0	4	0	0	14	35	2	1	.250

AL Batter	Team	BA	HR	RBI	SB	CS	G	AB	R	BB	OBP
Easley, D.	Cal	.215	6	30	4	5	88	316	41	29	.288
Edmonds, J.	Cal	.273	5	37	4	2	94	289	35	30	.343
Eenhoorn, R.	NYA	.500	0	0	0	0	3	4	1	0	.500
Elster, K.	NYA	.000	0	0	0	0	7	20	0	1	.000
Espinoza, A.	Cle	.238	1	19	1	3	90	231	27	6	.258
Fabregas, J.	Cal	.283	0	16	2	1	43	127	12	7	.321
Felix, J.	Det	.306	13	49	1	6	86	301	54	26	.372
Fermin, F.	Sea	.317	1	35	4	4	101	379	52	11	.338
Fielder, C.	Det	.259	28	90	0	0	109	425	67	50	.337
Flaherty, J.	Det	.150	0	4	0	1	34	40	2	1	.167
Fletcher, S.	Bos	.227	3	11	8	1	63	185	31	16	.296
Fox, E.	Oak	.205	1	1	2	0	26	44	7	3	.255
Franco, J.	ChA	.319	20	98	8	1	112	433	72	62	.406
Frye, J.	Tex	.327	0	18	6	1	57	205	37	29	.408
Fryman, T.	Det	.263	18	85	2	2	114	464	66	45	.326
Gaetti, G.	KC	.287	12	57	0	2	90	327	53	19	.328
Gagne, G.	KC	.259	7	51	10	17	107	375	39	27	.314
Gallego, M.	NYA	.239	6	41	0	1	89	306	39	38	.327
Gates, B.	Oak	.283	2	24	3	0	64	233	29	21	.337
Gibson, K.	Det	.276	23	72	4	5	98	330	71	42	.358
Gomez, C.	Det	.257	8	53	5	3	84	296	32	33	.336
Gomez, L.	Bal	.274	15	56	0	0	84	285	46	41	.366
Gonzales, R.	Cle	.348	1	5	2	0	22	23	6	5	.448
Gonzalez, A.	Tor	.151	0	1	3	0	15	53	7	4	.224
Gonzalez, J.	Tex	.275	19	85	6	4	107	422	57	30	.330
Goodwin, T.	KC	.000	0	0	0	0	2	2	0	0	.000
Grebeck, C.	ChA	.309	0	5	0	0	35	97	17	12	.391
Green, S.	Tor	.091	0	1	1	0	14	33	1	1	.118
Greenwell, M.	Bos	.269	11	45	2	2	95	327	60	38	.348
Greer, R.	Tex	.314	10	46	0	0	80	277	36	46	.410
Griffey Jr, K.	Sea	.323	40	90	11	3	111	433	94	56	.402
Guillen, O.	ChA	.288	1	39	5	4	100	365	46	14	.311
Hale, C.	Min	.263	1	11	0	2	67	118	13	16	.350
Hall, J.	ChA	.393	1	5	0	0	17	28	6	2	.452
Hamelin, B.	KC	.282	24	65	4	3	101	312	64	56	.388
Hamilton, D.	Mil	.262	1	13	3	0	36	141	23	15	.331
Hammonds, J.	Bal	.296	8	31	5	0	68	250	45	17	.339
Harper, B.	Mil	.291	4	32	0	2	64	251	23	9	.318
Haselman, B.	Sea	.193	1	8	1	0	38	83	11	3	.230
Hatcher, B.	Bos	.244	1	18	4	5	44	164	24	11	.292
Helfand, E.	Oak	.167	0	1	0	0	7	6	1	0	.167
Hemond, S.	Oak	.222	3	20	7	6	91	198	23	16	.280
Henderson, D.	KC	.247	5	31	2	0	56	198	27	16	.304
Henderson, R.	Oak	.260	6	20	22	7	87	296	66	72	.411
Hocking, D.	Min	.323	0	2	2	0	11	31	3	0	.323
Hoiles, C.	Bal	.247	19	53	2	0	99	332	45	63	.371
Howard, C.	Sea	.200	0	2	0	0	9	25	2	1	.250
Howard, D.	KC	.229	1	13	3	2	46	83	9	11	.309
Howitt, D.	ChA	.357	0	0	0	0	10	14	4	1	.400
Hrbek, K.	Min	.270	10	53	0	0	81	274	34	37	.353
Hudler, R.	Cal	.298	8	20	2	2	56	124	17	6	.326
Huff, M.	Tor	.304	3	25	2	1	80	207	31	27	.392
Hulett, T.	Bal	.228	2	15	0	0	36	92	11	12	.314
Hulse, D.	Tex	.255	1	19	18	2	77	310	58	21	.305

AL Batter	Team	BA	HR	RBI	SB	CS	G	AB	R	BB	OBP
Ingram, R.	Det	.217	0	2	0	1	12	23	3	1	.240
Jackson, B.	Cal	.279	13	43	1	0	75	201	23	20	.344
Jackson, C.	Tex	.000	0	0	0	0	1	2	0	0	.000
Jackson, D.	ChA	.312	10	51	7	1	104	369	43	27	.362
Jaha, J.	Mil	.241	12	39	3	3	84	291	45	32	.332
James, C.	Tex	.256	7	19	0	0	52	133	28	20	.361
Javier, S.	Oak	.272	10	44	24	7	109	419	75	49	.349
Jefferson, R.	Sea	.327	8	32	0	0	63	162	24	17	.392
Johnson, L.	ChA	.277	3	54	26	6	106	412	56	26	.321
Jose, F.	KC	.303	11	55	10	12	99	366	56	35	.362
Joyner, W.	KC	.311	8	57	3	2	97	363	52	47	.386
Karkovice, R.	ChA	.213	11	29	0	3	77	207	33	36	.325
Kelly, P.	NYA	.280	3	41	6	5	93	286	35	19	.330
Kirby, W.	Cle	.293	5	23	11	4	78	191	33	13	.341
Knoblauch, C.	Min	.312	5	51	35	6	109	445	85	41	.381
Knorr, R.	Tor	.242	7	19	0	0	40	124	20	10	.301
Koslofski, K.	KC	.250	0	0	0	0	2	4	2	2	.500
Kreuter, C.	Det	.224	1	19	0	1	65	170	17	28	.327
LaValliere, M.	ChA	.281	1	24	0	2	59	139	6	20	.368
Lee, M.	Tex	.278	2	38	3	1	95	335	41	21	.319
Leius, S.	Min	.246	14	49	2	4	97	350	57	37	.318
Levis, J.	Cle	1.000	0	0	0	0	1	1	0	0	1.000
Lewis, M.	Cle	.205	1	8	1	0	20	73	6	2	.227
Leyritz, J.	NYA	.265	17	58	0	0	75	249	47	35	.365
Lind, J.	KC	.269	1	31	9	5	85	290	34	16	.306
Listach, P.	Mil	.296	0	2	2	1	16	54	8	3	.333
Litton, G.	Bos	.095	0	1	0	0	11	21	2	0	.091
Livingstone, S.	Det	.217	0	1	0	0	15	23	0	1	.250
Lofton, K.	Cle	.349	12	57	60	12	112	459	105	52	.412
Lovullo, T.	Sea	.222	2	7	1	0	36	72	9	9	.309
Macfarlane, M.	KC	.255	14	47	1	0	92	314	53	35	.359
Mack, Q.	Sea	.238	0	2	2	0	5	21	1	1	.273
Mack, S.	Min	.333	15	61	4	1	81	303	55	32	.402
Maldonado, C.	Cle	.196	5	12	1	1	42	92	14	19	.333
Martin, N.	ChA	.275	1	16	4	2	45	131	19	9	.317
Martinez, E.	Sea	.285	13	51	6	2	89	326	47	53	.387
Martinez, T.	Sea	.261	20	61	1	2	97	329	42	29	.320
Matheny, M.	Mil	.226	1	2	0	1	28	53	3	3	.293
Matos, F.	Oak	.250	0	2	1	0	14	28	1	1	.267
Mattingly, D.	NYA	.304	6	51	0	0	97	372	62	60	.397
Mayne, B.	KC	.257	2	20	1	0	46	144	19	14	.323
McCarty, D.	Min	.260	1	12	2	1	44	131	21	7	.322
McDowell, O.	Tex	.262	1	15	14	2	59	183	34	28	.355
McGwire, M.	Oak	.252	9	25	0	0	47	135	26	37	.413
McLemore, M.	Bal	.257	3	29	20	5	104	343	44	51	.354
McRae, B.	KC	.273	4	40	28	8	114	436	71	54	.359
Meares, P.	Min	.266	2	24	5	1	80	229	29	14	.310
Melvin, B.	ChA	.158	0	1	0	0	11	19	3	1	.200
Melvin, B.	NYA	.286	1	3	0	0	9	14	2	0	.286
Merullo, M.	Cle	.100	0	0	0	0	4	10	1	2	.250
Mieske, M.	Mil	.259	10	38	3	5	84	259	39	21	.320
Miller, K.	KC	.133	0	0	0	0	5	15	1	0	.133
Mitchell, K.	Sea	.227	5	15	0	0	46	128	21	18	.324
Molitor, P.	Tor	.341	14	75	20	0	115	454	86	55	.410

AL Batter	Team	BA	HR	RBI	SB	CS	G	AB	R	BB	OBP
Munoz, P.	Min	.295	11	36	0	0	75	244	35	19	.348
Murray, E.	Cle	.254	17	76	8	4	108	433	57	31	.302
Myers, G.	Cal	.246	2	8	0	2	45	126	10	10	.299
Naehring, T.	Bos	.276	7	42	1	3	80	297	41	30	.349
Neel, T.	Oak	.266	15	48	2	3	83	278	43	38	.357
Newfield, M.	Sea	.184	1	4	0	0	12	38	3	2	.225
Newson, W.	ChA	.255	2	7	1	0	63	102	16	14	.345
Nilsson, D.	Mil	.275	12	69	1	0	109	397	51	34	.326
Nixon, O.	Bos	.274	0	25	42	10	103	398	60	55	.360
Noboa, J.	Oak	.325	0	6	1	0	17	40	3	2	.357
Nokes, M.	NYA	.291	7	19	0	0	28	79	11	5	.329
O'Leary, T.	Mil	.273	2	7	1	1	27	66	9	5	.329
O'Neill, P.	NYA	.359	21	83	5	4	103	368	68	72	.460
Olerud, J.	Tor	.297	12	67	1	2	108	384	47	61	.393
Ortiz, J.	Tex	.276	0	9	0	1	29	76	3	5	.329
Ortiz, L.	Bos	.167	0	6	0	0	7	18	3	1	.182
Owen, S.	Cal	.310	3	37	2	8	82	268	30	49	.418
Palmeiro, R.	Bal	.319	23	76	7	3	111	436	82	54	.392
Palmer, D.	Tex	.246	19	59	3	4	93	342	50	26	.302
Paquette, C.	Oak	.143	0	0	1	0	14	49	0	0	.143
Parks, D.	Min	.191	1	9	0	1	31	89	6	4	.242
Pasqua, D.	ChA	.217	2	4	0	0	11	23	2	0	.217
Pena, T.	Cle	.295	2	10	0	1	40	112	18	9	.341
Perez, E.	Cal	.209	5	16	3	0	38	129	10	12	.275
Perez, R.	Tor	.125	0	0	0	0	4	8	0	0	.125
Perry, H.	Cle	.111	0	1	0	0	4	9	1	3	.357
Phillips, T.	Det	.281	19	61	13	5	114	438	91	95	.409
Pirkl, G.	Sea	.264	6	11	0	0	19	53	7	1	.286
Polonia, L.	NYA	.311	1	36	20	12	95	350	62	37	.383
Puckett, K.	Min	.317	20	112	6	3	108	439	79	28	.362
Raines, T.	ChA	.266	10	52	13	0	101	384	80	61	.365
Ramirez, M.	Cle	.269	17	60	4	2	91	290	51	42	.357
Reboulet, J.	Min	.259	3	23	0	0	74	189	28	18	.327
Redus, G.	Tex	.273	0	2	0	0	18	33	2	4	.351
Reed, J.	Mil	.271	2	37	5	4	108	399	48	57	.362
Reynolds, H.	Cal	.232	0	11	10	7	74	207	33	23	.310
Ripken, B.	Tex	.309	0	6	2	0	32	81	9	3	.333
Ripken, C.	Bal	.315	13	75	1	0	112	444	71	32	.364
Rodriguez, A.	Sea	.204	0	2	3	0	17	54	4	3	.241
Rodriguez, C.	Bos	.287	1	13	1	0	57	174	15	11	.330
Rodriguez, I.	Tex	.298	16	57	6	3	99	363	56	31	.360
Rowland, R.	Bos	.229	9	20	0	0	46	118	14	11	.295
Royer, S.	Bos	.111	0	1	0	0	4	9	0	0	.111
Sabo, C.	Bal	.256	11	42	1	1	68	258	41	20	.320
Saenz, O.	ChA	.143	0	0	0	0	5	14	2	0	.143
Salmon, T.	Cal	.287	23	70	1	3	100	373	67	54	.382
Samuel, J.	Det	.309	5	21	5	2	59	136	32	10	.364
Sasser, M.	Sea	.000	0	0	0	0	3	4	0	0	.000
Sax, S.	Oak	.250	0	1	0	0	7	24	2	0	.250
Schaefer, J.	Oak	.125	0	0	0	0	6	8	0	0	.125
Schofield, D.	Tor	.255	4	32	7	7	95	325	38	34	.332
Seitzer, K.	Mil	.314	5	49	2	1	80	309	44	30	.375
Shumpert, T.	KC	.240	8	24	18	3	64	183	28	13	.289

AL Batter	Team	BA	HR	RBI	SB	CS	G	AB	R	BB	OBP
Sierra, R.	Oak	.268	23	92	8	5	110	426	71	23	.298
Silvestri, D.	NYA	.111	1	2	0	1	12	18	3	4	.261
Singleton, D.	Mil	.000	0	0	0	0	2	0	0	0	.000
Smith, D.	Bal	.311	3	12	0	1	28	74	12	5	.363
Smith, D.	Cal	.262	5	18	2	3	45	122	19	7	.300
Smith, L.	Bal	.203	0	2	1	0	35	59	13	11	.333
Smith, M.	Bal	.143	0	2	0	0	3	7	0	0	.143
Snow, J.	Cal	.220	8	30	0	1	61	223	22	19	.289
Sojo, L.	Sea	.277	6	22	2	1	63	213	32	8	.308
Sorrento, P.	Cle	.280	14	62	0	1	95	322	43	34	.345
Spiers, B.	Mil	.252	0	17	7	1	73	214	27	19	.316
Sprague, E.	Tor	.240	11	44	1	0	109	405	38	23	.296
Stanley, M.	NYA	.300	17	57	0	0	82	290	54	39	.384
Steinbach, T.	Oak	.285	11	57	2	1	103	369	51	26	.327
Strange, D.	Tex	.212	5	26	1	3	73	226	26	15	.268
Surhoff, B.	Mil	.261	5	22	0	1	40	134	20	16	.336
Sveum, D.	Sea	.185	1	2	0	0	10	27	3	2	.241
Tackett, J.	Bal	.226	2	9	0	0	26	53	5	5	.317
Tartabull, D.	NYA	.256	19	67	1	1	104	399	68	66	.360
Tettleton, M.	Det	.248	17	51	0	1	107	339	57	97	.419
Thomas, F.	ChA	.353	38	101	2	3	113	399	106	109	.487
Thome, J.	Cle	.268	20	52	3	3	98	321	58	46	.359
Tingley, R.	ChA	.000	0	0	0	0	5	5	0	0	.000
Tinsley, L.	Bos	.222	2	14	13	0	78	144	27	19	.315
Tomberlin, A.	Bos	.194	1	1	1	0	17	36	1	6	.310
Trammell, A.	Det	.267	8	28	3	0	76	292	38	16	.307
Turang, B.	Sea	.188	1	8	3	1	38	112	9	7	.242
Turner, C.	Cal	.242	1	12	3	0	58	149	23	10	.290
Valentin, J.	Bos	.316	9	49	3	1	84	301	53	42	.400
Valentin, J.	Mil	.239	11	46	12	3	97	285	47	38	.330
Valle, D.	Bos	.158	1	5	0	1	30	76	6	9	.256
Valle, D.	Mil	.389	1	5	0	1	16	36	8	9	.522
Vaughn, G.	Mil	.254	19	55	9	5	95	370	59	51	.345
Vaughn, M.	Bos	.310	26	82	4	4	111	394	65	57	.408
Velarde, R.	NYA	.279	9	34	4	2	77	280	47	22	.338
Ventura, R.	ChA	.282	18	78	3	1	109	401	57	61	.373
Vizquel, O.	Cle	.273	1	33	13	4	69	286	39	23	.325
Voigt, J.	Bal	.241	3	20	0	0	59	141	15	18	.327
Walbeck, M.	Min	.204	5	35	1	1	97	338	31	17	.246
Ward, T.	Mil	.232	9	45	6	2	102	367	55	52	.328
Wedge, E.	Bos	.000	0	0	0	0	2	6	0	1	.000
Whitaker, L.	Det	.301	12	43	2	0	92	322	67	41	.377
White, D.	Tor	.270	13	49	11	3	100	403	67	21	.313
Willard, J.	Sea	.200	1	3	0	0	6	5	1	1	.333
Williams, B.	NYA	.289	12	57	16	9	108	408	80	61	.384
Williams, G.	NYA	.291	4	13	1	3	57	86	19	4	.319
Wilson, D.	Sea	.216	3	27	1	2	91	282	24	10	.244
Winfield, D.	Min	.252	10	43	2	1	77	294	35	31	.321
Wrona, R.	Mil	.500	1	3	0	0	6	10	2	1	.545
Young, E.	Oak	.067	0	3	0	0	11	30	2	1	.097
Zupcic, B.	Bos	.000	0	0	0	1	4	4	0	0	.000
Zupcic, B.	ChA	.205	1	8	0	0	32	88	10	4	.237

FINAL 1994 AVERAGES •

AMERICAN LEAGUE: PITCHERS

AL Pitcher	Team	W	L	SV	ERA	Ratio	GS	IP	H	BB	K
Abbott, J.	NYA	9	8	0	4.55	1.453	24	160.1	167	64	90
Acre, M.	Oak	5	1	0	3.41	1.398	0	34.1	24	23	21
Aguilera, R.	Min	1	4	23	3.63	1.500	0	44.2	57	10	46
Alvarez, W.	ChA	12	8	0	3.45	1.293	24	161.2	147	62	108
Anderson, B.	Cal	7	5	0	5.22	1.495	18	101.2	120	27	47
Appier, K.	KC	7	6	0	3.83	1.316	23	155.0	137	63	145
Armstrong, J.	Tex	0	1	0	3.60	1.100	2	10.0	9	2	7
Assenmacher, P.	ChA	1	2	1	3.55	1.212	0	33.0	26	13	29
Ausanio, J.	NYA	2	1	0	5.17	1.404	0	15.2	16	6	15
Ayala, B.	Sea	4	3	18	2.86	1.200	0	56.2	42	26	76
Bailey, C.	Bos	0	1	0	12.46	3.000	0	4.1	10	3	4
Bankhead, S.	Bos	3	2	0	4.54	1.221	0	37.2	34	12	25
Barnes, B.	Cle	0	1	0	5.40	2.025	0	13.1	12	15	5
Belcher, T.	Det	7	15	0	5.89	1.691	25	162.0	192	78	76
Belinda, S.	KC	2	2	1	5.14	1.551	0	49.0	47	24	37
Benitez, A.	Bal	0	0	0	0.90	1.300	0	10.0	8	4	14
Bere, J.	ChA	12	2	0	3.81	1.412	24	141.2	119	80	127
Bergman, S.	Det	2	1	0	5.60	1.698	3	17.2	22	7	12
Boever, J.	Det	9	2	3	3.98	1.463	0	81.1	80	37	49
Bohanon, B.	Tex	2	2	0	7.23	1.607	5	37.1	51	8	26
Bolton, T.	Bal	1	2	0	5.40	1.800	0	23.1	29	13	12
Bones, R.	Mil	10	9	0	3.43	1.254	24	170.2	166	45	57
Bosio, C.	Sea	4	10	0	4.32	1.432	19	125.0	137	40	67
Boskie, S.	Sea	0	1	0	6.75	1.875	1	2.2	4	1	0
Brewer, B.	KC	4	1	3	2.56	1.190	0	38.2	28	16	25
Briscoe, J.	Oak	4	2	1	4.01	1.439	0	49.1	31	39	45
Bronkey, J.	Mil	1	1	1	4.35	1.548	0	20.2	20	12	13
Brow, S.	Tor	0	3	2	5.90	1.862	0	29.0	34	19	15
Brown, K.	Tex	7	9	0	4.82	1.612	25	170.0	218	50	123
Brumley, D.	Tex	0	0	0	16.20	3.300	0	3.1	6	5	4
Burrows, T.	Tex	0	0	0	9.00	2.000	0	1.0	1	1	0
Butcher, M.	Cal	2	1	1	6.67	1.888	0	29.2	31	23	19
Cadaret, G.	Det	1	0	2	3.60	1.650	0	20.0	17	16	14
Cadaret, G.	Tor	0	1	0	5.85	2.050	0	20.0	24	17	15
Campbell, K.	Min	1	0	0	2.92	1.054	0	24.2	20	5	15
Carpenter, C.	Tex	2	5	5	5.03	1.508	0	59.0	69	20	39
Casian, L.	Cle	0	2	0	8.64	2.400	0	8.1	16	4	2
Casian, L.	Min	1	3	1	7.08	1.746	0	40.2	57	12	18
Castillo, T.	Tor	5	2	1	2.51	1.426	0	68.0	66	28	43
Clark, M.	Cle	11	3	0	3.82	1.390	20	127.1	133	40	60
Clemens, R.	Bos	9	7	0	2.85	1.166	24	170.2	124	71	168
Cone, D.	KC	16	5	0	2.94	1.113	23	171.2	130	54	132
Converse, J.	Sea	0	5	0	8.69	2.342	8	48.2	73	40	39
Cook, D.	ChA	3	1	0	3.55	1.303	0	33.0	29	14	26
Cornett, B.	Tor	1	3	0	6.68	1.742	4	31.0	40	11	22
Cox, D.	Tor	1	1	3	1.45	0.804	0	18.2	7	7	14
Cummings, J.	Sea	2	4	0	5.63	1.609	8	64.0	66	37	33
Darling, R.	Oak	10	11	0	4.50	1.425	25	160.0	162	59	108
Darwin, D.	Bos	7	5	0	6.30	1.665	13	75.2	101	24	54
Darwin, J.	Sea	0	0	0	13.50	2.750	0	4.0	7	3	1
Davis, S.	Det	2	4	0	3.56	1.458	0	48.0	36	34	38
Davis, T.	Sea	2	2	2	4.01	1.682	1	49.1	57	25	28

AL Pitcher	Team	W	L	SV	ERA	Ratio	GS	IP	H	BB	K
DeJesus, J.	KC	3	1	0	4.72	1.500	4	26.2	27	13	12
DeLeon, J.	ChA	3	2	2	3.36	1.269	0	67.0	48	31	67
Deshaies, J.	Min	6	12	0	7.39	1.734	25	130.1	170	54	78
Dettmer, J.	Tex	0	6	0	4.33	1.593	9	54.0	63	20	27
DiPoto, J.	Cle	0	0	0	8.04	2.362	0	15.2	26	10	9
Doherty, J.	Det	6	7	0	6.48	1.658	17	101.1	139	26	28
Dopson, J.	Cal	1	4	1	6.14	1.636	5	58.2	67	26	33
Dreyer, S.	Tex	1	1	0	5.71	1.615	3	17.1	19	8	11
Eckersley, D.	Oak	5	4	19	4.26	1.421	0	44.1	49	13	47
Eichhorn, M.	Bal	6	5	1	2.15	1.211	0	71.0	62	19	35
Eldred, C.	Mil	11	11	0	4.68	1.374	25	179.0	158	84	98
Erickson, S.	Min	8	11	0	5.44	1.674	23	144.0	173	59	104
Fajardo, H.	Tex	5	7	0	6.91	1.476	12	83.1	95	26	45
Farr, S.	Bos	1	0	0	6.23	2.077	0	13.0	24	3	8
Farr, S.	Cle	1	1	4	5.28	2.217	0	15.1	17	15	12
Farrell, J.	Cal	1	2	0	9.00	1.923	3	13.0	16	8	10
Fernandez, A.	ChA	11	7	0	3.86	1.256	24	170.1	163	50	122
Fernandez, S.	Bal	6	6	0	5.15	1.361	19	115.1	109	46	95
Fetters, M.	Mil	1	4	17	2.54	1.500	0	46.0	41	27	31
Finley, C.	Cal	10	10	0	4.32	1.375	25	183.1	178	71	148
Finnvold, G.	Bos	0	4	0	5.94	1.734	8	36.1	45	15	17
Fleming, D.	Sea	7	11	0	6.46	1.863	23	117.0	152	65	65
Fossas, T.	Bos	2	0	1	4.76	1.500	0	34.0	35	15	31
Frohwirth, T.	Bos	0	3	1	10.80	2.213	0	26.2	40	17	13
Garagozzo, K.	Min	0	0	0	9.64	2.357	0	9.1	9	13	3
Gardiner, M.	Det	2	2	5	4.14	1.295	1	58.2	53	23	31
Gibson, P.	NYA	1	1	0	4.97	1.517	0	29.0	26	17	21
Glinatsis, G.	Sea	0	1	0	13.50	2.813	2	5.1	9	6	1
Gohr, G.	Det	2	2	0	4.50	1.676	6	34.0	36	21	21
Gordon, T.	KC	11	7	0	4.35	1.455	24	155.1	136	87	126
Gossage, G.	Sea	3	0	1	4.18	1.310	0	47.1	44	15	29
Grahe, J.	Cal	2	5	13	6.65	2.123	0	43.1	68	18	26
Granger, J.	KC	0	1	0	6.75	2.036	2	9.1	13	6	3
Grimsley, J.	Cle	5	2	0	4.57	1.585	13	82.2	91	34	59
Groom, B.	Det	0	1	1	3.94	1.438	0	32.0	31	13	27
Guardado, E.	Min	0	2	0	8.47	1.765	4	17.0	26	4	8
Gubicza, M.	KC	7	9	0	4.50	1.415	22	130.0	158	26	59
Gullickson, B.	Det	4	5	0	5.93	1.604	19	115.1	156	25	65
Guthrie, M.	Min	4	2	1	6.14	1.656	2	51.1	65	18	38
Guzman, J.	Tor	12	11	0	5.68	1.656	25	147.1	165	76	124
Hall, D.	Tor	2	3	17	3.41	1.295	0	31.2	26	14	28
Hammaker, A.	ChA	0	0	0	0.00	0.750	0	1.1	1	0	1
Haney, C.	KC	2	2	0	7.31	1.694	6	28.1	36	11	18
Harris, G.	Det	0	0	1	7.15	1.588	0	11.1	13	4	10
Harris, G.	Bos	3	4	2	8.28	1.839	0	45.2	60	23	44
Harris, G.	NYA	0	1	0	5.40	1.800	0	5.0	4	3	4
Helling, R.	Tex	3	2	0	5.88	1.538	9	52.0	62	18	25
Henke, T.	Tex	3	6	15	3.79	1.184	0	38.0	33	12	39
Henneman, M.	Det	1	3	8	5.19	1.788	0	34.2	43	17	27
Henry, D.	Mil	2	3	0	4.60	1.787	0	31.1	32	23	20
Hentgen, P.	Tor	13	8	0	3.40	1.260	24	174.2	158	59	147
Hernandez, R.	ChA	4	4	14	4.91	1.343	0	47.2	44	19	50
Hernandez, X.	NYA	4	4	6	5.85	1.775	0	40.0	48	21	37
Hesketh, J.	Bos	8	5	0	4.26	1.447	20	114.0	117	46	83

AL Pitcher	Team	W	L	SV	ERA	Ratio	GS	IP	H	BB	K
Hibbard, G.	Sea	1	5	0	6.69	1.835	14	80.2	115	31	39
Higuera, T.	Mil	1	5	0	7.06	1.909	12	58.2	74	36	35
Hill, M.	Sea	1	0	0	6.46	1.732	0	23.2	30	11	16
Hitchcock, S.	NYA	4	1	2	4.20	1.561	5	49.1	48	29	37
Honeycutt, R.	Tex	1	2	1	7.20	1.920	0	25.0	37	9	18
Horsman, V.	Oak	0	1	0	4.91	1.398	0	29.1	29	11	20
Howard, C.	Bos	1	0	1	3.63	1.185	0	39.2	35	12	22
Howe, S.	NYA	3	0	15	1.80	0.875	0	40.0	28	7	18
Howell, J.	Tex	4	1	2	5.44	1.419	0	43.0	44	16	22
Hurst, B.	Tex	2	1	0	7.11	1.816	8	38.0	53	16	24
Hurst, J.	Tex	0	0	0	10.13	2.344	0	10.2	17	8	5
Hutton, M.	NYA	0	0	0	4.91	1.091	0	3.2	4	0	1
Ignasiak, M.	Mil	3	1	0	4.53	1.364	5	47.2	51	13	24
Jimenez, M.	Oak	1	4	0	7.41	2.088	7	34.0	38	32	22
Johnson, D.	ChA	2	1	0	6.57	2.189	0	12.1	16	11	7
Johnson, R.	Sea	13	6	0	3.19	1.221	23	172.0	132	72	204
Kamieniecki, S.	NYA	8	6	0	3.76	1.509	16	117.1	115	59	71
Karsay, S.	Oak	1	1	0	2.57	1.250	4	28.0	26	8	15
Key, J.	NYA	17	4	0	3.27	1.381	25	168.0	177	52	97
Kiefer, M.	Mil	1	0	0	8.44	2.156	0	10.2	15	8	8
King, K.	Sea	0	2	0	7.04	2.543	0	15.1	21	17	6
Klingenbeck, S.	Bal	1	0	0	3.86	1.571	1	7.0	6	4	5
Knudsen, K.	Det	1	0	0	13.50	3.375	0	5.1	7	11	1
Krueger, B.	Det	0	2	0	9.61	2.237	2	19.2	26	17	17
Langston, M.	Cal	7	8	0	4.68	1.466	18	119.1	121	54	109
Leary, T.	Tex	1	1	0	8.14	1.810	3	21.0	26	11	9
Lefferts, C.	Cal	1	1	1	4.67	1.788	0	34.2	50	12	27
Leftwich, P.	Cal	5	10	0	5.68	1.509	20	114.0	127	42	67
Leiper, D.	Oak	0	0	1	1.93	1.071	0	18.2	13	6	14
Leiter, A.	Tor	6	7	0	5.08	1.719	20	111.2	125	65	100
Leiter, M.	Cal	4	7	2	4.72	1.500	7	95.1	99	35	71
Lewis, S.	Cal	0	1	0	6.10	1.871	0	31.0	46	10	10
Lilliquist, D.	Cle	1	3	1	4.91	1.466	0	29.1	34	8	15
Lima, J.	Det	0	1	0	13.50	2.100	1	6.2	11	3	7
Lloyd, G.	Mil	2	3	3	5.17	1.426	0	47.0	49	15	31
Lopez, A.	Cle	1	2	0	4.24	1.588	4	17.0	20	6	18
Lorraine, A.	Cal	0	2	0	10.61	2.196	3	18.2	30	11	10
Magnante, M.	KC	2	3	0	4.60	1.511	1	47.0	55	16	21
Magrane, J.	Cal	2	6	0	7.30	1.973	11	74.0	89	51	33
Mahomes, P.	Min	9	5	0	4.72	1.533	21	120.0	121	62	53
Martinez, D.	Cle	11	6	0	3.52	1.228	24	176.2	166	44	92
McCaskill, K.	ChA	1	4	3	3.42	1.386	0	52.2	51	22	37
McDonald, B.	Bal	14	7	0	4.06	1.316	24	157.1	151	54	94
McDowell, J.	ChA	10	9	0	3.73	1.287	25	181.0	186	42	127
Meacham, R.	KC	3	3	4	3.73	1.283	0	50.2	51	12	36
Melendez, J.	Bos	0	1	0	6.06	1.837	0	16.1	20	8	9
Mercedes, J.	Mil	2	0	0	2.32	1.290	0	31.0	22	16	11
Merriman, B.	Min	0	1	0	6.35	2.118	0	17.0	18	14	10
Mesa, J.	Cle	7	5	2	3.82	1.370	0	73.0	71	26	63
Milacki, B.	KC	0	5	0	6.14	1.599	10	55.2	68	20	17
Mills, A.	Bal	3	3	2	5.16	1.522	0	45.1	43	24	44
Minchey, N.	Bos	2	3	0	8.61	2.522	5	23.0	44	14	15
Miranda, A.	Mil	2	5	0	5.28	1.435	8	46.0	39	27	24

AL Pitcher	Team	W	L	SV	ERA	Ratio	GS	IP	H	BB	K
Mohler, M.	Oak	0	1	0	7.71	1.714	1	2.1	2	2	4
Montgomery, J.	KC	2	3	27	4.03	1.433	0	44.2	48	15	50
Moore, M.	Det	11	10	0	5.42	1.581	25	154.1	152	89	62
Morris, J.	Cle	10	6	0	5.60	1.656	23	141.1	163	67	100
Moyer, J.	Bal	5	7	0	4.77	1.329	23	149.0	158	38	87
Mulholland, T.	NYA	6	7	0	6.49	1.575	19	120.2	150	37	72
Murphy, R.	NYA	0	0	0	16.20	1.800	0	1.2	3	0	0
Mussina, M.	Bal	16	5	0	3.06	1.168	24	176.1	163	42	99
Nabholz, C.	Bos	3	4	0	6.64	1.786	8	42.0	44	29	23
Nabholz, C.	Cle	0	1	0	11.45	3.000	4	11.0	23	9	5
Nagy, C.	Cle	10	8	0	3.45	1.346	23	169.1	175	48	108
Navarro, J.	Mil	4	9	0	6.62	1.717	10	89.2	115	35	65
Nelson, J.	Sea	0	0	0	2.76	1.488	0	42.1	35	20	44
Nunez, E.	Oak	0	0	0	12.00	2.400	0	15.0	26	10	15
Ogea, C.	Cle	0	1	0	6.06	1.959	1	16.1	21	10	11
Ojeda, B.	NYA	0	0	0	24.00	5.667	2	3.0	11	6	3
Oliver, D.	Tex	4	0	2	3.42	1.620	0	50.0	40	35	50
Ontiveros, S.	Oak	6	4	0	2.65	1.084	13	115.1	93	26	56
Oquist, M.	Bal	3	3	0	6.17	1.903	9	58.1	75	30	39
Orosco, J.	Mil	3	1	0	5.08	1.538	0	39.0	32	26	36
Pall, D.	NYA	1	2	0	3.60	1.514	0	35.0	43	9	21
Patterson, B.	Cal	2	3	1	4.07	1.238	0	42.0	35	15	30
Patterson, K.	Cal	0	0	0	0.00	0.000	0	0.2	0	0	1
Pavlik, R.	Tex	2	5	0	7.69	1.887	11	50.1	61	30	31
Pennington, B.	Bal	0	1	0	12.00	2.833	0	6.0	9	8	7
Perez, M.	NYA	9	4	0	4.10	1.289	22	151.1	134	58	109
Phoenix, S.	Oak	0	0	0	6.23	1.385	0	4.1	4	2	3
Pichardo, H.	KC	5	3	3	4.92	1.670	0	67.2	82	24	36
Plantenberg, E.	Sea	0	0	0	0.00	1.714	0	7.0	4	7	1
Plunk, E.	Cle	7	2	3	2.54	1.408	0	71.0	61	37	73
Poole, J.	Bal	1	0	0	6.64	2.115	0	20.1	32	11	18
Pulido, C.	Min	3	7	0	5.98	1.518	14	84.1	87	40	32
Quantrill, P.	Bos	1	1	0	3.52	1.391	0	23.0	25	5	15
Reardon, J.	NYA	1	0	2	8.38	2.069	0	9.2	17	3	4
Reed, R.	Tex	1	1	0	5.94	1.500	3	16.2	17	7	12
Reyes, C.	Oak	0	3	1	4.15	1.500	9	78.0	71	44	57
Rhodes, A.	Bal	3	5	0	5.81	1.576	10	52.2	51	30	47
Righetti, D.	Oak	0	0	0	16.71	3.286	0	7.0	13	9	4
Righetti, D.	Tor	0	1	0	6.75	1.425	0	13.1	9	10	10
Risley, B.	Sea	9	6	0	3.44	0.955	0	52.1	31	19	61
Rogers, K.	Tex	11	8	0	4.46	1.339	24	167.1	169	52	120
Ruffcorn, S.	ChA	0	2	0	12.79	3.158	2	6.1	15	5	3
Russell, J.	Bos	0	5	12	5.14	1.571	0	28.0	30	13	18
Russell, J.	Cle	1	1	5	4.97	1.263	0	12.2	13	3	10
Ryan, K.	Bos	2	3	13	2.44	1.333	0	48.0	46	17	32
Salkeld, R.	Sea	2	5	0	7.17	2.068	13	59.0	76	45	46
Sampen, B.	Cal	1	1	0	6.46	1.957	0	15.1	14	13	9
Sanderson, S.	ChA	8	4	0	5.09	1.348	14	92.0	110	12	36
Scanlan, B.	Mil	2	6	2	4.11	1.447	12	103.0	117	28	65
Schullstrom, E.	Min	0	0	1	2.77	1.462	0	13.0	13	5	13
Schwarz, J.	Cal	0	0	0	4.05	1.650	0	6.2	5	6	4
Schwarz, J.	ChA	0	0	0	6.35	2.206	0	11.1	9	16	14

AL Pitcher	Team	W	L	SV	ERA	Ratio	GS	IP	H	BB	K
Sele, A.	Bos	8	7	0	3.83	1.458	22	143.1	140	60	105
Shuey, P.	Cle	0	1	5	8.49	2.229	0	11.2	14	12	16
Small, A.	Tor	0	0	0	9.00	3.500	0	2.0	5	2	0
Smith, D.	Tex	1	2	0	4.30	2.045	0	14.2	18	12	9
Smith, L.	Bal	1	4	33	3.29	1.174	0	38.1	34	11	42
Smithberg, R.	Oak	0	0	0	15.43	3.000	0	2.1	6	1	3
Spoljaric, P.	Tor	0	1	0	38.57	6.000	1	2.1	5	9	2
Springer, R.	Cal	2	2	2	5.52	1.467	5	45.2	53	14	28
St. Claire, R.	Tor	0	0	0	9.00	3.000	0	2.0	4	2	2
Stevens, D.	Min	5	2	0	6.80	1.756	0	45.0	55	23	24
Stewart, D.	Tor	7	8	0	5.87	1.628	22	133.1	151	62	111
Stidham, P.	Det	0	0	0	24.92	3.692	0	4.1	12	4	4
Stottlemyre, T.	Tor	7	7	1	4.22	1.450	19	140.2	149	48	105
Swan, R.	Cle	0	1	0	11.25	2.500	0	8.0	13	7	2
Tapani, K.	Min	11	7	0	4.62	1.436	24	156.0	181	39	91
Tavarez, J.	Cle	0	1	0	21.60	4.200	1	1.2	6	1	0
Taylor, B.	Oak	1	3	1	3.50	1.252	0	46.1	38	18	48
Thigpen, B.	Sea	0	2	0	9.39	2.217	0	7.2	12	5	4
Timlin, M.	Tor	0	1	2	5.18	1.575	0	40.0	41	20	38
Trlicek, R.	Bos	1	1	0	8.06	2.149	1	22.1	32	16	7
Trombley, M.	Min	2	0	0	6.33	1.593	0	48.1	56	18	32
Turner, M.	Cle	1	0	1	2.13	1.816	0	12.2	13	7	5
Valdez, S.	Bos	0	1	0	8.16	2.302	1	14.1	25	8	4
Van Poppel, T.	Oak	7	10	0	6.09	1.714	23	116.2	108	89	83
Vanegmond, T.	Bos	2	3	0	6.34	1.539	7	38.1	38	21	22
Viola, F.	Bos	1	1	0	4.65	1.645	6	31.0	34	17	9
Vosberg, E.	Oak	0	2	0	3.95	1.537	0	13.2	16	5	12
Wegman, B.	Mil	8	4	0	4.51	1.452	19	115.2	140	26	59
Welch, B.	Oak	3	6	0	7.08	1.791	8	68.2	79	43	44
Wells, B.	Sea	1	0	0	2.25	1.250	0	4.0	4	1	3
Wells, D.	Det	5	7	0	3.96	1.249	16	111.1	113	24	71
Wertz, B.	Cle	0	0	0	10.38	2.308	0	4.1	9	1	1
Whiteside, M.	Tex	2	2	1	5.02	1.590	0	61.0	68	28	37
Wickman, B.	NYA	5	4	6	3.09	1.171	0	70.0	54	27	56
Williams, W.	Tor	1	3	0	3.64	1.331	0	59.1	44	33	56
Williamson, M.	Bal	3	1	1	4.01	1.396	2	67.1	75	17	28
Willis, C.	Min	2	4	3	5.92	1.702	0	59.1	89	12	37
Witt, B.	Oak	8	10	0	5.04	1.666	24	135.2	151	70	111